CUBA IN TRANSITION

Volume 5

Papers and Proceedings of the

**Fifth Annual Meeting
of the
Association for the Study of the Cuban Economy (ASCE)**

Miami, Florida
August 10-12, 1995

Cuba in Transition volumes may be ordered from:

The Association for the Study of the Cuban Economy
6321 Walhonding Road
Bethesda, Maryland 20816, USA
Tel. (301) 229-8921
Fax (301) 229-8921

PREFACE

This volume contains selected papers and commentaries presented at the Fifth Annual Meeting of the Association for the Study of the Cuban Economy (ASCE). The Fifth ASCE Annual Meeting was co-sponsored by the North-South Center, University of Miami, and held at the James L. Knight Center, Miami, Florida, on August 10-12, 1995.

The papers and commetaries contained in this volume cover a wide range of subjects related to Cuba's transition to a free-market economy, among them: recent economic reforms; trade; investment and financial markets; markets in the Cuba of today and of the future; macroeconomic and legal issues; expropriation and privatization; the environment; citrus and sugar markets; sociological issues; banking; and United States policy toward Cuba.

Preparation of the papers and commentaries for publication has been done by a group of ASCE members: José F. Alonso, Armando M. Lago, Lorenzo Pérez and Jorge Pérez-López. Lorenzo Pérez also chaired the Program Committee for the Fifth Annual Meeting. To these generous colleagues and friends, our heartfelt thanks.

Armando M. Lago
President

TABLE OF CONTENTS

ASSOCIATION FOR THE STUDY OF THE CUBAN ECONOMY (ASCE)

Fifth Annual Meeting
University of Miami, James L. Knight Center, Hyatt Hotel
Miami Florida
August 10-12, 1995

CONFERENCE PROGRAM

Panel Discussion: The Current Situation

José F. Alonso (USIA-OCB-Office of Research, Radio Martñ)

Alvaro Alba (Consultant)

Enrique Baloyra (University of Miami)

Recent Economic Reforms in Cuba

Markets, the State and Corruption in a Reform Process: Cuba
Roger Betancourt (University of Maryland)

Julio Carranza and Pedro Monreal on Economic Change in Cuba: A Critique
Ernesto Hernández-Catá (International Monetary Fund)

Institutional Requirements for Successful Market Reforms
Luis Locay (University of Miami)

Coveting Beijing, but Imitating Moscow: Cuba's Economic Reforms in Perspective
Jorge F. Pérez-López (U.S. Department of Labor)

Evaluation of Changes in Economic Policy in Cuba
Jorge Sanguinetty (DEVTECH, Inc.)

Panel: The Trade Impact — Florida After a Free Cuba

Teo Babún (T. Babún Group)

Trade, Investment, and Financial Markets

Financing the Economic Reconstruction of Cuba While Rebuilding the Financial Sector: Perspectives on Development Banking
Manuel Lasaga (Strategic Information Analysis, Inc.)

Discussant: Ricardo C. Martínez (Inter-American Development Bank)

Banking in Transition
Alberto Luzárraga (Amerinvest Corp.)

Discussant: Lorenzo L. Pérez (International Monetary Fund)

Markets in the Cuba of Today and of the Future

Markets Redux: The Politics of Farmers' Markets in Cuba
Juan Carlos Espinosa (University of Miami) .

Discussant: Antonio Gayoso (World Council of Credit Unions)

On the New Economic Geography of Havana's Food and Paladar Markets
Joseph L. Scarpaci (Virginia Tech University)

Discussant: Nicolás Crespo (Cuban Society of Tourism Professionals)

Small Business Development in Post-Transition Cuba
Joseph M. Perry, Louis A. Woods, Jeffrey W. Steagall (University of North Florida)

Discussant: José M. Ruisanchez (World Bank, Retired)

Macroeconomic and Fiscal Issues

A First Approximation Model of Money, Prices and Exchange Rates in Revolutionary Cuba
José F. Alonso (Radio Martí) and Armando M. Lago (Consultant)

Discussant: Fernando Alvarez (Babson College)

La crisis de las finanzas públicas en Cuba
Evaldo Cabarrouy (Universidad de Puerto Rico)

Discussant: Joaquín Pujol (International Monetary Fund)

The "New" Cuban Economic Model
Rolando H. Castañeda and George Plinio Montalván (IDB)

Discussant: Jorge F. Pérez-López (U.S. Department of Labor)

Legal Issues

Legal Policy for a Free Cuba: Lessons from the Civil Law
Néstor Cruz, Esq. (Carr, Morris and Graeff, P.C.)

Discussant: Luis Figueroa, Esq.

The Present Legal Status of Property Rights in Cuba
Juan Consuegra-Barquín, Esq. (Attorney in Private Practice)

Discussant: José M. Hernández (Georgetown University-retired)

Recommended Features of a Foreign Investment Code for Cuba's Free Market Transition
Matias F. Travieso-Díaz, Esq. (Shaw, Pittman, Potts and Trowbridge)

Discussant: José D. Acosta, Esq. (OAS, retired)

Luncheon Address

Mr. Xavier L. Suárez, Esq. (Shutts & Bowen, and former Mayor of Miami)

Expropriation and Privatization Issues

Economic Factors in Selecting an Approach to Expropriation Claims in Cuba:
Rolando Castañeda and George Plinio Montalván (IDB)

Discussant: Ralph Galliano (Institute for U.S.-Cuba Relations)

Restitution versus Compensation: Their Effects on the Pace of Privatization
Luis Locay and Agdem Ural (University of Miami)

Discussant: Roger Betancourt (University of Maryland)

The Ethics Foundation of Private Property
Alberto Martínez-Piedra (Catholic University of America)

Discussant: José M. Hernández (Georgetown University-retired)

Environment and Socioeconomic Indicators

Cuba's Environmental Law
    Ralph Barba and Amparo E. Avella: (Environmental Site Assessments, Inc.)

The Special Period and the Environment
    Sergio Díaz-Briquets (Casals and Associates)

Statistical Comparison of Cuban Socioeconomic Development
    Jorge Luis Romeu (State College at Cortland, NY)

Discussant: Armando M. Lago (Consultant)

Round Table on Sociological Issues

The Achievements of the Cuban Revolution: Sociological and Psychological Costs
    Maida Donate (Sigma Dos, Madrid)

Cuba's Refugees: Manifold Migrations
    Sylvia Pedraza Bailey (University of Michigan)

Philosophical Inquiry and the Crisis of Cuban Public Life
    Robert Vichot (Florida International University)

El otro testimonio: literatura carcelaria en Cuba
    Rafael E. Saumell (Sam Houston University)

Round Table on Banking Policies for a Democratic Cuba

Agustin Batista Falla (Asociación de Bancos de Cuba)
    Alberto Luzárraga (Amerinvest Corp.)

Round Table Discussion on the Sugar Sector in Cuba

José F. Alonso (OCB, Radio Martñ, Office of Research)

Alvaro Carta (Sugar Consultant)

José E. Lima (IPS Consultants)

Sugar and Citrus Markets

The Transformation of the State Extensive Growth Model in Cuba's Sugarcane Agriculture
    José Alvarez (University of Florida) and Lazaro Peña (Centro de Investigaciones de la Economia Mundial, La Habana)

Discussant: José F. Alonso (OCB, Radio Martí, Office of Research)

Cuba and the International Sugar Market
    Oscar Echevarría (EISCA)

Discussant: José Antonio Rivero (Amerop Sugar)

Cuban Citrus Production in a Post-Transition Economy
    Joseph Perry, Louis Woods & Jeffrey Steagall (University of North Florida)

Discussant: William Messina (University of Florida)

Round Table on the Status and Future Needs of Environmental Impact Assessments in Cuba

The Economic Dimension of EIA in the Transition from a Centrally Planned Economy to a Truly Participative Market Based Economic System
    René Costales (Inter-American Development Bank)

Walter Arensberg (Center for International Development and Environment)

The Process of Environmental Impact Assessment in Cuba
    Amparo Avella (Environmental Site Assessments, Inc.)

Lic. Amanda Barraza (Fundación Promar-Panamá)

Aspectos Esenciales sobre la Mitigación de los Desastres Naturales en Cuba
José Carlos Lezcano (Meteorologist/Physical Geographer)

United States Policy Toward Cuba

A Road Map for Restructuring U.S. Relations with Cuba
C. Richard Nelson (The Atlantic Council)

Discussant: J. P. Rathbone (World Bank)

Background on the Potential Impact of the Helms/Burton Act on Castro's Rule over Cuba
Ernesto Betancourt (International Development and Finance)

Discussant: Alfredo Cuzán (University of West Florida)

The Helms and Burton Bills: Myth and Reality
Robert E. Freer, Jr., Esq. (Freer & McGarry)

Discussant: Pamela Falk (ex-Staff Director, House Inter-American Committee)

Transition and Other Issues

Preliminary Analysis of Retirement Programs for the Personnel in the Ministry of the Armed Forces and the
Ministry of Interior of the Republic of Cuba

Ricardo Donate-Armada, A.S.A. (Towers Perrins Actuaries)

Issues of Legitimacy and Constitutionalism in the Cuban Transition
Mario A. Rivera (The University of New Mexico)

Discussant: Roger Guerra (Georgian Court College)

Economic Education for a Market Economy: The Cuban Case
Jorge Sanguinetty (DEVTEC Inc.)

JULIO CARRANZA AND PEDRO MONREAL ON ECONOMIC CHANGE IN CUBA: A CRITIQUE

Ernesto Hernández-Catá[1]

Since 1990, the Cuban economy has been coping with the effects of a massive withdrawal of external resources resulting from the elimination of Soviet subsidies and the collapse of Cuba's trade with former communist countries. The resulting problem could not be addressed in the way that is generally viewed as most appropriate, i.e., by combining adjustment and financing, because the financing part of the solution was not available. Cuba could not count on the support of multilateral financial institutions, from which it had withdrawn in the 1960's; financing from private or from official bilateral sources was unavailable, among other things because the Cuban government had built up a large stock of external arrears; and Russia did not have the resources or the political will to continue subsidizing the Cuban economy, even on a reduced scale. So the country had to adjust in full to the external shock.

Still, important options were open to Cuba's policy makers. The process of adjustment to the external shock could have been addressed by cutting domestic expenditure; by increasing output; or by a combination of the two. In the first phase, which covered roughly the period 1990-92, the Cuban economy ad-justed essentially by brute force: in other words by squeezing domestic expenditure through generalized rationing. National income plunged,[2] imports dropped in relation to gross domestic product (GDP) from 25 percent in 1989 to 11 percent in 1992, and the trade deficit shrank from 8 percent of GDP to 3 percent (Table 1). According to Julio Carranza,[3] this policy of forcing external adjustment by repressing domestic demand—if it was indeed a coherent policy—was aimed at "an equitable sharing of the burden of adjustment" but also at avoiding a rise in inflation and a surge in unemployment. But these goals were not achieved.

The maintenance of massive domestic subsidies in spite of the loss of external resources led to a sharp rise in the budget deficit from approximately 4 percent of GDP in 1989 to 24 percent of GDP in 1992, and these deficits were financed largely by monetary expansion. In part, the inflationary consequences were repressed by continuing to control prices at levels that were increasingly away from equilibrium. This resulted in the involuntary accumulation of monetary balances by the population, thus creating the potential for a future surge in prices. The coun-

---

1. An earlier version of this paper was presented at the workshop on "The Future of Economic Reforms in Cuba" organized by Shaw, Pittman, Potts & Trowbridge, Washington, D.C., April 10, 1995. The views expressed in this paper are the author's and not necessarily those of the International Monetary Fund.

2. Estimates of the cumulative drop in GDP between 1989 and 1992 range between 23 and 39 percent. This paper uses an estimate published in the 1994 *Economic Report* of the National Bank of Cuba which puts the drop in GDP near the lower limit of that range. From 1989 to 1984, GDP probably fell somewhere between 34 percent and 48 percent.

3. Julio Carranza, "Los cambios económicos en Cuba: Problemas y desafíos," *Cuadernos de Nuestra América*, Vol XI, No. 22 (julio-diciembre 1994).

Table 1. Cuba: Selected Macroeconomic Indicators

	1989	1990	1991	1992	1993	1994
In Percent of GDP						
Government revenue	35	43	46	50	52	69
Government expenditure	43	49	62	74	80	77
Budget balance	-4	-6	-16	-24	-28	-8
Exports	17	17	13	9	6	7
Imports	25	24	18	11	11	11
Trade balance	-8	-6	-5	-3	-5	-3
In billions of pesos						
Real GDP (1981 prices)	19.6	19.0	17.0	15.0	12.8	12.9
Budget balance	-1.4	-2.0	-3.8	-4.9	-5.0	-1.4
Trade balance	-2.7	-2.0	-1.3	-0.5	-0.9	-0.6
Percentage changes						
Real GDP	0.3	-3.0	-10.7	-11.6	-14.9	0.7
Black market prices	3	2	157	98	201	12
Black market exchange rate (negative sign=depreciation)	-27	-51	-84	-20	9	50

Sources: Jorge Pérez-López, *op. cit.*; data provided by Armando Lago and José Alonso; Cuban National Bank, *Economic Report, 1994;* Ministry of Economy and Planning, National Statistical Office; and author's estimates.

Note: Estimates of Cuba's nominal GDP are subject to an extraordinary margin of uncertainty as suggested by the counterintuitive behavior of the implicit GDP price deflator (for example, the deflator falls in 1991, a year of strong inflationary pressures in parallel and back markets). Accordingly, estimates expressed in percent of nominal GDP should be interpreted with considerable caution and should be used only to provide rough orders of magnitude.'

terpart of this excess supply of money was, of course, an excess demand for goods, which was eliminated by rationing in various forms, including queues and forced interruptions of water and power supply to the population. But high inflation was not avoided: part of the pressure resulting from monetary expansion found its way in parallel and black markets were prices increased at an average annual rate of about 150 percent in the period 1990-93.[4] Neither was the rise in unemployment avoided: it was merely disguised, with enterprises often shouldering the burden of keeping idle employees on the payrolls.

In late 1993 and 1994, the government adopted a seemingly more rational approach to adjustment. First, it restrained aggregate demand by raising excise taxes and cutting subsidies, thus reducing the need to resort to rationing, forced saving and the inflation tax, Second, it provided some incentives to expand production through a partial liberalization of agriculture and the legalization of some forms of self-employment.[5] The measures succeeded in reducing financial imbalances: the budget deficit, which had peaked at almost 30 percent of GDP in 1993, dropped to 8 percent of GDP in 1994. The monetary overhang was reduced and inflation in parallel and black markets apparently subsided. Third, a favorable treatment was given to foreign investment in certain sectors, particularly tourism, and residents were allowed access to specially designated, government controlled stores were they were authorized to spend the foreign currency they obtained from rela-

---

4. Based on data provided by José Alonso and Armando Lago.

5. For a summary of these measures, see Jorge Pérez-López, "The Cuban Economy in 1995," *Association for the Study of the Cuban Economy Newsletter* (June 1995).

tives in the United States or from certain transactions with non-residents. But the structural reforms were too timid, subject to too many restrictions and limitations, to yield a sufficiently strong supply response, and real GDP stagnated at a low level in 1994. Moreover, the policies adopted in 1993-94 have created a dual economy with a number of distortions and inequalities—between those who have access to foreign currency and those who do not, between the self-employed and those employed in the state sector, and between farmers and city-dwellers.

* * *

Where will the Cuban economy go from here? A strategy aimed at achieving a lasting improvement in the standard of living of the Cuban population would have to combine continued adjustment on the demand side through a tight fiscal policy with a decisive effort to boost the supply of output by eliminating distortions and providing incentives to work and to produce. The proposals presented by Julio Carranza and Pedro Monreal[6] in their recent articles and in their oral presentations at the April 1995 meeting in Washington, D.C., with a group of Cuban-American economists are not consistent with this strategy. At times the authors do emphasize the need to increase economic efficiency, to base enterprise behavior on considerations of profitability and to expand the role of markets. But in the end their program envisages the maintenance of central planning (although it will be planning of a different nature, we are told), of major distortions and obstacles to the functioning of markets, and the perpetuation of a large state-controlled enterprise sector insulated from competitive pressures.

Their apparent affection for distorting policies is revealed most clearly in their brief reference to industrial policy (on page 3 of the "Proposals for discussion"), where they envisage the use of "economic tools such as duties and import permits, selective

credit policies, direct allocation of hard currency, legally sanctioned monopolies, export subsidies, state orders, direct state investment in dynamic sectors, etc..." This reads like a collection of the policies that have distorted resource allocation and hindered growth in so many developing countries for so many years; and these policies are inconsistent with the authors' professed interest in the efficiency and the productivity of the economic system. Even if the scope of state control over the economy were to be reduced in the period ahead and the role of decentralized decision-making expanded, the use of instruments such as import permits and the direct allocation of credit and hard currencies will lead to rent-seeking behavior and lobbying by special interest groups, thus jeopardizing both efficiency at the micro level and financial discipline at the macro level.

Yet, efficiency and stability are the authors' stated goals. But throughout their writings these goals clash with their specific policy recommendations. This is particularly striking in Julio Carranza's proposals for enterprise reform. In his article titled "Los cambios económicos en Cuba," he states that enterprises should operate under a system of hard budget constraints ("régimen financiero fuerte") that provides the right incentives to maintain profitability. This is very encouraging. But is it consistent with Carranza's view of Cuba's future enterprise sector? He does envisage that the small, and most of the medium-size enterprises will be profit-oriented (although he adds, ominously, that they "will have to account for their economic results before the structures of Popular Power," whatever that might be). However, the large and medium-size enterprises "which have a major impact on overall economic relations" must be centralized and remain subject to the direct control of the government.

The word 'profitability' does not appear in the discussion of these large, state-controlled enterprises which, we are told, must remain the "central axis" of

---

6. See Carranza, *op. cit.*; and Pedro Monreal and Manuel Rúa del Llano, "Apertura y reforma de la economía cubana: Las transformaciones institucionales (1990-1993)," *Cuadernos de Nuestra America.*, Vol XI, No. 21 (enero-junio 1994). See also Carranza and Monreal, "Cuba: La reestructuración de la economía. (Una propuesta para el debate)," presented at the workshop on "The Future of Economic Reforms in Cuba," April 1995.

the economy. Presumably, this means that these enterprises—most of which are probably loss-making, have a redundant labor force and operate at dismally low levels of capacity—will not be subject to hard budget constraints. There is not a word about a plan to take a serious look at these enterprises to determine which ones should be restructured and which ones should be closed. And there is not a word about privatization. So, presumably, these enterprises will be kept afloat through budgetary transfers and centralized credits. And so they will continue to be a burden for the population and, as the experience of the former Soviet Union strongly suggests, a threat to macroeconomic stability. Cuba's budget deficit is still around 10 percent of GDP, and monetary financing on that scale is incompatible with low inflation.

Julio Carranza is understandably concerned about the monetary overhang in Cuba. He is also concerned about the fragmentation of the economy into a dollar sector and a peso sector—a fragmentation that distorts prices and wages and contributes to the misallocation of resources. His proposal to unify the currency is sensible. Moreover, I have no difficulty with the proposal of eliminating the dollar from circulation by exchanging it for the national currency. But this misses the point. The source of the distortions is not the fact that the dollar is allowed to circulate: it is the fact that it can only be used in specified sectors of the economy where the national currency cannot be used, and the fact that the two currencies cannot be freely exchanged for one another. Therefore, free convertibility of the national currency, together with unification of the official and free market exchange rates, is the real solution to the problem.

Similarly, the authors propose a currency reform as a solution to the problem of excess liquidity. This is a possible solution; I suspect its interest derives from the fact that it allows the confiscation of monetary balances above a specified threshold and therefore it

can be used as an instrument of social policy. This is a double-edged sword because it will have obvious implications for the credibility of the government as a debtor. But more to the point, monetary reform by itself will not eliminate the distortions created by disequilibrium prices. The way to eliminate these distortions and also to get rid of the monetary overhang once and for all is to liberalize prices. The authors agree that this is part of the solution, but they assert that "the process of price liberalization necessarily must be partial and gradual." [7] They recognize that the coexistence of free prices and controlled prices will give rise to "tensions." That's putting it mildly. They should bear in mind the experience of Russia and the outcome of Gorbachev's disastrous attempt at partial and gradual decontrol of prices. In January 1992, Egor Gaidar freed all prices with one stroke of the pen, not because he had a taste for big bang solutions, but because goods had disappeared from the markets.

* * *

To conclude, the basic problem faced by the authors results, I believe, from a *fundamental ambiguity at the level of strategic objectives*. On the one hand these objectives are defined as the achievement of "high rates of growth of output and employment, low inflation and external balance." But this must be done, we are told, "without jeopardizing the socialist essence" of the economic system. And in case there is any doubt, we are told that "planning is an essential instrument within a strategy aimed at the country's economic and social development in the medium and long term."[8] These objectives are mutually inconsistent.

I have read what Pedro Monreal said about the "complex learning process" through which the various economic and political leaders must go through,[9] and I understand his feeling that he must adopt a cautious approach to reform. I am not in a position to give tactical advice to those who influence economic policy in today's Cuba. I can only urge them

---

7. Carranza, *op. cit.*, p. 30.

8. Carranza, *op. cit.*, p. 38.

9. Monreal and Rúa del Llano, *op. cit.*

to look reality in the face and state clearly and unambiguously what I believe is wrong and must be changed.

Central planning has failed worldwide as a system because it has proved unable to provide for a lasting improvement in the standards of living of the population. It did not work well in Cuba, even when the government was able to provide social benefits at the expense of the Russian tax payer. I don't see why it should work now that the party is over. If the goal is to achieve lasting growth of output and employment as Carranza and Monreal tell us it is; if their cherished goal of social equity is to involve sharing prosperity—and not only sacrifices and poverty—then the reform program will have to be much more ambitious. It will have to pursue a genuine solution to the problem of large scale enterprises through a combination of restructuring and privatization, and to improve efficiency and avoid the perpetuation of subsidies that the population cannot afford to pay. It will have to seek the replacement of central planning by market mechanisms as the principal mode of resource allocation and realize that the only price reform that will work is full price liberalization. It will have to insist on freedom for the Cuban people to work, produce, and invest, and on their right to appropriate the benefits of their efforts. And it will have to call for a much more fundamental withdrawal of the state from economic life.

INSTITUTIONAL REQUIREMENTS FOR SUCCESSFUL MARKET REFORMS

Luis Locay

As the title of my paper suggests, my comments will focus on institutions. Specifically, I wish to emphasize that what we refer to as an economic system is a set of institutions, so that economic restructuring essentially involves institutional change. In this paper I will discuss some of the institutional requirements of a market economy and consider whether the changes occurring in Cuba are a substantial move in that direction or simply a public relations ploy to improve the Castro government's image abroad.

INSTITUTIONAL REQUIREMENTS OF MARKET ECONOMIES

Markets are social arrangements by which people, either as individuals or as parts of larger organizations, exchange goods and services. The exchange itself directly increases wealth by transferring goods and services to those who value them most. More importantly, markets allow us to take advantage of scale economies and to exploit the gains from specialization and the division of labor. These gains can be amplified by physical and human capital, so that the role of markets in generating growth and wealth is as important for developed countries, where both types of capital are high, as it is for developing ones.

Unfortunately market exchange is costly. When the costs of transacting are very high, markets either do not function well or do not exist. What are these costs of transacting? Let me illustrate with a mundane example most of us are familiar with. Imagine a person who is interested in buying a computer. Such a purchase normally begins by a search process by which the customer determines the type of computer

he wants, perhaps what brands are acceptable, and where he can get a good price. This search may involve looking at computer magazines, searching newspapers for sales, listening to advertisements on the radio or television, talking to friends, or visiting computer stores. Once the search is complete the customer must arrange for payment and delivery. If anything goes wrong he may have to return the computer to have it serviced or to obtain a replacement.

As can be seen, even a relatively simple purchase can involve a significant expenditure of time and resources. What is important is that a society's institutional structure determines to a considerable extent the magnitude of these transaction costs. Suppose computer stores were not allowed to advertise. Our imaginary buyer would have found his search more difficult. Or suppose computer stores were restricted to a few locations, as were, for example, all businesses in the black townships of South Africa under apartheid? What if the computer purchaser had to operate in a highly inflationary environment, where he kept very low money balances on hand? He would have had to incur the additional transaction costs associated with converting some of his assets into money. If the government taxes the transaction heavily, that also discourages the exchange from taking place. And what if the computer is faulty and does not work? We can imagine a system where the customer has to either accept the loss or take matters into his own hands and try to get his money back. Such a problem is not a major concern in the United States, as there is a system of contract law—and courts and police to enforce them—that reduce enormously enforcement costs for the typical customer. If the customer chooses to finance his purchase, banking institutions and credit agencies, as well as the legal system that supports them, come into play.

Imagine now much more complicated transactions such as financing and building a power plant, discovering and marketing new drugs, or developing virgin land that contains endangered species, and you can quickly see just how important is the institutional structure that supports these transactions. In general, for markets to exist and to function reasonably well, they require an institutional structure that reduces as much as possible the costs of transacting of all affected parties.

Most so called developing countries have not had institutional structures whose purpose is to facilitate market exchange and encourage productive activities. In my opinion this is the main reason such countries have not developed. Their institutions create large transaction costs in an attempt to achieve a distribution of wealth that is different from that which would arise through the functioning of low cost markets. Their governing coalitions have grabbed a bigger a share of the pie at the expense of making the pie smaller for everyone. And the tools by which this has been achieved has been the countries' institutions. The epitome of this approach have been the centrally planned economies. In their purest form, centrally planned economies outlaw the private ownership of most types of productive assets and most types of economic activities and organizations. Their institutions are designed not to reduce, but to rather create, large barriers to market exchange in order to redistribute wealth to the ruling coalition, a distribution that could not be maintained in a market economy.

TOWARD A MARKET ECONOMY OR TINKERING WITH SOCIALISM?

Since a change in economic structure involves changing institutions, the question naturally arises, are the recent economic reforms in Cuba a move toward a more market friendly institutional structure? In a simple minded way, the answer must be yes. Cuba has been so hostile to markets, that practically any change must be toward greater market friendliness.

But have there been significant institutional changes? The answer to me is clearly no. Let us consider the legalization of self-employment and the creation of agricultural cooperatives as examples.

At first glance the legalization of self-employment appears to be a significant step in reducing the barriers to a type of market that is important in poor countries. On more careful examination it looks quite different.

First of all, as others have pointed out, many of the large number of laid-off government workers would probably have moved into self-employment informally in the absence of legalization. This could only be prevented through the expenditure of considerable resources on greater repression, and the Cuban government is currently in no position to do this. Besides, what does it gain by creating a large number of desperate people with nothing to lose?

Secondly, by legalizing self-employment the government can hope to raise some revenues through licensing fees and taxes. Thirdly, through heavy regulation it can focus its resources on preventing the types of economic activities it does not want, namely successful ones. Consider the case of home restaurants, the "paladares." Despite their very limited nature, some proved successful, and the government's first reaction was to make them illegal. I understand they are legal again, but the episode shows the opportunistic nature of the government, instability in the rules of the game, and lack of commitment to true reform. If the Cuban government was serious about expanding the role of markets, it would have made self-employment legal, subject to some simple regulations. Instead it has amended the penal code to make it easier to prosecute "profiteers," and it has limited the success people can achieve by such restrictions as not allowing the hiring of employees. Earlier this year, *The Miami Herald* reported that the Cuban Government had imposed millions of pesos in fines in the first quarter of the year for violations of the self-employment law. The government's message is clear: if you need to engage in self-employment to survive, do so, but do not go beyond survival or you'll be punished.

The new system of agricultural cooperatives sounds similar to what China had before it changed to private property. That which the Cuban government would consider as a major reform, the adoption of a system of agricultural production that was used by the Chinese more than twenty years ago when their economy was centrally planned, tells us a great deal about just how centralized the Cuban economy has become.

The motivation for the shift from state farms to cooperatives seems to me to be similar to the motivation for allowing limited self-employment: to offset to some extent the immediate impact of the external shocks Cuba has experienced with the fall of the Soviet Union. The availability of foodstuffs can not decline so much that the survival of the regime is threatened.

While I would not be surprised if the cooperatives show some improvement relative to the state farms, at least in the short run, we should not exaggerate how different the two are. Both share many of the problems common to socialist methods of production, and both are consistent with central planning. The literature on the Chinese cooperatives identifies many potential incentive problems and several reasons for why resources may have been used inefficiently. When the Chinese shifted to private land ownership agricultural output rose substantially, as did the rate of growth of productivity. The lesson most of us would draw from the Chinese experience is that if you are serious about increasing farming output, you liberalize agricultural markets and move to a system of private land ownership. The lesson drawn by the Cuban government seems to be that private land ownership will create some very successful farmers, which are to be as feared as the successful self-employed.

These examples illustrate that the implemented reforms do not involve a change toward an institutional structure that supports markets. In the presence of a legal code that punishes economic success, and a demonstrated willingness to enforce it, even retroactively, future "legalization" of other forms of economic organizations, such as small firms, are meaningless. The Cuban government's view of economic reform is to tinker with socialism at the edges—permit a few very restricted markets, decentralize decision making slightly—but not the sort of institutional restructuring that would compromise the socialist nature of the economy. This should not surprise us. Important members of the government, such as Raúl Castro and Alarcón, as well as lesser spokesmen have repeatedly stated that the purpose of the reforms is to restructure socialism—to make it more productive and efficient—and not to pave the way toward a market economy.

Even if the reforms are yet not substantial, some may argue that their tentativeness is natural at this stage. As those in favor of reform as well as those against it struggle, the result is likely to be slow and confused, and we may even see temporary changes of direction. Are we really witnessing the first steps to what ultimately will be dramatic reform? I believe not, and the reason lies in the nature of the regime and the situation its leaders find themselves at home and within the international community. To see this we need to digress a bit.

INSTITUTIONAL CHANGE AND DEMOCRATIC REFORM

It is often argued that any economic reforms in Cuba aimed at greater reliance on markets and the lessening of centralized decision making will be unsuccessful if unaccompanied by democratic reform. Since the current economic reforms are not accompanied by political liberalization, by this argument the reforms will fail. I do not agree with this view. The historical experience, especially in the post-war period does not support the notion that democracy is necessary for successful, market oriented institutional reform. In fact, it may well be that authoritarian regimes are in a better position to implement such reforms. Chile, China, Singapore, South Korea, and Taiwan, are all examples of economies that have experienced major market friendly institutional change and rapid economic growth under authoritarian regimes. Even Hong Kong and Japan have had much of their institutional structure imposed on them from the outside. Meanwhile, democracy in the transition economies of Eastern Europe has sometimes hindered institutional change toward market economies.

Nevertheless, when one looks across all countries, democracy appears to be positively related to economic growth and with the types of institutional structures that are necessary for markets to function well. I believe the primary line of causation, however, runs from economic reform to democracy. There are at least three reasons for this. First of all, institutional restructuring aimed at reducing transaction costs and encouraging productive activity generates increases in wealth and more rapid growth. With higher incomes people demand a greater say in how they are governed. Secondly, they have greater means at their disposal to challenge the power of the government. This is particularly so if some individuals are very successful and accumulate some wealth, becoming pockets of power separate from the government. This is one reason the Cuban government cannot tolerate individual economic success. Thirdly, the freedom of movement, the decentralization of control of the means of production, and an improved system of communication which are necessary in a market economy, make the logistics of a challenge to the government easier.

If this analysis is correct, the Cuban government is between a rock and a hard place. If it does not liberalize its economy, the grossly inefficient structure of central planning, in the absence of Soviet subsidies, imperils the regime. If it makes real reforms and moves toward a market economy, it also sows the seeds of its own destruction.

One may ask why Cuba cannot follow the Chinese example of genuine market reform without political liberalization? I believe the answer lies in the simple fact that China is a powerful country with a large market, and Cuba is not. Economic reform in China was followed by calls for democracy and greater political freedom, culminating in the demonstrations of Tiananmen Square. These demonstrations were brutally crushed, with relatively mild protests from the international community.

Imagine a similar uprising in a more market oriented future Cuba still controlled by the Castro regime. Even if the repressive apparatus of the state is successful in squashing the rebellion, it cannot be expected that the reaction of the rest of the world will be a mild as it was following Tiananmen Square. At a very minimum the U.S. would push, probably successfully, to extend the embargo to include Europe and Latin America. I think a naval blockade by the U.S. would not be out of the question, and neither would be outright military intervention. Cuba's small size, its proximity to the U.S., and the presence here of a large and vocal exile community, pose risks to the Castro regime from economic liberalization that the Chinese leaders never faced.

While Cuba cannot follow the Chinese example, it certainly is not following that of the Soviet Union. Cuba's economic reforms may resemble those of the ex-Soviet Union, but in Cuba there has been no political liberalization. The ruling class in the ex-Soviet Union may have believed it could open up the system politically and remain in power. If so, it was partially wrong. I say "partially" because while the old regime collapsed, many in the nomenklatura have retained positions of political and economic power. Even Mikhail Gorbachev has not done badly for himself. I understand he heads an international environmental organization. But in Cuba the revolution is too recent, and a political transition is not likely to be so kind to its ruling class. Can any of us imagine an ousted Fidel Castro heading efforts to save the rain forest, or just simply enjoy his wealth in peace on the Costa Brava?

DESPERATE TACTICS OR LONG-RUN STRATEGY

The economic reforms that Cuba has implemented are not going to create the sort of institutional change that will move that country toward a market economy. The Cuban government admits this. In fact, its spokesmen go out of their way to assure those elements in Cuban society that depend on its paternalism, and in turn provide it with political support, that the system is not going to radically change.

The reforms refer to entities such as firms, banks, and NGOs, that we find in market economies. These entities, however, have little resemblance to the real things. It is as if the Cuban government claimed to have copied a foreign car based solely on a photograph of the exterior. It may look like a car from the outside, but the internal mechanisms that make a car what it is, would be absent. Economic entities in market economies exist within an institutional structure that makes them possible and rational. That structure is completely missing in Cuba, and in my opinion is not likely to be created by the current regime. The current reforms simply recycle known forms of socialist economic organization. I see no reason to believe that they will function any better in the Cuban context than they have elsewhere. The best the regime can hope for is a marginal improvement that will allow it to survive the present crisis.

Government spokesmen have claimed that the reforms are part of a long-term strategic restructuring of the Cuban economy. I am extremely skeptical. The reforms all smack of a tactical response to the immediate problems caused by the cut-off of Soviet aid. I have this image—I am sure it is wrong in its particulars, but perhaps correct in its essence—of the Cuban leadership sitting around wondering if the stop-gap measures they have been forced to take could be used to their advantage. Someone then suggests that if they can be packaged as part of a grand design to restructure the Cuban economy—making sure, of course, that nothing fundamental is changed—it can be used to improve Cuba's image abroad. "Cuba is no longer rigidly dogmatic," the plan seems to say, "we are primarily interested in productivity and efficiency, just like all you potential investors out there." Who knows, if properly marketed, maybe it could even help remove the American embargo.

In closing, if we judge the reforms as to how significantly they will shift Cuba toward a market economy, I believe they will turn out to be a complete failure. If they are viewed as a new way of substantially increasing productivity and improving efficiency within the socialist framework, again I believe they will fail. As an aid for the regime to survive the current crisis, they may well succeed. As a means by which the regime can improve its image abroad, the reform package may also prove useful. In my opinion, they are not the first tentative steps toward a market oriented Cuba. I do not believe we are witness a child who is starting to crawl and will eventually, after many falls and scrapes, learn to walk. Down that path is disaster for the current leadership. I believe they understand that very well.

COVETING BEIJING, BUT IMITATING MOSCOW: CUBA'S ECONOMIC REFORMS IN A COMPARATIVE PERSPECTIVE

Jorge F. Pérez-López[1]

In mid-1995, in the throes of an economic depression and with no generous allies to turn to after the dissolution of the Soviet Bloc, it is incontrovertible that Cuba has to make substantive changes in order to find a niche in the international economic system. The question, then, is not whether Cuba should reform its economy and polity, but rather how does Cuba do it? What model does it adopt? What path does it follow?

It can be argued that the current Cuban government seeks a reform model that will bring about rapid economic growth while maintaining the Cuban Communist Party and its current leadership in political control. That is, the Cuban government seeks the best of two worlds: vigorous economic growth—with its attendant potential to improve income levels and standards of living of its population and strengthen national security—under a socialist system controlled by the current *nomenklatura*.

China's record of rapid economic growth under a communist regime is, of course, appealing to Cuba. In the 1980s, the Chinese economy grew at an average annual rate of over 10 percent; double-digit growth rates have continued into the 1990s, with the economy reportedly growing at a rate of about 13 percent in 1992 and 1993 ("China" 1994, p. 96) and 11.8 percent in 1994 (Tyler 1995, p. A9), one of the

fastest growth rates in the world. At the same time, the ruling Chinese government—one and the same with the Chinese Communist Party—has managed to hold on to power. When challenged by those seeking political pluralism in 1989, the Chinese government confronted them squarely, and brutally, at Tiananmen Square. The Chinese government continues to exercise political control and suppress dissent.

Cuba covets Beijing's ability to achieve economic growth while the Communist Party remains in power. Relations between Cuba and China have become closer in the 1990s (Fernández 1993 and 1994). In 1994, China became Cuba's third largest trading partner, with two-way bilateral trade of about $250 million, and further expansion of economic relations are contemplated ("China estudia" 1995). Cuba has sent official missions to China to study the Chinese model and to explore how some of the policies the Chinese have implemented might be applied in Cuba (Benjamin 1994, p. 51).

Despite the appeal that the Chinese model might have for the Cuban leadership, in practice, policies implemented by Cuba since 1990 differ significantly from Beijing's model. As I argue in this paper, Cuba's economic policies are closer to those associated with *perestroika* in the former Soviet Union during

---

1. An earlier version was presented at the workshop "The Future of Economic Reforms in Cuba," sponsored by Shaw, Pittman, Potts & Trowbridge, Washington, D.C., April 10, 1995. The paper presents only the personal views of the author.

the government of Mikhail Gorbachev. The upshot of those policies, as has been amply documented, was not to bring about economic growth and stability to the Soviet Union, but rather to promote a series of economic imbalances that resulted in a veritable economic crisis. So far, the outcome of the implementation of similar policies in Cuba has also been chaotic. Moreover, there is no basis for assuming a different—and more positive—outcome in Cuba in the longer term as a result of implementation of *perestroika*-like reforms.

CHINA—ECONOMIC LIBERALIZATION AND POLITICAL CONTROL

Generally speaking, China has pursued partial and more gradual reforms than has been the case in Eastern European countries in transition to market economies. Since 1978, China has introduced market-oriented behavior in certain sectors of the economy while preserving, in principle, a socialist, centrally planned system. China's reform strategy was based on the judgement that "by opening the door to the outside world, China could absorb foreign investment, trade, and technology while spurning the cultural and political influences, or bourgeois liberalization, that would challenge Communist Party rule" ("China: Is Prosperity" 1994, p. 96).

China's efforts at economic reform began with the Great Leap Forward (1958), which, among other actions, decentralized some economic decision-making by increasing the authority of local governments over the supply of raw materials and over certain types of investment. It also gave local governments responsibility for the great majority of enterprises formerly managed by central government ministries, and reduced the role of the central planning apparatus. Another series of modest decentralization measures were adopted in 1979 in accord with the slogan "delegating power to lower levels is a revolution" (Burki 1988, p. 46).

In the aftermath of the Cultural Revolution, a more far reaching set of reforms was introduced in 1978 and implemented in earnest in 1979 under the shorthand name of the "Four Modernizations," a reference to the four areas (agriculture, industry, science and technology, and national defense) that were tar-

geted for extensive reforms (Perkins 1989; Prybyla 1990). One of the basic tenets of the Chinese approach to reform has been an emphasis on competition rather than ownership as the key factor in stimulating production and economic efficiency.

Agriculture: In the agricultural sector, the reforms began a process of recreating markets for agricultural output, reestablishing agricultural research activities, importing modern technologies, raising prices for agricultural output procured by the state, and dismantling the system of communes (Burki 1988, p. 47). Communes gave way to a "contract responsibility system," whereby land and other inputs were allocated to workers; the obligations of these workers was the payment of taxes, the fulfillment of production quotas, and contributions to social welfare funds.

Through the "contract responsibility system," the beneficial impacts of privatization on efficiency and output in the agricultural sector have been obtained without an actual legal transfer of property. Agricultural communes were broken up and land turned over to individuals on a long (15 to 25 year) lease basis, provided farmers sold a share of output to the state and, in some instances, agreed to plant specific commodities. The contract responsibility system has been largely responsible for the phenomenal growth in Chinese agricultural output since the beginning of the reforms. One study suggests that three quarters of the increase in agricultural productivity in China between 1978 and 1984 can be attributed to the incentive effects of the responsibility system and one quarter to higher procurement prices (McMillan et.al. 1987).

Industry: In industry, state enterprises have been granted greater decision-making autonomy, the scope of compulsory deliveries has been reduced, and a two-tier system of sales and prices has been introduced (Balassa 1991, pp. 411-415). Since the 1980s, enterprises have been allowed to retain a share of their profits; enterprises have also been allowed some latitude in procuring inputs and in producing and selling goods outside of the plan (Rawski 1994, p. 272). In the mid-1980s, the contract responsibility system was extended to medium and large industrial enterprises (Koo 1990), allowing them to retain any surplus after meeting "contract responsibility" production and financial obligations. China also initiated a "two-track" or "dual-price" system under which output produced outside of the plan could be sold without government control (Rawski 1994, p. 272).

To compete with state-owned enterprises, China stimulated the establishment of rural industries in the form of locally-managed township and village enterprises (TVEs) (Singh 1992; "When China" 1991). Although technically "collectives," TVEs are controlled by township and village leaders; these leaders designate the managers of TVEs, with local residents not possessing a "right of ownership" or workers any rights to participate in TVE management (Naughton 1994, p. 267). Several studies (Naughton 1994, p. 267) show that township and village officials, in their official capacity, possess all of the key components of property rights: control of residual income, the right to dispose of assets, and the right to appoint and dismiss managers and assume control.

Foreign Investment: Another important element of China's economic reform was the passage of a joint venture law in 1979 and the opening of the first four Special Economic Zones in 1980. Pursuant to the joint venture law, foreign direct investment poured into China, financing economic development and bringing with it foreign technologies and management practices. China also decentralized foreign trade activities, allowing the creation of foreign trade corporations (Harrold 1992, pp. 15-17). Formation of joint ventures with foreign investors, especially in the so-called special economic zones (Sklair 1991), has been another form of *de facto* privatization in China.

The effect of these policies on the structure of the Chinese economy are quite remarkable. It is estimated that in 1994, about half of China's industrial output and as much as 75 percent of its total output were produced by private or "collective" firms; at least 30 million Chinese were working in privately-owned businesses; TVEs employed another 90 million persons and accounted for over one-third of industrial output ("China's Communists" 1994, pp. 19-20).

China's impressive economic reforms have not been accompanied by political change. According to the U.S. Department of State (1995, p. 555), China is an authoritarian state in which the Chinese Communist Party monopolizes decisionmaking authority, with almost all top civilian, police, and military positions at the national and regional levels held by party members.

SOVIET UNION—PERESTROIKA'S FAILED PARTIAL REFORMS

Mikhail Gorbachev ascended to the post of General Secretary of the Communist Party of the Soviet Union in March 1985. He inherited a troubled economy: growth rates had slowed down considerably and commodity shortages were rampant. The diagnosis of experts was that the economic malaise resulted from overplanning and overadministration of the economy (Desai 1989, p. 27). Under the very structured Soviet system, firms and farms had very little autonomy, and there were very few incentives to increase production and efficiency.

Perestroika (restructuring) was Gorbachev's strategy to reform the Soviet economy within the framework of a socialist economic system. Adoption of certain elements of *perestroika* began in 1986, and the full program came into effect in 1988. By 1990, in the midst of a chaotic economic and political situation, *perestroika* was abandoned and replaced with a more radical set of policies aimed at transforming the Soviet Union into a market economy (Aslund 1991, p. 2). The main elements of *perestroika* included:

Agriculture: One of the earliest policy changes associated with *perestroika* was the Decree on Agricultural Management of March 1986, also known as the Law on Collective Farms. The decree allowed collective farms some management autonomy and established a system of production incentives. Collective farms were given the ability to sell a certain amount of their above-quota surpluses in cooperative and private outlets where prices were generally higher than official prices. The decree also allowed households on the collective farm to band together and undertake various activities, a mild version of the contract responsibility system used in China, intimating that collective farms would be eventually dissolved as private contracts took over (Desai 1989, pp. 34-38). The 1988 Law on Cooperatives (see below) formally abolished plan targets for collective farms, while the Law on Leasehold (1989) allowed long-term leases (for up to 50 years) of land to farmers (Aslund 1991, p. 104).

Self-Employment: Unlike in Hungary, Poland, East Germany, and even China, where self-employment was common and the hiring of labor by private entities was allowed, these activities were severely restricted in the former Soviet Union.

The Law on Individual Labor Activity, passed in 1987, was intended to liberalize self-employment and stimulate private sector activity. The Law set out lists of professions that henceforth could be performed by individuals, identified branches of the economy in which private enterprise could operate, and established criteria for licensing entrepreneurial activities. However, the application process for self-employment was long and difficult, with local authorities having numerous opportunities to turn down applications. Special taxes (both a lump sum tax and a progressive income tax) were imposed on the self-employed.

Aslund (1991, p. 167) described the significance and results of the Law on Individual Labor Activity as follows:

> Although many principles of the Law on Individual Labour Activity were quite liberal, and the official attitude positive, the ideological perception of individual enterprise had not been revised. Private enterprise was only allowed as a part-time family business. It was both difficult and expensive to enter the legal private sector. Licensing and high taxes rendered private enterprise exclusive. The law impresses with the insight that many conditions cannot possibly be regulated in the disorderly Soviet shortage economy. The limitation of enterprise size was at least one guarantee that the earnings of private monopolists would not be limited. Individual labour activity remained very limited, only involving 300,000 people in 1989.

Enterprise Management: The Law on State Enterprises, adopted in June 1987, granted state-owned enterprises—all units in the state sector engaged in production, processing, financing, distribution, and

trade—some freedom from the straitjacket of the central plan. The Law called for self-management of state enterprises, with enterprise managers and directors to be elected by their workers; a work council, also elected by workers, would have some say over each enterprise's plans.

Perhaps the most significant contribution of the Law on State Enterprises was the changes it made to the working arrangements among state production units. It relaxed the very strict system that obliged state enterprises to produce specific outputs and sell them to other state enterprises at pre-determined prices. Under the new Law, state enterprises were given the flexibility to develop their own production plans based on contracts with other economic actors, except for important products for which enterprises were given "state orders." In practice, "state orders turned out to be old commands under a new name and tended to cover 100 percent of the production capacity of most enterprises" (Aslund 1991, p. 108), undermining the enterprise autonomy intended by the Law.

The Law on Cooperatives, adopted in 1988, was perhaps the most liberal of the *perestroika* policies. It allowed the formation of cooperatives in any sector of the economy, including areas such as banking and foreign trade. Cooperatives would be owned by members and be self-managed, self-financed, and profit-oriented. Forming a cooperative required a minimum of three members; cooperatives could not hire paid workers, but could get around this limitation by employing an unlimited number of non-members on a contract basis. Technically, cooperatives did not require special permission from local authorities although in some places, compulsory registration was required. The new cooperatives also benefitted from low tax rates on revenue and members paid lower income tax than self-employed individuals (Aslund 1991, pp. 167-170).

External Sector: The main policy changes that affected the foreign sector were those that allowed some enterprises to engage in foreign trade and provided guidelines for foreign investment in the Soviet Union. Prior to *perestroika*, the central government of the Soviet Union maintained a monopoly on foreign trade, with a central foreign trade organization (the Ministry of Foreign Trade) responsible for conducting all exports and import transactions. The new policy granted direct trading rights to 20 ministries and to 70 production associations and enterprises. As an incentive to increase exports, enterprises were allowed to retain a certain percentage of their foreign exchange earnings to buy machinery and inputs abroad (Desai 1989, p. 40).

A law authorizing foreign investment in the Soviet Union in the form of joint ventures went into effect in 1987. This was a significant step for the Soviet Union, as most other socialist countries—including China—had passed such legislation much earlier on. The creation of free economic zones, enclaves where foreign investors could operate in Soviet soil but outside of the Soviet system, were considered as part of the overall reforms of the foreign sector, but were too controversial and were not implemented during the *perestroika* period (Aslund 1991, pp. 144-145).

Implementation of *perestroika* failed to jump start the stagnant Soviet economy. In 1989, the economy ground to a halt and, in 1990, the economy underwent further deterioration so that the question was whether a breakdown of the economy was imminent. Aslund (1991, p. 182-201) argues that the *perestroika* policies were responsible for the Soviet economic crisis of 1990 because they aggravated the worst features of a centrally planned economic system: shortages of goods, fiscal and monetary imbalances, tensions in enterprise management, foreign trade imbalances. That is, the imposition of the *perestroika* reforms on a centrally planned economy were a recipe for disaster. As Aslund (1991, p. 182) succinctly puts it, "although the economic system was not the immediate cause of the economic crisis, the features of the malaise were specific for a command economy out of gear."

Campbell (1991) has examined the experiences of centrally planned economies that attempted to reform while maintaining a socialist system. He refers to countries such as Yugoslavia, Poland, China, and Hungary in the late 1980s as "semi-reformed economies," a sort of "half-way house" between the old "administrative-command" system and a market-

driven, price-regulated, private property system. Semi-reformed economies are unstable; in addition to the well known problems that plague centrally planned economies, market reforms superimposed on a centrally planned economy create a hybrid system that has distinctive new problems of its own. As Campbell (1991, pp. 165-166) puts it:

> It is clear that the semi-reformed economy is still burdened with much of the allocative ineffectiveness and incentive defects of the old system, along with some special problems all of its own. These problems can be solved only by moving farther in the direction of reform. ... On a reform thermometer calibrated by the experience of the other socialist countries, economic *perestroika* in the USSR by the end of the eighties had brought the system barely above the freezing point. It is not yet to the half-way house. It is sometimes thought that the USSR could learn from the experience of the smaller socialist countries and telescope the two stages, going much more directly to a fully reformed, marketized economy.

CUBA—LATE AND MODEST REFORMS

In the first half of the 1990s, Cuba has been experiencing an economic depression. Cut off from its normal sources of foreign trade and financing by the demise of communism in the former Soviet Union and Eastern Europe, the Cuban economy went into a tailspin after 1989 from which it has not yet fully recovered. The island's national product reportedly shrank by about one-half, and foreign trade turnover by about three-fourths, between 1989 to 1993 (Terrero 1994). There is no compelling evidence that the economic situation improved markedly in 1994; Cuban official Carlos Lage has announced that economic growth in 1994 was about 1 percent ("Lage Announces" 1995), suggesting that the economic slide may have reached bottom, but detailed data to support such conclusion have not been made available.

In the 1990s, during the so-called "special period" (*período especial en tiempo de paz*), Cuba has experimented with a set of policy initiatives aimed at breathing life into the economy. Adoption of new measures picked up speed in the summer of 1993, when several initiatives were announced, and slowed again in 1994. Another bundle of measures was implemented in the second half of 1994. Relatively little activity regarding economic policy changes has occurred in the first half of 1995.

Looking through the lens of reforms of other socialist countries, Cuba's economic policy initiatives of the 1990s are late in their adoption and quite modest in terms of breadth and depth of implementation. As will be discussed below, Cuba's recent economic policy initiatives resemble the *perestroika* economic program implemented in the former Soviet Union during 1988-90 and fall short of reform measures in other Eastern European socialist countries and China.

Timing: In the mid-1980s, as Poland and Hungary were gradually transforming their socialist systems by introducing market-oriented reforms, the Soviet Union was setting the foundation for *perestroika*, and China was *de facto* privatizing its economy, Cuba was also making important economic policy changes. However, unlike the other socialist countries, where changes were aimed at increasing flexibility and promoting decentralization in economic decisionmaking, Cuba moved in the opposite direction.

The so-called "rectification process," which began to be implemented formally in 1986, has been characterized by Mesa-Lago (1989, p. 98) as economic counter-reform, "a reversal of the previous direction, away from decentralization and the use of market mechanisms." Among the victims of rectification were the farmers' free markets and artisan markets that had been authorized in the early 1980s as a way to stimulate production and serve consumption needs of the population.

The objectives, methods, and outcomes of rectification have been discussed elsewhere (e.g., Mesa-Lago 1989 and 1993; Pérez-López 1990) and need not be revisited here. For purposes of this paper, the important point is that rectification at best froze the introduction of, and experimentation with, further market-oriented economic techniques in Cuba for a period of at least five years, and at worst brought the economy closer to the orthodox centrally planned system that operated in Cuba in the early 1970s. Because of the policy paralysis or regression associated with rectification, when Cuba began to implement its current reforms in the early 1990s, the country was less well prepared institutionally to assimilate the changes than other socialist economies at the same stage of reform.

Breadth and Depth: In comparison with the policy retrenchment or retrogression associated with rectification, the economic reforms that Cuba has implemented in the 1990s appear quite significant. They are modest, however, in comparison with reform programs put in place by other countries in transition. Cuba's reforms—legalization and liberalization of self-employment, changes in the agricultural sector that converted state farms into cooperatives, reauthorization of farmers' free markets and artisan markets, some managerial reforms, encouragement of incoming foreign investment—bear a strong resemblance to the *perestroika* program, although the Cuban reforms fail to include measures that stimulate a domestic private sector, such as those embodied in the Soviet Law on Cooperatives, and grant state enterprises freedom to manage their own affairs. Like *perestroika* in the Soviet Union, but unlike the Chinese reforms, Cuba has not undertaken meaningful price reforms and has not created free economic zones to attract investors.

Cuban reforms lack depth, and their implementation often negates the positive contribution they are intended to make. The decree legalizing and liberalizing self-employment, for example, establishes onerous registration requirements (including having to prove "honorable social behavior") and forbids physicians, teachers, and most professionals with a university-level degree from legally practicing their trade. Cuba still does not allow self-employed workers to hire helpers and form small, private businesses. Agricultural cooperatives created in the former state farms clearly have more autonomy in managing their activities than was the case before, but still have to follow instructions from the state on which crops to plant and where to sell their output.

Cuba has also back-tracked on reforms. Shortly after the enactment in September 1993 of the decree legalizing and liberalizing self-employment, private restaurants known as *paladares* sprung up in private homes throughout the island. In December 1993, the government ordered the shutdown of the *paladares* on the basis of a legal interpretation that the decree did not foresee the creation of private restaurants. In reality, the *paladares* were shut down because some of them were too successful. President Castro decried the "excesses" that had occurred as a result of the implementation of the legalization and liberalization of self-employment in several interventions before the December 1993 session of the National Assembly. For example, he said ("Castro Addresses" 1993, pp. 5-6):

> This happened in a Havana neighborhood. A restaurant was opened with 25 tables and 100 chairs and a cabaret. Some guy found himself a spot and charged 15 pesos to let people in. ... He charged in dollars, pesos, and what not. He had all the clients he needed. People from abroad would come in and bring friends and even family. I have already calculated how much the happy owner was making. He was making no less than 1000 pesos a day. And this is a conservative estimate. At least 1000 pesos a day. And all this because things had opened up a bit.

Concerned about the possibility that liberalization associated with the economic reforms would bring about the enrichment of some individuals, effective in May 1994 the penal code was amended to facilitate the prosecution of "profiteers." The law granted the government sweeping powers to confiscate all cash, goods, and assets of individuals found guilty of profiteering and provided for retroactive application of sanctions for this offense. Decisions of the Ministry of Finance to confiscate cash, goods, or assets are not subject to judicial review.

Grudgingly, the government authorized *paladares* in mid-June 1995, placing very severe limitations on their operation to prevent the successes that Castro had so vehemently criticized. A government decree authorized self-employment related to the production and sale of foods and beverages in an individual's home provided: 1)tables and chairs were limited to no more than 12 persons; and 2) subject to the payment of a stiff monthly fee of 400 pesos in national currency or 300 pesos in convertible currency. The decree restated that those self-employed in this line of work would have to meet all requirements un-

der existing law (including demonstrating "honorable social behavior") and be properly licensed. Moreover, according to the decree, self-employed workers engaged in the preparation and sale of foods and beverages in their own homes could only be aided by family members and could not hire others. Finally, when required by authorities, operators of eating establishments in their own homes would have to justify "the origin of the products used to perform the activity" ("Joint Resolution" 1995, p. 5).

Writings by Cuban economists suggest that additional economic reform measures within a socialist system are under consideration (Carranza 1995; Carranza and Alonso 1994; Monreal and Rúa del Llano 1994). However, the nature and timing of such reform measures are not known to the general public or to researchers.

CONCLUDING REMARKS

The current Cuban government seeks a reform model that will bring about vigorous economic growth while maintaining the Cuban Communist Party and its current leadership in political control. Simultaneous achievement of these two goals is extremely difficult, with China being perhaps the only example where it has been accomplished to date. Rather than replicating the Chinese reform model, however, Cuba's policymakers have steered closer to the *perestroika* model implemented in the former Soviet Union under Gorbachev which resulted in a chaotic economic situation. Cuban economic reforms to date are modest and have been implemented half-heartedly. As with other partial reforms, economic recovery is unlikely.

The Cuban people have paid a heavy price in the 1990s in terms of their standards of living, consumption levels, and quality of services they receive. Between 1989 and 1993, per capita gross domestic product shrank by about one-half; merchandise exports fell by 69 percent; and merchandise imports declined by 75 percent. Consumption of food and both durable and nondurable goods was sharply reduced, with rationing reinstated for a wide range of staple foods and personal hygiene and clothing items, and monthly allowances scaled back. Electricity shortages and blackouts became commonplace, and transportation services were sharply curtailed. Public health and education, two of the sacred cows of the Cuban regime, were also scaled back, and the quality of services deteriorated (Pérez-López 1995, p. 11).

In the 1990s, Cuba faces its worst economic crisis since independence (Ritter 1994, p. 67). The roughly 50 percent reduction in national product per capita is unprecedented in the nation's post-World War II history and extremely high by international standards. An examination of national statistics collated by international organizations does not show contractions in national product over a five-year period of the magnitude of Cuba's. It is tempting to set out the proposition that the island's drop in economic activity over 1989-93 represents a contemporary (negative) world record of sorts. Such a categorical statement cannot be made, however, since the appropriate data are not available for Cambodia (Kampuchea) and Laos, two economies that are known to

have shrunk sharply in the 1970s because of wars and the pursuit by their leaders of radical economic policies.

To conclude, a case could be made that the Cuban economy, and the Cuban people, have paid the price of the most severe type of "shock therapy"— arguably a recipe worst than that prescribed by the International Monetary Fund—without attaining the potential benefits associated with systemic transformation. Cuba's *perestroika*-like reforms of the 1990s seem to have been successful only on one count: prolonging the rule of Fidel Castro and the communist party *nomenklatura*. Fidel Castro has now overtaken General Alfredo Stroessner of Paraguay as the longest-lasting head of state in contemporary Latin America, a (dubious) achievement in terms of longevity, but one that does not put food on the table or improves the material situation of the overwhelming majority of the Cuban people.

REFERENCES

Aslund, Anders. 1991. *Gorbachev's Struggle for Economic Reform.* Ithaca: Cornell University Press.

Balassa, Bela. 1991. "China's Economic Reforms in a Comparative Perspective." *Journal of Comparative Economics* 11:3 (September):410-426.

Benjamin, Medea. 1994. *Cuba: Talking About Revolution—Conversations with Juan Antonio Blanco.* Melbourne, Australia: Ocean Press.

Burki, Shahid Javed. 1988. "Reform and Growth in China." *Finance and Development* 25:4 (December):46-49.

Campbell, Robert W. 1991. *The Socialist Economies in Transition.* Bloomington: Indiana University Press.

Carranza, Julio. 1995. "Los cambios económicos en Cuba: Problemas y desafíos." *Cuadernos de Nuestra América* 11:22 (July-December):26-40.

_____, and Aurelio Alonso. 1994. *Economía cubana: Ajustes con socialismo.* La Habana: Editorial de Ciencias Sociales.

"Castro Addresses 28 December ANPP Session." 1993. Havana Radio Rebelde Network (29 December), as reproduced in *FBIS-LAT-93-249* (30 December):2-10.

"China estudia ampliación de comercio con isla." 1995. *El Nuevo Herald* (17 March):13A.

"China: Is Prosperity Creating a Freer Society?" 1994. *Time* (6 June):94-99.

"China's Communists: The Road from Tiananmen." 1994. *The Economist* (4 June):19-21.

Desai, Padma. 1989. *Perestroika in Perspective.* Princeton: Princeton University Press.

Fernández, Damián J. 1993. "Cuba's Relations with China: Economic Pragmatism and Political Fluctuation." In *Cuba's Ties to a Changing*

World, ed. Kaplowitz, pp. 17-31. Boulder: Lynne Rienner.

____. 1994. "Continuity and Change in Cuba's International Relations in the 1990s." In *Cuba at a Crossroads*, ed. Pérez-López, pp. 41-66. Gainesville: University Press of Florida.

Goldman, Marshall I. 1987. *Gorbachev's Challenge.* New York: W.W. Norton.

Gorbachev, Mikhail. 1987. *Perestroika: New Thinking for Our Country and the World.* New York: Harper & Row.

Harrold, Peter. 1992. *China's Reform Experience to Date.* Discussion Paper No. 180. Washington: World Bank.

"Joint Resolution Addresses Self-Employment Activities." 1995. Havana Tele Rebelde and Cuba Vision Networks (15 June), as reproduced in *FBIS-LAT-95-115* (15 June):5-6.

Koo, Anthony Y.C. 1990. "The Contract Responsibility System: Transition from a Planned to a Market Economy." *Economic Development and Cultural Change* 38:4 (July):797-820.

"Lage Announces 1 Percent Growth at World Economic Forum." 1995. Havana Radio Rebelde Network (28 January), as reproduced in *FBIS-LAT-95-020* (31 January):4.

McMillan, John, John Whalley, and Zhu Li Jing. 1987. "Incentive Effects of Price Rises and Payment-System Changes on Chinese Agricultural Productivity Growth." National Bureau of Economic Research Working Paper No. 2148 (February).

Mesa-Lago, Carmelo. 1989. "Cuba's Economic Counter-Reform (*Rectificación*): Causes, Policies, and Effects." *The Journal of Communist Studies* 5:4 (December):98-139.

____. 1993. "Cuba's Economic Policies and Strategies for Confronting the Crisis." *In Cuba After the Cold War,* ed. Mesa-Lago, pp. 197-257. Pittsburgh: University of Pittsburgh Press.

____. 1994. *Are Economic Reforms Propelling Cuba to the Market?* Coral Gables, Florida: North-South Center, University of Miami.

Monreal, Pedro, and Manuel Rúa del Llano. 1994. "Apertura y reforma de la economía cubana: Las transformaciones institucionales (1990-1993)." *Estudios Internacionales* 27:107/108 (July-September/October-December):542-569.

Naughton, Barry. 1994. "Chinese Institutional Innovation and Privatization from Below." *American Economic Review* 84:2 (May):266-270.

Pérez-López, Jorge F. 1990. "Rectification at Three: Impact on the Cuban Economy." *Studies in Comparative International Development* 25:3 (Fall):3-36.

____. 1995. "Castro Tries Survival Strategy." *Transition* 6:3 (March) 11-14.

Perkins, Dwight H. 1989. "Reforming China's Economic System." *Journal of Economic Literature* 26:2 (June):601-645.

Prybyla, Jan S. 1990. "Economic Reform of Socialism: The Dengist Course in China." *The Annals of the American Academy of Political and Social Science* 507 (January):113-122.

Rawski, Thomas G. 1994. "Chinese Industrial Reform: Accomplishments, Prospects, and Implications." *American Economic Review* 84:2 (May):271-275.

Ritter, Archibald R. M. 1994. "Cuba's Economic Strategy and Alternative Futures." In *Cuba at a Crossroads*, ed. Pérez-López, pp. 67-93. Gainesville: University Press of Florida.

Singh, Inderjit. 1992. *China: Industrial Policies for an Economy in Transition.* Discussion Paper No. 143. Washington: World Bank.

Sklair, Leslie. 1991. "Problems of Socialist Development: The Significance of Shenzhen Special Economic Zone for China's Open Door Policy." *International Journal of Urban and Regional Research* 15:2, pp. 197-215.

Terrero, Ariel. 1994. "Tendencias de un ajuste." *Bohemia* 85:22 (28 October):B30-B39.

Tyler, Patrick E. 1995. "Chinese Leader Says `Mistakes' By Government Fueled Inflation." *The New York Times* (6 March):A1, A9.

U.S. Department of State. 1995. *Country Reports on Human Rights Practices for 1994*. Washington: U.S. Government Printing Office.

"When China Wakes." 1991. *The Economist* (28 November), Survey Section.

EVALUATION OF CHANGES IN ECONOMIC POLICY IN CUBA

Jorge A. Sanguinetty

In order to evaluate Cuba's movements towards some forms of market economics, let us first identify the conditions that characterize a market economy in its most ideal state. Then we will be able to determine the magnitude and significance of the deviations between the model and the practice, actual or projected.

DEFINITION OF A MARKET ECONOMY

In its purest state, a market economy can be defined as one that cannot be affected by the decisions or actions—mainly purchases or sales—of a single agent or decision-maker. This implies that no agent has the power, economic or otherwise, to significantly alter the workings of such an economy. The quantities of the goods and services transacted in a market economy, and their corresponding prices, are determined by the simultaneous and continuous decisions of innumerable agents pursuing their self-interest.[1]

One central characteristic of a market economy is the freedom with which individuals can make decisions and express preferences about consumption and production alternatives. A consumer, for instance, reveals his or her preferences in a market by choosing what he or she wants within a budget constraint. A worker, on the other hand, expresses his preferences in the labor market by choosing how much time to dedicate to work and how much to other activities. Entrepreneurs choose production technologies, and production factors and resources (mainly labor and capital) to produce what they expect consumers will buy. If they produce what consumers want, they will be rewarded; if they make a mistake in this regard, they may lose their businesses and leave their workers unemployed. All individuals, either as consumers, workers or entrepreneurs (a special category of worker) also make decisions about how much to consume and how much to save for future use or investment. This involves decisions on how much to hold as wealth and what to do with it. Private property rights are derived from these freedoms and represent one of the pillars of a market economy.

In other words, free choice and decentralized power are vital characteristics of a market economy. Without them, all production and distribution activities become distorted and less efficient. In order to maximize social welfare, an economy should work under these conditions. The role of government should never include intervention in markets (prices, levels of production, etc.), but be limited to providing the rules of the game; guaranteeing property rights, contractual security, and competition; and making provisions for the supply of public goods (national security, public order, etc.)

First Tier Imperfections of the Theoretical Model

The ideal market economy would be in what economists call long-term competitive equilibrium. It depends on virtually perfect flows of information among decision-makers. At the same time, long-run competitive equilibrium can only be achieved when there is no innovation of any form, Thus, in reality,

---

1. Self-interest does not exclude altruistic behavior, but implies that individuals make decisions on their own, without any external coercion to behave as if they were altruistic.

even the most efficient market systems are always operating around equilibrium positions but they manage to grow and provide increasing levels of welfare to its members. One possible deviation of the market system arises when there are monopolies, or rent-seeking coalitions, that distort prices preventing them to respond to regular supply and demand conditions. However, these deviations can be controlled—or at least their impact can be minimized—when the government intervenes in behalf of freedom and competition. But the reverse does not hold.

Government Induced Deviations

When governments intervene on the premise that they can correct "market imperfections" and also improve efficiency and equity of a market economy, economic theory demonstrates, and practice teaches us, that distortions are severe and welfare loses instantly occur. The reason for this is relatively simple: no government has the wherewithal to gather and process the amount of information that a market system requires to be efficient. No computer system or algorithm managed by a group of bureaucrats can replace the versatility and capacity of millions of decision makers pursuing their own interests. The more centralized the government is, the worse the information glut it creates and the more serious become the deviations from a market system.

Privately Induced Deviations

Governments are not the only actors who create distortions in a market system. Rent-seeking individuals or coalitions may exercise influence to have legislation enacted creating certain privileges, such as protective tariffs and quotas, monopolies, etc. A society committed to a market economy will have a government capable of monitoring these phenomena and enforcing the rules of the game to guarantee fair practices in competition. This implies that having or not having a market economy is a social contract not simply a matter of decision by a single government.

THE CUBAN DEVIATIONS

Cuban deviations from a market economy were extreme with the installation—formally although not in reality—of a Stalinist centrally planned economy. In 1960, as the country started building a socialist economy, the country lost its traditional markets, its investors, and its entrepreneurs. It also started losing its production capacity in almost every single industry. The Soviet subsidies hid for three decades the Cuban inability to produce. Their disappearance uncovered a sad reality: Cuba not only destroyed a market-based economic system that, despite its problems, provided a degree of welfare and independence to the country, but also failed to develop a socialist economy with at least a mediocre productive capability.

In adopting a socialist economic system, the Cuban Government imposed itself an internal embargo on all productive activities of the country. In adopting a policy of confrontation and antagonism with the United States, besides the massive expropriations of U.S. holdings, it provoked the external embargo by the United States that has lasted for over three decades. The Cuban Government adopted a myopic attitude towards the U.S. embargo until it realized, even before the demise of the Soviet Union, that the embargo was a liability for the country. What they never have realized is that the main problem is the planning system they adopted. The U.S. embargo obviously exacerbates the problem, but its unilateral lifting is not the complete solution to Cuban economic problems.

The process of dismantling the pre-1960 Cuban economic system that took centuries to developed can be summarized as follows: a) a virtual total loss of free choice for consumers, workers, and other economic agents; b) an extreme centralization of economic power in one single person, Fidel Castro; c) a dramatic loss of the closest and most natural external markets for Cuba's imports and exports; d) a deviation of economic resources to wage war and finance subversion in other countries; e) complete secrecy, total lack of transparency on the use of funds by the government; and f) loss of Cuba's best human resources, especially entrepreneurs, and consequent loss of productive and investment capabilities.

CURRENT CHANGES IN CUBA: HOW FAR FROM A MARKET ECONOMY?

The Cuban Government does not seem to have a master or game plan to install a market economy, or even a mixed economy. The first piece of evidence is the repeated public utterances of president Fidel Castro when he declares his commitment to Marxist values and socialism and expresses his criticisms of market economies at large.

The current changes seem to obey a strategy of slow retreat as, first, foreign investment, second, the efforts to develop tourism, and third, the reluctant liberalization of self employment and farmers markets, fail to produce the economic recovery that the country desperately needs.

If the Cuban Government were serious about genuine economic reforms it would try to relax the political system to some degree. It is simply inconceivable that a market economy or even a mixed economy can coexist with the current degree of political absolutism present in Cuba. A one-man government does not provide sufficient guarantees to foreign investors and traders. Even if we accept the need to have a strong executive to implement profound economic changes in a country, the current situation in Cuba is ridiculous.

There is no middle ground between a market economy and a centrally planned system that can be justified on arguments of efficiency or equity. The evidence of the reduced efficiency of state enterprises is overwhelming and cannot be ignored by serious scholars. The so-called achievements of the Cuban revolution in matters of health and education can be maintained by a market economy through a well-designed tax and fiscal expenditure system or by other means, without having to sacrifice economic freedoms. The fact is that social gains must be affordable

and therefore based on an efficient economic system. The social "conquistas" of the revolution were funded by the Soviet system, therefore they were not real achievements. Anybody knows how to spend; few know how to create wealth.

A more efficient economic system must be de-politicized. Economic considerations, not political ones, must prevail in economic decision making. In order to achieve this, economic agents (consumers, workers, investors, etc.) must have sufficient freedom of choice and economic power, even if their political choice is still constrained. Economic changes in Cuba are so far cosmetic in essence, simply because the government refuses to give a role to the Cubans.

Finally, the U.S. embargo undoubtedly constrains the development of the Cuban economy, but not more so than the current economic and social systems in Cuba. Such systems, combined with the lack of transparency in the management of fiscal matters in Cuba, determine that the advantages to the Cuban population of an eventual lifting of the embargo are severely limited. Fidel Castro today would be the main beneficiary of the lifting of the embargo, while the Cuban population would only receive token benefits. More than thirty years of experience in the mismanagement of public affairs sustain this proposition. The current economic crisis has halted Fidel Castro's ability to finance subversion outside Cuba. Without fundamental changes (in personnel as well as in structure) in the Cuban political system, little positive can be expected on behalf of the Cuban public interest.

FINANCING THE ECONOMIC RECONSTRUCTION OF CUBA WHILE REBUILDING THE FINANCIAL SECTOR: PERSPECTIVES ON DEVELOPMENT BANKING

Manuel Lasaga

Since the 1950s, development banks have evolved from their role as banks for everyone, usually funded by the Central Bank at subsidized terms, into that of specialized financial intermediaries, though still government-owned, but now lending primarily through commercial banks, under market-determined terms and conditions. Those countries that have succeeded in transforming the role of development banks along these lines, benefitted by the existence of a long-standing and viable banking system, which was able to efficiently assume those activities which had previously been performed by the development banks.

Because it lacks a financial sector infrastructure, Cuba is currently not equipped to implement an effective development financing strategy. Unfortunately, the liberalization of the economy, when it does occur, will require drastic and immediate action in certain areas, while a gradual and flexible approach in others, and as a consequence, it may not be possible to achieve the desired sequencing of first, rebuilding the financial sector, and second, implementing an economic reconstruction program. The final outcome may be somewhere between a big bang and a big bust.

Following the initial efforts at economic stabilization, which could actually trigger unstable reactions, the government will need to implement a comprehensive strategy to rebuild the economy's productive capacity, with a focus on the development of a viable financial system and the privatization of existing government enterprises. This paper reviews some of the critical issues dealing with the establishment of efficient development financing vehicles, which, at the same time, could serve as the catalyst for the development of the financial sector under private sector initiative. While some recommendations are made to assist in the development of private sector commercial banks, the principal focus of this paper is the role of development banks during the transition. This is not meant as a comprehensive analysis of all the relevant financial sector issues affecting the reconstruction and development of the economy, but rather a discussion of some highly relevant aspects. While some reference is made to experiences in Eastern Europe and the ex-Soviet republics with development banks and financial sector reforms, Cuba's experience is more likely to resemble that of its neighboring Latin American economies, but under a more severe case of disequilibrium and with greater haste in getting reforms through.

STABILIZATION IN AN UNSTABLE ENVIRONMENT

The starting point for any sustainable structural reform program should be an acceptably stable economic environment The design of the structural reform program should in turn depend on the country's initial conditions. For example, a pre-condition for the implementation of investment banking and capital market reforms should be the existence of a strong commercial banking sector, supported by a solid money market, and supervised by highly qualified regulators and responding to an autonomous and credible Central Bank as manager of monetary policy. If none of these conditions are present at the start of the a structural reform program, its design needs to be very simple and should focus on very few basic policies. Because of inadequate initial conditions, Cuba will be at a major disadvantage whenever the Government initiates any fundamental reform program. After more than 35 years of almost total Government control over the economy, where the official economy has operated in the absence of any (legal) market mechanisms, the return to a free market economy will be overwhelmingly difficult. This point has been articulated extensively in numerous academic studies on the subject, and clearly demonstrated by the experience of the ex-Soviet republics.[1]

The Cuban economy's dire initial conditions are likely to defy any attempts at stabilization, at least for a number of years. By a stable economy we usually mean a combination of low inflation, facilitated by a small fiscal deficit, and stable international reserves, which in turn will hinge on a normal response of exports and imports to market signals under a suitable currency management policy. During 1991-94, the economy suffered an unprecedented collapse, whereby production in the official market fell to about 20-25 percent of capacity.[2] At the same time, domestic prices as well as the price of the currency have been practically frozen since the early 1960s. Under these circumstances, the implementation of market reforms is bound to create an almost chaotic economic environment. There is no compelling evidence of any attempt to implement similar changes in other countries that have not produced major economic disruption. In some cases, a dramatic stabilization program accompanied by aggressive structural reforms has actually veered off the scale and worsened economic conditions, and thus further delayed the return to normal conditions. One of the more pertinent examples of this adverse response to reforms is the imple-

mentation of price liberalization which can unleash a hyper-inflationary spiral such as occurred in Russia after 1990. Inevitably these negative experiences raise the question of whether the ends justify the means. Should the objective of establishing a market-based economy override all costs incurred during the transition. Can the government adequately compensate all those adversely affected by the reforms? Or does it have the political capital to withstand widespread discontent and possibly social disorder?

In view of the great obstacles to change, the organization of stabilization and structural reform programs will be an extremely difficult task. As a pioneer of structural reform lending, the World Bank has learned many lessons in the design of sustainable structural reform programs. Two of the Bank's lessons which are of particular relevance to Cuba are: (i) when there are multiple distortions in the economy, the design of an optimal sequence of reforms is very difficult; and (ii) reforms that require the development of institutions and adequate human capital should proceed very cautiously.[3] On both of these counts, Cuba's prospects appear dim. Unraveling decades of distorted economic linkages in order to hastily design comprehensive structural reform programs will very likely produce highly undesirable results, and inflict severe hardship on the Cuban people. Because of its vulnerability to sudden changes in the economic environment, the financial sector will thus be exposed to a very high risk of collapse during the critical stabilization period.

A QUICK FIX COULD BE DEVASTATING

One of the buzz words in stabilization policies is shock treatment. The premise for this approach is that a radical change in the rules of the game would immediately produce a new desirable economic environment, and would thus wipe out any memory or any excess baggage from the past. If a reform-bound government were to decree free markets, after having

---

1. For additional references see Association for the Study of the Cuban Economy, *Cuba in Transition,* Volumes 2, 3 and 4, 1992, 1993 and 1994 respectively.

2. See Manuel Lasaga, "Dollarization: Scrambling for Foreign Exchange," in *CubaNews,* The Miami Herald, September 1993.

3. See Vittorio Corbo, Stanley Fisher, and Steven B. Webb, eds., *Adjustment Lending Revisited,* The World Bank, 1992.

exerted absolute control over the economy for many years, the shock therapy approach predicts that the morning after, economic agents will begin to operate efficiently using market signals as their *modus operandi*. In a comparative static analysis, this predicted outcome would appear to be a reasonable scenario. However, when we introduce a dynamic adjustment process in an unstable environment, the simplistic approach could be more harmful than the *status quo*. In this regard, the multilateral lending agencies have learned many lessons on the hazards of economic restructuring. Unfortunately, entrepreneurs are not created by simply legislating their existence. In fact, entrepreneurs are a very small minority within the business community, even in highly developed economies, and adding to their numbers is a slow evolutionary process.

In recent years the establishment of a fixed exchange rate regime, accompanied by the "dollarization" of the economy, with a monetary board which makes sure that every unit of local currency is backed by dollars, has been gaining popularity in countries that have experienced high inflation and severe international liquidity problems, and which seek a quick solution to these problems. This has been proposed as one of the economic stabilization mechanisms that Cuba could apply when it initiates a fundamental reform process. The fixed exchange rate mechanism as managed by a monetary board in effect represents a draw back to the days of the gold standard as it was applied to the currencies of the then existing colonies. Unfortunately the gold standard monetary system failed because of the lack of discipline by the member countries. The appeal of the fixed exchange rate mechanism lies in its simplicity. However, its sustainability calls for an exceedingly high level of fiscal, monetary, and economic discipline by all economic agents, which will be far beyond the reach of Cuba when it embarks on a perilous path to stabilization.

One of the risks of "dollarization" of the economy is that it could create a false sense of stability in thinking that the relative strength of the dollar would solve Cuba's economic problems, and that the stability and strength of the U.S. economy would be extended to

Cuba through this currency linkage. The negative experience of Liberia and Panama with "dollarization" has diminished the credibility of this mechanism. While Panama survived major political and economic upheaval during the late 1980s, the existence of a dollarized economy did not prevent those problems from surfacing.

On the other hand, the use of a fixed exchange rate might be expedient under certain conditions, as when the monetary authorities seek to stabilize domestic prices, but only for a temporary period. The problem arises when the government locks in the mechanism, as if it could place economic management on automatic pilot, and refuses to change it even when the currency becomes grossly overvalued.

Because of its complexity, the financial system is highly vulnerable to rapid structural economic changes. Financial intermediation is a highly leveraged low-margin business where the primary determinant of profitability is the risk-adjusted interest rate margin. In the case of open economies, the banking system is exposed to yet another and sometimes devastating source of risk through currency fluctuations and highly volatile capital flows. Drastic changes in interest rates caused by dramatic shifts in economic policy could inflict irreparable damage on the operations of a financial intermediary. As a consequence, the use of quick fix or simplistic mechanisms could seriously undermine the stability of the financial sector. For example, locking in the value of the currency with respect to the dollar, could create a false sense of security as banks fund dollars overseas and then make dollar denominated loans to local companies. However, their borrowers could be totally un-hedged. A collapse of the financial system brought on by sudden shifts in the economic environment would result in a severe liquidity crunch in the economy that could then trigger a major depression.

FLOWING WITH THE CURRENT

The possibility that the Cuban economy will enter a period of instability during the transition to a market-based system, combined with the vulnerability of the financial sector to unpredictable events, would support the use of a flexible approach in setting transition policies. Proper sequencing of structural reforms is essential, but sometimes it may be necessary to put aside the logical structures and pursue a more eclectic approach. At other times gradual changes may be more appropriate than shock treatment. The pitfall of policy makers would be to try to fit the Cuban economy into a rigid model that is inconsistent with the initial conditions.

Emphasis should be placed on the quality of the economic management team and its ability to navigate in a tumultuous climate. Economic advice should be taken only after careful consideration of Cuba's unique situation, specially its unstable initial conditions. One of the lessons from reform programs in other countries is that the design of structural reforms should be determined on a case-by-case basis. Economic models based on the experiences of other countries that have adopted dramatic economic reforms should be referenced in making policy decisions; but at the same time, these models should be discarded if they lead to undesirable consequences. Once again, the economic management team will have to decide when to change the course, even if it means changing the course for structural reforms that may take many years to produce the expected results, and yet the government does not have the luxury of time to see the final outcome. Successful passage through the transition to a market-based economy will mean that Cuba will have written its own textbook on the reform process.

ECONOMIC POLICY GUIDELINES OF RELEVANCE TO THE DEVELOPMENT OF THE FINANCIAL SECTOR

This discussion does not attempt to identify all the components of a comprehensive economic reform program, but to present those elements of importance to the development of the financial sector, and more specifically, to the establishment of a viable development banking institution(s). Satisfactory management of these policy areas is a basic requirement for the sustainable expansion of the financial sector and thus the transition from a viable development banking led reconstruction of the economy to a sustainable private sector led commercial banking system.

Price and interest rate liberalization

Price and interest rate liberalization will perhaps be the most unpredictable and potentially disruptive element of a stabilization program. In an ideal situation, domestic prices should be market-determined. The fact that prices have been set rigidly for decades, raises the potential of a hyper-inflationary spiral during the transition period. The ability to curtail the fiscal deficit while shrinking the role of the government in the economy will be a critical factor in the success of any price stabilization strategy. No enduring progress will ever be achieved in the financial sector without first drastically reducing the fiscal deficit, and second, instituting a credible monetary authority, so that price stability can be reasonably assured. The importance of controlling the fiscal deficit in achieving price stability can never be over-emphasized. Even with satisfactory progress in the implementation of stabilization policies, the lack of supply responses to price signals, inherent in a collapsed economy in which the government has controlled all decisions, and which lacks the basic corporate unit of economic organization, is bound to intensify inflationary pressures from any price liberalization.

Chronic inflationary problems will impede the development of the financial sector by exacerbating economic volatility, which will thus discourage domestic financial savings, and by raising real interest rates to unsustainable levels, will severely limit access to credit as well as threaten the quality of the newly emerging banks' portfolios.

In addition to price stability, one of the basic conditions for an efficient financial system is the existence of market determined interest rates. However, during the transition period, there may not be a feasible market mechanism for determining interest rates. The government may have to assume an interventionist role by setting interest rates, preferably by use of a formula which would assure that rates reflect a reasonable return to savers, or that they compensate for the time value of money adjusted by the level of risk in the financial system. Once the market mechanisms to negotiate interest rates are put in place, liberalization of rates should be phased in.

Clear rules of the game

The safety and soundness of the financial sector will hinge on the reconstruction of Cuba's legal and regulatory infrastructure. A credible constitution, along with a basic body of laws governing, among others, commercial and banking activities, are primordial conditions. The question of property rights and pending resolution to property claims dating back to the time of the 1959 revolution would have to be resolved quickly. The establishment of a land registry which allows the issuance of valid titles will be an essential ingredient for the development of mortgage-based lending. If the lengthy process associated with the passage of economic reform legislation in other Latin American countries is an indication, then the establishment of these basic legal ingredients for the development of a rudimentary market-based capitalist system in Cuba will pose a major challenge to the government during the transition.

Effective enforcement of the rules

The passage of appropriate legislation governing economic activity and its regulation is only a first step towards sustainable economic development. The key to success is in the adequacy of enforcement mechanisms. The recent episodes of financial sector crises in Latin America can be attributed in part to excessive risk taking resulting from inadequate supervision. For example, Mexico had made important changes in its banking legislation during 1990-91, which set the stage for the subsequent privatization of the banks that had been nationalized in 1982. Nevertheless, the banks failed to implement adequate risk management procedures, and the authorities failed to respond to these problems until after a full-fledged financial crisis had erupted.

Cuba lacks both the legal infrastructure and the supervisory capabilities that will in turn support the development of a financial sector. There are no laws supporting the establishment of corporations to do business, no generally accepted accounting standards, no property rights, and the current government has

no experience in managing a market-based economy.[4]

One of the more troublesome issues in the enforcement of new laws and regulations will be the ability of the government to control black-market or criminal activities. There is practically no information on the current size and scope of the black-market in Cuba. In view of the recent collapse of the official economy, the absence of famine or other serious health problems would indicate that the black market is thriving. People are able to survive by engaging in so-called criminal activities. If the government were to liberalize the economy and allow free markets, would the economic agents in the illegal markets then have an incentive to participate in a formal economy where they would have to pay taxes and to abstain from certain questionable practices? The answer to this question will depend on the present value of their expected profits under the new system compared to their expected profits from continuing to engage in illegal market activities, where the benefits from engaging in illegal franchises would have to be adjusted by the expected value of potential penalties if any are to be enforced. Criminal forces may also be able to resist attempts by a legitimate government to eliminate their illegal activities. Due to the lack of information on the size of the black market or its activities, there are no good answers to these questions.

Currency liberalization with selective foreign exchange controls

During the transition period the peso will be subjected to maxi-devaluations as domestic prices begin to catch up to market realities and the government seeks to promote a competitive economy supported by a dynamic export sector. At some point it may be desirable to manipulate the value of the currency in order to combat inflationary pressures. Foreign exchange controls could be used selectively. Another option would be the use of tariffs to indirectly adjust the value of the currency by increasing the cost of imports and the benefits to exports. The use of a dual

---

4. There are a limited number of special purpose corporations such as of joint ventures with foreign investors, and those that engage in international trade.

currency market could provide some temporary relief for essential goods. Whatever mechanisms are chosen, their departure from generally accepted market-determined operating procedures should be viewed as a temporary phenomenon. Unfortunately experience amply demonstrates that once a government deviates from the pro-market approach to economic policy, it is very difficult to reinstate market principles. Nevertheless, there is no easy solution to the problem of getting the currency to float near a stable equilibrium. A drastic liberalization of the currency could have the undesirable result of adding three digits to the exchange rate without moving closer to equilibrium.

While the government may decide to actively manage the currency during the transition, the trading of the currency should be dispersed extensively via the financial sector in preparation for an eventual liberalization of the currency markets. For this reason, banks should be allowed to trade in foreign exchange, and not have a separate entity such as the foreign exchange houses which may be more difficult to supervise, and which have a tendency to lure transactions that evade foreign exchange controls.

Privatization

Following the initial phase of stabilization and economic liberalization, the government will need to implement a comprehensive strategy to rebuild the economy's production capacity, with a focus on the privatization of existing government enterprises. The establishment of a privatization agency charged with the implementation of the government's privatization strategies should be a high priority. This agency could become the financial agent in charge of preparing the necessary valuations and initial public offering documentation, and subsequently conducting the sale of the shares, whether directly to individual investors or through a public auction.

External Debt

Access to the international financial markets hinges on the borrower's economic performance as well as on current and past status regarding debt service payments. Relations between Cuba and the international financial community deteriorated sharply during the 1980s. The economic collapse, triggered by the with-

drawal of Soviet aid in the early 1990s, was also caused by Cuba's inability to obtain other sources of financing due to its record of non-payment on external debt. The bulk of the current external debt is owed to Russia, formerly the Soviet Union. Since a good part of this debt is denominated in rubles, the disintegration in the value of the ruble in dollar terms has created an opportunity for Cuba to repay all its Russian debt at a pittance in dollar terms, but this would have to be done before the peso is allowed to float, and thus before the resulting change in the cross-rate between the peso and the ruble make this debt expensive once again. With respect to its hard currency debt, Cuba will need to initiate negotiations with its creditors, since the participation of foreign banks in the reconstruction of the economy hinges on a satisfactory settlement of existing obligations.

One of the debt reduction mechanisms, which was developed during the debt crisis of the 1980s, is the debt-equity swap. Cuba has already been utilizing this facility to attract foreign investments from Europe and the Western Hemisphere. The use of debt-equity swaps, whenever these are properly managed in terms of exchange ratios and monetary consequences, should be continued.

AN EMBRYONIC FINANCIAL SECTOR

Because of its unique condition, there is no ready-made paradigm for the rebuilding of Cuba's financial system. While the lessons of other comparable countries will provide useful insights, the development of Cuba's financial sector will be driven by its own political-economic environment, and as a consequence, the final outcome will not only repeat the mistakes of others, but will also give rise to many new ones, just as it will also create new innovative mechanisms to deal with the challenges of financing the reconstruction of the economy while developing the financial sector. Sometimes the lessons from a country could actually become the mistakes for another. For example, recommending that the monetary authorities of a country assure that domestic interest rates reflect a positive margin over the inflation rate, could backfire in a country which is receiving a large inflow of foreign capital, since the higher domestic interest rates would further intensify the capital inflows and thus complicate the management of the monetary aggregates.

The issues raised by this paper deal primarily with the embryonic stage in the development of Cuba's financial sector, whenever the government decides to implement a fundamental economic reform program as described above. The three principal players during this initial transition period would be the *Banco Nacional de Cuba* (BNC) as Central Bank, a strong development bank, and a limited number of private sector commercial banks. As proposed by the Cuban Banking Study Group, the development of the private banking sector during the transition period could be accomplished by the establishment of a banking consortium comprised of the government's development bank, foreign commercial banks, and the previously expropriated banks, whose owners would have the right to apply for reactivation of their banking licenses.[5] The development of the capital markets, which would include investment banking, insurance, and pension funds would follow in a subsequent phase.

This proposal thus emphasizes the need for sequencing in terms of the principal institutional structures. Doing everything at once, without appropriate mechanisms and controls, could lead to unstable conditions. Proponents of an immediate open house for all financial services base their recommendation on the presumption that this would create a dynamic environment for financial innovation driven by competitive forces. However, the validity of their conclusions would depend on the freedom of entry and exit, on the availability of experienced professionals, on responsible behavior by all players, and on the existence of viable market mechanisms. In a country where markets have not functioned for more than 35 years, the notion that an entrepreneurial financial sector culture could be created overnight is not a realistic assumption. For this reason, the development of the financial sector will need to follow a sequential process with a strong role for development banks during the transition. While another option would be for the government to allow foreign banks to practically divvy up Cuba's financial sector among themselves, this would not be a politically viable solution, and one which no other country has found acceptable.

Current Status of the Financial Sector

The expropriation of all commercial banks in 1960, marked the end of the formal banking system in Cuba.[6] Subsequently, the Central Bank, *Banco Nacional de Cuba* (BNC) became the principal financial intermediary with more than 200 branches throughout the country. In effect the BNC assumed the dual role of Central Bank and commercial bank. In 1983, the government established a new entity called *Banco Popular de Ahorros* with more than 500 agencies and branches throughout the country accepting savings accounts from small savers, and offering consumer and mortgage loans. In addition, *Banco Financiero Internacional,* was established as an offshore banking vehicle to manage the government's international trade accounts, and to act as agent bank for foreign corporations operating under joint venture partnerships in Cuba. Since 1984, foreign banks have been allowed to establish representative offices in Cuba. Several European banks have opened representative offices mostly to serve their home country clients doing business in Cuba, and to finance Cuban exports, in which case they use the export commodities as collateral for the loans.

The current financial system is in a primitive stage of development. Operating procedures are inadequate, and thus the quality of the financial system's assets are highly questionable. Reliable information on the financial condition of the above mentioned banks is almost non-existent. Under these conditions, it is reasonable to conclude that after the expropriation of

---

5. The idea to create a private sector consortium of domestic banks, through the reactivation of the banking licenses of the confiscated banks, and with the participation of foreign banks was proposed in *The Creation of UNIBANCO, A Consortium of National and International Banks*, by the Cuban Banking Study Group, Inc., November 1994.

6. For more information see *Cuba: Past, Present and Future of its Banking and Financial System*, Cuban Banking Study Group, Inc., 1995.

the banks in 1960, financial intermediation basically disappeared, except for international trade, which is dependent on the expertise of *Banco Financiero Internacional*. Because of the poor state of the banking system as it exists today, this proposal recommends the establishment of *de novo* institutions rather than attempting to retrofit the current insolvent institutions, with the exception of BNC, which would go back to serving its role as the Central Bank.

Central Bank as credible manager of monetary policy

The rebuilding of Cuba's financial system will need to begin with the reinstatement of *Banco Nacional de Cuba's* (BNC) original charter as the nation's central bank functioning as an autonomous entity.[7] The rebuilding of the Cuban economy should be based on prudent economic management implemented by a credible monetary authority under the auspices of the BNC.

The traditional functions of a central bank have been associated with the management of monetary policy through regulation of the monetary aggregates, and to a limited extent, with the supervision of the financial system. Even though the basic functional structure is the same, central banks differ in their institutional framework across all countries, whether industrialized or developing nations. The three principal instruments of monetary policy have been the following:

1. **Reserve requirements.** Under the fractional reserve system, the central bank regulates the amount of liquidity in the system which, at the same time, needs to be compatible with an appropriate level of reserves necessary for the stability of the financial system.

2. **Rediscount facilities.** If additional liquidity is needed over an above what is provided through the other instruments, the central bank can extend credit to financial intermediaries in the form of rediscounts of eligible instruments. The rediscount facility, or window, is also available as a source of funds for institutions that may be experiencing liquidity problems.

3. **Open market operations.** Through the purchase or sale of financial instruments, principally government securities, the central bank can control the amount of funds in the system. This instrument is easier to apply and has a more immediate effect on liquidity than the others. However, the capacity to use open market operations as an instrument to control the monetary aggregates is dependent on the depth and degree of development of the domestic money and capital markets. The development of a viable domestic money and capital market in Cuba may not be realizable until a later stage of development. During the transition period, BNC may have to limit its open market operations to the establishment of a special money desk to manage the purchase and sale of government securities directly with commercial banks via telephone lines.

Since foreign assets represent one of the components of the monetary aggregates, the central bank should be designated as the guardian of international reserves, and act as the regulator of the foreign exchange market.

A revamped BNC should not extend credit to the economy, but only use its rediscount window as an instrument of monetary policy, or for temporary support for banks experiencing liquidity problems. In this regard, BNC's existing branching network should be downsized considerably, and many of the branches could be transferred to the development bank as well as to the newly emerging commercial banks. The existing loan portfolio could be transferred to a Government Trust, which would then contract with the development bank or commercial banks to perform the loan servicing function. In effect, the government would eventually assume any losses from these loans.

---

7. For further discussion see M. Lasaga and Jorge Salazar-Carrillo, *The Reorganization of the Cuban Central Bank in a Post-Castro Cuba*, August 1993.

Not only should BNC avoid interfering with the banking system's credit allocation mechanism, but it should not intervene in the setting of interest rates. However, during the potentially unstable transition period, when there is likely to be a severe liquidity constraint, BNC might prefer to set interest rates on a very selective basis, with the understanding that within a specified timetable, rates would become market determined.

A strong development bank as protagonist of the reconstruction process

With the new wave of economic reforms in Latin America that followed the debt crisis in the 1980s, the role of the development bank has been firmly recasted as a facilitator in the development process, with the principal intermediary role assigned to private sector financial institutions. Prior to the debt crisis, development banks had become a type of bank for all which provided, in many cases, highly subsidized loans which were funded on-demand with loans from the central banks. Many were designed to have a monopoly over long-term financing, on the assumption that commercial banks were unwilling to take that type of risk. The lending criteria applied by development banks was mostly inadequate and subject to political influence, and thus their portfolios were cluttered with doubtful loans. Few achieved sustainable profitability, and in fact many were eventually liquidated.

The fact that development banking institutions, as previously structured, had failed to achieve their objectives does not necessarily justify their elimination. At the same time, the persistence of market failures still hinders the ability of private sector financial institutions to assume the dual role of commercial and development banking. The recent financial crises throughout Latin America also point to a lack of maturity in the financial sector which applies to both public and private sector intermediaries.

Despite the errors of the past, development banks are still a very important part of the financing equation. Having learned from experience, governments have restructured development banks to play a supporting role to private sector financial intermediaries. Development banks can address the following market needs:

- Limited Access to financing: Micro-, small- and some medium-scale enterprises typically have great difficulty in obtaining financing from the commercial banking sector.[8]

- Lack of long-term funding: In order to grow, a company needs to invest in fixed assets. However, medium- and long-term financing is very scarce due in turn to the commercial banks' limited access to medium- and long-term deposits and borrowing, both domestic and foreign.

- Problem of information and transaction costs: financial intermediaries have a comparative advantage in managing credit risk due to their ability to obtain critical information on the financial position of their borrowers. However, the lack of credit history and other relevant operating information on prospective clients is much harder to obtain in the case of small- and medium-sized companies, or in markets which have not yet developed a reliable information network. At the same time, the cost of underwriting a loan may be greater than the actual amount of the loan if the borrower is a micro-scale enterprise whose borrowing requirements are very small.

In the case of Cuba, these market imperfections are greatly magnified. The primitive stage of development of the financial sector, not to mention the absence of a client base, since there is no viable private sector, would necessitate the use of a strong development banking institution to serve as catalyst for the reconstruction of the financial sector. Simultaneously, the government would need to institute a special purpose vehicle capable of organizing a viable commercial banking sector that would eventually assume the leading financial intermediary role. A banking consortium which would include both foreign and domestic banks could serve as the catalyst for the de-

---

8. One exception would be small- to medium-sized companies that are part of a large and profitable holding company.

velopment of the private banking sector. During the transition, the development bank could serve as the principal funding vehicle, which would then on-lend these resources via the banking consortium to the final borrowers. A critical element of the Cuban Banking Study Group's recommendation is that the banking consortium have a limited life. After an acceptable transition period, the operations of the consortium would be phased out, and the participating banks would then be expected to become independent banking entities, having gained valuable market experience as part of the consortium. Nevertheless, once the consortium is phased out, any qualified entity should be allowed to apply for a banking license.

Organization of BANFOR

A National Bank for Reconstruction and Development (BANFOR) could assume the initial responsibility, along with a private sector banking consortium, to finance the reconstruction of the economy and to promote the development of the banking sector.[9] BANFOR would serve as the bridge between the current communist-based de-capitalized economy, and a market-based private sector led sustainable recovery. During the transition period BANFOR would play a dominant role in securing financial resources for the reconstruction of the economy.

This proposal calls for the establishment of a *de-novo* development banking entity. In line with the recommendation to downsize BNC's banking activities, the other government bank, *Banco Popular de Ahorros*, should likewise be downsized with most of its branches transferred to BANFOR, and its loan portfolio also transferred to a Government Trust, while the servicing of the portfolio would be performed by BANFOR or the commercial banking consortium. BANFOR would be a joint venture between the public and private sectors. It would serve as the principal vehicle to allocate external development credits from bilateral and multilateral agencies, as well as from the government's own resources, to support infrastruc-

ture and private sector development. All credit lines extended to BANFOR would be guaranteed by the government.

The bank could be structured as a mezzanine-type financial organization that would operate through the private banking system, or during the transition period, through the above mentioned consortium of commercial banks. BANFOR would thus serve as a financial intermediary that would source funds overseas as well as in the domestic capital market, and channel these funds to final borrowers through the commercial banking system. Under this arrangement, the commercial banks would assume the risk of the final borrower. In effect, BANFOR would provide loans, priced under market conditions, through participating financial institutions to private sector enterprises. The final credit decisions would be made by commercial banks, while BANFOR would manage its own risk through supervision of the loan processing by the banks and through its selection of participating banks that are deemed to be creditworthy.

The objectives of BANFOR would include: (i) to assist with the reconstruction of the Cuban economy by allocating economic aid from the international community to the private sector; (ii) to participate in the privatization of public sector enterprises; (iii) to support the government's economic development policies, including support of the development of efficient and competitive enterprises in the private sector; (iv) to provide financial resources to micro- and small-scale enterprises; and (v) to contribute to the development of the private banking system through the establishment of a bank training institute.

The initial capital of the bank would consist of an amount to be determined by the government, and to be subscribed by both the public sector and private financial institutions. The government would maintain 51 percent ownership of the bank, while private commercial banks would own the remaining 49 per-

---

9. Some of the material in this section was first developed in Alberto García Tuñón, José Garrigo, and Manuel Lasaga, *Cuba's Development Financing: National Bank for Reconstruction and Development (BANFOR)*, October 1994, prepared for the Cuban Banking Study Group.

cent. In order to qualify for participation in BAN-FOR's financing facilities, a private commercial bank would have to be a stockholder in BANFOR.

The Board of BANFOR would consist of nine directors: five public sector, and four private commercial bank representatives. It is important that both public and private sectors work jointly in the promotion of private sector enterprises. The government's majority control would result from its role in determining economic development policies, as well as its position as final guarantor for BANFOR's lines of credits. Private sector participation on the Board would assure critical input in the areas of credit policy and management philosophy of the institution. It would also strengthen BANFOR's knowledge of the marketplace.

Activities of BANFOR

During the initial phase of economic reconstruction, BANFOR would play an active role in channeling economic assistance to priority sectors of the economy. It would become the public sector's financing vehicle to support private sector development. However, from its creation, BANFOR would be prohibited from providing any type of lending, directly or indirectly, to the public sector, except when involved in the privatization of government enterprises. Nor would it be allowed to underwrite guarantees on behalf of the government. As the principal source of funds for the economy during the initial transition period, BANFOR would have to adhere strictly to checks and balances, and to policies and procedures that would ensure the safety and soundness of the financial system. Lending to the government or in response to government directives would compromise the goal of promoting an efficient private sector-led banking system.

One of the critical elements of a structural reform program will be the privatization of government entities. Most of the major transactions during the transition period involving some type of financing are bound to be associated with the sale of government interests. BANFOR could play an active role in this process as the agent for the government. Once the government identifies a candidate for privatization, it could proceed along the following steps: (i) the enter-

prise would be incorporated; (ii) the government would deposit its shares with BANFOR; and (iii) acting as agent, BANFOR would arrange for the valuation of the company's assets, prepare the public offering documents, supervise the bidding and select the best offer. BANFOR could also provide financing for the purchase of the shares. At the same time, the proceeds from privatization could be used to support the lending activities of BANFOR. Under this scheme BANFOR would issue medium- and long-term bonds denominated in foreign currency that would be exchanged with the government for the proceeds from the privatization of government-owned enterprises.

BANFOR could provide local as well as foreign currency denominated loans. Its sources of funds would include loans from bilateral and multilateral agencies' under the guarantee of the government; lines of credit from domestic and foreign financial institutions; and issuance of its own obligations in the domestic and international capital markets. BANFOR would lend only to participating domestic financial institutions which, in turn, would assume the credit risk of loans made to final borrowers, except when under government guarantees. As administrator of multinational lines of credit, BANFOR would be responsible for supervision of its credits to participating banks, and periodic accounting of all relevant information on the distribution and impact of loans made under each credit facility.

BANFOR would provide medium- to long-term financing for both fixed assets and permanent working capital. Participating financial institutions would be able to discount individual loans, or, based on a predetermined loan approval limit, discount a group of loans, or simply work under a line of credit directly from BANFOR. All loans would be priced at market determined interest rates. In the case of dollar based funding, BANFOR would be expected to pass through the exchange rate risk to the final borrower, except during the initial reconstruction phase, when the government may find it necessary to assume such a risk directly in order to entice private sector investment.

During the period of economic reconstruction and rebuilding of the financial sector, BANFOR may need to pay special attention to the needs of the micro- and small-scale enterprises as well as to the availability of financing in the rural context. The lack of capital and collateral is bound to forestall the growth of all newly created enterprises, both large and small. At the same time, financial intermediaries will not be able to make good credit decisions without predictable earnings or prior track record for potential borrowers. In the case of micro- and small-scale enterprises, these same obstacles will be much greater. In this regard, BANFOR may need to make available special facilities to support lending to these small entities. It may have to subsidize the information and transaction costs via technical assistance to micro- and small-scale enterprises to perform project evaluations and to prepare the loan applications. Some creative but effective mechanisms will have to be developed to substitute for the lack of credit history and limited amount of capital and collateral by loan applicants.

Due to the lack of a formal nationwide branching network with access to rural areas, BANFOR could assume the responsibility for establishing a rural credit bureau. In order to promote the participation of private commercial banks in lending to the rural sector, BANFOR loans to small companies through its rural credit bureaus could be limited to medium-term tenor, without the possibility of refinancing or new lines of credit. After an initial period, performing loans could be packaged and placed with commercial banks, thus facilitating the transition both for the borrower, who would then achieve access to the formal banking sector, and for the commercial banks, which would then be able to acquire loans that have a performance record.

Nurturing a banking sector while operating in a high risk environment

The development of a dynamic banking industry in Cuba will take time. Even in some Latin American countries with more than a century of banking expe-

rience, major structural problems persist. Cuba will be no exception. A stable macroeconomic environment is a primordial condition for a healthy banking system. However, the ability of private sector financial intermediaries to channel resources from savings into investment, while managing risks efficiently, will hinge on the development of a critical mass of environmental factors which include the following: (i) a legal infrastructure in terms of the banking and commercial codes; (ii) adequate human capital in the terms of experienced and knowledgeable bankers; (iii) ample supply of financial market instruments; (iv) existence of acceptable forms of collateral; and (v) comprehensive and effective supervision. By serving as the focal point for all government banking activities, BANFOR could play a useful role in the development of these requisite environmental factors during the transition.

One of the traditional roles of development banks has been the training of banking professionals.[10] Through access to foreign-based technical assistance on risk management techniques and efficient financial intermediation, development banks have been able to pass on this expertise to its personnel, who in turn pass on these techniques to other commercial banks with whom they participate, or who may themselves eventually move on to private sector financial institutions, and thus apply the expertise they had acquired as development bankers.

Because of the absence of commercial banking activity for more than 35 years, there is a shortage of local banking personnel in Cuba. In order to speed the adjustment process during the transition, BANFOR could establish a technical banking institute that would offer a formal program in banking. The faculty for these training programs could be comprised of BANFOR Banking Institute staff, local University professors, local bankers, and international experts in the field of banking.

One of the obstacles to the financing of Cuba's reconstruction will be a lack of domestic financial savings. Even though commercial banks will begin to of-

---

10. See Mario Rietti, *Money and Banking in Latin America*, Praeger Publishers, 1979.

fer savings and time deposit instruments at supposedly adequate interest rates, which would be considered to be positive in inflation adjusted terms or would be considered a favorable rate when compared to the return on foreign based assets, depositors may not feel comfortable with these newly created financial institutions. For that reason, BANFOR could act as a facilitator by issuing investment certificates which would be used to attract local savings, and then make these funds available to participating commercial banks.

FROM DEVELOPMENT BANKING TO COMMERCIAL BANKING

Because of the likelihood of economic instability, of policy back-tracking or inappropriate quick fix policies, of inadequate structural underpinnings, the management of the financial sector development should be based on a sequential process. This proposal calls for a two-stage process in the rebuilding of Cuba's banking system. During phase I, the development bank (BANFOR) would assume the lead role in the financing of Cuba's reconstruction as well as in the development of the banking system. After a clearly defined transition period, which would allow sufficient time to launch a self sustaining commercial banking system under adequate supervision, phase II would begin with the gradual conversion to home-grown and foreign-owned private sector banks. The length of the transition would depend on the success of the proposed banking consortium in preparing its participating private sector intermediaries to assume the role of independent banks.

Since the mid-1980s, the design of structural reforms in Latin America has featured the private sector as the principal protagonist of the financial sector. This proposal does not contradict these developments, it supports an identical strategy for Cuba, except during the initial transition period when a development bank, with the government as majority and the private sector as minority shareholders, will assume a broad scope of responsibilities.

Analysis of development banking failures have led to the conclusion that most development financing functions should be managed by private sector commercial banks which are supposed to be market-driven and thus more efficient. However, these conclusions may be lopsided in that they fail to address similar risk problems within the private banking system. Some of the most spectacular bank failures in recent history, Chile in 1982, Venezuela in 1994, and Mexico in 1995, have originated within the private sector.[11] In this regard, the issue of banking system risk may go much beyond the question of public versus private sector ownership, and thus deserves further analysis. In fact, there are many profitable public sector enterprises.

The recent history of public and private sector banking failures points to the lack of adequate regulatory supervision as one of the principal problems.[12] If a banking system operates under strict adherence to the principles of safety and soundness, and if regulators assure compliance with these basic rules of the game, then the principal source of risk to the banking system would only be local and global market risks. Ideally, through diversification, banks would be able to reduce local risk and, in the end, be exposed to non-diversifiable global market risk. And if appropriate asset/liability management polices are implemented, banks could further reduce their risk and thus enhance their possibilities for profit maximization. The financial crises in Latin America that began with the onslaught of the debt crisis in the early 1980s repeatedly point to a lack of regulatory supervision, and to excess risk taking on the part of the banks, which, absent any deviant management behavior, can be traced back to the banks' directors and to the shareholders they represent. Therefore, in a well structured and properly supervised financial sector environment,

---

11. The term failure is used in the technical sense, since in the named examples the government assumed the financial cost of a technically insolvent situation.

12. For the importance of a proper regulatory framework see Joseph E. Stiglitz, "The Design of Financial Systems for the Newly Emerging Democracies of Eastern Europe," in C. Clague and G. Rausser, eds., *The Emergence of Market Economies in Eastern Europe*, Blackwell Publishers.

both public and private sector banks should make credit decisions under the same creditworthiness standards. Their objective functions may differ, but their intermediation techniques would be the same.

Phase I: Development bank as the lead intermediary

During Phase I, the development bank (BANFOR) would assume a leadership position in both the financing of Cuba's reconstruction and in the development of the banking sector. This should in no way detract from the very important task of setting in motion a viable private sector banking system. However, this proposal envisions BANFOR as acting as the principal financial intermediary during the transition period. The length of the transition period will depend on how much damage is incurred as a result of the initial steps towards a market-based economy, and on how quickly either the private sector consortium or other private banking entities can get their operations rolling on a profitable path. The critical element in this proposal is that Phase I will have a limited time span, and that inevitably the banking sector will be dominated by private sector intermediaries.

The principal objectives of Phase I would be: (i) to ensure an effective flow of resources from bilateral donors and from multilateral agencies aimed at rebuilding the country's infrastructure; (ii) to provide resources to local enterprises to finance investment where the funding for those loans originates with multilateral lending agencies; (iii) to maximize the benefits from privatization in terms of revenues generated for the public sector and of jobs created through the newly privatized companies; and (iv) to build the human capital skills necessary to support the development of a home-grown banking network. The time frame for the achievement of these objectives could be well defined given that their outcomes are quantifiable. On the other hand, once the private sector banks begin to expand in a sustainable fashion, they should develop much greater appetite for lend-

ing, and would thus surpass BANFOR in market share, so that initially the private banks' share of the market might be as low as 20 percent, as measured by total assets, and, by the beginning of Phase II would reach two-thirds share.

It may be necessary for BANFOR to act as a direct lender during Phase I, although these activities could be limited through the bank's credit policies. Initially, some projects might be too large for the embryonic banking sector, however, BANFOR could underwrite the credit and then sell participations to other banks. A government-owned bank that dominates the banking sector could help to reduce the possibilities of a banking collapse. Hardy and Lahiri conclude in their analysis of Eastern Europe that a dramatic change in the economic structure could trigger the collapse of a very inexperienced banking sector.[13] In this regard, Phase I could serve as a bridge during the critical period of economic instability with one intermediary firmly in control, and thus helping to build depositors' confidence, while giving time for the new commercial banks to get their operations firmly established.

Phase II: Home-grown and foreign-owned banks take the lead

Historically, the government has played a major role in the development of the financial sector in Latin America. Unfortunately, its involvement, though well intentioned, was detrimental to the healthy development of private sector financial intermediaries. Distorted macroeconomic policies such as over-valued currencies and controls over interest rates, combined with cheap and bountiful central bank credits to the commercial banks, produced inefficient, non-competitive and highly risky financial intermediaries. This proposal considers Phase II as the critical point in the development of Cuba's financial sector. If successful, Phase I will have established a sound structure made up of commercial banks that will have proven their ability to intermediate efficiently in a rapidly emerging market. During Phase II, BAN-

---

13. See Daniel C. Hardy and Ashok Kumar Lahiri, "Bank Insolvency and Stabilization in Eastern Europe," in *IMF Staff Papers*, December 1992.

FOR would assume a secondary role in the financial system with most of its lending activities by then channelled through the banking system.

The commercial banking system should evolve in an open environment which allows both domestic and foreign-owned banks to compete on a level playing field. Nevertheless, during the transition, domestic banks should be given some preference in terms of their ability to capture market share, as has been done by all countries whether big or small, industrialized or newly emerging. For example, recent reforms in Latin America to open the local markets to foreign bank participation have emerged only after their own home-grown institutions have enjoyed a near absolute monopoly for many years.

The success of Phase II will hinge on the development of an effective Superintendency of Banks with a legal mandate and adequate resources to supervise the banking system. Both public and private sector banks should be subject to the same regulatory requirements. The status of an autonomous agency would reinforce the Superintendency's credibility and effectiveness. Nevertheless, some overlapping of functions between the Superintendency and the Central Bank might be useful, since the Central Bank's technical expertise in financial markets and foreign exchange management could strengthen the Superintendency's supervisory function.

Phase III: The unfinished agenda

As stated earlier in this proposal, the immediate goals of the Government during a transition to a market-based economy should be to rebuild the commercial banking system. Undoubtedly the development of the equity markets, insurance, and pension funds are essential for the sustainability of economic growth and development. In that regard efforts should be undertaken from the start to institute the legal groundwork for the establishment of capital markets. However, the successful development of a credible Central Bank, an efficient development bank, a competitive commercial banking system, and an efficient money market should take priority over the development of the other capital market components. The risk of a collapse is much greater when everything is done at once, specially when it will all have to be built from the ground up.

COMMENTS ON

"Financing the Economic Reconstruction of Cuba While Rebuilding the Financial Sector: Perspectives on Development Banking" by Manuel Lasaga

Ricardo C. Martínez 1/

This paper looks into one of the thorniest, and most crucial, subjects in the study of economic development, namely the role of financial intermediation, or of how the financial system transforms a country's savings into the flow of investment that the economy needs in order to grow and develop. Mr. Lasaga adds complexity to this issue by looking at it in the context of a future Cuban economy in transition from Marxism to a free-market system. In my view, three issues raised by this paper merit further exploration.

The *first issue* can be viewed as a version of that old riddle of folk wisdom: "who came first, the chicken or the egg?" This is because the author's proposal for rebuilding Cuba's banking system features a first phase in which a new, mixed, state/private entity— the proposed development bank named BANFOR—would provide most financial intermediation services in the economy, thus allowing a privately owned banking system to develop, strengthen, and ultimately, in phase II, take over the main intermediation role in the economy. On the other hand, the description of the BANFOR entity itself often refers to functioning private financial institutions, and even to a capital market, as essential in the organization and early functioning of BANFOR. So which came first, the chicken or the egg?

Actually, the riddle in this case may be more apparent than real. This is because Mr. Lasaga's paper makes very little reference to the financial system which exists under Castro's dictatorship. Whatever the constitution and functioning of that system are now, it will necessarily have to provide one of the few building blocks available for the transition. For example, existing branches of the Cuban central bank, suitably reorganized, and possibly privatized, could be the origin of a commercial banking system, even during "Phase I" in Mr. Lasaga's definition. In any case, this topic is worth exploring in greater depth, prefaced by a brief explanation of the organization and functioning of the country's existing financial system.

The *second issue* is that Mr. Lasaga's paper has very little to say about the role that foreign banks and financial intermediaries could play in the Cuban transition. These entities could make critical contributions of capital and technology in phase I of the transition, when the new Cuban commercial banks would still be in embryonic form. This is particularly true of the multinational banks, which have experience operating in a wide variety of countries and conditions. However, two problems come to mind with respect to these institutions:

1/ The views expressed in this comment are entirely and solely the author's, and should in no way be construed to represent the views of the Inter-American Development Bank, its Governors, Management, or staff.

1. Can they be persuaded to come in, given the high level of risk involved in an early entry into the Cuban market, and, if so, how?

2. If they in fact do come in, how can the country avoid their using their vast resources and advanced technology to prevent domestic competitors from growing? (It is assumed here that the national objective would be to develop Cuban-owned financial institutions to the point where they have the lions's share of the country's financial market).

The *third issue* refers to government policy. After a critique of various approaches to structural reform of the economy of the paper discusses the economic policy guidelines which the author deems advisable for the development of the financial sector. It is remarkable that the list omits both fiscal policy, particularly taxation and deficit financing, and monetary policy, with the exception of interest and exchange rates. Both of these sets of policies would direct-ly affect the development and role of the financial sector. The core issue in this regard boils down to two related questions: (a) what is the best macroeconomic policy framework for the development of the financial system?; and (b) what role will the financial system itself play in that same framework? This paper is not quite definite about answers to either question.

In *summary*, these comments have dealt mostly with issues which were not, in my opinion, sufficiently discussed in Mr. Lasaga's paper, but which would have enhanced that work if they had been so taken up. As it stands the paper makes a very useful contribution to understanding the difficulties a future Cuban economy in transition would face in building up a new financial system, suitable for its growth and development. One final *caveat*: in a paper that deals with a subject as complex as this one is, a "summary and conclusions" section would have been very useful.

A CONCEPTUAL SKETCH OF THE
NEW FINANCIAL AND DEVELOPMENT INSTITUTIONS
FOR THE CUBA IN TRANSITION AND THE FUTURE CUBA

Alberto Luzárraga

The title of this paper reveals its content. The lack of concrete facts on the Cuban economy, particularly the State deficit and that of its enterprises, renders a serious quantitative analysis an almost impossible job. It is best then to work on a conceptual level. Common sense and the experiences of other countries should allow us to reach some logical conclusions.

To start let us say that the financial work to be done has to be governed by the concept of *Reconstruction*. Only as this process advances may we consider financial transactions normal and commonplace. "Ab initio" we must think of a hybrid state of affairs where public, private and semi-public entities will co-exist. The design of banking legislation, including a Central Bank law, rules and regulations, etc., is a laborious and indispensable assignment, but not extremely difficult as this subject is well studied and adaptation to the Cuban reality is all that is required. The difficult assignment will be to diagnose the depth of the Cuban problem and to provide a balanced and forward looking remedy that avoids the excesses and mistakes we have seen elsewhere.

Let us accept then that the reconstruction will be truly the work of Romans, particularly if one includes the worthy objective of cooperating to make the Cuban people the owner of the fruit of its labor. This latter concept merits emphasis. The Cubans in the island must be integrated quickly to a normal life and be able to feel that they own something including stock ownership of the company for which they work. Many models may be designed but the objective is the same: to bond and to give incentives. This is indispensable in order to promote social peace and is also the best vaccine available to counter 35 years of brainwashing.

If all that Cubans can aspire to is to be mere employees of a foreign company or of companies controlled by Cuban exiled capital, we will have created an excellent prescription for the demagogues. They will then be able to exploit comfortably the owner versus proletarian antagonism that underlies the Marxist rhetoric and indeed human nature in general.

We must open new avenues to channel the energy and aspirations of the Cuban people through institutions that facilitate a better future, and thus insure a process of social cohesion and national unity directed to a common objective: the peaceful reconstruction of Cuba. As I see it the former is not just a beautiful ideal but an eminently practical objective. Without social peace, investment will not take place and Cuba will not be an attractive country to live in. Thus, the exile community has the unavoidable duty to think first on how to *reconstruct,* which is not the same as to *regain* its property. A well directed reconstruction will furnish great opportunities to all those that want to work, invest and even regain property, but through consensual and juridical processes, where there is agreement amongst the parties.

A successful reconstruction process requires patience, flexibility and the will to make mutual concessions in order to create a new reality that may be first viable and second better than the one that preceded it. Japan and Germany are two good examples.

Since space and time do not allow a detailed analysis, let us then examine the most pressing financial problems and sketch possible solutions. A warning is in order: Banking is only the reflection of the society in which it operates and will not function efficiently in the transitional Cuba unless many problems are solved a priori.

Central Bank

Cuba's Central Bank must be independent if it is to be useful. However, in the beginning it must work very closely with the Cuban Treasury as it will need to walk a tightrope to take care of transfer payments and the deficits of the state enterprises; and all of this without unleashing a galloping inflation. The Central Bank cannot issue without limit.

This is an appropriate moment to make a general consideration applicable to the whole reconstruction effort. State deficits cannot be absorbed financially unless successful private businesses exist, earn profits and pay taxes. The financial problem has to be seen as a whole. The disastrous business of agrarian and industrial socialism has to be dismantled and substituted by a profitable normality. This profitable normality shall be obtained more quickly in certain sectors, as tourism, that must finance the reconstruction of the more complicated sectors, such as the sugar industry.

The process will require an open and free foreign exchange policy with a free flotation of the peso. There is no other choice for an exporting country that will maintain close relations with a vast community located in the United States. Mexico, with a similar situation, attempted an exchange control and we know the result, it lasted less than a year. An exchange control in Cuba will only result in a black market, absurd and inefficient rationing of imports and in a source of scandals and corruption. This is not a gratuitous statement. I have observed this phenomenon for 30 years in Latin America and only now (finally) has it been dismantled.

PRIVATE VERSUS STATE BANKING

There are no great doubts here. The banking system must be private if it is to effectively serve depositors and borrowers. The supervision of public banking more often than not suffers from political interference that eventually degenerates into favoritism and, in the worst of cases, in the purchase and sale of influence. Experience shows that a good part of the State Banks fail "de facto" if not "de jure" and that the State must replenish their capital.

However, initially in Cuba one must be prepared to accept the coexistence of private banks with certain specialized entities necessary for the reconstruction process. The need arises simply because many of the risks will not be suitable for private commercial banks due to the fact that an information base for the borrowers, as well as competent management, legislation, courts, etc., will not be created overnight, and in the meantime the country cannot remain at a standstill.

The special entities that will be mentioned later may assume higher risks than the private banks, but must have a common denominator, i.e. the presence of independent private persons in their boards and a limited term established by law after which they would be liquidated. And this, to avoid the creation of bureaucratic monsters that would intervene in everything, restraining liberty and the rights of citizens. *They must be transitional entities, period.* Some entities such as Development Banks may be useful at a later stage, but in that case a specific new approval should be required and private capital should participate in some measure in order to insure a balanced operation.

One could then ask: what is the function of the private banks? The answer is: The most ample one that can possibly be authorized within a strict system of supervision and regulation focused on what are capital risks and what are loan risks.

At the inception of a transition Cuba cannot allow itself the luxury of authorizing a multitude of poorly capitalized commercial banks that may lend imprudently and fail with the attendant loss to their depositors. The effect on a population that would only then be emerging from Marxist arbitrariness would be as devastating as it is unacceptable. Some will say that deposit insurance would solve this problem but this is not really true. If deposit insurance is extended to all banks without strict criteria as to quality of management, capitalization, etc., we will witness the same phenomenon that has taken place elsewhere, i.e. the proliferation of banks often managed by incompetent people or, in the worst case, people with low moral standards. Banking is a concession to invest other people's money and the state cannot offer its guarantee to everybody.

Deposit insurance would have to be very demanding as to who may deserve it and who is worthy of continuing to have it and at what price. This approach may solve a problem but may create another one, i.e. the concentration of banking in entities that are very well capitalized, and that probably would be mostly foreign owned. From a purely technical standpoint some will say this is irrelevant. But it is not convenient for a country to depend almost a 100% on foreign entities in an industry as essential as banking; particularly a country such as Cuba that has seen itself subject to the insistent exaltation of its nationalism, with political ends if you wish, but perhaps with the beneficial effect (provided it is constructively channeled) of the consolidation of its national identity.

In any case, the answer to the dilemma is not an antiquated and inoperative market reserve a la Mexico that would fall by its own weight, but a gradual opening where licenses are granted to all the foreign banks that had one prior to 1959 or to new ones in the absence of those, and to the well capitalized Cuban banks that have competent personnel. In this last case, the association of Cuban capital and of Cuban capital with that of foreigners is a sensible answer. The by-laws of Cuban/foreign capitalized entities could have well known provisions that will ensure the agreement of the Cuban nationals for certain management decisions.

As the disaster is remedied new licenses can be granted and deposits will flow from the public sector to the private sector. There is really no other way. In Cuba the ratio of money to Gross Domestic Product is so low that it is not enough to allow many banks to function. The Cuban people must have first a stable currency and second earn enough to be able to save and invest. Without saving, investment and private companies there cannot be a private banking system that is worthy of its name as it would lack the necessary diversification of loans and deposits. Experience shows that banks fail due to loan concentrations with a few borrowers as well as by liquidity crises brought about by a badly diversified deposit base. Bank regulators all over the world are aware of this fact, but what they cannot do is to control the problem if the market does not of itself furnish the necessary diversification.

Add to this the need to create commercial legislation, impartial courts and the training of competent bank regulators and it is easy to see that commercial private banking cannot but follow the national course of the privatization of the economy, assuming in a gradual form the financial activity that at inception must be accomplished by specialized financial entities and this only as worthy borrowers emerge.

What one could authorize with broader criteria is the operation of investment banks as long as they operate with their own capital, that is risk capital, as in the end this is what the country needs. At the beginning of the process most of the transactions (perhaps with the exception of exports) are going to be risk capital and thereby not suitable for commercial banks lending depositors' money.

MUTUAL FUNDS—STOCK MARKET

This is a topic that raises a keen interest due to its success in the United States and other markets. Mutual funds are an excellent conduit to raise capital and privatize, but at the inception of the process their sale to the Cuban public and commercial banks (as opposed to investment banks) should be strictly regulated. The excesses and frauds that have taken place in Russia and elsewhere, taking advantage of the public's ignorance, should not be repeated in Cuba. On the other hand, the participation of the Cuban people in stock ownership of new and privatized companies is very desirable. In the latter the preferred method, although not the only one, should be the soft loan amortized through salary withholdings and with the prohibition to sell the shares for a certain period in order to avoid premature sale due to ignorance. This has functioned well in Chile and has the advantage of creating a supply of stock that in the future could be acquired by the mutual funds. The objective must be to create a sound mutual fund industry even if it takes longer.

Needless to say, the mutual funds industry is dependent on the existence of a stock market with the proper regulations and personnel. The topic needs separate treatment. Suffice to say that this is yet another institution to be designed soundly and allowed to operate only as a trustworthy information base becomes available.

SOCIAL SECURITY—PENSION FUNDS — HEALTH CARE

This is another monumental financial problem inasmuch as the Cuban State does not have enough funds to run the system and pay reasonable salaries and benefits. The issue is so vast that we will only attempt to put it in a financial conceptual frame. Withholding at the source would have to be implemented combined with the employers' participation. The deficit must be absorbed with public funds until the retirement funds are viable and can be reverted to the private sector a la Chile. The same can be said about health care. We will have to revert in part to HMO's and mutualist associations, but in the meantime expenses must be met.

All of the above implies public financing and this affects the banking industry. It will have to voluntarily purchase government bonds or accept a system of directed investment. Certainly not an ideal solution, but a common one in crisis situations which brings forth vividly how complicated the beginning of banking in Cuba will be. There will be many needs to be addressed, few sources of money and as we said before, the Central Bank cannot issue without limits.

SPECIAL ENTITIES BY SECTORS
Housing

Cuba's housing deficit is well known. Worse, we know that the existing housing stock is in a state of disrepair. If the Cubans of the island lack adequate housing, needless to say that if the exiles wanted to go and live there tomorrow they would have to be content with a prolonged "camping" experience. There is simply no room for so many.

The problem has two solutions; new construction and repair of the existing housing stock. But as we know all existing housing is occupied and much of it has its original owner living in exile. A logical question would be: How can one conciliate the rights of the original owners with the possession by a third party that in many cases has been told by the government that he is the owner though the payment of rents? There is a possible solution and it is the creation of a *Bank for the Reconstruction of Real Estate Property* that would do two things:

a. Facilitate the reconstruction of existing housing.

b. Construct new housing.

However objective (b) would be linked to objective (a). The person that wishes to recoup and reconstruct his original house, now occupied by a third party, could do it on the basis that the Bank would furnish a new house or apartment to the occupant giving him a priority. This priority would be justified by the contribution of foreign currency by the person paying for the restoration. In that way, a constructive activity would be fostered, i.e. find an exiled Cuban willing to do such a transaction.

The financial engineering design, sources of capital for the Bank's deposits, etc. is not the subject of this paper. Suffice to say that the design is feasible and that it can be done without massive monetary issuance.

Agrarian Problem - Financial Impact

There are two problems. The sugar problem with characteristics of industrial reconversion and the general agrarian problem centered on the property of land and diversification of crops.

Many years before Fernando Ortíz wrote his famous *"Cuban Counterpoint of Sugar and Tobacco"* the topic of diversification was in vogue. Much had been done in the fifties. Cuba exported winter fruits and vegetables to the United States (today a big business), was almost self sufficient in rice, etc. The regime threw us back to the days of a one crop economy, and committed Cuba to the role of sugar bowl for the communist bloc. And of course without the slightest regard for costs.

The present system of harvesting cane is very deficient and results in very poor saccharose yields. Add the obsolescence of the industrial plant and compare then Cuba's situation to that of other sugar producing countries that:

a. Protect their internal prices.

b. Are better equipped industrially.

Further, most countries with acceptable rainfall produce beet or cane sugar. The export sugar industry is in a good part a marginal industry that offsets the deficits produced by unpredictable climate related events. This means that in the future Cuba there will be no role for inefficient sugar mills that produce at costs in excess of the world market price. It is well known that Cuba has optimal conditions for the growing of sugar cane. The sugar industry will always play an important role in the economy but it cannot exist as a subsidized activity that generates huge deficits to be covered by monetary issuance. This would unleash a vicious circle of issuance-inflation at a prohibitive cost for the country.

The post-Trujillo experience in Santo Domingo is indicative. Therefore, Cuba must create an *Institute of Reconversion and Return to Private Management of the Sugar Industry.* The Institute must attack the economic-financial problem coordinating with the Central Bank and the Ministry of Finance and do the following:

a. Determine the optimum size of the industry.

b. Determine which units are obsolete and which can produce more efficiently.

c. Develop a transition plan in order to place excess workers and pay them an unemployment benefit during this period.

d. Develop an agricultural plan determining the supply roles, ownership and possession of land and cane price as a percentage of its sugar con-

tent, taking into account the maximum extension of land that a country with a relatively small territory can dedicate to this crop. A new version of the *"Ley de Coordinación Azucarera"?* Perhaps it would be the best solution.

e. Develop the financial plan.

The financial component of the process is as vast as it is difficult. The state must pay the wages of excess personnel until they find gainful employment, and it will have to absorb operating losses until the units go back to the private sector. For bankrupt units to go back to the private sector it is necessary first to clean them up. Nobody is going to pay for past losses. This has been the experience in other countries.

What we can foresee in the sugar sector is a classic investment banking activity where the units go to those that can guarantee an adequate operation of the business. Here we face a difficult problem of conciliation of interests. There are valid claims of United States citizens properly registered, as well as the rights of Cuban nationals who suffered confiscations. But the problem is complicated because without cane there are no mills, without mills there is no cane and without peace in the possession of land and people to work it, there is nothing. It is the classic difficulty of an agro-industrial business that faces the challenges of both activities.

The issue must be viewed as a whole. Harmonic solutions must be found which may result in many combinations, including the association of the owners with new investors or with labor, the return of the units to the old owners that can operate them or proper and viable compensation if the former is not possible. The details of how to do this are not the subject of this paper, suffice it to say that in all probability certain basic criteria imposed by reality will exist, namely:

a. Need to produce at an internationally competitive cost and therefore to create healthy industries that can be of interest to the private sector.

b. Need to provide juridical safety to new investors, and to conciliate the interests of growers, workers, mill owners through a fair system.

c. Need to find ways to finance the industrial conversion.

I feel this is feasible albeit complex. Without juridical stability and industrial peace the banks are not going to be very keen on doing much. Assume we obtain both things. Then we must determine if there is a capital base upon which one may grant credits and more importantly, is there sufficient cash flow? Loans are paid with cash flow and not with liens. The value of liens is a function of the productivity of the business. Banks are not going to be interested in foreclosures in a country in transition. A lien on produced sugar can be a good source of loans, but if there are operating losses these loans solve nothing. The losses must be covered and eventually the same result obtains, insolvency and foreclosure in more or less time.

I repeat, the only solution is: Clean up the industry, bring in new capital and then loans are feasible. If there are doubts I would invite you to study the processes of industrial reconversion in Europe and Latin America. There are no brilliant inventions in these matters. Accounts balance or they don't balance.

Other Industrial Sectors

Concurrent with the handling of the sugar problem, Cuba must create a financial institution dedicated to develop other crops with high export potential as well as those necessary for the sustenance of the population. Cattle ranching must also be included.

Export sectors that have competitive advantages are:

a. Citrus

b. Tropical fruits and winter vegetables.

c. Tobacco

d. Light manufactures derived from agriculture

Compared to the sugar problem this is a less difficult challenge. Land and climate are the main factors and investment in equipment is much smaller per production unit. The main issue here is how to create a viable borrower. The present government is organizing cooperatives and they will have to be reckoned with, without forgetting that generally the best farmer is the one that owns his land.

Today there exists a small base of private farmers. We should begin right there, supporting the best so that they extend their arable land and production. Let us emphasize that agriculture and/or cattle lending requires constant attention. Here, cash flow can evaporate quickly if there is a lack of care to the day to day needs of crops and cattle, not to mention climate which may change everything. A team of agronomists that supervise the investment of loan process is essential. Agricultural loan programs do not work with bankers sitting in their offices listening to their clients. Fortunately Cuba has many agronomists, frustrated by the insanity of the past, that could find here useful employment. The organization and funding of the agricultural financial sector can follow many models, including an important role for credit cooperatives.

Industrial Reconversion (excluding Sugar Industry)

A Bank or *Institute of Reconversion of Industry and Mining* must support this process and do the following:

a. Close the obsolete loss leader industries created by the government and

b. Sell the viable ones to private enterprise.

c. Return to its owners the industries that can operate efficiently provided the owners have economic and management capacity. If they lack it, they could form partnerships with those that have it or receive the compensation that is appropriate and viable. Within this process, the participation of workers in the stock ownership of companies should be promoted by reserving, when viable, a portion of the capital that could be paid with a soft loan a la Chile. Undoubtedly, this idea will be criticized by some but, if well managed, it should facilitate rather than hinder the privatization process. What should remain clear is that management must be independent and that one or more control shareholders must exist. Otherwise we are dealing with utopia.

d. Develop a general plan to start new industries facilitating their creation and operation. Cuba has a great future in service industries (tourism aside) such as informatics, data processing, offshore banking (really the province of the Central Bank), distribution and warehousing centers, as well as those that provide added value, i.e., maquila., etc.

Service and added-value industries create many jobs and at inception should be the engine that propels a good part of the economy. Within this special entity, tourism merits a discrete organization. Cuba's privileged geographic location, its beaches, natural beauty and climate are a coveted asset in a world with a limited availability of such resources. Therefore, one of the first things to do is to revise all the abusive and disadvantageous agreements that have been made, and place at auction at a fair price that which has been sold or given as a concession for very little. And let us not even speak now of the labor claims that should and must arise due to the ridiculous salaries paid to the workers of this sector by those that exploit tourism. Karl Marx would blush at the present scheme which by the way extends also to mining and industry in general.

EXTERNAL DEBT

A quick reference is in order due to the debt's financial impact. A special section of the Ministry of Finance must be created so that it, together with the Central Bank, may handle the task of renegotiating the debt.

Cuba is probably the country with the highest per capita debt in the world. The political-economic debt with Russia is unpayable in its greatest part, and Russia knows this well enough. The debt with other Western countries that lent, very imprudently, to the Marxist outpost in the Americas must suffer a much greater discount than the one granted to Mexico, Poland, Brazil, etc. Cuba will have to pay something but on very, very comfortable terms. The creditors know it, and the only reason for settling this matter is to normalize commercial relations so that Cuba may earn enough to pay what is agreed to and obtain a positive commercial balance.

As to the conversions of debt into capital effected with some of our neighbors in the American continent and with others, a careful revision is in order.

We must apply the same principles of valuation of assets and transparency that were applied by those countries when they accepted debt conversions. This is fair and just. Sales at very low prices and without transparency or with pressure can be nullified according to all the civil codes of the world.

CONCLUSION

The present Cuban government is attempting reform and has announced drastic measures, such as the firing of 800,000 workers that will receive up to 60% of their meager salaries (for a limited time), provided they are not suitable for agricultural work. This is really tragic. The application of harsh measures without incentives to the population, and without the massive capital infusions that are generally only available from investors that would demand the guarantees offered by the Rule of Law, are not going to produce great results.

The financial problems that we have described are of such enormity that a satisfactory resolution cannot be anticipated without the participation of capital that has a long term development objective rather than short-term exploitation. The investors that Cuba needs will only invest if there exist clear rules of the game that cannot be changed by one or a few people without transparency or accountability.

Today's joint ventures pay salaries in dollars to the Cuban State for the workers that the State furnishes, allowing it to earn an exchange differential as the Cuban government pays the workers in pesos. It would seem that the Cuban government learned well the lesson of the "plusvalía" that Marx so harshly criticized. Economically speaking, the policy is clumsy. Miserly salaries do not allow for consumption, without it there is no internal market and without the internal market, the capital of many investors will never arrive.

The model as designed is only good for a plantation economy focused on exports and on cheap and harshly controlled labor. In itself it is a very fragile design. Many export businesses need the support of the internal markets to cover costs which then allows them to compete internationally at good prices. Further, cheap labor is the weakest of competitive advantages in a world where technology, marketing skills, state of the art equipment, etc., are crucial. The hope of Cuba's government is that the United States blockade will be lifted and that the U.S. consumers will be content to buy products made by slave labor only 90 miles away. I believe they misjudge greatly the good instincts and fairness of the American people.

Cuba is losing the best part of the process of change while implementing a regressive policy, wherein it demands sacrifice without providing means to make it worthwhile. The so called "opening" has all the characteristics of an operation to gain time and hold on to absolute power for a few more years. No doubt, many thoughtful and capable people that work in the administrative apparatus of the regime see this and know that in the end things must be different, that brute force and productivity do not march hand in hand, but circumstances prevent them from speaking out. Further, the regime manages skillfully the old adage "après moi, le déluge" . . . and it doesn't have to be that way because the immense majority of the exiled Cubans want to see Cuba prosper peacefully.

This is why I close with a thought for all. *For Cuba to progress we must unite the Cubans that lost their land to preserve their liberty with those that kept their land but lost their liberty.* This can only be obtained within a State subject to the Rule of Law, with independent courts, a freely elected Congress that legislates for the good of its constituents and not against them and by an elected executive that respects the law.

In any case, like it or not, the blinding pride of those that do not want to yield anything or yield only the strictly necessary will fail, because the aspiration to liberty is irrepressible and then, with optimism and energy we may work together to create a Cuba "With all and for the good of all."

SUMMARY

The paper attempts to present a conceptual sketch of the financial problems facing the post-Castro Cuba, and to present possible solutions.

An attempt is made to outline practical alternatives based on the author's experience of investing and running businesses in Latin American economies that have gone through similar processes.

To be practical one must have both feet firmly anchored in reality and this includes the social and historical reality of Cuba. In this context it is imperative to bring the people of Cuba into the reconstruction process fully and enthusiastically. The latter can only be obtained by allowing them to participate as much as possible in the ownership of the new enterprises to be created. as has been done in the one Latin American country that has attained the greatest degree of success and social stability, i.e. Chile.

Social peace is indispensable for reconstruction. To attain it will require great flexibility, imagination coupled to the willingness to work patiently and create a number of transitional institutions. Of necessity this will mean a radical change vis a vis the status quo ante.

Castro's scheme for a plantation economy where he is foreman for life and where selected foreign partners exploit the Cuban people is reactionary. However, a mitigated version of the same shrouded by the cloak of a weak democracy and tainted capitalism a la Russia is also reactionary, and does not constitute a viable alternative. Cuba must be Cuba, break the vicious circle of tyranny/liberty that has plagued its history and finally become a country —"Con todos y para el bien de todos" — "With all and for the good of all."

COMMENTS ON

"A Conceptual Sketch of the New Financial and Development Institutions for the Cuba in Transition and the Future Cuba" by Alberto Luzárraga

Lorenzo L. Pérez[1]

Mr. Luzárraga's paper presents a sketch of the financial and developmental problems facing the post-Castro Cuba and makes a number of proposals to address these problems. The paper touches upon many important issues including the importance of creating an efficient financial system in Cuba, the promotion of capital markets, the establishment of a viable social security system, and the development strategy for key sectors of the economy. There is much I agree with in Mr. Luzárraga's paper and given the limitation of time, I will limit my remarks to areas of the paper that I feel should be highlighted or where some of the conclusions of the paper can be questioned.

In analyzing the problems of the public finances and the role that a central bank can play in a post-Castro Cuba, I would have stressed more the limitations that a central bank has in providing financing to the public sector. At the outset the basic objectives of the central bank should be to protect the value of the currency and its international reserves to ensure that an appropriate framework of price and external stability is fostered under which economic development can occur. It might be unavoidable that the central bank provide credit to the public sector for a transitional period, particularly if the central bank continues to receive most of the deposits of the financial system. However, this should not detract from serious efforts to strenghten the finances of the public sector which is one of the major challenges facing Cuba today.

Mr. Luzárraga proposes that initially in the reconstruction period we must be prepared to accept the coexistence of private banks with certain specialized entities necessary for the reconstruction process. Some of the possibilities that the author discusses are a housing bank, an agricultural bank, and an industrial bank. He feels that the need arises because many of the risks with granting credit in Cuba will not be suitable for private commercial banks due to the lack of credit records, legislation, courts, etc. I am not sure, however, that the creation of state banks is the solution to these problems even with private individuals in their board of directors. A fear I have is that these institutions tend to perpetuate themselves, are not usually transitory as Alberto envisages them, and can be the source of corruption. An alternative that should be given serious consideration is establishing portfolio requirements for private banks for an initial period to try to channel credit to some socially desirable endeavors. The availability of official or multilateral credits from abroad could also make possible

---

1. The views expressed herein are those of the author and in no way represent the official views of the International Monetary Fund.

on-lending operations through private banks without necessarily creating state banks.

The author emphasizes that banking licenses have to given out with very strict criteria, while allowing a wide range of action for banks. I believe that we can support this proposal and that it has to be accompanied by a modern banking supervision which emphasizes the valuation of the loan portfolio of banks and that ensures that banks are appropriately capitalized. I agree with the author that deposit insurance is not substitute for properly capitalized and well run banks. Deposit insurance has to be limited to a reasonable amount per depositor per financial institution taking into account the income per capita level of the country and the size of the financial market. In this context, I agree with the author that it would be better for Cuba if a strategy is designed to allow the operation of both foreign banks and domestic banks. Competition on this sector would be very important to ensure that credit is available at reasonable costs.

MARKETS REDUX: THE POLITICS OF FARMERS' MARKETS IN CUBA

Juan Carlos Espinosa

The purpose of this paper is to discuss the decision to re-open Farmers' Markets in Cuba in 1994 and to assess their significance in the context of the policy changes and reforms that began in the summer of 1993. To this end, the *Mercados agropecuarios* (MAs) will also be compared to the *Mercados libres campesinos* (MLCs) of the 1980s, the only other instance that the Cuban State resorted to market mechanisms to try to resolve the problems of agricultural production and food distribution. The process of interest group and institutional politics that led to the opening, and later closing of the MLCs is particularly instructive for an understanding of economic policy changes in Cuba. Comparing the two market 'experiments' might also indicate important changes in the process that one scholar has called "the blackest of all black boxes": decision making in Cuba (Fernández 1992, p. 53).

The MAs and the MLCs emerged in very different economic, social and political situations. The disparate circumstances also affect the attitudes of the political leadership towards the markets. A discussion of the politics of the Farmers' Markets must be placed in the context of the evolution of Cuba's economic policies, the Revolution's ideological orientation, as well as the nature of politics and decision making in Cuba. They are the product not only of Cuba's economic predicament and its international position, but of domestic political factors that have helped create a different set of supporters and detractors for the market experiments.

This preliminary study is limited by the availability of information on the decision making process in Cuba, the uncertain fate of the current market reforms, as well as by the brief time the MAs have been in operation, less than a year at the time of writing. Despite these limitations, even a speculative exercise may prove valuable as a starting point for an analysis of conflict resolution and decision making in the Castro regime. Two underlying assumptions must be revealed at the very beginning. The author believes that interest-group conflicts over policy do occur in Cuba, albeit within the severe constraints imposed by *personalismo*, ideology, and economic circumstances. The second assumption is that even in opaque areas such as decision making in Cuba, some light can be shed on the meaning of policy moves (or consequences) by identifying actors, interests, and interactions, and by studying the trajectory between initial conditions and outcomes.

ECONOMIC POLICY AND DECISION MAKING IN CUBA

One of the constants of the Cuban Revolution has been the tension between ideological and pragmatic approaches to economic policy (Mesa-Lago 1989, pp. 187-188). Pedro Pablo Cuscó, a Cuban economist, recently referred to the process of internal debate as a '*contrapunteo*' between these two approaches.[1] There is a general consensus over the

---

1.   Pedro Pablo Cuscó, interview, Miami, July 29, 1995. *Contrapunteo* literally means 'counterpoint.'

periodization of the policies that recognizes at least seven discrete stages (see Appendix). We can characterize the general approach to economic policy taken during these periods as either *Fidelista*, reformist/pragmatic or mixed/unclear.[2]

Two brief, but important periods of communist Cuba's economic history are typified by *Fidelismo*: 1966-1970 and 1986-1990.[3] Political considerations overrode economic rationality during those years. These periods were characterized by tendencies toward centralization of power and decision making, greater utilization of sectoral plans over more global planning, emphasis on voluntarism and mass mobilization, moral incentives and egalitarianism, as well as anti-market and anti-private initiative campaigns. Significantly, these periods have been followed by severe economic downturns. The periods denoted *Fidelista* have also been called as orthodox or ideological by other authors (Mesa Lago 1989, Rosenberg 1992a, *inter alia*).[4]

The years 1971-1986, were characterized to varying degrees by reformist tendencies. The period was typified by moves toward decentralization, the use of Soviet-style central planning with some market features, the use of material incentives, and increased social and wage differentiation.[5] The period can be divided into three discrete phases: (1) Redefinition (1971-1974), which involved the assessment of the disastrous dislocations engendered by the pharaonic attempt at a 10 million metric ton sugar harvest and the redirection of economic policy under the aegis of Soviet-bloc economists and technicians. The predominant approach in economic policy could still be categorized as mixed or unclear; (2) Institutionalization (1975-1984), which saw an attempt to create

Soviet-style institutions and implement the reforms that typify this period. It can be argued that this nine-year phase is the only time that Cuba actually tried to follow an economic model although it never fully implemented the reforms and economic decision-making never devolved from the highly centralized purview of Fidel Castro and his inner sanctum; and (3) Recentralization (1984-1986), which was the period of retreat from reform. The SDPE was dismantled and there were increasingly ideological attacks on *merolicos* as the newly-prosperous farmers and middlemen were called. The MLCs came under extreme duress only to be abolished in 1986. In fact, the Rectification Process can be said to have begun at this time, or at the very least was presaged by the anti-market, ascetic rhetoric that emerged.

"Mixed" or "unclear" periods were those when either a debate over models was taking place (e.g. 1964-1966) or when there seemed to be no clear direction or model indicated. Economic policy in the first few years of the Revolution, in the immediate post-1970 *zafra* period and during the Special Period, can be placed in this category. These periods have seen the closest thing to open debate in economic policy, albeit within the parameters described in the decision-making framework described below. They have also been periods of uncertainty and flux, both in policy and in personnel. It is during these times more than any other that the personalistic influence of Fidel Castro is most acute. Policy-participants court his attention à la Mandarin emperor and a single utterance from Castro can send policy spinning in different directions.

Pragmatic reformists, those who have encouraged the use of market-like mechanisms, have been most in-

---

2. The term "*fidelista*" as used here is not inconsistent with Eduardo González's definition and later use of the term, i.e. (1) propensity for maximalism, (2) primacy of objective over subjective factors, (3) penchant for revolutionary action and elitism, (4) disdain for political organization, (5) preference for personalistic leadership, etc. See González (1974, p. 83 and pp. 146-167).

3. The first period is called "Sino-Guevarist" because of the dominant influence of Che Guevara and of Chinese-style mass mobilization. The latter period is known as the Rectification Period or RP.

4. The term "orthodox" has been the source of some confusion. As used in Cuba, it refers to Soviet-style policies such as those of 1971-1986. Other scholars working outside Cuba have used the word to describe ideologically charged periods when Cuba has actually had policies contrary to those of the Soviet Union. The term is avoided or qualified in this paper.

5. These policies have been associated with "reform-communism" models (see Kornai 1992, *inter alia*).

fluential during phases of the Soviet Reform Model (1971-1986) and of the Special Period (mid-1993 to the present). Although they have never had complete control over policy making, on both occasions they have been able to control important sectors or aspects of Cuba's economy. Their hold has been tenuous; in fact during the Institutionalization Phase of the Soviet Reform Model, the trend was mixed. It was increasingly characterized by compromises that diminished the role of markets (especially after the restrictions placed on the MLCs in 1982), and the status of the reformers within policy circles.

Despite Fidel Castro's well-documented aversion to them, markets and market-like mechanisms have appeared twice after the consolidation of the Revolution, in the late 1970s - early 1980s and again after the summer of 1993. These 'moves to the market' were taken with the approval of the leadership but were initiated by more pragmatic functionaries working within the state's economic policy circles. For the purposes of discussion, we will extrapolate political tendency from policy approach. In that case, the tension between approaches also exists between identifiable groups of people.

As noted above, markets appeared only during periods when reformists were most influential. That is not to say that the *Fidelista* tendency lost or that reformists were in control of economic policy making. That has consistently remained in the hands of the top leadership. Instead, on both occasions, the market features that emerged were the result of a process of compromise which allowed Fidel and the orthodox group ultimate control even as the reformist experiments were carried out.

DECISION MAKING IN CUBA

Underlying almost every dispute or controversy in Cuban studies is the question of the nature of the Castro regime and its *modus operandi*.[6] It is really a question about politics and how decisions are made that is colored by the almost inevitable bias of the scholar. There is also an unfortunate tendency to try

to explain political phenomena by any other disciplinary means except politics. These kinds of approaches, from the psychological-biographical to the economic structuralist, are informative and occasionally interesting, but fail to give an adequate explanation of the full scope of politics in Cuba. Hungarian economist János Kornai recommends a political-economic approach that is more holistic. He writes that "the key to an understanding of the socialist system is to examine the *structure of power*" (1992, p. 33). This holds true for Cuba's socialist economy as well. An elaborate analysis of the regime is beyond the scope of this brief paper, but a short discussion of the decision making process is crucial to an understanding of the market experiments.

Damián J. Fernández identified four major views of the decision making process of the Cuban State that approximate the contending approaches alluded to above: (1) Fidel Castro as the sole decision maker; (2) a rational actor approach; (3) a structuralist *dependentista* model; and (4) an amalgam of domestic institutional, bureaucratic and elite politics approaches. Fernández finds all four approaches inadequate if used alone and integrates them.

> The framework of decision making can be conceived as four concentric circles. The smaller inner circle, at the center, is that of Fidel Castro, the principal decision making unit. His ideology and his authority exert predominant influence over Cuba's domestic and international activities. The actors closest to the center circle have authority to make decisions, while peripheral actors implement decisions (1992, p. 60).

This simple model recognizes the centrality of Fidel, the existence of distinct agendas among ideological and bureaucratic elites, the influence of the external environment, and the intricacies of domestic politics. This framework can also be used to look at the process of decision making in economic policy.

Figure 1, adapted from Fernández, illustrates a model of the structure and process of economic decision making in Cuba related to food and agricultural poli-

---

6. See for example the exchange between Susan Eckstein and Carmelo Mesa-Lago on the Rectification Process in several issues of the journal *Cuban Studies*.

cy. At the center, in circle 1, is Fidel Castro. The second circle is inhabited by his closest advisors such as Carlos Lage, José Luis Rodríguez and Raúl Castro. The third circle is divided into State and the Party halves. These two sections are "interweaved" (Kornai 1992, p. 38) and consist of the ministries such as Agriculture (MINAGRI), and Food Production (MINALIM), and party institutions such as the Central Committee. The outer circle consists of agricultural producers, the National Association of Small Farmers (ANAP), the State bureaucracies, provincial and municipal authorities in charge of implementing food and agricultural policy, Communist Party activists, and consumers. Academics who are not a part of the "in" advisory group of the third circle, but who nevertheless function in institutional settings, are included in the outer circle.

Ideas and policy options percolate toward the center. The role of the second circle, made up of specialized institutions of the state and the Communist Party, is to present policy options to the leadership, but sometimes ideas start from the outer circles. The scope of the policy options are limited by political constraints. Their ultimate fate is determined by their ability to find a 'sponsor' close to the center and of course, the disposition of the "principal decision making unit."

Tzvi Medin's metaphor of "Ravelization" is a colorful, yet insightful description of this process. Referring to the dissemination of the "revolutionary message" in order to shape a new political culture, Medin writes: "I call this phenomenon the 'Ravelization' of the message, in the sense that, as in Ravel's *Bolero*, a certain motif begins to creep in and gradually develops into a crescendo through numerous channels (instruments), increasing in volume until it finally dominates the piece completely (1990, p. 11)."

In the case of both the MLCs and the MAs, the option to open the markets began as a theme that moved through the policy orchestra until it was taken up by more powerful voices. Yet even after the MLCs became the policy, to continue Medin's musi-cal image, an inversion of the 'markets' motif was introduced fugue-like into food and agricultural policy. This counter-theme won out in the end.

Of course there are other less artistic explanations of decision-making in communist economies that rely more on structural dimensions such as Kornai's, but they are inadequate because they underestimate the role of agency, particularly the impact of the maximum leader in the economic policy decision making arena.

The demise of the MLCs in 1986, however, demonstrated that: (1) political imperatives, often cloaked by ideology, carried more weight than economic rationality or ideological consistency; (2) markets and the relations they engender encouraged linkages which fostered independence from the State and thus, were perceived as inherently threatening to the integrity of the regime; and (3) that the ultimate fate of all policies is decided by Fidel Castro and others in the center of the concentric circle of decision-making and policy implementation in Cuba.

THE *MERCADO LIBRE* CAMPESINO [7]

"Creo que el mercado libre campesino va a pasar sin glorias y habiéndonos dejado una gran lección y no pocos daños, no sé cuántos millonarios hay por ahí. Rectificaremos lo que incuestionablemente fue una decisión equivocada; es de sabio rectificar, y cuanto más pronto se rectifique mejor" (Castro 1986d, pp. 57-58).

Problems in Cuba's domestic food sector led to the introduction of the *Mercados libres campesinos* in May 1980. The MLCs were sites where small private farmers, cooperativists, state farm workers and owners of small plots and gardens could sell their surplus produce directly to consumers, with prices set by supply and demand, albeit under significant restrictions.[8]

According to Medea Benjamin, the idea of allowing private farmers to sell their surplus was discussed as early as the mid-1970s by the party leadership.

---

7. This section relies heavily on the work of Benjamin, et. al. (1984) and Rosenberg (1992a 1992b).

8. The farmers would first have to satisfy their production quota with the State (the *acopio*), before they could sell at the markets.

Figure 1. Economic Decision-Making in Cuba
(Food and Agricultural Sectors)

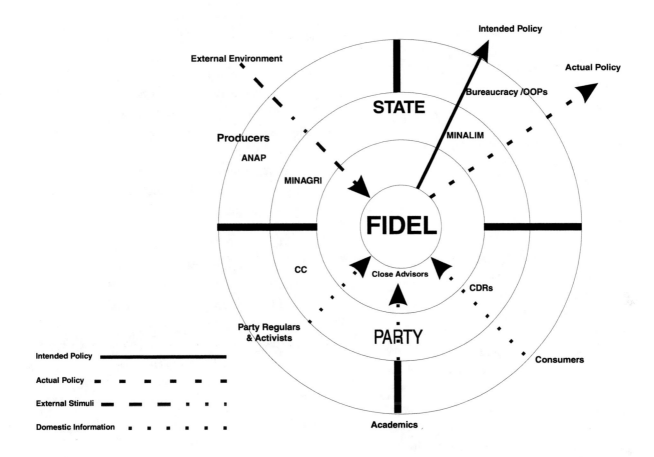

Figueroa and García report that "the creation of a non-state market to commercialize a portion of agricultural production" was discussed in the First Congress of the Cuban Communist Party in 1976. Proponents of the markets, such as Carlos Rafael Rodríguez, saw them as a way to satisfy consumer demand for increased variety and quality, while at the same time providing farmers with material incentives to increase production. Additionally, they were seen as a way to subvert the black market.[9] Opponents of the markets were concerned that private farmers would "seek individual gain rather than the common good" and that by making private farming more attractive, the markets would discourage farmers from joining the producer cooperatives the government was encouraging. The political impasse meant that the idea was "shelved" until 1980 when "further pressures finally turned the tables in their favor (Benjamin, et. al. 1984, p. 62)."

Jonathan Rosenberg's (1992a and 1992b) study of the *Mercados libres campesinos* argues that the rise and fall of the MLCs is best understood as the outcome of political conflict between the two groups identified by Benjamin, a struggle between advocates of "orthodox" and radical approaches to socialist devel-

---

9.   Figueroa and García (1984, p 46) noted that the MLCs were a response to low levels of efficiency and production in the agricultural sector, inability to satisfy consumer demand, and to provide material incentives for farmers.

opment.[10] The formation of the MLCs was the result of compromises between the two approaches.

The dispute was more than a difference between two socialist development models; it was a dispute over policy among actors with clear political interests in the success or failure of liberalizing reforms. For supporters, the MLCs provided increased importance in the domestic political economy and credit for a policy that would increase support for the Revolution. "For opponents, successful MLCs threatened their continued domination of the domestic political economy by focusing the credit on the agrarian private sector and on the technocratic elites" (Rosenberg 1992a, p. 85).

Rosenberg claims that the original impetus for the MLCs began among Soviet and Bulgarian advisors at the Agriculture Ministry in the 1970s. The private marketing of agricultural surpluses was allowed in some of the other Socialist countries with some success. In time, the main supporters of the MLCs were the institutions most identified with Soviet-style reforms[11] such as the State Planning Ministry (JUCE-PLAN), and later, the Economic Management and Planning System (SDPE). By 1980, the National Association of Small Farmers (ANAP), the Agriculture Ministry (MINAG), the State Committee for Finance and Statistics, and the Cuban Institute for the Investigation and Orientation of Internal Demand (ICIODI) were also identified as institutional supporters.

Opponents of the MLCs included the provincial party first secretaries, the Agriculture Cooperatives Associations (CPA), Arnaldo Milián (the Central Committee member responsible for the MINAG), and Fidel Castro. The cast of proponents and detractors changed over time as the MLCs came under increasing attack from consumers and from the radical anti-market leadership.

The years 1980-82 were characterized by early optimism, but mounting problems (see for example, Martínez 1981a, 1981b, 1982). Consumer complaints about high prices and accusations of illegal activities (such as the use of middlemen, profiteering, and diversion of *acopio* products to the MLCs) provided the backdrop for a crackdown in February 1982 (Operation Bird-on-a-wire or *Pitirre en el alambre*), increasingly hostile comments from Fidel (see Castro 1982a, 1982b) and a restrictive reform of the MLC law in 1983.

Rosenberg concluded that the MLCs were designed to fail. The author cited an interview with a former official (José Luis Llovio-Menéndez) to claim that the MLCs were doomed and subverted from the start for political reasons. In December 1980, a secret accord was produced for the second Cuban Communist Party (PCC) Congress that claimed support for the CPAs and outlined a plan for the disintegration of the MLCs. The plan was passed along to MLC opponents and supporters. It reportedly said that MLCs would collapse on their own and that the Party intended to allow that to happen. The accord's conclusions did not require supporters to become active opponents, but it also made it politically unwise to actively support MLCs (Rosenberg 1992a, p. 72).

Opponents whittled away at the initial support enjoyed by the MLCs. High prices and lack of accessibility were the major complaints of consumers, particularly those from the popular sectors.[12] These complaints were amply documented in the Cuban press and in other sources (see Benjamin, et. al. 1984, Martínez 1981b). Rather than accede to demands for

---

10. "Orthodox" approaches are identified with Soviet-style reforms, while radicals are refered to as *fidelistas* in this paper.

11. These reforms included the introduction of market mechanisms such as credit, interest, rational pricing, budgets, monetary controls, and taxes. Decentralization of economic decision making and the use of economic indicators that focused on profits as well as output, productivity, quality and cost (Mesa-Lago 1981, p. 29).

12. High prices were expected at the beginning, but they were supposed to decline as market forces operated. The price decrease predicted by Fidel when he announced the opening of the MLCs never occurred (Alonso, J. 1992, p. 175).

price controls, [13] the government focused its energy on demonizing and punishing "intermediaries," greedy farmers, and others who appeared to be getting rich from their activities in the MLCs and in the black market (Rosenberg 1992a, p. 384). Other supporters began to distance themselves from the markets in the wake of Operation Bird-on-a-wire.

The additional measures taken in 1983 also narrowed the base of support for the MLCs among the agricultural sector. Access to the markets was limited to private farmers who were members of ANAP and who worked their own land, explicitly excluding co-operatives (Burnhill 1985, p. 23). CPA members and private farmers not only had different interests and perceptions, but had different cost/benefit relations to the MLCs. "The CPA members adopted the anti-market attitude growing within the top echelons of the party, the CPA national movement and ANAP, while private farmers advocated more liberal market regulations that would allow them to take better advantage of strong consumer demand" (Rosenberg 1992a, p. 386).

Humberto Pérez (JUCEPLAN minister) and the pro-MLC ANAP president José Ramírez Cruz were dismissed in 1985. In May 1986, Castro announced the closing of the MLCs using strong language and the kind of moral, anti-market rhetoric that would characterize the Rectification Period: "The liquidation of the MLCs is the beginning of the end of the weeds that are the remnants of capitalism, it is a great blow in the crusade that our society has embarked upon against all manifestations of privilege, deviation, *blandenguería*, or weakness that can blunt revolutionary principles (Pozo & Martínez 1986, p. 4)." Free small farmers, the last supporters of the markets, were politically isolated and found themselves without a powerful representative among the political elites or an institutional base from which to defend their interests.

At the Fourth Party Congress (1991) Fidel revealed that he never supported the initiative, "We committed a big mistake by creating the MLCs, but we are a Party governed by democratic centralism and we have to abide by it. The Party leadership approved it, although I had my own opinion, I respected that of the others (in "El campesinado" 1991).

ORIGINS OF THE *MERCADO AGROPECUARIO*

As it entered the most serious crisis in its history, euphemistically called the "Special Period in Time of Peace" (SP), Cuba chose a hybrid strategy which combined elements of a Chinese-style opening to the world market with the autarky model of North Korea. While it would be difficult to speak about an economic blueprint during the Special Period, the main policies can be summarized as follows: austerity measures aimed at conserving energy and reducing imports of raw materials; increasing domestic food production; attracting foreign investment; expanding markets for Cuba's traditional and non-traditional exports such as biotechnology; an emphasis on the development of tourism; and some limited managerial and structural reforms at the enterprise or ministerial level (Pérez-López 1995, p. 128). In any case an increasing use of market-like features in the Cuban economy can be seen from the announcement of the Special Period in August 1990 to the present.

We can divide the SP into three approximate phases: the Dual Strategy Phase (August 1990 to mid-1993); the Domestic Reform Phase (mid-1993 to August 1994); and the Mixed-Market Phase (September 1994 to the present). [14]

---

13. "By drastically limiting the pool of potential sellers and refusing to regulate prices, Fidel had practically guaranteed that MLC prices would remain high. And the rise in taxes, from an easily circumvented 3% to a carefully enforced 20%, restored some of the incentives for black market activities (Rosenberg 1992a, p. 451)."

14. Measures were introduced as necessary actions in order to address specific problems such as capital accumulation and investment (*inversión extranjera* and *empresas mixtas*), excess liquidity or budget deficits (*saneamiento de finanzas internas*), stimulate production (*mercados* or UBPCs) or create employment (*auto-empleo*). However, these measures have been encumbered by high levels of regulation and in the case of self-employment, high entry costs for individuals.

The Dual Strategy Phase was a period of "mixed" approaches. The formal economy consisted of a market-oriented external sector and a command-style domestic sector. By the end of 1990, a two-tiered economic policy was set where external policies were increasingly connected to the world market economy and domestic policies were based on austerity and autarkist measures.[15] The external economy emphasized the cultivation of new trade partners, export diversification, tourism, and foreign investment (Mesa-Lago 1994a). The domestic economy continued to be characterized by Guevarist strategies such as the ambitious *Programa Alimentario* [Food Program], the return of moral incentives and voluntary mass mobilizations.[16] This situation created strong contradictory effects, such as a boom in the black market and an increase in crime ("Régimen," 1992; Whitefield 1991, 1992). The intention of this policy was to insert Cuba into the world market economy while keeping the world of the market out of Cuba's domestic economy.

EL LLAMAMIENTO

In March 1990, the Central Committee of the Cuban Communist Party invited Cubans to participate in mass meetings to discuss important issues. The "llamamiento" [convocation] to the Fourth Party Congress was made for the purpose of "deepening the process of rectification" and to "permit the perfecting of society" starting with the Party itself. The first round of meetings held in April was abruptly canceled by the Party leadership who complained about the lack of sincerity and real debate.

The Party reconvened the meetings in the summer after establishing the bounds of discussion: the one-party system, the socialist nature of the economy, and the leadership of Fidel Castro (Pérez-Stable 1994, p.169). This time, citizens felt free to express themselves. One of the most popular changes requested was the return of the free peasant markets— the MLCs (Gómez 1992, p. 13; Pérez-Stable 1994, p. 169; later confirmed in deliberations at the Party Congress in October 1991 in "El campesinado" 1991; but not mentioned in discussion of "salient points" of the "Llamamiento" in Reed 1992, pp. 17-18).[17]

On the fourth day of the Congress, Manuel Alvarez, a delegate from Pinar del Río, brought up the MLCs. *Granma* obliquely reported, "he emphasized that he had gathered some opinions that criticized the situation that the markets had disappeared and that effective measures had not been taken against the black market, because people now don't go to the market, but to the countryside where they pay higher prices" ("El campesinado" 1991).

The response against the MLCs was strong. Delegate after delegate rejected the markets and underscored that the only solution to the problem of agricultural production and distribution was the Programa Alimentario (Food Program). One delegate, a CPA member, said he "felt ashamed to speak about the MLCs again. We can never go back to them because they didn't resolve anything. They only accomplished one thing: to make unscrupulous men rich." Another delegate said, "To allow the MLC would not only be a betrayal of the peasant, but to the people as a whole" ("El campesinado" 1991). Finally, Fidel addressed the delegates and rejected the MLCs

---

15. Ritter (1995) writes that Cuba has a "bifurcated economy" divided into a socialist and an internationalized spheres.

16. One of the centerpieces of the strategy to confront the Special Period was the Food Program. The program was started in 1990 and had two major goals: to make the country self-sufficient in tubers, vegetables and other food products and to increase the production of export crops such as citrus and sugar. To achieve its aims, the program required massive mobilization of labor from the cities to the countryside, the employment of vast resources to house, feed and clothe workers, the importation of irrigation equipment, trucks, machinery, seed, fertilizers, pesticides, and the building of a network of dams and irrigation fields (Mesa-Lago 1994a, p. 24).

17. The return of the MLCs was also one of the demands made by dissident groups. *La Carta de los Diez*, signed by members of the group *Criterio Alternativo* included it in its list of requested reforms.

calling them an unsuitable idea borrowed from abroad and a source of corruption.[18]

By mid-1992, it became obvious that the Food Program had been a failure. Many of the features designed to support the program such as the building of rural housing and new dams were canceled. The main reason cited by the regime was the drastic decline in imports of fertilizer, pesticides and fuel (see Pérez-López 1995, p. 131). Despite some modest gains in output in the period 1990-1992, e.g. tubers 16%, there were declines in the production of beef, pork, poultry and milk. The sugar harvest also experienced a drastic decrease: the 1992-1993 zafra yielded 4.2 million tons, while the year before it had reached 7 million tons (Pérez-López 1995, p. 133).

The black market became an important alternative to a population whose monthly rations were inadequate. "The black market rapidly expanded, became dollarized, and was increasingly supplied by goods stolen from the state sector and by foodstuffs illegally sold by private farmers" (Mesa-Lago 1994b, p. 25). Party and government officials continued to publicly oppose any liberalization of the agricultural sector. The regime responded by cracking down on economic crimes in police actions with names like "Operation Bell-the-Cat" (Whitefield 1991, 1992). "It isn't moral or proper to pilfer from society what it is due and later dedicate those resources to dealing in the black market for profit," reported the Cuban Press Agency (in "Régimen" 1992).

The dual approach had not stopped the precipitous decline of the economy and by mid-1993, the Cuban regime began to introduce market-oriented reforms into sectors of the domestic economy (Bussey 1993; Mesa-Lago 1994b). The most important measures were taken in the summer of 1993, which marks the beginning of the Domestic Reform Phase, included the legalization of hard currency (known as dollarization), the approval of limited self-employment and the creation of the UBPCs.[19]

The domestic reforms initiated in the summer of 1993 addressed some of the concerns, but it appears that they may have exacerbated existing tensions and were creating increasing inequality (ANEIC 1995a). They also revealed the increasing strength of a reformist tendency within the government willing to allow the play of market-oriented mechanisms in the economy. The changes introduced came with extensive restrictions and some observers noted that the regime was trying to "regulate" the reforms "to death" (Mesa-Lago 1994a).

The fidelista side, led by the maximum leader, stymied fiscal and structural reforms promoted by Finance Minister José Luis Rodríguez and others in the National Assembly of Popular Power in late 1993.

> "Fidel Castro led the chorus against capitalism and the 'excesses' of the profit motive and called for assemblies (parlamentos obreros) in workplaces and neighborhoods to discuss the package. Raúl Castro lambasted 'reformist bureaucrats' who did not have the 'real interests of the masses' in mind (Pérez-Stable 1995, p. 15)."

In an apparent victory for hardliners, the "parlamentos obreros" supported the Castros' call for caution with reforms in the Spring of 1994. At about the same time, the regime launched Operation Girón 94, a clampdown on illegal commerce of all kinds. This was accompanied by measures that placed limitations on the self-employment reforms of the year before,

---

18. After the Congress, Party leaders continued to trumpet the Food Program. They also dismissed the MLC as an insignificant contributor of only 2-3% of produce to consumers. At the same time that they decried it because it had a negative effect on agricultural production (see interview with Raúl Castellanos, member of the CC of the PCC in Gómez 1992).

19. *Unidades Básicas de Producción Cooperativa* (UBPCs) are production cooperatives formed from state farms in both the sugar and non-sugar sectors, authorized in September 1993 by the Council of Ministers. Some Cuban economists refer to the UBPCs as "the third agrarian reform" (e.g. lecture by Pedro Pablo Cuscó at the University of Miami, July 26, 1994). For different perspectives on the UBPCs, see Mesa-Lago (1994a.)

the closing of *paladares*[20] (which had actually started in December 1993), a crackdown on *jineteras* and *jineteros* [prostitutes and hustlers], black market profiteers nicknamed *macetas* and a campaign against illegal enrichment [enriquecimiento ilícito] (ANEIC 1995d; Alfonso 1994a; Mesa-Lago 1994b). In May 1994, the National Assembly agreed to what appeared to be a compromise package of measures that addressed the fiscal and budgetary problems of Cuba without taking actions that could be called "capitalist" or "neo-liberal."[21] The imminent opening of the markets had been rumored since the July party meetings (see Alfonso 1994b, Whitefield 1994a).

The MLCs were not mentioned in the press, but the "crisis of agricultural production and distribution" became almost a code phrase for indirectly discussing the issue. Part of the problem was that farmers were either cutting back on production or withholding production from the acopio in order to sell on the black market. ANAP president Osvaldo Lugo discussed it in a July 11, interview in *Trabajadores*. He suggested opening agricultural markets which could help in the areas of "distribution, regulation, and above all, encouraging peasants to produce more (quoted in Malapanis & Walters 1995)."

Raúl Castro had begun to take greater role in managing the crisis late in 1993. By the summer of 1994, his involvement became more important. He led three regional party conferences in July where he proclaimed "to satisfy the food needs of the people was the number one objective" ("Satisfacer" 1994). Raúl also delivered the speech at the 41st anniversary of the assault on the Moncada Barracks where he reiterated "today, the principal economic and political task, is the production of food, including sugar" (Castro, R. 1994).

Despite the straight-forward goal, contradictory measures exacerbated the tension and confusion on the island. As 1994 progressed, the crisis atmosphere intensified. Shortages, long and frequent electricity blackouts, and a deepening sense of hopelessness, especially among the youth. The result was an increase in illegal emigration, defections abroad and in foreign missions in Havana, an epidemic of street crime and a general disdain for order. The informal or second economy grew to make up for the receding Cuban State. A Cuban economist is quoted as saying during this period, "there is no clear government economic policy. Everything is vague. You don't know exactly what is permitted" (Slevin 1994).

The regime was unable to head off the climax of the crisis: the violent anti-government street demonstrations in Havana of August 5 (the Maleconazo[22]). The disturbance was quickly quelled, and the regime resorted to one of its traditional 'safety valves' for discontent by allowing Cubans to leave on almost anything that would float.[23] The *Maleconazo* proved to be a turning point in the policy debate allowing the more pragmatic tendencies to come to the fore and reintroduce markets as a way to encourage production and to address other problems of the economy.

The Mixed-Market Phase emerged in September 1994 in the wake of the events of the summer with the announcement of the opening of the *mercado agropecuario* which the Cuban people had openly requested during the 1990 *llamamiento*. Had the regime been planning to open the markets all along? If yes, the *Maleconazo* and the *Balsero* crisis delayed the

---

20. *Paladares* are small- to medium-sized private restaurants usually run out of people's homes. They are named after the name of a restaurant chain featured in a Brazilian soap opera broadcast in Cuba in the early 1990s (ANEIC 1995b). Current regulations limit them to no more than 12 chairs.

21. The trade union newspaper *Trabajadores* said that some the proposed measures "looked neoliberal or capitalist" and urged caution, echoing Fidel and Raúl.

22. From *Malecón*, the name of the seawall along the Havana littoral. It is also the name of the street that follows its path. The disturbances occurred along the *Malecón* and in the streets of Central Havana.

23. Approximately 37,145 Cubans left the island by sea in 1994. Over 32,000 left between August 1 and September 13, 1994, when the Cuban government began to enforce the migration agreement signed with the United States (Mesa-Lago 1995, p. 6). For more information on who the *balseros* were, see Ackerman (1995).

planned announcement of the markets (Mesa-Lago 1995, p. 17). However, at least one knowledgeable Party activist resident on the island, claims that there were no definite plans. She credits the August riot and government concern over popular discontent expressed by the rapid departure of over 30,000 people (telephone interview, May 3, 1995). Bert Hoffman also notes this coincidence and points to the accelerating rhythm of change after August (Hoffman 1995, p. 99).

The National Association of Independent Economists of Cuba (ANEIC) came to another conclusion. They opined that it was the potential impact of the Clinton Administration's restriction of remittances from the United States that finally forced the regime hardliners to open the MAs, not primarily a fear of a social explosion:

> "Concientes de toda esta situación y percatados de que la medida tomada por el presidente de los Estados Unidos, William Clinton parece definitiva, el Estado comienza a buscar soluciones de emergencia que no estaban contempladas en la línea inicial de acción ya que van en contra de los principios fundamentales que trataba de mantener. . . consideramos que el mercado agropecuario surge en última instancia como consecuencia de la afectación de la entrada de divisa que ha tenido el país . . . lo cual ratifica indiscutiblemente las posibilidades de quedarse sin las reservas y sin poder de importaciones (ANEIC 1995c, p. 14)."

Raúl Castro confirmed in September that the *mercado* had been discussed at three regional party conferences held in July that he had chaired (Báez 1994, see also Alfonso 1994b).[24] A review of Raúl's announcement of the opening of the MAs revealed that the debates over the summer were intense, but does not reveal if a decision to reopen markets was taken at these meetings (Batista Valdés 1994).

After the Cuba-U.S. agreement stanched the rafter exodus, the balance of power shifted toward the reformists who were now free to try a mixed-market strategy. The market-oriented measures of this stage were to be accompanied by reforms of the tax system, a new foreign investment law, the restructuring of state entities (*redimensionamiento*) and the massive dismissal of over 500,000 state employees (*racionalización de plantilla*), but these moves have been delayed.

THE *MERCADO AGROPECUARIO*

"Si hay comida para el pueblo no importan los riesgos" —Raúl Castro[25]

The Announcement

The opening of the *Mercado agropecuario* was announced in an interview with Raúl Castro published in the Communist Party daily *Granma* on September 17, 1994.[26] In it he declared, "the country's main political, military and ideological problem today is to feed itself . . . in order to alleviate the situation, [we] expect to open farmers markets soon" (Báez 1994, p. 6). The news came at the end of a difficult summer and after long discussions within the party and government regarding the crisis of agricultural production and distribution (see Alfonso 1994b; R. Castro 1994; "Satisfacer " 1994).

Within days, a special meeting was called to explain the move to those who would be involved in its implementation and administration.[27] According to Raúl, prices at the new markets would be set by supply and demand, and their operations would be regulated and taxed by the government. He explained that if the measure was carried out systematically, it

---

24. The imminent opening of the markets had been rumored since the July party meetings (see Alfonso 1994b; Whitefield 1994a).

25. "If there is food for the people, the risks don't matter" (Raúl Castro in Báez 1994).

26. The *Mercado Industrial y Artesanal* (MIA) opened on December 1, 1994. Vendors at the MIAs can sell non-primary products to the public at prices set by supply and demand (Rodríguez Fernández 1994). This was followed by the re-authorization of *paladares* and a small expansion in the list of permitted self-employment categories.

27. Among those reported in attendance were Politburo members, provincial government leaders, party cadres, administrators from the ministries of agriculture and of internal commerce, as well as leaders of the National Association of Small Farmers (ANAP) (Pagés 1994a).

would help stimulate production (Pagés 1994b). Other stated objectives of the new measure included: to combat the negative effects of the black market, to increase the variety of products available to the public, to make the surpluses from self-consumption plots available at the markets, to encourage the cultivation of fallow land and to give consumers additional choices (Pagés 1994a).

On October 1, 1994, approximately 130 *Mercados Agropecuarios* opened throughout Cuba (Pagés 1994d). Although leaders played down the immediate impact of the markets, the crowds that greeted them on the opening weekend were enthusiastic despite the high prices.[28] The Cuban press was restrained in its coverage: "We can't expect the opening of the markets to become a magic fix" (Pagés 1994e), but the foreign press was more effusive in its reporting (see for example Vicent 1994, Whitefield 1994b).

Producers could sell their surplus yields once they fulfilled their monthly quota to the state procurement system (*acopio*). Prices were set by supply and demand. The following products could not be sold at the markets: potatoes, rice, beef, horse, mule or donkey meat, fresh milk, coffee, tobacco, cacao or their derivatives. The Provincial Assemblies of Popular Power would administer the markets and be in charge of granting permits, doing inspections and collecting rents and taxes.

The resolution regarding the operation of the markets authorized 8 kinds of sellers: State farms and enterprises, non-sugar producing UBPCs, CPAs, the farms of the Youth Workers' Army (EJT), the Credit and Services Cooperatives (CCS) representing their individual members, independent small farmers, state enterprises with plots for their self-consumption, individuals who produce in parcels for the self-consumption of their families, and people who produce in their yards and in small plots (see "Decreto y resolución" 1994).

All of the entities may select "representatives" to sell their products in the markets except those in the last two categories.[29] This is a major difference from the MLCs of the 1980s where producers could only sell what they grew on their own land (Rosenberg 1992b, p. 253).[30] ANAP president Orlando Lugo noted, "a lot of them [peasants] do not like to go to the markets. We're better off having the farmer producing on the farm instead of selling in the market (Borrego 1994b)." The distinction between "representative" and "middleman" other than their legal status is not very clear.

Under the original MLC legislation, farmers were to sell in their own municipalities and could not sell outside of it. The MLCs were was the difficulty of transporting produce to the predominantly urban markets (Rosenberg 1992a). The original MLC ban was intended to discourage the employment of drivers and middlemen and to keep producers from concentrating in large cities, particularly Havana. This problem was solved for the MAs with a decree liberalizing the rules allowing the leasing of vehicles announced on October 7, 1994. Once drivers completed their required assignments, they were free to lease their trucks, tractors and other vehicles to agricultural producers. The fee was to be arrived at by mutual agreement of the contracting parties. The decree even allowed military farms to lease their off-duty vehicles for this purpose (Vicent 1994).

On the first weekend the seller with the highest volume of sales in Havana was the EJT, followed by the UBPCs and the CPAs (Pagés 1994e). By November 17, *Granma* reported $187 million pesos in sales since their opening. The MAs were averaging $4.7

---

28. The Ministry of Internal Commerce estimated that there were $14.5 million pesos in sales and over $700,000 pesos in taxes collected in the first two days (Pagés 1994e).

29. All others are apparently limited to one representative per entity (Lee 1995d).

30. This did not stop the emergence of "intermediaries"- middlemen who sold produce at the MLCs. The controversy over "intermediaries" becoming rich by selling products they did not produce was a major point of attack for Fidel Castro when he banned MLCs in 1986.

million pesos per day by early November. The article also asserted that 70% of the sellers were small farmers, although they made up only 30-35% of produce on sale (Calzadilla 1994).[31] At year's end the MAs had brought in more than $468 million pesos in sales, $47 million pesos in taxes and had the participation of an average of 4,000 vendors nationally. Agriculture Vice Minister Miguel Angel Casa praised the MAs and reported that producers had increased their plantings due to the incentive of the market. The ANAP president announced that because of their earnings in the MA, 180 CPAs would retire their debts with the National Bank by 1996 (de la Rosa 1995).

There were reports that CCS, private farmers and *parceleros* were reluctant to participate because of their past experience with the MLCs and more recent experiences with the campaigns against *macetas* and illegal enrichment. ANAP president Lugo was interviewed by Radio Rebelde on October 1, 1994 as he visited small farmers in order to encourage their involvement.

The most extensive review of the performance of the MAs in the Cuban press was a three-part series published in *Granma* in late March (see Lee 1995b, 1995c, 1995d). The articles reprised the most common consumer complaints: high prices and the stark contrast between mostly empty state-run *placitas* and bustling *agromercados*.[32] People do complain, but the writer says that if consumers were asked if the MAs should be eliminated, their answer would be a definite 'no.'

As of late March 1995, there were 211 MAs in Cuba, 29 of them in Havana. Approximately 19% of all agricultural products were sold through MAs. Havana's markets account for 56% of sales income, 32% of products sold. The MAs are still accessible to a limited portion of the population that can afford its prices. An increase in the participation of the state farms,

the EJT and the UBPCs in the MA are among the measures being studied in the hopes that their greater involvement will act as a price regulator (Lee 1995c, 1995d).

By Spring 1995, the cost of many products at the MAs had reportedly declined. The price of pork dropped between 25%-50% from October and other reductions were reported in the price of tubers, vegetables and grains. At the same time, a decrease in sales volume was also reported indicating a reduction of spending power, i.e. a decline of 19,000 quintals for the first week in April, compared to the first week in March. Another explanation for the decline in price and in sales was the improvement in the quality and quantity of goods for sale at cheaper state-run *placitas*. *Juventud Rebelde* reported that some sellers, mostly small peasants, were so concerned about the dropping prices that they were trying to band together to fix a floor price for their products (González, A. 1995).

THE *MERCADOS* COMPARED

The MLCs and the MAs shared many similarities such as the requirement that producers prove the fulfillment of their *acopio* quota, and the ban on sales of export cash crops and beef. The law authorizing the MA addressed many of the limitations of Decree 66—the MLC law. For example, the list of eligible sellers was increased so that virtually anyone who produces an agricultural product may participate if they meet the requirements and get the permission of the local authorities. Producers may also employ "representatives," hire transportation and sell in any municipality that authorizes them (see "Decreto" 1994; Rosenberg 1992b).

The most important policy change is who can sell? The MLC permitted sales by private and state sector producers. Participation by the state sector was discouraged and later banned after Operation Bird-on-a-wire. So far, the MAs have seen an opposite trend;

---

31. An economist living in Cuba said in a conversation that in Havana, location of the largest and most lucrative markets, the state sector made up 70%, while the private agricultural sector made up 30% (11/14/94).

32. Susana Lee synthesizes the complaint as follows: "Pero... las placitas están vacías y los mercados llenos en cantidad y variedad" (Lee 1995b).

the state sector is being encouraged to increase its involvement in the market as a way to self-finance the
operation of enterprises (Bordón & Roque 1995; Lee
1995c) and to help regulate prices (Lee 1995d). The
military is also very involved through its farms, the
EJT, and military-administered enterprises. This is
not surprising in light of the increasing militarization
of the Cuban economy including agriculture (Lee
1995b). The Ministry of Interior's farm system
which uses prison labor to grow crops for the ministry's commisaries, may soon be selling their surplus
on the MAs as well.

The private sector was reluctant at first to participate
in the MA (ANEIC 1995b) no doubt because of earlier experiences with the regime's drastic policy
swings. There was also an underlying fear that many
sellers and producers had about being labeled *macetas*
and losing everything in light of the very public anti-
illegal enrichment campaign in the Spring of 1994
(Bordón & Roque 1995, p.5). Their fears appear to
have subsided because of the large presence of the
state sector especially the EJT.

The private farmers found that the state sector
soaked up a substantial portion of the excess liquidity
of pesos in the first six months. Their large presence
in some markets gives the state sector price-setting
powers. Reports indicated that the State and para-
State vendors constituted between 10-35 % of sellers,
but accounted for approximately 70% of sales. However, a recent CEPAL report noted that 70% of sellers were peasants. This discrepancy reflects differing
definitions of peasant. The CPAs, the UBPCs and
the other entities have lower costs and can spread any
losses among members. Individual private farmers
may not have that option.

Consumers complained bitterly about high prices at
the MLCs. Popular demands for price controls were
dismissed by Fidel as interference in the market. The
MLC reforms of 1983 actually made matters worse.
Reducing the number of sellers and not regulating
prices virtually guaranteed that prices remained high
until the end (Rosenberg 1992a). There have also
been complaints about the prices at the MAs but
consumers seem reticent about complaining (Lee

1995b, 1995d), especially after what happened to the
MLC.

The proportion of consumers who have regular access to the MAs is limited to between 10%-20% because of prices (Bordón 1995, p. 2; Bordón & Roque
1995, p. 6). The State showed concern about the
contrast between abundant MAs and empty shelves
at State *libreta* stores. This encouraged the regime to
redirect potatoes, cabbage and other greens to the
placitas (González, A. 1995). An increase in the availability of some foodstuffs at state stores and the large-
scale involvement of the state sector has also helped
bring down prices in the MAs. Lower prices might
help placate low-income consumers who Fidel
claimed to speak for when he banned the MLCs in
1986.

IDEOLOGICAL *CONTRAPUNTEO*

Elite support or rejection of the MLCs was described
above. Rosenberg quotes José Luis Llovio-Menéndez
about a secret report circulated among party and
ministry elites in 1980 that in effect, sabotaged the
MLCs just after they opened. This would explain the
sparse support the MLCs received from the *nomenklatura*. Political elites have also been reluctant to
show support for the MAs. Perhaps it is still to early
to tell but some determinations about the actual political and institutional supporters of the MAs is possible.

ANAP president Lugo and Finance Minister Rodríguez appear to have encouraged Raúl to discuss
market approaches to solving the problem of agricultural production and distribution, as well as the fiscal
and monetary problems Cuba faced in 1994 at the
July party conferences. Raúl also announced the
opening of the MAs and appeared as the front man
for the market option (Báez 1994; Borrego 1994b).
It would have been unseemly for Fidel to announce
such a drastic turnaround, especially after his vituper-
ative attacks on the MLCs at the Fourth Party Congress. This is not to say that the MAs returned because of the victory of a *raulista* faction. There is no
evidence for the existence of such a faction. Raúl's involvement was both tactical and cosmetic.

The main institutional supporters of the MAs appear to be the National Association of Small Farmers (ANAP), the Agriculture Ministry (MINAG), the Finance and Prices Ministry, the Interior Commerce Ministry, the Provincial Popular Power governments, and possibly the military. Other supporters include farmers and medium-higher income consumers. Opponents of the MAs have accepted their operation if only as a transitory measure to deal with the food and financial problems facing Cuba. They probably include Fidel and some of his closest ideological colleagues such as José Machado Ventura, Armando Hart, Ricardo Alarcón, as well as party and government functionaries involved in the *acopio* and the central resource distribution system who lose power and prestige as the markets begin to function.

The array of detractors, now muted by current necessities, does not bode well for the MAs if the food problem is alleviated enough for the regime to feel more secure about the population's nutrition and quiescence. The fate of the MAs, like the fate of the MLCs, depends on the political arrangements of friends and foes that can develop around them.

CONCLUSION: POLITICS AND MARKETS

The story of the rise and fall of the MLCs and the emergence of the MAs, are emblematic of the struggle between two different approaches to socialist economics. The opening of the MAs are evidence of the failure of Cuba's socialist experiments and of its leadership. The MA also represents the legalization (and to some extent the manipulation by the state) of the Cuba's functioning market economy, the black market.[33]

The *contrapunteo* between ideology and pragmatism intensified as the economic crisis of the SP worsened. In an important sense, the MAs are part of a struggle for policy dominance of three different approaches among Cuban political and economic elites: one *fidelista* and ideological and two more pragmatic tendencies. By mid-1993, these distinct tendencies were discernable: a hardline *fidelista* group led by Fidel Castro wedded to Guevarist moral economic policies and opposed the use of market mechanisms; a Conjunctural-Pragmatic tendency that favored limited reforms and the strategic use of markets in a centrally planned economy, a "*mercado en la economía;*" and a Structural-Reformist option which supported major structural changes that would lead to a form of market-socialism, an "*economía con mercado.*"

It is not the intention of any of these tendencies to "propel" Cuba to market capitalism, but to "save" the Revolution and its accomplishments. In the Cuban case, reform refers to changes within the system (conjunctural) or to a model of reform-communism (structural) not to a Velvet Revolution.

Like the MLC, the *Mercado Agropecuario* is the result of a compromise between *Fidelista* orthodoxy and reform. However, this time, the reformists were in a stronger position to project their policy options.

The *fidelista* group is led, not surprisingly, by Fidel Castro himself. They justify the changes by blaming external forces for Cuba's predicament (e.g. collapse of the Soviet Union, the embargo, weather). They highlight the moral dangers and human costs of reforms in terms of increased inequality, privilege, corruption, and foreign influences.[34]

The group has been resistant to the changes by slowing their implementation, imposing restrictions, appealing to the egalitarian values of the Revolution, and relying on "*el genio colectivo del pueblo* [the collective genius of the people]." Fidel and other leaders

---

33. "If the state experiences difficulties in meeting foreign debt obligations or import requirements, it is likely to turn to the black market to tap its resources" (Los 1990, p. 217).

34. *Granma*, perhaps tongue-in-cheek, referred to the danger of the "black market of ideas" in an article criticizing the plot of a popular television soap opera from Japan called Oshin, "the formerly battleworthy peasant leader Kota confesses his *desmerengamiento* on screen, and says that it has not been worthwhile to struggle for the unreachable goals of yesterday. The prudent thing to do is to dedicate himself to business and free competition... the Japanese *maceta* is in drag disguised as an honorable businessman!" (Pita Astudillo 1994). *Desmerengamiento* literally means the collapse of a baked merengue; the collapse of something frothy and full of hot air; like a pack of cards.

recognize that the MA and other market features are "capitalist elements" but insist that only an "idiot" would say that Cuba is moving toward capitalism.[35] Fidel and others often give the impression that the reforms are transitory measures and can be reversed whenever the extraordinary conditions are overcome. This viewpoint is held by Fidel, members of the historic leadership, and other Communist Party functionaries.

The other two groups represent the pragmatic side of the dichotomy. They differ mostly as to pacing and in their final objective. One group is defined by a pragmatic conjunctural approach that favors limited reforms and the strategic use of markets in a centrally planned economy controlled by a "capable State" (Alonso, A. 1993, p. 88), a "*mercado en la economía* [a market in the economy]." The conjuncturalists prefer a slow and calibrated economic opening with as little political impact as possible. They present reform as a technocratic exercise consonant with socialism.

The Chinese and Vietnamese models appeal to this group because they allow for an economic opening toward the outside while the political regime can remain unchanged. This group received a boost when on a visit to Paris in 1994, Fidel quipped that Cuba was interested in the Chinese model. The intensification of the Cuba-Vietnam relationship is also evidence that this is an option being studied closely. Nevertheless, some the reforms announced by Lage and Rodriguez in late 1993 were panned as "neo-capitalist" or "neo-liberal" by Fidel, Raúl and other hardliners. The measures were either postponed or altered to reflect orthodox concerns. Their proposals do bear some resemblance to IMF structural adjustment plans and show the influence of the Solchaga Report ("El informe secreto" 1992). They also encouraged the study of China and Vietnam and their amalgam of Asian despotism and enclave capitalism.

The other reformist tendency can be called "structuralist" in that it recognizes the need for systemic

change without neccesarily giving up on socialism. Proponents are the policy makers who represent a compromise between stagnation and reform. Their point-of-view is shared by individuals that come from academic, finance or non-party backgrounds. They possibly have support among those who have a stake in the new market arrangements (e.g. ANAP President Lugo, other producers) or in the emerging State capitalist sector of mixed-enterprises, many of whom are former military, former party cadre hacks or the scions of *nomenklatura* families. They assert that reforms were justified for the main purpose of generating the economic resources to maintain "independence, social justice, and human solidarity" (Lage 1994). In their view, the solution is the promotion of growth and production, (Rodríguez Derivet 1995) with the State intervening where needed. Like the other pragmatic tendency, they claimed that the reforms are "inevitable" or "irreversible" (Alonso, A. 1993; see also interview with José Luis Rodríguez by Rodríguez Derivet 1995).

The Structural-Reformist option supports structural changes that would lead to a form of market socialism, an "*economía con mercado* [an economy with markets]." They see the MAs as part of overall decentralization of decision making on production and distribution of foodstuffs. They believe markets can be regulated but while positive aspects of markets should be encouraged (see Carranza interview in González, L. 1995). Pedro Monreal writes, "economic reform implies fundamental change in Cuba's social and political structures" (1993, p. 10). Julio Carranza of the Center for the Study of America (CEA), an apparent structuralist, says that "socialism is, in the best of cases, the last of mercantile societies and as such, the place of markets in it must be recognized" (1992). They also acknowledge that "economic reform [is] a political process (Monreal 1993, p. 11)," and not just a technocratic exercise.

This tendency finds support mainly among academics, particularly younger economists. Some of their

---

35. Fidel prefers to interpret the MA in terms of production not marketization: "Nosotros hemos establecido que un 20% de la producción se lleve libremente al mercado---" ("Entrevista" 1995).

views were expressed at the recent 4th Congress of the National Association of Cuban Economists (ANEC). Some ANEC economists called for "urgent structural changes" especially the decentralization of business management and the restructuring of state enterprises. National Institute of Economic Research director Arturo Guzmán said, "the reform and reorganization process within the state enterprise must allow for the creation of an autonomous public trading business" (Costa 1995). Some economists urged that cooperatives and small private businesses be allowed to expand in order to cope with the coming crisis of mass unemployment (Costa 1995).

The truth is that there is little distance between the conjuncturalists and the structuralists. They both agree on a strategy: "to pursue long-term goals of economic reform under state control" (Monreal 1993, p. 11). They agree on the role of a strong state and on the importance of sustaining the Revolution's "achievements." Their differences are more on a theoretical level.

The intellectual and policy debate is narrow. It is being carried out within very restricted parameters (see for example Carranza, Monreal & Gutiérrez 1995). The basic limits have not changed: the Party, Socialism and Fidel. If the leadership perceives a challenge or the potential for one, conjuncturalists and structuralists can end up outside the circle of influence, economic policy dissidents like the members of the National Association of *Independent* Economists of Cuba (ANEIC).

The three tendencies presented here are by no means Cuba's only options; they are just the ones that originate from within the regime itself. There are other kinds of models and approaches represented by the democratic opposition on the island: a vague socialism "with a human face," Christian-inspired Social Economy, New Institutionalism, Neo-Liberalism, free-market capitalism and many others.

The reforms, the *Mercados* in particular, are timid and are obtained *"a regañadientes"* [grudgingly] from the top leadership. One of the effects of the compromised reforms has been that corruption and other economic crimes have increased, partly as strategies

to get around the restrictions. This reality has brought the expected moral outcry from Fidel and other hardline leaders seen in the last few months. The regulations and restrictions imposed on the market-oriented reforms such as the MAs and self-employment, are dampening the potential positive effects of the changes.

ANEIC economist Orlando Bordón makes a convincing argument that the reforms are actually just strategies to resolve conjunctural problems intended to maintain and preserve the model. He challenges the notion that the changes being made are reforms much less evidence of an opening. He writes, "perhaps we are in the presence of conjunctural capitalist patches that can be removed when the present crisis has been overcome" (Bordón 1995, p. 3)."

There is a sense that there is a race against time going on. The reformers may not get the opportunity to make the structural changes they desire unless something changes at the top. The orthodox position appears untenable in today's world, but there is no scarcity of models that combine the economic efficiency of the market with authoritarian political regimes. Markets do not automatically translate into liberty and democracy. Markets are not the same as capitalism, and while a market economy seems a prerequisite for democracy, a democratic system is not required for the operation of a market system. However optimal we may consider the combination of democracy and free markets, the Asian "models" are more attractive not only to the old *fidelistas*, but to the new state-capitalist entrepreneur of Cuba, the former party hack or military official who has found the pallid reforms personally rewarding. This may be the essence of an emerging Cuban model. It does not augur well in the short-run for democracy.

However, we should not discount the unintended consequences of the reforms either. The truth is that the "conjunctural capitalist patches" Bordón writes about appear to have taken a stronger hold than before; 1995 is not 1985. Marta Beatriz Roque writes that the seeds of a true market system are germinating in the MA, even among people who work for State enterprises.

These "seeds" are also sprouting as weeds in different sectors of the economy in the form of corruption, egoism, and misanthropy. The rampant abuses seen in the market enclaves in the Cuban economy (and in peripheral "market" activities such as prostitution, drug trafficking and the fencing of stolen goods) are also part of this sprouting.

The timid reforms may be intended to sustain basic needs and keep Fidel and the party in power, but they could lead elsewhere, maybe even to a real market and a real political opening. If this is where they end up, it will not be because of conjuncturalists or structuralists but because people are finding that they can "*resolver*" for themselves.

APPENDIX

Table 1 — Summary Characterization of Economic Periods — Predominant Approaches			
Period	**Fidelista**	**Mixed/Unclear**	**Reformist**
(1) Elimination of Capitalist System 1959-1960		●	
(2) Attempt to Introduce Orthodox / Stalinist Model 1961-1963		●	
(3) Debate over Models 1964-1966		●	
(4) Sino-Guevarist Period 1966-1970	●		
(5) Soviet Reform Model 1971-1986			●
Phases (a) Redefinition 1971-1974		✔	
(b) Institutionalization 1975-1984		✔	→ ✔ (MLCs)
(c) Re-centralization 1984-1986	✔		
(6) Rectification Process 1986-1990	●		
(7) Special Period 1991-1995		●	
Phases (a) Dual Strategy 1991-1993		✔	
(b) Domestic Reform 1993-1994		✔ →	✔
(c) Mixed Strategy 1994-1995			✔ (MAs)

Legend: ● - period ✔ - phase → - trend

Sources: Based in part on Mesa-Lago 1994b, Rodríguez 1990.

REFERENCES

ANEIC. 1995a. "Un retrato social." *Boletín de la Asociación Nacional de Economistas Independientes de Cuba.* 1 (1) January: 9-11.

ANEIC. 1995b [1994]. "Los mercados agropecuarios (primera parte)." *Boletín de la Asociación Nacional de Economistas Independientes de Cuba.* 1 (3): 13-15.

ANEIC. 1995c [1994]. "Las finanzas internas y el mercado agropecuario." *Boletín de la Asociación Nacional de Economistas Independientes de Cuba.* 1 (3): 16-18.

ANEIC. 1995d [1994]. "Enriquecimiento ilícito y los mercados agropecuarios." *Boletín de la Asociación Nacional de Economistas Independientes de Cuba.* 1 (3): 18-20.

Ackermann, Holly. 1995. "A Demographic Profile of Cuban *Balseros*, 1991-1994." University of Miami, unpublished paper.

Alfonso, Pablo. 1994a. "Marcha atrás a la dolarización." *El Nuevo Herald* (Miami). 3 May: 1A.

Alfonso, Pablo. 1994b. "Mercado libre agrícola regresa a Cuba en medio de crisis total." *El Nuevo Herald* (Miami). 22 September: 4A.

Alonso, Aurelio. 1993. "Las reformas cubanas y la introducción de la lógica de mercado en el sistema económico. Apreciaciones sobre los efectos sociales." Presented at the conference Social Aspects of the Logic of the Market in Societies of the South: Perspectives and Alternatives, University of Louvain, Belgium, 19-20 November. Reprinted in *Cuba en el mes, Dossier #4 (Cuba: transformaciones económicas)*, Elsa Barrera López, ed. January 1994.

Alonso, José F. 1992. "The Free Farmers Market: A Rejected Approach But A Possible Solution." In *Cuba in Transition, Volume 2.* Miami, FL: Latin American and Caribbean Center, Florida International University.

Báez, Luis. 1994. "Entrevista a Raúl Castro." *Granma.* 17 September: 3-6.

Batista Valdés, Pastor. 1994. "¿Es lógico seguir pensando igual? En torno a las reuniones con Raúl." *Granma.* 21 September: 2.

Benjamin, Medea, Joseph Collins and Michael Scott. 1984. *No Free Lunch: Food & Revolution in Cuba Today.* San Francisco, CA: Food First Books.

Bordón, Orlando. 1995. "Reformas o estrategias ¿Qué cree usted?" *Boletín de la Asociación Nacional de Economistas Independientes de Cuba* 1 (4) May-June: 1-2.

Bordón, Orlando and Marta Beatriz Roque. 1995. "Orígenes, desarrollo y perspectivas del mercado agropecuario." *Boletín de la Asociación Nacional de Economistas Independientes de Cuba* 1 (3): 5-6.

Borrego, Juan Antonio. 1994a. "Analiza Lage experiencia en venta liberada de productos." *Granma.* 27 September: 8.

Borrego, Juan Antonio. 1994b. "El plan como principio sagrado." *Granma.* 1 October: 3.

Burnhill, Lauren A. 1985. "The Private Sector in Cuban Agriculture, 1958-1985: A Socio-Economic Study." Occasional Paper No. 8. Washington, D.C.: Central American and Caribbean Program, School of Advanced International Studies, The Johns Hopkins University.

Bussey, Jane. 1993. "Castro opens Cuba's door to capitalism a crack." *The Miami Herald.* 1 August: 1K.

Calzadilla Rodríguez, Iraida. 1994a. "Mercados agropecuarios: ventas diarias por más de cuatro millones de pesos." *Granma.* 17 November: 2.

"El campesinado está íntimamente comprometido con la Revolución y sabe de sus beneficios; admitir el mercado libre campesino sería traicionar al campesino y al pueblo." 1991. *Granma.* 15 October: 4-6. (From Day 4 of IV Congress of the Cuban Communist Party).

Carranza, Julio. 1992. "Cuba: los retos de la economía." *Cuadernos de Nuestra América* 9 (19) July-December: 131-123.

Carranza, Julio, Pedro Monreal and Luis Gutiérrez. 1995 (forthcoming). *Cuba: la restructuración de la economía (una propuesta para el debate).* Havana: Editorial de Ciencias Sociales.

Castro, Fidel. 1982. "Discurso en el VI Congreso de la ANAP." *Bohemia* 74 (22) 28 May: 68-79.

Castro, Fidel. 1986a. "The Interests of the Country, of the Population Will Not Be Sacrificed for the Sake of the Interests of a Group That Wants to Take the Easy Way Out, Get Easy Bonuses, Look for Easy Profits." *Granma Weekly Review.* May 18: 3-4.

Castro, Fidel. 1986b. "El principio del fin de la mala yerba." *Bohemia* 78 (21) 23 May: 4-9.

Castro, Fidel. 1986c. "Unanimous Call for End to Free Peasant Market." *Granma Weekly Review.* 1 June: 2-4.

Castro, Fidel. 1986d. "En el II Encuentro Nacional de Cooperativas Agropecuarias." *Cuba Socialista* 6 (5): 49-76.

Castro, Fidel. 1986e. "No Matter How Important Profits May Be, Enterprises Must Think Above All of the Interests of the Country and Society." *Granma Weekly Review.* 6 July: 2-3.

Castro, Fidel. 1986f. "Discurso en la clausura de la sesión diferida del III Congreso del Partido." *Trabajadores.* 8 December: 1-8.

Castro, Raúl. 1994. "Discurso en el acto central nacional por el aniversario 41 del asalto a los cuarteles Moncada." *Granma.* 27 July: 4-5.

"Clausuró Carlos Lage seminario sobre mercado de productos industriales." 1994. *Granma.* 10 November: 2.

Costa, Dalia. 1995. "Economists call for reversal of business policy." *InterPress Service.* 22 March.

"Decreto y resolución sobre el mercado agropecuario." 1994. *Granma.* 21 November: 3.

de la Rosa Labrada, Amado. 1995. "Se confirma validez del mercado agropecuario." *Opciones.* 5-11 February.

"Entrevista a Fidel." 1995. *Granma.* 8 February: 3-14.

Fernández, Damián J. 1992. "Opening the Blackest of Black Boxes: Theory and Practice of Decision Making in Cuba's Foreign Policy." *Cuban Studies* 22: 53-78.

Figueroa, Victor M. and Alberto Averhoff. 1986. "Desarrollo de la producción agropecuaria y su repercusión en el mejoramiento del nivel de vida de los trabajadores del campo cubano en veinticinco años de revolución socialista." *Economía y desarrollo* 90 (January-February): 51-68.

Figueroa, Victor and and Luis A. García. 1984. Apuntes sobre la comercialización agrícola no estatal." *Economía y desarrollo*: 34-61.

Gómez, Andrés. 1992. "Peleándola como gallos finos. Entrevista a Raúl Castellanos, Miembro del Comité Central del Partido Comunista de Cuba." *Areíto* 3-Segunda Epoca (10-11): 5-15.

González, Ana Margarita. 1995. "Mercado agropecuario: los precios bajan. . . ¿Por qué?" *Juventud Rebelde.* 16 April.

González, Edward. 1974. *Cuba under Castro: The Limits of Charisma.* Boston: Houghton-Mifflin Company.

González, Luis Jesús. 1995. "Cuba ante el laberinto del mercado: entrevista a Julio Carranza." *El Habanero.* 27 January.

Hoffman, Bert, ed. 1995. *Cuba: apertura y reforma económica. Perfil de un debate.* Caracas: Instituto de Estudios Iberoamericanos de Hamburgo/Editorial Nueva Sociedad.

"El informe secreto (El informe Solchaga)." 1992. *Esta Semana* (San José, Costa Rica). 22-28 February: 18.

Kornai, János. 1992. *The Socialist System: The Political Economy of Communism.* Princeton, NJ: Princeton University Press.

Lage Dávila, Carlos. 1994. "Discurso en la inauguración de la XII Feria Internacional de La Habana, ExpoCuba." *Granma.* 1 November: 3.

Lee, Susana. 1995a. "A casi seis meses de funcionamiento de los mercados agropecuarios (1): lapso adecuado para echarles una ojeada." *Granma.* 30 March: 2.

Lee, Susana. 1995b. "Perfeccionamiento empresarial en las FAR." *Granma.* 11 March.

Lee, Susana. 1995c. "A casi seis meses de funcionamiento de los mercados agropecuarios (2): aún no hay más producción pero sí mayores siembras que lo posibilitarán." *Granma.* 31 March.

Lee, Susana. 1995d. "A casi seis meses de funcionamiento de los mercados agropecuarios (3): el sí y el no de los precios y los resultados de una inspección." *Granma.* 1 April.

Los, Maria, ed. 1990. *The Second Economy in Marxist States.* New York: St. Martin's Press.

Malapanis, Argiris and Mary-Alice Walters. 1995. "Agricultural Markets Raise Expectations that Food Scarcity May Ease in Cuba." *The Militant.* Posted 21 January in IGC:militant.news.

Martínez, Magda. 1981a. "Consideraciones en torno al Congreso Agropecuario." *Bohemia* 73 (27) 3 July: 36.

Martínez, Magda. 1981b. "Abaratar los mercados." *Bohemia* 73 (30) 24 July: 33.

Martínez, Magda. 1982. "Un tema de actualidad." *Bohemia* 74 (13) 26 March: 58.

Medin, Tzvi. 1990. *Cuba: The Shaping of Revolutionary Consciousness.* Boulder, CO: Lynne Rienner Publishers.

Mesa-Lago, Carmelo. 1989. "The Cuban Economy in the 1980s: The Return of Ideology." In *Cuban Communism* (Seventh Edition), Irving Louis Horowitz, ed. New Brunswick, NJ: Transaction Publishers.

Mesa-Lago, Carmelo. 1994a. *Are Economic Reforms Propelling Cuba to the Market?* Miami: North-South Center, University of Miami.

Mesa-Lago, Carmelo. 1994b. *Breve historia económica de la Cuba socialista: Políticas, resultados y perspectivas.* Madrid: Alianza Editorial.

Mesa-Lago, Carmelo. 1995. "Cuba's Raft Exodus of 1994: Causes, Settlement, Effects and Future." *North-South Agenda Papers* 12 (April). Miami: University of Miami, North-South Center.

Monreal, Pedro. 1993. "To market, to market. . ." *Hemisfile* 4 (3) May-June: 10-11.

Pagés, Raisa. 1994a. "Mercado agropecuario: abrirán paulatinamente a partir del primero de octubre." *Granma.* 21 September: 1.

Pagés, Raisa. 1994b. "Clausuró Raúl el seminario sobre mercados agropecuarios." *Granma.* 22 September: 1.

Pagés, Raisa. 1994c. "Una medida necesaria y realista que debemos asumir con audacia." *Granma.* 24 September: 3.

Pagés, Raisa. 1994d. "Comienza hoy nueva etapa en la comercialización agricola." *Granma.* 1 October: 1.

Pagés, Raisa. 1994e. "Recógense primeras experiencias de los mercados agropecuarios." *Granma.* 4 October: 1.

Pérez-López, Jorge F. 1995. *Cuba's Second Economy: From Behind the Scenes to Center Stage.* New Brunswick, NJ: Transaction Publishers.

Pérez-Stable, Marifeli. 1994. *The Cuban Revolution: Origins, Course and Legacy.* New York: Oxford University Press.

Pérez-Stable, Marifeli. 1995. "Politics, Crisis, and Transformation in Cuba: Perspectives and Prospects (Draft)." Presented at the symposium "Toward a New Cuba?" Princeton University, 7-8 April.

Pita Astudillo, Félix. 1994. "¿Mercado negro de ideas? La otra Oshin." *Granma.* 12 November: 4.

Pozo, Alberto and Magda Martínez. 1986. "El pricipio del fin de la mala yerba." *Bohemia.* 21 (May 23): 4-9.

Reed, Gail. 1992. *Island in the Storm: The Cuban Communist Party's Fourth Congress.* Melbourne, Australia: Ocean Press.

"Régimen cubano fustiga mercado negro agrícola." 1992. *The Miami Herald.* 16 May: 3A.

Ritter, Archibald R. M. 1995. "The Structural Bifurcation of Cuba's Economy in the 1990s: Causes, Consequences and Cure (Preliminary Draft)." Presented at symposium "Toward a New Cuba?" Princeton University, 7-8 April.

Rodríguez, José Luis. 1990. *Estrategia del desarrollo económico en Cuba.* Havana: Editorial de Ciencias Sociales.

Rodríguez Derivet, Arleen. 1995. "La solución es producir." *Juventud Rebelde.* 26 February. [Interview with José Luis Rodríguez].

Rodríguez Fernández, Alberto. 1994. "A partir de mañana mercado industrial y artesanal." *Granma.* 30 November: 1.

Rosenberg, Jonathan. 1992a. "Cuba's Free Market Experiment: *Los mercados libres campesinos,* 1980-1986." *Latin American Research Review* 27 (3): 51-89.

Rosenberg, Jonathan. 1992b. "Politics and Paradox in the Liberalization of a Command Economy: The Case of Cuba's Free Peasant Markets, 1980-1986." Ph.D. diss. University of California at Los Angeles.

"Satisfacer las necesidades alimentarias de la población, objetivo número uno de la actividad económica y política actual." 1994. *Granma.* 23 July: 2.

Slevin, Peter. 1994. "Cubanos pronostican duros años de transición." *El Nuevo Herald* (Miami). 19 June: 1A, 20A.

Vicent, Mauricio. 1994. "Un sueño de ajo y boniato." *El País* (Madrid). 24 October: 10.

Whitefield, Mimi. 1991. "In trying times, Cuba puts black marketeers on trial." *The Miami Herald.* 10 December: 1A, 21A.

Whitefield, Mimi. 1992. "Cuba zeros in on 'closet capitalists.'" *The Miami Herald.* 20 April: 1A, 14A.

Whitefield, Mimi. 1993. "Cuba eases hand on farms to boost output." *The Miami Herald.* 16 September: 16A.

Whitefield, Mimi. 1994a. "Cuba OKs farmers markets." *The Miami Herald.* 18 September: 1A, 23A.

Whitefield, Mimi. 1994b. "In Cuba, a sweet smell of success: New farmers' markets are drawing crowds and rave reviews." *The Miami Herald.* 13 October: 21A.

THE EMERGING FOOD AND *PALADAR* MARKET IN HAVANA[1]

Joseph L. Scarpaci

Since its economic free-fall spurred from the collapse of the socialist trading system, Cuba has been embroiled in a 'Special Per8iod in Peace Time.' New pressures brought on by the search for convertible currencies have buffeted the Cuban economy (Mesa Lago 1994). The nation's economic bind has placed 'food' at the head of the list of Cuban household needs, replacing the long-standing concern over housing. Despite some free-market tinkering with private food markets between 1980-1986 (Rosenberg 1986), the Cuban government scuttled market-regulated mechanisms for distributing, selling and preparing food. Recently, though, numerous food-preparation occupations and restaurants have been legalized ("Cubanos vuelven a tener paladares" 1995; "Cuba's revolutionary restaurants" 1995; "Paladares" legalized 1995). However, there has be no in-depth investigation to date of Havana's emerging food and *paladar* market.

This paper examines one segment of the new food market—speak-easy restaurants called *paladares*[2]—in an attempt to better understand the emerging market economy in Havana. Divided into four sections, I begin with the legal context and brief history of these growing neighborhood eateries in Cuba. The following two sections sketch profiles of these new entrepreneurs, and presents a brief case study of one paladar businesswoman. The fourth section considers the relationship between food prices on the black market, and the effect imposed by the recently sanctioned state agricultural markets. Finally, the paper concludes with some new observations about Havana's emerging economic geography and the role of the *paladares* in Cuba's transition to a new post-socialist economy. We begin with the legal context.

PALADARES: THE LEGAL FRAMEWORK
Problems with State Food Provision

The state rationing system of food and basic-household goods is inadequate in the Special Period. Rationing in Cuba is monitored by the booklet, the *libreta* (*control de venta de productos alimenticios*). Each Cuban household receives one for buying highly-subsidized products at local state food stores (*bodegas*). By law it must be turned in or modified i) within 10-days of the death of a household member, ii) hospitalization, iii) old-age institutionalization, iv) incarceration, or v) leaving the country.

The *libreta* lists the age composition of the household by the cohorts < 2, 2-6, 7-13, 14-64, and 65 years and older. Non-food items normatively include

1. This paper is part of a larger chapter on the nature of work in Havana, and is greatly modified from Segre, R., Coyula, M. and Scarpaci, J. forthcoming. *Havana: Two Sides of the Antillean Metropolis.* New York and London: John Wiley and Sons. My thanks to Gilda de los Angeles Machín, Lawrence Grossman, and Jorge Pérez-López for their comments on an earlier draft. All errors and omissions are mine alone.

2. The term *paladar* literally means "palate" but comes from a Brazilian soap opera that played in Cuba in the early 1990s. In this *telenovela*, the protagonist migrates to Rio de Janeiro and sells sandwiches on the beach. So successful is the venture that she returns to her humble residence and establishes a restaurant out of her home. Not only is this term used widely among Cubans, but the actual license granted by Cuban authorities to operate a home-based diner is called, *Licencia de Paladar*.

Table 1.   Products Available at Selected State-run Food Stores (*Bodegas*) in Three Municipalities, Havana, 1995

Generally Available	Price	Generally Unavailable
Rice	.24 per lb.	vegetable oil
Black Beans (*Frijoles Negros*)	.30 per lb.	lard
Sugar	.14 per lb.	canned tomatoes
Baby Food (*Compota*)	.25 per can	body soap
Coffee	.12 per two oz.	laundry detergent
Cigarettes (*Fuertes And Suaves*)	2 /6 pesos pack	toothpaste
Peas (*Chícharos*)	.11 per lb.	vinegar
Rum	20 pesos/750 ml.	meat

Data source: Author's field notes.

fuel (kerosene, pre-heated kerosene, liquid gas, charcoal, firewood), laundry soap, body soap, cigarettes, rum and beer. *Bodegas* post prices on a chalkboard, along with the period in which the price is valid, and whether or not the product is available.

In June 1995 I documented prices at a half dozen *bodegas* in the municipalities of Plaza de la Revolución, Centro Habana, and Habana Vieja. My aim was to determine which products had been available most of the time during that calendar year (Table 1). As can be seen, more items were generally unavailable, and the latter were not products of conspicuous consumption. Among those items available, most were allocated by temporal dimensions and strictly controlled portions. For example, each *libreta* allocates 5 lbs. of rice per person and just under two pounds of beans per person (Table 2).

In brief, although the state system of food allocation is heavily subsidized and affordable even for households earning between 120-200 pesos monthly, it lacks variety and regularity. This penty up demand for alternative food sources.

The Rise, Fall and then Resurrection of the *Paladar*

Fidel Castro announced the legalization of more than 100 private-sector jobs on the 40th anniversary of the attack against the Moncada Barracks. This date, 26 July 1993, marked the first of a series of market liberalizations which, among other reforms, sanctioned the dollar's circulation, and proposed setting up savings and checking accounts in dollars. *Paladares* were

Table 2.   Monthly Food Allocation by Household or Person, According to the Cuban *Libreta*, Selected Items, 1995

Item	Monthly Allocation	Per Unit
Rice	5 lbs.	Person
Black Beans	30 oz.	Person
Sugar (white)	3 lbs.	Household
Sugar (brown)	3 lbs.	Household
Chicken	3 oz.	Person
Fish (various)	One (6-9 oz.)	Person
Soy Meal (*picadillo de soya*)	Varies	Person
Salt	8 oz.	Person

Source: Author's field notes.

also granted legal space to operate and their legal operators now form part of a larger private job sector of some 170,000 self-employed (*CubaNews* 1995c).

The first round of *paladares* was short lived, however. In February 1994, a police raid on more than 100 *paladares* in the Havana metropolitan area ensued. Allegedly, police raided only certain *paladares* that were operating illegally. These establishments were accused of illicit enrichment. My interviews with more than a dozen *paladar* operators reveal that most of them had legal permits to operate. They claimed that the police harassed them and then stole and confiscated their wares. The indirect message to civil society, according to some restaurateurs, was that many operators were making too much money too fast. Because these were neighborhood-based operations, the word got out to *Habaneros* that conspicuous profiteering among the new entrepreneurial class would not be tolerated by the Cuban state. In May 1994 the penal code was amended to ease the prosecution of 'profiteers,' thereby giving the government *ex post facto* powers to confiscate assets and apply sanctions (Pérez-López 1995b, p. 27). Those same *paladar* operators stated that they were back in business anywhere from three days to three weeks later.

Minister of Finance Manuel Millares Rodríguez and Minister of Labor and Social Security Salvador Valdés Mesa issued Resolution No. 4/95 on June 8, 1995 which once again 'legalized' *paladares* ("Resolución conjunta" 1995). In doing so, it eliminated the following self-employed occupations: producer of 'light' foods, processors of dairy products, maker of conserves that originated on a farm, and cook. The new law identified the tax payments each self-employed profession in the food-preparation business would make according to the size of the operation and whether or not alcohol was served (Table 3). Most of these self-employed professions pay a flat monthly rate (*cuota fija mensual mínima*). This flat charge is contentious because it requires a market forecast by the entrepreneur to determine whether she or he will in fact generate sufficient revenue to cover the monthly tax. Instead, all *paladar* owners with whom I have spoken would prefer to pay a sales tax that is based on actual sales. Those who charge in dollars must remit monthly quotas to the government in that same currency.

My fieldwork shows that most *paladares* cater largely to Cubans, and charge mainly in Cuban pesos. No one I interviewed could identify a *paladar* operator who paid the dollar license fee; though an occasional tourist paying in dollars was always welcome, such revenue would not be reported to government officials. To situate these monthly fees by the purchasing power of an average salary, let us suppose a worker is earning 180 pesos monthly. The lowest monthly quota requires workers to put forth 55% of their monthly paycheck, merely to sell food and drink at the retail level. Most *paladares* fall under category c) in Table 3, "Preparer-seller of food products and non-alcoholic beverages through dining services." In that case, they must place more than 200% of an average monthly wage 'up front,' to operate their family restaurant. The dollar-run *paladar* faces even stiffer start-up costs. At a monthly income of 180 pesos and buying dollars on the black market at 40 pesos per dollar (as of June 1995), means a prospective owner must invest nearly 67 months (about five and a half years) of wages into that business. Such an investment, though, would just cover the first month's business tax. To be sure, overtly dollar-run *paladares* need to have direct access to capital in order to operate legally. Most likely, that hard currency comes from overseas remittances by family members.

Table 3. Minimum Payment Criteria for Self-Employed Restaurant Owners (*Paladares*)

Occupation	Minimum Monthly Quota In Pesos	Minimum Monthly Quota In Dollars[a]
a) Preparer-seller of food products and non-alcoholic drinks at retail level (outside residence)	100 pesos	not applicable
b) Preparer-seller of food products and non-alcoholic drinks (inside residence)	200 pesos	100 US dollars
c) Preparer-seller of food products and non-alcoholic beverages through dining services	400 pesos	300 US dollars
d) Preparer-seller of food products and alcoholic beverages through dining services	500 pesos	400 US dollars

a.   The official listing states "*Cuota mínima en moneda libemente convertible cuando proceda su aplicación*" which for all purposes, is the U.S. dollar. Data source: Modified after "Resolución conjunta" 1995.

Other parameters in Resolution No. 4/95 shape the nature of the *paladar* operation. For example, there can be no more than 12 place settings in any given restaurant. Permanent residents of Cuba can also enter the trade. However, only family labor can be employed and it is illegal to hire by wage or salary non-family members. The law is vague about whether one can remunerate family labor. The kitchen, serving area, and private residences of each *paladar* must pass a sanitation inspection by the local Ministry of Public Health. Once the health inspection is approved and the license is secured, each restauranteur must sign up at the Central Business Register *(Registro Central Comercial)* administered by the Ministry of Internal Commerce. Those preparing food for retail sale are expected to sell their goods at cultural or recreational events, and only in public spaces designated for retail sale. All food providers—regardless of the currency they use or whether they dispense alcoholic beverages—must get their inputs at dollar-run state stores *(diplotiendas)*, agricultural markets *(mercados agropecuarios)*, or through their own livestock and private gardens. However, "in all cases [operators] are required to justify to the appropriate authorities the origin of the products used in their enterprise" (Article 7, Resolution No. 4/95). My sources claim that this is the legal loophole to close down any operator since only dollar stores give receipts for purchases on a regular basis.

Paladar owners face other restrictions. They are forbidden to sell horse meat or beef, and shellfish and other fish which are illegal to catch. Owners claim that restrictions on horse meat concern problems of hygiene, aesthetics and the likelihood of increasing horse thievery in the countryside. The state targets tourism for beef production and those on special medical diets (the latter receiving food through physician-approved notations made in the libreta). Cuba's yield of beef per head of cattle has deteriorated from 40 kg. to 30 kg. between the mid-1970s and 1988, the last date of available data (Figueras 1994, p. 69). Lastly, only milk purchased in dollar stores may be sold, and no food bought from state-run food stores *(bodegas)* or other restaurants[3] can be resold in *paladares*.

LA SEÑORA DE LA COCINA

Profiles of Havana's Upcoming Entrepreneurs

Since 1992, I have visited 12 *paladares* on a regular basis, mostly as a participant observer, though sometimes as a customer. In a series of five focus groups over the past three years, I gathered in-depth information about the respective twelve owners. Ten of these 12 operators were female and half of the twelve had either been recently laid off, or else they gave up going to work because it was not worth their while to earn so little. The other half who were not previously employed were working mothers in the home (i.e., housewives).

Each owner had an array of sources for their inputs. If the state-run agricultural markets *(mercados agropecuarios,* or *los agros)*, in operation since October 1994, lack products that the owners seek, then they resort to the black market. All twelve have violated Article 3 of Resolution No. 4/95 which prohibits hiring non-family workers. At the very least, they required errand runners *(mensajeros)* to scout out an occasional food item at the market, or track down a lead about food availability or price on the black market. About half regularly employed someone to work in the kitchen while the host or hostess attended to the clients dining in the living room; if only to keep an eye on their own furnishings. As the apartments were fairly small, the clients were never out of the owners' hearing range. A time consuming task during evening meal hours—the main period of activity— is answering the door by the frequent (Cuban) inquirers coming by to see what the evening fare was, and at what price.

---

3. Restaurants accepting pesos and catering only to Cubans have always existed in Revolutionary Cuba, though they were less common in the early 1990s than they are today. A whole host of small pizza and sandwich kiosks have sprung up in Havana in 1995. However, they opeate with hard currency and are owned by larger joint-venture tourist companies. See Dávalos Fernández (1993) on joint ventures.

Echoing Hays-Mitchell's (1989, 1993, 1994a, 1994b) studies of street vendors and small entrepreneurs in Peru, the *paladar* operators with whom I have spoken express satisfaction in the occupational independence that their job provides. Although only half of the twelve actually planned on getting a license for a *paladar*, those same individuals had already secured a license to prepare food in the home, but not to sell it in a restaurant-like setting. Each of the 12 vendors had at some time contracted cooks, messengers, and dishwashers, or else swapped kitchen labor for meals. Deciding to operate legally carries clear risks and benefits that operators must assess (Table 4).

Table 4. Benefits and Detriments of the Illegality of *Paladares*

Benefits

- Avoiding Licensure Fees and Bureaucratic Snares (Hygiene Certification)
- Less Corruption Payments to Public Officials
- Evading Labor Laws
- Evading Taxes

Detriment

- Fear of Fine and Incarceration (Social Deviant or Counter-Revolutionary or Dangerousness or *peligrosidad*)
- Police Shake Down and Confiscation of Food, Beverages and Wares (tables, chairs, cassettes, televisions, stereos, etc.)
- Inability to Advertise Widely

Concern about getting arrested for not having the proper papers has abated. The proliferation of private enterprise gives them 'cover' from prying government officials in this new free-market frenzy. Instead, operators' main concern is screening out clients who look like they might not pay, or cannot show cash 'up front.' Operators never boast about their successes for fear of gaining the attention of prying government officials. Although an occasional tourist passes by and pays in dollars, the clientele is mostly Cuban. Several *paladares* can put out a 'pleasant spread' for the tourists, including fine dinnerware and a table cloth. A smaller group serves local rum and foreign distilled spirits as well as an array of Cuban cigars for after-dinner pursuit. Take-out orders are common; patrons either bring their own containers (usually a plastic tub or bucket) or use take-out boxes, plastic containers, or dinner ware provided by the owner. Three of the 12 had purchased non-descript cardboard-boxes—bought on the black market by suppliers who had stolen them from state warehouses—that could be assembled for take-out orders.

The experience of one *paladar* owner and operator typifies the ways in which these new entrepreneurs assess market opportunities, perceive risk, and operate in Cuba's unfolding free-market economy.

The Case of Doña Rosa

Rosa (a pseudonym) entered this profession by default. At the age of 33, she found herself single, childless, and with a dead-end job at a state medical agency. Her work had not always been disappointing. Recently, though, it had been disrupted by changes in her work site. Up until quitting her job in May 1995, her job description had been changed five times because of government downsizing, a common force in driving Third World workers into informal and semi-legal occupations (Scarpaci and Irarrázaval 1994; Portes and Benton 1984; Portes and Borocz 1988). Her last reassignment entailed traveling across metropolitan Havana from her Vedado home. However, there was no bus service to that work site and she felt unable (or was unwilling) to bicycle such a long distance. When she did make it to work, often times there were no prepared lunches in the workplace *comedor*. Thus, like many Habaneros, she simply stopped going to work. Food shortages rise to dangerous levels in the hot summer months when workers are on vacation and school children at home stretch household ration books to the limits. Witness, for example, the 5 August 1994 riot on the Malecón seaside promenade which stemmed in part from a lack of food (Farah 1995). Rosa, though, stated she is pleased to be able to avoid the 'no lunch' sign at her workplace because her new trade keeps a good supply of food in her kitchen.

Before quitting her steady job, she had prepared and sold a few meals on the weekends and evenings to neighbors, friends, and an occasional stranger who had a referral by a friend or family member. About a year ago, she secured a license to prepare confectioneries in her home; usually sweets, caramels, and candied fruits. They gave her—in her own words—a "legal pretext" to store supplies in her home. It also explained why callers come to her door at all hours should the authorities inquire about that. She told state officials that the license would be in her mother's name because friends had said that the authorities tended to frown upon letting young workers move into these kinds of jobs. Any meddling or intervention by the authorities into her business, she feels, stems from the rapport she maintains with the local Committee for the Defense of the Revolution (CDR, *Comité de Defensa de la Revolución*). Luckily for her, Rosa has exceptionally good relations with the local CDR because she went to school with the son of the committee head. This echoes sociologist Francisco León's (1995) observation that the Cuban 'buddy system' (*sociolismo,* or *socio*) may be just as important as credit, entrepreneurial skills, state approval, and marketing. She entered the *paladar* business 'full time' after deciding not to return to her workplace across town.

At first, Rosa had no idea how to price her meals, and during the first month she lost money (in national currency). After securing a loan from a family member, she purchased more supplies and materials for her second month's operation. Her goal was not only to 'survive' but to make repairs to the spacious, street-level apartment her mother had occupied since migrating to Havana in 1957 from Ciego de Avila. A friend told her that she should always try to make a 50% return on her investment. When asked how that figure was derived she said that she did not know, but that her friend had worked long and hard in selling second-hand wares. She simply trusted her friend's judgment. After serving several meals on credit but never having the debt repaid, she imposed a cash-only business. Moreover, she now charges everyone for the meals. In the beginning, friends and neighbors would come around at the end of the night and chat. Later, she discovered that the real motivation was to see if there were any leftovers (*sobras*), or even passing a harmless comment like seeing if there was any burnt rice at the bottom of the pan (*raspa*); a treat among some Cubans.

As a single woman, Rosa takes special precautions. First, she cannot depend on a steady income from a male partner, and wishes to save her money for emergency expenditures. Second, she refuses to sell alcohol except to tourists who come recommended by trustworthy Cubans. Alcohol, claims Rosa, breaks down semi-formal relations between her and the clients, and that can lead to trouble (e.g., sexual advances by male customers, people asking for credit, rowdy behavior, snooping police and CDR members). Third, she has a tendency to trust people, a value she claims was instilled in her by the Revolution. In the free-market, she argues, such trust can be a liability.

Market forces fluctuated within the three months of a full-time *paladar* operation. In late June, 1995, business was down somewhat, as was the exchange rate of the dollar and the circulation of cash (pesos). Her market draws largely on two demographic groups: young, single adults in their late teens or 20s who tend not to work at full-time state jobs, but rather engage in casual work in the tourist industry. A second steady clientele—consisting of 20% of her gross sales—comes from single, elderly people who may not have sufficient fuel, cooking oil, or condiments to prepare meals to their liking. Since Rosa has all of the above and is known in the neighborhood as a particularly good cook, these elderly diners seek her out often. In return for their steady business, she lowers her prices by as much as 30% if she knows she can count on them. The elderly send younger neighbors or family members to pick up the meals. Rosa, moreover, refuses to buy processed foods such as frozen croquettes and makes all her meals from scratch.

Food is not cheap in Havana for Cubans. For 10 pesos (only 25 cents U.S. but the equivalent of 5.5% of an average monthly wage of 180 pesos), a customer can take away a dish of *congrí* (rice and beans), cabbage salad (*ensalada de repollo*; lettuce is rare), and a *vianda* (potato, *boniato* [sweet potato], *yuca* [cassava] or *ñame* [yams]). Fish or meat—depending on the quality and quantity—almost always doubles or trebles the price, respectively.

Paladar Inputs

As Rosa learns more about pricing, client relations, and planning, she is able to increase her rate of profit.

Her profit margins increase markedly when she can buy in bulk: rice, ham, chicken, eggs, and oil are perfect for wholesale purchases. Saving up enough capital is difficult. Her first recourse in securing inputs is from the municipal *mercados agropecuarios*. There are two such markets in every municipality of the Province of the City of Havana. Rosa likes to cruise the market stalls late in the day, right before closing time, hoping that vendors will drop their prices to make a last-minute deal. If she has transportation (a friend with a car), she will venture out to the large Cuatro Caminos market in Cerro, where the quantity and quality are more favorable than at the small market near her home. When the state markets fail to supply her, she turns to the black market. Some black-market providers are generic, and well known to all households. For instance, bakeries (*panaderias*) are state run but many individuals use them for buying vegetable oil, since they always have large quantities in stock.

The purchasing and retail behavior of this aspiring entrepreneur deviate from the contours of a normative market economy. No mid-level and high-order wholesalers exist for her. Buying-in-bulk means striking ad hoc deals with individual retailers that do not pass on to her—in her words—"*grandes ahorros*" (i.e., economies of scale). Although large purchases help her out, they do not generate the discounts she would like to receive. Furthermore, it is difficult to map out the location of these and other *paladares* because they are so recent and because telephone directories and tourist literature do not list them.

Rosa is optimistic about the future "Cubans are very resourceful, and I am the most creative of all' (*El cubano es muy inventor y yo soy la más creativa de todos!*). Rosa's new career in post-socialist Cuba does not break through the traditional gender-defined roles since she is wedded ever more to the kitchen (Scarpaci 1993). Nonetheless, she is moving forward to secure a category C license for her *paladar* which will let her sell food and non-alcoholic drinks. Still, she will continue to sell beer to tourists and charge in dollars whenever possible, and she does not greatly fear state sanctions. A first review of the cleanliness of her kitchen by the public-health inspector was positive. Although that state agency is not too prone to bribes, she may have to pay a small one to get her name on the Central Business Register in a timely manner. Alas, she explains, she has no *socios* working there.[4]

THE ROLE OF *MERCADOS AGROPECUARIOS*, THE BLACK MARKET, AND THEIR INFLUENCE ON INPUTS IN *PALADARES*

Before the present liberalization of the agricultural and food markets, Cuba tinkered with private farmer's markets in the mid-1980s. However, like the *paladares* in their early months, these markets were closed because middle-men were thought to acquire too much wealth, too quickly. Thus, until late 1994, farmers' produce had to be secured through tightly controlled state outlets (Alvarez and Puerta 1994). As of March 1995, there were approximately 1,479 agricultural cooperative units in Cuba, of which 486 (one-third) reported a profit (*CubaNews* 1995a). These cooperatives are permitted to sell their goods to the new *mercados agropecuarios*, though it is likely that two-thirds of those noted above are not meeting their state quotas (*acopio*)—a prerequisite for selling goods in the private market. For a variety of reasons, therefore, most cooperatives provide few inputs to Havana's legal food markets. *Paladar* operators and other citizens who are unable or unwilling to seek fruits, meat and poultry, and vegetables through that outlet have no recourse but to turn to the black market. In this section we briefly visit some prices of commodities that prevailed in mid-1994, and then consider how the new *mercado agropecuario* markets have influenced the price of food products in Havana.

---

4. In June 1996 doña Rosa had secured business cards with her name and phone number, the name of her establishment, and had a formal 'name' for her *paladar*. Moreover, she had decided to secure a *paladar* license for selling food in pesos. She expanded her patio and installed a bar with lights. On one visit in June, 1996 I counted 16 foreigners dining there, and a half dozen Cubans. She had both exceeded her 12-person maximum and was charging all 22 customers in dollars. The fare for the evening: lobster dinners for $6.

Between 1992 and late 1994, I periodically monitored black-market food prices. Figure 1 shows the purchasing power required to secure selected items on Havana's black market according to four income scenarios: worker, professor, physician, and taxi driver. Significantly, all workers except the taxi driver are paid in pesos.

Figure 1 reveals considerable variation in purchasing power. Perhaps the most controversial aspect for Cubans and foreign analysts is that the Special Period has placed material incentives on par with the traditional moral incentives that had driven the Revolution. A taxi driver, or any other Cuban formally or informally affiliated with the tourist trade (e.g., *jinetera*), has access to a wide array of basic foods and household products. A physician or college professor would have to sacrifice much to buy those items. For example, while a taxi driver would only have to spend about 1% of her/his wage on a pound of pork, a worker would forgo nearly half a month's wage for the same item.

Here lies a deep contradiction in the new market reforms, and one for which Cuban authorities have few patent replies. Put differently, the Cuban government has codified basic foods and household staples in a way that is not only unprecedented in the 36 years of the Revolution, but anathema to a social system based on common ownership of the means of production (Bradshaw 1991; Callinicos 1991; Forbes and Thrift 1987).

Figure 1. Percentage Monthly Wage Required to Purchase Black-Market Items, Havana, July 1994

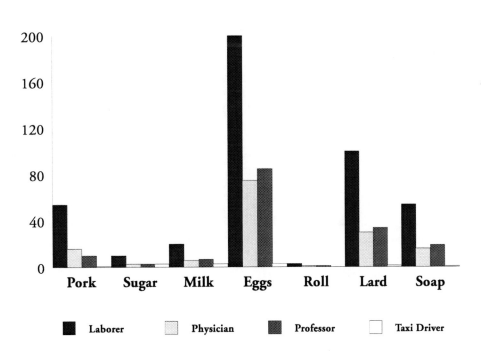

Data source: Author's fieldwork. *Notes:* 'pork' and 'sugar' prices per pound; 'lard' usually sold in one-liter recycled rum bottles; 'milk' refers to a can of condensed milk since fresh milk is uncommon in black markets because of perishability; 'eggs' are sold in trays of 30; 'roll' means a single portion; 'soap' usually means a four-ounce bar but prices show considerable variability based on size, fragrance, country of origin and brand name.

Recall, however, that the above black market items prevailed before *mercado agropecuarios* were legalized four months later. As a result of this new source of food sales, black market prices have plummeted. In fact, in June 1995 I was unable to gather any consistent pricing on most of the items shown in Figure 1, though by June 1996 prices were much more stable. The only items not regularly sold in the new state markets are soap, milk, and bread products. In brief, the legalization of the *agros* has lowered black-market prices. However, this statement assumes nothing about the general population's ability to acquire these goods. Both the decriminalization of dollars and the legalization of many black-market activities allows the Cuban government to resolve its foreign exchange problems (Pastor and Zimbalist 1995, p. 709).

SUMMARY AND CONCLUSIONS

Just a decade ago, Cuba suffered from a kind of apartheid where foreigners and their non-Revolutionary ideas were carefully segregated from the general population. Much has changed since then. Since 1993, a host of private-sector self-employed ventures have proliferated in Havana and elsewhere, albeit with erratic 'stops' and 'gos,' as the Cuban government defines and re-defines what can only be described as new type of *criollo* Keynesian economics. To some Cuban analysts, there is a way out Cuba's quagmire, and its formula sounds much like those drawn from neoclassical economics. The prescription is as follows:

> Una nueva estructura económica, más dinámica, más diversificada, menos dependiente de un solo producto, con un turismo internacional muy activo, cientos de empresas mixtas y asociaciones productivas funcionando y docenas de nuevos artículos manufactureros y agrícolas exportándose, puede ser el panorama de Cuba en los finales de este siglo (Figueras 1994, p. 181).

While few observers inside and outside Cuba would dispute the value of such a panorama, the macro-policy constraints placed on the simplest of enterprises —*paladares*— begs the question about whether such a prospect for the year 2000 is realistic. An increase in government regulation to equalize income distri-

bution may dampen all self-employed enterprises (Alonso 1995; Locay 1995). As Pastor and Zimbalist (1995, p. 705) note, "the recent spate of halfhearted measures...has likely worsened distributional inequities, distorted incentives, and failed to improve the macroeconomy."

Distortions in the *paladar* market stifle the kinds of multiplier effects we might envision in a less restrictive setting. At the national level, Cuba lacks what the Chilean business community calls *transparencia*: clarity about norms, regulation and information that is unrestricted by cumbersome regulation. Like de Soto's (1989) description of pre-Fujimori Peru, state regulations hinder more than help Cuba's fledgling cottage industry. At the service-delivery level, the case study of Rosa in this paper revealed that she is operating in an imperfect market that lacks economies of scale. No wholesaling inputs exist for her, and her inputs stem mainly from retail sources. While it is perhaps not surprising that the normative features of a market economy have not yet taken hold in Havana, future research should monitor the evolution of this particularly economic geography. In doing so, we will be able to situate Havana's informal and second economies in a broader Latin American and Third World context (Pérez López 1995a; Rakowski 1994; McGee 1974). In the meantime, *paladares*—Cuba's new speak-easy restaurants— provide operators with autonomy, the potential of increased cash flow, and a chance to exercise dormant business skills in a newly dollarized economy.

Qualitative research of a small group of *paladar* operators reveals that state guidelines are both costly, onerous, and even unnecessary. As this new market takes form, unspoken rules, rumors and a buddy-system (*sociolismo*) play an important role in the decision-making process. Those constraints notwithstanding, *paladar* operators continue to search out low-cost inputs for their speak-easy restaurants. They face the same concerns micro-enterprises elsewhere must cope with: pricing, advertising, return business, buying in bulk, and access to credit. In this regard, this reservoir of a new business class plots along, building their firms, and incrementally improving their entrepreneurial learning curve. *Paladar* owners welcome their new-found occupational independence, and desire less of what the government wishes to impose over all self-employed: "greater discipline and control" ("Si de cuenta" 1995). Perhaps the only obstacle in their horizon will be a battery of new government guidelines should *paladares*—as past experience indicates—prove to be too profitable in the eyes of Cuban authorities.

REFERENCES

Alonso, J.F. 1995. "The path of Cuba's economy today." *ASCE Newsletter*, Spring - June, pp. 18-23.

Alvarez, J. and Puerta, R. 1994. "State interventions in Cuban agriculture: Impact on organization and performance." *World Development* 22:1663-1675.

Bradshaw, M. 1991. *The Soviet Union: A new regional geography?* London: Bellhaven.

Callinicos, A. 1991. *The revenge of history: Marxism and the East European revolutions.* Oxford: Polity Press.

"Cuba's revolutionary restaurants." *Washington Post*, 15 September 1995, A-28.

CubaNews. 1995a. "Facts and Stats." page 3 (July).
_____. 1995b. "Paladares legalized.: page 5 (July).
_____. 1995c. "Private job list grows." page 5 (July).

"Cubanos vuelven a tener paladares" 1995. *El Nuevo Herald.* 15 June, p. 1-A, 9-A.

Dávalos-Fernández, R. 1993. *Las empresas mixtas: Regulación jurídica.* Madrid: Consultoria Jurídica Internacional.

de Soto, H. 1989. *The other path: The invisible revolution in the Third World.* New York: Harper Row.

Farah, D. 1995. "Summertime, and Havana is uneasy." *The Washington Post*, July 21, p. 23, 24.

Figueras, M.A. 1994. *Aspectos estructurales de la economía cubana.* Havana: Editorial de Ciencias Sociales.

Forbes, D. and Thrift, N. 1987. *The socialist Third World: urban development and territorial planning.* Oxford: Blackwell.

Hays-Mitchell, M. 1989. "Taking to the streets." *Grassroots Development* 13:25-30.

_____. 1993. "The ties that bind. Informal and formal sector linkages in streetvending: the case of Peru's ambulantes." *Environment and Planning* 25:1085-1102.

_____. 1994a. "Streetvending in Peru." *National Geographic Research & Exploration* 10:354-365.

_____. 1994b. "Streetvending in Peruvian cities: The spatio-temporal behavior of *ambulates.*" *Professional Geographer* 46:425-438.

Locay, L. 1995. "Institutional requirements for successful market reforms." Paper presented at the 'Cuba in Transition' workshop, Shaw, Pittman, Potts & Trowbridge, Washington, D.C., April 10, mimeo.

León, F. 1995. "Socialismo y sociolismo: Los actores sociales en la transición cubana." Paper presented at the conference, "Toward a New Cuba: Legacies of Revolution." Princeton University, April 8, mimeo.

Mesa-Lago, C. 1994. *Are economic reforms propelling Cuba to the market?* Miami: North-South Center, University of Miami.

McGee, T.G. 1974. *The persistence of the proto-proletariat: Occupational structures and planning for the future of Third World cities.* Los Angeles: School of Architecture and Urban Planning, UCLA.

Pastor, M. and A. Zimbalist. 1995. "Waiting for change: Adjustment and reform in Cuba." *World Development* 23:705-720.

Pérez-López, J. 1995a. *Cuba's Second Economy.* New Brunswick: Transaction Books.

_____. 1995b. "The Cuban economy in 1995." *ASCE Newsletter,* Spring - June, pp. 24-29.

Portes, A. and Benton, L. 1984. Industrial development and labor absorption: A reinterpretation. *Population and Development Review* 10:589-611.

Portes, A. and Borocz, J. 1988. "The informal sector under capitalism and state socialism: a preliminary comparison." *Social Justice* 15: 17-28.

Rakowski, C.A. 1994. *Contrapunto: The informal sector debate in Latin America.* Albany, SUNY Press.

"Resolución conjunta No. 4/95." 1995 *Granma* June 14, p. 2.

Rosenberg, J. 1992. Cuba's free market experiment: 1980-1986. *Latin American Research Review* 27 (3) 51-89.

Scarpaci, J. 1993. "Empowerment strategies of poor women under the Chilean dictatorship." In M. Turshen and B. Holcomb, Eds., *Women and Development Policy in the Third World.* Westport, CT: Greenwood Press, pp. 33-50.

Scarpaci, J. and Irarrázaval, I. 1994. "Decentralizing a centralized state: Local government finance in Chile within the Latin American context." *Public Budgeting and Finance* 14 (4):120-136.

"Si de cuenta propia se trata..." 1995. *Granma,* 15 June p. 2.

SMALL BUSINESS DEVELOPMENT IN POST-TRANSITION CUBA

Joseph M. Perry, Jeffrey W. Steagall and Louis A. Woods

Small businesses form the productive foundation of most mixed economies around the world. They provide an effective outlet for entrepreneurial initiative and ability, they fill market niches that are not profitable for larger firms, and they create jobs in a wide variety of occupations. The encouragement of small business growth has been a major concern of both governmental and non-governmental organizations in many developing countries.

Cuba will face some special problems in developing its small business sector again after the transition. Some such issues will be made easier by studying the lessons of the transitions in Eastern Europe. Among these topics are the re-establishment of entrepreneurial incentives and rationalization of the price system. Other issues are particular to the Cuban experience. These include developing a small-business sector from a position of essentially no commercial small businesses and access to capital. This study attempts to outline the issues involved and to provide an initial analysis of the potential solutions to the problems.

The paper first briefly describes small business operations in the United States to highlight their important role in job creation and market expansion. The conditions necessary for small business success are then contrasted with the actual birth and death rates of U. S. firms. Out of this comparison comes a picture of an extremely dynamic process.

The paper next focusses on small business conditions in Belize, using available data from a variety of sources, to show that Belizean entrepreneurs face many of the same dynamic market conditions found in more developed countries. A description of the critical role played by key governmental and non-governmental organizations follows. Different market conditions and challenges facing Belizean entrepreneurs are then explained, along with their implications.

The final section of the paper addresses the special problems that the Cuban economy will face as it begins to create a small-business sector in the transition. The required legal, social, and incentive structures are identified.

SMALL BUSINESSES IN THE UNITED STATES

In order to provide a foundation for considering Cuba's small business sector, this section analyzes the world's leading small business sector, that of the U. S. This discussion provides an introduction to the data available on small businesses, highlighting several of the data problems that exist even in the information-intensive American economy. One especially important concept is the volatility inherent in this segment of the economy, with individual firms entering and exiting the market with amazing frequency. This issue will prove to be daunting in the Cuban case. The reasons for failure of American small businesses are also exposited. Again, these topics will be of considerable importance to Cuba.

Defining and Counting Small Businesses. A critical first step in analyzing small businesses is to define them so that they may be counted. Over the years, many different definitions have been used by Federal, state, and local governments in the United States. One widely-accepted current approach is that used by the Small Business Administration (SBA). The classification scheme developed by the SBA is used primarily for identifying small businesses which may be given preferential treatment in government procurement programs.

The SBA considers a small business to be "any concern organized for profit that, including its affiliates, is independently owned and operated, is not dominant in [its] industry," and meets any special criteria the SBA imposes. The size criteria used by the SBA may differ from one industry to another, as defined by the U. S. Department of Commerce Standard Industrial Classification (SIC) codes. For all practical purposes, however, any firm that has fewer than 500 employees, and meets the other criteria noted above, is a small business.[1]

Counting the number of businesses in a large, developed country is a rather daunting task. Probably the best indirect measure available in the United States is the number of income tax returns filed by business establishments. In 1992, 21.3 million business firms filed tax returns. Of this total, about 14,000 had 500 or more employees. The remaining firms, by definition, were small businesses.

Out of the 21.3 million businesses, 5.7 million reported having employees. Almost 60 percent of these firms reported fewer than five employees; over 89 percent of the firms had fewer than 20 employees. A perhaps surprising corollary is that, in 1992, 15.6 million business concerns were single person firms, comprised of entrepreneurs working part-time or full-time in their chosen field.

Another striking characteristic of the small business sector in the United States is its dynamic nature. Although the number of small firms with employees has been increasing since 1986 at an annual rate of about 2 percent, this net figure reflects substantial

business birth and death rates. Typically, about 15 percent of all firms terminate or go out of business every year. At the same time, the number of new firms grows annually by about 15 percent. Another 2 to 3 percent of all firms, called "successor firms" are taken over by new or other existing firms. The 17 percent growth figure, minus the 15 percent termination figure, yields the net growth rate of 2 percent.

These percentages reflect substantial absolute numbers of business firms. In calendar year 1992, for example, government records show a total of 871,001 new and successor firms being formed. Over the same period, 818,756 other firms went out of business. This pattern of change is reflective of what Joseph Schumpeter called "creative destruction," a process in which entrepreneurial activity not only feeds economic growth, but is also the source of economic fluctuations.[2]

Small businesses also tend to concentrate in specific industrial sectors in the United States. Table 1 shows the distribution of small businesses for 1992, ranked in declining order of concentration. As common sense would suggest, small businesses were most common in those sectors where a low capital-to-labor ratio is found, and where individual enterprise is most easily rewarded.

Job Creation by Small Businesses. Contrary to popular belief, the small business sector in the United States tends to be an active producer of new jobs. Between 1988 and 1990, for example, small businesses generated almost all of the net new jobs created in the United States. Analysts believe that about 70 percent of the new jobs that will appear in the country's fastest-growing industries will be generated by small business expansion. Taking into account all anticipated job growth to the year 2005 (about 23.3 mil-

---

1. See, for example, Office of the President, *The State of Small Business: A Report of the President, 1993* (Washington, D. C.: U. S. Government Printing Office, 1993), p. 295. The President's Report is bound together with the Annual Report on Small Business and Competition and the Annual Report on Federal Procurement Preference Goals of the U. S. Small Business Administration.

2. The data in this section come from *The State of Small Business*, pp. 36-37, and Small Business Administration, *Handbook of Small Business Data: 1994 Edition* (Washington, D. C.: U. S. Government Printing Office, 1994), pp. 36 and 62. See also Joseph A. Schumpeter, *The Theory of Economic Development* (Cambridge, Mass.: Harvard University Press, 1934), pp. 56-62 and *Business Cycles* (New York: McGraw-Hill Book Company, 1964), pp. 46-104.

Table 1. Small Business in the United States, 1992

U. S. Industrial Sector	Small Businesses as a Percent of All Businesses in the Industry
Construction	88.01
Wholesale Trade	66.86
Services	60.15
Retail Trade	54.92
Finance, Insurance, Real Estate	44.27
Mining	39.76
Manufacturing	37.66
Transportation, Communication, Utilities	35.39

Source: *The State of Small Business*, p. 53.

lion new positions), projections show small businesses creating about 66 percent of those positions.[3]

Small Business Success and Failure. Periodic surveys by the firm of Dun and Bradstreet document the tenuous existence of most small businesses. The reasons for small business failure are equally easy to document. Analyses by Dun and Bradstreet identify the following specific drawbacks of entrepreneurs or poor decisions the entrepreneurs make:

- Lack of experience
- Lack of capital
- Poor location
- Too much inventory
- Excessive purchasing of fixed assets
- Poor credit granting practices
- Unwarranted personal expenses
- Unplanned expansion

- Faulty attitudes[4]

Any one of these items could prove troublesome to the businessperson. Typically, the small business that fails, and fails early, suffers from several of these problems. Dun and Bradstreet offer the following suggestions to the entrepreneur as pragmatic strategies to keep a business alive and growing:

1. Recognize your limitations, and stay within them.

2. Plan ahead. It is wise to sit down and write out your policies.

3. Keep enough records, but no more than necessary.

4. Watch the balance sheet, as well as the income statement. Especially watch your liabilities.

5. Investigate first, not after. Don't take pigs in pokes.

6. Establish good relationships with suppliers and banks.

7. Learn all that you can about your business and its market.

8. Seek professional advice if you need it: lawyers, bankers, and accountants, for example

9. Watch your health.

These suggestions clearly constitute a counsel of perfection.[5]

A slightly different approach is used in the tabulation of business failures. For calendar year 1992, Dun and Bradstreet analyzed the demise of business firms to identify the proximate and primary causes of their failure. Obviously, the deeper, underlying causes listed previously are reflected in this tabulation. Table 2 presents the data. Some business failures understandably result from unforeseen market conditions or unfavorable changes in the economic environment.

---

3. *Handbook of Small Business Data: 1994 Edition*, p. 1.

4. Dun and Bradstreet, *The Pitfalls in Managing A Small Business* (New York: Dun and Bradstreet), p. 16.

5. *The Pitfalls in Managing A Small Business*, pp. 16-19.

Most of the causes listed under the categories of neglect, fraud, experience, finance, and strategy are traceable, at least in part, to the lack of experience and ability of the businessperson. The clear implication is that additional training, education and experience would help businesspersons mitigate or avoid many of these terminal business conditions.

The tenuous life of American small businesses is further emphasized by Dun and Bradstreet figures showing business failures by age of firm. Table 3 presents these observations for 1992. The figures show that, during the given year, almost 36 percent of all business firms that failed were no more than five years old. Two thirds of all failing firms were no more than ten years old. And many of those surviving the ten-year mark would fail before seeing fifteen years. A corollary of this record is that small businesses may create short-term jobs, unlike the jobs generated by a government bureaucracy or a large, oligopolistic manufacturing firm. Employees of small businesses (including the entrepreneurs) can therefore expect some job turnover during their working careers.

All of these data suggest that the picture of a business sector dominated by large conglomerates is somewhat misleading. Although a handful of large corporations accounts for over 60 percent of the output of the U.S. economy, numerically these firms are dwarfed by small business concerns that occupy more specialized niches in the marketplace. Most of the business firms that are born every year in the United States are one-person operations, reflecting the will and the desire of an entrepreneur to produce a good or service that customers will appreciate and buy, thereby generating profit. The training, experience, and judgment of these entrepreneurs are critical to the survival and persistence of their firms, as the preceding Dun and Bradstreet data clearly show.

Because a market economy permits, and even demands, risk-taking and experimentation, failure is also a normal part of business experience. It is a seeming paradox that, without business failure, there would probably be little business success. Both are by-products of the competitive market process. How well an economic system prepares its entrepreneurs

Table 2. Causes of Business Failure in the United States: 1992

Major Causes and Subcategories	Percent of all
1. Neglect Causes	3.70%
Business conflicts	2.10%
Family problems	0.40%
Lack of commitments	0.30%
Poor work habits	0.90%
2. Disaster	4.50%
3. Fraud	2.20%
4. Economic Factors Causes	64.10%
High interest rates	0.00%
Inadequate sales	2.60%
Industry weakness	22.70%
Insufficient profits	37.70%
Inventory difficulties	1.00%
Not competitive	0.60%
Poor growth prospects	0.20%
Poor location	0.20%
5. Experience Causes	0.80%
Lack of business experience	0.20%
Lack of line experience	0.30%
Lack of managerial experience	0.30%
6. Finance Causes	23.90%
Burdensome institutional debt	5.00%
Heavy operating expenses	16.60%
Insufficient capital	2.30%
7. Strategy Causes	0.90%
Excessive fixed assets	0.10%
Over expansion	0.20%
Receivables difficulties	0.60%

Source: Dun and Bradstreet, Business Failure Record, 1992.

Table 3. Business Failures by Average Age of Business Firm, 1992

Age of Business Firm	Percent of All Business Failures
One year or less	1.70%
Two years	6.20%
Three years	9.90%
Total Three Years or Less	17.90%
Four years	9.40%
Five years	8.70%
Total Five Years or Less	35.90%
Six years	8.20%
Seven years	7.40%
Eight years	6.10%
Nine years	4.80%
Ten years	3.90%
Total Six to Ten Years	30.40%
Over ten years	33.70%

Source: Dun and Bradstreet, Business Failure Record, 1992

for the critical decisions that must be made for firms such as these, helps to determine the growth path of the economy.

In the United States, extensive help is available both to businesspersons contemplating a new venture and to those entrepreneurs who already manage a going concern. The SBA, in conjunction with many universities throughout the United States, including the University of North Florida, provide training, technical assistance, problem-solving help, and aid with financing. Other, more specialized organizations, such as the Institute for Business and the International Council for Small Business, provide various types of aid, some of it fee-based. Many trade organizations mount training programs for firms in their industry. And local Chambers of Commerce are frequently the source of small business aid consulting. There is even an academic journal, the *Journal of Small Business Management*, that addresses the specific problems of small firms.[6]

Even with such extensive aid, many U. S. firms fail with great regularity, just as new firms are coming into existence to replace them. The Schumpeterian process of "creative destruction" thus lends variety, freshness, and change to the marketplace, and helps it adapt better to the needs of the consuming public.

SMALL BUSINESSES IN BELIZE

In order to understand the likely post-transition Cuban experiences with the development of its small business sector, it is useful to consider a reasonably well-functioning analog in another developing country. The choice here is Belize, a geographically small Central American country with a population of less than 200,000. Examining Belize is sensible in that the climates and crops of Belize and Cuba are largely similar. Belize also provides examples of both the potential positive and negative activities that can affect the small business sector.

Defining and counting small businesses in Belize is more difficult than performing that task in the United States. National small business statistics have not been collected by the government, either routinely or periodically. In addition, the transitional segments of the economy, where entrepreneurs are moving their operations into the market system, are difficult to identify and measure. Casual empiricism, based upon extensive in-country travelling since 1981, suggests that a high percentage of Belizean business firms are individual proprietorships, managed and operated by their owners. These firms are lightly capitalized, and typically service local or regional markets.

Periodic surveys of registered factories by the Belizean Labour Department provide the employment patterns reported in Table 4. These figures, although

6. For a listing of small business resources, see, for example, Joseph R. Mancuso, *Mancuso's Small Business Resource Guide* (New York: Prentice Hall, 1988), or Office of Management and Budget, *Catalog of Federal Domestic Assistance* (Washington, D. C.: U. S. Government Printing Office, 1994).

not comprehensive, provide a clear indication that the typical (or modal) Belizean factory is a small business. Factory categories include sawmills, sugar factories, distilleries, garment factories, bakeries, aerated water firms, machine shops, printing firms, fruit processing firms, corn mills, cigarette factories, ice plants, furniture shops, aluminum products firms, and flour mills. The details of the reports also suggest some changes in the pattern of factory employment over time. Corn mills appeared in double digits for all reported years. Bakeries also showed consistently high numbers. In contrast, garment factories increased from 1 to 7 over the period, reflecting one of the growth (and export-oriented) sectors of the economy.

Table 4. Size of Work Force in Registered Factories in Belize, 1986-1988, 1990

	1986	1987	1988	1990
Work Force Under 10	66	48	79	55
Work Force Under 25	16	13	17	15
Work Force 25 and Over	13	5	31	19

Source: Annual Report of the Labour Department, 1986, 1987, 1988, and 1990.

A survey carried out by Planning Innovations, Inc., in November, 1988, attempted to develop a profile of small-scale enterprises in Belize. Researchers visited all nine major urban or town centers in Belize, where they interviewed 189 business owners and managers, representing 18 different business sectors. Small-scale enterprises were defined as "all small business enterprises engaged in manufacturing, processing, assembly, or repair and servicing activities." Additional criteria limited the number of employees

to less than five, and the value of the firm's fixed assets to no more than BZE$50,000.00.[7]

Auto repair firms constituted the largest segment of surveyed firms, accounting for 20.6 percent of the total. The latest available data show over 20,000 vehicles of all types registered in Belize, all of them imported, and most of them older models. Woodworking and furniture firms made up another 15.3 percent, reflecting the exploitation of Belize's extensive forest resources. Ninety-one percent of all the surveyed firms were owned by men. The firms owned by women were concentrated in beauty care services, dressmaking, and food processing.

Business owners reported a median equity invested of BZE$1,500.00 at business start-up. Two-thirds of the owners used their own savings as startup capital. Only 5.3 percent indicated that they had borrowed funds from commercial institutions. Median annual gross sales for the surveyed firms was BZE$10,000.00 in 1988. The median annual wage bill was BZE$4,160.00 for those firms paying wages.[8]

Government publications report that small enterprises in Belize include "the manufacture of metal doors and windows, furniture, concrete blocks, bricks, clothing, boat building, soft drink bottling, brewing, cigarette manufacture, tyre recapping, the production of flour and animal feed, wire and paper products, an agricultural fertilizer plant, matches, plywood and other meat products, a meat packing plant, food processing operations and the manufacture of rolled steel bars for the construction industry."[9]

A less formal survey, presented in a commercial publication, lists some of the largest private employers in Belize, with figures derived from records of the Belize Chamber of Commerce and Industry and the In-

---

7. The Belizean national currency, the Belize dollar, is denoted by the symbol, BZE$. Since 1974, the Belize dollar has enjoyed a fixed exchange rate of BZE$2.00 = US$1.00.

8. Planning Innovations, Inc., *Small-Scale Enterprises in Belize: A Survey. Part I*, Report prepared under USAID Contract No. 505-0000-C-00-8701 (Washington, D. C.: Planning Innovations, Inc., December, 1988), pp. E-1 to E-5. For vehicle registrations, see Ministry of Economic Development, *Abstract of Statistics: 1993* (Belmopan: Government Printery, 1994), Table 9.4.

9. See Belize Information Service, *Fact Sheet: Belize* (Belmopan: Government Printery, 1994), p. 7.

come Tax Department. The figures in Table 5 may be subject to considerable error, and hence are suggestive, rather than definitive. They also suggest an upper bound to the employment levels of Belizean firms.

Table 5. Estimated Employment of Some of the Largest Belizean Business Firms

Name of Business Firm	Number of Employees
Citrus Company of Belize, Ltd.	800
Williamson Industries	690
Belize Sugar Industry, Ltd.	625
James Brodies	580
Belize Telecom	486
Belize Food Products, Ltd.	300
Tropical Produce, Ltd.	300

Source: Country Business, 1991-1992, pp. 9 and 15.

While other firms that employ several hundred workers may be identified, the clear implication of these figures is that there are no very large firms in Belize, measured by the standards that would be applied in countries such as Germany, Canada, or the United States. The business sector in Belize, according to all indications, is a small business sector, with all of the opportunities, strengths, and flaws of small businesses elsewhere. There probably is a relatively high turnover rate, especially among the smallest concerns in the country.

Belize and CBI II. An indirect measure of the high turnover rate of Belizean small businesses comes from recent amendments to the Caribbean Basin Initiative. Reconsideration of CBI by the U.S. Congress led to passage of the Caribbean Basin Economic Recovery Expansion Act of 1990 (CBI II). This revision of the 1983 legislation contained two very important changes: CBI was made a permanent program of the U. S. Government, with no termination date; and both Belize and the Eastern Caribbean countries were targeted for special efforts to encourage wider use of CBI preferences.[10]

The special targeting of Belize for encouragement is based partly upon a CBI participation level that did not meet U. S. expectations. From 1984 to 1989, Belizean exports to the United States under CBI ranged between $42 million and $50 million per year, basically without a positive growth trend. In contrast, U. S. exports to Belize rose steadily after 1986, reaching $101 million in 1989. The United States has been and is the single most important trading partner of Belize, buying over 40 percent of all Belizean exports in 1989, and supplying about 50 percent of the goods and services then imported into Belize.[11]

Further concern was generated by the 1988 and 1990 Caribbean Basin Investment Surveys. Carried out by the U.S. Department of Commerce, the 1988 survey identified those firms in CBI countries that had invested in a new foreign exchange generating operation between January 1, 1984, and December 31, 1987. The 1990 update identified firms that had made such investment between January 1, 1988, and December 31, 1989. The 1988 data from Belize showed 34 firms that met the criteria. By 1990, half of those firms, representing 148 jobs and $28 million in assets, had gone out of business. An additional eight firms met the 1990 survey criteria. Total annual export sales for the reporting firms amounted to $6.2 million, based upon $30.5 million of assets, and

10. See U. S. Department of Commerce, *1989 Guidebook: Caribbean Basin Initiative* (Washington, D. C.: U. S. Government Printing Office, October, 1988), for a broad outline of the CBI program, and *1991 Guidebook: Caribbean Basin Initiative* (Washington, D. C.: U. S. Government Printing Office, November, 1990), for details on the amended legislation.

11. See *1991 Guidebook*, pp. 55-56, and U. S. Department of Commerce, *1990 Caribbean Basin Investment Survey* (Washington, D. C.: U. S. Government Printing Office, February, 1991), pp. 16-17.

a full-time work force of 976 persons.[12] In short, this restricted sample of firms showed a fifty-percent mortality rate over a two-year period. The addition of eight more firms (a positive growth rate of almost 24 percent) fell far short of compensating for the loss.

Tourism and the Hospitality Industry. Because tourism has been targeted for special encouragement by the Government of Belize, and because small businesses (bed and breakfast concerns, small hotels, guide operations, travel agencies) can both exist and thrive in this sector, some observations about recent changes in facilities are warranted. Between 1981 and 1993, the gross value added by hotels and restaurants in Belize increased by 189 percent, mirroring an increasing inflow of tourists, particularly after 1985.[13]

Over the past decade, the flow of foreign tourists into Belize has approximately trebled, from about 67,000 per year to about 220,000 per year.[14] As the data in Table 6 show, the business response to the growing flow of foreign tourists has been positive. From 1991 to 1994, according to Belize Tourist Board data, the number of hotel rooms in Belize rose by almost 36 percent, reflecting a net increase of 119 lodging establishments over the period. The strongest growth occurred in the cayes, in Cayo District, and in Stann Creek District, responding to a growing interest in ecotourism activities inland and the complex of diving and fishing activities around the barrier reef.

Examination of the underlying details for Table 6 brings two important conclusions to the fore. First of all, the net increase in hotel rooms was accomplished by the process of "creative destruction" noted above. Some hotels went out of business, others came into being, while yet others either expanded or contracted. The process was very dynamic, even over a short time span. Table 7 details those changes.

Secondly, many of the smaller hotel operators discovered that renting rooms will not cover all expenses. The hotel business, particularly for smaller operators, is seasonal. In an economy with a limited market and strong competition for tourist dollars, small hotel owners and operators therefore diversified their activities. Some introduced restaurants or eating facilities, that might also draw neighborhood customers. Others provided travel services, acted as guides, or sold souvenirs and crafts. In short, instead of specializing solely in the provision of lodging, they broadened their market appeal by engaging in other, related activities.

This latter point is of special importance, since much anecdotal evidence suggests that Belizean small businesses often have so limited a market that they cannot provide a living for the entrepreneur who operates them. Instead, the entrepreneur must find other remunerative activities during the slack periods of the year.

The Formal Sector/Informal Sector Dichotomy. Another way of analyzing business organization in developing countries is based upon the perceived dualistic nature of Third World urban economies. Many agencies and organizations in those countries categorize firms as belonging either to the formal sector or to the informal sector. Jan Breman summarizes the classification scheme as follows:

> The "formal sector" is taken to mean wage labour in permanent employment, such as that which is characteristic of industrial enterprises, government offices and other large-scale establishments. This implies (a) a set number of inter-related jobs which are part of a composite, internally well-organized labour structure; (b) work situations which are officially registered in economic statistics; and (c) working conditions which are protected by law. Some authors therefore speak of the organized, registered or protected sector. Eco-

---

12. *1990 Caribbean Basin Investment Survey,* pp. 5-6, 16-17, and 55. Appendix J of this publication includes a complete listing of all business firms included in the surveys,

13. Central Statistical Office, *National Accounts Bulletin, 1980-1993* (Belmopan: Government Printery, 1994), pp. 34-37.

14. Because of large numbers of border crossings by returning Belizean nationals and short-term visitors from Guatemala and Mexico, the tourism data are approximations. See Central Statistical Office, *Abstract of Statistics, 1993* (Belmopan: Government Printery, 1994), tourism/immigration tables.

Table 6.   Belizean Lodging Places and Rooms, 1991 and 1994

Location	1991		1994	
	Number of Establishments	Number of Rooms	Number of Establishments	Number of Rooms
Belize District	52	855	60	896
Ambergris Caye	38	560	51	704
Cayo District	32	337	61	561
Caye Caulker	20	185	29	289
Other Cayes	16	126	23	207
Stann Creek District	26	223	54	396
Toledo District	10	81	31	212
Corozal District	7	124	11	163
Orange Walk District	10	106	10	101
Totals	211	2,597	330	3,529

Source: Hotel Directory compiled by the Belize Tourist Board from periodic survey.

nomic activities which do not meet these criteria are then bundled under the term "informal sector", a catchword covering a considerable range of economic activities which are frequently marshalled under the all-inclusive term of "self-employment." This is employment of a sort that is very little organized if at all, which is difficult to enumerate and is therefore ignored by official censuses and, finally, employment in which working conditions are rarely covered by legal statutes.[15]

Breman goes on to criticize the looseness of the definition of the informal sector. He points out that the definition is usually supplemented by a listing of typical informal sector members, such as street vendors, newspaper sellers, shoeshine boys, stall-keepers, prostitutes, and beggars, or, as he concludes, "the exten-sive collection of small tradesmen, the loose and unskilled workers and other categories with low and irregular incomes who lead a laborious, semi-criminal existence on the margins of the urban economy."[16]

Breman argues that the impossibility of demarcating the informal sector as an "isolated sector of the urban economy" supports an alternative approach that views an economic system as a continuum of business organizations, ranging from "a capitalist sector which is narrowly linked with the international economy" at its more organized end, to "a sector composed of pre- or non-capitalist modes of production" at the other extreme.[17]

---

15. See Jan Breman, "A dualistic labour system? A critique of the 'informal sector' concept," in Ray Bromley, ed., *Planning for small enterprises in Third World cities* (Oxford: Pergamon Press, 1985), p. 43. For a comprehensive discussion in the context of Indian society, see N. Vijay Jagannathan, *Informal Markets in Developing Countries* (New York: Oxford University Press, 1987), *passim.*

16. Breman, "A dualistic labour system?", pp. 43-44.

17. Breman, "A dualistic labour system?", p. 53.

Table 7. Number of Hotels, Number of Hotel Rooms, and DFC Loans for Tourism in Belize, 1974-1992

Year	Number of Hotels	Number of Hotel Rooms	Value of DFC Loans for Tourism (000 BZ$)
1974	61	618	
1975	71	759	
1976	82	798	332.90
1977	81	799	155.00
1978	94	854	438.50
1979	118	1,076	346.50
1980	120	1,166	661.30
1981	143	1,352	370.30
1982	141	1,377	110.60
1983	153	1,481	535.00
1984	153	1,485	345.70
1985	146	1,441	1197.80
1986	157	1,519	44.50
1987	163	1,653	1662.00
1988	188	1,891	237.00
1989	201	2,168	122.00
1990	210	2,115	1657.00
1991	248	2,784	1397.00
1992	271	2,896	637.00

Source: Central Statistical Office, Abstract of Statistics, various issues; Development Finance Corporation (DFC), 29th Annual Report, 1992.

When the formal/informal classification scheme is used, it implies that entrepreneurs in the informal sector will require greater assistance to create, operate, and maintain their business firms than entrepreneurs who have moved into the formal sector. Since the Belizean economy is in a state of structural transition, in which non-market, or barter, activities are gradually moving into organized markets, agencies in that country that support economic units have also used these terms in their approach to analyzing small business. In particular, the National Development Foundation of Belize has begun to focus on "formalizing the informal sector."

Jeffrey Ashe focussed on the "micro-entrepreneurs" in Third World countries, as part of a survey to identify their credit and technical assistance needs. The term emphasizes the smallness of the enterprises involved. Ashe distinguished among three levels of micro-entrepreneurs, each with separate needs:

> At the lowest level (Level One) people do whatever they must do to subsist. They do not perceive themselves as entrepreneurs, nor do they conceive of their money-making activities as "business opportunities." Activities are often ephemeral—selling chewing gum or cigarettes on a corner, or colas and sweets during parades.

People at the next level (Level Two) have a fundamental understanding of business practices and have a viable going concern. They may make tortillas, or sew clothes . . ., or hawk an assortment of clothing or toys, or sell prepared food. Level Two entrepreneurs will invest whatever resources are available—be it capital, raw materials, skills, effort, time or ingenuity—into their businesses.

At Level Three, business owners have better skills. They understand the basic principles governing their markets better and are flexible enough to expand when the opportunity arises. Examples of businesses at this level might be a shoemaker with a small rented shop who has an assistant, or a family of tailors who divide their living area with a cloth to create a workshop.[18]

The entrepreneurs at Level One are best helped by community assistance programs, that include not

---

18. Jeffrey Ashe, "Extending credit and technical assistance to the smallest enterprises," in Ray Bromley, ed., *Planning for small enterprises in Third World cities* (Oxford: Pergamon Press, 1985), p. 279.

only support for the development of formal business enterprises, but also education, health, nutrition, and sanitation. In other words, these programs may address the entire life style of the entrepreneur, as part of an integrated community development effort. Level Two enterprises that are already generating income may be aided by a more focussed approach, emphasizing the need for credit and technical assistance, and often setting up groups of like-interest businesspersons to exchange information and support. At Level Three, entrepreneurs are operating well-developed firms that can generally qualify for loans from established financial institutions, in spite of their small size.[19] Ashe's classifications roughly coincide with the formal/informal categories. Level Three firms would probably be classified as the formal sector, in spite of their small size, while Levels One and Two would correspond to the informal sector.

These classification schemes not only provide an intellectually satisfying way of understanding small businesses, but they also emphasize the differing needs of small businesses at various stages of development. In the Belizean case, the evidence suggests a wide spectrum of small businesses, ranging from the ephemeral, one-person, seasonal retail or service activity at one extreme, to the well-established, well-connected business firm at the other extreme. In Belize City, the nation's capital, street vendors are ubiquitous in the downtown business district, coexisting and competing with the retail firms that line the streets. In the district towns, such as Punta Gorda or Belmopan, the same phenomenon in observed, especially on long-established "market days." The vendors form a fluid group that is never the same from week to week. In order to meet the diverse set of needs posed by such a broad spectrum of entrepreneurial activity, either helping institutions must offer a broad variety of support activities, or there must be a broad group of complementary institutions, each offering some of the needed activities.

Support for Small Business Growth in Belize. Belize has developed a complex of support organizations and agencies for small businesses, reflecting the wide range of entrepreneurial experience and developmental level shown by those firms. Entrepreneurs can receive training, financial support, and operational guidance, and are encouraged to do so by the Belizean government. The major financing and training agencies are described below.

The Development Finance Corporation (DFC) is a government development bank (a "body corporate with limited liability established by the Development Finance Corporation Act, Chapter 226 of the Laws of Belize").[20] It provides technical assistance and financing for firms in agriculture, tourism, and manufacturing. In Belize, it has been in operation since 1973. As of 1992, the DFC had a capital base of about BZE$50 million, coming from a variety of sources, including the Caribbean Development Bank, the Commonwealth Development Corporation, the European Investment Bank, and USAID. From 1973 to 1992, the DFC has loaned BZE$123.8 million on 16,011 projects.

The DFC has focussed on larger projects and larger loans. Almost 50 percent of the loans made during the 1973-1991 period were for BZE$50,000 or greater. The percentage was even higher in 1992. Nevertheless, small businesses have not been forgotten.

Over 12,000 loans have been made with face amounts of BZE$5,000 or less. Another 1,409 loans were made for amounts ranging between BZE$5,001 and BZE$15,000. While these loans account for only 11 percent of the total dollars lent by the DFC, they have been of critical importance to the small business sector in Belize, particularly since the commercial banks in Belize normally extend trade credit, rather than longer-term loans for investment purposes.

---

19. Jeffrey Ashe, "Extending credit and technical assistance," pp. 279-280.

20. Belize Development Finance Corporation, *29th Annual Report: 1992* (Belmopan: Development Finance Corporation, 1993), Appendix page 5.

Table 8 highlights the wide distribution of DFC loans to Belizean firms, showing the importance of DFC funds to sugar cane producers, citrus producers, and other agricultural interests. In addition, housing and student loans have subsidized Belizean students studying abroad as well asBelizeans moving up to better housing.[21] A complementary organization exists, however, that fills the need for assistance to the smaller firms in the economy. It has gradually developed a network of helping organizations, that tie together government agencies, trade organizations and cooperatives, and financing agencies.

The National Development Foundation of Belize (NDFB) was founded in 1983 to provide support for small enterprise in the country. It owes its existence to the U. S. Alliance for Progress initiative aimed at providing non-traditional funding and training assistance for small businesses in developing countries of this hemisphere. Both USAID and the Government of Belize supported NDFB in its initial stages. The UDP government thereafter (1984-1989) provided subsidized loan funds of BZE$520,000. Private-sector support has come from 66 Belizean business firms and businesspersons, at last count, who have contributed about BZE$300,000.[22]

NDFB basically makes loans to entrepreneurs who do not have the resources to finance the beginning and operation of a small business. The organization also provides technical assistance, management training, and marketing assistance to entrepreneurs. From the point of view of NDFB, small business includes legal activities in the fields of farming, fishing, retailing, ecotourism, manufacture, and trade. Instead of defining small business specifically in terms of sales level or number of employees, NDFB uses the more pragmatic approach of itemizing the characteristics of small businesses, as follows: limited capital, assets, and employment; non-access to bank loans; family owned and managed; capable of providing low-cost employment to the owners and others. NDFB argues that small businesses produce more than fifty percent of the annual GDP in Belize.

Since beginning operations in 1983, NDFB has made about 3,500 loans, with an aggregate value of BZE$15 million. Ninety percent of the loans were for less than BZE$10,000. Twenty percent of the loans went to women entrepreneurs, and 40 percent to small farmers. Loans are available from a minimum of BZE$500 to a maximum of BZE$25,000. Loans may finance up to 100 percent of project cost.[23]

Several other organizations that focus on small business activity are closely related to the NDFB. The Small Business Association of Belize (SBA/BZE) is an organization composed of businesspersons who represent small or non-formal businesses. Most of the members are clients of NDFB. The organization was begun on June 10, 1992, as one of the initiatives coming from the CARICOM Regional Small Business Consultation held in Port of Spain, Trinidad and Tobago, on March 25-27, 1991.

The SBA/BZE mobilizes the efforts of small business owners and operators to provide mutual support for business development. The group exerts political influence to support legislation, identifies credit sources, conducts or supports research studies on small business, refers members to appropriate helping agencies, and provides liaison with other NGO's and agencies, including the Small Sector Development Council (SSDC) and the Confederation of Co-operatives and Credit Unions of Belize (CCC-B).[24] Two

---

21. United States Department of Commerce, *Andean and Caribbean Basin Financing Directory* (Washington, D. C.: U. S. Government Printing Office, October, 1992.), p. 97.

22. This section relies upon National Development Foundation of Belize, *NDFB At A Glance* (Belize City: NDFB, no date); NDFB, *Ninth Annual General Meeting Report, 1991/1992* (Belize City: NDFB, 1993), *passim*; and an informational letter from NDFB to prospective supporters, dated February, 1994.

23. *Andean and Caribbean Basin Financing Directory*, p. 97.

24. Small Business Association of Belize, *Agenda for the Development of Small Business in Belize*, a report prepared by Michael M. Seepersaud (St. Lucia: Financial and Management Services, October 8, 1992).

Table 8. Loans Approved by the Development Finance Corporation, 1991-1993, BZ$ 000

ACTIVITY	1991		1992		1993	
	Number	Value	Number	Value	Number	Value
1. Agriculture	1,406	5,568	792	8,637	1,553	4,823
Sugarcane	734	642	567	760	1,055	1,267
Citrus	21	811	31	2,038	148	1,385
Bananas	5	2,384	6	2,705	1	700
Livestock	6	327	7	60	17	218
Poultry	1	6	4	2	12	47
Agro Industry	-	-	2	51	-	-
Fishing	2	12	1	500	6	149
Rice	3	35	107	88	143	490
Corn	9	208	4	2	12	87
Vegetables	4	13	-	-	5	22
Mixed Farming	3	28	7	115	11	36
Peanuts	-	-	1	3	-	-
Beans	213	225	12	8	114	249
Other	405	877	43	2,305	29	173
2. Tourism	5	1,397	5	637	3	592
3. Industry	3	1,697	7	649	9	1,310
4. Services	4	265	9	1,152	14	526
5. Student	38	214	74	517	116	868
6. Housing	69	1,441	117	3,794	131	4,228
TOTALS	1,525	10,582	1,004	15,386	1,826	12,347

"-" indicates zero; "r" indicates a revised figure

Source: Development Finance Corporation, Belmopan, Belize

specific programs targeted by SBA/BZE include Women Enterprise and Entrepreneurial Development (WEED), and Youth Enterprise Services (YES).

- The Small Sector Development Council of Belize (SSDC) was founded on October 2, 1992. Its membership includes representatives from the following organizations and agencies:

- National Development Foundation of Belize (NDFB)

- Belize Fishermen Cooperative Association (BF-CA)

- Small Business Association of Belize (SBA/BZE)

- Association of National Development Agencies (ANDA)

- Trade Union Congress (TUC)

- Council of Voluntary Social Services (CVSS)

- Belize Honey Producers Federation (BHPF)

- Belize Federation of Agricultural Cooperatives (BFAC)

- Credit Union League (CUL)

Four government ministries also have representatives on the Board of directors of SSDC: the Ministry of Economic Development, the Ministry of Agriculture and Fisheries, the Ministry of Social Development, and the Ministry of Housing, Cooperatives, and Industry.[25] The SSDC is a broad-based organization that tries to encourage intersectoral communication and growth, and to keep interest groups in contact with appropriate governmental agencies and ministries.

While not specifically targeting small businesses, several government programs do facilitate the development of small export enterprises. The Export Processing Zone Act of 1990 sets up EPZ's for investors, permitting free inflow and outflow of materials and funds, with no import or export license required. The Fiscal Incentives Act of 1990 is intended to encourage business growth through tax breaks and other incentives. Foreign investment is "particularly welcome" when it uses Belizean labor and raw materials, helps produce for the export markets, is environmentally sound, and increases the nation's capital stock.[26]

SMALL BUSINESS DEVELOPMENT IN EASTERN EUROPE: LESSONS FOR CUBA

The other experience relevant to the consideration of the development of Cuba's small business sector in the transition is that of the Eastern European economies. While this topic is too broad to consider in detail here some, the main problems are identified below.

First, one difference between the former East Bloc countries and Cuba is that most European countries already had relatively prosperous and organized small-business industries in place when the transition began. Although political reality relegated the true

entrepreneurs to the underground economy, many small businesses operated profitably, and some even flourished, despite the Soviet-style economic regimes. Thus, for these countries, the transition has been merely a matter of adjusting to the increased market pressures, rational pricing structures, and decreased government interference in the business sector that accompanied the transition.

Unfortunately for Cuba, the analogous sector ceased to function in the 1960's as a major player in the economy because of the substantial shortages and lack of raw materials available in Cuba. This lack of a head start will jeopardize the Cuban transition for more reasons than simply the dearth of enterprises. For example, the lack of a strong small business sector now implies that many would-be entrepreneurs lack the management skills and experience that are essential for avoiding business failures. In addition, the lack of businesses has driven down demand for loanable funds. When the demand begins to increase, therefore, transactions costs are likely to be extraordinarily high for a period of time.[27]

Fortunately, a few options for improving access to capital are available for Cuba. First, Cuba does have the decided advantage of a huge pool of available capital in the hands of expatriates living in Miami. Presumably, much of this pool will return to Cuba once the "rules of the game" are clearly defined by the transition government. Unfortunately, the Eastern European experience also illustrates that transition governments often fail to understand the issues that are critical to a well-functioning market economy. Ambiguity in one such issue, property rights of current versus pre-Castro landowners, promises to be sticky. A resolution of ownership rights could easily extend for years, slowing the flow of capital into Cuba.

Another possible solution for providing capital to export-oriented firms is that of "forfaiting," which in-

---

25. NDFB, *The Non-Formal/Small Sector on the Move* (Belize City: NDFB, no date).

26. Belize Ministry of Economic Development, *Belize Investment Guide* (Belmopan: Government Printery, 1994), p. 1.

27. See Gregory Rand "Foreign Financial Intermediation in Cuban Transition," University of North Florida working paper, August, 1995, and the references contained therein for a fuller discussion of capital availability issues.

volves government guarantees of loans to foreign companies that wish to purchase capital equipment. Because the return on capital investment is spread over time, many firms that wish to import capital equipment are unable to make desired purchases due to cash flow problems. Banks in several European countries, notably France, have addressed this market failure by having governments guarantee the loans. If European banks and governments can be convinced of the investment-worthiness of Cuba, forfaiting might well become the method of choice for importing physical capital.[28]

CCONCLUSIONS

There are several requirements for the existence of a strong, dynamic small business sector in a mixed economy. First, a well-defined, established set of property rights is essential for providing entrepreneurs the proper incentives to take risks. Rational pricing by market forces is also required. This will likely be the most important and daunting problem faced by Cuba in the transition. Conflicting claims by expatriates and non-expatriates could tie up courts and cast a long shadow of uncertainty over Cuba's private sector for many years. A necessary condition for a successful small business sector is the resolution of these conflicts.

Second, Cubans, like Eastern Europeans, must learn to accept the inherent instability of a market economy. This dynamism is especially evident in the small business sector, where even in the well-informed American market some 15% of small businesses fail every year. This Schumpeterian "creative destruction" is an essential part of a healthy economy, but it does create hardships. Cubans must fight the inevitable pessimism that business failures create.

Third, the lack of practice at managerial and entrepreneurial skills will imply that Cubans will initially make unsophisticated, and inaccurate, decisions about starting small businesses. In this case, too, the only solution is time and experience. One bright spot is the ample supply of managerial and entrepreneurial experience just north of Cuban waters. These businesspeople will be able to substantially improve the business decisions made early in the transition. Native entrepreneurs will then be able to learn the required skills relatively quickly, especially as contrasted with the Eastern European experience.

Fourth, availability of capital, both physical and human, will hurt Cuba in the initial stages of transition. Imprecise property rights will exacerbate this problem. However, there are two potential solutions: forfaiting activity by European banks and investment by Americans and Cuban-Americans.

All things considered, small business is likely to be the backbone of the Cuban transition. Its success must be a top priority for the transition government. Although Cuba has been cursed with some unique problems, it is also blessed with potential solutions that have been unavailable to other transition economies. Given the nature of the Cuban people, it is likely that small business will succeed there.

REFERENCES

Ack, Anita. "Community-Based Tourism Initiatives in Belize." *Belize Today* VIII:5 (May, 1994), 14-16.

Bauer, P. T. *Economic Analysis and Policy in Underdeveloped Countries.* Durham, N. C.: Duke University Press, 1957.

---

28. For a complete discussion of forfaiting, see Yatin Bhagwat "Forfaiting: A Technique to Increase Trade Between NAFTA Countries." Paper presented at "Economic and Financial Cycles and NAFTA: Issues and Analysis of Micro and Macroeconomics" symposium, Mexico City, June 7, 1995.

Belize. Central Statistical Office. *National Accounts Bulletin, 1980-1993.* Belmopan: Government Printery, 1994.

Belize. Export Processing Zone Act, 1990.

Belize. Fiscal Incentives Act, 1990. Chapter 45 of the Laws of Belize, as revised.

Belize. Information Service. *Fact Sheet: Belize.* Belmopan: Government Printery, 1994.

Belize. Ministry of Economic Development. *Abstract of Statistics: 1993.* Belmopan: Government Printery, 1994.

_____. *Belize Investment Guide.* Belmopan: Government Printery, 1994.

_____. *Investment Advantages and Opportunities for You in Belize.* Pamphlet. No pace of publication, no date.

Bghawat, Yatin. "Forfaiting: A Technique to Increase Trade Between NAFTA Countries." Paper presented at "Economic and Financial Cycles and NAFTA: Issues and Analysis of Micro and Macroeconomics" symposium. Mexico City. June 7, 1995.

Bromley, Ray, editor. *Planning for small enterprises in Third World cities.* Oxford: Pergamon Press, 1985.

Coase, Ronald H. "The Nature of the Firm." *Economica* 4 (November, 1937), 386-405.

Country Business. *Country Business, 1991-1992.* San Ignacio: Country Business, 1992.

Dun and Bradstreet Corporation. *Business Failure Record.* New York: Dun and Bradstreet, 1992.

Delaney, William A. *So You Want To Start A Business!.* Englewood Cliffs, N. J.: Prentice-Hall, Inc., 1984.

Development Finance Corporation (Belize). *Twenty-Ninth Annual Report: 1992.* Belmopan: Development Finance Corporation, 1992.

Díaz-Briquets, Sergio, and Sidney Weintraub, editors. *Migration, Remittances, and Small Business Development: Mexico and Caribbean Countries.* Boulder, Colo.: Westview Press, 1991.

Jagannathan, N. Vijay. *Informal Markets in Developing Countries.* New York: Oxford University Press, 1987.

McMorrow, Maura. "When You're Hot, You're Hot!" *Belize Currents* (Winter, 1989), 7-9.

Meissner, Frank. *Seeds of Change: Stories of IDB Innovation in Latin America.* Washington, D. C.: Inter-American Development Bank, 1991.

National Development Foundation of Belize. *NDFB At a Glance.* Pamphlet. Belize City: NDFB, no date.

_____. *Ninth Annual General Meeting Report, 1991/1992.* Belize City: NDFB, 1993.

Perry, Joseph M., and Louis A. Woods. "Mennonite Agricultual Enclaves and Economic Growth in Belize." Paper presented at the Annual Meetings of the Association of American Geographers, San Diego, April 18-22, 1992.

Planning Innovations, Inc. *Smallholder Farms in Belize: A Survey. Part II.* Report prepared under US-AID Contract No. 505-0000-C-00-8701. Washington, D. C.: Planning Innovations, Inc., May, 1989.

_____. *Small-Scale Enterprises in Belize: A Survey. Part I.* Report prepared under USAID Contract No. 505-0000-C-00-8701. Washington, D. C.: Planning Innovations, Inc., December, 1988.

Rand, Gregory. "Foreign Financial Intermediation in Cuban Transition." University of North Florida working paper. August, 1995.

Schumacher, Ernst Friedrich. *Small Is Beautiful: Economics as if People Mattered.* New York: Harper and Row, 1973.

Schumpeter, Joseph A. *Business Cycles.* Abridged, with an introduction by Rendigs Fels. New York: McGraw-Hill Book Company, 1964.

_____. *The Theory of Economic Development.* Translated by Redvers Opie. Cambridge, Mass.: Harvard University Press, 1934.

Seepersaud, Michael M. *Small Business Association of Belize: Agenda for the Development of Small Business in Belize.* St. Lucia: Financial and Management Services, October 8, 1992.

_____. *The Pitfalls in Managing A Small Business.* New York: Dun and Bradstreet.

United States, Department of Commerce, International Trade Administration. *Andean and Caribbean Basin Financing Directory.* Washington, D. C.: U. S. Government Printing Office, October, 1992.

_____. *1991 Guidebook: Caribbean Basin Initiative.* Washington, D. C.: U. S. Government Printing Office, November, 1991.

United States. Office of the President. *The State of Small Business: A Report of the President, 1993.* Together with the Annual Report on Small Business and Competition and the Annual Report on Federal Procurement Preference Goals of the U. S. Small Business Administration. Washington, D. C.: U. S. Government Printing Office, 1993.

United States. Small Business Administration. Office of Advocacy. *Handbook of Small Business Data: 1994 Edition.* Washington, D. C.: U. S. Government Printing Office, 1994.

Woods, Louis A., and Joseph M. Perry. "Regional Integration, Foreign Trade, and Economic Development: CARICOM and Belize." Paper presented at the Fourth Annual Studies on Belize Conference, Belize City, Belize, October 25-27, 1990.

A FIRST APPROXIMATION MODEL OF MONEY, PRICES AND EXCHANGE RATES IN REVOLUTIONARY CUBA

José F. Alonso[1] and Armando M. Lago

INTRODUCTION

This paper traces the interrelationship between money, black market prices and black market exchange rates in Revolutionary Cuba, that is, in the post-1958 Cuban economy. The research was originally designed as a study of foreign exchange rates, with the objective of developing predictive equations of foreign exchange rates of the Cuban peso. The predictive functions of exchange rates were to be used in adding the economic contributions of the foreign and domestic sectors of the Cuban economy in the context of a model of foreign aid requirements of the Cuban economy (Alonso & Lago, 1994). However, the interrelationships between black market exchange rates and black market prices made us abandon the initial objective to develop a single- equation model of foreign exchange rate determination in favor of the more complex multi- equation model presented in this paper.

Numerous data problems complicated the research design and its execution. For example, black market prices in Cuba are considered sensitive information and have never been published by the Cuban government. Our effort to collect black market prices was only partially successful, since black market prices were assembled for only 14 years in the post-1958 period.

Other problems encountered were conceptual in nature. The Cuban authorities and Cuban professional journal articles use solely currency in circulation and savings deposits of the household sector to define money supply, completely ignoring the enterprise sector's demand for money in the broadest sense of the money supply definition. Credits to state enterprises and foreign credits are typically ignored by Cuban analysts when analyzing trends in money aggregates, so that data on the monetary mass and its components are never published in Cuban official statistics. It would seem as if the Cuban government does not recognize that price inflation can occur from excess credits in the state enterprise sector. The lack of data on the components of the monetary mass became a significant handicap to this research study on the interrelationship of money, prices and exchange rates. Because of data problems and the conceptual difficulties with the Cuban monetary statistics alluded above, this research can be deemed as a first approximation.

---

1. No discussion, interpretation, results or comments contained herein can be attributed to the U.S. Government or any of its Agencies, including the U.S. Information Agency, Office of Cuban Broadcasting, Radio Martí Program. The authors accept responsibility for any errors of omission or commission. The authors would like to acknowledge the assistance of Ms. Inés Bustillo of ECLAC's Washington Office and Mrs. Janice Snow Rodríguez, Mrs. Ellen B. Zeytoun and Ms. Bonnie Kunkel of Radio Martí's, Information Center. We also benefitted from talks and discussions on unemployment and black market prices with Ms. Marta Beatriz Roque-Cabello of the Associación Nacional de Economistas Independientes de Cuba (ANEIC).

A CONCEPTUAL OVERVIEW
OF MONETARY POLICY IN SOCIALIST
CUBA

As discussed in greater detail in the International Monetary Fund's Study of the Soviet Economy (IMF, 1991), monetary and financial policy in the former Socialist bloc (and as well in Socialist Cuba) played a secondary and subordinate role to the detailed quantitative enterprise production targets contained in the Central State Plan. This subordination was explicitly designed so that there would be no feedback from monetary policy to the production targets. Thus, the role of monetary policy (Unanue, 1985) was to ensure that liquidity in the economy would correspond to the production targets and fixed prices contained in the Central State Plan.

As discussed by several Cuban analysts, such as Infante (1986) and by Chaviano, Rico and López (1986), the Global Financial Plan is the counterpart of the Central State Plan. The Global Financial Plan groups incomes/revenues and expenses from the Budget (prepared by the Comité Estatal de Finanzas), the Credit Plan (prepared by the Banco Nacional), the Balance of Income and Expenditures of the Population and the Balance of Payments (both prepared by JUCEPLAN), so that some attempt is indeed made at achieving financial balance. But this may be misleading, since Infante (1986) complains that little attention is actually paid to achieving material-financial equilibrium in the enterprise/state sector of the economy.

To ensure that monetary policy would have no feedback effect on production and prices, the supply of credit to the state enterprises and their financial flows are kept completely separated from the household sector money flows and credit. The financial flows to enterprises are regulated through the Credit Plan (Unanue, 1985), which groups and adds the planned demand for credit at the enterprise level, whereas the household financial flows are regulated through the Cash Plan. Currency can be withdrawn by state enterprises only for payroll purposes and cash-holding by enterprises is severely limited, if not actually prohibited. The credit extended to the enterprise sector is mainly of a short-term nature, designed to finance

working capital. Investments are financed through budget allocations and the enterprises must remit most of the profits to the State budget. Enterprises face a soft budget constraint (Kornai, 1980 and 1982), so that credit repayment shortfalls are covered from budgetary transfers. Kornai also mentions the problem of intra-enterprise transactions, which are generally unpaid in times of shortages and which are usually absorbed by the government deficit. The enterprise demand for money depends on the quantitative requirements contained in the Central State Plan (transaction demand) and on the opportunity costs of holding money in terms of inventories (as a store of value), since inventories substitute for money in times of shortages in socialist economies (Kornai, 1980)

That socialist enterprises accumulate larger inventories than their free-market counterparts has been documented by several other authors. Fogel and Rosenthal (1994) mention that large strategic reserves of food, spare parts and machinery and equipment are kept in Cuba under the control of several government organizations, including the Instituto Nacional de Reservas del Estado (INRE), the reserves of the Ministry of Armed Forces, the reserves at the Provincial level under the control of the officials of the Poder Popular, and the special reserves under the direct control of the commander-in-chief, Fidel Castro himself. According to the above referenced authors, at the beginning of the decade of the eighties, Cuba had a two-year strategic reserve of spare parts, and of machinery and equipment replacements.

The Cash Plan focuses mainly on household financial flows and specifies the factors that contribute to the growth of currency in circulation and its flow into the banking sector. Households can hold saving deposits, but currency is the only means of payment. Households are not allowed to purchase enterprise securities nor to receive loans from the enterprise sector. The Cash Plan is reflected in the Balance of Money Incomes and Expenditures of the Population, reported annually in the *Anuario Estadístico de Cuba* (Comité Estatal de Estadísticas, 1989), in contrast to the information on enterprise credits, which is rarely reported. The reader should appreciate by now that there is some degree of liquidity in the short-term financial assets of the household sector, in contrast to the low degree of liquidity in the enterprises's financial assets.

It is important to note the impacts of monetary expansion, that is, of excess demand for money in socialist economies. Since official prices are controlled and foreign exchange operations restricted, excessive money growth leads to general merchandise shortages throughout the official economy and to price inflation in black market transactions and deterioration in black market exchange rates. The socialist government authorities have always believed that the merchandise shortages induced by excessive money growth can be dealt with through administrative procedures with no feedback on the rest of the economy, but as will be seen in this paper, that is not the case in Cuba.

While the information contained in the Credit Plan (enterprise credits) and in the Cash Plan (currency in circulation and household savings deposits) in principle cover the components of the monetary mass, in practice statements by Cuban authorities on stabilization policies focus solely on the Cash Plan when analyzing the monetary overhang of the economy. It is as if enterprise credits played no role in overheating the Cuban economy.

Unanue (1985) complains about the insufficient search for material-financial equilibrium and balance between JUCEPLAN, the Banco Nacional de Cuba and the Comité Estatal de Estadísticas and proposes a system of national income accounting identities to achieve the material-financial balance. According to Unanue (1985) the material-financial balance requires that the sum of: 1) consumption for social purposes, 2) net investments, 3) social security pensions and transfers, and 4) salaries paid in the non-productive sphere be equal to a) changes in household liquidity, b) the net balance of payment imbalance, plus c) what socialist economists call the "plusproducto", or the excess of national income over the addition of salaries paid in the productive sector plus income of the non-state sector plus consumption of agricultural products at the farm. The reader should note the lack of the usual monetary

concepts in Unanue's model, which won a Cuban award.

All the discussions and econometric models of monetary circulation in Cuba—that is, including those of Martínez Fagundo (1989), Espinosa and Quintana (1989) and Alpízar (1992)—focus solely on the component flows into the Balance of Incomes and Expenditures of the Population, completely ignoring the "quasi-money" inter-enterprise transactions and credits. For example, Mejías (1985) looks into the interrelationship between monetary issue and budgets deficits, but only recognizes as increases in money supply those transactions which result in higher incomes and salaries of the population, reductions in household taxes and user charge payments and reductions in household expenditures. One of the few analysts to recognize the importance of the state enterprise sector is Echeverría (1992), but he has yet to formulate a precise quantitative economic model.

Disequilibrium and Shortage Views in Socialist Economies

Traditional views of inflation in socialist economies have maintained that the demand for money in these societies is of little relevance to the functioning of the economy, since money holdings are not a subject of choice, but merely the by-product of the Central Plan. Thus, it is argued that the households' money holdings are somewhat involuntary and unwanted, the result of forced savings. As a consequence, it is claimed that there is a "monetary overhang" in the economy. To bring market equilibrium, prices would have to be set free and would have to rise substantially, contributing to the conclusion that there is "repressed inflation" in socialist societies; that socialist economies are in persistent disequilibrium under central planning.

A variation of the traditional view, called the disequilibrium school (Portes, 1987, and Portes and Winter, 1980), argues that due to central planners' mistakes in a closed economy, or foreign trade shocks in an open economy, when aggregate demand exceeds aggregate supply in the presence of rigid or sticky prices, then the economy is indeed subject to repressed inflation. However, if aggregate demand and aggregate supply are in equilibrium, excess supply or excess demand in some markets only requires adjustment to relative prices but no changes in the overall price level.

A competing view is that socialist economies are economies operating under chronic shortages (Kornai, 1980 and 1982) and that households accumulate monetary balances because they have a shortage of goods in which to spend their earnings. The shortage theorists point out that in socialist economies there are often large unofficial markets—free agricultural markets and black markets—where the household consumer can purchase goods unavailable at official rationed markets and can also substitute for the goods originally desired. Kornai (1980) mentions that shortages may lead to "forced spending" on other goods, particularly since goods also play a role as a store of value in the midst of shortages. It is also argued that in the presence of the chronic shortages, the households amass monetary balances as a precaution, artificially increasing their savings rate. The end result of the discussion between the two schools is that the size of the forced saving may overestimate the amount of genuine macroeconomic disequilibrium. More on this discussion is presented in later sections of this paper.

A BRIEF SYNOPSIS OF POST-1958 DEVELOPMENTS IN MONEY, PRICES AND EXCHANGE RATES

As a way of background into the subjects of money, prices and exchange rates in Cuba, a brief summary of developments and events in the post-1958 period are discussed next.

Created in 1948, the Banco Nacional de Cuba maintained, since its inception, a freely-convertible Cuban peso at par with the U.S. dollar. Prices were stable previous to the onset of the Revolution, growing at 1.9% annually from 1955 to 1958 according to the general price index compiled by the Banco Nacional de Cuba (1957-1958, p.198) and there were no undue pressures on the Cuban peso which remained at

par with the dollar. However by the late fifties Cuba began to experience a deterioration in its balance of payment due to a boom in imported consumer durable goods that remained basically unchecked until the revolutionary government led by Fidel Castro took power by force of arms on January 1, 1959.

Almost from its beginning, the Castro government sought the monopoly of foreign exchange and trade. Once the government took over control of the economy, it increased the money supply and imposed foreign exchange controls. This led to the development of a black market for Cuban pesos as early as 1959. The controls enforced by the central bank consisted of declaring illegal for any citizen to own and trade gold and foreign currency and to have bank balances abroad. In addition, international trade of goods and services remained the exclusive domain of the government. By December 31, 1959, (Figure 1), the peso was trading at 1.67 per dollar in the black market[2] (Pick's, 1970). By March 1961, the year when the entire banking sector was nationalized without compensation, the gold reserves of the Banco Nacional were exhausted, and the value of the peso plunged to 6.25 per U.S. dollar in the black market. Since then the peso has become a non-convertible currency worldwide.

As the government applied its expansionary monetary policy, inflation and foreign exchange deterioration became apparent during the early years of the Revolution. The Cuban monetary mass, defined as comprising money in circulation plus bank deposits of both households and enterprises, grew from 1,342.7 million pesos in 1958 to 1,765.2 million pesos in 1960 (Grupo Cubano de Investigaciones Económicas, 1963). Using Dudley Seers' (Seers, Bianchi, Joy and Nolff, 1964) general price indexes, the price inflation rate was 3.5% in 1960 and 16.13% in 1961, that is, the previous record of price stability had been broken.

---

2. These black market rates for foreign exchange refer to trades and/or un-licensed transfers to international financial centers. They are generally higher than the black market rates for small volume transactions inside Cuba. See *Pick's Currency Yearbook* (1970) for explanations.

In August 1961 the Cuban government instituted a currency reform, issuing new bank notes which replaced all the previously-circulating paper money. Since the currency reform stipulated that no individual was allowed to exchange more than 200 pesos, it achieved a major reduction in circulation. In fact, the currency in circulation dropped from 1,045 million Cuban pesos in 1960 to 478 million pesos in 1961, while the peso appreciated in black markets to 5.0 pesos per dollar by September 1961. But soon afterwards the slide of the peso continued and by September 1962 the dollar traded at 11 pesos per U.S. dollar in the black markets for Cuban currency.

The aftermath of the Cuban missile crisis generated further transactions in the currency black markets, as the repatriated Soviet bloc technicians and armed forces exchanged pesos for dollars to take home under the very noses of the Cuban state security agents that would not arrest them for these otherwise illegal activities. In March 1963, the black market rates for the Cuban pesos reached 25.0 pesos per U.S. dollar and stayed at this rate for the rest of 1963. (Figure 1). By the end of 1964, the peso had appreciated slightly to 23.0 pesos per U.S. dollar and remained at 22.0 pesos per dollar up to the Spring of 1967. Currency in circulation during this period was 540 million pesos in 1964 (654 million pesos if currency, notes and savings deposits are included in the monetary mass) and 811 million pesos (including, currency, notes and savings deposits) in 1966 according to Rodríguez (1990).

By the end of 1967, black- and free-market transactions in Cuban pesos declined. The black market currency premiums declined sharply and the value of the peso appreciated to 8.0 pesos per dollar in December 1967, 5.0 pesos per dollar in December 1968 and 6.0 pesos per dollar in December 1969. The sources of these reduced levels of foreign exchange transactions, not exceeding a few thousand dollars per week, were Cuban delegates attending meetings abroad and Soviet bloc technicians and forces returning to Eastern Europe after the completion of their duties in Cuba. The population did not participate in these transactions since foreign currency trading was illegal. However, the economy also showed deterioration and exhaustion. This period coincided with the failure of the grand plan to produce ten million tons of sugar for the purpose of cornering the international sugar market. This event not only delivered the "coupe de grace" to the chosen economic model but depleted all available resources, forcing the leadership to publicly admit economic failure.

Cuba began in the mid-sixties to increase its outstanding debt and economic dependency on the Soviet Union. Mesa-Lago (1981) has reported that trade with the Soviet Union set a record in 1967 and trade deficits began to rapidly increase. By 1969 the trade deficit reached more than half billion pesos. Money in circulation began to increase, according to Pick's (1975), from 850 million pesos at the end of December 1968 to 3,478 million pesos (with savings deposits included) in 1971. By 1969, Cuba owed its trading partners close to 10.0 million tons of sugar. Therefore, the political leadership was caught confronting a serious economic deterioration resulting from a colossal "sugar" mistake, the exhaustion of the economic model and being politically at odds with the Soviet Union, as Cuba openly criticized the invasion of Czechoslovakia in the summer of 1968. As a result of the serious fracas with the Soviet leadership, oil shipments were halted beginning in 1968. However, as the Soviets began to reconsider the amount of economic assistance provided, the black market boomed in 1969-70 in response to the crisis. The peso/dollar black market exchange rate in December 1970 was 7.0 pesos per U.S. dollar and it kept climbing until September 1972 when it hit 10.15 pesos per dollar.

In order to positively respond to the economic crisis of the late sixties and earlier seventies, the leadership installed a new economic model suggested by the Soviet economic advisors. This model required a complete reorganization of the politico-economic relationships in the country. The new model known as the SDPE (Sistema de Dirección y Planificación Económica) was very similar to the Soviet centrally planned model known as "Calculi Económico". Cuba's SDPE model was implemented under the guidance of Humberto Pérez, the head of JUCEPLAN, the Central Planning Board. As the country embarked in a new experiment, expectations improved, economic activity revived and by 1972 money supply decreased to 2,648 million pesos. The black market exchange rate reflected the economic improvement, with the peso appreciating to 9.0 pesos per dollar by 1973 from its early trading of 10.15 pesos in September 1972. However, sugar did not recover as fast as others sectors and the country began to accumulate sugar deficits with the Soviet Union, made up by purchasing sugar in the world market (USIA, 1988).

Currency in circulation was estimated by Pick's (1975) at 850 million pesos at the end of December 1968, growing to 3.478 billion pesos (with households savings deposits included) in 1971 and then falling to 2.648 billion pesos in 1972. In 1974 the Banco Nacional's gold reserves were close to US$ 474.0 million, an increase of 127% over 1973, in great part due to increases in short-term debt with overseas creditors. Early in 1973, the U.S. dollar suffered a 10.0 percent devaluation and, as a consequence, the Cuban peso appreciated to 9.0 pesos per dollar in the black market.

There were irregular variations in the black market value of the peso in 1974 and 1975, but by early 1976 the dollar traded at 8.45 pesos per U.S. dollar. Black market transactions were still small in volume, seldom exceeding a few hundreds pesos per week and still involved mostly Soviet bloc personnel.

In addition to the implementation of the new economic model and the resumption of Soviet aid, several events during the early seventies affected Cuba's international financial transactions. Among those were:

1. the floating of the U.S. dollar in August 1971, and its devaluation in December 1971, which lead to a slight appreciation of the peso,

2. the 10.0 percent further devaluation of the U.S. dollar on February 13, 1973,

3. the increased indebtedness of Cuba, via short term loans and trade credits, with hard currency countries, mostly West Germany and other western European countries and

4. the rise in sugar prices from U.S. $0.03 / lb. at the end of 1968 to U.S. $0.09/ lb. at the end of 1972, to U.S. $0.63 / lb. in November 1974, only to descend to U.S. $0.27 / lb. in early 1975.

Figure 1. Cuba: Free market foreign exchange rate

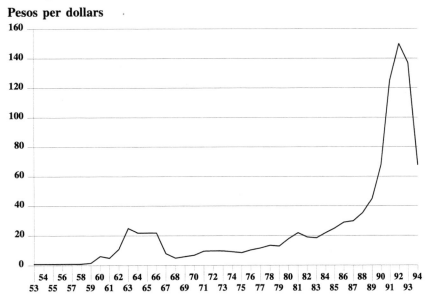

Source: Pick's Currency Yearbook

However, as was the case of 1963-64 and later in 1980-81, these increases in sugar prices contributed to the worsening of the balance of payments deficits and to the growth of short-term foreign debt.

The sugar price decline in 1977 to U.S. $0.05 / lb. reduced foreign trade in hard currency, forcing Cuba to borrow in the international market. By 1977 the country's hard currency debt with the West had grown to US $1.4 billion dollars; its servicing of U.S. $400.0 million annually comprised 44.0 percent of Cuba's hard currency export earnings. The debt was the result of short term borrowing during the early-and mid-seventies (Table 1). In addition, Soviet debt and trade credits began to increase. As a result of the borrowing and increase in economic activity, bank notes in circulation increased 202.0 percent in 1977 and the value of the Cuban peso deteriorated in the black market to 11.74 pesos per dollar. By September of 1979, it had achieved a low of 15.0 pesos per U.S. dollar.

Cuba's outstanding debt has three principal components: 1) development assistance and credits in convertible currency and transferable rubles from the Soviet Union, 2) trade credits from Eastern Europe, the former CMEA (Council of Mutual Economic Assistance) countries, and 3) credits from the West in convertible currency. From 1960 to 1975, the Cuban debt to the Soviet Union was mostly the result of development assistance and trade financing, as was the debt with the rest of the CMEA countries. Cuba's debt to the Soviet Union exceeded U.S. $5,000 million in 1976 (Mesa-Lago, 1981). In the meantime, the convertible currency debt with capitalist countries began to rise in the mid-seventies and continued growing until 1986. Convertible currency debt grew from 1975 to 1986, as shown in Table 1, and was mostly used for purchasing capital equipment and intermediate goods. This debt exceeded $4,900.0 million of U.S. dollars in 1986. In addition, Soviet debt during this period exceeded 20.0 billion transferable rubles as a result of trade subsidies and credits, including oil sales on the Soviet account for convertible currency (Rodríguez, 1992). However, faced with the impossibility of repaying the hard currency debt, in September 1982 Cuba halted payments, declaring a moratorium. In May 1982 the dollar sold at 23.50 pesos per dollar in the Cuban black markets and continued to lose in value during the eighties in spite of the flow of foreign tourists into Cuba; by December 1989 the dollar traded at 45.0 pesos per dollar. The risk associated with Cuban loans although high was not exorbitant. In 1983 Cuba was borrowing at LIBOR + 2.25% rates from European and central banks, rates which declined to LIBOR + 1.88% in 1984, and to LIBOR + 1.50% in 1985 according to José Luis Rodríguez (1990). These rates pale in comparison to the current 1995 LIBOR + 8% rate charged Cuba by the Dutch "ING Bank" to finance the purchase of inputs for the 1995-96 sugar harvest.

A word is in order about the behavior of black market prices in Cuba during the eighties. A price index of black and parallel market prices (using 1980 commodity basket weights) revealed only slight inflationary pressures during this decade. The black market price index $P_{89} = 100.00$, behaved as follows: $P_{80} = 90.31$, $P_{83} = 91.15$, $P_{85} = 90.98$, $P_{86} = 89.98$, $P_{87} = 100.09$ and $P_{88} = 97.55$; that is, a growth of only 10% during a ten-year period. These low price inflation rates were the result of large increases in the supply of goods through the massive Soviet foreign aid program and the government fiscal discipline during this period. While no budgetary information has been published for the pre-1978 period, the data published since reveals that government deficits never exceeded 2% of GDP from 1978 to 1986. By 1988, the government fiscal discipline had begun to wane, with budget deficits (including public enterprise deficits) rising to 6% of GDP in 1988 and to 7.2 % of GDP in 1989. The result of this fiscal constraint and massive foreign subsidies was a remarkable price stability up to 1989.

The decline in trade subsidies and foreign aid from the former USSR and the socialist bloc resulted in a major drop in Cuba's ability to import the raw materials, oil, and machinery needed to run its economy, and as a consequence Cuba's gross domestic product (GDP), measured in current pesos, dropped 48.28% from 1989 to 1993 (Table 2). With the Cuban government's precipitous announcement of a 0.7% recovery in 1994, GDP declined 47.92% from 1989 to 1994. These declines measured in current pesos pale when compared with the declines in constant pesos, considering that by 1993 the index of black market prices had increased by a multiple of 15.5 times compared to the 1989 black market price levels. As the Cuban economy plunged, tax revenues decreased appreciably and the government was unable to hold on to its precarious fiscal discipline. The government deficit rose to 26.33% of GDP in 1991, to 39.72% of GDP in 1992 and peaked at 50.50% of GDP in 1993. The liquid assets owned by households grew both as the result of the increased government deficit and as a consequence of the drop in the available supply of goods (both domestic and foreign). Liquidity, comprising currency in circulation and household saving deposits, which in 1989 stood at 21.5% of GDP, grew to 49.8% of GDP in 1991, to 69.5% of GDP in 1992 and actually outstripping GDP, to 120.0% of GDP in 1993. The net result of the lack of fiscal discipline and the drop in supply was the significant inflationary precess that Cuba is still trying to control today.

The end of Soviet foreign aid to Cuba after 1990 accelerated the deterioration in the value of the peso, which successively dropped to 68.0 pesos per dollar in December 1990, to 125.0 pesos per dollar in December 1991, and to 165.0 pesos per dollar in June 1993. On 13 August 1993, the government enacted Law Decree 140 decriminalizing the use of foreign currency by citizens to conduct domestic transactions. The passage of this law signals the end of currency transaction controls. But, controls remain imposed in international trade and buying and selling of gold. In July 1993, the Cuban government estimated that US $200.0 millon were circulating in Cuba (Fogel and Rosenthal, 1994). José L. Rodríguez confirmed this high rate of dollar holdings in Cuba (*Cuba-Business,* Jan/Feb. 1995), stating that 21.0 percent of cuban households admitted having access to U.S. currency.)

A few weeks later, in September 1993, the Cuban government legalized self-employment (trabajo por cuenta propia) for selected categories of employment. In August 1994, the government announced a series of stabilization measures to reduce the excess demand in the economy. These stabilization measures included some increases in taxes and user fees, as well as reductions in the deficits of state enterprises. In August 1994, the U.S. government prohibited the sending of remittances in dollars to the Cuban relatives of U.S. residents. The combined result of the Cuban government stabilization policies has been to reduce the government deficit, thereby dampening price inflation and improving the value of the Cuban peso in black market transactions. Thus, the value of the peso appreciated to 137.0 pesos per dollar in December 1993 and to 68.0 pesos per dollar in December 1994. By January 1995, the dollar sold for 66.0 pesos in Cuban black markets.

Commodity prices in black markets exhibited similar behavior. By 1990 black market prices were still stable enough, only 2.4% above 1989. But the end of foreign aid and trade subsidies from Russia and the loss of fiscal discipline (noted above) had a dramatic adverse effect on increasing demand while decreasing the supply of goods and services, and as a result, prices began to grow appreciably in black markets. The black market price index $P_{89} = 100.00$ rose as follows: $P_{90} = 102.43$, $P_{91} = 263.43$, $P_{92} = 509.84$, $P_{93} = 1552.54$, $P_{94} = 1396.48$.[3] Black market prices probably peaked in September 1994 and have been diminishing since as a consequence of the Cuban government stabilization policies (Figure 2). On October 1, 1994, the Cuban government authorized the re-opening of free farmers markets, which had been closed since the mid-eighties, and whose opening provided a legal outlet for purchasing goods not available in the rationing cards. By the end of 1994, Cuba's stabilization policies had reduced the budget deficit to 14.0% of GDP, while a combination of increased taxes on liquor and tobacco, higher rents and

---

3. These prices indexes are slightly larger than the un-weighted indexes presented by Mirta Rodríguez Calderón in *Bohemia.* (1993). Rodríguez Calderón's indexes add individual commodity prices without any commodity basket weights.

Table 1.   Cuba: Outstanding convertible currency debt - selected years 1969-1994
In million of dollars

Year	Total debt	Official bilateral	Official multilateral	Suppliers	Financial institutions	Other credits
1969	291.0	n/a	n/a	n/a	n/a	n/a
1975	1338.0	n/a	n/a	n/a	n/a	n/a
1978	2883.8	n/a	n/a	n/a	n/a	n/a
1979	3267.3	n/a	n/a	n/a	n/a	n/a
1980	3226.8	1353.6	7.9	27.0	1837.1	1.2
1981	3169.6	1293.7	15.2	33.4	1334.9	0.9
1982	2668.7	1275.8	18.2	46.8	1327.3	0.7
1983	2789.7	1332.5	25.0	96.7	1334.9	0.7
1984	2988.8	1578.7	17.2	228.5	1164.2	0.2
1985	3621.0	1820.4	21.5	433.2	1345.7	0.2
1986	4985.2	2082.1	23.3	1129.1	1750.5	0.2
1987	6094.3	2656.9	23.2	1365.9	2048.1	0.2
1988	6605.5	2905.5	47.5	1496.7	2108.7	47.1
1989	6165.2	2817.4	60.7	1408.0	1837.0	42.1
1990	6686.6	n/a	n/a	n/a	n/a	n/a
1991	n/a	n/a	n/a	n/a	n/a	n/a
1992	6377.0	2914.0	n/a	1338.0	2125.0	n/a
1993	8784.7	4046.8	438.3	1867.1	2405.5	27.0
1994	9082.8	3991.7	502.5	2057.8	2501.4	29.4

Sources: For years 1969, 1975 and 1980 to 1992 see: José Luis Rodríguez, "La Deuda Externa Cubana: Una Evaluación Actual (II), *Boletín de Información Sobre Economía Cubana*, Centro de Investigación de la Economía Mundial (CIEM), Vol.1, No. 11/12, Noviembre/Diciembre, 1992, p.8. and for other years A.R.M. Ritter, "Cuba's convertible currency debt problem," *Cepal Review* No. 36, December, 1988, p.120. and for 1993 and 1994, Banco Nacional de Cuba (August 1995).

uses charges and higher prices in the black markets, also contributed to decrease household liquidity to 97.3% of GDP. The consequence of these policies was to reduce the rate of inflation, while the Cuban peso appreciated in black markets in the island and abroad. Based on newspaper articles in *The Washington Post* and in *The Miami Herald,* and on information provided by the Instituto Cubano de Economistas Independientes (1996), we have estimated that black market prices fell to P_{95} = 1282.55 by March 1995 and P_{95} = 739.64 by December 1995. These price indexes indicate that the Cuban population is now paying a multiple of 7.4 times the 1989 level of commodity prices with no comparable adjustment in wages and salaries.

The task at hand is to develop predictive relationships that explain these financial results and events in Cuban black markets.

MARKETS IN SOCIALIST CUBA

There are at least four types of markets in socialist Cuba: 1) government-run official rationed markets, 2) government-run parallel market stores, 3) free

Table 2. Cuba: selected macroeconomic indicators 1989-1994

(All figures in millions of current pesos, unless otherwise specified)

Year	Gross Domestic Product	Executed Government Deficit	Liquidity	Black market Price Index	Black Market Foreign Exchange Rate (Pesos/Dollar)
1989	19335	1403.4	4163	100.00	45
1990	18735	1958.1	4986	102.43	68
1991	14051	3764.8	6663	263.43	125
1992	12084	4869.0	8361	509.84	150
1993	10000	5050.6	11043	1552.55	137
1994	10070	1421.4	9940	1396.48	68

Note: Black market foreign exchange rate as of December 31st of each year. Liquidity includes currency in circulation plus household saving deposits.

Source: Appendix A and Banco Nacional de Cuba (August 1995).

farmers' and artisan markets, and 4) the unofficial black markets that have always existed in Cuba irrespective of repression and coercion by the Cuban Government. A brief discussion of these markets is in order before getting immersed with the formulation of the economic model.

In response to shortages and inflationary pressures in the early years of the Revolution, food rationing was introduced in Cuba in 1962. The introduction of rationing in effect created two markets in Cuba: the official rationed market and the ever- present black market. Dumont (1971) compared official rationed and free black market prices in 1969, confirming the strength of the black markets in spite of all of the government efforts to suppress them. To minimize the importance of the black markets, the government created a state-controlled parallel market in the seventies which charged prices more attuned to production costs and supply/demand conditions. By 1977-78, the prices charged at parallel market stores were three to eight times greater than the official rationed and subsidized prices (Mesa-Lago, 1981)

The State-owned parallel market stores assisted in soaking up the excess liquidity resulting from expan-

sionary monetary policies, but did not displace the black markets altogether. Because of problems of poor work quality and absenteeism, deemed by government authorities as related to the lack of outlets for spending the excess liquid assets accumulated by the households, a decision was taken by the government to open free farmers' markets in April 1980. According to Deere and Meurs (1992), more than 200 free farmers' markets were operating across the island in 1981, resulting in significant increases in the supply of agricultural products.

The free farmers' markets of the early eighties were opened as a result of an increasing consumer demand for better quality and more abundant agricultural produce and goods. The consumer had accumulated excess liquidity as a result of the government inability to provide sufficient goods. Therefore, to alleviate the shortage of supplies and to increase production, the government authorized the farmers' markets to begin functioning. The farmers' markets charged prices which sometimes were above or similar to the parallel market prices. The results were an increase in supplies which benefitted consumers and producers. However, producers and other market operators began to accumulate earnings which created income in-

111

equalities and the government disliked those results. The income inequalities created favored mostly the small farmers and other operators, but that was not to be tolerated. By 1982, complaints arose and Fidel Castro and other leaders began to criticize the operations of the farmers' market. In addition, regulations were enacted to tightly control market operations. Among those regulations were: a tax increase on sales, documentary evidence to prove compliance with "acopio" and limiting access to ANAP members, excluding the cooperatives. By the middle of 1982, the end of he free farmers' markets was evident. The government was no longer in favor of the experiment. In May of 1986, the free farmers' market were closed, supposedly because of many complaints by ordinary consumers who had limited access to the market, but also because basically the State could no longer sustain competition, not wanting to allow prices to fluctuate and not letting the market determine agricultural production without state interference.

After the end of the free farmers' market experiment, the black markets for agricultural produce and other scarce goods continued to exist and became the only source of additional agricultural produce and other

supplies for the consumer. Soon, the Socialist Bloc (CMEA) ceased to exist. By November 1989, the countries of Eastern Europe became politically- and economically-free and after their liberation all economic assistance to Cuba ceased. Only Russia continued to fulfill the previously promised assistance. Supplies after 1991 became scarce, as the ration card no longer could provide a minimal quantity of necessity items. Consequently, the black markets grew in importance. Economic activity declined dramatically in a short period of time and shortages of all sorts of goods became apparent. Supplies were difficult to obtain for the average citizen. Prices in the black market suddenly increased to unprecedented high levels while wages did not keep pace with inflation. Inflation became a reality in socialist Cuba and real income has severely declined.

In the meantime, the leadership had to confront problems of several dimensions. It had to control the budget and the excess liquidity, it needed to reduce the size of the employed labor force and increase production and productivity to curtail the free fall in economic activity. In order to address the difficult economic situation, respond to the supply difficulties and the excessive amount of money in the hands of

Figure 2. Cuba: Black Market Price Index

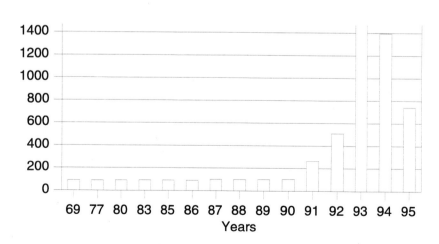

Source: Appendix A

the consumer, the government introduced new taxes and authorized the re-enactment of a free farmers' and other markets which included other type of stores such as hardware, artisans and special stores known as "shoppins" which only operated with convertible currency and sold specialized goods.

The new farmers' and other markets introduced in October 1994, were created to achieve a multitude of political-economic goals and participation is more open than in the previous market. It now includes the UBPC (Unidades Básicas de Producción), the Army cooperatives and anyone in the private agricultural sector. The functioning of the market is controlled by the central government and the local governments and is restricted to sales in domestic currency only. Among those economic goals are: a) to reduce money in the hand of the consumer, b) to increase budget revenues, c) to increase production and productivity, and d) to make an attempt to introduce private property rights. However, in order to achieve the desired goals, participants must provide goods at reasonable prices. Until now few of those necessary conditions have been attained and these markets can only be qualified as a partial success. In the meantime, the black market still operates and attracts people engaged in prohibited commercial activities or farmers/operators who seek dollars for their produce rather than domestic currency. In addition the black market is an outlet to obtain goods not available in the special government stores such as the "shoppins"or any other official outlets.

There is a wide discrepancy in the estimates of the relative shares of the official rationed, parallel and free farmers' markets in the Cuban economy. Deere and Meurs (1992) quote Eugenio Rodríguez Balari's (then Director of the Instituto de Estudios de la Demanda) estimates that by 1980 the parallel market accounted for 70% of all expenditures in consumer goods and that free farmers' markets accounted for the following shares of expenditures in food: 1980: 8.8%, 1981: 9.8%, 1982: 6.2%, 1983: 2.9%, 1984: 3.9% and 1985: 3.4%.

These shares are different than those from other sources. The United Nations' Economic Commission for Latin America and the Caribbean (1984, pp.

248) published the following shares of total consumer expenditures for 1983 and 1984: for free farmers' markets: 1983: 1.0% and 1984: 1.3%; for parallel markets: 1983: 54.5% and 1984: 58.7% and for the official rationed market: 1983: 44.5% and 1984: 40.0%.

Finally the 1988 *Anuario Estadístico de Cuba* (Tables X.18 through X.20) presents another different set of market shares for the government-run parallel market stores. The shares of total retail sales reported by the Comité Estatal de Estadísticas in the above referenced publication are: 1982: 1.1%, 1983: 10.3%, 1984: 14.0%, 1985: 15.2%, 1986: 15.4%, 1987: 15.6% and 1988: 16.0%. The *Anuario Estadístico* also reports different figures for food retail sales, but these are not presented here since there is no need to over-stress the point.

This wide discrepancy in the shares of the three types of markets affected the research design. It was decided not to attempt to develop a general consumer price index of the Cuban economy (combining official rationed, parallel and free farmers' markets), but instead to concentrate solely on the black market prices which now dominate the Cuban scene in 1995. As a result the authors decided to use the official GDP deflators for the Pre-1989 period, but to use black market price indexes after 1989. The development of the black market price indexes is explained in Appendix A.

A REVIEW OF THE LITERATURE ON THEORIES AND APPROACHES TO EXCHANGE RATE DETERMINATION

Before immersing ourselves in the details of specifying the first approximation model, a short review and background on the theories of exchange rate determination is in order. The old traditional view of exchange rate determination is that exchange rates equilibrate the international demand for flow of goods. This view was reflected in the classic Biderdicke-Robinson-Metzler model (Krueger, 1983), according to which the exchange rate is determined by the flow of supply and demand for foreign exchange.

Closely related to the traditional view is the purchasing power parity theory of exchange rate determination, which in its absolute version states that the equilibrium exchange rate equals the ratio of domestic to foreign prices. The more reasonable relative version of the purchasing power parity theory states that exchange rates are simply related to changes in the price ratios. We dispense here with all the arguments on which foreign price index to use, foreign consumer prices vs. foreign wholesale prices vs. foreign GNP price deflators (Frenkel, 1976).

A third viewpoint on exchange rate determination is the monetary asset view (Dornbusch, 1976), in which monetary factors predominate. According to this theory, exchange rates are determined as the result of balancing portfolios of domestic and foreign currency so as to equilibrate the rates of return on holdings of foreign and domestic currency. Exchange rates thus equilibrate the international demand for stocks of assets. The real rate of return on assets, so claims this theory, will be equal and independent of the currency denomination of the assets. This postulate is referred to as the interest rate parity, and in its simplest formulation argues that interest rate differentials are paramount in the determination of exchange rates. In these portfolio models the nominal rate of interest will be equal to the real rate of interest plus the expected rate of inflation, a proposition that will lead us later to the last theory of exchange rate determination, which depends on expectations of rates of return on domestic and foreign assets.

Within the monetary asset theory of exchange rate determination there are two variants depending on the degree of price and wage flexibility of the economy. When prices are flexible, there is a positive relationship between nominal interest rates and exchange rates, since when domestic interest rates rise relative to foreign rates, it is due to the fact that the domestic currency is expected to lose value through inflation and depreciation. In these conditions of price flexibility, the demand for domestic currency falls relative to foreign currency, which causes it to depreciate instantly. This view appears to be valid when inflation differentials are large, as in the German hyperinflation of the twenties.

When prices and wages are sticky, a negative relation emerges between nominal interest rate differentials and exchange rates. This result comes about because under sticky prices and wages, changes in nominal interest rates no longer reflect changes in the expected inflation rate, but instead reflect changes in the tightness of monetary policy. Thus, when domestic interest rates rise relatively to foreign rates, it is due to a contraction in domestic supply without a matching fall in prices, with these higher domestic interest rates attracting capital inflows which cause the domestic currency to appreciate. This variation is applicable to scenarios where inflation differentials are small.

The final view of exchange rate determination takes into account the special role of expectations (Frankel, 1979), where demand for domestic and foreign money depend—like the demand for any other asset—on the expected rates of return. Thus, current values of exchange rates incorporate market expectations concerning the future course of events. A modern variation of this viewpoint is the rational expectations theory (Bilson, 1978), in which market price and exchange rate expectations will be equal to the actual predictions of the underlying models being estimated.

The applicability of all these theories to the Cuban situation is analyzed below. However, at the outset the peculiarities of the Cuban scenario must be recognized. Prices, wages, domestic interest rates and official exchange rates have remained fixed in Cuba for long periods of time. Until July 26, 1993 it was illegal for Cuban citizens to hold foreign currency and the citizens have remained barred from participating in international trade transactions up to this point. The presence of exchange controls and exchange restrictions has led to the development of black markets for foreign money and for the sale of goods and commodities at prices different than the subsidized rationed market. The exchange rate and the commodity prices in the black market are freely determined by market forces and respond to disequilibria in the domestic money market and to changes in the supply of goods throughout the economy. Since official exchange rates are administratively determined by the government, the differential between the official rate and the black market rate provides an incentive for the additional inflow of dollars into the black market. Because of the stickiness of prices and wages in Cuba, black market exchange rates have no effect on domestic interest rates, nor on the official exchange rates.

Since the stock of U.S. dollars held by Cuban households is large, with 21% of Cuban households having access to U.S. dollars (see José Luis Rodríguez, *Cuba Business*, January-February 1995), the analysis of black markets for foreign exchange in Cuba can proceed in the fashion of a dual exchange rate market with elements of currency substitution and portfolio diversification between domestic and foreign currencies. However, one of the key differences between the dual exchange model with portfolio and currency substitution elements (Lizondo, 1987 and Calvo and Rodríguez, 1977) and the Cuban scenario is that foreign currency in Cuba is used for purchasing goods and services in black markets as well as for capital-type transactions, and thus the first approximation model specified in this paper must include a proviso that covers current account transactions in the black markets.

THE MACROECONOMIC MODEL

This section formulates a macroeconomic model that traces the short-term interactions between government monetary policies and black markets for prices and exchange rates in Cuba. The macroeconomic model incorporates elements of all the theories of exchange rate determination but relies, to some extent, on purchasing power parity, currency substitution and forward-looking rational expectations concepts.

The inclusion of expectation variables in the macroeconomic model translates into the assumption that the results of government stabilization policies have an impact beyond the quantitative magnitudes of the policies announced. The macroeconomic model follows the "monetary approach to the balance of payments" (Polak, 1957 and IMF, 1977) in the sense that excess money supply plays a key factor in determining black market prices and exchange rates. Unfortunately, the lack of comprehensive definitions of the Cuban monetary mass by the Cuban authorities and the lack of published data on the components of the monetary mass do not allow us to trace all the in-terrelationships between the excess money supply and output.

The macroeconomic model contains several component modules, namely: output and supply, balance of payments, liquidity, prices and foreign exchange rates. Each of these modules is discussed next.

OUTPUT AND SUPPLY MODULE

The output module begins with a variation of the production function estimated earlier by the authors (Alonso and Lago, 1994). The new production function estimated in this paper explicitly recognizes the significant role played by the Cuban balance of payment crisis in lowering output. Thus, apart from the usual labor and capital variables, we include two new explanatory variables: the addition of fuel and intermediate imports as one variable, and food and consumer goods imports as a second variable. Imports of fuel, raw materials and intermediate products have a direct effect on output, since factories and farms cannot be operated efficiently without raw materials, fertilizers and insecticides and fuel. Imports of food have a less direct effect on output, since they affect the labor supply and labor productivity through absenteeism and shoddy work quality. The new production/output function to be estimated is of the type:

$$(1a) \quad Y_t = A_0 K^{\alpha}_t LABOR^{1-\alpha}_t IMFOOD_t (IMOIL_t + IMINT_t)^{\Gamma}$$

where:

Y_t = real gross domestic product in constant pesos in year t.

K_t = stock of real capital, inconstant pesos during year t.

$LABOR_t$ = labor employed in year t.

$IMFOOD_t$ = food imports in constant pesos in year t.

$IMOIL_t$ = oil imports in constant pesos in year t.

$IMINT_t$ = imports of raw materials and intermediate products in constant pesos in year t.

A_0 = costant (intercept) to be estimated.

α, β, Γ represent output elasticities to be estimated

An aggregate demand model, adapted from Khan and Knight (1981), will also be researched to estimate the change in gross domestic product [$\Delta(Y_t)$] as function of changes in household liquidity balances [$\Delta(L_t)$], lagged values of capacity utilization ($CAPUTIL_{t-1}$), exports (X_t), gross investments (I_t), and changes in the import variables noted above. This formulation is expressed in equation (1b), presented next:

(1b) $\Delta(Y_t) = f_{01b}[\Delta(L_t), CAPUTIL_{t-1}, \Delta(IMOIL_t + IMINT_t), \Delta(X_t), I_t]$

where $\Delta(Y_t)$ denotes the change in output, IMMACH$_t$ represents machinery and equipment imports and f_{01b} represents the aggregate income function to be estimated. The employment level is estimated through the substitution of equation (1b) into equation (1a). The capital stock is estimated from:

(1c) $K_t = K_{t-1} + I_t - D_t$,

where:

$I_t =$ investments in constant pesos during year t.

$D_t =$ depreciation charges in constant pesos during year t (default value = 2% of capital stock).

The annual flows of investments are estimated as function of machinery imports, the terms of trade, and accelerator variables (Alonso & Lago, 1994) in the following manner:

(1d) $I_t = f_{01d}[\Delta(Y_{t-1}), IMMACH_t, (PSUGAR_t/POIL_t)]$

where $POIL_t$ represents the price per ton of Cuban oil imports, $PSUGAR_t$ denotes the price per ton of Cuban sugar exports, and f_{01d} represents the investment equation to be estimated.

Both total exports and total imports contain components in transferable rubles and in convertible currencies. Imports in convertible currencies are considered endogenous, whereas all the exports and the imports in transferable rubles are considered exogenous. The following definitions apply:

(1e) $X_t = X^c_t + X^r_t$

(1f) $IM_t = IM^c_t + IM^r_t$

where X_t and IM_t represent total exports and total imports respectively, while the superscript **c** denotes transactions in convertible currencies and the superscript **r** denotes transactions in transferable rubles.

Because of the role that aggregate supply plays in the determination of prices and liquidity in Cuba, we define two supply variables to be tested in the macroeconomic model, namely: 1) absorption, which was used by Lipschitz (1984) in the analysis of demand for money and price inflation in Korea and 2) marketed supply, used by Sundarajan (1984) in the analysis of money and prices in India.

(2) $ABS_t = Y_t + IM_t - X_t$

(3) $SU_t = Y_t + IM_t$

where:

$ABS_t =$ absorption, measured in constant pesos during year t.

$SU_t =$ aggregate supply of goods and services, measured in constant pesos during year t.

$IM_t =$ total imports in constant pesos during year t.

$X_t =$ total exports in constant pesos during year t.

Exports (X_t) are assumed exogenous to the Cuban economy in this first approximation, whereas imports in convertible currency (IM^c_t) are deemed endogenous and their estimation explained in the balance of payments module presented next.

Balance of Payments Module

The balance of payment module covers international transactions and estimates the volume of imports and their composition, and the changes in foreign reserves. The first start is the import equation specified through the following identity:

(4) $IM_t = X_t + F_t + \Delta(R_t)$

where:

$F_t =$ net foreign capital flows in constant pesos during year t.

$\Delta(R_t) =$ net change in international foreign reserves, in constant pesos during year t,

and all the other variables as specified above in equation (2).

The net foreign capital flows (F_t) are deemed exogenous in the model, but the annual change in international foreign reserves in convertible currencies $\Delta(R^c_t)$ are considered endogenous. Ordinarily, a monetary approach to the balance of payments (Khan and Knight, 1981) would estimate equations where changes in foreign reserves would be estimated as functions of gross domestic product, exchange rates, lagged real money supply, current and lagged price indexes, expected price inflation and balance of payment deficits among other variables. Similarly, Ottani and Sassanpour (1988) estimate changes in foreign reserves as function of domestic assets of the banking system, lagged foreign reserves, interest rates, lagged money supply and gross domestic product. But these free-market specifications do not fit the Cuban case. In Cuba, imports and changes in foreign reserves are determined through administered allocation methods by the Cuban authorities, mostly JUCEPLAN and the Banco Nacional, so that the conventional monetary variables do not play a part in the Cuban exchange control system.

Because of the existence of foreign exchange controls in Cuba, a different specification must be chosen. Lipschitz (1984) presents an interesting formulation where desired reserves are calculated as the product of average reserves to import ratios times peak imports divided by import prices. But even this formulation fails in Cuba, where imports have currently dwindled to one quarter of their peak 1989 values. As a consequence we specify a foreign reserve equation where changes in foreign reserves are estimated as function of lagged values of foreign reserves, current values of exports and foreign capital flows, lagged ratios of foreign reserves to imports, lagged money supplied, terms of trade and overseas interest rates. The equation to be estimated, which is specified next, is close to the foreign exchange control allocation equation specified and estimated by Hemphill (1974). The proposed equation is:

$$(5)\ \Delta(R^c_t) = f_{05}[\ R^c_{t-1}, X^c_t, L_{t-1}, F_t, (\ R^c_{t-1} / IM^c_{t-1}), oi_t, (PSUGAR_t / POIL_t)]$$

where:

$\Delta(R^c_t) =$ First difference of series of international foreign reserves in convertible currencies, in constant pesos.

$R^c_{t-1} =$ level of international foreign reserves in convertible currency, in constant pesos, during year $t-1$.

$L_{t-1} =$ lagged household liquidity

$oi_t =$ overseas interest rates during year t, and

f_{05} represents the function that needs to be estimated, while the superscript c denotes transactions in convertible currency.

To complete the balance of payments module all that remains is to estimate the imports of food, oil and intermediate products, and the imports of machinery. The import components are estimated via the following equations that specify ratchet effects:

$$(6)\ IMFOOD_t / IM_t = f_{06}(\ IM_t, IM_t / IM_{peak})$$

$$(7)\ IMMACH_t / IM_t = f_{07}(\ IM_t, IM_t / IM_{peak})$$

where $IMMACH_t$ represents the imports of machinery and equipment (in constant pesos) during year t, while the subscript peak denotes the peak year value of the subscripted variable during the years on or previous to the observation year. Functions f_{06} and f_{07} are to be estimated later. The imports of oil, raw materials, chemicals and intermediate products are estimated as residuals in the following expression:

$$(8)\ (IMOIL_t + IMINT_t) / IM_t = 1 - [\ (IMFOOD_t / IM_t) + (IMMACH_t / IM_t)],$$

where all the variables have been defined earlier.

The import components are estimated as having ratchet effects, that is, the adjustment paths of the import components are different when the economy is growing than when it is contracting; this is accomplished through the use of the variable "peak year" values of imports.

Liquidity Module

This section begins by reiterating the discussion on the unavailability of estimates of the monetary mass in Cuba. Thus, the usual definition of "broad" money as in equation (9) cannot be estimated except for a handful of years. This broad money supply definition is given by:

$$(9)\ \Delta\,(M_t) = GDEF_t + \Delta(ENTCRED_t) + \Delta(HHCRED_t) + \Delta(PRIVCRED_t) + \Delta(R_t)$$

where the increases in broad money $\Delta\,(M_t)$ are the results of adding the strictly-government budget deficit $(GDEF_t)$ to changes in government enterprise credits $\Delta(ENTCRED_t)$, plus changes in household credits $\Delta(HHCRED_t)$, plus changes in credits to private farmers $\Delta(PRIVCRED_t)$, plus changes in foreign reserves $\Delta(R_t)$. Only data on the government deficits are available regularly. The losses of the government enterprise sector are included in the government deficit, but since 1989 have not been published. The data on enterprise credits, household credits and credits to the small private sector are available only for a handful of years in the mid-eighties. Thus, it is virtually impossible to estimate the broad money definition presented in equation (9).

The only recourse we have left is to estimate the liquidity of the household sector, the so-called balance of income and expenditures of the population, which has been estimated using statistical methods by several Cuban researchers (Espinosa and Quintana, 1989; and Martínez Fagundo, 1989, among others). According to the monetary definitions used in Cuba, the annual net result of the balance is equal to the changes in currency in circulation and household bank deposits at the Banco Popular de Ahorros during the year in question. The Cuban models of the balance of incomes and expenditures of the population include several sources of income and expenditures and are estimated with pre-1989 data. However, these models estimated in Cuba are not structural in any sense of the word. They have jointly-dependent variables as explanatory variables and contain a mish-mash of variables included for the sake of high correlations. To complicate the matter, the Cuban government has not released any data on components of the balance of incomes and expenditures of the population since 1989. After 1989, the Cuban government has only published the net results of the balance of income and expenditures of the population and not its components. Because of these mone-

tary data limitations, we turn our attention to the estimation of changes in household liquidity, that is, the changes in the balance of income and expenditures of the population (or the sum of changes in money in circulation held by households and household saving bank deposits).

Changes in household liquidity in socialist economies have been researched by several authors. Cottarelli and Blejer (1992) studied changes in the balance of expenditures (household consumption) which were estimated as functions of the rate of growth of output, the difference between domestic interest rates and inflation rates (as proxy for the opportunity costs of holding money balances), dependency ratios (defined in terms of the proportions of pensioners and children under 16 years old), ratios of black market prices to rationed prices, lagged values of household liquid assets, lagged values of household wealth (including housing) and benefit ratios (defined as the ratio of wages to the social payments paid to non-workers). In his analysis of household's demand for money in Poland, Lane (1992) used the following explanatory variables: the expected rate of inflation, the expected changes in consumption lagged one-year, the percent changes in official prices and black market prices and lagged values of liquid assets. Another pertinent study is one by Charemza and Ghatak (1990) on the demand for money in Hungary and Poland, in which changes in real per capita household liquidity are estimated as function of changes in real income, differences between interest rates and expected inflation rates and ratios of consumption and of private investments to national income. What is important from these earlier studies is their use of portfolio concepts (i.e, the opportunity costs of holding money), black market prices and of price expectations in affecting the demand for money. Another further comment is their lack of inclusion of shortage concepts, such as Sundararajan's (1986) use of marketed output and Lipschitz' (1984) use of an absorption variable, to reflect the effect of shortages on the household demand for money.

We now turn our attention to the specification of the demand for money in developing countries. Olgun (1984) uses expected inflation rates and real income to estimate the demand for money in Turkey, while Sundarajan (1986) uses expected inflation rates and marketed output to specify the demand for money in India. Khan and Knight (1981) use expected inflation rates and current and lagged values of income for a cross-section study of the demand for money in developing countries. Haque, Lahiri and Montiel (1990) add current interest rates and lagged values of the money mass to the earlier specification. Lipschitz (1984), as mentioned earlier, adds absorption, whereas Agénor (1990) specifies a demand for money equation that includes a variable to measure the expected rate of return on foreign currency-- this variable is defined as the difference between the expected devaluation rate in the black market foreign exchange market and the expected changes in world price inflation. Agénor's formulation, which is among the first to recognize the effect of foreign exchange rates and holdings of foreign money, also includes the expected rate of inflation, as well as current and lagged values of income among the explanatory values of the demand for money.

Two alternative formulations are presented of household liquidity. The most standard formulation, following Agenor (1990), specifies that household liquidity (L_t) adjusts with a lag to the difference between desired demand (L^d_t) in the current period and the actual money holdings at the begining of the period (L_{t-1}).

$$(10a) \quad \Delta L_t = v (L^d_t - L_{t-1})$$

where v is the speed of adjustment.

The desired demand for money balances is a positive function of household incomes measured by their proxies (i.e. current government deficits, enterprise loses and current gross domestic product) and depends negatively on current and expected of rate of price inflation and the expected devaluation rate.

$$(10b) \quad L^d_t = \alpha_0 + \alpha_1 (GDEF_t + ENTLOSS_t) + \alpha_2 (Y_t) - \alpha_3 (\Delta PBM_t) - \alpha_4 [E (\Delta PBM_t - i_t)] - \alpha_5 [E (e_t - \Delta PW_t)]$$

substitition of (10b) into (10a) results in :

$$(10c) \quad \Delta L_t = \beta_0 + \beta_1 (GDEF_t + ENTLOSS_t) + \beta_2 (Y_t) - \beta_3 (\Delta PBM_t) - \beta_4 [E (\Delta PBM_t - i_t)] - \beta_5 [E (e_t - \Delta PW_t)] - \beta_6 (L_{t-1})$$

where:

$\Delta (L_t) =$ changes in the real balance of incomes and expenditures of the population during year t.

$L_{t-1} =$ lagged values of real household liquid assets, measured in constant pesos as currency in household circulation plus and household savings bank deposits in year t-1.

$Y_t =$ real gross domestic product, in constant pesos, during year t.

$ABS_t =$ absorption of goods and services, in constant pesos during year t (an alternative to this shortage-related variable is to use aggregate supply (Su_t), defined earlier).

$PBM_t =$ index of black market prices during year t.

$i_t =$ real interest rate paid on savings deposits at the Banco Popular de Ahorros during year t.

$\Delta (BM_t) =$ annual change in the black market price index during year t.

$E(e_t) =$ expected black market exchange rate in terms of Cuban pesos per US dollar in year t, based on the information available in year t-1.

$E (\Delta(PBM_t)) =$ expected price inflation rate in the black market during year t, based on information available in year t-1,

$E (e_t) =$ expected foreign exchange depreciation rate in year t, based on information available in year t-1.

$E (\Delta PW_t) =$ expected world price inflation in year t, based on information available in year t-1.

A second formulation specifies the components of the exchange in household money balances. On the one hand increases in liquidity assets arise from the current government deficit, enterprise losses and the current gross domestic product. Decrease in household liquidity assets occur because of household expenditures, which themselves are a function of the current and expected rates of inflation, the expected devaluation rate and the supply of marketed commodities. The addition of the marketed supply -represented by the absorption variable- denotes that in situation of scarcity households spends liquid assets only if goods are indeed available for consumption. The second specificiation is:

$$(10d)\ \Delta L_t = \zeta_0 + \zeta_1\ (GDEF_t + ENTLOSS_t) + \zeta_2\ (Y_t) - \zeta_3\ (\Delta PBM_t) - \zeta_4\ (ABS_t) - \zeta_5\ [E\ (\Delta PBM_t - i_t)] - \zeta_6\ [E\ (e_t - \Delta PW_t)] - L_{t-1}.$$

whose variables have been defined earlier.

The liquidity modules to be estimated reflect concepts of currency substitution between the Cuban peso and the U.S. dollar, portfolio concepts (such as the opportunity costs of holding money balances and of holding foreign currency) and forward-looking rational expectations; that is, expectations formed in year t conditionally based on the information available in year t-1. Also included are measures of shortages (such as changes in supply of marketed output and/or changes in absorption) and measures of monetary disequilibrium (such as ratios of household liquidity to gross domestic product).

Note that the difference between the domestic rate of interest and the price inflation rate measures the opportunity cost of holding domestic money balances, while the difference between the expected foreign exchange devaluation rate and the expectations of world prices measure the opportunity cost of holding foreign currency.

Price Module

As discussed earlier, official prices in Cuba are controlled and correspond to official rationed markets. Because the rationed markets are hardly ever able to satisfy the demand for goods and services in the Cuban economy, the unsatisfied demand spills over into the black markets, where transactions are more in tune with demand and supply conditions. The task at hand is to develop predictive relationships that trace interaction between monetary conditions, exchange rates and prices in conditions approximating free markets as in the Cuban black markets.

Studies of black market prices in developing countries are few and far between, among them Olgun's (1984) study of Turkey shows that among the key variables affecting black market prices in Turkey are the black market exchange rates, the level of foreign prices, the real stock of money and the ratio of money to income. Agénor (1990) adds to the above variables the excess demand for money, the expected rate of inflation and the official exchange rate.

In Korea, Lipschitz (1984) considers capacity utilization and lagged absorption as important variables explaining price inflation, also adding the usual stock of price-explanatory variables: lagged real money stock, lagged price levels and changes and lagged import prices. In their study of Singapore, Ottani and Sassanpour (1988) related price inflation to lagged real money stock, interest rates, and price changes in exports, imports and wholesale domestic price indexes. Khan and Knight (1981) used lagged real money stock, current income, expected inflation rates, current and lagged black market exchange rates, lagged foreign prices, and lagged domestic price levels in their estimation of price equations. Aghevli and Sassanpour (1982) added the ratio of prices of tradable goods to the prices of non-tradeable goods to the following explanatory variables: lagged real money stock, current income, and changes in import price levels and wholesale price indexes. Finally Sundararajan's (1986) added marketed output to expected inflation rates and to the current and lagged real stock of money in explaining price inflation in India.

The following discussion relies on Olgun's (1984) black market price model, to which we have made changes to reflect concepts of shortage economies. The percentage rate of change in the domestic price level ($\Delta \ln P_t$) is the weighted average of the percent change in the price of internationally traded goods ($\Delta \ln PT_t$) and the percent change in non-traded goods ($\Delta \ln PNT_t$).

$$(11)\ \Delta\ln P_t = r\ (\Delta \ln PT_t) + (1- r)\ (\Delta \ln PNT_t)$$

where r is the share of internationally-traded goods in total expenditure, ln denotes natural logs, and Δ represents first differences.

The percent price change of internationally-traded goods ($\Delta \ln PT_t$) is a function of the exogenously- determined percentage changes in the world price of traded goods ($\Delta \ln PW_t$) and a weighted average of the rate of change of the official exchange rate ($\Delta \ln oe_t$) and the rate of change in the parallel or black market ($\Delta \ln e_t$), such as:

$$(12)\ \Delta \ln PT_t = \Delta \ln PW_t + s\ (\Delta \ln oe_t) + (1 - s)\ (\Delta \ln e_t),$$

where s denotes the proportion of transactions carried out at official exchange rates. However, the officially-fixed foreign exchange rate in Cuba is not relevant to the determination of market prices of traded goods, so that s approximates s = 0 for current conditions in Cuba, where only a small group of privileged communist party-connected importers have access to the official rate.

The demand for the non-traded goods is assumed dependent on the money supply (monetary disequilibria) and on the aggregate supply of goods and services and/or absorption (both shortage concepts) as well as on forward looking future price expectations, that is, price expectations for year t formed on the basis of information available in year t-1. Thus, home prices are determined by domestic supply and demand. A disequilibrating increase in the money supply should affect prices according to the capacity for increasing output or imports and thereby raising real absorption. Because of the inadequacy of Cuban monetary statistics regarding the definition of the monetary mass, we use two related variables: household liquidity (L_t) defined as the sum of household's money in circulation plus household savings deposits, and the total government deficit ($TGDEF_t$) defined to include the deficits of the state enterprises (ENTLOSS$_t$) and the strictly-government deficit (GDEF$_t$), as in:

$$(13)\ TGDEF_t = ENTLOSS_t + GDEF_t,$$

whose terms have been defined previously.

The price equation for non-tradeable goods is then given in equation (15) as follow:

$$(14)\ \Delta \ln PNT_t = \Lambda_0 + \Lambda_1\ (\Delta \ln TGDEF_t) + \Lambda_2\ (\Delta \ln L_t) + \Lambda_3\ (\Delta \ln ABS_t) + \Lambda_4\ E(P_t)$$

where $E\ (P_t)$ = expected price inflation in time t, based on information available in time t-1.

Finally equations (12) and (14) are substituted into equation (11), rendering a function in which the rate of change in domestic prices is a function of official (oe$_t$) and black market exchange rates (e$_t$), the rate of change in the prices of imports ($\Delta \ln PW_t$), current [$\Delta(L_t)$] and lagged changes in household liquidity [$\Delta (l_{t-1})$], the total government deficit (TGDEF$_t$), including the deficits of the state enterprises, the aggregate supply SU$_t$, (or its absorption alternative, ABS$_t$) and the expected rate of price inflation $E\ (P_t)$. The resulting price equation is:

$$(15)\ \Delta \ln P_t = \varepsilon_0 + \varepsilon_1\ (\Delta \ln TGDEF_t) + \varepsilon_2\ (\Delta \ln L_t) + \varepsilon_3\ (\Delta \ln ABS_t) + \varepsilon_4\ E\ (P_t) + \varepsilon_5\ (\Delta \ln PW_t) + \varepsilon_6\ (\Delta \ln oe_t) + \varepsilon_7\ (\Delta \ln e_t).$$

where equation (15) represents the price equation to be estimated, while the other variables have been defined earlier. The reader should note that if we assume that the bulk of the transactions take place in the parallel or black market, as is the case of Cuba today, then s approximates the value of s = o, and the black market prices can be substituted for the rationed official domestic price level in the above formulation, as is probably the case of Cuba today.

The Foreign Exchange Module

The last module to be considered is the foreign exchange module, which essentially completes this first approximation of the interrelationship between money supply, and prices and foreign exchange rates in the black market. We approach the design of the foreign exchange module with some trepidation and modesty, since recent research on the predictive ability of foreign exchange models have shown them not to have better predictive abilities than random walk models (Meese and Rogoff, 1983). A short review of the literature on the prediction of black market exchange rates is provided below before entering into the specification of the foreign exchange equation to be estimated.

Early approaches to the estimation of predictive equations of foreign exchange followed a simple single-equation formulation. Culbertson (1975), developed a single-equation that predicted black market exchange rates in India, the Philippines and Turkey using as independent variables: official exchange rates, variables which reflected purchasing power parity concepts (such as the ratio of domestic price indexes to world price indexes), the percent change in foreign reserves and the ratio of foreign reserves to the domestic assets of the Central Bank. Gupta (1980) developed another single equation model of foreign exchange valuation of the Indian rupee, which used as explanatory variables the price of gold and silver, domestic interest rates, the real monetary stock, gross domestic product, and the U.S. GNP price deflator. Blejer's (1978) single equation model predicted the foreign exchange rates of Brazil and Chile as function of current and lagged values of the rate of change of domestic monetary assets of the Central Bank net of the rate of change in money balances and net of the world rate of inflation.

Portfolio concepts related to the opportunity cost of holding foreign exchange were introduced by Dornbusch et al. (1983) in their Brazil study, which approximated this opportunity cost through interest rate differentials adjusted for devaluation (by adding foreign interest rate in dollars to the rate of devaluation of the cruzeiro net of the domestic interest rate in cruzeiros). Closely related to the Dornbusch et al. model is the work of Phylaktis (1992) for Chile, which predicted changes in the black market exchange rate premia as function of changes in money and demand deposits, purchasing power parity ratios (using the U.S. consumer price index), values of total wealth expressed in dollars, changes in official exchange rates and changes in interest rate differentials adjusted for devaluation. Other variables used by Phylaktis included changes in import tariffs, travel allowances, repatriation of profits and preferential rates on foreign loans.

In one of the few studies of demand for money in the Soviet bloc, Charemza and Ghatak (1990) estimated real black market exchange rates in Hungary and Poland as function of real incomes, real money balances, the ratio of domestic interest rates to expected inflation rates, and the ratios of private investments and consumption to income. Ottani and Sassanpour

(1988) used lagged values of black market exchange rates, ratios of foreign prices to domestic prices (i.e. a purchasing power parity concept) and ratios of foreign to domestic assets of the Central Bank to predict foreign exchange rates in Singapore. Edwards' (1988, 1989) massive cross section studies of exchange rates in developing countries considers the following variables as affecting real exchange rates: excess credit (measured as the differential between the rate of growth of domestic credit and the rate of growth of gross domestic product), the rate of growth of domestic credit, the lagged ratio of the fiscal deficit to the money supply M1, the terms of trade, the ratio of tariff revenues to imports, the real rate of growth of gross domestic product, the changes in nominal exchange rates, the lagged real exchange rate, capital inflows and the ratio of government consumption in non-tradeable goods to gross domestic product.

One of more important works, important because of its multiple-equation black market linkages is Olgun's (1984) study, which used official exchange rates, expected inflation rates and purchasing power parity (using the U.S. consumer price index) to predict black market exchange rates in Turkey. Finally, we focus on Agénor's (1990) cross-section study which uses as explanatory variables forward-looking expected inflation rates, purchasing power parity ratios, the rate of change in money balances, the changes in gross domestic product, the official exchange rate and the differential between the expected rate of devaluation and the rate of foreign inflation. Agénor's formulation contains just about every factor applicable to Cuba, except for the lack of concepts related to a shortage economy.

The formulation of the foreign exchange module begins by distinguishing stocks from flows in the foreign exchange market following Kharas and Pinto (1989), and Lizondo (1987). The stock of foreign exchange is held as part of a diversified wealth portfolio that includes domestic liquid assets, foreign exchange stocks, housing and other wealth. The equilibrium conditions for the stock of foreign exchange have been worked out by Phylaktis (1992) among others and they are the usual equilibrium condition for an asset. Phylaktis assumes the stock demand for black market dollars to be proportional to total wealth (which includes non-dollar assets evaluated at the existing black market rate of exchange) and to interest rate differential adjusted for the rate of depreciation of the domestic currency in the black market. The equilibrium conditions (Phylaktis, 1992) for the stock of dollars requires that the rate of change in the black market premium be equal to the interest rate differentials adjusted for devaluation minus a function of the ratio of wealth in domestic assets to wealth in foreign assets. However we do not pursue the analysis of the stock of dollars held- for which there is no data available- and instead pursue the analysis of the flow market for foreign exchange.

In Cuba, the flow market for foreign exchange arises from family remittances from the Cuban exiles, tips from tourists visiting the island, from transactions of foreign personnel stationed in Cuba (specially those from the former Soviet bloc) and from corruption by the Cuban authorities. In July 1993 the government estimated that as much as US $200 million were freely circulating in Cuba (Fogel and Rosenthal, 1994), figures which at the existing rate of 100 pesos per U.S. dollar were double the liquid assets of the Cuban households. This high rate of foreign currency holding in Cuba is validated by José Luis Rodríguez' statement (*Cuba Business*, January-February 1995) that 21% of Cuban households had access to U.S. dollars, figure which rises to 25.5% in Havana. Following Olgun (1984), the flow supply function for foreign exchange is assumed to be dependent on the level of spread between official and black market exchange rates, that is, family remittances are assumed to be a function of the spread between the two exchange rates. The flow supply is also

assumed to depend on the other important source of foreign exchange that is, tourist expenditures (or the number of tourists visiting the island, because the information on tourist expenditures is sometimes not available for recent years). The flow supply function is given by:

(16) $\Delta \ln FES_t = f_{16} [(e_t / oe_t) , TOUR_t]$,

where $\Delta \ln FES_t$ represents the rate of change of the supply of foreign exchange, $TOUR_t$ represents tour-

ists expenditures in year t, oe_t denotes official exchange rates and e_t is the exchange rate in the black market.

The flow demand for foreign exchange in the black market arises because of the use of foreign currency as a medium of exchange in the black markets, since the government authorities cannot satisfy the total demand for goods and services in the economy. The flow demand is assumed to be dependent on the level of liquid assets (L_t), on deviations of domestic prices from foreign prices evaluated at the black market rate (i.e. a purchasing power parity concept), on the level of shortages in the economy [measured in terms of aggregate supply (SU_t) or of absorption (ABS_t)], on gross domestic product (Y_t), on the opportunity cost of holding domestic money, which is equal to domestic interest rates (i_t) minus the expected domestic inflation rate [$E (\Delta P_t)$], assuming that expectations are formed at time t-1 for period t and on the opportunity costs of holding foreign money, defined as the difference between the expected rate of devaluation and the expected rate of world inflation [$E (\Delta Pw_t)$].

(17) $\Delta \ln FED_t = f_{17} \{ L_t , Y_t , ABS_t , (P_t / PW_t),$
$E [i_t - (\Delta \ln P_t)] , E [(\Delta e_t / e_t) - (\Delta PW_t)] \}$

where $\Delta \ln FED_t$ represents the flow demand for foreign currency, $E [(\Delta e_t)/e_t]$ represents the forward-looking expectation of foreign exchange depreciation. All the other term have been defined earlier.

Agénor (1990) presents an interesting formulation whereby both the flow demand and flow supply functions are introduced into the equilibrium conditions in the stock for foreign currency to develop a reduced-form equation to predict the foreign exchange rate in black markets. Borrowing literally from Agénor (1990), the following reduced-form function is proposed:

(18) $e_t = \gamma_0 + \gamma_1 (oe_t) + \gamma_2 (ABS_t) + \gamma_3 (L_t) + \gamma_4 (TOUR_t) + \gamma_5 (Y_t) + \gamma_6 (P_t / Pw_t) + \gamma_7 E [i_t - (\Delta \ln P_t)] + \gamma_8 E [(\Delta e_t / e_t) - (\Delta PW_t)]$

where equation (18) is the foreign exchange function to be estimated. This function combines elements of currency substitution, portfolio approaches, shortages concepts and rational expectations, but before the estimated results are analyzed a brief discussion of estimation methods is in order.

ESTIMATION METHODS

Estimation of the model specified earlier presented two main difficulties. The first difficulty concerned the presence of endogenous variables among the regressors in several of the equations. For example, the black market prices (P_t), foreign exchange (e_t) and household liquidity (L_t) variables are all simultaneously-determined, necessitating the use of simultaneous equation estimation techniques. In addition, both gross domestic product (Y_t) and household liquidity (L_t) are jointly determined. In this paper the technique used for estimating equations with jointly dependent variables is two-stage least squares. However, as will be described later, we were unable to estimate statistically-significant coefficients for black market exchange rates—a jointly-dependent variable--in the price module (equation 15), which negated one of the reasons for using simultaneous equations estimation techniques. We also ended up redefining the liquidity variable to include both lagged liquidity (L_{t-1}) plus the government budget deficit ($GDEF_t + ENTLOSS_t$), in effect redefining liquidity as an exogenous variable and annulling its joint-dependency with gross domestic product (Y_t).

Another difficulty concerns estimating the (unobserved) rational expectation variables.[4] These variables measure expectations of events in year t, expected on the basis of information available in the year before, that is, year t-1. These expectation variables are assumed to follow rational expectations, and are equal to actual (realized) values plus a stochastic error term. There are two general approaches for the estimation of rational expectations models. The most obvious and common sense approach is the substitution method, in which the rationally-expected variables are replaced by their forecasts. Thus, in the substitution approach, unrestricted reduced-form equations of the expectation variables are estimated and their predicted forecasts are substituted for the unobserved expectations. However, this otherwise common sense approach had to be abandoned because it leads to inconsistent and not fully efficient estimation unless the estimation approach follows cumbersome non-linear estimation methods with constraints placed on the parameters to be estimated (Wallis, 1980).

In view of the above referenced difficulties, the approach chosen relied on errors-in-variables formulations, and estimated the coefficients of the expectations variables through instrumental variables techniques. In the errors-in-variables approach, the expected variables are replaced by the realized (observed) values of the expected variables. Instrumental variables chosen in this paper are: all the exogenous variables lagged one year, values of all the endogenous variables during the previous year, plus the constant/intercept term. Care was taken to insure that an expected and a realized value of the same variable do not appear in the same equation and that an endogenous variable and its expected value also do not appear in the same equation (Wickens, 1982).

Rational Expectation Variables

Two rational expectations variables were analyzed, namely: 1) the rate of return on domestic currency ($RRDOM_t$), and 2) the rate of return on foreign currency ($RRFORG_t$), with both of these variables incorporating portfolio concepts into the demand for money, prices and foreign exchange. The rate of return on domestic currency ($RRDOM_t$) is defined as the percent annual interest rate on savings deposits at the Banco Popular de Ahorros minus the percent annual rate of domestic price inflation. The rate of return on foreign currency ($RRFORG_t$) is defined as the percent annual rate of black market foreign exchange rate depreciation minus the percent annual rate of import price inflation. Both of these portfolio-type variables show negative values on selected

---

4. Some critics will be amused at the mere thought of rational expectations in Cuba and will call the application of this concept to Cuba to be an oxymoron, that is, a contradiction in terms. However, the rational expectations variables used in this paper apply only to household liquidity and to black market exchange rates, and not to government-run processes, where the application might indeed be construed as an oxymoron.

years and as a consequence do not appear in logarithmic form in the equations estimated in Table 3.

The rational expectation variables: E (RRDOM$_t$,) and E (RRFORG$_t$,) represent expectations about these portfolio variables for year t, formed on the basis of expectations formed in year t-1. These rational expectation variables are estimated via instrumental variables techniques, as explained earlier.

ANALYSIS OF ESTIMATED MACROECONOMIC, BALANCE OF PAYMENTS, MONEY, PRICES AND EXCHANGE RATE EQUATIONS

The following paragraphs describe and analyze the modules and functions estimated, which are displayed in Table 3. The data sources used are described in detail in Appendix A. The original data series is not uniform. Data is available only for specific time periods that vary depending on the module analyzed. For example, all the modules and equations that require data on government budgets and deficits are necessarily constrained to the post-1978 period, since the Cuban government has not published any government budget data for the pre-1978 period (Mesa-Lago, 1994). Similarly no data on international foreign reserves have been published previous to 1977 and after 1990, restricting the data based used in the estimation of demand for foreign reserves to the period 1977- 1990. Finally, the data on components of imports are not available (with the exception of 1970) for the period previous to 1975, thereby restricting the historical period analyzed in the production, investment and import functions to the period 1975-1994.

Estimation of Output and Supply Equations

The production function estimated in equation (1a) of Table 3 is of the Cobb-Douglas type, which assumes constant elasticity of output as functions of inputs. The variable I$_t$, representing gross investment, had to be used in lieu of the capital stock figures (K$_t$) because of difficulties with the highly erratic capital depreciation figures used in the Cuban material product accounting system. The investment capital share of output is 43%, with the labor share (100% - 43% = 57%) accounting for the remainder of out-

put. The capital share is slightly larger than the one previously estimated by the authors (Alonso & Lago, 1994), but still within the ranges of the Latin American developing countries (Bruton, 1967). But what is interesting about the production function estimated in Table 3 is the influence of imports on the Cuban output level. It is not surprising that the imports of oil, raw materials and intermediate products affect output, but what is noteworthy is that the imports of food and consumer goods also significantly affect labor productivity, especially in these recent times of food shortages. The plausible influence of food and consumer goods on labor productivity had already been mentioned in the Report of the Task Force on Cuba (Banco Nacional, 1989), but this is the first time that it has been measured. Because of the presence of multi-colinearity between the two import categories used in the production function, it became necessary to express the influence of the food and consumer goods imports on output through the ratio shown in equation (1a) in Table 3.

Machinery imports also affect output through their impact on gross investments, as shown in equation (1d). Again as in our previous modeling work (Alonso & Lago, 1994), we were unable to estimate statistically significant coefficients for the investment accelerator variable (ΔY_{t-1}). Perhaps the lack of flexibility implicit in the development of multi-year investment plans in socialist economies precludes the importance of accelerator variables in driving annual investments. Our investment formulation is borrowed from Adelman and Chennery (1966) who, while successfully estimating investment functions in open economies - like Greece - also failed to develop statistically significant coefficients for the accelerator variable.

The aggregate demand function, presented in equation (1b) of Table 3, portrays the significant effect on aggregate income of lagged household liquidity (L$_{t-1}$) plus the government deficit (GDEF $_t$ + ENTLOSS$_t$), as a proxy for money supply. In fact, in other simultaneous-equations estimated (but not shown in Table 3), a current household liquidity (L$_t$) variable was estimated as a significant quadratic variable, denoting that up to a certain point the effect of money on income is positive, but that after the maximum effect is reached any other increases in money supply result in decreases in real income because of the adverse effects of money on the rate of inflation, a topic to be discussed later. The other two variables in the aggregate demand equation are the usual exogenous macro- economic variables of gross investments (I_t) and total exports (X_t). Capacity utilization was not used as a variable because published values are available for only two recent years.

Estimation of Balance of Payment Equations

The demand for annual changes in foreign reserves in convertible currencies is estimated in equation (5) as functions of lagged reserves, exports and net payments and capital inflows in convertible currency, and lagged levels of household liquidity, among others. In addition, the import component shares estimated in equations (6) and (7), show the presence of ratchet effects that take into account the fact that the time-paths of adjustment are different when total imports are growing than when they are contracting. As a general rule, the share of food and consumer goods imports grows when the economy is in the downswing and diminishes during economic recovery and growth. The opposite is true of machinery imports.

We also estimated Hemphill's (1974) import-predictive function for economies with foreign exchange controls and, to our surprise, Hemphill's formulation fits better the Cuban data than do any of the other developing countries in his sample. Hemphill's equation is not used in this study because its alternative [equation (5)] proved to be superior in all respects, including the statistical significance of its coefficients and the tests of serial correlation of residuals.

Estimation of Liquidity Equations

Household liquidity, measured as currency in circulation and household saving deposits at the Banco Popular de Ahorros, is specified as an endogenous variable in the model and estimated in equations (10c) and (10d) in Table 3. Equation (10c) estimates the annual changes in liquidity as function of the government budget deficit, the price level (P_t), and lagged levels of liquidity (L_{t-1} / P_{t-1}). Equation (10c)

uses the original series (not the first difference) and substitutes real gross domestic product (Y_t / P_t) for the lagged levels of liquidity (L_{t-1} / P_{t-1}). What is interesting about this equation is that it reflects both shortages and monetary disequilibria views. It shows that the so-called "monetary overhang" is partly due to shortages (i.e., supply scarcities reflected in the variable ABS_t) and to subsidized prices (i.e reflected in P_t) as well as due to the usual monetary expansion variables, such as lagged liquidity (L_{t-1} / P_{t-1}) and government budget deficits ($GDEF_t + ENTLOSS_t$). The two rational expectations variables reflecting the rates of return on domestic currency holdings [$E(RRDOM_t)$] and foreign currency holdings [$E(RRFORG_t)$] were found not to be statistically significant.

Estimation of Price Equation

Equation (15) estimates prices (P_t) as a function of the government budget deficit ($GDEF_t + ENTLOSS_t$), import prices (Pw_t), absorption (ABS_t) and lagged household liquidity (L_{t-1}). It is interesting to note the importance of the absorption supply variable (ABS_t) in affecting prices, denoting that the balance of payments influence the level of prices through its effect on imports, and thereby on supply. We were unable to estimate a statistically-significant foreign exchange rate (e_t) variable as affecting prices, thereby throwing some doubt on our ex-ante hypothesis of the joint-simultaneity of prices and foreign exchange rates. However, it is still too early in this research to abandon our hypothesis of simultaneity of prices and exchange rates, more research awaits the final conclusion of this issue. We did not include any forward looking expectation variables that made the current inflation rate dependent on expectations about next year's inflation rate because this procedure implies that the error terms follow a moving average of order 1 and would result in biased standard errors of the coefficients (Agénor, 1990).

Estimation of Foreign Exchange Rate Equation

Two alternative foreign exchange rate equations are presented in Table 3. In equation (18a) the foreign exchange rate (in pesos per U.S. dollar) is estimated

Table 3. Estimated Aggregate Demand, Balance of Payments, Money, Price and Exchange Rate Functions

OUTPUT AND SUPPLY MODULE

Production Function Equation:

(1a) $\ln (Y_t / P_t / LABOR_t) = -1.4917 + 0.4292 \ln [(I_t / P_t) / LABOR_t]$
$\qquad\qquad\qquad\qquad\qquad (0.7316) \quad (0.0975)$

$\qquad + 0.4521 \ln [(IMOIL_t + IMMINT_t) / P_t] + 0.4947 \ln [IMFOOD_t / (IMOIL_t + IMINT_t)]$
$\qquad (0.1101) \qquad\qquad\qquad\qquad (0.1519)$

($R^2 = 0.9972$; D. W. $= 1.8066$; N = 18 observations from 1977 to 1994)

Aggregate Demand Equation:

(1b) $Y_t / P_t = 1.0649 (I_t / P_t) + 2.4752 (X_t / P_t) + 0.2393 [(L_{t-1}/P_{t-1}) + (GDEF_t + ENTLOSS_t)/P_t]$
$\qquad\qquad\quad (0.4735) \qquad\quad (0.3355) \qquad\quad (0.0721)$

($R^2 = 0.995273$; D. W. $= 1.6982$; N = 17 observations from 1978 to 1994)

Investment Equation:

(1d) $(I_t / P_t) = 3.4689 + 1.6232 (IMMACH_t / P_t) + 59.0464 (PSUGAR_t / POIL_t)$
$\qquad\qquad (85.9545)(0.0376) \qquad\qquad (10.6995)$

[$R^2 = 0.9918$; D. W. $= 2.0691$; N = 20 observations from 1975 to 1994--

The serial correlation of residuals in the original data set was adjusted through maximum likelihood iterative techniques (RHO autocorrelation coefficient is equal to

- 0.2452)]

BALANCE OF PAYMENTS MODULE

Demand for International Reserves Equation:

(5) $\Delta \ln (R^c_t / P_t) = 20.3209 - 1.0673 \ln (R^c_{t-1} / P_{t-1}) + 0.7716 \ln [(X^c_t + F^c_t) / P_t] - 2.7527 \ln (L_{t-1}/P_{t-1}) + 0.9389 \ln (PSUGAR_t / POIL_t$
$\qquad\qquad\qquad (5.4074) \quad (0.1796) \qquad\qquad\qquad (0.2408) \qquad\qquad\qquad (0.5874) \qquad\qquad (0.3437)$

$R^2 = 0.8875$; D. W. $= 1.8230$; N = 13 observations from 1978 to 1990, and where the superscript c denotes convertible currency transactions)

Food and Consumer Goods Import Equation:

(6) $\ln (IMFOOD_t / IM_t) = 1.9604 - 0.4298 \ln (IM_t / P_t) - 0.1600 [(IM_t / P_t) / (IM_{peak} / P_{peak})]$
$\qquad\qquad\qquad\qquad (0.5200) \quad (0.0597) \qquad\qquad (0.0150)$

($R^2 = 0.8991$; D. W. $= 1.6438$; N = 17 observations from 1977 to 1993)

Machinery Imports Equation:

(7) $\ln (IMMACH_t / IM_t) = -0.0653 - 0.1224 \ln (IMMACH_t / P_t) + 0.2700 \ln [(IM_t / P_t) / (IM_{peak} / P_{peak})]$
  (0.5576) (0.0646) $\qquad\qquad\qquad$ (0.0596)

$(R^2 = 0.8422 ; D.W. = 2.2083 ; N = 19$ observations from 1975 to 1993)

Liquidity Module

(10c) $\Delta (L_t / P_t) = 2068.640 + 0.5409 [(GDEF_t + ENTLOSS_t) / P_t] - 132.422 P_t - 0.7485 (L_{t-1} / P_{t-1})$
  (714.86) $\quad (0.3116)$ $\qquad\qquad\qquad\qquad$ (41.3359) $\quad (0.2645)$

$(R^2 = 0.4660 ; D.W. = 1.2774; N = 17$ observations from 1978 to 1994)

(10d) $\ln (L_t / P_t) = 3.6491 + 0.0001986 [(GDEF_t + ENTLOSS_t) / P_t] + 0.4414 \ln (Y_t / P_t) - 1.1032 \Delta \ln (ABS_t / P_t) - 1.2461 \Delta \ln P$
  (0.2437) (0.00003886) $\qquad\qquad\qquad\qquad$ (0.0260) $\qquad\quad (0.3954)$ $\qquad\qquad (0.5048)$

$(R^2 = 0.9780 ; D.W. = 1.1493 ; N = 17$ observations from 1978 to 1994)

Price Module

(15) $\ln P_t = 8.5494 - 0.9175 \ln (ABS_t / P_t) + 0.0693 \ln [L_{t-1} / P_{t-1} + (GDEF_t + ENTLOSS_t)/P_t] + 0.6989 \ln PW_t$
  (0.2317) (0.0135) $\qquad\quad (0.0280)$ $\qquad\qquad\qquad\qquad\qquad$ (0.0648)

$(R^2 = 0.9981 ; D.W. = 1.8000 ; N = 17$ observations from 1978 to 1994)

Foreign Exchange Rate Module

(18a) $\ln e_t = 12.1828 + 2.1756 \ln (L_t / P_t) - 1.3495 \ln (P_t / Pw_t) - 2.6655 \ln (ABS_t / P_t) + 0.004152 E (RRFORG_t)$
  (3.0174) (0.1227) $\qquad\quad (0.3062)$ $\qquad\qquad (0.2912)$ $\qquad\quad (0.0008351)$

$(R^2 = 0.9945 ; D.W. = 2.1687 ; N = 17$ observations from 1978 to 1994. The serial correlation of residuals in the original data set was adjusted through the Cochrane-Orcutt iterative technique after two iterations, Rho autocorrelation coefficient = - 0.0710)

(18b) $\ln e_t = 0.3596 \ln (Y_t / P_t) + 3.2637 \ln oe_t + 0.9349 \ln (P_t / Pw_t) - 0.8680 LEGAL_t + 0.006535 E (RRFORG_t)$
  (0.0078) $\qquad\quad (0.4054)$ $\qquad (0.0657)$ $\qquad (0.3741)$ $\qquad\quad (0.001750)$

$(R^2 = 0.9760 ; D.W. = 2.3952 ; N = 17$ observations from 1978 to 1994. The serial correlation of residuals in the original data set was adjusted through the Cochrane-Orcutt iterative technique after two iterations, Rho autocorrelation coefficient = - 0.3527)

Notes: R^2 represents the square of the multiple correlation coefficient. D.W. represents the Durbin-Watson coefficient for testing the serial correlation of residuals. Δ represents the first difference series of the variable in question, while ln denote natural logarithms. Figures inside parentheses represent the standard errors of individual regression coefficients.

VARIABLE DEFINITIONS USED IN TABLE 3:

$ABS_t =$ absorption, in millions of pesos in year t. ($ABS_t = Y_t + IM_t - X_t$).

$e_t =$ black market exchange rate, in pesos per U.S. dollar as of December 31 of year t.

$ENTLOSS_t =$ public enterprise losses financed out of the budget, in millions of pesos in year t.

$E(RRFORG_t) =$ expectations of percent rate of return on holdings of foreign currency in year t given the information available in year t-1.

$F^c_t =$ net foreign capital and payment flows in convertible currency, in millions of pesos in year t.

$GDEF_t =$ government budget deficit, in millions of pesos in year t. (excludes ENTLOSS$_t$)

$I_t =$ gross investments, in millions of pesos in year t.

$IM_t =$ total imports, in millions of pesos in year t.

$IMOIL_t =$ imports of oil and oil products, in millions of pesos in year t.

$IMINT_t =$ imports of raw materials and intermediate products, in millions of pesos in year t.

$IMFOOD_t =$ imports of food, beverages and consumer goods, in millions of pesos in year t.

$IMMACH_t =$ imports of machinery and equipment, in millions of pesos in year t.

$L_t =$ currency in circulation and household savings deposits, in millions of pesos in year t.

$LABOR_t =$ labor, in thousands of employed persons in year t.

$LEGAL_t =$ proportion of no. of months in year t during which it was legal to hold foreign currency.

$oe_t =$ official exchange rate, in pesos per U.S. dollar as of December 31 of year t.

$PSUGAR_t =$ price per ton of exported sugar, in pesos in year t.

$POIL_t =$ price per ton of imported oil, in pesos in year t.

$P_t =$ price deflator index for the gross domestic product, in year t. ($P_{1989} = 100.0$)

$PW_t =$ import price index during year t. ($P_{1989} = 100.0$)

$R^c_t =$ international foreign reserves in convertible currency, in millions of pesos in year t.

$RRFORG_t =$ rate of return on holdings of foreign currency, measured as the difference between the percent annual devaluation rate and the percent annual rate of inflation in import prices, in time t.

$X_t =$ total exports, in millions of pesos in year t.

$X^c_t =$ exports in convertible currency, in millions of pesos in year t.

$Y_t =$ gross domestic product, in millions of pesos in year t.

as a function of purchasing power parity concepts (P_t / Pw_t), monetary-related influences (L_t / P_t), supply-related variables, such as absorption (ABS_t/P_t), and expectations on the rate of return on holdings of foreign currency [E ($RRFORG_t$)]. The significance of the absorption variable reflects the fact that the Cuban households take dollars from the stock under their mattresses when there are goods available to be bought. An expectations variable representing expectations on the rate of return on domestic currency E ($RRDOM_t$) was estimated as statistically significant but with an incorrect sign and is therefore excluded from the final formulation.

A second formulation of the foreign exchange rate equation is presented in equation (18b) and estimates exchange rates as functions real gross domestic product (Y_t / P_t), official exchange rates (oe_t), purchasing power parity (P_t / Pw_t), expectations on the rate of return on holdings of foreign currency [E (RRFORG$_t$)] and on the legalization of holding foreign currencies in Cuba (LEGAL$_t$). Another dummy variable denoting the August 1994 Clinton Administration restrictions on remittances to Cuba was estimated with the correct sign but was found to be statistically insignificant. Perhaps the flow of remittances through third countries has made the Clinton Administration restrictions less effective than originally thought. The expectations variable about the rate of return on holdings of domestic currency [E (RRDOM $_t$)] was estimated as statistically significant, but with an incorrect sign. Equation (18b) was estimated without an intercept because in the presence of official exchange rates equal to one (oe_t = 1), the data matrix is singular and cannot be inverted to estimate the relevant coefficients. A selection between these two equations for forecasting purposes must await the results of policy simulations to be conducted in a subsequent second approximation study by the authors.

OPERATION AND HIGHLIGHTS OF THE FIRST APPROXIMATION MODEL

The First Approximation Model of Money, Prices and Foreign Exchange Rates has been changed from its original simultaneous-equation design into a recursive system of equations. The recursive nature of the model was specified because of the failure to estimate statistically-significant simultaneous equation linkages between prices and foreign exchange rates. Thus, prices were found to affect foreign exchange rates via purchasing power parity concepts, but the reverse, namely that foreign exchange rates affect domestic prices, could not be estimated with any significant degree of confidence. In addition, due to the problems of defining monetary mass in socialist Cuba, we opted for an exogenous measure of liquidity that included lagged levels of liquidity plus the current government budget deficit. At the end, none of the equations estimated required simultaneous equation estimation techniques, except for those functions which contained rational expectations, which were estimated via instrumental variables.

The application of the First Approximation Model is relatively easy and requires performing the following analytical steps:

Step One: Exogenous exports, payments and capital flows, lagged levels of liquidity and international reserves are used to estimate the change in reserves in equation (5). Next, total imports are estimated from equation (4) and the import components are estimated from equations (6), (7) and (8).

Step Two: Machinery imports, previously estimated from equation (7), and the exogenous ratio of sugar to oil prices are used to predict gross investments from equation (1d); while gross investments, exports, lagged levels of liquidity and the exogenous government budget deficit are used to forecast aggregate income from equation (1b). Finally employed labor is estimated from the production function estimated in equation (1a).

Step Three: Absorption [estimated from equation (2)], lagged levels of liquidity, the exogenous government budget deficit, and the exogenous import price level are used to forecast prices in equation (15).

Step Four: Lagged levels of liquidity, absorption, prices, gross domestic product and the exogenous government budget deficit are used an inputs to estimate the forecasts of household liquidity in equation (10d) or the change in liquidity in equation (10c).

Step Five: The expected rate of return on foreign currency holdings is forecasted as function of all of the rest of the variables in the model (after a one-year lag) and along with purchasing power parity, household liquidity and absorption is used to project foreign exchange rates in equation (18a).

We have postponed the exercise of simulating the effects of Cuban government policy initiatives because the model is still in its initial stage. In addition, care must be exercised in selecting policy initiatives to be simulated, since our objective is not to provide advise to the Castro government. In summary, we do not want to help "build the bridge over the river Kwai."

To summarize, imports of food and consumer products were found to affect labor productivity (equation 1a) and some of the decline in labor productivity in recent years is partly due to the scarcity of food and consumer products. The allocation of foreign exchange for import food, machinery, oil and other import components follows a "ratchet effect," with the shares of import components varying significantly depending on whether the economy is in an upswing or downswing (see equations 6 and 7). Household liquidity, sometimes referred to as the monetary overhang, depends on shortage concepts-- like changes in supply (i.e., absorption) and price inflation-- as well as monetary disequilibrium (such as government budget deficits). The reader is referred to equation (10d) for the analysis of household liquidity. The black market price level (see equation 15) is affected not only by liquidity considerations and government budget deficits, but also the supply variables, such as absorption. That is, an increase in supply leads to reductions of black market prices. Finally, monetary considerations, purchasing power parity ratios, supply variables (such as absorption) and rational expectation about the rate of return on foreign currency holdings affect the foreign exchange rate (equation 18a), providing an eclectic combination of several theories of exchange rate determination. In summary, money, expectations, government budget deficits and supply considerations do matter even in a socialist non-market economy like Cuba.

Appendix A
DATA SOURCES AND DATA DEVELOPMENT PROCEDURES

This section describes the data base assembled and the procedures used in their development.

BLACK MARKET EXCHANGE RATES

The black market exchange rates come from Pick's Currency Yearbook and from its successor, the World Currency Yearbook. These black market exchange rates are compiled from currency transactions conducted in international money exchange centers and as such they are different from the black market exchange rates observed in currency exchange transactions inside Cuba. While the sources of the currency information exchange services are proprietary and confidential, we noted that one of the earlier issues of Pick's mentioned that the black market exchange rates were compiled from currency transactions data in Zurich, Paris, London, New York, Mexico and Miami. A long 1959-1994 time series is available from observations on currency transactions outside Cuba.

Black Market Prices

The basket of commodities is a 1980 consumption basket assembled from several sources: most of the commodity weights come from Brundenius (1984), complemented by weights from

Pérez-López's (1987) production figures net of exports. A few of the 1980 commodity weights also come from several issues of the U.N. Economic Commission for Latin America and the Caribbean's (ECLAC) *Economic Survey of Latin America*. The commodity basket includes foods, drinks and tobacco, clothing, textiles and miscellaneous consumer industrial products (television and radio sets, refrigerators etc.) and covers 91 commodities.

Individual black market commodity prices come from several sources. Pre-revolutionary prices for 1953 come from Oshima (1961) and from Oscar Lewis (1977), while 1957 prices are available from Sánchez-Herrero (1995). The 1969 black market prices come from René Dumont (1970) and from Lewis (1977). The 1977-78 commodity prices come

from Mesa-Lago (1981) and from the World Bank (Hultin, 1979), while the 1980 prices come from Brundenius (1984). The 1983 prices come from Medea Benjamin et al. (1986) and from ECLAC's *Economic Survey of Latin America* (1983). Black market commodity prices for the period 1985-1989 and for 1990 come from ECLAC's *Economic Survey of Latin America* (1988, 1989, and 1992).

Other 1989 black market prices come from Juan Clark (1990) and from observations collected by José F. Alonso, who also contributed some price observations for the period 1992-1994. Price observations for 1993 were complemented by data contributed by Marta Beatriz Roque-Cabello (1993) of the Asociación de Economistas Independientes de Cuba (ANEIC) and by data contributed by the Partido Pro-Derechos Humanos de Cuba (1993). The black market price observations in 1994 were assembled mostly from ANEIC's 1994 expenditure surveys, complemented by data from issues of the magazines *Contrapunto* (1994 and 1995), Areíto (1995), and from reports in *The Washington Post* (Farah, 1995) and *The Miami Herald* (Pérez, 1995). December 1994 black market prices also come from Marta Beatriz Roque-Cabello (1995) of ANEIC. Black market price data for 1995 are available from Sánchez-Herrero (1995), and from articles in *The Miami Herald* (Alfonso, 1995 and Alvarez, 1995) and from *Contrapunto* (1995). The Instituto Cubano de Economístas Independientes (ICEI, 1996) supplied December 1995 price data from their surveys of black market prices.

The price indexes were estimated using 1989 as the base year, since 1989 is the year for which the largest amount of individual price information is available. Pair-wise comparisons of individual commodity prices were conducted comparing the 1989 commodity price with the commodity price for the year in question. If one of the commodity prices in the pair-wise comparison years was not known, both prices were set equal to zero to estimate pair-wise compared ex-

Table A-1. Comparison of Gross Domestic Product, Price Deflator Index with Black Market Price Index- 1969-1994

Years	Black Market Prices		Official GDP Price	Price Index Used
	Index	No. Pairwise Matches	Deflator	in this Study
1953	12.66	9	n/a	n/a
1957	9.56	9	n/a	n/a
1969	90.08	30	91.55	91.55
1970			92.25	92.25
1973			98.18	98.18
1974			99.38	99.38
1975			100.09	100.09
1976			98.75	98.75
1977			93.17	93.17
1978	88.79	16	97.13	97.13
1979			97.96	97.96
1980	90.31	11	104.14	104.14
1981			102.36	102.36
1982			102.69	102.69
1983	91.15	15	103.93	103.93
1984			102.98	102.98
1985	90.98	13	101.49	101.49
1986	89.98	14	97.55	97.55
1987	100.09	14	97.92	97.92
1988	97.55	14	98.74	98.74
1989	100.00	Not applicable	100.00	100.00
1990	102.43	13	100.89	102.43
1991	263.43	31	84.73	263.43
1992	509.85	23	82.34	509.84
1993	1552.55	24		1552.55
1994	1396.48	32		1396.48
1995	739.64	36		

Notes: Black market price indexes are based on comparisons of prices of identical products/goods between each respective year and 1989. Source: See text in appendix A.

penditures. The estimation of annual consumer expenditures used the 1980 commodity weights mentioned earlier. The black market price indexes and the number of commodity pair-wise price comparisons are presented in Table A1.

Total Exports, Imports and their Components

The pre-1990 figures of exports, imports and the components of imports come from the *Anuario Estadístico de Cuba* (1990). The post-1989 exports and imports totals come from Ariel Terrero's *Bohemia* article (1994), while the components of imports from 1989 to 1993 come from the Central Intelligence Agency (1994). Imports and exports data for 1994 come from the Comité Estatal de Estadísticas (Agence France Press, 1995).

International Trade in Convertible Currency

Figures for international trade in convertible currency for the periods 1970-1979 and 1981-1983 come from Turits (1987), while the 1980 figures come from CEPAL (1989). International trade figures for 1984 were estimated by the authors from the *Anuario Estadístico de Cuba* (1989), while the source of the trade figures in convertible currency for the period 1985-1989 is CEPAL's *Notas para el Estudio Económico de América Latina y el Caribe 1989: Cuba* (CEPAL, 1991)

The trade figures for 1990 and 1991 come from a combination of sources, including the Central Intelligence Agency (CIA, 1994) and from José Luis Rodríguez (1993). The CIA's (1994) international trade estimates were used for years 1992 and 1993.

Foreign Monetary Reserves

The source of foreign monetary reserves in convertible currency for the period 1977-1982 is the United Nations Conference on Trade and Development (United Nations, 1984). Total reserves (which include reserves in transferable rubles) and convertible reserves for 1981 come from Turits (1987) and from the Banco Nacional de Cuba (1982). For the period 1982-1989, data on total reserves and on reserves in convertible currency come from CEPAL's Notes (1991). For 1990, the authors were forced to use--for the lack of better figures-- those for June 1990 presented by the Banco Nacional de Cuba's *Informe Económico Semestral* (June 1990).

Gross Domestic Product (GDP)

The GDP series (in both constant and current prices) assembled by Hidalgo and Tabares (1992) was used for the period 1975-1989. For 1971-1974, the series comes from the Banco Nacional de Cuba (1982) after adjusting for overlapping with the more extensive and more recent Hidalgo and Tabares' (1992) series. GDP for the period 1961-1971 was estimated by assuming that the annual rate of change in the gross material product estimated by Mesa-Lago (1981) would be the same for the GDP. This assumption is reasonable, since the gross material product of socialist national income accounting is the closest concept to the gross domestic product. GDP figures for the period 1958- 1960 were taken from José Luis Rodríguez (1985), while the figures for the pre-revolutionary period come from the Banco Nacional de Cuba (1958).

Finally, GDP figures for the more recent period 1990-1993 come from information published in *Bohemia* (Terrero, 1994), while the 1994 GDP estimate takes at face value[5] the January 27, 1995 precipitous announcement in Davos, Switzerland by Cuban pediatric psychiatrist and Minister Carlos Lage, MD (*Cuba Business*, April, 1995 and Evans, 1995) in charge of economic policy, to the effect that Cuba had experienced growth of 0.7% in GDP at constant prices during 1994.[6]

GDP Price Deflators

Hidalgo and Tabares (1992) are the source for the GDP price delator series for the period 1975-1989. The post-1989 price deflators were estimated from Terrero's (1994) current GDP figures and from the constant GDP figures presented in Consultores Aso-

---

5. The Cuban government has begun to correct Lage's precipitous announcement. Thus, in a Radio Taíno interview of June 28, 1995 two Cuban journalists, Fernando Dàvalos of Radio Taíno and Osvaldo Rodríguez of *Bohemia* refer to a lower 0.4% growth rate for 1994. We should not be surprised that when all the adjustments are done the rate of growth will turn to a slight rate of further decline.

6. This practice of having medical doctors in charge of the Cuban economy is not new. In the early sixties, Ernesto "Che" Guevara, MD, became Minister of Industry and President of Banco Nacional de Cuba. This period was characterized by a disastrous management of Cuba's economy . Therefore, this revolutionary practice of putting a psychiatrist in charge of the Cuban economy should not be missconstrued to mean that the Cuban economy is necessarily a "crazy" economy, that is, an economy in need of psychiatric therapy.

ciados S.A. (CONAS, 1994) and Oficina Nacional de Estadísticas (1995). The price deflators for the GDP series for the pre-1975 period come from the GSP deflators published by José Luis Rodríguez (1990) and from Cardoso and Helwege (1992). Since the post-1989 GDP price deflators were found unreliable and non-sensical, they were substituted for the black market price index after 1989. The reader should note that the price inflation rates that result from the use of Hidalgo and Tabares (1992) GDP price deflators are very different from those quoted by Mesa-Lago (1994) based on gross social product (GSP) price deflators.

Because the GDP price deflators published in Cuba show an erratic behavior in the post-1990 period, the black market price index is substituted for the GDP price deflator in some of the equations estimated. This precaution was taken because the official GDP price deflators show a declining trend after 1990, in marked contrast to the black market price inflation amply corroborated by journal articles and even official statements from the Cuban authorities.

Gross and Net Investments

The investment figures used throughout this study exclude inventory changes. Gross investments for years 1958, 1959 and 1961 come from Felipe Pazos (1961, 1962), the founder and first President of the Banco Nacional de Cuba. The 1960 figure comes from Pérez-López (1987) and covers solely public investments.

Gross investment and productive depreciation for the period 1962-1974 come from Brundenius (1984) with two exceptions concerning the 1971 and 1972 depreciation charges, whose values were not published and were imputed at 2% of capital values. Gross investments and depreciation for the years 1975-1989 come from the *Anuario Estadístico de Cuba* (1990). The post-1989 investment figures have not been published officially and had to be imputed from references in the literature. Gross investments in 1990 were estimated as declining 6% from the peak year 1989, a decline which corresponds to the reduction in imports of machinery and transport equipment published by the CIA (1994). Gross investments in 1991 and 1992 come from Casanova

(1994) and differ from the earlier 1991 estimates by Carranza (1993) used in our previous research (Alonso & Lago, 1994), and from the 1992 estimates published by the government-run Consultores Asociados S. A. (CONAS, 1994). The 1994 gross investment estimates come from José Luis Rodríguez' December 20, 1994 speech to the Asamblea Nacional del Poder Popular (Foreign Broadcast Information Service, January 1995).

Depreciation for the missing years was estimated as follows. The depreciation for the pre- revolutionary period 1949-1957 was estimated from the Banco Nacional de Cuba as comprising 1.2% of capital values, clearly an underestimation of depreciation, but by 1957, the annual depreciation figure was 1.75% of capital values. As a consequence the depreciation for the missing years 1958- 1961 and 1971-1972 was estimated at 2.0% of capital, the same rate used in our previous work (Alonso & Lago, 1994). The 2.0% depreciation charge fits closely the depreciation charges during the revolutionary period 1962-1970 published by Brundenius (1984). The Cuban authorities increased the depreciation charges annually to 4.22% of capital values in 1979 and to 4.90% in 1989. Accordingly, the missing value for the 1990 depreciation charge was imputed at 4.90% of capital values, then lowered to a more reasonable 4.0% of capital for the post-1990 period of economic decline. The average depreciation charge for the entire period 1958-1994 that results from the mix of actual figures and our estimates is 4.0% of capital values. The Cuban government has not published any depreciation figures since 1989.

Sugar Prices and Oil Prices

Sugar and oil prices per ton for the pre-1989 period come from the *Anuario Estadístico de Cuba* (1990) and correspond mainly to the trade with the Soviet Union. The sugar and oil prices for 1990 and 1991 come from José Luis Rodríguez (1992). After 1991, all the figures are expressed in world market prices. The world sugar prices come from GEPLACEA (1995) and from the U.S. Department of Agriculture (1994). The oil prices come from the World Bank (IBRD, 1994).

Labor and Employment

The pre-1980 employment figures come from Mesa-Lago (1981) and the 1980-1989 come from CEPAL's several publications, including Notas..... (1990) and the *Economic Surveys of Latin America and the Caribbean*. (Selected 1ssues 1983-1990). Mesa-Lago's pre-1980 employment figures were adjusted to reflect the private farm labor estimates presented by Ghai, Kay and Peek, (1988). The 1992 and 1993 employment figures come from the Concertación Democràtica Cubana (1993) and from the Asociación Nacional de Economistas Independientes de Cuba (ANEIC, 1994)[7]. The 1994 employment estimate comes from the Reuters' interview with the Cuban union leader Pedro Ros Leal (Kerry, 1995). Labor figures for the year 1990 were imputed assuming changes proportional to the GDP change for that year. Labor estimates for 1991 were projected in between the above figures. Labor figures for June 1995 come from Salvador Valdez (1995), while unemployment rates and labor figures for 1989 originate from Enid Felipe (1995).

Foreign Trade Price Indexes

Unit values of Cuban imports estimated by Mesa-Lago and Pérez-López (1991) for the period 1975-1987 were used as the primary source for world prices facing Cuba's imports, an important exogenous variable for the prediction of both black market prices and black market exchange rates. This index was projected for the period 1988-1989 from the Russian export unit values reported in the IMF's Study of the Soviet Economy (IMF, 1991). For the earlier pre-1975 period, the unit value indexes for Russian exports to the CMEA countries (Marer et al., 1992) were used as the basis for interpolating backwards in time the later Mesa-Lago and Pérez-López' indexes. Post-1989 import prices were projected proportional to the Russian oil prices charged to Cuba for 1990 and to the world oil price for the period 1991-1994.

Interest Rates

The interest rates on savings accounts offered by the Banco Popular de Ahorro (BPA) of Cuba for saving deposits under 1,000 pesos are used as proxy for interest rates available to households. The source of the interest rate data previous to 1993 is the Banco Nacional de Cuba's Report by the Task Force to Cuba (1989). The post-1992 data comes from Marta Beatriz Roque-Cabello of the ANEIC.

Budgetary Expenses, Taxes and Deficits

According to Mesa-Lago (1994), no budgetary data has been published for the period 1966-1977. Figures on government expenses, taxes and deficits for the period 1978-1989 are available from CEPAL's *Economic Survey of Latin America and the Caribbean* (Several issues). Figures solely on the deficit are presented for the period 1981-1993 in CEPAL's *Cuba: Evaluación económica durante 1993* (Junio 1994), while budgetary deficit figures for 1990-1993 are available from *Bohemia* (Terrero, 1994). Deficit figures for 1990 to 1992 are available from Casanova (1994) and for 1992- 93 from José Luis Rodríguez' Radio Progreso interview (1994). Finally, deficit figures for 1994 come from *Cuba Business* (Jan/Feb 1995) and from the Economic Press Service (Diciembre 1994, and Enero 1995).

Household Liquidity: Money in Circulation and Savings Deposits

Household liquidity figures, covering both money in circulation and savings deposits, are available from 1975 to 1990 from Alpízar (1992). The components of the balance of income and expenses of the household sector are presented from 1975 to 1989 in the *Anuario Estadístico de Cuba* (1990). The sums of money in circulation and savings deposits (but not data on the components) are available from *Bohemia* (Terrero, 1994) for the period 1990-93, while similar data for 1994 are available from Economic Press Service (Enero 1995). Household liquidity figures, sometimes called the monetary surplus, are available without details on the components for the period

---

7. Employment figures for 1992 were supplied by Marta Beatriz Roque-Cabello of the ANEIC based on the research of Angela Fauriol of CIEM in La Habana

1970 - 1978 from Mesa-Lago (1981), whereas the monetary surplus for the period 1961-1988 are available (in aggregate form) from José Luis Rodríguez (1990). Earlier monetary data for 1959 and 1960 and for the pre- revolutionary period are available, with details on the components, from the Grupo Cubano de Investigaciones Económicas (1963).

BIBLIOGRAPHY

Acciaris, Ricardo. "La Dette Cubaine Envers L'Ouest". *Le Courier des Pays de L'Est*. No. 284. Mai 1984. pp. 50-65.

Adelman, Irma and Hollis B. Chennery. "Foreign Aid and Economic Development: The Case of Greece". *The Review of Economics and Statistics*. 48. February 1966. pp. 1 - 19.

Agence France Press, "Cuba's 1994 GDP rises, but still a shadow of 1989 figure," Havana, July 6, 1995.

Agénor, Pierre Richard. "Stabilization Policies in Developing Countries with a Parallel Market for Foreign Exchange" *IMF Staff Papers*. Vol. 37. September 1990. pp. 560-592.

Aghevli, Bijan B. and Cyrus Sassanpour. "Prices, Output and the Trade Balance in Iran". *World Development*. Vol. 10. No. 9. 1982. pp. 791-800.

Alfonso, Pablo. "Gobierno Paga Dólares a Ciertos Obreros Cubanos". *El Nuevo Herald*. March 30, 1995.

Alonso, José F. and Armando M. Lago. "A First Approximation of the Foreign Assistance Requirements of a Democratic Cuba". *Cuba in Transition. Vol. 3*. Papers and Proceedings of the 3rd Annual Meeting of the Association for the Study of the Cuban Economy (ASCE). Washington D.C. 1994. pp. 168-219.

Alonso, José F. . "The Free Farmers Market: A Rejected Approach, but a Possible Solution". *Cuba in Transition. Vol. 2*. Papers and Proceedings of the 2nd. Annual Meeting of the Association for the Study of the Cuban Economy (ASCE). Miami, Florida: Florida International University. 1993. pp. 166-185.

Alpízar, Osvaldo. "La Liquidez Monetaria en la Economía Cubana: Reseña Estadística." *Boletín de Información sobre Economía Cubana*. Vol. 1. No. 4. Abril 1992. La Habana: Publicación Mensual del Centro de Investigaciones de la Economía Mundial. pp. 19-23.

Alvarez, Lizette. "Farmers Markets: Oasis of Food for the Hungry". *The Miami Herald*. March 28, 1995. pp. 4-A

Alvarez, Lizette. "Castro Tries Using Capitalism to Save Socialism." *The Miami Herald*. March 28, 1995. pp. 1-A and 4-A.

Areíto. "Hay màs Chaùcha: Los nuevos mercados agropecuarios". Volume 5 No. 17. Enero 1995. pp. 16 - 19.

Asociación Nacional de Economistas Independientes de Cuba (ANEIC). "Encuesta sobre Ingresos y Gastos de la Población". ANEIC Documento No. 12. La Habana: ANEIC, 14 de noviembre de 1994. (Mimeo).

Benjamin, Medea, Joseph Collins and Michael Scott. *No Free Lunch--Food and Revolution in Cuba Today*. New York, Grove Press Inc., 1986.

Bilson, John F. O. "Rational Expectations and the Exchange Rate." in J. Frenkel and H. Johnson, editors. *The Economics of Exchange Rates*. Reading, PA: Addison-Wesley. 1978

Blejer, Mario I. . "Exchange Rate Restrictions and the Monetary Approach to the Exchange Rate" in *The Economics of Exchange Rates: Selected Stud-*

ies, edited by Jacob A. Frenkel and Harry G. Johnson. Reading, Pennsylvania: Addison-Wesley. 1978. pp. 117-128.

Brundenius, Claes. *Revolutionary Cuba: The Challenge of Economic Growth with Equity,* Boulder, Colorado: Westview Press, Inc. 1984.

Calvo, Guillermo A. and Carlos A. Rodríguez. "A Model of Exchange Rate Determination under Currency Substitution and Rational Expectations." *Journal of Political Economy.* Vol. 85. June 1977. pp. 617-625.

Cardoso, Eliana and Ann Helwege. *Cuba After Comunism.* Cambridge, MA: MIT Press. 1992.

Carranza Valdés, Julio. "Cuba: Los Retos de la Economía" *Cuadernos de Nuetra América.* Publicación del Centro de Estudios sobre América. (CEA). Vol. 19, 1993.

Casanova Montero, Alfonso y Juan Triana Cordoví. "La Economía Cubana en 1994: Coyuntura, Reformas y Perspectivas". *Areíto.* Vol. 5, No. 17. Enero 1995. pp. 8 -15.

Casanova Montero, Alfonso. "La Economía de Cuba en 1993 y Perspectivas para 1994". *Prensa Latina.* Marzo 21 de 1994.

Central Intelligence Agency. Directorate of Intelligence. *Cuba: Handbook of Trade Statistics: 1994.* Report ALA 94-10011. Langley, VA: CIA. August 1994.

Charemza, Wojciech W. and Subrata Ghatak. "Demand for Money in Dual-Currency, Quantity-Constrained Economy: Hungary and Poland, 1956-1985." *Economic Journal.* Vol. 100. December 1990. pp. 1159-1172.

Chaviano Saldaña, Noel, Angel V. Rico García y Manuel López García. "Características del Sistema Financiero-Crediticio de la República de Cuba." *Finanzas y crédito.* Año 1986. No.6. Abril-Junio 986. pp. 72-115.

Clark, Juan. *Cuba: Mito y Realidad: Testimonios de un Pueblo.* Caracas, Venezuela: Ediciones Saeta. 1990.

Concertación Democràtica Cubana. "Nivel de Desempleo en la Sociedad Cubana". La Habana: 1993. (mimeo).

Consultores Asociados, S.A. (CONAS). *Cuba: Inversiones y Negocios.* La Habana, Cuba: Ediciones Pontón Caribe S.A. 1994.

Contrapunto. "Mercados Agropecuarios. Cuba pone los pies en la Tierra." Miami, Florida: Año 5, No. 12. Edición No. 48. Diciembre 1994. pp. 15-20

Contrapunto. "Mercado Agropecuario". Miami, Florida: Año 6, No. 3. Edición No. 51. Marzo 1995. pp. 50-54.

Cooper, Richard N. "Monetary Theory and Policy in an Open Economy". *The Scandinavian Journal of Economics.* Vol. 78. 1976. pp. 146-163.

Cottarelli, Carlo and Mario I. Blejer. "Forced Saving and Repressed Inflation in the Soviet Union. 1986-90: Some Empirical Results". *IMF Staff Papers.* Vol. 39. No. 2. June 1992. pp. 256-286.

Cowitt, Phillip P. . *World Currency Yearbook.* Brooklyn, New York: International Currency Analysis, Inc. Selected Annual Issues.

Cuba Business. Vol. 9 No. 1. January/February 1995.

Cuba Business. Vol. 9, No. 3. April 1995.

Culbertson, William Patterson Jr. "Purchasing Power Parity and the Black Market Exchange Rates". *Economic Inquiry.* Vol. 14 . 1975. pp. 287-296.

Deere, Carmen Diana and Mike Meurs. "Markets, Markets Everywhere? Understanding the Cuban Anomaly." *World Development.* Vol. 20 No. 6. 1992., pp. 825-839.

Dornbusch, R. "Expectations and Exchange Rate Dynamics". *Journal of Political Economy.* Vol. 84. 1976. pp. 1161-1176.

Dornbusch, Rudiger, Daniel Valente Dantas, Clarice Pechman, Roberto de Rezende Rocha and Demetrio Simoes. "The Black Market for Dollars in Brazil". *Quarterly Journal od Economics.* Vol. 98. February 1983. pp. 287-296.

Dumont, René. *Cuba, Socialisme et Développement.* Paris, France: Editions du Seuil. 1994.

Dumont, René. *Cuba: Es Socialista?* Caracas, Venezuela: Editorial Tiempo Nuevo, 2nd. ed., 1971.

Echeverría Vallejo, Oscar. "Apuntes para una Discusión sobre el Sistema Financiero Cubano". *Boletín de Información sobre Economía Cubana.* La Habana, Cuba: Publicación Mensual del Centro de Investigaciones de la Economía Mundial. Vol. 1. Enero-Diciembre 1992. pp. 10-19.

Economic Press Service. Información Quincenal sobre Cuba. "Finanzas: Programa de Saneamiento mejoró Salud Financiera." La Habana: Año 7, No. 24. 31 de Diciembre de 1994.

Economic Press Service. Información Quincenal sobre Cuba. "Economía Global: Un Vistazo Económico a 1994." La Habana: Año 8, No. 1. Enero de 1995.

Edwards, Sebastian. *Real Exchange Rates, Devaluation and Adjustment.* Cambridge, Massachussetts: MIT Press. 1989.

Edwards, Sebastian. "Real and Monetary Determinants of Real Exchange Rate Behavior: Theory and Evidence from Developing Countries." *Journal of Development Economics.* Vol. 29. 1988. pp. 311-341.

Espinosa Martínez, Estela y Didio Quintana Mendoza. "Evolución de los Ingresos y los Gastos Monetarios de la Población. Su pronosticación a Largo Plazo." *Cuba Economía Planificada,* Año 4, No.4, Octubre-Diciembre, 1989, pp. 71-95.

Evans, Robert. "Cuba Bids at Business Meet for Foreign Investment". Reuters Limited. January 30, 1995.

Farah, Douglas. "Farmers' Markets Help Ease Cuba's Pain". *The Washington Post.* January 23, 1995. pp. A-1 and A-15.

Felipe, Enid. "Apuntes sobre el Desarrollo Social en Cuba". Boletín Informàtico No. 20 del Centro de Investigación de la Economía Mundial. Marzo - Abril 1995.

Fogel, Jean-Francois and Bertrand Rosenthal. *Fin de Siglo en la Habana.* Bogotà, Colombia: Tercer Mundo Editores. 1994.

Foreign Broadcast Information Service. FBIS-LAT-95-003-S. "Finance Minister addresses morning session of 20 December 1994 of Asamblea Nacional del Poder Popular. Reported by TeleRebelde Network on 21 December 1994. Washington D.C.: FBIS. 5 January 1995.

Frankel, Jeffrey A.. "On the Mark: A Theory of Floating Exchange Rates based on Interest Rate Differentials." *American Economic Review.* Vol. 69. 1979. pp. 610-622.

Frenkel, Jacob A.. "A Monetary Approach to the Exchange Rate". *The Scandinavian Journal of Economics.* Vol. 78. 1976. pp. 200-224.

GEPLACEA. *Boletín GEPLACEA.* Vol. X, No. 2. February/Febrero 193 and Vol. XI, No. 2, February/Febrero 1994.

Ghai, D., C. Kay and P. Peek. *Labour and Development in Rural Cuba.* International Labour Organization. London: McMillan Press. 1988.

Grupo Cubano de Investigaciones Económicas. *Un Estudio sobre Cuba.* Miami, Florida: University of Miami Press. 1963.

Gupta, Sanjeev. "An Application of the Monetary Approach to Black Market Exchange Rates: India." *Weltwirtschaftliches Archiv.* Vol. 116. 1980. pp. 235-252.

Haque, Nadeem U., Kajal Lahiri and Peter J. Montiel. "A Macroeconometric Model for Developing Countries". *IMF Staff Papers.* Vol. 37. September 1990. pp. 537-559.

Hemphill, William L. . "The Effect of Foreign Exchange Receipts on Imports of Less Developed Countries". *IMF Staff Papers.* Vol. 21. November 1974. pp. 637-677.

Hidalgo, Vilma y Lourdes Tabares. "La Evolución Estimada del PIB en la Economía Cubana entre 1975 y 1989". *Boletín de Información sobre Economía Cubana.* La Habana, Cuba: Publicación Mensual del Centro de Investigaciones de la Economía Mundial. Vol 1. No. 4. Abril 1992. pp. 10- 19.

Hooper, Peter and John E. Morton. "Fluctuations in the Dollar: A Model of Nominal and Real Exchange Rate Determination." *Journal of International Money and Finance.* Vol. 1. 1982. pp. 39-56.

Hultin, Mats. "World Bank Cuba-Education Study Mission. Full Report." World Bank Office Memorandum. Washington D.C. February 14, 1979.

Infante Ugarte, Joaquín. "Comentarios sobre la Elaboración del Plan Financiero Global del Estado" *Finanzas y Créditos.* Año 1986. No. 5. Enero-Marzo 1986. pp. 10-40.

Instituto Cubano de Economistas Independientes. "Encuesta de Precios, Diciembre, 1995." La Habana, 24 de Enero de 1996.

International Bank for Reconstruction and Development. International Trade and International Economic Division. *Market Outlook for Major Primary Commodities. Vols. I and II.* Washington D.C.: The World Bank. Selected Issues.

International Monetary Fund. *The Monetary Approach to the Balance of Payments.* Washington D.C. : IMF. 1977.

International Monetary Fund, The World Bank, Organization for Economic Co-operation and Development and Europen Bank for Reconstruction and Development. *A Study of the Soviet Economy.* Vol. No. 1. Paris: OECD. February 1991.

Kerry, Frances. "Cuba's Workers have to be Flexible—Union Boss". Reuters Asia Pacific Business Report. February 19, 1995.

Khan, Mohsin S. and Malcom D. Knight. "Stabilization Programs in Developing Countries: A Formal Framework". *IMF Staff Papers.* Vol. 28. March 1981. pp. 1-53.

Kharas, Homi and Brian Pinto. "Exchange Rates Rules, Black Market Premia, and Fiscal Deficits: The Bolivian Hyperinflation". *Review of Economic Studies.* Vol. 56. July 1989. pp. 435-447.

Kornai, Jànos. *Economics of Shortage.* Volume B. North Holland Publishing Company. Amsterdam. 1980.

Kornai, Jànos. *Growth, Shortage and Efficiency: A Macrodynamic Model of the Socialist Economy.* Berkeley, CA: University of California Press. 1982.

Krueger, Anne O. *Exchange-Rate Determination.* Cambridge Surveys of Economic Literature. Cambridge, United Kingdom: Cambridge University Press. 1983

Lane, Timothy D. . "Household Demand for Money in Poland". *IMF Staff Papers.* Vol. 39, No. 4. December 1992. pp. 825-854.

Lewis, Oscar, Ruth M. Lewis and Susan M. Rigdon. *Four Men.* Champaign, Illinois: University of Illinois Press. 1977.

Lindbeck, Assar. "Approaches to Exchange Rate Analysis--An Introduction." *The Scandinavian Journal of Economics.* Vol 78. 1976. pp. 133-145.

Lipschitz, Leslie. "Domestic Credit and Exchange Rates in Developing Countries: Some Policy Experiments with Korean Data". *IMF Staff Papers.* Vol. 31. December 1984. pp. 595-635.

Lizondo, J. Saul. "Unification of Dual Exchange Markets". *Journal of International Economics.* Vol. 22. February 1987. pp. 57-77.

Lizondo, J. Saul. "Exchange Rate Differentials and Balance of Payments under Dual Exchange Rates". *Journal of Development Economics.* Vol. 26. June 1987a. pp. 37-53.

MacDonald, R. "Exchange Rate Economics: An empirical Perspective". in R. Bird, editor. *The International Financial Regime.* London: Surrey University Press. 1990. pp. 91-144.

MacDonald, Ronald and Mark P. Taylor. "Exchange Rate Economics: A Survey". *IMF Staff Papers.* Vol. 39. No. 1. March 1992. pp. 1 - 57.

Marer, Paul, Janos Arway, John O'Connor, Martin Schrenk and Daniel Swanson. *Historically Planned Economies: A Guide to the Data.* Washington D.C.: The World Bank. 1992.

Marquetti Nodarse, Hiram. "El Comercio Exterior de Cuba en 1993". *Cuba: Economía y Administración.* La Habana, Cuba: Centro de Estudios de la Economía Cubana. Año 1. No. 1. Julio-Agosto-Septiembre 1994. pp. 6 - 8.

Martínez Fagundo, Carlos. "Aproximación al Anàlisis y Proyección de la Circulación Monetaria. Un Modelo para Cuba". *Cuba Economía Planificada.* Año 4, No. 2, Abril-Junio, 1989, pp. 40 - 77.

Meese, R. and K. Rogoff. "The Out-of-Sample Failure of Empirical Exchange Rate Models" in J. Frenkel, editor. *Exchange Rates and International Economics.* Chicago: University of Chicago Press. 1983 pp. 3-24.

Mejías Ribes, Aledio. "Existe Relación entre el Déficit Presupuestario y la Emisión Monetaria". *Finanzas y Crédito.* Año 1985. No. 1. Enero-Mayo 1985. pp. 114-145.

Mesa-Lago, Carmelo. *Breve historia económica de la Cuba socialista.* Madrid: Alianza Editorial S.A. 1994.

Mesa-Lago, Carmelo and Jorge Pérez-López. "Cuban Economic Growth in Current and Constant Prices 1975-88: A Puzzle on the Foreign Trade Component of the Material Product System". In James W. Wilkie and Carlos Alberto Contreras, editors. *Statistical Abstract of Latin America.* Vol. 29, Part 1. Los Angeles: UCLA Latin American Center Publications, University of California. 1991. pp. 599 - 615.

Mesa-Lago, Carmelo. *The Economy of Socialist Cuba.* Albuquerque, New Mexico: University of New Mexico Press. 1981.

Mesa-Lago, Carmelo and Jorge Pérez-López. "A Study of Cuba's Material Product System, Its Conversion to the System of National Accounts, and Estimation of Gross Domestic Product per Capita and Growth Rates." *World Bank Staff Working Papers.* No. 770. Washington D.C.: The World Bank. 1985.

Moreno, Juan Luis . "Una Política o un Sistema Monetario Optimo". *Cuba in Transition. Vol. No. 2.* Papers and Proceedings of the Second Annual Meeting of the Asociation for the Study of the Cuban Economy (ASCE). Miami, FL : Florida International University. 1993. pp. 221-240.

Naciones Unidas. Comisión Económica para America Latina y el Caribe (CEPAL). *Notas Para el Estudio Económico de America Latina y el Caribe, 1989 : Cuba.* México D.F. : CEPAL. 16 de enero de 1991.

Olgun, Hasan . "An Analysis of the Black Market Exchange Rate in a Developing Economy--The Case of Turkey". *Weltwirtschaftliches Archiv.* Vol. 120. June 1984. pp. 327-347.

Oshima, Harry T. "A New Estimate of the National Income and Product of Cuba in 1953". *Food Research Institute Studies.* Stanford University. November 1961. pp. 213 - 227.

Otani, Ichiro and Cyrus Sassanpour. "Financial, Exchange Rate, and Wage Policies in Singapore 1979-86". *IMF Staff Papers.* Vol. 35. September 1988. pp. 474-495.

Partido Pro-Derechos Humanos de Cuba. "Listado de Productos o Artículos en el Mercado Negro". (Mineo). La Habana, Cuba: 20 de Mayo de 1993.

Pazos, Felipe . "Desarrollo Insuficiente y Depauperización Económica". *Cuadernos: Suplemento.* (Paris, Francia). Marzo-Abril 1961. pp. 46-64.

Pazos, Felipe . "Comentarios a Dos Artículos sobre la Revolución Cubana". *El Trimestre Económico.* Vol. XXIX (1), No. 113. Enero-Marzo 1962. pp. 1 - 18.

Pérez, Lisandro. "The Good Malanga" *The Miami Herald.* January 22, 1995. p.1-M and 4-M.

Pérez-López, Jorge F. . *Measuring Cuban Economic Performance.* Austin, Texas: University of Texas Press. 1987.

Phylaktis, Kate. "The Black Market for Dollars in Chile." *Journal of Development Economics.* Vol. 37. 1992. pp. 155-172.

Pick, Franz. *Pick's Currency Yearbook.* New York.: Pick Publishing Corp., various issues.

Pitt, Mark M. . "Smuggling and the Black Market for Foreign Exchange." *Journal of International Economics.* Vol. 16. 1984. pp. 243-257.

Polak, J. J. . "Monetary Analysis of Income Formation and Payment Problems". *IMF Staff Papers.* Vol. 6. November 1957. pp. 1-50.

Portes, Richard and David Winter. "Disequilibrium Estimates for Consumption in Centrally Planned Economies". *Review of Economic Studies.* Vol. 47. January 1980. pp. 137-159.

Portes, Richard. "Macro-economic Planning and Disequilibrium: Estimates for Poland 1955-1980." *Econometrica.* Vol. 55. January 1987. pp. 19-41.

República de Cuba. Banco Nacional de Cuba. *Economic Report, 1982.* La Habana: Banco Nacional de Cuba, 1983.

República de Cuba, Banco Nacional de Cuba. *Economic Report, 1994,* La Habana: Banco Nacional de Cuba, August 1995.

República de Cuba. Banco Nacional de Cuba-Comité Estatal de Estadísticas. *Cuba: Informe Económico Semestral, Junio 1990.* La Habana: Banco Nacional de Cuba. 1990. pp. 1 - 30.

República de Cuba. Comité Estatal de Estadísticas. (CEE). *Anuario Estadístico de Cuba .* La Habana, Cuba: Selected Issues 1985-1989.

República de Cuba. Banco Nacional de Cuba. *Report by the Task Force to Cuba.* October 1989. pp19.

República de Cuba. Banco Nacional de Cuba. *Memoria 1957-1958.* La Habana, Cuba. 1958. pp. 198.

República de Cuba. Oficina Nacional de Estadísticas, *La Economía Cubana en 1994,* La Habana, Junio de 1995.

Ritter, A. R. M. "The Cuban Economy in the 1990s: External Challenges and Policy Imperatives". *Journal of Interamerican Studies and World Affairs.* Vol. 32 No. 3. Fall 1990. pp. 117-149.

Ritter, A.R.M. "Cuba's convertible currency debt problem," *Cepal Review*, No.36, December, 1988, pp.120.

Rodríguez, Carlos A. "The Role of Trade Flows in Exchange Rate Determination." *Journal of Political Economy.* Vol. 88. 1980. pp. 1148-1158

Rodríguez Calderón, Mirta. "Dedo en la Llaga". *Bohemia.* Noviembre 23 de 1994. pp. 40-42.

Rodríguez y García, José Luis. *Desarrollo Económico de Cuba, 1959-1988.* México D.F.: Editorial Nuestro Tiempo S.A. 1990.

Rodríguez, José Luis. "Las relaciones económicas entre Cuba y la antigua USSR: evaluación y perspectivas". *Cuadernos del Este.* (Madrid, Spain) Mayo de 1992.

Rodríguez, José Luis. "La Deuda Externa Cubana: Una Evaluación Actual (II)". *Boletín de Información Sobre Economía Cubana.* Centro de Investigación de la Economía Mundial (CIEM). Vol. 1, No. 11/12. Noviembre/Diciembre, 1992.

Rodríguez, José Luis. *Cuba: Revolución y Economía. 1959-1960.* La Habana: Editorial de Ciencias Sociales. 1985.

Rodríguez, José Luis. "The Cuban Economy in a Changing International Environment". *Cuban Studies* Vol. 23. Pittsburgh, PA: University of Pittsburgh Press, 1993. pp. 33- 47.

Rodríguez, José Luis. "Entrevista por Susana Lee de Noviembre 28 de 1994." La Habana: Radio Progreso.

Roque-Cabello, Marta Beatriz. "Libreta de Abastecimientos y Consulta Popular en la Ciudad de la

Habana". (penciled manuscript). La Habana, Cuba. Diciembre de 1993.

Roque-Cabello, Marta Beatriz. "Hablemos de la Economía Cubana". *Boletín de la Asociación Nacional de Economistas Independientes de Cuba*. Nùmero IV, Mayo-Junio 1995. pp. 3 - 7.

Sánchez-Herrero, Manuel. "La Crisis del Abastecimiento". *Boletín de la Asociación Nacional de Economistas Independientes de Cuba*. Nùmero IV, Mayo-Junio 1995 . pp. 8 - 12.

Seers, Dudley, Andrés Bianchi, Richard Joy and Max Nolff. *Cuba: The Economic and Social Revolution*. Chapel Hill, North Carolina: University of North Carolina Press. 1964.

Sundararajan, V. "Exchange Rates versus Credit Policy." *Journal of Development Economics*. Vol. 20. 1986. pp. 75-105.

Terrero, Ariel. "Tendencias de un Ajuste". *Bohemia*. 28 de Noviembre de 1994. pp. B-31.

Turits, Richard. "Trade, Debt and the Cuban Economy". *World Development*. Vol. 15, No. 1. January 1987 Special Issue. pp. 163-180.

U. S. Information Agency. Voice of America. Radio Martí Program. Office of Research and Policy. *Cuba Annual Report: 1985*. New Brunswick, New Jersey: Transaction Books. 1988.

U.S. Department of Agriculture. Economic Research Service. *Sugar and Sweetner: Situation and Outlook Report*. Washington D.C.: USDA. December 1994. pp. 1 - 55.

Unanue Hernàndez, Alberto. "La Planificación Financiera Global y su Utilización en la Economía Cubana." *Finanzas y Crédito*. Año 1985. No. 2. Abril-Junio, 1985. pp. 29-47.

United Nations Conference on Trade and Development. *Cuba: Economic Developments in 1983 and Future Prospects*. New York: United Nations. 1984. pp. 1 - 51.

United Nations. Economic Commission for Latin America and the Caribbean. *Economic Survey of Latin America*. Selected Issues 1983-1992. New York: United Nations.

Vaez-Zadeh, Reza. "Oil Wealth and Economic Behavior: The Case of Venezuela 1965-1981." *IMF Staff Papers*. Vol. 36. June 1989. pp. 343-384.

Valdez Mesa, Salvador. *Agenda Abierta*. Cuban TV Program of June 27, 1995. Reproduced in Foreign Broadcast Information Service. "Labor Minister on Employment Issues". FBIS-LAT-95- 128. Washington, D.C.: FBIS . 5 July 1995. pp. 9 - 12.

Vogel Jr., Thomas T. "Cuba Seeks to Revamp Its Defaulted Debt," *Wall Street Journal*, June 26, 1995, pp. C1 and C8.

Wallis, Kenneth F. . "Econometric Implications of the Rational Expectations Hypothesis". *Econometrica*. Vol. 48. January 1980. pp. 49 - 73.

Wickens, Michael R. "The Efficient Estimation of Econometric Models with Rational Expectations". *Review of Economic Studies*. Vol. 49. March 1982. pp. 55-67.

DIMENSION FISCAL DE LA
CRISIS ECONOMICA DE CUBA, 1986-1994

Evaldo A. Cabarrouy

La economía cubana confronta serios problemas económicos como resultado de diversos factores. Algunos de ellos son derivados de los cambios en el entorno internacional, pero la mayoría son resultados de problemas económicos internos de un sistema de economía dirigida. El proceso de transición de una economía es sumamente difícil pues se intenta, de manera simultánea, reestructurar el sistema económico, proteger el bienestar de los ciudadanos, estabilizar los precios, conseguir equilibrio en la balanza de pagos y reactivar la producción.

Al mismo tiempo, conviene recordar que los países denominados en sentido amplio como "economías en transición" constituyen un grupo bastante heterogéneo que iniciaron la transformación de sus economías en momentos diferentes. En el caso de Cuba, la complejidad del proceso se acentúa si se tiene en cuenta que los cambios económicos que se están implantando procuran en las nuevas circunstancias internacionales la viabilidad de un modelo de economía dual. Por un lado existe una economía emergente, sector constituido por empresas de diversas modalidades de asociación que operan con orientación de mercado en moneda convertible. Por el otro lado, contrapuesta a las fuerzas del mercado, la economía centralizada caracterizada por la acumulación de poder económico en manos del Estado. Sin embargo, nuestra exposición no pretende hacer un análisis detallado de todo el problema ni del debate implicado en los cambios actuales de la economía cubana, sino más bien, examinar el grave problema

de las finanzas internas que ha sido una de las dimensiones centrales de la crisis que comenzó en Cuba desde la segunda mitad del decenio de 1980.

En el proceso de cambio institucional fundamental, las economías en transición experimentan graves perturbaciones socio-económicas y un creciente desequilibrio macroeconómico. Debido al papel que desempeña el Estado en esas economías, la formulación y aplicación de la política fiscal es crucial para el objetivo doble de estabilizar la economía y avanzar hacia un sistema con orientación de mercado. Por lo tanto, la política fiscal ha constituido la piedra angular de los programas de reforma económica de las economías en transición. En las siguientes páginas se describe primero de forma breve los orígenes de las graves dificultades de las finanzas internas del país, seguido de un análisis de las implicaciones inflacionarias que conllevan los monumentales déficit fiscales. Finalmente, puesto que la sustitución de monedas es un producto derivado de la inflación elevada, se discute también la dolarización de la economía cubana y sus implicaciones en materia de política fiscal.

LAS FINANZAS PUBLICAS DE CUBA EN EL PERIODO DE 1986-1993

En un sistema de planificación centralizada, el Estado decide respecto a la asignación de recursos y como prácticamente controla toda la economía, las finanzas públicas son también de vasto alcance. Ello trae consigo intervenciones discrecionales masivas en la economía por medio —entre otras cosas— de las transferencias directas a las empresas estatales, los

Gráfico 1. Cuba: Saldo Fiscal

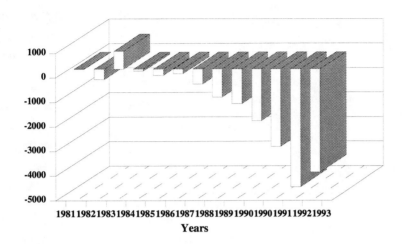

subsidios a los precios y los beneficios sociales. En Cuba, este sistema de financiación presupuestaria ha sido la fuente fundamental de financiamiento de la economía en lugar de los propios recursos de las empresas y de los créditos bancarios (autofinanciación). De hecho, los dos métodos a menudo se mezclaban pero hacia 1990 predominaba la financiación presupuestaria en la mayoría de las empresas.[1] Los ingresos del gobierno provienen principalmente de impuestos sobre la cifra de los negocios (impuestos de circulación), excedentes de las empresas y sobre el diferencial de precio de comercio exterior. A su vez, las empresas estatales y el sistema bancario apoyan las metas de la planificación centralizada mediante la subvención directa o indirecta del empleo, el consumo y la inversión bajo unas limitaciones presupuestarias favorables, entre la cuales se destaca la protección contra el riesgo de la quiebra.

Las dificultades de las finanzas internas de Cuba se ponen de manifiesto en la década de 1980 cuando la economía sufrió una severa recesión en 1987, con una caída de 3.5% en el producto social global a precios constantes, acompañada de una precaria disponibilidad de divisas de libre convertibilidad. Según la Comisión Económica para América Latina y el Caribe (CEPAL), la crisis se venía gestando antes, al agudizarse problemas más permanentes, que se habían reflejado en el deterioro del saldo comercial con los países socialistas y en el mantenimiento de un amplío déficit comercial con los países de economía de mercado. Como consecuencia de estos resultados, ya a mediados de 1986 el país había dejado de servir parte de los compromisos de la deuda externa, lo que tornó más difícil el dialogo con las fuentes crediticias externas. A raíz de esa menor capacidad para importar con divisas de libre convertibilidad, las autoridades adoptaron medidas dirigidas a comprimir la demanda interna de bienes importados desde mercados internacionales. Estas medidas, que fueron aplicadas en 1986, contribuyeron a desencadenar una contracción económica que se

---

1. En 1976-1985, el gobierno introdujo un modesto programa de reformas con alguna orientación de mercado (Sistema de Dirección y Planificación de la Economía, SDPE) donde la financiación de las empresas dejaría de depender del presupuesto del Estado y utilizarían algunos mecanismo de mercado como, entre otros, el uso de las utilidades como indicador principal de la eficacia empresarial. Se esperaba que la autofinanciación fuera sustituyendo gradualmente a la financiación presupuestaria en la economía cubana, pero la fecha límite para lograr este objetivo fue aplazándose y nunca se implementó completamente. En 1990 el IV Congreso del Partido ratificó el principio de autofinanciación, especialmente para las empresas que operan con moneda convertible (una minoría) pero permitió a la mayoría de las empresas seguir con la financiación presupuestaria. Véase a Carmelo Mesa-Lago (1994).

manifestó en casi todos los sectores de las actividades productivas.[2]

En términos de la ejecución del presupuesto del Estado, el resultado final puso en evidencia un grave problema de la economía del país. Los ingresos nominales del Estado fueron los más bajos del último quinquenio, mientras que los gastos totales declinaron a un ritmo inferior al de los ingresos. La combinación de estas dos tendencias determinó que el déficit presupuestario se ampliara a 609 millones de pesos, siendo más de tres veces mayor que el déficit del año anterior. En valores absolutos, el desequilibrio de las finanzas internas fue muy agudo, pero además cualitativamente resultó ser muy grave, al coincidir con una situación muy precaria de liquidez externa en moneda convertible. (Véase el Cuadro 1 y el Gráfico 1.)

En los dos años siguientes, los niveles del producto social registraron una ligera recuperación, pero el producto por habitante se mantuvo prácticamente estancado. Por otra parte, la brecha fiscal siguió ampliándose ya que mientras los ingresos caían en picada, los gastos retrocedieron sólo levemente. En 1988, el déficit de las finanzas estatales casi se duplicó mientras que el coeficiente respecto al producto social global aumentó al 4.4%. El aumento en el déficit fue consecuencia de la baja en la recaudación del impuesto de circulación de algunos productos y por el aumento en el gasto corriente debido al alza de los salarios y defensa. En 1989, el presupuesto del Estado registró un déficit fiscal que sobrepasó los 1,400 millones de pesos lo que representó el 7% del producto social global. Aunque el crecimiento de los ingresos fue significativo, los gastos totales acusaron una fuerte aceleración por concepto de subsidios de precios y del financiamiento de las empresas públicas no rentables.

Durante el bienio 1990-1991 se agudizaron las dificultades de la economía cubana que se venían experimentando desde la segunda mitad de los ochenta, vinculadas a la progresiva declinación

económica de los países integrantes del Consejo de Ayuda Mutua Económica (CAME). Estas formas de relación comenzaron a desaparecer en 1990 y se extinguieron totalmente en 1991, con lo que se redujo a la mitad la capacidad externa de compra del país, induciendo en consecuencia una aguda y sostenida contracción de la actividad productiva.[3]

Cuadro 1. Cuba: Saldo Fiscal

	Millones de pesos	Porcentaje del PSG
1981	4	3.5
1982	-421	0.7
1983	735	3.0
1984	-76	0.3
1985	-253	0.9
1986	-188	0.7
1987	-609	2.4
1988	-1147	4.4
1989	-1403	7.3
1990	-2105	10.0
1991	-3157	23.0
1992	-4800	32.7
1993	-4200	n.d.

Fuente: CEPAL, sobre la base de cifras oficiales

En 1992, el recrudecimiento del embargo económico impuesto por el gobierno de los Estados Unidos aunado a la caída del intercambio comercial con los países que anteriormente conformaban el área socialista y el deterioro de los precios de los principales bienes de exportación, condicionaron nuevamente la declinación del producto social global como de las importaciones de bienes y servicios. Al mismo tiempo, durante el período 1990-1992, el gasto público continuó aumentando debido a que los ingresos declinaron al tiempo que los gastos aumentaron. La disminución de los ingresos

---

2. Comisión Económica para América Latina y el Caribe (1988, p. 233).

3. Comisión Económica para América Latina y el Caribe (1992, pp. 177-184) y (1993, pp.169-177).

corrientes estuvo asociada a la contracción económica, mientras que en los gastos continuaron pesando las erogaciones por concepto de subsidios a las empresas públicas y de seguridad social.[4] Mientras tanto, durante este período, el déficit fiscal aumentó a 4,800 millones de pesos, siendo más de tres veces mayor que el ya abultado déficit de 1989 y representando el 33% del producto social. (Véase el Cuadro 1 y el Gráfico 1.)

En 1993 continuaron profundizándose los desequilibrios que enfrentaba la economía cubana prácticamente desde 1986 y se registró de nuevo un descenso de la actividad productiva. A mediados de año, ante el continuo desempeño económico adverso—en el que la escasez de divisas continuó siendo el obstáculo principal debido a la caída de la producción azucarera y la insuficiencia de insumos—el gobierno cubano introdujo una serie de medidas económicas internas con orientación de mercado. Entre las acciones de más importancia puestas en marcha se destacan las mayores facilidades a la inversión extranjera, el acrecentamiento de los servicios turísticos, la cooperitivización de las tierras estatales, la despenalización de la tenencia de divisas, la ratificación y ampliación del trabajo por cuenta propia y la reestructuración de los organismos de la administración del Estado.[5] Asimismo, se realizó un esfuerzo de ajuste fiscal que se reflejó en una reducción del déficit fiscal de 12% en términos nominales. Sin embargo, la producción cayó de nuevo en alrededor del 10%, frente al declive del 14% del año anterior, y se registraron elevados niveles de los déficit fiscal y comercial mientras que la proporción de la deuda externa fue alta con respecto a las exportaciones.[6]

Las mejoras obtenidas en el saneamiento de las finanzas internas se lograron en un contexto en que los ingresos declinaron con menor celeridad que los gastos. Estos últimos se redujeron gracias a las medidas de ahorro y austeridad implantadas por el gobierno central, pero resultaron todavía cuantiosos a raíz de los altos subsidios a las empresas públicas y a la política de preservar los servicios básicos a la población. De acuerdo con la CEPAL, en 1993 los gastos nominales por conceptos de subsidios, seguridad social y salud pública fueron mayores en 70, 33 y 10% respectivamente que en 1989. Ahora bien, no obstante la disminución de la brecha fiscal, ésta aún todavía representaba tres veces el nivel absoluto alcanzado en 1989 y posiblemente se mantenía en un elevado porcentaje con respecto al producto social global.[7]

Para terminar esta sección, cabe mencionar brevemente que en la primera semana de mayo de 1994, la Asamblea Nacional del Poder Popular consideró otras medidas para reducir el enorme déficit presupuestario del país, entre las que sobresalen: el establecimiento de un nuevo sistema tributario, estimulo al ahorro privado, incrementos selectivos de precios y tarifas (en particular los cigarrillos y las bebidas alcohólicas, pero también los precios de la gasolina, de la electricidad, del agua, así como las tarifas de los servicios postales y telefónicos), mejoras en la eficiencia y reducción de las subvenciones millonarias para las empresas públicas deficitarias, y aplicación de requisitos más estrictos en torno al respaldo financiero para todas las operaciones económicas.[8]

DEFICIT FISCALES E INFLACION

Uno de los aspectos fundamentales de la política fiscal es la gestión del déficit del sector público. Aunque los déficits en sí mismos no plantean automáticamente problemas macroeconómicos, la forma en que se financien determinará en gran medida el impacto que tendrá sobre la economía. Tanto en las economías de mercado como en las de

---

4. Ibid.

5. Bert Hoffmann (1995).

6. Comisión Económica para América Latina y el Caribe (1994a).

7. Ibid.

8. Asamblea Nacional del Poder Popular, Acuerdo IV-24 con propuestas de las medidas para el saneamiento de las finanzas (1994).

Cuadro 2. Cuba: Liquidez Monetaria

				Millones de pesos		
	Efectivo	Depósitos de Ahorro	Liquidez Total	Efectivo	Variaciones en Ahorro	Liquidez
1981	1653	888	2541	309	138	447
1982	1573	1086	2658	-80	198	118
1983	1567	1160	2727	-6	75	68
1984	1656	1276	2931	89	116	205
1985	1701	1396	3097	45	121	166
1986	1529	1658	3187	-172	262	90
1987	1521	1662	3184	-8	4	-3
1988	1816	1819	3635	295	157	451
1989	2103	2061	4164	288	242	529
1990	2141	2645	4786	38	584	622

Debido a que a veces se redondean las cifras, los datos no siempre suman el total correspondiente.

Fuente: Osvaldo Alpizar, "La liquidez monetaria en la economía cubana: reseña estadística" Boletín de Información sobre la Economía Cubana No. 4 Abril 1992.

planificación centralizada, un déficit puede financiarse con recursos internos (ahorros de la población y emisión de moneda), recursos externos (préstamos extranjeros) o con una o combinación de ambos. Con respecto al financiamiento interno, hay que distinguir básicamente entre el financiamiento por medios inflacionarios y el financiamiento mediante fuentes no inflacionarias. El no inflacionario se asocia generalmente con los bancos comerciales y el sector no bancario mientras que en el financiamiento inflacionario la fuente interna de financiación es el banco central. Ahora bien, como lo que específicamente nos interesa es examinar las finanzas inflacionarias, el déficit fiscal adquiere una importancia especial cuando origina una expansión monetaria. Esta relación entre el déficit fiscal y la inflación surge del efecto que el déficit puede tener sobre la creación de dinero.

La vinculación entre el financiamiento del déficit y la expansión monetaria puede ocurrir de diversas maneras. En una economía de mercado, por ejemplo, el gobierno puede emitir y vender bonos al público, inclusive a los bancos comerciales, y el banco central, a su vez, puede comprarlos al público. En este caso, la vinculación entre el financiamiento del déficit y la expansión monetaria no es inmediata ni directa, pero el resultado final podría ser inflacionario. Ahora bien, en una economía de planificación centralizada donde una gran parte de la intermediación financiera se efectúa a través del presupuesto, el banco central puede otorgar crédito a empresas estatales a tasas de interés muy favorables, o el gobierno puede decidir financiar sus déficits fiscales creando dinero, es decir, emitiendo moneda y gastándola. En todos estos casos, el resultado neto sería un aumento en términos nominales de la cantidad de dinero en circulación. Si la economía está creciendo en forma acelerada y la elasticidad-ingreso de la demanda de dinero es alta, su crecimiento irá acompañado de un aumento en la demanda de dinero; por lo tanto, parte de la expansión monetaria satisfará esta demanda adicional sin conducir necesariamente a aumentos de precios. Sin embargo, cuando la tasa de creación de dinero

Gráfico 2. Cuba: Liquidez Monetaria

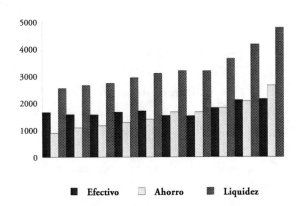

- Efectivo   ☐ Ahorro   ■ Liquidez

Gráfico 3. Cuba: Liquidez Monetaria y Déficit Fiscal 1981-1990

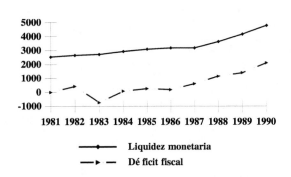

—♦— Liquidez monetaria
—►— Dé ficit fiscal

nuevo sobrepasa al crecimiento de la demanda de dinero, el resultado más probable será la inflación.[9]

En Cuba, después de la recesión de 1987, la liquidez monetaria se amplió en forma significativa, superando la expansión del producto social global en términos corrientes. De hecho, como consecuencia de la escasez de divisas debido al amplio déficit comercial con los países de economía de mercado, a mediados de 1986 el país ya había dejado de servir parte de los compromisos de la deuda externa, lo que tornó más difícil el financiamiento con fuentes crediticias externas. Para financiar los crecientes déficits fiscales las autoridades recurrieron a la emisión monetaria, así como a los remanentes de las empresas y fondos de reparación acumulados en el Banco Nacional. Así pues, en 1988 las dificultades de financiamiento del presupuesto obligaron al Banco Nacional de Cuba a emitir alrededor de 450 millones de pesos.[10] Entre 1987 y 1990, la expansión monetaria como resultado del financiamiento del creciente déficit fiscal, provocó un aumento en la liquidez total acumulada del 31% en 1989 con respecto a 1987, aumentando en 50% en 1990 con respecto a ese mismo año. (Véase el Cuadro 2 y el Gráfico 2.) El Gráfico 3, mientras tanto, ilustra la estrecha relación a partir de 1987 entre el crecimiento en el déficit fiscal y el sustancial incremento en la liquidez total acumulada.

Comienza así una tendencia nefasta para la economía cubana: a medida que el déficit fiscal se acrecentaba, la creación de dinero era cada vez mayor, alimentando de este modo la inflación. A finales de 1990, Fidel Castro afirmaba que había demasiado dinero en manos de la población y luego de haber señalado los muchos inconvenientes que tenía esta abundancia preguntaba: "¿Qué debemos hacer con todo este dinero en manos de la población?"[11] Se estima que a partir de agosto de 1990 cuando los desequilibrios financieros internos tendieron a agudizarse, el excedente monetario creció en 822.2 millones de pesos en un sólo año. Por otro lado, en el primer trimestre de 1992, el nivel de cuentas de ahorro alcanzó 3,246 millones de pesos, lo cual significó un incremento del 22.7% sobre el saldo existente a finales de 1990.[12] En síntesis, el principal origen del excedente de liquidez en Cuba radicaba en el gigantesco déficit fiscal, financiado en más del 60% con emisiones monetarias (señoreaje). El señoreaje del gobierno se convirtió por lo tanto en un "impuesto de la inflación" implícito.

---

9. En las economías donde hay libre convertibilidad de la moneda y tipos de cambio fijo, la inflación hace que se pierdan reservas de divisas al cambiar la gente la moneda nacional que no desean por moneda extranjera.

10. Comisión Económica para América Latina y el Caribe (1989, p. 295).

11. Fidel Castro, "Discurso de Clausura del Congreso de la FEU," Granma, Suplemento especial, 31 de diciembre de 1990, p. 4, citado en Carmelo Mesa-Lago (1992/93, p. 92).

12. Osvaldo Alpizar (1992, pp. 20-21).

LA SUSTITUCION DE MONEDAS EN LA ECONOMIA CUBANA

Pese al crecimiento de la masa monetaria, la tasa de inflación manifiesta en Cuba, medida por índices de precios oficiales, fue probablemente la más baja de América Latina. Según las cifras oficiales, la tasa anual media de inflación fue de solamente 0.7% en el período de 1986 a 1988. Esto por supuesto refleja la ubicuidad del sistema de control de precios que efectivamente "reprimió" la inflación subyacente y con toda probabilidad evitó que los mercados alcanzaran sus niveles de equilibrio.[13] Cabe señalar que en las economías de planificación centralizada cuando las pérdidas de las empresas estatales son cubiertas con el déficit presupuestario y la creación de dinero, las personas frecuentemente mantienen saldos monetarios excesivos (excedente de liquidez) por falta de otros instrumentos financieros. Así pues, dada la escasez de mercancías, el dinero no puede utilizarse para comprar bienes a precios controlados, a no ser que se permita la aparición de una economía paralela. En tal caso, el dinero se filtra al mercado paralelo y eleva los precios del "sector informal" de la economía. Pero generalmente en las economías centralizadas el mercado paralelo es insuficiente para eliminar el excedente de liquidez.

En Cuba, los mercados paralelos creados en 1973 y los mercados libres campesinos introducidos en 1980 y hasta su desaparición en 1986, fueron instrumentos que intentaron en alguna medida aminorar las distorsiones del sistema de control de precios. A principios de los años noventa, con el empeoramiento de los desequilibrios internos y también externos, el mercado paralelo había desaparecido y eran pocos los bienes al margen de racionamiento en que gastar el dinero. La severa escasez de artículos de consumo junto al exceso de liquidez en manos de la población propició la expansión de la economía informal; esto, a su vez motivó la decisión de aplicar aumentos de precios en algunos productos agropecuarios y a diversos bienes y servicios no considerados de máxima prioridad. Aun cuando no se dispone de datos oficiales, se estima que el índice de precios al consumidor subió en términos moderados en la economía formal, mientras el alza del nivel de precios fue muy superior en la economía informal que en 1992 representaba ya cerca del 50% de la circulación mercantil minorista.[14]

Una vez el proceso inflacionario se puso en marcha a finales de los años ochenta el pueblo cubano, ante la insuficiencia de la producción de bienes de consumo y la notable contracción de las importaciones, comenzó a dejar de usar la moneda nacional como medio de cambio sustituyéndola principalmente dólares estadounidenses (dolarización) para poder adquirir artículos en el mercado negro que habían sido robados de la economía formal o que provenían de agricultores privados.[15] La aceleración de la inflación reprimida, provocada por el alto excedente de liquidez resultante de los déficit fiscales insostenibles, se reflejó claramente en el mercado informal de divisas. Antes de agosto de 1993, cuando se penalizaba la tenencia de divisas, los dólares llegaban a Cuba principalmente a través de turistas, inversionistas extranjeros, ciudadanos cubanos empleados en el extranjero, envíos ilegales del exterior o en visitas de exiliados. Aunque el tipo de cambio oficial era de un peso por dólar estadounidense, de 1990 hasta mediados de 1992, el precio del dólar subió de 8 a 20 pesos por dólar.[16] A partir de agosto de 1993, cuando este mercado se "blanquea" en tanto se despenaliza la tenencia de

---

13. En Cuba la mayoría de los precios empezaron a fijarse centralmente en 1962 y en el mismo año se inició la asignación física de bienes de consumo mediante el racionamiento.

14. Comisión Económica para América Latina y el Caribe (1992, pp.169-177).

15. El uso de moneda extranjera como medio de cambio en países con alta inflación no es nada nuevo. En América Latina donde el dólar estadounidense tiene amplia aceptación en las transacciones se emplea comúnmente el término dolarización al referirse al fenómeno de la sustitución de monedas. La expresión también se usa con frecuencia para describir el uso de una moneda extranjera como unidad de cuenta y reserva de valor. Véase a Guillermo Calvo y Carlos A. Végh (1993, pp.34-37).

16. Carmelo Mesa-Lago (1994, p. 164).

divisas, el cambio era de 60 pesos y a fines de ese año el dólar había subido a 80 pesos. El precio del dólar sin embargo alcanzó su momento culminante en el verano de 1994, cuando subió a 100 pesos por dólar en junio y luego llegó a valer entre 120 y 135 pesos durante la "crisis de los balseros" en agosto. De manera que a medida que se disparaba la inflación reprimida, perdía valor el peso y se dolarizaba más la economía cubana.

Al finalizar el año 1994, la política fiscal orientada a reducir el déficit arrojaba algunos resultados positivos mediante una ampliación de los ingresos corrientes y una disminución de los gastos. Se registró un incremento en las recaudaciones tributarias a consecuencia del aumento en los precios de productos no esenciales (tabaco, alcohol y combustible) y de los servicios públicos. Asimismo, se ha incrementado la tributación directa sobre ingresos de los empleados por cuenta propia, campesinos y cooperativistas. Al mismo tiempo, se disminuyeron los gastos eliminando servicios gratuitos, simplificando la estructura del gobierno central y se redujeron subsidios. El saneamiento de las finanzas internas se reflejó en una disminución de la liquidez acumulada y una desaceleración del ritmo de aumento de los precios. En el sector informal, que representa una notable proporción de la circulación minorista, se observó una moderada disminución de los precios, como resultado del decrecimiento de la liquidez acumulada y de la liberación del mercado agropecuario. En los primeros meses de aplicación de estas medidas (junio a octubre) se registraron contracciones equivalentes a 21% de la liquidez, lo que se tradujo en una apreciación de la moneda nacional en el mercado informal de divisas.[17] En el verano de 1995 el dólar se cotizaba entre 35 pesos en La Habana y 40 pesos en el interior del país.

Lamentablemente, es difícil cuantificar el grado de sustitución de monedas en Cuba, dado que todavía no hay datos publicados sobre la cantidad de dólares que circulan en la economía. Sin embargo, no hay dudas de que el proceso de dolarización continúa extendiéndose aun después de la tendencia decreciente de la inflación. En otras palabras, el proceso de dolarización parece mostrar síntomas de "histéresis," o irreversividad en el sentido de que el coeficiente de dolarización (relación entre dólares en circulación y el acervo monetario en sentido amplio) no baja aun después de un considerable descenso en la inflación. Puesto que en Cuba las tenencias de divisas se mantienen principalmente para fines de transacción en vez de por consideraciones de cartera, cabría esperar a que el coeficiente de dolarización respondiera al diferencial entre la viabilidad de comprar bienes y servicios con dólares o con moneda nacional. En otras palabras, es muy probable que esta irreversibilidad del proceso de sustitución de monedas podría estar relacionada a la facilidad con que la gente pueda adquirir mayor cantidad y variedad de bienes y servicios con dólares que con moneda nacional.

Si bien es cierto que la legalización de la posesión de divisas ha producido beneficios importantes para la economía del país como la acumulación de reservas internacionales, ciertas consecuencias negativas son inevitables.[18] Por un lado, la capacidad de las autoridades para formular política monetaria puede verse considerablemente reducida porque el componente de moneda extranjera de la oferta total de dinero (en sentido amplio) que circula en la economía no se puede controlar directamente. En segundo lugar, la posibilidad de cambiar de la moneda nacional a la moneda extranjera le proporciona a la gente un medio barato y eficaz de evadir impuestos sobre los saldos en moneda nacional. Por último, la sustitución de monedas limita la capacidad del gobierno para continuar financiando el déficit fiscal emitiendo moneda nacional. A medida que la dolarización se refleje en un alejamiento de la moneda nacional, la importancia relativa de la base monetaria, y por consiguiente del financiamiento que se puede lograr mediante la emisión de moneda, se reduce. Ello

---

17. Comisión Económica para América Latina y el Caribe (1994, p. 24).

18. Véase también Lorenzo L. Pérez (1994).

implica que se agravarían las consecuencias inflacionarias de un determinado déficit fiscal. Así pues, como la sustitución de monedas es el resultado del financiamiento del déficit presupuestario por la vía de la inflación, irónicamente hace más costoso para el gobierno la monetización de su déficit.

RESUMEN Y CONCLUSIONES

Para un país que está en proceso de efectuar una delicada transición de una economía de planificación centralizada a una en la que se permite cada vez más la intervención de las fuerzas del mercado, la formulación y aplicación de la política fiscal es un problema difícil e importante. Para una economía como la cubana, que se enfrenta a graves desequilibrios macroecómicos de corto plazo caracterizados por una inflación reprimida y un producto que ha disminuido vertiginosamente, una política fiscal apropiada y un programa de reforma estructural constituyen prioridades impostergables.

Uno de los aspectos más importantes de la política fiscal es la gestión del déficit presupuestario, es decir, el exceso de su gasto con respecto a su ingreso. Un déficit puede financiarse con recursos internos (ahorro privado y ahorro público), recursos externos (préstamos del exterior), emisión de moneda o una combinación de los tres métodos. Una presión demasiado grande sobre cualquiera de estas fuentes de financiamiento puede crear desequilibrios macroeconómicos. En Cuba, el excesivo recurso a la

creación de dinero estimuló una mayor inflación reflejada en un alto crecimiento de la liquidez acumulada. Con la despenalización de la tenencia de divisas en el verano de 1993 se legalizó un proceso de sustitución de monedas que venia ocurriendo desde hace algun tiempo.

En conclusión, la dolarización de la economía cubana ha sido una de las manifestaciones de los desequilibrios macroeconómicos que se reflejan en los déficits fiscales crónicos. La experiencia de América Latina indica que la política de desalentar la sustitución de monedas con medidas artificiales como la conversión forzosa a moneda nacional de los activos en divisas (desdolarización) ha tenido a menudo efectos contrarios a los que las autoridades pretendían y con frecuencia estos han sido contraproducentes.[19] En Cuba, la desdolarización forzosa empujaría la economía dolarizada, que es una gran proporción del sector informal, a la clandestinidad (mercado negro) y ciertamente contribuiría meramente a una inflación más alta y volátil. En otras palabras, es posible que atacando los síntomas de la enfermedad en vez de sus causas se empeore la situación. Por lo tanto, la política a seguir sería la de abordar los desequilibrios macroecómicos básicos atacando la causa de la inflación (el déficit fiscal) en vez de los síntomas (la sustitución de monedas).

BIBLIOGRAFÍA

Alpizar, Osvaldo. "La liquidez monetaria en la economía cubana: reseña estadística." Boletín de Informacion sobre Economía Cubana No. 4 (abril 1992): 19-23.

Asamblea Nacional del Poder Popular. Acuerdo IV-24 con propuestas de las medidas para el

saneamiento de las finanzas. Gaceta Oficial No. 8 (2 mayo 1994).

_____. Ley No. 73 del Sistema Tributario. Gaceta Oficial. No. 8 (5 agosto 1994).

Banco Mundial. Informe sobre el Desarrollo Mundial 1988. Washington, 1988.

---

19. Véase a Ratna Sahay y Carlos A. Végh (1995, pp. 34-37).

Calvo, Guillermo y Végh, Carlos A. "Sustitución de monedas en países con inflación alta." *Finanzas y Desarrollo* 30 (Marzo 1993): 34-37.

Cardoso, Eliana y Helwege, Ann. *Cuba after communism.* Cambridge, Mass.: The MIT Press, 1992.

Carranza Valdés, Julio. "Los Cambios económicos en Cuba: problemas y desafíos." *Cuadernos de Nuestra América* XI, 22 (julio-diciembre de 1994): 26-40.

Comisión Económica para América Latina y el Caribe. *Estudio Económico de América Latina y el Caribe,* 1987-1992. Santiago de Chile: Naciones Unidas, 1988-1993.

_____. Cuba: *Evolución económica durante 1993.* LC/MEX/R.477 (7 de junio de 1994).

_____. "Balance preliminar de la economía de América Latina y el Caribe 1994." *Notas sobre la economía y el desarrollo* N° 556/557 (diciembre de 1994).

García Lorenzo, Tania. "El mercado informal de divisas en Cuba." *Economía Cubana / Boletín Informativo* No.19 (enero-febrero de 1995): 21-27.

Hoffmann, Bert. ed. *Cuba: apertura y reforma económica.* Perfil de un debate. Caracas: Editorial Nueva Sociedad, 1995.

Kopits, George y Offerdal Erik. "La política fiscal en economías en transición: problema difícil e importante." *Finanzas y Desarrollo* 31 (Diciembre 1994): 10-13.

Mesa-Lago, Carmelo. "Cuba: un caso único de reforma antimercado. Retrospectiva y perspectiva." *Pensamiento Iberoamericano* 22/23, tomo II (1992/93): 65-100.

_____. Carmelo. *Breve historia económica de la Cuba socialista. Políticas, resultados y perspectivas.* Madrid: Alianza Editorial, 1994.

Pérez, Lorenzo L. "The implications of currency substitution experiences in Latin America and in Eastern Europe for Cuba." En *Cuba in Transition,* Volume 4. Washington, 1994.

Sahay, Ratna y Végh, Carlos A. "La dolarización en las economías en transición." *Finanzas y Desarrollo* 32 (Marzo de 1995): 34-37.

Solchaga, Carlos. "Invertir en Cuba (I)." *Actualidad Económica* (1 de mayo de 1995): 112-113.

Tanzi, Vito y Blejer, Mario I. "Los déficit fiscales y el desequilibrio de la balanza de pagos en los programas de ajuste del FMI." En *Ajuste, condicionalidad y financiamiento internacional,* comp. Joaquín Muns, 128-48. Washington, D.C.: Fondo Monetario Internacional, 1983.

THE "NEW" CUBAN ECONOMIC MODEL
(OR SOCIALISM WITH CUBAN CHARACTERISTICS)[1]

Rolando H. Castañeda and George Plinio Montalván[2]

"The 'two-track' approach ('governing the market'), as for instance pursued in China, seems to be more effective policy than moving directly from one extreme (central planning) to the other (a capitalist market economy)."

"In more general terms it looks as if the present transition—the one leap "big bang" transition—is too abrupt and too extreme. Eastern Europe should look East rather than West, i.e., should study the East Asian model rather than the OECD model of the 1980's."

"It is difficult, if not impossible, to reach the two objectives of political democracy and economic efficiency simultaneously. If the two can only be reached in sequence, then it would seem that economic restructuring, development and efficiency should come first."

— Louis Emmerij, *Eastern Europe in a Development Perspective*, 1995, pp. 31-32.

INTRODUCTION

Cuba has passed the first half of the 1990's with a wave of economic and political change, social tension, disillusionment and threatening conflicts. It faces a convergence of moral, social, economic and political crises that derive mainly from the failure of its economic and political systems and also as a result of external pressures: the tightening of the U.S. embargo and the end of the annual US$500 per capita Soviet subsidies. The existing socioeconomic system and, above all, the values on which it is based have lost the support and confidence of most Cubans, especially the young. [3] While, this period is about the terrifying collapse of the existing order, it also presents yet undefined and not fully understood opportunities that can lead Cuba to a new, more dynamic, progressive, participatory and democratic order, both economically and politically. Cuba has *much* to gain

---

1. It is beyond the scope of this paper to analyze political reform in Cuba or whether political reforms should precede or follow economic reforms. As we have indicated elsewhere, we believe that a path of negotiated, gradual and simultaneous political and economic reforms is best for Cuba. A political and economic path of systemic and comprehensive reforms cannot be accomplished quickly, but instead as a result of a gradual process, because of the lack of democratic and market institutions and because the development of these institutions takes years. Cuba urgently needs a strong accord for a steady, peaceful and integral transformation from a dictatorial command organizational structure to a democratic market-oriented society.

2. The views expressed herein are those of the authors and in no way represent the official views of the Inter-American Development Bank. The authors thank Mr. Jorge Pérez-López for his comments and suggestions.

3. An alternative view is held by Tad Szulc: "Castro's pilgrimage marks the successful completion of the latest phase in the history of the revolution he had launched in Cuba on Jan. 1, 1959, when his guerrillas defeated the forces of Fulgencio Batista, the old-style dictator. It was the phase in which Cuba made the painful and perilous transition from the nearly total dependence on the Soviet Union, which ended with the Soviet collapse, to today's relative self-reliance—at low living standards—and the beginning of efforts to attract foreign support for the strange Chinese-style 'socialist market economy' that Castro is striving to introduce." (*Washington Post*, October 22, 1995, p. C4).

from the emerging system, and *much* to lose if it fails to act decisively to put it in place.

Young Cubans, discontent with the present and worried about the future, feel that they are the last generation of an old system and the first generation of a new one. At the end of 1995, traditional communists are seen as remote, uninspiring, "conservative rightists," a reactionary group led by tired elderly men imbued with a failed and irrelevant nineteenth-century theology, and who have already seen their best days. Reformers are viewed as radicals, "leftists" trying to provide for a brighter future. In the recent past, especially in 1968 and in 1986, the politically powerful state sector had marginalized or wiped out small entrepreneurs in agriculture, services and handicrafts, and own-account workers. It is clear that poor domestic policies (misallocation of resources, inefficient investment, discrimination against exports) rather than external pressures have been the main cause of present failures. These failures have ignited a process of deep soul-searching among Cuban intellectuals.

There is a widening gap between dynamic change taking place in the world, generalized modernization, globalization of the economy with increasing competition—e.g., the creation of free trade areas such as the NAFTA and the liberalization of trade of the WTO—and the slow change of the present Cuban politics and government. While there are extensive changes in the world and more intensive, deep and complex links among countries, in Cuba there is an ineffective status-quo, immobilized by the application inappropriate economic principles and obsolete institutions and policies. The Cuban Communist Party's selfishness and self-centeredness organize rear-guard actions against market mechanisms and true decentralization and empowerment of citizens, about which it knows less and less. It still considers itself entitled to a monopoly on solving problems and

helping Cuba make structural reforms, although cosmetically, timidly and slowly, instead of the required major substantive and systemic transformations and modernization truly based and centered on the people *that are inevitable.*

Cuba's level of national income is unusually low for the level of education and health of its people. [4] Cuban policymakers should begin to look strategically thirty years ahead, about the kind of nation they would like Cuba to be and the path the nation should take during the first quarter century of the new millennium to use its full potential, even if it is engaged in very difficult immediate tactical problems.[5] Cuba's failure to think about the long run also risks missteps and tragedy. The new economic model should avoid preserving a generally unworkable present as well as restoring an outmoded and remote past. The new system should be based on new and fresh ideas, values, institutions and structures that yield economic results based on individual responsibility and flexibility. This is very important because the swift pace of events and high-speed economic and political change in the region (a generalized free trade area for the Western Hemisphere by the year 2005) and in the world at large (e.g., the newly created WTO) and its acceleration will affect all countries, including Cuba.

It is the prospect that Cubans could be drawn into a reform process by default rather than design in this period of epochal change and sharp challenges that has stirred renewed interest on the part of the Cuban leadership and intelligentsia ("official" NGOs) in devising a strategy for the transition. Indeed the time has come for a more comprehensive reform and transformation. Not everything in the past was mistaken and not all in the present is hopeless. The jeopardy argument of reforms simply cannot be applied to a country where it is impossible to endanger previ-

---

4. Although it ranks very high in most social indicators, Cuba's per capita GDP was so undeniably low by 1990 that its "Human Development Index" was 12th in Latin America and the Caribbean. See United Nations Human Development Programme, *Human Development Report 1993* (New York: Oxford University Press, 1993), Table 1, p. 135-137. In 1995 its ranking is far lower due to the plummeting GDP.

5. For example, Malaysia started its vision for the year 2020 in 1993, establishing guidelines to reach Switzerland's standard of living by that year. It is time for Cuba to look forward to define its vision of the future, and define the strategy for getting there.

ous and recent progress as such progress was not based on solid grounds. The task for our generation is to ensure that the Cuban economy works; today it does not.

After five years of major economic decline and implosion, facing the brink of financial insolvency and international trade barriers, burdened by administrative inefficiencies and excessive defense spending, the Cuban authorities started some stabilization and structural reform measures, if only in a narrow field and without a clear framework or general success. In our view, the government squeezed the economy when it was contracting. The overall economic prospects remain grim. We consider the recent reforms irreversible, a historic watershed from which retreat is all but impossible. Others consider them only a mirage and a dangerous one. More open markets and foreign investment have barely reached the bottom dwellers, by some measures as destitute as ever. Still no transformation so recent can be called sustainable, particularly with Castro long accustomed to broad swings and abrupt economic-policy reversals as the ones in 1968, 1975, 1986 and 1993. Thus there is potential yet again for bitter disappointment. Uncertainties surrounding the transition to a new generation of leaders to succeed Castro also affect decisions. His likely successors are reluctant to assert themselves while he is still alive.

Cuba is at a crossroads. The wrong turn may indeed have a serious impact on its social and political make-up. The legitimacy of the system is increasingly questioned as the government continues to postpone measures and reforms to satisfy the needs of the large masses of its citizens who are deprived of productive employment and find difficult to cover their most basic needs. Unevenness in sharing the benefits of the recent incipient recovery, high unemployment, abolition of workers' basic rights, scant housing, and deteriorating education, health and sanitation are lead-ing to a stressful social situation. It is likely that many countries will rightly resist allowing Cuba to enter the regional integration agreements without further political and market-based economic reform.

In this paper we analyze the recent proposal for the restructuring of the Cuban economy advanced by Cuban economists Carranza, Gutiérrez and Monreal's (CGM) [Carranza, Gutiérrez and Monreal, 1995]. This proposal has been greeted with a mixture of uneasiness and misgivings because it is a marked metamorphosis of their previous position, it is still characterized by some unyielding features, and because the authors do not apparently share our convictions in a market economy, unlimited civil liberties, pluralistic political system, open government and limitation of police powers. [6] Although we have some important, and often deep, differences of opinion with them, they have advanced the most significant departure from the Stalinist model of society from within Cuba, as well as the most complete and ambitious attempt inside Cuba from quasi official sources to analyze current government failures and present the first coherent proposal for transition to a more market-oriented economy. They are willing to admit with candor policy errors and the infeasibility of the current system. They vigorously address some structural problems in the economy and the need to dismantle the pervasive disincentives and distortions of extreme statism, though at times in fumbling fashion. They rightly assert that without real economic growth, there is nothing Cuba can do to improve the well-being of its people. They have raised the toughest questions about the design of the current policies and institutions and present a convincing case for substantial and comprehensive market-based reforms that could bring at least some of the changes the Cuban people want. The CGM proposal entails Cuba continuing to open the economy internally and to

---

6.   We envision a political system for Cuba based on the free competition of ideas, freedom of speech, freedom of the press, freedom of assembly and freedom of association. The role of the state must be reduced, with the government authorities subject to control by the law, a legislature and mass media. These freedoms and regulations contain in themselves the abolition of the one-party system, freedom for alternative parties to organize and free elections for the legislative and executive branches of government. In general we consider that the state should not decide for the individual.

the outside world in line with requirements for entry to such arrangements as NAFTA and the WTO.

The CGM proposal represents a very significant step towards a more market-oriented, people-based and open economy but it is still far from the Chinese and Vietnamese model or the Asian market socialism model (AMSM) that Castro promised to follow in his "prepared" speech of July 26, 1995 and after his visit to China and Vietnam in December 1995. After analyzing and submitting the proposed "new" model and framework for change and reform to rigorous and skeptical questioning, we offer some counterproposals to kick off the intellectual debate called for CGM that must occur, i.e., we hope that the CGM proposal is the beginning of the reform debate rather than the end of it. A new strategy is needed to return Cuba to a path of modernization and sustained, long-term economic and social development. Once the CGM model and framework is fully understood, it is evident that additional and deeper steps are needed to handle some of their omissions and commissions. A much more systematic and complete approach is required to make the imperative and decisive breakthrough to shape the future that lies ahead, to direct it, rather than to let the Cuban nation be victimized by it. Both Cuban academicians and émigrés can best serve the Cuban cause by discarding the narrow and parochial bounds of ideology. Our goal in this paper is not to settle the issues, but rather to raise some unconventional thoughts.

In the second section we present the main elements and characteristics, as well as some important omissions, of the CGM proposal or "new" Cuban economic model and will analyze the principal differences and similarities between the AMSM and the new Cuban model, both for the main microeconomic reforms, institutions and strategies and for the macroeconomic policies, institutions and strategies. In the third section the likely outcomes in relation to growth and equity from the application of the new Cuban model are diagnosed. The next section includes five recommendations for a more effective model for self-sustaining and lasting growth with social equity and effective participation. In the fifth section the main conclusions are summarized and

some final reflections are presented. The main features of the AMSM are analyzed in Appendix I, showing that it is feasible to introduce markets in a centrally-planned Stalinist economy in a gradual way.

THE "NEW" CUBAN ECONOMIC MODEL AND THE AMSM: SIMILARITIES AND DIFFERENCES

"The disasters that have happened in the countries of the Soviet Union ... compared to the impressive successes of China and Vietnam, clearly indicate what can and what cannot be done if one wants to save the revolution and socialism."

— Fidel Castro, July 26, 1995 as quoted by the *Financial Times*, November 27, 1995, p. 4.

"The real difficulty in changing the course of any enterprise lies not in developing new ideas but in escaping from old ones."

— John Maynard Keynes

Principal Elements and Characteristics of the CGM Proposal

The "new" Cuban economic model has two main purposes, now that the Cold War has ended and Cuban socialism has arrived at a stage when it is unable to survive in its non-market fashion. One is to revive the Cuban economy from the deepest depression in its history. The other is to formulate a cautious medium-cum-long-term economic reform program to modify the socialist nature of the economy, reflecting the inclinations of the Cuban leadership for political continuity and social control. Until now, the authorities have been extremely vague about basic economic objectives and policies. The propelling factors for change lie in the generalized pessimism about the economy, the current stagnation trap, the fundamental strains in Cuban society and the demonstration effect of reform in market socialist economies in Asia.

The CGM proposal for restructuring the Cuban economy involves three stages:

- Stage I, reestablishment of financial equilibria and search for efficiency, has two phases: improvement of internal finances (Phase A) and initiation of economic restructuring and hard budget constraint (Phase B).

- Stage II, transition to a regulated market (decentralized marketization of state enterprises (SEs)) and

- Stage III, decentralization of the economy. The last two stages place more emphasis on structural reforms.

The CGM proposal covers two microeconomic areas:

1. Reform of SEs and

2. Redefinition and establishment of other forms of property and economic organizations.

It also covers seven macroeconomic areas:

1. social security,

2. price and wage policies,

3. budget,

4. public investment,

5. exchange rate policies,

6. foreign trade and

banking, monetary and credit policies (see Table 1).[7] As we shall see further on, in many ways the CGM proposal is long on laying out principles and short on specific policies.

The CGM proposal shows some flexibility, albeit insufficient, and skips the nuances and subtleties of some complex issues in setting market-based policies and reforms to modify many earlier positions. Hence, it stifles efficiency and growth potentials and, if followed, will prove incapable of meeting effectively the nation's need for self-sustaining, long-term growth and equity. While in most cases the proposed reforms are steps in the right direction, they neither go far nor deep enough, especially in the microeconomic and institutional areas. They also have some unintended, though predictable, consequences and perils. If the market-based reforms are not well-designed, they will not be able to create sufficient supply expansion and could create a reaction against further reforms. Additionally, some of Cuba's longstanding obstacles to reassuming self-sustaining growth remain unaddressed. These include, inter-alia, the excessive reliance on foreign capital to propel growth; the lack of implementation of market reforms necessary to dismantle the maze of regulations and distortions accumulated during of 35-plus years of heavy statism, make the Cuban economy run more efficiently and provide it with more resilience to compete in international markets; and its omission of the fact that the physical infrastructure and the environment have deteriorated significantly while sugar has become obsolete from a technical point of view, is undercapitalized, and its comparative advantage has eroded. Notwithstanding all this, the CGM proposal could contribute to the improvement of the Cuban economy in the near future.

The proposed reforms are not temporary capitalist measures or concessions, but are presented as a true initiation of systemic transformations. CGM realize that change is inevitable and their prescriptions define the scope and the terms of some market-based reforms. However, the CGM proposal is far less fundamental than the AMSM. It has some of the institutional weaknesses of the AMSM but not some of the latter's dominant microeconomic strengths. CGM should look closer at the AMSM to gain insights. The static analysis in the CGM proposal about the role of a hyperactive state is wrong in economic terms. It fosters dependency on bureaucratic direction and inflexibility rather than on cooperation and opportunity with impersonal market forces. We see it as a serious failure of strategy. Even in a socialist market economy, the role of the state is more focused than in the CGM proposal, and the structure of incentives for the private sector is more appealing.

If Cuba is beginning the transition from a system of central planning towards one with a greater use of markets, market signals and associated incentives, it

---

7. We have changed the order of the macroeconomic topics in the CGM for organizational purposes.

Table 1. The Carranza-Gutiérrez-Monreal (CGM) Proposal for Restructuring the Cuban Economy[a]

	STAGE I:Reestablishment of financial equilibria and search for efficiency.		STAGE II: Transition to a regulated market (decentralized marketization for SEs).	STAGE III: Decentralization of the economy.
	Phase A: Improvement of internal finances (stabilization, 1 month).	Phase B: Initiation of economic restructuring and hard budget constraint (1 year).		
Special concerns and features	Monetary reform. Problem of financial liberalization prior to monetary reform.	Need to create dynamic of growth. Increase efficiency of state enterprises (SEs). Increase agricultural production.	Priority to administration of SEs and to budget control.	Emphasis on the diversification of property forms, not their appropriate composition.
Microeconomic Reforms				
1. Reform of public sector enterprises.		Economic incentives for SEs to improve their performance. Wage bonuses related to cost reductions and increases in production, both in quantity and in quality. More strict labor discipline. Eliminate unnecessary workers. Cooperativization of assets and SEs or privatization through sales, leases and administrative contracts.	Allow retention of profits for investments and decentralization of their accountability to local levels. Strengthening of hard budget.	Government directives concentrated in SEs. SEs will normally finance their expansion with own profits.
2. Redefinition and establishment of other forms of property and economic organizations.		True decentralization of UBPC. Small private enterprises and cooperatives, including privatization of existing assets and enterprises. Establishment of production quotas. Allow small private firms to provide services to SEs. Allow hiring of workers by private enterprises and own-account workers. Flexibilization of own-account workers, intermediaries, including professionals. Bankruptcy law for private enterprises and cooperatives.	Strengthening of private services, including professional services. Bankruptcy law for SEs.	Some sectors and activities are restricted to SEs. Partial privatization of some SEs through sale of stocks.

a. Based on: Julio Carranza Valdés, Luis Gutiérrez Urdaneta and Pedro Monreal González, Cuba: *La restructuración de la economía,* (La Habana; Centro de Estudios sobre América), unpublished draft, January 1995.

Table 1. **The Carranza-Gutiérrez-Monreal (CGM) Proposal for Restructuring the Cuban Economy[a] (Continued)**

	STAGE I:Reestablishment of financial equilibria and search for efficiency.		STAGE II: Transition to a regulated market (decentralized marketization for SEs).	STAGE III: Decentralization of the economy.
	Phase A: Improvement of internal finances (stabilization, 1 month).	Phase B: Initiation of economic restructuring and hard budget constraint (1 year).		
Macroeconomic Reforms				
3. Price and wage policies.	Keep ration system for necessities but with higher prices; allow parallel markets and some free markets for non essential goods.	Establish more rational prices both for outputs and inputs. Price ceiling for agriculture goods. Wage differentials and bonuses.	Gradual expansion of price liberalization. Decentralization of wage determination.	Elimination of rationing. Market-determined prices but with price ceilings.
4. Social security.	Direct income transfers to the poor and vulnerable to compensate for the retail price increase.	Labor training. Work for the unemployed in community activities. External sale of services. Promotion of assembly plants for exports.	Adjust direct income transfers to the poor and vulnerable.	Minimum wages established and adjusted.
5. Budget.	Increase retail prices to eliminate the fiscal deficit.	State restructuring. Income tax and social security payments on UBPC, cooperatives, private farms, own-account-workers and land tax on UBPC. Hard budget and elimination of subsidies for SEs. Indirect taxes on luxury items and remittances.	Emphasis on tax administration. VAT. Decentralization to local governments.	
6. Public investment.		Investments in infrastructure for exports and export activities.		
7. Exchange rate policies.	Limited convertibility; free convertibility for foreign firms and trade-oriented SEs. Dual exchange rate with preferential rate for tourism and remittances.	Limited convertibility. Dual and competitive rate adjusted periodically. Use of tariffs instead of other restrictions to control imports. Orderly opening.	Mini-devaluations or crawling peg. Partial convertibility. Some exchange controls to avoid capital flights.	Unification. Full convertibility in the current account except for a few transactions.

Table 1. The Carranza-Gutiérrez-Monreal (CGM) Proposal for Restructuring the Cuban Economy[a] (Continued)

	STAGE I:Reestablishment of financial equilibria and search for efficiency.		STAGE II: Transition to a regulated market (decentralized marketization for SEs).	STAGE III: Decentralization of the economy.
	Phase A: Improvement of internal finances (stabilization, 1 month).	Phase B: Initiation of economic restructuring and hard budget constraint (1 year).		
8. Foreign trade.		Demonopolization of foreign trade. Debt swaps. Trade accords. Orderly and gradual opening. Use of tariffs instead of other restrictions to control imports.	Gradual reduction of tariffs.	Selective protection through fiscal, monetary and trade instruments.
9. Banking; monetary and credit policies.	Monetary reform to eliminate the monetary overhang. De-dollarization and limitations on dollar circulation.	Separation of Central, commercial and developing banking. Interest rate for loans to the private sector. Individual savings accounts in dollars.	Differential interest rates.	Use of selective credit. Institutionalization of "public" capital markets.

can consider seriously the experience of other countries, such as China and Vietnam. Further, Cuba can skip steps and avoid the mistakes or detours of those two trailblazers. The AMSM has shown that the transition from central planning to the market can best be accomplished by establishing an efficient incentives regime and then relying on the decentralized decision-making of households and firms based on market prices. The economy will develop more successfully if the incentives structure for domestic producers is brought more in line with that for foreign investment. In addition, the authorities should play a major role in establishing the legal, regulatory, and policy environment conductive to growth of a free and competitive market.

The CGM proposal is much more growth, outward-looking and future oriented in its basic objectives than in its means. Cuba's tradable sector, based on an outward-looking strategy in which non-sugar expansion will be the engine of economic growth and development, is central to the restoration of growth. This outward orientation is a necessity arising from the smallness of the domestic market and limited natural resources. It also requires a production system able to follow the international rhythm of technical progress, a more liberal trade regime likely to impose discipline on the domestic producers, and a reorientation toward a structure of production in line with the country's comparative advantages, in order to compete internationally. Gradual, but continuous and decisive, opening of the economy to foreign trade and competition is an intrinsic component of a robust transition to a market economy and its integration into the world economy. Consequently, a more determined trade policy and reform instruments to achieve than the one proposed are necessary to reap the benefits of specialization and modernization and to maximize efficiency and factor productivity.

Microeconomic aspects of the CGM Proposal
While the CGM proposal improves the incentives regime for state enterprises (SEs), private enterprises (PEs) and own-account work, the microeconomic part of the proposal barely makes a dent in the dominant role of the state in the Cuban economy. There remains a disturbing tendency on the part of the authorities in trying to micromanage, perform lots of tasks and make decisions. No solutions are proposed

to address the need for transparency in this critical area. CGM have neither fully accepted the principle of decentralized decision-making by households and firms nor that competition is an essential market force. The proposed microeconomic reforms need significant rethinking. This is the time to change the proportions among what is permitted, what is restricted and what is banned for the private sector to do in order to develop and implement a strategic approach that is focused largely on domestic efforts to raise savings and factor productivity.

The CGM proposal is not likely to provide entrepreneurs enough space and confidence to invest in real production and jobs, essential elements for economic recovery and prosperity. Cuba will grow if it can establish a clear and efficient division of labor between the public and private sectors, as well as competition between them to improve the public sector. The public sector in the CGM proposal will still crowd the private sector out of a range of activities that the latter could well undertake and do much more efficiently than the state. The authorities need to define state activities more sharply and to give greater scope and size to the private sector as China, Vietnam and Laos PDR have done successfully. CGM define a vision that cannot transcend a false choice of what the government should do for the people instead of what people must do for themselves and for the country. Here our differences with CGM are not about gradualism in the implementation of the proposed measures as they suggest, but about intensity and comprehensiveness of the measures.

The CGM proposal also needs to include more market reforms to improve the incentives structure for saving, investment and production by households and firms through reforms of the investment and trade regimes, the financial system and the legal infrastructure. CGM calls for gaining some advantages from the market without actually relinquishing centralized control.[8] Cuba has to rebuild its institutions to the decentralized realities of cyberspace and the

Information Age to promote individual initiative, entrepreneurship and opportunity. However, massive regulations generally result in a lethargic public sector, a private sector motivated by rent-seeking, corruption, and efforts to gain monopolies from government favors, income inequality and a growing underground economy. Cuba has to move from a culture of redundant economic controls and scrutiny to a culture of economic results.

Great emphasis is placed by CGM on improving the performance of SEs, eliminating poorly-performing SEs and disguised employment, and prescribing the renovation for the operational conditions of capable firms. These steps are insufficient to generate the supply response needed in the Cuban economy. The hard budget constraint, hard loans and proper taxation of SEs should improve the macroeconomic conditions but will not solve the supply problems of the Cuban economy. Even by granting SEs more autonomy, and by enforcing hard budgets, hard loans and bankruptcy, they will continue to waste resources because of political intervention, the absence of discipline, inefficient management, and the absence of clear property rights. Those who really want an enhanced role for the market, must allow more room for formal private activities, increasingly free entry and exit, individual entrepreneurship, private property and competition. Only a radical extension of the private sector creates favorable conditions for the expansion of production.

In the CGM proposal, the agricultural cooperatives —that did not work well elsewhere, especially in socialist countries—are the proposed predominant form of organization for agriculture and other economic activities. There is only limited decentralization without private ownership. This basic idea seems emotionally-inspired rather than rationally-determined. The Yugoslav cooperative experience constituted an attempt—albeit a highly imperfect one— to move socialism away from the exclusive reliance on the state and the bureaucracy and on the private

---

8. "The market shall be subordinated to the plan in order 'to force' development and to guarantee the primacy of the state sector and the political power in the hands of the people" (CMG, 1995).

sector, private property and the market.[9] This proposal is unrealistic and unworkable, hence failure is inevitable because it maintains a highly restrictive organization unlikely to produce tangible dividends, has little support outside the Cuban intelligentsia and lacks a positive experience as its foundation.

One of the strengths of the CGM proposal is that it refers for the first time in socialist Cuba to the need for a comprehensive legal framework for the economic system in general and for the restructuring or liquidation of insolvent SEs and PEs in particular. Policy changes to reverse the command system without an appropriate legal framework may be sufficient to initiate the transition, but are not enough for long-term development. However, still missing are fair and credible laws for real property, intellectual property, domestic investment, contracts and dispute resolution so that the incentives regime will work properly within the legal framework of a market economy. Also, a labor code for a market economy is needed to include, inter-alia, protection of employer and *employee* rights and obligations, microregulation of labor contracts, social insurance, the right to strike and a labor arbitration mechanism truly independent from the government. The strong distortions created by the government intermediary by hiring workers for foreign enterprises at salaries charged in dollars but paid in pesos should be eliminated. They reduce the degree of international competitiveness of the Cuban labor force and tend to stymie employment-creation.

Considerations regarding transparency and accountability in decision-making and in conducting the affairs of state—which are marked weaknesses of the AMSM—are starkly absent in the CGM proposal. The principles of good government, respect for human rights, accountability and the role of law, have value in their own right as well as relevance to the process of economic development.

It is easy to dismiss some of the microeconomic commissions and omissions of the CGM proposal as routine rhetoric, short on specifics and long on discourse. Of course there is a political rationale for them. CGM are faced with dramatic policy dichotomies and conflicting objectives of transformation needs that might undermine the interests of the Communist party hierarchy and its constituency.[10] However, problems exist on two levels. The first is in the microeconomic reform debate itself. The CGM proposal's deceptive, but crisp and contentious, rhetoric might frustrate the imperative reforms, when they ought to be within reach, by hardening positions. The larger danger of their situational microeconomic proposals, is that they tend to vindicate public cynicism of economic leadership. The CGM proposal's rationale or basis is that people do not notice untruths. But, of course, they ultimately do, and in the long run, this makes effective government harder.

Macroeconomic aspects of the CGM Proposal

It is obvious that stabilization cannot continue forever. It cannot be justified for as long a period as 1990-1995, neither on account of the need to ensure price stability, nor to create the conditions to restructure the economy. The timetable is already overstretched. The required stabilization should be accomplished, once and for all, and in the shortest possible time. A longer timetable only makes the long-term effort more difficult. One month, as suggested by CGM for eliminating the imbalances both in the flow (slashing the budget deficit and bringing it under control) and in the stock (eliminating the monetary overhang) makes sense. We also agree with their emphasis on the need for a monetary reform. There is an excessive monetary overhang as the result of several years of fiscal deficits that has to be addressed either through monetary reform or by an increase in the general price level, or both.

---

9. Kornai (1995) considers that however noble the motives behind this model, it lacks coherence, due to the obvious absence of separate representation for capital.

10. For many communists, a prosperous Cuba is not and never has been the real goal. What they care about far more is staying in power and keeping political and social control. The recovery of the economy is only a means to this end.

However, it should be noted that since the fiscal deficit in 1994-1995 was eliminated via a price increase, the case for another increase of prices at the retail level for fiscal reasons is weak because it could be deflationary in an already very depressed economy. Excessive macroeconomic tightness could suffocate the supply response to the liberalizing microeconomic reforms. Macroeconomic stability is easier to achieve when growth is vigorous.

The basic concept underlying the proposed tax reform in the CGM proposal is to place the tax burden on income; however, more emphasis should be placed on indirect taxes to spur entrepreneurial activity. The backbone of the system should be an across-the-board value-added tax. On the expenditures side, the CGM proposal includes important but insufficient propositions to rationalize social expenditures, such as one to supplement incomes by direct transfers to the poor, instead of maintaining blanket subsidies through low prices for some essential goods. In general redistribution by taxes and transfers is more efficient than by direct interference in markets. Absent in the CGM proposal are reforms such as rationalizing social expenditures by eliminating unnecessary administrative and bureaucratic expenditures, as well as concentrating social expenditures on the poor and avoiding universal coverage for some services. Also, the government should use cost-benefit analysis to select public investments, establish public bidding for public procurement, and use NGO's to provide social services to the poor. Choice, competition and market incentives should be gradually introduced to the public sector through innovations such as public school choice, social services vouchers, and partial payment for some health expenditures. The Chinese and Vietnamese have privatized, at least partially, university education and health services. Many doctors and nurses practice privately in those countries.

We agree with CGM that the most important objectives of exchange rate policy must be to avoid significant overvaluation of the currency and make it predictable. The actual overvaluation of the exchange rate is preposterous and determines a severe anti-export bias that discourages both the growth and diversification of exports and creates an over-dependence on foreign capital. A real exchange rate with a competitive, stable value is a very important stimulant to export-led growth by providing a favorable environment for investment and marketing decisions. The recommended crawling peg, or depreciating the exchange rate at a pace that maintains external competitiveness—through small changes at frequent intervals mainly to compensate for differences in the rates of inflation—could be very important, with periodic adjustments to reflect internal and external factors. Likewise, if the tariffs are reduced step-by-step according to a clear and pre-announced schedule, all enterprises, both SEs and PEs, will have strong incentives to impose efficiency and adjust to increasing foreign competition.

The CGM proposal considers that if U.S. the embargo is lifted the conditions for the external sector will improve. We agree with this proposition, but the lifting of the embargo is neither a necessary nor sufficient condition for the self-sustaining improvement of the external sector. Many of the difficult structural obstacles that have inhibited growth must be addressed. Expectations will improve but "objective" economic conditions also have to improve. The incompetent management and inappropriate economic policies followed over the years, because they have not been rapidly corrected, as well as the current system and economic organization, have undoubtedly played a significant role and have been a fundamental cause of the vulnerability of the external sector, not their consequence. Cuba must improve internal organization and resource allocation if it is to overcome its external fragility and fully recover. In this sense change has to come mainly and mostly from within Cuba.

The CGM proposal placed a lot of emphasis on foreign direct investment through joint ventures. However, foreign private investors expect to earn a competitive rate of return, adjusted for risk, within an environment that provides international standards of investor protection and business services, which are usually taken for granted by foreign enterprises and are not available in Cuba. If that infrastructure is incomplete or missing, foreign investors will go elsewhere unless the opportunities for rent-seeking and establishing dominant market shares are considered to be sufficient to offset the increased risk of investment. The joint ventures already in place, mainly involving small capital flows, suggest that foreign investors are keeping a foot in the door for just such a development. Foreign direct investment is a lagging, not leading, variable in the transition process.

The CGM proposal does not pay attention to external debt management nor to the normalization of relations with the international community that could make Cuba once again an appealing place for real and financial investment. Cuba's foreign debt and U.S. compensation claims on confiscations of property tend to discourage foreign private investment. Negotiation and settlement of foreign claims and debt renegotiation (debt write-down, debt restructuring, debt service reduction, and a temporary moratorium) are needed to improve the credibility of the stabilization program with private investors and contribute to exchange rate, interest rate, and fiscal adjustments by diminishing the uncertainties about future policies and to smooth the path to market-oriented reform. The remittances from émigrés could also trigger a robust expansion pulled by externally-financed consumption.

There is still a need for an overall strategy to establish a reliable private financial system; otherwise the chances of achieving sustainability are virtually nil. The financial system's tasks during the transition are to raise and efficiently allocate resources, make payments, help finance the emerging private sector, help place a hard budget constraint on SEs, and perform corporate functions, both in public and private sectors. If the financial policy is correct, monetization will occur and monetary policy must accommodate a sustained increase in monetary demand. Policies should develop a genuine two-tier banking system, increase its integrity and make it accessible to non-traditional savers. The emphasis of the CGM proposal is on a public capital market that is unlikely to work; neither are the references to a positive real interest rate to private domestic savings, and the ability to attract financial capital movements.

CGM also recommend an industrial policy, but the emphasis appears to be only on SEs rather than on a selective export push for the private sector based on the acquisition, adoption and mastery of "best practice" international technologies and production organization methods.

LIKELY OUTCOMES OF THE CGM PROPOSAL ON GROWTH AND EQUITY

The main weakness of the CGM proposal, in contrast to the AMSM, is that it does not pay sufficient attention to the vitality and dynamism of some basic microeconomic policies that are essential to expand the aggregate supply and to generate a high and self-sustaining rate of growth. These include the proper liberalization and deregulation of private economic activities, the strengthening of incentives that link material reward to economic performance for individuals and enterprises, and the stimulation of private initiative and competition. One point that needs stress is that the proposed microeconomic reforms will generate a sluggish adjustment on the supply side given the starting conditions of the economy and the vast and comprehensive structural changes that are necessary. The proposed macroeconomic policies for stimulating savings are also limited.

One of the major strengths of the CGM proposal is that the authors attempt to reestablish macroeconomic equilibrium and provide a credible macroeconomic framework and instruments to manage aggregate demand and structural adjustment in desirable directions, through proper, though limited, policies (fiscal, monetary and external sector policies). Also, the proposed policies will institutionalize macroeconomic instruments for prompt and effective response to external shocks. Though real, our differences in this area are of degree and need, except for the financial sector. What is feasible and desirable macroeconomically depends, nevertheless, upon achievements in the microeconomic area. Unless the low efficiency at the micro level is improved, the macro unbalance will continue. The problem is just not of balancing aggregates but turning the aggregate supply around.

The reform recommendations by CGM may well trigger some immediate output expansion and put Cuba on a higher growth path than the current status quo allows. However, it is unlikely that Cuba will be able to achieve growth and social development with the new system of incentives and institutions, because it is clear that Cuban exports are not competitive. The point is that even some recovery will only reach a level that is far below what most consider Cuba could achieve. In this sense we consider that the CGM's recommendations constitute a transformation trap—or an unnecessary long detour—for high, self-sustaining and lasting growth with equity.[11]

The CGM proposal is comprehensive in the sense that it covers some of the main policy variables but it is not complete because it lacks the consideration, both in depth and breadth, of some key microeconomic institutions and macroeconomic variables. Yet it is full of paradoxes in relation to consistency. Internally the proposal is articulated because the effects of its measures are mutually supportive, but there are inconsistencies and discrepancies between extensive objectives and confined instruments; hence likely outcomes are based on hope rather than on design. The proposed new model of reformed socialism for growth and prosperity is partially based on market-oriented policies, international trade, foreign private investment and a smaller private sector, but lacks a sense of priority because of still too comprehensive and asphyxiating state sector. The proposal lacks a true vision for the country because it effectively disregards the situation and trends imposed by today's world markets. In the final analysis, CGM have yet to recognize that the world has changed profoundly and irrevocably.

The limitations on proper incentives and required institutions and the excessive role of the public sector, both directly and through regulatory mechanisms—with excessive and tight prohibitions, often contradictory microregulations and cumbersome and redundant controls—will harass and irritate private firms. Simplifying regulations is particularly important for investment promotion, both domestic and foreign. Unless higher rates of growth are achieved, the coverage and quality of social services that Cu-

bans became accustomed to in the 1980's will not continue.[12]

Finally, we consider that the CGM proposal can be improved both on growth and equity grounds. There are severe conceptual problems with the proposal even if its initial premises were correct. That is why, in the following section, we make five recommendations to spark more robust economic growth.

RECOMMENDATIONS FOR "UNMAKING THE CUBAN QUAGMIRE"

"It takes all the running you can do to keep in the same place. If you want to go somewhere else, you must run at least twice as fast as that."

— Carroll, *Through the Looking Glass*

"In the life cycle of growth and relative decline, the experiences of different countries show somewhat different features, as one factor in growth substitutes for another. But it is the vitality and flexibility giving way to rigidity that determines the pattern."

— Kindleberger (1995, p. 36)

It is obvious that Cuban stalinist socialism based on central planning and public property is dying and state-generated development is in retreat. Economic stagnation exists alongside political fragility. There is increasing tension between the internationalism required by global economics and the radical nationalism and chimera of isolationism and autarky that the island's communist leaders believe fosters internal political cohesion.

The core of the debate between CGM and us is not about the need to rebuild the shattered Cuban economy. The notion that many aspects of the economy must be overhauled in a number of different dimensions is mutually accepted. We also agree that Cuba requires a carefully considered, systematic and clear set of transition policies. There is, however, much less consensus in relation to the role and limits of the private and public sectors in the economy and about the speed, intensity, comprehensiveness, sequencing and sectoralism with which an orderly transition

---

11. In Kornai's words "...whichever of the grave problems it tries to resolve, it may exacerbate the others" (Kornai 1995, p. 217).

12. At the time annual transfers from the Soviet Union were approximately US$500 per capita.

strategy can be implemented realistically, and about microeconomic and institutional matters.

We consider that the basic economic goals of the Cuban people are to: (1) create an expanding economy that generates high levels of income and employment opportunities for the well-educated population; (2) maintain social coverage of basic public services (education and health) and a relatively even distribution of income; (3) create a truly decentralized economic system that allows for widespread participation and initiatives of the population; (4) reinsert Cuba into the world economy; and (5) have a smaller but effective and proactive state that orients and guides the transformation and modernization processes. These basic goals can be summarized as decentralized growth with social equity guiding the transition and transformation processes. The main reforms and policy measures should be constrained by them. Therefore, we are critical of extreme recipes, from both the "left"—those that consider all other alternatives neoliberalism—and the "right" that consider all other alternatives to be statism. We find this debate as gravitational pull away from center-based economics, anguished and polarizing and not in the best interest of Cuba. Both extremes are faulty in four fundamental ways: (a) they unnecessarily induce economic stagnation; (b) they incur in large and unnecessary social costs; (c) they weaken, instead of strengthening, civil society in general, and democratic institutions and organizations in particular; and (d) they confuse means and ends about the role and limits of the state and the objectives of privatization.

Our approach consists of putting more emphasis on five elements. **First**, the entire reform package must be designed by nurturing entrepreneurship and initiative based on individual rights and freedoms, market and competitive deepening, and institutional development with a view toward smooth path of recovery and resumed high, self-sustaining and lasting growth. **Second**, social policy must be redesigned and put in place to minimize the social costs of stabilization, liberalization and deregulation. **Third**, re-

form programs should be formulated and implemented as a result of the political interplay of representative organizations within the framework of increasing initiatives and participation of all members of society. **Fourth**, Cuba must joint international financial institutions (the World Bank, IMF and IDB) in order to sustain the reform and to mobilize external resources as a precondition to effective mobilization of private foreign capital. **Fifth**, a leaner but strong state should orient the entire transformation and modernization processes.[13]

For the analysis that follows, it will be assumed that a satisfactory solution to the external debt problem—consisting not merely of postponing payments, but of a significant and permanent reduction of the debt burden—can be found. This is also a precondition for finding new strategies that could return the country to a path of high and sustained economic and social progress. In addition to being assigned a lower priority, Cuba now suffers the consequences of its debt moratoria and a very poor credit rating. It must reach agreements with commercial and official creditors on debt relief and reduction, simultaneous with, and not following the required adjustment, and should include a lower level of servicing and improved terms for interest and principal payments that must be made, compatible with adopted targets.

The dimension of the task ahead is daunting and goes well beyond the realm of economics. We strongly support reforms aimed at stabilization, considered mainly as a reduction of the fiscal crisis and the elimination of the monetary overhang with all their attendant consequences. As opposed to CGM, we place stronger emphasis on an in-depth and immediate liberalization and deregulation of the main markets, as Vietnam did in 1989, especially for new PEs, or an increased reliance on national and international markets to allocate scarce resources to increase efficiency in an economy that is stagnant, monopolistic, overregulated and overprotected. Moreover, the settling of property rights and compensation for confiscation should not become a symbol of unresolved social

---

13. See Rolando H. Castañeda and George P. Montalván, *Cuba in Transition—Vol. 3.*

conflicts, and expanding privatization should be motivated by efficiency and by the proper long-term distribution of wealth and property rather than by the need to improve the short-term financial position of the state or to restore the pre-1959 distribution of wealth.

We envision an initial acceleration of price increases after a process of price decontrol with a slow and protracted process of low inflation that may take several years; a moderate decline in output and in employment in the short run and a strong recovery in the medium term; a rapid privatization of services, retail trade and small and medium agricultural and manufacturing activities coexisting with a slow and complex process of privatization of medium- and large-scale SEs in industry, public utilities and state-owned banks while there is a continued improvement in their operation; an induced improvement in the current account of the balance of payments and a reduction of the fiscal deficit in the short run and then a slow deterioration of both in the medium term to the extent there is a strong recovery.

Catalysts for growth

Development depends on growth and therefore market-based policies and reforms must be adopted based on export-led growth and internal competitive markets which will encourage initiative, entrepreneurial drive, savings and investment to make a real and lasting breakthrough. The net effect will be a stronger Cuban economy and higher incomes all around, which should be stabilizing. Two missing elements in the CGM proposal are a more effective incentives system to create strong growth performance and a more appropriate price structure to guide efficient resource allocation.

It is not necessary to make Cuban society wait to achieve absolute stability and structural transformation (liberalization and deregulation of internal and external markets) of its economy before launching into a strategy for sustained economic growth. The economy has been stagnant and there has been a steady increase in the gap with other regional developing countries in technical development, innovation and product quality. Economic growth is indispensable for social and political reasons and cannot

be delayed much longer. Sustained growth will depend primarily on Cuba's ability to generate private savings to finance investment. A good program of comprehensive and enhanced incentives for entrepreneurship and modernization and clear rules of the game are required in order for government policies to inspire credibility about long-term sustainability. Once investors and savers begin to benefit from new opportunities and the potential financial payback for them is clear, there will be little trouble raising the necessary capital. This is a precondition for debt renegotiation and mobilization of external resources from international financial institutions.

There are three key and related reasons why strong economic growth is critical and cannot be postponed any longer: (1) the existence of unsatisfied social services (especially housing and restoring the quality of health and education that more seriously affect the poor and disadvantaged, since they are unable to secure private services; (2) the unemployment compensation and other social safeguards; and (3) the capability to maintain a pattern of distribution of income and wealth without great disparities would otherwise be quite limited to assure long-term social peace and order in Cuba. Vigorous rates of broad-based growth are also needed to strengthen political democracy because of the social and political pressures that the movement toward democracy entails. Economic reforms will only survive politically if they show some benefits early on and if those benefits expand gradually encompass, larger and larger segments of society.

The main dilemma in the current situation is that substantial and sustained economic growth is needed, but the reforms and policies being presently pursued, or the better ones proposed by CGM, are not conducive to vigorous and sustained growth, assuring rather that it will not be forthcoming. Cuba has to put a new system in place capable of achieving a level of growth near the economy's potential through long-term capital accumulation. Economic theory and practical experience teach us that the combination of a skilled labor force, low real wages, proximity to a large and growing market, and the availability of financial resources should lead to growth.

Accepting the urgent need for a higher rate of economic growth, the question is how best to achieve it under the present circumstances, i.e., to create an attractive environment in Cuba for all individuals and enterprises, whether domestic or foreign. The proper incentives to work harder, save more and invest are needed, such as the ones established in China, Vietnam and Eastern Europe. We are especially concerned with the supply side, and seek to enlarge productive capacity by increasing mobility, adaptability, flexibility and efficiency in the utilization and allocation of resources among competitive uses. We consider that Cuba should seek to eliminate distortions in incentives, enhance the role of market forces, and improve microeconomic efficiency. The advantage of marketization lies not only in its allocative efficiency and factor productivity, but also in its facilitation of innovative and creative activity (technological change).

To boost the rate of economic growth, significant expansion of productive capacity through physical investment must be one of the primary objectives of the reform process. But equally important is the mobilization of adequate savings to ensure the realization of required investment and to make it more accessible to non-traditional investors. Institutional and legal changes are necessary to mobilize domestic and foreign savings and ensure a better allocation of it. A proper positive real interest rate policy can be critical in influencing not only short-run changes in spending, inflation, and external financing, but also in affecting longer-term accumulation of financial assets and the level, composition and productivity of investment. Two distinct supply-side forces should be freed by the market-based reforms: a rapid accumulation of capital stock and technology catch-up and, second, a powerful adjustment in the structure of saving incentives and in the variety of instruments. A set of attractive and secure savings instruments needs to be developed, such as bonds and stocks, pension funds, and mutual funds.

It will also take the concerted effort of government, individuals and businesses. Creating wealth demands cooperation. We have in mind that private foreign investment usually lags rather than leads growth. It enters when growth has already gained momentum and then tends to accelerate it. Increasingly entry into activities, internal competition, international trade based on outward growth orientation and application of up-dated technologies and organization can contribute substantially to improving both the allocation of resources and their productivity and, consequently, the international competitiveness of Cuba's exports. The state must play the strategic role of devising the policies and implementing the mechanisms to make the best use of these factors. There is need for continued absorption of up-dated and improved technologies and organization in the more traditional activities that still represent the backbone of production and exports (agriculture and tourism).

Social policy targeted to the poor

The adverse social effects of the stabilization and adjustment policy should be offset by the rationalization of the social expenditures and carefully focusing relief on the vulnerable and in investing in human capital to maintain the social safety net. A social policy designed to protect the vulnerable from the most distressing effects of economic restructuring and to distribute the fruits of progress evenly must be an intrinsic part of any reform strategy that seeks continued political support under increasingly democratic and participatory conditions. The degree of social and political support will determine the scale of reforms that can be sustained without derailing the entire transformation and modernization program. The recent experiences of Eastern Europe and Latin America suggest that the increase in social programs not only constitutes good economics but also makes political sense. If this is not done, there is a real danger that the reforms will stall and even that voters will once again favor the old order.

Reduction of waste, focalization and efficiency gains provide the most likely and immediate means for improvements in the public provision of social services in a hypertrophied welfare state. Greater reliance should be placed on private provision of some of these services or through NGO's.

We believe that a combination of high economic growth with a relatively even distribution of income, and not at its expense, is highly possible and desirable for Cuba. It tends to insure dignity to all citizens and prevents private concentrations of economic power from dictating economic policy. East Asian market economies have made a conscious effort to achieve "shared growth," that is, growth whose effects would be felt by as wide a segment of society as possible and they have achieved very successful results.

Democratization for true and effective participation

Institutions necessary for effective involvement, participation and democratic decision making should be put in place to breed cooperation, self-confidence and accord; they are important elements in maintaining support in favor of reforms and are most important for much wider reasons than narrow economic ones. Honest differences of opinions and wide participation "from below" in the introduction of the new policies are required to elicit and encourage the attitudinal changes and to address political corruption, a fixture of Cuban political life since independence, without which no reform can succeed. It should empower Cuban citizens to use the energies of their good education and health that are available waiting to be unleashed. We consider that if only fast and abrupt top-down changes are implemented, they are likely to prove counterproductive and unfeasible. There are strong pressures in Cuba today to evolve in the direction of individual rights, participation and pluralism, in order that political choices are voiced and made in a transparent, predictable, reliable, and comparatively inexpensive manner. It is crucial that a broad set of people—not just a few bureaucrats—participate in the debate about how important changes should be shaped, as well as in the design, administration and supervision of the programs. Then these will gain broader acceptance and become a reality.

Feedback and participation to define a sense of common purpose and shared burdens, is crucial for success, especially in a country where effective de-facto taxation is so high. People will serve the cause only by devising undertakings that command participation and can be sustained over time. Current domestic realities permit no other choice than to obtain clear and unambiguous backing. One of the most strategic choices that the government faces is whether to give some control and decentralize decision-making based on superior understanding of appropriate circumstances in return for a faster pace of development. Instead of trying to control most decisions, the government should concentrate on establishing an incentives regime that promotes efficient decision and true participation by households and enterprises both in economics and politics.

By establishing strategic alliances and partnerships with non-governmental and business sectors, the public institutions will be able to pursue a broader concept of governance. A strong and vibrant non-governmental participation is needed. This should include, inter-alia, new independent non-governmental and community-based organizations, professional and business groups and associations that will allow professionals and entrepreneurs in Cuba to stay in touch with advancements being made in their disciplines and enterprises. Open debate regarding economic policies should be allowed. For example, the government should encourage labor participation in enterprise reform.

Cuba and the international financial community

Cuba's active participation in international financial institutions—the IMF, World Bank and IDB—is an area that was not covered by CGM, but that in our opinion could play a significant role in making possible decentralized and sustainable economic growth with equity. It would facilitate reflection and could be decisive in the analysis of alternative proposals for systemic and structural market-based reforms and developing microeconomic policies to remove impediments to economic growth. Furthermore, international financial organizations can offer loans for economic development, possibly under advantageous (concessional) conditions, given Cuba's precarious situation, as well as facilitate technical cooperation and renegotiation of debt.

Foreign assistance could also stimulate the growth of private investment and provide the necessary assurance that the transition program will succeed. Cuban policymakers could then look ahead several years and consider how inflows of official development assistance and direct investment might contribute to development, within a context of sound and well-managed macroeconomic policies.

Role of the state during the transition

In contrast to the CGM proposal, we support a subsidiary role for the state in productive activities, getting out of activities that the private sector can perform in a more efficient way, shrinkage of government and demystification of the state. The continuing dominance of SEs in industry, foreign trade, banking and other sectors by CGM is a major impediment to competitiveness and capital accumulation necessary for the sound development of the economy.

Having so stated, we understand that boosting Cuba from stagnation to steady economic growth requires an important initial role for the state. Many of the transformations will not take place spontaneously. Rather, they will require a proactive state, particularly during the earlier phases of the transition. The goals of the transition can be best achieved by purposeful improvement and guidance of the market rather than by unfettered market forces. There is a need for reform of the state to address the downsizing of numerous ministries that are supposed to deal with economic issues in a command fashion.

The strong empirical evidence from the experience of East Asian market economies shows that the public sector has played a forceful and aggressive role in defining the growth strategy and implementing it, by fostering and stimulating entrepreneurship, ensuring a strong competitive framework and guidelines, and factor allocation in preestablished directions. This is based on the presence of externalities arising from large, coordinated investments in infrastructure and productive capacity, as well as the risks involved in substantial investment with long gestation periods. No local entrepreneurial groups, alone or in conjunction with foreign investors, foresaw the full potential of these sectors or appropriately discounted the future costs and benefits. However, the state did not intervene in the direct production of goods and services that the private sector is more efficient in producing nor did it interfere with the private sector's ability to do so. Market remedies should generally be used to treat and correct market distortions.

Government and the private sector are partners; they should not be adversaries locked in combat. They are supposed to be working toward the same goal: economic development.[14] Cuba needs critical macroeconomic balances, microeconomic guidance and institution-building in the transformation and modernization process, it should avoid market failures and support the development of small and medium enterprises, especially by improving access to capital, training, the transfer of technology and marketing. Additionally, effective state intervention is needed to establish and preserve competition, to regulate monopolies, to mobilize concessional resources and negotiate debt rescheduling and forgiveness, promote education, guide infrastructure, enforce laws, and for the protection of health, safety, the environment and overall natural resource management. The pursuit of self-interest unrestrained by suitable institutions carries no guarantee of anything except chaos and uncertainty, especially in financial markets where prudent regulation and supervision is needed. We support the public presence in economic activities that are regulatory in nature. We strongly reject a "do-nothing" position on the ground that competent state bureaucracies do not simply exist to administer such a role. That is precisely why Cuba should avoid government failures through unnecessary interventions in the production of goods and services, as well as problematic enforcement, rent-seeking activities and bureaucratic expansion.

What is needed is a professional, independent, and disciplined civil service that is prohibited from being active in politics, selected on merit through an examination system, protected from undue influence of business groups, operating on the basis of clear rules and written records and with promotion based on performance and merit. Bureaucrats should be pre-

---

14. "When markets and governments have worked in harness, the results have been spectacular, but when they have worked in opposition the results have been disastrous" (World Bank, 1991, p. 2).

vented from entering business or politics while in service. Political appointments and civil service positions should be clearly distinguished by law.

Dismantling the production of goods and services out of the public sector will facilitate the state's streamlining and strengthening, leading to a greater ability to administer the workings of the economy, to control and regulate economic activity where required without stifling private initiative, to provide basic income and social services for all instances in which the economy fails to provide for the most vulnerable, to make highly selective government intervention and work together and in close collaboration with the private sector, as partners in the development process.

FINAL REFLECTIONS AND CONCLUSIONS

At the beginning of 1995 it was widely known in U.S. academic circles that CGM had prepared a new development strategy for Cuba based on the AMSM. It was also assumed that the Cuban leadership was going to announce additional structural reforms to those enacted in 1993 and 1994 for the strengthening of the incipient recovery of the Cuban economy and its reinsertion into international markets based on the framework and guidelines of the CGM proposal. On July 26, 1995 Castro declared that Cuba would follow a strategy inspired on the AMSM and adopt "unquestionable elements of capitalism." In September 1995, with a remarkable coincidence of timing, the CGM proposal was finally published in Cuba. At the end of November, the Finance Minister announced an income tax on hard currency earnings, tax on boats and road tolls for two highways. However, as of February 1996, significant structural reforms proposed by CGM are yet to be disclosed and implemented in Cuba, as well as the initial trigger mechanism to effectively start the process for the needed recovery of the economy and its international reinsertion.

In Appendix I of this paper we analyze the AMSM and reach the conclusion that China was able to introduce gradual and piecemeal market-based reforms starting with a minimum bang in 1978 due to its unique initial macroeconomic stability-cum-moderate economic growth, but that Vietnam had to follow a faster and deeper approach, based on an initial "radical surgery" to stabilization and gradual structural reforms in 1989, because of its much more severe internal and external problems.

We are not able to assert confidently that the AMSM is the appropriate model for transition, but we consider that it holds very significant lessons for Cuba. Given the current difficulties in Cuba and the progress achieved by China and Vietnam, there is a strong case for the initiation of a Cuban version of the AMSM, similar to the faster and deeper approach that the Vietnamese started in 1989. Both China and Vietnam have allowed substantial private enterprise, starting with agriculture, small manufacturing, handicrafts, services and own-account work, that has extended across the whole economy even though they have reserved several activities (heavy industry, public utilities and natural resources) for the public sector or for joint enterprises with foreign participation. Both countries have adopted deregulating and liberalizing microeconomic reforms within a stable macroeconomic management framework that have encouraged investment, savings and productivity increases. They have been able to achieve high rates of economic growth, relatively low inflation, have maintained social expenditures and have induced massive foreign investment from émigrés. We hope Cuba can encourage the imagination and initiative of its people and combine a gradual but decisive economic opening with serious advances and modernization of political institutions.

The CGM proposal is a first, but still far distant, approximation to the AMSM. It does not support a more complete liberalization and deregulation of agricultural activities nor the increasing entry and competition into many economic activities as the Chinese and Vietnamese did when they started their market-based reforms. The CGM proposal does not have some of the most important microeconomic strengths of the AMSM, but it has most of its weaknesses, both economically and politically. Its likelihood of survival in the long run in its present form is a matter of serious doubt. It should be bolder and more daring in proposing genuine solutions sooner. This is not simply right. It is also necessary for the survival and prosperity of Cuba. The more similar feature of the new Cuban model and AMSM is on its political aims: there are neither proposals for significant political reforms, civil liberties and freedoms, nor political parties and pluralism. This silence was predictable.

CGM have presented a vision of Cuban society to which the transition process should be moving and have drawn a program of action which is coherent in its components parts and can serve as a stepping-stone for building the required accord for change. However, the economic reform prescriptions they have presented are still driven more by calculations of political convenience and effective social control than by the genuine requirements of economic need and growth. The effort to overregulate and control a broad range of private activities stems from a distrust of markets and competition and will determine a weak microeconomic setting vulnerable to external shocks. The economic reform process that they recommend will prove insufficient to produce any real prospect of self-sustaining and lasting recovery in living standards or new sources of growth and employment. It will not end the binding constraint on long-term growth of the economy; hence it is a transformation trap or an unnecessary long detour for high and sustainable growth with equity. However, the CGM proposal—even with all its limitations and contradictions—has established a basic framework which can subsequently be built upon. If their recommendations were implemented, it would constitute a remarkable, albeit inadequate and incomplete, accomplishment.

APPENDIX I
THE ASIAN MARKET SOCIALISM MODEL (AMSM)

"Our revolution is still in its first day. We have no real private property, no de-monopolization. We still have the same Soviet communist leaders in power... I want Russia to have not simply a market economy but an effective market economy, not simply an anti-totalitarian regime but a working democracy. I want to liberate the people from the previous system and from the quasi-democratic system we have today."

— Grigory Yavlinsky, *The Washington Post*, December 3, 1995, p. C3.

"What the Chinese have done to their economy is phenomenal. In 15 years, China has come from a poverty-stricken nowhere to the economic front. Real income has quadrupled, putting it on the course to become the world's largest economy..."

— Mortimer B. Zuckerman, "America's China Syndrome", in *U.S. News & World Report*, October 30, 1995, p. 110.

"More disturbing is the tendency to dismiss the Chinese experience as irrelevant or somehow phony. Indeed, this dismissal verges on a kind of physiological denial when carried out by individuals who have themselves been involved in policymaking in European socialist countries with rather mixed results. Thus, one commonly hears a wide range of far-fetched and mutually contradictory reasons why China's experience is irrelevant to other socialist countries."

— Barry Naughton, "China's Economic Success: Effective Reforms Policies or Unique Conditions?" in *The Evolutionary Transition to Capitalism*, Kazimiers Z. Poznanki, ed. (1995), p. 132.

TWO APPROACHES TO A MARKET-BASED ECONOMIC SYSTEM: "BIG BANG" VIS-A-VIS GRADUALISM

There are two principal approaches, in terms of the nature and pace of transition, from a centrally-planned to a decentralized, predominant market economy. One is the so-called "big bang" or "generalized shock therapy" (Lipton and Sachs, 1990, especially p. 99).[15] It advocates swift and comprehensive policy reform, some kind of an "all or nothing" or "quick-fix" approach, including simultaneous economic stabilization, liberalization of domestic and external markets, top-down privatization and institution building as necessary components of market-based reforms. It implies that unless the preconditions are created at once, the road to a market economy can never open up. This approach encourages initiating and completing all these measures within a relatively short period of time. In this approach, sequencing of reforms is practically irrelevant. It offers simple prescriptions, has no patience for the diversity, complexity and complications of dismantling the socialist system, and scarcely focuses on detailed microeconomic reforms that are necessary to eliminate the frictions and barriers of imperfect and segmentated markets. It implicitly assumes a strong and rapid market adjustment toward new equilibrium based on an extreme form of market clearing, that unemployment is a voluntary phenomena and that the role of economic policy in general is distorting and irrelevant as established by the new classical macroeconomic theory. It ignores that increased uncertainty in prices and employment reduces the market efficiency due to the lack of a proper coordination/communication mechanism. The market-based reforms undertaken in Eastern Europe and the former Soviet Union in the first half of the 1990's are prime examples of this strategy.

The big bang is expected to generate a "J-curve" effect on growth, i.e., that GDP will initially decline for a kind of creative destruction and to accelerate

---

15. Technically, shock therapy is a treatment propelling electric current through the body with the goal of stimulating nerve cells, thus altering the chemistry of the brain, to resume more normal functions. Following the convulsion, the cure is likely to become evident only gradually, if at all, over a protracted period of time. It is applied as a last resort to patients suffering from certain types of severe mental depression and catatonic schizophrenia by psychiatry departments in hospitals and related mental institutions. The effectiveness of the treatment is a matter of considerable controversy in the medical profession.

the natural selection, but soon be followed by a strong and robust recovery as a result of better economic policy, improved overall management and increased efficiency. It has been judged to be theoretically sound, rigorous and feasible in practice by the mainstream of the economics profession and the international financial institutions (the World Bank and the IMF). It is an interesting theory but not a proven method. It is the conventional wisdom or the economists' consensus of the moment which has so far overshadowed the design of alternative transitional agendas.[16] It is a leap of faith, rather than a conclusion based on hard evidence, because the idea that it will generate a growth takeoff represents a hope rather than a well-founded expectation. It has generated a sort of speculative bubble or a temporarily self-fulfilling prophecy, creating an initial mood of euphoria. However, typically a "reality check" comes and the bubble bursts, because of its high transition costs and because the technical design is not a good as its myth. In reality, the behavior of output followed, at least initially, an "L"-shaped pattern instead of a "J"-shaped one and the supply side has been so weak that the reduction in output in Eastern Europe in 1989-1993 "was on a massive scale and unprecedented since the Great Depression of 1929-1933." (UN/ECE, 1995, p. 10).[17]

In some cases, the radical change was carried out explicitly to shatter the former economic system, take the old guard out, and make the transition process irreversible, but it has also stopped further reforms, generating a very strong adverse reaction.[18] It has been more harmful than necessary. The sacrifice ratio of disinflation and the Okun's misery index (unemployment and inflation rates) have been very high. There has been a significant increase in poverty, un-

employment, inequality and a decrease in human welfare in general (Emmerij, 1994, pp. 19-21) evidenced by rising numbers of people below national poverty lines and serious deterioration in standards of health and mortality rates. Ordinary people face rising economic insecurity. The jobless rate in most East European countries is well over 10 percent of the labor force and has remained high, despite the emerging recovery of output. There has been only a small reduction in "excess employment" as indicated by the difference or similarity between the cumulative contraction in GDP and the cumulative compression in employment between 1989 and 1994. As more people remain without a job for a long time they will tend to drop out of the active labor force permanently because of a loss of skills. One especially worrisome fact is that there are more young people and school leavers among the unemployed.

There has been an institutional vacuum and generalized administrative weakness due to the problem of missing, weak or inappropriate state institutions or, at best to the transaction costs of making the change from one set of institutions to another. There has been a marked rise of organized crime that some authors consider is providing a service to economic development because it is "the only force interposed between the new economic boyars and the defenseless consumers and entrepreneurs of Russia."[19] Foreign direct investments have been rather modest, probably linked to systemic factors such as the uncertain legal, political and institutional environment.

The contrasting approach is the "gradual," "incremental," "evolutionary" or "organic" approach (Kor-

---

16. Summers, 1992, p. 112.

17. "by far the most helpful circumstance for the rapid propagation of a new revolutionary theory is the existence of an established orthodoxy which is clearly inconsistent with the most salient facts of reality." (Johnson, 1971).

18. Also, the advances in democracy and of a truly independent judicial system have several limitations, as the Josef Olesksy affair has shown in Poland. "In a little less than in two years, Poland has been transformed from a country headed by pro-Western leaders who risked their lives and well-being for democratic values into nation headed by leaders who collaborated with and had strong personal friendships with officials of a foreign power that dominated their country for half a century." (Article by Adrian Karensky, President of Freedom House, *The Wall Street Journal*, January 22, 1996, p. A12).

19. Edward M. Luttwak, "Russia's Pro-Capitalist" in *The Washington Post*, February 4, 1996, p. C2.

nai, 1990 and McKinnon, 1991).[20] It is partial, incremental, sequential, induced, often experimental and bottom-up. It characterizes the reform process that China started in 1978 and that Vietnam and Laos PDR initiated in 1986. However, countries differ with regard to its intensity. China has progressively introduced market forces, decentralized economic decision-making and strengthened material incentives and competition, often on an experimental basis, since 1978. It has shown the feasibility of gradually reforming a socialist economy, because with a quarter of the world's population, China has managed to record a growth rate of nearly 10 percent per annum since it started the market reforms—by far the fastest growth rate among major economies.

The gradual approach typically does not pursue privatization, especially large-scale privatization, but an increase in the free entry of PEs, improvements in the performance of SEs and competition, both among SEs and between SEs and PEs. Heavy industry, public utilities and natural resources have remained firmly the responsibility of the central government or of joint enterprises with foreign investment. Recent developments in these countries indicate that partial privatization of SEs is beginning to take place and is likely to expand soon.

Gradualism proceeds slowly, relying on the organic development of the private sector "from below"

through free entry, and transition from centralized controls over prices and output to a more decentralized market economy. Privatization of SEs in China has become less important, as SEs weigh less and less heavily in the overall economy. The gradual approach implies market-based reforms over a fairly protracted period of time. Major disruptions to the economy are avoided, as well as social unrest and conflicts that could derail the reform process. Pragmatism is much more of a driving force. It has sought to reform the existing institutional and organizational structures in a deliberate manner, rather than to dismantle them and build them from scratch, because the requisite institution-building is not a goal that can be reached overnight. It tries to avoid the propagation effects of major and rapid changes. In many aspects institutional and organizational reforms lag behind policy reforms.

As a method of liberalization, it is generally regarded as groundless social engineering and self-defeating by the mainstream of the economics profession, based on the failures of partial and half-hearted liberalization in Eastern Europe (i.e., the "Hungarian economic mechanism") and the Soviet Union ("perestroika") during the 1980's, and in Rumania during the 1990's. We agree with Pérez-López (1995) who implicitly distinguishes between "perestroika," a poor, limited and faulty decentralization based on

---

20. McKinnon (1991) had the ability to translate his vision into gradual measures to approach the transformation goals in stages. Kornai (1995), defends an "initial radical surgery" for some areas of economic policy and supports gradual measures in several areas. "For my part, I agreed with those who stress that a profound transformation of society in the area of coordination mechanisms and property forms cannot be brought about at a stroke, by aggressive state measures, that they necessarily take place as an integral development by evolutionary means." (Ibid, p. 214). "...this is an evolutionary process that wise government measures can speed up and stupid measures or indifference can slow down. Whatever the case, it will take several years to run its course." (Ibid, p. 72). Kornai strongly rejects market socialism. He considers that something is doomed to failure when countries mix elements of planned and market economies because of irreconcilable differences, contradictions and tensions. "...undivided communist political power and a capitalist economy cannot co-exist within a single robust, stable system in a permanent way, over a long historical period." (Ibid, pp. 19) It is "...a blind alley." (Ibid, viii.). Kornai also advocates "a general and comprehensive price reform which places the entire system on a market basis in a relatively short time" (Kornai, 1990, p 51).

improving SEs, and the AMSM as an adequate and increasing decentralization based on *expanding* PEs.[21] "Mainstream" economists also stress that Czechoslovakia and Poland which introduced faster and more comprehensive stabilization and price liberalization packages—have fared better than Hungary. "Gradualists" are portrayed as backsliding, lacking commitment to market reforms, aiming to restore the previous status quo, or preferring a more relaxed collectivism.[22] In contrast, gradualists consider that the "big bang" is not dictated by initial conditions but simply constitutes errors in policy and causes the interconnected socialist system to collapse. All market-based reforms are crammed into a tight time frame, so there are bound to be critical dislocations and malfunctions and a generalized chaos in economies with a virtual absence of factor markets and with low price elasticities of supply by SEs.

Unfortunately the debate between advocates of the "big bang" and "gradual" approaches has taken on an increasingly ideological and philosophical tone, along with escalation in rhetoric, each side suggesting rather demagogically that there is only one alternative, instead of analyzing whether one will get farther along the desired road by moving quickly or gradually in certain areas. We disagree with this sole dualistic choice; the question, rather, is which policies should be carried out gradually and which swiftly. Most economists will agree that certain reforms should be done more rapidly because of the effects of global distortions and the need for an initial "minimum bang" or an initial "radical surgery" to start a dynamic and sustainable growth process. Other reforms cannot or should not be done quickly. As a late developer Cuba can learn from the experiences of the trailblazers and should adopt successful policies to the extent feasible. In most democratic societies gradualism is the rule and the "big bang", shock or "cold turkey" policies the rare exceptions. Indeed, one of the major arts of democratic politics is to seek gradual solutions to conflicts of interest. Claims that bold liberalization is generally more sustainable than gradual programs are questionable given the considerable diversity of national experiences.

We believe that stressing exclusive reliance on one position or the other will ultimately be detrimental to the original transformation objectives and will not take advantage of lessons gained through experience. Transformation is an issue of political economy of normative economics, rather than simply a technical one. There is usually more than one way of carrying out reforms to attain a particular set of objectives in a specific set of historical, cultural, institutional and political circumstances.

Stabilization policies must be implemented quickly with great intensity, comprehensively and without sequencing or sectoralism, as Vietnam did in 1989. Also, fostering savings, productivity and private initiative in establishing new small and medium PEs—

---

21. There are three common characteristics in the AMSM and in perestroika: (1) maintenance of the ruling role of the Communist party, but with some mitigation of the repression and allowing a degree of freedom for alternative views; (2) the extensive role of state control and the subordination of the economy to the public sector; and (3) the importance of state ownership and lack of privatization of large SEs. However, there are marked differences between the AMSM and perestroika in two significant aspects: (1) an increasing role for the private sector and competition; and (2) using the market as the main integrator and coordinating mechanism of the economy which embraces decentralization, a degree of autonomy and partial liberalization of prices for SEs, and opening to trade and foreign investment. The way perestroika worked was an immediate and disorderly decentralization of SEs by giving more autonomy to enterprise managers with emphasis on soft-budgets for SEs and a limited role for the private sector. Perestroika got unconvincing and bad economic results because it did not create good fundamentals, in terms of bringing about a change that increasingly depended on the private sector and automatically reducing the inefficiencies of public sector. The initial expectation of the Soviet reformers was that, once the administrative system was decentralized, there would a momentary vacuum which would then be filled by the market mechanism, but they had no method for coordinating inputs and outputs and the result was chaos.

22. The experiences of Eastern Europe, the former URSS and Asian countries in 1989-1995 suggest the possibility that countries that retain the nomenklatura in political control may in fact move just faster by orderly progress to a market-based system than those attempting transition immediately and simultaneously on both the political and economic fronts. Political reformers who courageously struggled for rapid political and economic change (i.e., Lech Walesa in Poland) are often elbowed out in the process by the nomenklatura. The main beneficiary from rapid privatization is the nomenklatura.

which is possible in conjunction with small-scale privatization—and mobilizing these resources for carrying out the transformation process must be implemented as rapidly as circumstances permit, and it can lay the groundwork for vast improvements in allocation efficiency and factor productivity as well as for political support by spreading ownership broadly. However, the arguments frequently invoked by shockers that trade and financial liberalization cannot be introduced gradually are simply not true.[23] Neither history nor logic yield hard evidence to that effect. Even a casual reading of postwar history of Western Europe and of the recent East Asian and Chilean experiences demonstrates the lack of rigor of these arguments. Additionally, there are some reforms that are difficult and time consuming, among them large-scale privatization,[24] restructuring of SEs or the institutionalization of a healthy market economy, e.g., constructing an appropriate tax system.

Some authors (Gelb, et. al., 1993) suggest that the weakness of certain states precludes a gradual reform process because only strong states can maintain for a long time a large, relatively inefficient public sector with a small but dynamic and expanding private sector. On the other hand, a big bang reform will require, as a condition of success, a strong state. Weaker states should therefore restrict the scale and depth of changes and should therefore not risk an immediate erosion of their power base by allowing steps that estrange political allies. The need is for simultaneous

sustainability and completion of the reforms rather than a simultaneous start of the transition. It is also important to consider that although a minimal state might be the *goal* at the end of the transformation process, an activist state should be the *means* during the transition.

When the generalized shock treatment was adopted in Eastern Europe and the former Soviet Union in the first half of the 1990's, its abrupt and radical changes resulted in demolishing the bureaucracy and laying the opportunity to adopt a market economy in its place. However, an unexpectedly deep, widespread and persistent decline of GDP (called the "transformational recession" by Kornai, 1995) took place with at least persistent moderate inflation rates, but sometimes extraordinarily high and explosive ones, with all their speculation effects. Persistent moderate inflation seems to be caused chiefly by inflationary expectations, hystheresis and inertial mechanisms, such as indexation schemes for wages, pensions, foreign exchange, and periodic key commodity prices (mostly food and energy) adjustments.

This situation has unraveled in some countries, producing a spiral of self-reinforcing destructive responses and slowing down reform, lowering the propensity of SEs to restructure, to significant lay-offs of workers, and generating unsettling political and social conflicts.[25] SEs prefer to raise prices, protect employment and lobby heavily for government support and

---

23. "It is now generally agreed that resolving the fiscal imbalance and attaining some degree of macroeconomic reform should be a priority in implementing a structural reform. Most analysts also agree that trade liberalization should precede liberalization of the capital account and that financial reform should only be implemented once a modern and efficient supervisory authority is in place" (Edwards, 1995, p. 122).

24. Hasty large-scale privatization could become an unfair give-away of the country's wealth to a small group of privileged insiders or well-connected people, as happened in Russia and in some countries in Latin America, or a "quasi" privatization where the assets are transferred but there are no improvements in management or in the financial situation of the enterprise. A growing number of Russians refers to it as "grabitization." The speed in privatizing state assets has enabled many insiders from the old regime, bureaucrats and managers, to obtain capital assets very cheaply and thereby trade their power base in the party hierarchy for economic power in the emerging market economy. "Chubais had been roundly criticized for having conceived what is viewed here as a deeply flawed privatization program. It has been variously skewered as a giveaway of precious state resources and sweetheart deals for former managers of Soviet industries and other insiders who have grabbed valuable assets for a fraction of their real value." (The Washington Post, January 17, 1996, p. A21) However, a strong case can be made for restructuring to be carried out by individuals who are able to run enterprises, rather than by the bureaucrats who made the mess to start with.

25. A contrasting view is held by Sachs (1994, p. 145): "There is simply no evidence of a sharp drop in living standards in Eastern Europe...In fact, living standards may well have increased, when we consider the elimination of queues and the increased variety and quality of consumer goods."

assistance. In some countries there are attempts to reverse the changes made thus far. The general popular mood is one of "reform" fatigue, disillusionment and anger over rising unemployment, inflation, decreasing real wages, shrinking welfare arrangements, collapse of social services, loss of job security, deteriorating standards of living, and soaring crime. This mood has been reflected in election results favoring former communists in many countries, which has been generally interpreted as signifying opposition to further *rapid* market reforms or at least in favor of marketization with a "human face."

In contrast, in China in 1978-1995, even in the aftermath of the Tiananmen Square tragedy and the subsequent political repression, and in Vietnam with its *doi moi* policy[26] and in Laos PDR in 1986-1995, the shift from central planning toward a market economy has produced strong production growth combined with remarkable stability. They have been outstandingly successful, at least in the narrow economic sense, with respect to improvements in the general standard of living, reduction of absolute poverty, and increase in foreign trade. The difference in macroeconomic performance with Eastern Europe and the former Soviet Union is so enormous that it is now impossible to disregard. Chinese, Vietnamese and Laotian experiences illustrate that prolonged drops of GDP and employment with their associated high social costs and political resistance are not an inevitable consequence of the transition towards a decentralized market economy. In the 1990's China and Vietnam have defined their own system as "market socialism," or a combination of communist politics and market economics, and have placed more emphasis on accelerating the integration of their economies to the world economy. One could argue that the process followed in these Asian countries better equips the people for freedom.

Clearly one of the most impressive achievements has been a reduction of inflation rates to levels that are among the lowest in transitional economies together with the maintenance of positive real interest rates.

These three Asian countries have avoided the financial disintermediation seen in those transition economies in Eastern Europe. Furthermore, the three significant social and distributional benefits of socialist economies relative to market economies of a comparable income level have been retained: (a) high levels of education and health; (b) a relatively high degree of income security; and (c) low incidence of income aspects of extreme poverty. However, there has also been an absence of significant political reforms and a lack of civil liberties.

This striking difference in performance would suggest that China, Vietnam and Laos PDR have gotten some of their economic policies right while not others. While it is somewhat early to tell, it could be that their overall gradualism has been the proper choice, while the overall radicalism of Eastern European and Russian reforms might have been an excess coupled with some conceptual mistakes. It is likely that there are significant spillover and hysteresis effects on growth associated with what is done well or badly, including of prolonged periods of instability, in opening and liberalizing a highly centralized system. China, Vietnam and Laos PDR have had increasing microeconomic efficiency within a framework of macroeconomic stability.

It should be stressed that the initial conditions in China in 1978 did not show the severe internal and external macroeconomic imbalances that afflicted many other post-communist transition economies. China neither had marked inflationary pressures, a monetary overhang nor foreign debt; indeed, international reserves exceeded the foreign debt. Most of its foreign trade was conducted with market economies due to the Sino-Soviet split of the early 1960's. The economy was decentralized in the sense that local governments had a great deal of discretion. This decentralization made it possible to introduce piecemeal market-based reforms and allow experimentation without disrupting the whole economy. The authorities did not have a detailed blueprint for market-based reforms, but they did have a marked commit-

---

26. Renovation or reform policy; literally, new change or new road.

ment to modernize China and to integrate its economy to international markets.

In contrast, Vietnam accelerated its path towards a socialist market economy and outward-oriented development in 1989 because of the end of Soviet aid, by strengthening and deepening its commitment to *doi moi*[27] with widespread price decontrol, liberalization of the exchange rate and interest rate reform, coupled with cutting drastically the deficits of SEs (see Table 2). Vietnam was able to achieve some notable and quick successes despite a lack of international support. Uncertainty over where the economic policies were leading brought about an articulate policy more clearly and more consistent in the methods used.

Unlike the populations of many other transition economies undergoing market-friendly reforms, the majority of the Chinese and Vietnamese people benefitted immediately from the decollectivization of, and price liberalization in, agricultural activities. Also, China and Vietnam faced a more elastic supply of labor than other transition economies, where a larger percentage of workers were in heavily subsidized jobs in industry and hence had little desire to seek other employment.

The initial efforts at gradual reform have unleashed forces that 17 years later have brought China to the brink of a market economy. Socio-politically, the dynamics of the system have led to the emergence of new internal economic forces, powerful informal interest groups, and the tremendously powerful social force of consumerism. Individual freedom of choice has increased as a consequence of reform. The participation of tens of thousands of enterprises and millions of administrators, managers, owners and workers in decisions over the years of reforms has built a solid constituency and important countervailing pressures for market-directed change that appears

stronger than any official announcement could in theory have produced. There is a nascent and awakening civil society (professional, business and information associations) that is making its voice heard. In Vietnam, the private sector now dominates the economy, and its share is likely to grow in the future. However, at present the private sector remains largely a household one, and few large private enterprises exist.

Most of the Eastern European countries and Russia faced major internal and external imbalances at the beginning of the 1990's, were highly centralized and received a major trade shock from the elimination of the CMEA arrangements in 1991. Most of their reformers have a sort of religious faith in a nineteenth century liberalism or considered, as do CMG, that China was a unique case determined by its very special initial conditions. Brada (1995) considers that the conditions under reforms which have taken place in China seemed so much more favorable than those found in Eastern Europe or the former Soviet Union, that the model of gradual change is not feasible for other economies. However, Brada does not consider the successful experiences of Vietnam and Laos PDR in his analysis. He does not consider that what is needed is an adjustment to the Chinese model, as Vietnam and other socialist countries has done successfully in Asia, rather than to discard it completely.

THE MAIN FEATURES OF THE AMSM APPROACH

"We have already taken the most difficult and complicated policy decisions related to the shift towards a more market-oriented and open economy. In the coming years economic reforms will be more focused, and will be combined closely with public administration reform, and necessary improvements in the legal framework and institutional development."

---

27. The doi moi development process seems a coherent and consistent strategy based on two basic principles. A more people-centered approach of incentive environment designed to encourage people to realize their potential and use their own creativity, drive and imagination to improve their lives, which in turn benefits their communities and country or that "development is the result of the efforts by the people for the people;" and the open policy toward investment and trade as the basis for more dynamic and efficient development with a clear realization that to remain isolated from the global economy would retard rapid economic growth and social progress. These two principles, together with other reforms, are developing an economy which is more people-led than state-driven.

Table 2. Main Economic Reforms Approved in China and Vietnam and the CGM Proposal

Reforms	China	Vietnam	Cuba (CGM proposal)
Microeconomic Reforms			
Price reforms	Dual system enacted in 1986. Partial market determination enacted in 1986. Increasing deregulation. 70% of retail prices and 85% of output prices of SEs are market determined.	Dual system until 1989, when almost total deregulation occurred.	Price adjustment proposed for Stage I, Phase 1. Limited price liberalization proposed for Stage I, Phase 2.
Agricultural reforms	Started in 1978 with responsibility system. By the end of the 1980's basically back to household agriculture. Market determined in most agricultural products except grain, edible oils and cotton. Long term land leases. Transfers of land-use legalized in 1988. Use of public stocks to avoid wide fluctuations in a few important crops.	Started in 1986. By the end of the 1980's basically back to household agriculture. Long term land leases.	Proposed for Stage I, Phase 1. Basically it consists of the consolidation of UBPC.
Industrial reform	Started in 1979 with guidance prices for above quota output and access to material inputs thorough the market. In 1984 TVEs authorized. In 1987 contract responsibility adopted.		
Corporate governance	Started in 1978. Intensified after 1984. Expanding hard budgets. Firms retain a progressively growing proportion of the profits over which the managers are given discretion. The salaries and bonuses of the managers are linked to firm performance. The proportion of the workers' income paid in the form of bonuses has been increased.	Started in 1987. Intensified after 1989. Expanding hard budgets.	Proposed for Stage I, Phase 2.
Promotion of non-SEs. Free entry to activities.	Started in the early 1980's. Licenses are easier to obtain.	Started in the early 1980's. Intensified after 1989	
Privatization of small SEs	Indirectly through leases.		Proposed for Stage I, Phase 2.
Reforms of legal property rights		Enacted in 1989	Proposed for Stage I, Phase 2.
Bankruptcy and liquidation law	Enacted in 1987.		Proposed for Stage I, Phase 2.

Table 2. Main Economic Reforms Approved in China and Vietnam and the CGM Proposal

Reforms	China	Vietnam	Cuba (CGM proposal)
Anti-monopoly law			Proposed for Stage I, Phase 1.
Foreign investment law	Enacted in 1979. Opening of first special zones.	Enacted in 1987 and revised in 1989.	Enacted in September 1995.
Macroeconomic Reforms			
Fiscal reforms			
Tax reform	Direct and indirect taxes approved. Weak tax administration.	Direct and indirect taxes approved in 1990. Weak tax administration.	
Expenditure reform	Subsidies partly reduced.	Subsidies reduced considerably.	Proposed for Stage I, Phase 2.
Monetary reforms			
Interest rate liberalization	Not liberalized. Positive real interest most of the times.	Administered rates have been increased but not liberalized.	
Two-tier banking system	Enacted in 1985	Enacted in 1988	
Financial market development	Stock markets established in two cities.	Non-formal institutions.	
External sector reforms			
Exchange rate	Unification in 1984. Dual market reappeared later on. Competitive real exchange rate.	Unification in 1989. Deviation between official and parallel rate is small. Competitive real exchange rate.	Dual exchange rate proposed for Stage I, Phase 1. Movement toward unification starting in Stage I, Phase 2.
Controls over imports and exports	Controls of trade management greatly reduced.	Restrictions on trade have been reduced to some extent.	
Mobilization of resources from émigrés	Active promotion.	Active promotion.	Proposed for Stage I, Phase 1.
International Organizations	China returned to the World Bank and the IMF in 1978. China applied to GATT in 1991.		

— Socialist Republic of Vietnam, "*Report of the Government of the Socialist Republic of Vietnam to the Consultative Group Meeting,*" Hanoi, October 1994, p. 8.

In both the shock therapy and gradual approaches, the dynamism of the economy is driven by: (1) the swift entry of new, small and medium non-state enterprises to less regulated activities that induces the shift of resources from sectors of low productivity to more productive ones and provide employee incentives; (2) the correct price signals from relatively liberalized markets; and (3) the outward orientation of the economy.

Although it may account for a relatively small share of production, this plays a major role in improving supply and introducing property relations that conform to the market economy. The initial response of the economy to the entry of PEs permits large increases in output based on only minor investments. In the gradual approach, the older planned allocation system and the distorted macro-policy environment are not immediately disrupted, but gradually become unsustainable and are slowly relaxed in the face of challenges from non-state enterprises as well as from the autonomous or decentralized SEs. In China, the local governments or communities that established the town and village enterprises (TVEs) are moved by the goals of developing their areas and extending non-agricultural employment, and depend on the TVEs for a large share of their revenues. The TVEs have been a powerful engine of growth and are market-driven and outside the web of official price and output controls that still circumscribe the activity of the SEs. They receive bureaucratic support, as well as assistance in obtaining bank credit on commercial terms, etc. The interactions and linkages between the TVEs and the SEs have determined development patterns in the medium and long term. It would be incorrect to conclude that the SEs have crowded out the TVEs or the PEs.

The three key elements of the Chinese supply-side strategy that characterize it and clearly differentiate it from other reform strategies (i.e. perestroika or the big bang) are: (1) the *gradual* but continual and cumulative introduction of market prices and competi-tion over a broad range of the economy; (2) the *gradual* openness to the new entry of firms into sectors previously reserved to state monopoly control; and (3) the *gradual* openness to foreign trade and investment, the so-called "open door" policy. The strategy was also intended to retain the main elements of the planning and institutional apparatus and try to restructure SEs under this system. The opening began with the abandonment of the commune system in agriculture, own-account work and services, and later foreign trade and manufacturing.

The collective system, including cooperatives, was dismantled and agriculture was returned to the household production system to develop the initiative, enthusiasm, energy and dynamism of farm households. The state made appropriate investments to develop rural infrastructure, with active participation of local communities and institutions. Farms previously in traditional agricultural communes were broken up into small farms for lease, the so-called "household" or "contract responsibility system." State marketing agencies gradually raised procurement prices of agricultural products toward world-market levels, private plots were enlarged, diversification and specialization of agricultural production was encouraged and restrictions on prices, rural markets and non-agricultural activities were relaxed, as well as increasingly deregulated and less encumbered by red tape, all of which raised farm productivity. Land was deemed public rather than land being privatized or given to the former owners, the communal land within each village was more or less equally divided among the peasant households, but individuals could buy, sell and transfer long-term agricultural leases. Farmers received land leases initially for a limited period and later for up to 15 years, with permission for the transfer and inheritance of rights.

A major concomitant of market-oriented reforms has been the progressive decentralization of economic decision-making and expanding market incentives. The central driving force is intense competition between SEs, TVEs and PEs which, by eroding the profits of SEs, spurs them to reduce costs and innovate. Moreover, since profits constitute a key element of the tax base, reducing profits lowers tax revenue, thereby hardening the government budget constraint. The government has responded by reducing subsidies to SEs, forcing them to maintain the momentum of innovation and cost reductions.

These elements have been capable of dealing at the same time with the legacy of central planning and gearing the engine of economic growth. Thus, the emphasis is not so much on immediate improvement of static efficiency, both productive and allocative, but on determining and gradually strengthening and deepening the dynamic process of ingenious supply expansion, technological innovation and application, as well as permanent restructuring in response to changes in relative scarcities.

China and Vietnam have increasingly used a dual pricing system by which most of the goods have both a market price and an administered or official price as well. Under this scheme the role of state-controlled prices diminishes over time and that of market determined price increases. Additionally, the former would gradually be brought in line with the latter. By allowing above-plan production to be sold at market prices typically higher that those allowed for delivery commitments, the government created incentives to expand production. Dual pricing also forces SEs to compete and improve quality to please their customers. This linking of effort and rewards has resulted in a spectacular increase in production. The fact that the price received from the market is higher merely means that the firm is facing the equivalent of a lump-sum tax for production up to the level of compulsory quotas.

Price and wage reforms have consisted of gradual but cumulative adjustments to administered prices and wages as well as expanding price and wage liberalization. Government price and wage controls have become less effective as market forces and the private sector have grown in importance. The expanding private sector has been exerting positive influence on the state through filling spaces that the state was staying away from, but also by applying competitive pressures when their areas have overlapped. Also, the presence of a viable and vigorous private sector has allowed the planners to improve monitoring of SEs and to make them responsible for their profits and

losses. Apparently, these strategic mechanisms have been sufficient to kick off a virtuous cycle of powerful economic growth and dynamic flexibility for the entire economy.

In China, microeconomic reforms (price reform, agricultural reform, industrial enterprise reform except privatization and reforms of the legal framework under which enterprises operate) were adopted earlier than macroeconomic reforms (fiscal, monetary and foreign trade) but within a relatively stable macroeconomic environment. China has attained quick supply responses and developed increasingly efficient markets.

The AMSM approach has not disrupted production in the state sector. It achieved similar or better effects than the "big bang" approach in the non-state sector, but was able to avoid its economic costs on SEs and its major social and political costs to society. The efficiency of SEs has improved as they become more autonomous and begin moving toward more realistic relative prices, facing competition from the non-state sector and financial constraints ("hard budget constraints").

Because the reform process has been gradual, the people have had sufficient time to make adjustments to the new market structures and institutions. The AMSM approach acknowledges that new institutions require time and understanding, especially the behavioral parts—ethical standards of behavior, habits, attitudes—which will inevitably evolve slowly, through the learning-by-doing process and are constrained by local idiosyncracies. The majority benefits from the market-based reforms because the economy maintains strong growth throughout the whole process. This has played a central role in supporting the momentum of piecemeal but expanding market-based reforms. The gradual approach in China, Vietnam and Laos PDR has followed a path which has induced virtuous institutional innovations and turned increasingly free national markets into places of profitable learning.

Jefferson and Rawski (1994) see the dynamics of partial reform in China's industry as a succession of responses to imbalance by both enterprises and government in a similar fashion to Hirschman's response to disequilibria in *Strategy of Development* (1958). Hirschman argued that imbalances induce not only vibrant market reactions but also government action. The dynamics that transform partial and gradual reform into improved performance is self-sustaining, simple and direct:[28]

1. Partial reform measures have reduced the entry barriers, lowered the cost of many types of transactions and eroded market segmentation, thereby reducing barriers to new technologies and resource flows.

2. Reform intensifies competition in markets for industrial products. Small and medium enterprises particularly have appeared flexible enough and have reacted rapidly to the new market conditions.

3. Stronger competition erodes profits and curtails the growth of wages and fiscal revenues. Reduced profitability limits the growth of wages and bonuses for some firms and throws others into a position of financial loss. The erosion of profits limits the growth of revenues accruing to the local, provincial and central governments.

4. Enterprises react to market pressures by searching for financial gain through modernization, increasing factor productivity and cost reduction, realized through the acquisition and application of technology improvements.

5. On balance, government policy increases industry autonomy and market exposure and hardens budget constraints.

6. Feedback mechanisms amplify and extend the reform process through technical development, economizing efforts and incremental reform. Piecemeal reforms generate a momentum of their own. The basic approach to reforms has been remarkably consistent. China's decision to create a market-based economic system ("market socialism") is an endogenous outcome of the successful partial reform process that generated forces which led to further reform, a process that is continuing to the present.

McKinnon (1994) has pointed out that China was able to avoid the inflation tax by liberalizing agriculture, self-employment and services in 1978 and imposing hard budget constraints and maintaining price controls (to avoid monopolistic price rises) on the increasingly liberalized SEs. The price controls are also necessary to peg price levels in order to provide a nominal anchor among SEs with soft budgets. To start the evolutionary search for efficient organization and a fitting mix of the public and private sectors, an initial "minimum bang" was made toward establishing a new institutional and organizational dynamics and order. By 1984, the focus of rapid economic growth had shifted to rural light industry, which began to absorb much of the labor released by productivity improvements in agriculture. The first important decision was to permit rural communities to keep the bulk of their incomes as savings and invest them in non-agricultural activities. Mobilizing increased domestic resources added to the development momentum and spread development throughout the country. This stimulated a new class of entrepreneurs operating in the countryside. China at the same time retained price controls, restrained financial support for traditional soft-budget SEs, and set positive interest rates for savings deposits thereby creating incentives to households and enterprises to build up their financial assets and soaking up potentially excess household purchasing power. SEs have become major lenders to the state itself. High capital formation rates in China have been a response to abundant economic opportunities (high real rates of return) and looser economic controls.

---

28. In Vietnam the government introduced an initial set of measures to harden budget constraints of public firms, including the elimination of budgetary subsidies and interest rate reforms, that reduced implicit subsidies through the banking system, and the principle of equal taxation of state and private firms. These policies led to a rationalization of the sector, and several thousand loss-making enterprises were liquidated.

Other prominent features of the Chinese model are:

1. Liberalization of self-employment activities and of small and medium enterprises in trade, together with other services reforms took place early and quickly, generating a surge of services, entrepreneurial energy and savings.[29] These reforms placed greater emphasis on material incentives and allowed a larger role for the market.

2. There was strong commitment to a stable macroeconomic environment and management. Macroeconomic adjustment (stabilization and liberalization) was initiated under the "old" administrative system. Stringent fiscal and monetary policies were implemented. There was little bank credit to the newly liberalized sectors in agriculture, services or industry, and constrained financial support to traditional soft-budget SEs. The enormous growth in savings and stocks of financial assets allowed the liberalized sector to finance itself.[30] The exchange rate has been periodically adjusted to maintain a competitive real exchange rate. The state has also occasionally used large external balances at its disposal to cool down the economy with imports.

3. Controls and monitoring of SEs have continued, although increasingly focused on profitability rather than plan fulfillment. The size of the central plan is fixed in absolute terms, but the SEs are allowed to exceed planned goals. The bonus system stimulates workers and management to increase their production targets, prodding them to ensure firms operate efficiently. Profit and depreciation allowance retentions are permitted. Greater financial and decision-making autonomy was provided to enterprises to enable them to become more efficient and respond dynamically to changing market opportunities.

4. A liberal foreign investment policy was implemented. China provided generous incentives to foreign investors and did not establish any discrimination against Chinese émigré investors. The restrictions on foreign investment were eased not only in the special trade zones but also in the rest of the country. The émigré communities have played a crucial role in the export-led growth and in the large inflow of direct investment, technological catch-up, technical assistance, human capital and trade infrastructure, thereby enhancing the performance of the supply side of the economy. They have provided the quickest source of equity for private entrepreneurs and, given the shortage of working capital, this flow was essential for private sector development, the largest source of state-of-the-art foreign investment and technology, a major conduit for Chinese exports, and an invaluable source of commercial know-how for exporting to industrial market economies. There has been an incentive to domestic entrepreneurs to invent fictitious foreign partners or to work thorough foreign fronts. Special trade zones were established to eliminate or reduce the burdensome and slow internal administrative procedures to foreign investors. The distinction between "special economic zones" and the rest of the economy has gradually eroded. The resulting capital widening and deepening, especially improvements in the quality of the capital stock, have increased labor productivity and income at a faster rate than would have been possible otherwise.

5. There has been a gradual and step-by-step opening to foreign trade but with a clear outward growth orientation. Instead of close integration to the world economy, China has sought a strategic integration to the extent that it is conducive improving its economic growth and upgrading its industrial development. China has provided high margins of effective protection and has discouraged consumption of "non-essential and

---

29. In Vietnam national savings increased from 3.2 percent of GDP in 1989 to 16.3 percent in 1992. This was associated with the stabilization of the economy, strengthening of property rights, and improvements in the banking system.

30. One of the most positive features of Vietnam's financial sector reform has been the entry of new banks, mostly private, both domestic and foreign.

luxury imports." Not only were exports promoted strongly but imports were controlled, giving preference to importing the technology and capital goods that obsolete production facilities required. The government allocated directly a great deal of foreign exchange and preferential treatment was given to imports which are thought to best for China's industrialization drive. The Chinese approach to freeing foreign trade has been gradualist. Instead of a "big bang" that suddenly opened up the whole economy to international competition, world prices and capital movements, special trade zones somewhat outside the control of the traditional state trading monopolies were started in the provinces of Guangdong and Fujian in connection with the Hong Kong trade. Then these special zones were expanded to other areas within the Southern Coast region (Zhejiang and Jiangsu provinces) and became progressively more numerous and broader in scope. Inside such zones, exporters could retain all of their foreign exchange earnings while having freer access to imported materials, foreign capital, trading services and in general having far fewer regulations and restrictions. By the end of the 1980's, exports had become China's new engine of economic growth and the distinction between special trade zones and the rest of the economy had eroded as had the domestic economy's insulation from the world market. There are still many controls on imports and on capital movements.

6. External borrowing has remained low and predominantly medium and long-term from official sources. A substantial proportion of it has been on concessional terms.

7. The legal and institutional frameworks have not kept pace with economic progress and are still deficient and limited, especially in relation to ill-defined ownership property rights. China does not have a rule of law and the judicial system is not independent, but the authorities have kept and fulfilled their simple and clear economic promises and have continued and expanded the reform program. However, in the case of Viet-

nam it was very important to define and establish the rights of the local entrepreneurs to encourage foreign investment. Vietnam has introduced several laws since 1989 to implement market socialism and create an enabling environment for the private sector to formally engage in business in many areas. However, a deficient legal framework made up of cumbersome regulatory laws and uncertain substantive laws is perceived by the private sector as one of the most serious obstacles to its expansion.

The main strength of the AMSM is that it has been able to generate high and sustainable rates of economic growth through an expanding private sector based on a framework of microeconomic liberalization and deregulation of economic activities and on a relative stable macroeconomic management. The levels of political repression, while remaining unacceptable by international standards, have declined dramatically since the introduction of reforms in both countries. Besides the continued monopoly of the Communist Party, the lack of political reforms and pervasive official corruption, its major economic weaknesses are narrow legal and ill-defined property rights, slow or lack of privatization, and weak legal institutions for stable policies that make for uncertain economic development in the future. Undoubtedly, a more liberal economic and political system has much more flexibility.

THE IMPORTANCE OF STATE ENTERPRISE RESTRUCTURING

The "big bang" approach to SEs restructuring, which prevailed in the early transition in Eastern Europe, featured full and immediate exposure to free market forces (both internal and international) and privatization of large SEs, often heavily indebted and with tainted balance sheets and it appears to be based on some kind of public policy ineffectiveness proposition. It expected that the boost from decreasing real wages, the elimination of all subsidies, the boost of free trade and anti-monopoly legislation, would create a supply-side growth momentum, getting promising SEs in shape to compete and encouraging new PEs. The elimination of subsidies to SEs would lead to lower interest rates, less inflationary money creation, lower real wages, and very likely to a growing demand for PEs. It put more emphasis on getting the prices right than on making markets work efficiently. However, this approach was either irrelevant or injurious to the restructuring needs of SEs in light of the actual problems they were encountering. It is clear that the adjustment period should be long enough to avoid too sudden and large reduction in the economic viability of the enterprise, but not so long as to blunt the incentive to adjust.

Van Brabant (1995) considers this a de facto or disguised passive industrial policy, a thorough hands-off policy to facilitate specializing according to static comparative advantage, and that as such it has been ill-advised. Long-term problems of SEs include too-narrow product lines, weak management costs and information systems, low-quality production, outdated technologies and production methods, and obsolete capital equipment. Further, the SEs began to incur losses in a stagnant or shrinking macroeconomic environment. Generally the mainstream economic literature blames the "inertial supply" response of SEs on poor managerial motivation, politicized employee councils and general lack of discipline.

According to Amsden (1994), the task of restructuring SEs requires time—around 5 years—to upgrade the technologies by acquisition and application, along with quality improvement that are all fundamental to create competitiveness and cannot be accomplished simply by full, immediate exposure to free market forces or by "pseudo-privatization" (the transfer or "giveaway" of public assets to private owners without a real exchange of financial resources, skills and technological expertise). Amsden considers that the "supply inertia" has been due to flawed transition policies related to restructuring that hindered the SEs economic progress. Her analysis of the Polish and Hungarian "rough and tumble" experiences indicates little evidence that either worker militance or managerial myopia lay behind the "supply inertia." Instead, tight monetary policies severely weakened the financial structures of the great majority of inher-

ently viable SEs that were unable to find private buyers. The immediate liberalization of imports tended to devastate even promising SEs in certain import-competing industries. During the restructuring, given all the adverse externalities or "prisoners' dilemmas" involved, the solution inevitably requires a more cooperative, gradual approach, involving the government, the enterprises and private agents such as banks and professional consultants, giving firms time to restructure their productive processes and resulting in lower dislocation costs in the form of unemployment and bankruptcies. Such participation, therefore, needs to be systematically planned and carefully designed, implemented, monitored, assessed and fine-tuned. Further, it is very likely that there are economies of scale in both generating production quality and in acquiring and applying new technologies and production methods.

In a study of structural adjustment in nine economies in the Pacific Basin, Patrick and Meisner (1991) found different degrees of government intervention in market-driven economic restructuring, but they did not find any evidence of restructuring by market forces alone. Highly selective interventions simply led the market.

According to Taylor (1994) the difference between shockers and gradualists is whether SEs operations stimulate or retard PEs activity and capital formation; in other words, whether "SEs crowd PEs in or out." He indicates that shockers consider that if SEs are healthy they will increase borrowing requirements and consequently generate financial disarray, while gradualists consider that if SEs are healthy they will reduce borrowing requirements thereby avoiding financial disarray. Of course, he is being disingenuous, as his conclusions contradict most of the conventional wisdom about the SEs in the transition and, as a consequence, about how to proceed with the transformation. McKinnon (1991) had already argued that rapid privatization of large SEs may cause a sharp decline in budgetary revenues.

REFERENCES

Alice H. Amsden, Jacek Kochanowics and Lance Taylor, *The Market Meets Its Match*, Cambridge, Mass., Harvard University Press, 1994.

Pedro Aspe, *Economic Transformation the Mexican Way*, Cambridge, Mass., The MIT Press, 1993.

J. M. van Brabant, "Property Rights Reforms, Macroeconomic Performance, and Welfare" in *Transformation of Planned Economies*. Paris: Organization for Economic Cooperation and Development.

Julio Carranza, Luis Gutiérrez y Pedro Monreal, *Cuba: La Restructuración de la Economía* (La Habana: Centro de Estudios sobre América), preliminary draft, January 1995.

Rolando H. Castañeda and George P. Montalván, "Transition in Cuba: A Comprehensive Stabilization Proposal and Some Key Issues," *Cuba in Transition Volume 3*, Washington, D.C., 1993, pp 11-72.

Paul Cook and Frederick Nixson, ed., *The Move to the Market?*, London, St Martin's Press, 1995.

Louis Emmerij, *Eastern Europe in a Development Perspective*, paper presented to a conference on "East Europe: Between Western Europe and East Asia," May 19-21, 1994, Aaoborg University, Denmark.

European Bank Reconstruction and Development, *Transition Reports*, 1994 and 1995.

Roberto Frenkel, "Macroeconomic Sustainability and Development Prospects: Latin American Performance in the 1990's," United Nations Conference on Trade and Development, Discussion Paper No. 100, August 1995.

Alan Gelb, Gary Jefferson, and Inderjit Singh, "Can Communist Economies Transform Incrementally—The Experience of China," *NBER Macroeconomics 1993*, pp. 87-133.

Albert Hirschman, *Strategy of Development*, New Haven, Yale University Press, 1958.

Gary H. Jefferson and Thomas G. Rawski, "How Industrial Reform Worked in China: The Role of Innovations, Competition and Property Rights," *Proceedings of the World Bank Annual Conference on Development Economics*, 1994, pp 129-156.

Harry G. Johnson, "The Keynesian Revolution and the Monetarist Counter-Revolution," *American Economic Review*, May, 1971.

Charles P. Kindleberger, *World Economic Primacy: 1500-1990*, Oxford, Oxford University Press, 1995.

Janos Kornai, *The Road to a Free Economy*, New York, W.W. Norton, 1990.

Janos Kornai, *Highway and Byways*, Cambridge, Mass, The MIT Press, 1995.

Richard Kozul-Wright and Paul Reymond, "Walking on Two Legs: Strengthening Democracy and Productive Entrepreneurship in Transition Economies," United Nations Conference on Trade and Development, Discussion Paper No. 101, August 1995.

David Lipton and Jeffrey Sachs, "Creating a Market in Eastern Europe: the Case of Poland," *Brookings Papers on Economic Activity*, Vol. 1, 1990, pp. 75-133.

Ronald I. McKinnon, *The Order of Economic Liberalization: Financial Control in the Transition to a Market Economy*, Baltimore Md, John Hopkins University Press, 1991.

Ronald I. McKinnon, "Gradual versus Rapid Liberalization in Socialist Economies: The Problem of Macroeconomic Control," *Proceedings of the World Bank Annual Conference on Development Economics*, 1993, pp 63-94.

Hugh Patrick and Larry Meisner, ed., *Pacific Basin Industries in Distress: Structural Adjustment and Trade Policy in the Nine Industrialized Economies*, New York, Columbia University Press, 1991.

John Page, "The East Asia Miracle:Four Lessons for Development Policy," *NBER Macroeconomics 1993*, pp. 219-281.

Dwight Heald Perkins, "Reforming China's Economic System," *Journal of Economic Literature*, 1988, pp. 601-645.

Kazimiers Z. Poznanki, ed., *The Evolutionary Transition to Capitalism*, Boulder, Westview Press, 1995

Pradumna B. Rana, "Reform Strategies in Transitional Economies: Lessons form Asia," *World Development*, 1995, pp 1157-1169.

Jeffrey D. Sachs, "Comment on Gelb et al.," *NBER Macroeconomics 1993*, pp 137-147.

Ajit Singh, "The Plan, the Market and Evolutionary Economic Reform in China," United Nations Conference on Trade and Development, Discussion Paper No. 76, February 1995.

Ajit Singh, "How did East Asia Grow so Fast?," United Nations Conference on Trade and Development, Discussion Paper No. 97, February 1995.

Robert Skidelsky, *The World after Communism*, London, MacMillan, 1995.

Barbara Stallings, ed., *Global Change, Regional Response*, New York, Cambridge University Press, 1995.

Larry Summers, "Comment on Fischer," *Brookings Papers on Economic Activity*, No. 1, 1992, pp 112-116.

Lance Taylor, "Enterprise and the State", pp 129-157, Alice H. Amsden, Jacek Kochanowics and Lance Taylor *The Market Meets Its Match*, Cambridge, Mass., Harvard University Press, 1994.

World Bank, *World Development Report*, New York, Oxford University Press, 1991.

LEGAL POLICY FOR A FREE CUBA: LESSONS FROM THE CIVIL LAW

Néstor E. Cruz

It can truly be said that the magistrate is a speaking law, and the law a silent magistrate.

— Cicero (106 b.c. - 43 b.c.).

A republic [is defined] to be a government of laws and not of men.

— John Adams (1735 - 1826). Second president of the United States.

This short essay attempts to compare the Civil Law to the common law as alternative legal paradigms for a free Cuba. Although the author is a common lawyer and not a civilian lawyer, theory and experience has persuaded him the Civil Law model is superior to the common law model for reasons of cost, clarity, simplicity, and stability. The author would even attempt to persuade his colleagues in the United States that this country should convert to the Civil Law, if that were possible, but the weight of history cannot be overcome with logic. Cuba, on the other hand, was a civilian country before the revolution. Although the so-called "socialist" system prevails in Cuba, a return to the Civil Law, with some changes and adjustments would seem to be not only desirable, but almost inevitable. Nonetheless, the author believes such a paper as this is helpful to remind Cubans, in and out of Cuba, that the Civil Law system is quite respectable.

Codes are the heart of the Civil Law system. Precedents exist but only to fill the lacunae in the codes. Moreover, few precedents are used and only after they have been confirmed several times by the courts. Put another way, codes are drafted to cover systematically a whole area of law and they are the primary source of law. Precedent is purely secondary and of little importance in day to day practice. When a civilian attorney is confronted with a legal problem of a civil nature, the attorney reaches for the Civil Code and carefully studies the articles in the Code applicable to the problem. The attorney then applies the Code to the facts and comes up with the legal answer. In case of ambiguity, which is rare, the attorney would first consult a treatise explaining the Code and in the last instance the body of jurisprudence. Treatises often refer to the applicable precedent, if any. A treatise is generally more authoritative than an isolated case. Fortunately, precedents are hard to find and rarely well indexed or digested so as a practical matter they matter even less than in theory.

Although codes have existed since the times of Hammurabi, king of Ancient Babylon, modern codes owe their existence to Napoleon I. In fact, codification is probably one of the most enduring achievements of Napoleon and he even dictated to his secretaries the first drafts of some articles in his Code. Napoleon's theory was that the law should be available, without the intervention of lawyers, to the emerging French middle classes. This set the tone for subsequent codes throughout the Civil Law world. Codes should be comprehensive, clear, concise, to the point, simple, and terse. Legal problems should admit of only one answer after applying the codes to the facts. Although codes have always had a partial empirical basis, the logic of the legislator has been no less important. If the natural sciences can truly be said to be a marriage of induction and deduction (observations plus mathematics), the codes were supposed to be analogous. It is thus, as we shall see, that when John Keats (1795-1821) wrote that "a thing of beauty is a joy for ever" he could have been referring to the Colombian Civil Code.

In Civil Law jurisdictions those fields of law known in the United States as domestic relations, real property, contracts, torts, and others familiar to laymen are covered in one Civil Code. When the author interned in a Bogota law firm the summer of 1970, right after law school, the author only knew American law and Spanish (not that well). A client of the firm had a problem of easements ("servidumbres"), a common problem in real property. The senior partner gave the author the facts, literally threw at him the Civil Code, and instructed the author to come up with a solution pronto. The solution was easy, not because the author is a particularly able lawyer, not because his Spanish is particularly good, but because all the author did was look up "servidumbres" in the detailed table of contents, carefully study the relevant articles in the Code, apply the articles to the facts, and draft a memorandum of law offering a simple and elegant solution for the client. When the memorandum was discussed with opposing counsel, he agreed with our client's position, and the case was over before it started. Had that been an isolated instance, one could assume the outcome was pure luck. However, the author repeated the same process three more times using the Colombian Labor Code, the Venezuelan Tax Code, and the Venezuelan Labor Code. Clearly, more than luck was involved here. The Codes operated just as the legislators had intended. Were it not for the wonderful draftsmanship of the jurists who codified the law, the outcomes would have been complex, unstable, inelegant, couched in uncertain language, of limited value to the client, and, worst of all, might have resulted in interminable litigation. Next, the author will examine the American system and its completely opposite outcomes.

To fully understand the nature of American law, one must delve into English legal history. After the Battle of Hastings in 1066, William the Conqueror was faced with enormous administrative problems. He

attacked some with great tenacity. For example, he ordered minute and accurate surveys of all his new land, which were compiled in the Domesday Book. On the other hand, since there was no Parliament or legislature, the process of making law was left to the courts as they decided controversies on a case by case basis. This is what is meant by common law: judge-made law. Given this historical accident, judges in England and later in the United States were enormously powerful figures because they were literally legislators as well as adjudicators. The common law of England was imported wholesale to the American colonies and remained intact after the Constitution was adopted. In modern times, however, the common law approach has created at least two serious problems for the American legal system: first, the question of precedent and "Shepardizing"; second, the stubborn insistence by American judges and other adjudicators to make law in the common law tradition, even when a field of law has been codified.

Due to the doctrine of stare decisis, all reported cases are precedent. This might have worked when the number of reported cases was small. It does not work now because there are fifty states, D.C., several commonwealths, and an enormous body of Federal law. There are literally 3 or 4 million reported cases and they are all precedents. This brings us to the subject of "Shepardizing." When an American lawyer renders a legal opinion, litigates, or designs transactions, the lawyer must state that as of the moment in time when the opinion is rendered, the litigation starts, or the transaction closes, the underlying law is "good law". That means that every case on which the attorney relies must be "Shepardized". The process of "Shepardizing" is tedious, time-consuming, and, therefore, expensive. "Shepardizing" consists of taking any given case which was good law at the time it was decided, and looking up the case in a series of forbidding volumes known as Shepard's Citations. There one will find whether the case is still good law, or whether the case has been modified, reversed, superseded, vacated, criticized, distinguished, limited, questioned, or, most importantly, expressly overruled. Manual "Shepardizing" is the most boring thing an attorney must do. With the advent of computerized legal research, "Shepardizing" has now become a matter of pushing a button. However, to the author's knowledge, "Shepardizing" is not offered as an un-bundled service, so "button Shepardizing" is still beyond the means of the average client.

The second problem adverted to is the attitude of modern judges and other adjudicators. Some fields of American law have been either legislated or codified by the legislative branch. One would think that at that point, precedent would be relegated to a well-deserved oblivion. Such is not the case. American statutes or Codes are remarkably obscure compared to Civil Law Codes. This is probably because American legislators have no experience in drafting laws, because laws are sometimes intentionally vague if a majority cannot be found for a clear statement of the law, and because American legislators sometimes insist on covering every possible detail. Nevertheless, all these drafting problems aside, American adjudicators still believe themselves to be omnipotent common law judges. The outcome is complexity and uncertainty for the client. An example or two will suffice. The National Labor Relations Act, the labor code of the United States, is only about 20 pages long. The published decisions of the National Labor Relations Board, a quasi-judicial agency established in 1935 to administer the Act, run into more than 300 volumes of around 1000 pages each. All the decisions in those volumes are precedent, and each decision ever cited must be "Shepardized." If the Board had been true to its mission, it would have merely applied the Act to cases before it and published just a few important precedents. However, for fifty years the Board has been acting ultra vires, not out of malice but out of misperception of its proper function. The final irony of this saga is that upon researching the law in many different areas, the author has found "good law" cases on both sides of every issue. Judges and other adjudicators accomplish this dubious feat two ways: first, they simply ignore other cases and decide cases before them as they see fit; second, they "distinguish" inconvenient cases on the facts, even when the operative facts are identical. It is thus that an American lawyer can give the client sound advice one way, while opposing counsel can give the client sound advice going precisely the opposite way. The predictable outcome is the present litigation explosion where both parties can in good faith claim that they are legally correct.

This sad state of affairs brings us back full-circle to the wisdom of the Civil Law which virtually ignores precedent and sticks to the plain meaning of the Codes. In the common law setting the surplus of precedent means, in practice, that there are no precedents at all. One can only reach the realistic, but not cynical, conclusion that the common law method "is a tale told by an idiot, full of sound and fury, signifying nothing." Macbeth.

With respect to the law of evidence there are marked differences between the Civil Law and the common law, due to the presence of juries in the latter system. In the Civil Law there are few rules of evidence. Judges are given the power to freely evaluate the proof ("libre apreciación de la prueba"). That is why they are judges in the first place. In the common law, the law of evidence is a tangled web designed to keep facts from the jury. In other words, the common law treats jurors as a bunch of morons incapable of common sense or good judgment. The recognition of this anomaly led England to abolish juries in 99% of civil cases sometime ago; yet, even after our mother country saw the errors of its ways, we cling to juries in civil cases despite overwhelming evidence from both sides of the Atlantic, that the jury system is very expensive and inefficient. The author can offer no explanation for this anomaly, except, perhaps as a form of cultural isolationism. Needless to say, even in the face of a jury, it is very easy for a corrupt common law judge to throw a case by his rulings on objections, jury instructions, or the use of judgment non obstante veredicto.

With respect to civil and administrative procedure, the American system is theoretically superior. In practice both systems have problems. The guiding light of American procedure are the Federal Rules approved in the late thirties. The drafters, all jurists of some note, however, could not foresee that their straightforward code of procedure would be abused by attorneys and distorted by judges in the manner already discussed with respect to the National Labor Relations Act and other laws or codes. Almost every impartial authority on the subject has called for drastic reform and simplification of the rules of procedure. The rules were designed for the efficient administration of justice, but because of The Law of Unintended Consequences, the rules have become an almost insurmountable obstacle to that end. Reaching the merits in many civil and administrative cases has become nearly impossible because of procedural maneuvers. Attorneys can quite ethically, if not morally, use the rules to frustrate reaching the merits with highly technical devices, motions, and discovery abuse. Some judges are reluctant to interfere in the common law tradition of judge as referee, instead of the modern view of judge as active participant and litigation manager. In the Civil Law, on the other hand, civil and administrative procedure expressly require so many long written pleadings, that the average litigant cannot afford vindication of rights or defense of interests. Since most law, despite rumors to the contrary, is practiced as a tailor would craft a made to order suit and not simply by filling-in the blanks in off the rack forms, as many believe, the requirement of several detailed pleadings of fact and law, by nature labor intensive, make litigation prohibitive. A happy combination of both systems, with two short pleadings of fact and law and limited discovery, would seem to make more economic sense without sacrificing the quality of the ultimate decision. Put another way, the author suggests that drastic simplification of procedure (not to mention substance and evidence) would lower legal unit costs at a small cost in quality. In fact, the possibility even exists that quality would improve since parties and judges would concentrate on the important and not on the tangential.

In fact, if unit costs (and prices) decline significantly, one could assume that quantity demanded would increase, attorneys could still earn their target hourly rates, and consumers would have more affordable legal services. The author has always found specious the argument often heard that lawyer income is directly proportional to legal complexity. The author suggests, to the contrary, that income per lawyer is inversely proportional to legal complexity. Controlling for GDP per lawyer or population per lawyer, there is no reason why this suggestion might not be true. Arguing by analogy, in the long run real wages

grow at about the same rate as output per hour. Then, if through efficiency gains derived from demystifying law, the cost of one unit of law produced and consumed can be lowered sufficiently, real wages of attorneys, at the very least, should not suffer.

Perhaps the alternative dispute resolution (ADR) movement in the United States constitutes partial verification of the propositions in the previous paragraph. The most efficient ADR mechanism is final and binding arbitration. The parties submit to an arbitrator the issues to be decided with terms of reference containing the law and uncontested facts. The arbitrator holds hearings in which witnesses and documents are examined under very informal rules of procedure and evidence. At the end of the process, the arbitrator issues his or her award. The award is virtually incontestable in the courts. The parties obtain a swift resolution of their dispute, the attorneys earn their regular hourly fee, and the arbitrator earns his or hers. The total cost to the parties is a mere fraction of litigation in the courts. It is argued in opposition to arbitration, that the parties lose their right to appeal. This argument, however, is fallacious. Appeals in the courts are expensive and interminable. In fact, most decisions of trial courts are never appealed. Moreover, most trial court decisions are affirmed on appeal. Therefore, in practice, losing parties in the courts are no better off than losing parties in arbitration. ADR has grown organically, slowly but surely, perhaps because sophisticated consumers of law had tacit knowledge of the real legal world. ADR is now consciously and expressly pursued by many legal actors. The American Bar Association created an ADR section in 1994 and ADR courses are proliferating as part of continuing legal education. One of the temptations ADR advocates should avoid is replication of the regular legal system. The failure of the Federal Rules of Civil Procedure should give pause to those who forget the key word in ADR: "alternative." It is not too soon to worry. Ian R. Macneil, the author's contracts professor at Cornell Law School, has just published a five-volume treatise titled "Federal Arbitration Law." After all that has been discussed above, ADR and Professor Macneil's $645.00 treatise appear to be manifestly incompatible.

THE PRESENT STATUS QUO OF PROPERTY RIGHTS IN CUBA

Juan C. Consuegra-Barquín

The current Cuban situation shows just how difficult it will be for a future democratic government to commit to property restitution. Official statistics in Cuba reflect a significant shortage of family housing, an increasingly unsafe and deteriorating housing infrastructure, and a high density of families living under the same roof. Furthermore, Cuban exiles (mostly middle and upper class) were estimated to be over 10% of the total population by the end of 1961.[1] These, and other factors, have to be considered by any future democratic government aiming to establish an orderly public policy when considering restitution or compensation of property to former owners.[2]

The present status quo of property rights in Cuba is governed almost entirely by Cuban domestic Law. Whether Cuban nationals should be compensated for property expropriated by the Castro Regime, is also an issue to be resolved pursuant to domestic Law.[3] Nevertheless, as opposed to international law, which may play a role with respect to the compensation for property expropriated to non-Cubans, a study of Cuban domestic law is presently the sole source available in order to understand the status of property rights for Cuban nationals.

In addition, and after 36 years of government control, Fidel Castro undergoes an economic crisis caused by the disappearance of his communist allies. New types of economic reforms have been created to save the Cuban economy. Basically, these reforms authorize the creation of joint ventures between the government and foreign entities. The Cuban joint venture experiments guarantee that the foreigner will inject the hard currency needed to save the Cuban economy and, thus, ensure the government's survival.

Currently, the Cuban government, pursuant article 24 of the Constitution of 1976 (amended in 1992),[4] has made public its interest in creating a new type of property while selling it to foreigners.[5] Accordingly, this type of government action rises a numerous of interesting questions regarding how the purchase of

---

1. Hemilce Esteve, *El Exilio Cubano en Puerto Rico* 13-14 (1984).

2. Juan C. Consuegra-Barquín, *Cuba's Residential Property Ownership Dilemma: A Human Rights Issue Under International Law* 46.2 Rutgers Law Review 873, 875 (1994).

3. *Id.* at 887; *Banco Nacional de Cuba v. Sabbatino*, 307 F2d 845 (1962) at 861.

4. See, Consuegra-Barquín, supra note 2, at p.897. (note 105).

"The collapse of communism in the Soviet Union and Eastern and Central Europe brought Cuba's economy to bankruptcy. Seeking new forms of incentives to attract venture capital was one of the objectives of the 1992 amendments to the Socialist Constitution of 1976. New forms of property ownership were created as an incentive to attract joint ventures with foreign investors.

"Those amendments authorized the transfer of property title only in those cases where the transfer benefitted the economic development of the Cuban economy; and when the social, economic and political principles of the socialist State were not affected. Furthermore, a title transfers only with the approval of the Cuban Minister Council and Cuban Executive Committee." Id.

5. See Ariel Remos, *Institucionaliza Fidel Castro la Venta de Cuba*, El Diario las Américas, enero 24, 1995 at 1.

private property by a foreign entity affects the rights of present and former owners. Perhaps, among them, how does this action fit with the well recognized principle of international law which states that a successor government is bound to recognize all obligations incurred by the predecessor government?[6]

Today, it is still unclear whether a former owner could claim his property back. Since the issue is not solved, arguments to either position are well accepted. Nevertheless, it is the duty of every responsible legal scholar to avoid speculating on this issue, specially to guarantee and assure that properties confiscated will be returned or compensated. One thing is clear, however, the decision is a political question[7] that might be left for the politicians to decide and not for the Courts. Thus, and until the time comes, we will keep updating, studying, analyzing and comparing different or newly emerged theories of law, in order to help and assist the next transitional government during its imminent transformation to a free market economy and to a democratic system of government. Likewise, we also assist in answering the political

question of whether the properties confiscated must be returned to their former owners.

A considerable portion of this paper is a brief and an update of the law review article *Cuba's Residential Property Ownership Dilemma: A Human Right Issue Under International Law*, published at the Rutgers Law Review and written by this author. Such article analyzes, inter alia, the current domestic law regarding property rights and the possible related controversies that will arise in the transitional process.

THE REVOLUTION AS A SOURCE OF LAW OR "FUENTE DE DERECHO"

When analyzing the current property rights in Cuba, the first question to answer is whether the triumph of the 1959 Revolution was powerful enough to overrule the Constitution of 1940. In other words, whether the Revolution was a legit Source of Law or "Fuente de Derecho." This question has been hotly debated by multiple law scholars in the exile.[8]

The general rule regarding revolutions is that a successful revolution has the power to annul the existing

---

6. The controversial Cuban Liberty Act, S. 381 H.R. 927, will not only have to deal with this principle, but will have to address the following issues: whether the act of the state doctrine forbids a State to adjudicate the acts of another sovereign State performed within its territory; whether the United States has the authority to espouse the claims of United States citizens who were Cuban nationals at the time of the takings; whether the United States has territorial or personal jurisdiction to govern the transactions executed outside the United States between the sovereign government of Cuba and a private entity of another foreign State; whether the United States has the power under international law to adjudicate and enforce this Act; what alternatives the United States has in order to harmonize this Act with other bilateral or multilateral treatise as the North America Free trade Agreement (NAFTA) or the General Agreement of Tariffs and Trade (GATT); whether the method of compensation in the FCSC shall be similar to the traditional international standard of compensation, "prompt, adequate and effective", or merely "appropriate" compensation, according to articles 24 of the 1940 Cuban Constitution and the Cuban Fundamental Law of 1959; whether this Act deteriorates the ability of the United States to espouse legitimate claims of persons who were United states citizens prior to the property takings; and others.

7. Emilio Cueto, one of the scholars who has study the issue thoroughly, has classified the property issue as a political question "with no real solution." Emilio Cueto, *Property Claims of Cuban Nationals*, in Papers and Proceedings of the Cuban Transition Workshop, organized by the Law Firm of Shaw, Pittman, Potts & Trowbridge, Washington DC, January 26, 1995 at 4. [hereinafter RESOLUTION OF PROPERTY CLAIM WORKSHOP].

   "[t]he Cuban property claims will not, I believe, be fully resolved in a Court of Law which will carefully weigh the legal arguments on both sides of the issue. The problem is of such complexity that Law alone cannot be expected to solve it. Thus the 'resolutions' of these claims will be 'political,' in the broadest sense of the term, and will take place in a particular context which, I suspect, will emphasize National Reconciliation and Social Peace while recognizing existing reality, the scarcity of resources, and the search for viable, sustainable options." Id.

8. See: Consuegra-Barquín, supra note 2; Matías Travieso, *Some Legal and Practical Issues in the Resolution of Cuban Nationals Expropriation Claims Against Cuba*, in Resolution of Property Claim Workshop, supra note 7; Cueto, supra note 7; Nicolás Gutiérrez, Jr., *The De-Constitutionalization of Property Rights: Castro's Systematic Assault on Private Ownership in Cuba*, in Resolution of Property Claim Workshop, supra note 7; Nestor Cruz, *Legal Issues Raised by the Transition: Cuba from Marxism to Democracy, 199_-200_?*, in Cuba in Transition, Papers and Proceedings of the Association for the Studies of the Cuban Economy (ASCE) (1992)[hereinafter CUBA IN TRANSITION]; José D. Acosta, *El Marco Jurídico Institucional de un Gobierno Provisional de Unidad Nacional en Cuba*, in Cuba in Transition, supra; and others.

constitution with a new set of legal norms.[9] Matías Travieso, citing a case from the High Court of the State of Lesotho, states the appropriate test to determine whether a revolutionary government is lawful.[10] The test inquires, inter alia, if the government is firmly established, if the government administration is effective, and whether the majority of the people behaves according to the new government.[11]

Whether we like it or not, it seems that in 1959 the Cuban Supreme Court did its own research and concluded that the Cuban Revolution was legit. The Cuban historical context show that on January 1, 1959, after Fulgencio Batista, then president-dictator of Cuba, fled the country and consequently surrendered control of the Cuban government, a Resolution by the Cuban Supreme Court held that the Revolution was a legit source of law.[12] The facts indicate that

"according to the 1940 Constitution, whenever the presidential position is vacant and there is no legitimate substitute available, the most senior justice of the Supreme Court should be appointed as the next President of the Republic.[13] As a result of the demise of the Batista government, the Cuban Supreme Court confronted the specific question of the Revolution's legitimacy. Justice Carlos M. Piedra, the Supreme Court's most senior incumbent Justice, brought forth a petition to assume the presidency, based on the constitutional presidential vacancy clause.[14]

"The Cuban Supreme Court in a January 1, 1959 resolution, decided instead that the Revolution was the legitimate 'government' under the law. *It also indicat-ed that the actual situation was not the one contemplated under the 1940 Constitution, being the revolutionary movement the original cause of the Batista regime collapse, and therefore a legitimate Revolution.* As a direct result of this ruling, Manuel Urrutia Lleó, the Revolution's candidate, was recognized as the legitimate new president of Cuba."[15]

However, questions of recognition by other governments arise whenever a new government assumes power through a revolution or a military coup d'etat. Such recognition involves a combination of international law and international politics.[16] In recent years, two major approaches were developed in order to recognize a foreign government: the traditional approach and the Estrada Doctrine.[17]

Basically, the traditional approach seeks to determine: "(1) whether the government is in de facto control of the territory and in possession of the machinery of the state; (2) whether the government has the consent of the people, without substantial resistance to its administration, that is, whether there is public acquiescence in the authority of the government; and (3) whether the new government has indicated its willingness to comply with its obligations under international law..."[18] The second requisite of this traditional approach, the consent of the people, is very controversial.[19] Even though most of the states interpret such requisite to mean the people's acquies-

---

9. Matías Travieso, supra note 8, at 26. (Citing a number of legal authorities stating, inter alia, that "when revolutions are successful and their actions meet with the habitual submission from their citizens, they acquire the power to overturn prior constitutions.")

10. *Id.* at 27 (note 63).

11. Id.

12. Ramón M. Barquín, *El Dia que Fidel Castro se Apoderó de Cuba*, Annex 23-A (1978).

13. Constitution of 1940 at art. 141-149.

14. Barquín, supra note 12.

15. Consuegra-Barquín, supra note 2, at 898. (Our emphasis).

16. L.T. Galloway, *Recognizing Foreign Governments* (1978), reprinted in Barry E. Carter & Phillip R. Trimble, *International Law* at 421 (1991).

17. Id.

18. Id.

19. Id. at 422.

cence to the new government, policy makers state that the concept of actual consent is meaningless.[20]

The second approach developed is the Estrada Doctrine. This doctrine was created by the Mexican Foreign Minister Don Genaro Estrada in 1930.[21] Basically, the doctrine postulates that states only recognize new states and not new governments since "when a new government comes to power either through constitutional means or otherwise, its relation with outside states remains unchanged."[22] The Estrada Doctrine makes no distinction between a government of bullets and a government of ballots. It "embraces to the principle of unfettered national sovereignty and rejects interferences with the domestic affairs of one state by another through the granting or withholding of recognition."[23]

An unsuccessful third approach to recognizing foreign governments, known as the Tobar or Betancourt Approach, emerged in Ecuador pursuant to a multilateral treaty signed by five Central American states.[24] The approach attempted to "encourage democratic and constitutional government by refusing to recognize any government that comes to power by extra-constitutional means until a free election is held and new leaders elected..."[25]

Castro's Revolution was immediately recognized by the majority of the states, including the United States. Thus, to analyze the Revolution's recognition would be practically unnecessary. However, in the event the Cuban Revolution's recognition needs to be analyzed, I have no doubt that the Revolution would satisfactorily comply with either of the two

prevailing and international recognized approaches (the traditional or the Estrada approach). It is hard to support the theory, however, that the present Cuban regime is not legit under international law with a status of crisis and disorder.[26] Castro's government has been in power over 36 years, and throughout this period it has proven to be politically stable and consistent in maintaining power.[27]

Since Fidel Castro's revolution came into power, three constitutions have ruled over Cuba. The first constitution, the one Castro found when he came into power, was the Constitution of 1940, the second constitution was known as the Fundamental Law (Ley Fundamental) of 1959, and the third, and current constitution, is the Socialist Constitution of 1976[28].

To support the theory that the Cuban Revolution's source of law did not possess enough power to repeal the Constitution of 1940 would not seem very helpful in practice. It might cause chaos and lead to collective disorderly conduct, not to mention legal confusion to follow within the judiciary.[29]

WAS THE PROPERTY EXPROPRIATED OR ABANDONED[30]

Is the act of departing a country for political reasons, and thus, leaving property behind, an act of abandonment? Why should property be reverted to its former owner from someone who possesses a legit title, recognized by a sovereign state, for a period of over 36 years? Such questions represent one of the most complex issues to be resolved by the next Cuban transitional government. Perhaps, in order to

---

20. Id.

21. Id.

22. Id.

23. Id.

24. Id.

25. Id.

26. See Consuegra-Barquín, supra note 2, at 906.

27. Id.

28. Amended by the Constitutional Reform Law of July 13, 1992.

29. Consuegra-Barquín, supra note 2, at 899.

30. See Id. at 904-907, for a detailed explanation of this topic.

understand the issue, the following paragraph briefly explains the historical situation during the first years of the Revolution.

"During the first years of the Revolution, political persecution was intense and political assassinations rampant. There were many well documented political trials with total disregard for due process in which sentences of anywhere from 30 years to life were handed down to the more fortunate. For the not so lucky, military style executions were organized for public entertainment and consumption in a manner not unlike an early Roman circus."[31]

Abandonment is "the act whose consequences and effects are to forsake property."[32] In order for an act to become an abandonment it must have been a voluntary act.[33] The owner has to forsake its property voluntarily, or in a noncontentious manner.[34] Once the requisites are established, the abandonment has been consummated.[35]

Can there truly have been a "voluntary" abandonment of property in those cases where an owner fled Cuba for political reasons?[36] It would be difficult and unjust to believe that those political emigres voluntarily abandoned their belongings.[37]

The Cuban migratory group which owned property in Cuba was pressured, at least emotionally, to leave the country.[38] They had well founded reasons to fear a political system which was hostile to them.[39] In many cases they suffered actual political persecution from the repressive forces of the system.[40] The required test would be to ask whether it was reasonable for a normal person, confronting an imminent danger of this nature, to emigrate and voluntarily enter political exile from his or her country with the hope of returning once the crisis ends and normality is reestablished.[41]

THE EXPROPRIATION LAWS RELEVANT TO THE PROPERTY RIGHTS ISSUE

As stated before, three constitutions have ruled over Cuba, since the Revolution took control:[42] The Constitution of 1940, the Fundamental Law (Ley Fundamental) of 1959, and the third and current constitution, the Socialist Constitution of 1976, amended in 1992.

The Fundamental Law[43] empowered the creation of the Law for the Recovery of Misappropriated Properties to recover all economic goods embezzled by the former regime[44] or its collaborators.[45] The government extended the power of confiscation to those properties owned by persons who in order to avoid the jurisdiction of the Revolutionary Courts, abandoned the country.[46] Furthermore, this Law permit-

---

31. Id. at 904.

32. I. Rivera García, *Diccionario de Términos Jurídicos* 1 (1985) (our translation).

33. See: M. Albaladejo, *Derecho Civil III* 223 (1st Vol., 5th Ed. 1983); A. M. Morales Moreno, *Posesión y Usucapión* 321 (1972).

34. Consuegra-Barquín, supra note 2, at 905.

35. Albaladejo, supra note 33, (our translation).

36. Consuegra-Barquín, supra note 2, at 905.

37. Id.

38. Id.

39. Id.

40. Id.

41. Id.

42. The issue of whether the expropriation laws were constitutional or null and void, will not be addressed in this paper. For a discussion of this issue, see Consuegra-Barquín, supra note 2, at 895-907.

43. Fundamental Law, art. 24.

44. Law 112 of February 27,1959. Amended by the Law 151 of March 17,1959.

45. Law 438 of July 7, 1959. Amended by Law 746 of February 19 of 1959.

46. Law 664 of December 23, 1992.

ted the confiscation of property owned by any person considered to be a conspirator against the Revolutionary Government.[47]

The Agrarian Reform[48] expropriated privately owned property, giving it free of charge to the persons who lived on the land and worked it.[49] Likewise, the Urban Reform Law[50] gave property title to every tenant, sub-tenant or any person who possessed property. The legislative intent expressed a number of reasons for its creation including the housing crisis that characterized every underdeveloped country, the incredibly high demand for housing that existed during Batista's rule, the increase in the number of unemployed persons, and the exodus from the countryside to the cities in search of better economic opportunities.[51] The revolutionary program's stated objective was to guarantee housing to every Cuban family.[52]

The 989 Law,[53] better known as the Confiscation of Abandoned Property Law, was enacted in order to confiscate properties owned by those persons who left the island because of their disagreement with the Castro regime.[54] Through this law, the Cuban government accomplished three goals: punish the "traitors" who left, provide disincentives for other Cuban professionals who might be thinking of leaving the country, and avoid an even deeper economic crisis.[55]

THE "USUCAPION" IN THE CIVIL LAW[56]

Cuba inherited its civil legal system from Spain since its days as a Spanish colony. Even though a communist government has controlled Cuba for more than 36 years, the civil code (in modified form) still operates as the basis of Cuba's legal system. However, during this period the communist government amended all of Cuba's civil codes so they could respond to the interest of a socialist order.

The civil law's adverse possession concept is known in the Civil Law as the "usucapión" [known in latin as "usucapio"]. Even though the Cuban Civil Law System has gone through a vast number of changes, the institution of the usucapion is still in existence under the communist government.

In essence, usucapión gives title to any person who possesses a property, or a right over a certain period of years and complies with certain requisites provided by the code.[57] Also, it is defined as the possessor's acquisition of an unowned property title, without the need for the real property owner to participate in the legal proceeding of title purchasing.[58]

In civil law, properties that can be adverse possessed under usucapion are those that are legally susceptible to appropriation.[59] However, in the Cuban socialist regime, socialist personal properties are the only type of property legally subject to appropriation.[60]

---

47. Consuegra-Barquín, supra note 2, at 900.

48. The Agrarian Reform, Law of May 17, 1959. This Law will not be discussed in this article since this land is not classified as residential property.

49. Consuegra-Barquín, supra note 2, at 901

50. The Urban Reform, Law of October 14, 1960.

51. Consuegra-Barquín, supra note 2, at 901

52. Id.

53. Law 989 of Dec. 6, 1961.

54. Consuegra-Barquín, supra note 2, at 903.

55. Id.

56. See Id. at 912-923.

57. Id. at 913.

58. Id.

59. Id. at 914. Also, see id. at 907-912 (explaining the types of property recognized under the socialist constitution of 1976).

60. Id. at 914.

The 1976 Constitution established that all land belongs to the state with the exception of the holdings of small farmers and/or their cooperatives.[61] The inclusion of housing as socialist personal property needs further clarification, however, since it is somewhat unclear whether the land under the house is personal or State property.[62] Because of the constitutional definition of State property, all land is irreversibly State property except that belonging to small farmers or their cooperatives, it is logical to conclude that the land under a house must be considered state property.[63] Therefore, it must first be resolved what is considered personal property or State property under the domestic law in order to determine whether anything could be transferred by usucapion.[64]

Ancient and modern scholars[65] have explained that the purpose of the usucapion was that "ownership of property should not remain uncertain for too long a time."[66] "In this way a title could be proved by giving its history for a limited time, instead of for an indefinitely long time."[67] Moreover, society and its legal order benefit from the usucapion's objectives,[68] since the State and public interest is to maintain the certainty of property rights[69] and to secure the confidence in the trade of property and its related commerce.[70]

Under Civil Law, usucapion can be achieved in two ways: through the possessor's good faith[71] or through the possessor's bad faith.[72] A good faith, or bona fide possessor, is a holder who is unaware of a flaw in his property title.[73] On the other hand, a bad faith possessor is one who has full knowledge of the flaw on the property title or knows that by his action he is possessing a property which does not belong to him.[74]

The stated requisites for usucapion are the following: (1) there must be continuous possession without interruption, (2) under "quiet or peaceful enjoyment" possession, (3) acting in an ownership capacity, and (4) with public and open possession.[75] Good faith usucapion, however, adds two more requirements for the possessor: (1) the possession has to be in good faith--bona fide, and (2) it must be with a just title ("justo título").[76] Following, we will first define the terms of the four requirements that apply to both types of possessions, bad and good faith, and then the two additional requirements for good faith usucapion.

---

61. Id. at art. 15.

62. Id. at 911.

63. Id.

64. Id.

65. William C. Morey, *Outlines of Roman Law* 309 (1890); H. F. Jolowicz, *Historical Introduction to Roman Law* 253 (1953); W. Burdick, *The Principles of Roman Law and Their Relation to Modern Law* 342-343 (1938); W. Hunter, *A Systematic and Historical Exposition of Roman Law in Order of a Code* 265 (4th ed., 1903); Puig-Brutau, *Fundamentos de Derecho Civil* 360 (1978); Albaladejo, *supra* note 33, at 165.

66. Gaius, II.44.

67. M. Radin, *Handbook of Roman Law* 362 (1927).

68. Consuegra-Barquín, supra note 2, at 913.

69. *See:* Id.; Spain Supreme Court Judgments made on Apr. 27, 1925; Sept. 26, 1927; Jun. 29, 1935; April 21, 1958; June 11, 1960; May 5, 1961; Dec. 14, 1967. (cited by Albaladejo, supra note 33, at 165).

70. Puig-Brutau, supra note 65, at 360.

71. 1889 Civil Code, art. 1940.

72. Id. at art. 1959.

73. Consuegra-Barquín, supra note 2, at 914.

74. Id.

75. Id.

76. Id.

1. *Continuous Possession.* The possession needs to be continuous, with no interruption. However, the owner has the right to interrupt the statute of limitation of such possession. Interruption of possession is defined as the "proprietor's act which stops the usucapion's statute of limitation."[77] The 1889 Civil Code recognizes three types of interruption[78], civil interruption, natural interruption, and the voluntary recognition by the possessor. When the possessor voluntarily stops possessing the property for a year or more, the interruption will be natural.[79] Voluntary interruption occurs when the possessor voluntarily recognizes that the possession has been interrupted.[80] Lastly, civil interruption takes place through a legal or personal summon.[81]

2. *"Quiet or Peaceful Enjoyment".* The possessor shall control the property under a quiet enjoyment capacity or under a peaceful degree,[82] and cannot engage in any violent action whose purpose is to possess the property or to control it.[83]

3. *Ownership Capacity.* The possessor must possess in an ownership capacity. Ownership Capacity has a different definition for good faith possessions and bad faith possessions.[84] In the good faith possession, ownership capacity is when the possessor has reasonable cause, or good faith, to believe that the property he is possessing was legitimately and legally transferred to him.[85] How-

ever, in the bad faith possession, ownership capacity is determined by community belief that the possessor is the legitimate owner, even when the bad faith possessor knows that the property he is possessing is not his.[86] Of course, in both types of usucapion the possessor must possess with the intent of making the property part of his proprietorship.[87]

4. *Public and Open Possession.* Another usucapion requisite is that it has to be public and open. The possessor cannot hide or live clandestinely, and neighbors must see him actually possessing the property.[88]

The good faith usucapion has two more requisites which obviously do not apply to the bad faith usucapion. As mentioned before, the two requisites are the possessors obligation to have a just title and to be a bona fide possessor.

1. *Good Faith or Bona Fide Possessor.* The 1889 Civil Code defines a good faith possessor as one who ignores that he holds a flawed title, or any defect that makes his title invalid.[89] The possessor must believe that the person he obtained the title from was the legitimate proprietor.[90]

2. *Just Title.* The 1889 Civil Code defines "just title" as anything required by law to transfer a property right, or a property domain, from one

---

77. J. R. Vélez Torres, *Los Bienes, Los Derechos Reales* 25 (2nd vol., 1983).

78. See the 1889 Civil Code at art. 1943-1948.

79. Id. at art. 1944

80. Id. at art. 1948.

81. Id. at art. 1945-1947.

82. Id. at art. 1941.

83. Puig Brutau, supra note 65, at 370-371.

84. Consuegra-Barquín, supra note 2, at 915.

85. 1889 Civil Code, art. 1950.

86. Consuegra-Barquín, supra note 2, at 915.

87. Id.

88. Id.

89. 1889 Civil Code, art. 433.

90. Puig Brutau, supra note 65, at 363.

person to another.[91] At the moment of the transaction the purchaser must have believed that the proprietor had real title and domain over the property.[92] The purchaser will not be a bona fide possessor if at the moment of the transaction he had doubts about the proprietor's ownership title.[93]

CHANGES TO THE "USUCAPION" INSTITUTION BY THE NEW SOCIALIST CIVIL CODE OF 1988 AND ITS IMPLICATIONS.

The Civil Code of 1889 (inherited from Spain) and the Socialist Civil Code of 1988 are the two civil codes used by the Revolutionary Government. The 1889 Civil Code was active until the year of 1988 when the new Socialist Civil Code expressly repealed it.[94] In order to protect the socialist order, the Revolutionary Government needed a code that could respond to the interests of the proletariat and not to a capitalistic society.[95]

The Civil Code of 1889 recognized the good faith usucapion. The code provided good faith usucapion, however, with two different statutes of limitation: First, a 10 year term to adverse possess a property against a proprietor living in the Cuban jurisdiction (a "present proprietor"); and, second, a 20 year term against a proprietor not living in the Cuban jurisdiction (an "absent proprietor").[96]

However, the Socialist Civil Code of 1988 prohibited any person to adverse possess against State property or farm land. Moreover, the new Code changed

the good faith statute of limitations to a 5 year term against either type of proprietor, present or absent.[97]

On the other hand, the old civil code stated that in order to adverse possess through the bad faith usucapion, the possessor needed to possess the property for a period of 30 years.[98] The possessor did not need to be a bona fide possessor nor hold a just title.[99] Furthermore, the 30 year statute of limitation for bad faith usucapion did not distinguish between absent or present proprietor.[100]

Currently, bad faith usucapion is not recognized under the new Cuban Socialist Civil Code. Framers of the 1988 Socialist Civil Code simply did not include this type of adverse possession in order to tacitly repeal it from existence.[101]

It seems that these changes have generated a rather curious situation, which can be explained as follows:

"The Socialist Civil Code became the law of the land effective October 12, 1988. That is, exactly 29 years, 8 months and 12 days after the Castro Revolution came into power--January 1, 1959. Was there a relation between the 30 year statute of limitation for bad faith usucapio and the timing of the code's repeal? If not, why did it take so long for communist Cuba to enact a Civil Code that could respond to the country's socialist postulates?"[102]

By eliminating the institution of bad faith usucapion, the Cuban Regime only protects the former owners, who in their majority are now living in exile. The implication is of such magnitude that the former owner

---

91. 1889 Civil Code at art. 1952.

92. Consuegra-Barquin, supra note 2, at 916.

93. Vélez Torres, supra note 77, at 229.

94. Consuegra-Barquín, supra note 2, at 916.

95. See 1988 Civil Code at 3.

96. See Id. at art. 1957.

97. See 1988 Civil Code at art. 185.1.

98. See 1889 Civil Code at art. 1959.

99. Consuegra-Barquín, supra note 2, at 917.

100. Id.

101. Id.

102. Id. at 917-918.

might have a new chance to reacquire their property back. In the event that the confiscatory laws are declared unconstitutional or null and void, and held that the present possessors are not possessing in a bona fide capacity, then the present possessor not only will lose title of the property, but will not be able to acquire title under the argument of usucapion.

This author cannot understand the reasons why the Cuban Regime eliminated the bad faith usucapion institution from the Cuban Legal system three months and eighteen days prior to the 30th anniversary of the Revolution without analyzing its implications. However, it seems that the act might be another one of Castro's blind copying of the former Soviet Law,[103] which does not recognize such institution.

REQUIRED CONDITIONS IN ORDER TO COMPUTE THE USUCAPION TERMS

In the event the laws that expropriated the property in question are declared unconstitutional or null and void, the occupant or possessor will have to prove that he owns the house through usucapion.[104] Arguments can be made in favor of both, the former owner or the present possessor, however, the stronger case lies in favor of a good faith usucapion against the former owner.[105]

As previously discussed, good faith usucapion requires the possession to be continuous and without interruption, in an ownership capacity, public and notorious, by a bona fide possessor, and with a just title ("justo título"). It seems, however, that the most probable controversial of these requirements to the Cuban property issue are the continuous possession

without interruption, the just title, and the good faith or bona fide possessor classification.[106]

Nevertheless, under the premise that the State's acts were unconstitutional or null and void, the present possessor cannot be blamed for such state actions since the acts of states are presumed to be executed in good faith.[107] Moreover, a well recognized principle in international law is that the State which executes a confiscation owing to its own law cannot be said to possess in bad faith under its own laws.[108]

The possessor was given property title by the State, which was absolutely legitimated through a resolution of the Cuban Supreme Court[109] and through the Revolution's source of law faculties. Under these circumstances, these possessors had no knowledge, or reason to suspect, of any flaw or defect in the title given by the government that made the title invalid.

> "It is the view of this author, that the possessor will be a bona fide possessor until the law that gave him the title is declared unconstitutional [or is declared null and void]. To date, none of these laws have been declared unconstitutional. Therefore, the possessor should have no reason to believe that he holds a flawed property title."[110]

Thus, in the event the confiscatory laws are declared unconstitutional or null and invalid, the actual possessor is a good faith possessor. In other words, a possessor who receives a confiscated property from the State, will never get to be a bad faith possessor.[111]

In order to determine which of the usucapion terms apply, the first step is to establish whether property owner is an absentee or a present proprietor. Since a

---

103. Id. at 917. (In Soviet Law "[t]he proprietor is given a term to regain the property illegally possessed. If the statute of limitations expires before, the proprietors' legal action will be dismissed and the property automatically will pass to the hands of the State." Id.)

104. Id. at 919.

105. Id.

106. Id. at 919-920.

107. Id. at 920.

108. M. Bogdan, *Expropriation in Private International Law* 43 (1975).

109. See Barquín, supra note 12.

110. Consuegra-Barquín, supra note 2, at 921.

111. Id. (for a detailed explanation of this issue, see Id. at 920.)

former proprietor living in exile is an absentee proprietor, the statute of limitation for a good faith possessor is 20 years. However, in those cases with a similar scenario but with the former proprietor still living in the Island (present proprietor), the statute of limitation is 10 years.

Did the former property owner have an opportunity to interrupt such statute of limitation? Were the political obstacles confronted by the Cuban exile community relevant to determine whether any former owner could interrupt the usucapion's statute of limitation? Even though these questions will be hotly debated, once again, arguments from both sides are equally valid and welcome.

In fact, even where an interruption was never sought by a former owner, and thus not achieved, the political circumstances provide a very reasonable cause to

justify that former owner's inaction.[112] However, scholars have argued that in order to interrupt the statute of limitation period, a simple advertisement[113] is enough to "warn in advance all potential buyers of the expropriated goods in order to make it impossible for them to invoke later their good faith."[114]

This approach was recently adopted by a number of organizations representative of the Cuban exile community when the Castro Regime, in order to survive, began the economic experiment of creating joint ventures with foreign entities in connection with the properties confiscated.[115] The validity of such advertisements may be questioned because: (1) the organization must have a standing to claim such proper-

---

112. Id. at 921.

113. Id. at 921 (quoting from Bogdan, supra note 108, at note 35.)

114. Id.

115. On May 1992, eleven widely disparate Cuban exile groups (Comisión Nacional Cubana, Coordinadora Social Demócrata de Cuba, Cuba Independiente y Democrática, Cuban American National Foundation, Cuban Committee for Human Rights, Directorio Revolucionario Democrático Cubano, Ejército Rebelde en el Exilio, Ex Club Asociación de Prisioneros y Combatientes Cubanos, Libertad y Vida, Partido Pro Derechos Humanos de Cuba y Union Liberal Cubana) signed an open letter directed to all foreigners investing in Cuba. The letter was published in the most recognized newspapers worldwide. Part of the letter states, in relevant:

"The undersigned have every intention of encouraging and providing appropriate protection for private investments in a democratic Cuba, and intend to deal with its legitimate international debt obligations in a responsible manner. However, *it is our position that investments made in Cuba under the present circumstances should not benefit from any laws passed by a future Cuban government for the protection of private property.* We feel that these investments should be considered as state property and disposed accordingly..." Id. (Our emphasis).

Likewise, see the approach adopted on January 14-15, 1994 by the National Association of Cuban Sugar Mill Owners, Sugar Cane Growers, Sugar Industry Workers, Cattlemen, Mineral and Petroleum Right Holders, Bankers, Tobacco Growers, Attorneys, Architects and Journalists, who published a notice of warning in the Wall Street Journal to any foreign investors purchasing assets which were the product of confiscation, without compensation and through the use of force, by the Revolutionary Regime.

However, another well recognized principle in international law is that the acts executed by a sovereign and legit state must be internationally recognized by its successor government.

"It is an established principle of international law that changes in the government or the internal policy of a state do not as a rule affect its position in international law. A monarchy may be transformed into a republic, or the republic into a monarchy; absolute principles may be substituted for constitutional or the reverse; but, though the government changes, the nation remains, with rights and obligations unimpaired." (Lehigh Valley R. Co. v. State of Russia, 21 F2d 396, 401 (2d Cir, 1927) (quoting Moore, Digest of International Law, vol. 1, p. 249)." *Jackson v. People's Republic of China*, 550 F.Supp. 869, 972 (N.D. Ala. 1982), rev'd on other grounds, 596 F.Supp. 386 (1984), aff'd, 794 F.2d 1490 (11th Cir. 1986), cert. denied, 480 U.S. 917 (1987).

If the government of Cuba sells private property to a foreign entity, would the successor government be bound to recognize this type of state action under international law? If a successor government is obliged to recognize the acts of its predecessor, then why bother paying for a worldwide advertisement? Should there be compensation or restitution of the properties at issue? What would be the standard of compensation? Prompt, adequate and effective compensation or appropriate compensation? Fascinating question may be raised when discussing this issue.

ty;[116] and (2) the advertisement must describe the location of the property in issue. In this way, the former owner guarantees due process and avoids a general fishing expedition.

To not declare an adverse possession in favor of the present possessors would be a ruling contrary to the purpose for which the legal concept was established under Roman Law, which was to maintain continuity and certainty in property ownership and hence to accomplish the good administration of land and property rights, especially for the confidence of society's property trade and commerce.[117] As Cueto points out,

"[t]he spirit behind 'adverse possession' is not so much the weighing of the circumstances which may have prompted the original owner to leave the property but, instead, the notion that uncertainty as to title cannot be tolerated for an indefinite period of time. (Like the proverbial show, 'Life must go on.')"[118]

The good faith usucapion's statute of limitation will be a term of 20 years, because of the proprietor's absence from the country, and 10 years if the former proprietor lives within the island. These terms apply only until 1988, when the statute of limitation term changed to 5 years, a much easier period in which to adverse possess through usucapion.[119]

The bad faith usucapion statute of limitation will never be reached unless the possessor started to adverse possess before October 12, 1958.[120] Currently, no one could legally adverse possess through usucapio with bad faith because of its non-recognition in the 1988 Socialist Civil Code.[121] Therefore, if an expropriation law is declared unconstitutional, or null and void, and the possessor is possessing in bad faith, the legitimate proprietor would still be the former owner.[122] Nevertheless, this does not imply that a bad faith possessor could not accumulate more years in his possession when the institution of bad faith usucapion is reestablished in connection with the private property right.[123]

CONCLUSION

Under the current Cuban law, the present possessors are owners of the property they possess. This analysis should not be a cause for concern to current possessors, or occupants, since presently the confiscation and expropriation laws have not been declared unconstitutional nor null and void.[124] However, even though the property rights issue regarding nationals is governed entirely by Cuban law, the Cuban Government still has the legal duty and moral obligation to compensate those nationals for property expropriated or confiscated.

Finally, the purpose of the usucapion, according to the Romans, is to maintain continuity and certainty in property ownership and to accomplish the good administration of land and property rights, especially for the confidence of society's property trade and commerce. Even though the usucapion applies to the issue of whether property confiscated should be returned to former owners, it may not be used to solve the dispute because of its political implications and interests. Therefore, we will leave such political questions for the successor Cuban government to decide.

---

116. In this case, an association standing may satisfy the standing qualification question since the Cuban organizations represent a legit party in interest.

117. Consuegra-Barquín, supra note 2, at 921.

118. Cueto, supra note 7, at 19 (note 44).

119. Consuegra-Barquín, supra note 2, at 922.

120. Id.

121. Id.

122. Id.

123. Id.

124. Id.

RECOMENDED FEATURES OF A FOREIGN
INVESTMENT CODE FOR CUBA'S FREE-MARKET TRANSITION

Matias F. Travieso-Díaz and Alejandro Ferraté

INTRODUCTION

Foreign investment, and foreign direct investment in particular, has in recent times been the driving force behind the growth and restructuring of formerly sheltered economies, and has also served as a vehicle for the internationalization of many of the world's economies. Even though its economy remains under tight government controls, Cuba has recently joined the global trend towards encouraging foreign investment. Cuban officials, as well as students of Cuban affairs on the island and abroad, point to foreign investment as an important source of hard currency, and as one of the principal mechanisms on which the current government relies to stem the decline in the country's economy.

New laws, regulations and practices implemented in the last few years have succeeded in attracting some foreign investment into Cuba. Foreign investment in Cuba has bolstered certain economic sectors, particularly tourism, and has served to strengthen the island's economic relations with other countries. The impact of foreign investment in Cuba is, however, limited by the country's political and economic program, which restrains foreign investment in a number of significant respects.

As Cuba's transition to a free-market economy progresses, foreign investment will play an increasingly important role in the island's economic reconstruction. Cuba's laws affecting foreign investment will need to be updated as the transition unfolds in order to effectively regulate and foster foreign investment in the country.

This paper seeks to identify what should be the objectives of Cuba's foreign investment legislation during its transition to a free-market economy, and to describe the main features that such legislation should contain in order to maximize direct foreign investment in the island. Since foreign investment laws must be integrated with other economic development legislation, the paper also seeks to identify some of the key areas of interaction between foreign investment laws and other transition period legislation.

There is no "ideal" foreign investment code which could be copied for use in Cuba. Even if such legislation existed, it would probably be to a large extent inapplicable to Cuba due to the unique circumstances that will exist during the country's market transition. Certain features in the legislation, however, are recognized as creating an attractive climate for foreign investment. These favorable features have been analyzed by scholars and incorporated into general guidelines for investment legislation, such as the World Bank Guidelines on the Treatment of Foreign Direct Investment (hereinafter "World Bank Guidelines"). In addition, the successes and failures of countries making the transition from a command to a free-market economy provide insights into the probable results of particular elements of the foreign investment laws. These experiences need to be kept in mind for their potential applicability to Cuba.

The discussion in this paper reflects the above considerations. The second part describes the foreign investment legislation that is in place in Cuba today and summarizes its main shortcomings. The third part defines what the objectives of foreign investment legislation for Cuba should be in order to support the country's orderly transition to a free-market economy. The forth part draws upon the preceding ones to define the recommended features and requirements of foreign investment legislation for Cuba during its free-market transition. The fifth part discusses the relationship between Cuban foreign investment legislation and other transition period laws. Lastly, the sixth part provides some pertinent conclusions and recommendations.

FOREIGN INVESTMENT LEGISLATION IN CUBA TODAY

1. The 1982 foreign investment law: opening the door to foreign investment

After over twenty years of negligible foreign investment in Cuba, the Cuban government started to open the door to foreign entrepreneurs through Decree-Law No. 50 of February 15, 1982 ("Law 50"). This legislation allowed foreign investors to enter into joint ventures with state-owned enterprises in the development of specific projects, and authorized the repatriation of profits or dividends in convertible currency. The law, however, imposed many restrictions on investors. For example, it limited a foreign investor's share in a joint venture to 49%, although investors could negotiate operational control of the project.

The 1982 foreign investment law, not surprisingly, failed to attract much foreign investment to the island. Indeed, the first foreign investment project in Cuba since the Revolution was completed in 1990, eight years after Law 50 went into effect.

2. The post-1989 liberalization of foreign investment in Cuba

The year 1989 marked a watershed for the communist world: the iron curtain collapsed and the countries of the Soviet bloc started to make their transitions to democracy and free-market systems. That year also witnessed the beginning of the disintegration of the Soviet Union itself. The collapse of communism in Europe brought about a steep decline in the Cuban economy, which was dependent on favorable trade relations with the nations of the Soviet

bloc. In addition, all economic aid from the former Soviet Union was suspended in 1992 and trade was dramatically curtailed. As a result of these developments, Cuba's economic output declined by 40% between 1989 and 1992. During that period, the country's exports declined by 70%, and imports dropped by 80%.

In response to the economic crisis, Cuba turned to foreign direct investment as the cornerstone of its strategy to lift the economy out of its depression. In order to attract such investment to the island, the government significantly liberalized its foreign investment practices. Amendments to the Cuban Constitution in 1992 eliminated some important restrictions on foreign investment. As amended, the Constitution permits property ownership by mixed enterprises and the transfer of state property to joint ventures with foreign capital.

These constitutional amendments enabled the institution of a more liberal foreign investment regime within the framework of Law 50. As set up after 1992, the foreign investment regime had the following salient features:

- Foreign ownership of up to 49% of an enterprise's shares. (In special cases, such as tourism, mining, and Latin-America based investments, foreigners were allowed to own 51% or more of an enterprise's shares.)

- Total exemption of taxes on gross income, personal income, and the transfer of real estate and business. The only taxes levied were 30% on profits and 25% on the payroll, to cover social security benefits for Cuban employees. Even those taxes could be waived or deferred at the discretion of the government.

- Elimination of customs duties for necessary imports of equipment and inputs.

- Unrestricted repatriation in hard currency of dividends, profits, and the salaries of foreign employees.

- Freedom in hiring foreign executives and technical personnel.

- State handling of the labor force, including disciplining of workers, a ban on strikes, and relatively low wages (to be paid in hard currency by the investor) for Cuban labor.

- State insurance covering lost profits due to accident, non-payment of merchandise, and non-fulfillment of terms of contracts due to political conditions.

- Availability of government support in areas such as legal, economic, accounting, and information services.

In addition to the general arrangements described above, the Cuban government sought to negotiate special deals in which foreign investment played an important role. Cuba also signed bilateral investment treaties (BITs) —agreements containing, inter alia, promises not to expropriate investors' property and to allow repatriation of investors' profits—with several countries, such as Britain, China, Colombia, Germany, Italy, Russia, and Spain. These guarantees are intended to provide further assurances to foreign venturers that their investment is secure.

3. Recent foreign investment experience in Cuba

The entire Cuban economy, with the exception of health care and education, was declared open to foreign investment in 1994. The main sectors where significant foreign investment has taken place include tourism, light industry, medical equipment and medicine production, mining, oil exploration, construction, and agro-industry.

Up to the present time, foreign investments in Cuba have been restricted to one of three types of business organization permitted under Cuban law:

- Joint ventures, in which a Cuban partner and a foreign partner invest jointly in a project. (This option includes management contracts, in which the foreign venturer provides the management skills to run the enterprise, and the Cuban partner provides all or most capital assets—an arrangement particularly common in the tourism industry.)

- Production agreements, in which Cuba supplies the labor and facilities and the foreign partner supplies equipment and materials, or provides advance credit. The foreign partner often becomes an exporter or distributor.

- Joint accounts, in which the foreign partner manufactures and distributes abroad products designed in Cuba, assuming the risks, but reaping the profits.

The most commonly used format has been the formation of joint ventures between the foreign party and a Cuban enterprise which is either an existing state instrumentality or a "private" SA formed by the Cuban government. Over 200 such ventures have been established in the last five years. While the foreign investor is generally not allowed to assume a majority interest in a joint venture, there have been a number of instances in which majority ownership by the foreign venturer was approved.

Despite the post-1989 liberalization of Cuban foreign investment law, foreign investors still have had to cope with an abundance of risks and red tape. One of the shortcomings of Law 50 was that the joint ventures it authorized between foreign investors and state entities required approval by a special commission of the Council of Ministers, which reviewed projects on a case by case basis. In addition, Cuban laws failed to provide explicit guarantees against expropriation, an important omission given the uncompensated expropriation of more than $2 billion worth of foreign-owned assets in 1959 and 1960. Foreign investors also had to contend with the possibility that the Cuban government might unilaterally terminate a venture—as apparently happened in one case—or that an enterprise could become subject to a restitution claim deriving from the expropriation of foreign assets after the 1959 revolution.

CUBA'S NEW FOREIGN INVESTMENT LAW
1. Introduction

As of the writing of this paper in August 1995, Cuba was reported to be ready to enact a new foreign investment law, which shall be referred herein as Law No. XX of 1995 ("Law XX"), which will replace Law 50. Predictably, Law XX does not represent a fresh start but follows an evolutionary approach to Cuba's foreign investment regime: the new law retains many of the provisions, and the generally restrictive investment climate, of Law 50. However, Law XX (in its current form, which may be modified when the law is finally passed) contains some significant improvements from the previous law, which may help liberalize the island's basic economic structure.

2. Major Similarities to Law 50

Law XX retains the basic structure of Law 50. The familiar forms of business organization in Law 50 (joint ventures, production agreements, and joint accounts) are retained in the new law, although Law XX includes one new important form of business organization, the "enterprise with entirely foreign capital." Such enterprises are described in the next subsection.

Approval of investments is still done on a case-by-case basis. A new entity, the Ministry of Foreign Investment and Economic Cooperation (MINVEC), is charged with supervising foreign investment activities, receiving foreign investment applications, and submitting them for approval to the Executive Committee of the Council of Ministers or a Commission appointed by that Committee. A decision on whether to approve an application must be reached within sixty days from the date of the application, and is not appealable.

The new law sets up a centralized system by granting MINVEC primary authority to process the investment applications. Nevertheless, the approval procedure is likely to remain onerous because authorization from other interested state entities will still be required. Other Cuban government institutions which have jurisdiction over foreign investments may be reluctant to relinquish their power and allow the establishment of a true centralized approval system. The result is likely to be a continuation of the cumbersome and unpredictable approval process now in place.

The provisions on profit repatriation remain basically the same. Since the new foreign investment law contains provisions (discussed below) that guarantee compensation in the event of expropriation and allow foreign investors to sell their shares in joint ventures, Law XX lists moneys received pursuant to those provisions among the authorized forms of profit repatriation. The new law also authorizes the repatriation in hard currency of any amounts received upon the winding up of the enterprise.

The new law generally retains Law 50's system of labor regulation for foreign investments. Enterprises with entirely foreign capital must still hire workers indirectly, that is, they must contract labor from a pool of Cuban workers designated by the state. As in the old law, foreign investors are free to employ foreigners in upper management and technical positions. The state is still responsible for disciplining workers and for regulating relations between foreign investors and their employees. Employee salaries will still be paid in national currency and foreign employees will continue to be able to repatriate their salaries in hard currencies. The new code, however, creates a potentially wide exception to the official labor regime by stating that a foreign investor may be authorized to utilize a different labor arrangement from that specified in the code.

Finally, Law XX generally maintains the existing tax structure for foreign investors. Foreign investors must pay taxes on net profits at 30% and payroll taxes at 25% to cover social security benefits. The tax rate on profits for investments that exploit renewable or non-renewable natural resources can be increased by the Cuban government up to 50%, depending on the natural resource being exploited.

The Ministry of Finance, in consultation with the MINVEC, can declare a foreign investment temporarily exempt from all or some of the applicable taxes. Likewise, although the tariff structure is not specified in the new law, special reductions in any applicable tariffs may be granted to certain foreign investors by Cuba's Customs Service. Thus, the tax regime for foreign investors under Law XX remains as vague and subject to the discretion of the Government as it was under Law 50.

3. Significant New Provisions in Law XX

Perhaps the most significant new provision in Law XX is an express guarantee against uncompensated expropriation of the property of foreign investors. The state also promises to reimburse the investor for the cost of any property involved in the venture which is subsequently subject to a successful claim to title by a third party. Compensation for expropriation is to be given in a convertible currency, although the amount and type of currency are left to be determined by a Cuban court, with the minimum value of the compensation to be set by an experienced "international organization" chosen by the foreign investor in conjunction with MINVEC.

Another important new provision allows investment by "enterprises with entirely foreign capital"—that is, investment without Cuban participation. The types of business organization allowed under the enterprise with entirely foreign capital provision are also new. Such enterprises can be established in two different ways: 1) by the foreign individual or entity registering in its own name with the Chamber of Commerce of Cuba; or 2) by setting up a wholly-owned Cuban subsidiary of a foreign entity.

Allowing foreign investors to operate as sole proprietorships or wholly-owned subsidiaries not only expands the types of business organizations available to foreign investors, but also moves Cuba's foreign investment legislation closer to internationally-recognized standards for foreign investment legislation. Experience in other countries shows that allowing 100% foreign ownership of enterprises is one of the elements of foreign investment legislation necessary to attract substantial amounts of foreign investment, particularly to countries with economies in transition. If enterprises wholly owned by foreign investors are allowed to acquire the assets of state-owned enterprises, this could signify the start of the process of privatization of state enterprises in Cuba.

The possibility that the Cuban government will allow the acquisition of state-owned assets by foreign investors raises issues regarding the status of title to properties expropriated after the 1959 Revolution. Cuban nationals and foreigners have outstanding claims on expropriated property totaling billions of dollars. The U.S. claims certified by the Foreign Claims Settlement Commission alone total $1.8 billion, before interest. The possibility that state-owned assets subject to expropriation claims could be acquired by foreign investors could complicate the resolution of the expropriation claims and delay the lifting of the U.S. trade embargo against Cuba, since the resolution of the property claims of U.S. nationals is one of the conditions necessary to lift the embargo.

Another provision enables foreign investors to acquire interests in real estate, but only in limited situations. Investments in real estate can only be made in structures intended as personal dwellings, vacation homes of non-resident foreign individuals, or residences of managers or corporate offices. It is unclear whether the acquisition of structures also includes the acquisition of the underlying land. More importantly, the term "acquisition" is not defined, and the terms and conditions under which real estate can be acquired are left to be set in the authorization issued to the foreign investor and are therefore subject to ad-hoc determination by the Cuban authorities.

Finally, the new Cuban foreign investment law establishes a system of "duty-free and industrial park zones," which apparently are some form of Export Processing Zones ("EPZs"). Special incentives may be granted to enterprises located in these zones. These incentives, again, are not defined in the law, but they are said to relate to "customs, exchange rates, taxes, labor, immigration, public order, investment and foreign trade." The types of activities which may be carried out in the duty-free zones include importation, exportation, storage, product modification, re-export and financial operations.

The duty-free zones probably will not attract large amounts of foreign investment. The worldwide record on the success of EPZs is mixed at best. In addition, the success of EPZs, particularly in the Caribbean, depends to a large extent on trade concessions from importing countries, which stimulate foreign investors to establish export manufacturing facilities ("maquiladoras") in the EPZs. A good example of this is the success of the Dominican Republic's EPZs in attracting apparel maquiladoras which take advantage of reduced quotas and import duties for their products under the US's Caribbean Basin Initiative ("CBI") program. Cuba presently is not eligible for CBI benefits, and it will continue to be ineligible as long as current U.S. policy remains in effect. In addition, even if Cuba were eligible for CBI benefits, the conclusion of NAFTA and the phasing out of the Multi-Fiber Agreement quotas under the Uruguay Round of the GATT have severely impaired the value of CBI benefits as investment incentives in beneficiary countries.

CURRENT CONSTRAINTS ON FOREIGN INVESTMENT IN CUBA

The present state of Cuba's foreign investment law is not unlike that of similar laws in Central and Eastern European countries, such as Hungary, the former Czechoslovakia, and Poland, prior to their transition to free-market economies. The constraints on foreign investment in Cuba today stem from both the internal controls that are still being imposed by the Cuban government, and by external factors that prevent the widespread entry of foreign investment. These constraints will be summarized next.

1. Constraints Placed on Foreign Investment by Cuba

Despite the post-1989 liberalization of Cuba's foreign investment law, there remain a number of specific restraints imposed by Cuba on foreign investment. These restrictions stem from the Cuban government's determination to maintain control over economic activity in the country. The following significant restrictions are still in effect:

- Foreign joint ventures still have to be individually authorized by the Cuban government, in a process that in the past has been protracted and has involved successive reviews by several agencies, ending up with Fidel Castro as the ultimate decision-maker in the approval of the venture. It does not appear that the new foreign investment law will do anything to alleviate this problem.

- Until recently, ventures were only permitted in selected areas of the economy; other areas, like the sugar industry, were considered off-limits. Investment in sugar is now starting, but is still limited to the pre-financing of sugar crops rather than the acquisition of productive assets. Even under the new law, investments in the sugar sector must be approved by Cuba's Council of Ministers.

- Since the objective of encouraging foreign investment is to secure foreign exchange via exports, investments directed at developing the internal Cuban market are generally not allowed.

- Foreign investors are still not permitted to acquire title to the properties in which they invest.

- A joint venture can still be terminated by the Cuban government essentially at will, with all property in Cuba involved in the venture remaining in the hands of the state.

- Contacts between the foreign investor and the internal economy of the country, and the population at large, are rather limited. As a general proposition, foreign venturers cannot hire labor directly, but must choose from a government-selected pool of candidates. The joint venturer must pay the Cuban agency that supplies the labor relatively high salaries in convertible currency, while the agency pays workers low salaries in pesos.

Although the new foreign investment law appears to provide an improved framework for foreign investment in the island today, it continues to suffer from such vagueness that the Cuban Government is free to exercise total control over the investment process and interfere with it arbitrarily by dictating the terms under which each investment is authorized. For those reasons, Cuba's transition to a free-market economy will require radical changes to the country's foreign investment regime.

2. External Constraints on Foreign Investment in Cuba

In addition to the internal constraints on foreign investment presented by Cuba's current regulatory environment, foreign investment is hampered by two main types of external constraints. First, Cuba is largely isolated from the international monetary and financial system because of its massive external debt burden, which denies it access to international credit. Second, Cuba is cut off from the U.S. market because the United States maintains a stringent trade embargo against Cuba and actively seeks to discourage trade and investment on the island by other nations. While a detailed discussion of these constraints is outside the scope of this paper, brief mention will be made of them to complete the picture of the foreign investment outlook in Cuba.

2a. Cuba's external debt

Cuba's external debt situation is bleak. Even before the collapse of the Soviet Union, Cuba owed about $7 billion (not counting accrued interest) to international private and public lenders in the West, and had defaulted on its loan obligations. As a result, Cuba is not eligible for credit from Paris Club members or private lenders. Also, Cuba owes Russia, as successor to the Soviet Union, about $30 billion in loans that it has never repaid.

Cuba is also not a member of the IMF and does not receive export credits from foreign governments except for Spain and France, which are actively encouraging their nationals to do business in Cuba. The country's inability to secure credit from the world's financial institutions restricts its ability to finance projects and limits both the number of investors and the types of investment projects that can be undertaken.

2b. The U.S. Trade embargo

The U.S. trade embargo is also a factor that greatly restricts foreign investment in Cuba. The embargo prohibits U.S. individuals and companies, and their foreign subsidiaries, from doing business in Cuba. Moreover, the U.S. pursues a policy of actively seeking to discourage third country entrepreneurs from investing in Cuba.

One of the arguments used by the U.S., sometimes effectively, to discourage third country investors from going into Cuba is that many of the joint ventures solicited by Cuba involve properties that were confiscated from U.S. citizens. The U.S. warns that investment in such properties could lead to litigation against the investors now or in the event of a change of government in Cuba. Also, it is sometimes said that those investing in Cuba might be subject to adverse action by a successor government coming to power on the island.

There is proposed legislation currently pending before the U.S. Congress (the LIBERTAD Act) that would greatly increase the potential for litigation in the U.S. against third country investors in Cuba, and would subject such investors to sanctions in the areas of immigration, trade, and financing. This legislation, if enacted, could further cloud the picture for third party nationals contemplating investing in Cuba.

OBJECTIVES OF A FOREIGN INVESTMENT CODE FOR A COUNTRY IN TRANSITION

1. Introduction

Foreign investment legislation can seek two goals which are largely contradictory: on the one hand, enabling and fostering the entry of foreign investment; on the other, regulating and controlling such investment to minimize its adverse impacts on the host country. Which of these two goals is pursued at a given time depends on the philosophy of the government then in power, as well as on prevailing political and economic conditions.

Until the last decade, a "provider mentality" pervaded most developing countries. This mentality was based on the belief that having an ample stock of natural resources was what made a country rich and its products competitive. This mentality caused many countries to effectively close their doors to perceived exploiters—investors from industrialized countries and multi-national corporations. Thus, countries enacted laws that emphasized the regulatory and exclusionary aspects of foreign investment legislation and thereby tended to discourage, rather than stimulate investment.

Other countries, particularly those in the Pacific rim, started some time ago to shrug off the provider mentality and open their markets to foreign investment. The results have been dramatic. Countries like Malaysia have become active and successful participants in the global marketplace. Their experiences are living proof of the wisdom of opening the door wide to foreign investment. Likewise, the successful experience of Central and Eastern European countries underscores the critical role foreign investment legislation of the "enabling" type plays in the rebuilding of the economies of countries in transition.

213

2. Fundamental pillars of foreign investment legislation

The main objective of an "enabling" type of foreign investment code is to create a legal and regulatory regime attractive to foreign investors. In order to achieve this goal, the foreign investment framework needs to meet at least three criteria: 1) it must provide for non-discriminatory or "national" treatment of foreign investors; 2) it must grant adequate protection to the foreign investors' property, and 3) it must establish streamlined foreign investment regulations and procedures. These criteria provide the fundamental pillars of successful foreign investment legislation.

a. Non-Discriminatory or "National" Treatment of Foreign Investors

"National treatment" is a crucial element of a hospitable foreign investment regime. National treatment means that foreign investors should not be put at a competitive disadvantage versus domestic investors regarding access to permits or authorizations necessary to conduct operations in the host country. At the same time, the laws should not give foreign investors a competitive advantage over national investors, absent compelling circumstances. In other words, the laws should apply fairly and equally to all investors.

b. Protection of Foreign Investors' Property

Adequate protection of the investors' property is also a fundamental pillar of a favorable foreign investment climate. Such protection has several elements. The most obvious and important one is a guarantee against the uncompensated taking of the investors' property by the state.

Another type of protection that must be given to foreign investors is the avoidance of excessive taxation and other forms of regulation that diminish the value of the investment. Foreign investors should also be free from discriminatory treatment, and should receive the same protection of their persons and property (including intellectual property rights) as that accorded to nationals.

3. Streamlined Foreign Investment Regulations and Procedures

The third fundamental pillar of a favorable foreign investment regime is a regulatory process free from bureaucratic impediments to investment. The concept of "one-stop shopping" has been postulated as the ideal method for streamlining foreign investment regulations. Under this concept, there is a central office where foreign investors can register and satisfy all other requirements to set up their enterprises. The obvious benefits of such a central office are time and transaction costs savings for foreign investors. Other advantages of the central office concept are the reduction of administrative costs, the elimination of duplicative government structures, and the minimization of conflicting requirements and interpretations of existing laws. An indirect, but perhaps important advantage of the establishment of a central agency to deal with foreign investors is that it gives the investors a single contact with whom to deal to obtain advice and resolve problems as they arise.

SPECIFIC OBJECTIVES OF FOREIGN INVESTMENT LAWS IN COUNTRIES IN TRANSITION

1. Introduction

In addition to the "fundamental pillars" on which successful foreign investment regimes rest, conditions in countries making a transition from socialism to a free-market society warrant that additional objectives be fostered by the foreign investment codes and related legislation. Following is a discussion of four such additional objectives. The continued relevance of these specific objectives depends, of course, on the conditions that exist in a country as the transition unfolds.

2. Promotion of Rapid Investment in the Country's Infrastructure

After years of communist rule, important elements of the infrastructure of countries in transition are likely to be in a state of disrepair. In Cuba, early foreign investment will be required to rebuild, enhance and modernize critical areas of the infrastructure, such as energy production, telecommunications, and transportation. These sectors of the economy are not only crucial to the welfare of the population, but their upgrading is required to attract foreign investment. Given the importance of rapidly modernizing Cuba's infrastructure, foreign investment legislation should not unduly burden investments in this area but, to the contrary, encourage the participation of foreign investors in these "strategic" sectors.

3. Promoting the Transfer of Modern Technology
Recent experience in Central and Eastern European countries in transition suggests that foreign investment has, at least in the short run, helped reduce the gap between the state of technological development in those countries and conditions in the rest of the industrialized world. Foreign investors have consistently installed the latest (or near-latest) technologies in their facilities in Eastern and Central Europe. Foreign investment legislation, therefore, should foster investments that will introduce state-of-the-art technologies during the transition period, and should provide adequate protection of the foreign investors' technology to encourage its importation into the country. Such protection should be afforded by the foreign investment code and other laws, particularly the intellectual property laws.

4. Fostering Employment-Creating Enterprises
An important objective of foreign investment legislation of countries in transition is to encourage the creation of new sources of employment for the population during the transition to a market economy. There are two reasons for this importance.

First, one of the effects of the transition process is a rise in unemployment as inefficient state enterprises shut down and the government bureaucracy is culled. The experience in many Central and Eastern European countries (and some Latin American countries implementing radical economic reform packages) is that the rise in unemployment leads to social instability and popular backlash against the economic reform process. To minimize these phenomena, foreign investment in employment-creating enterprises should be encouraged as a way to promote social stability and ensure the orderly implementation of economic reforms.

Second, employment in foreign-owned enterprises exposes the domestic labor force to modern work practices that improve productivity. Typically, much of the work force in countries in transition lacks the skills and discipline necessary to improve productivity and compete in the global marketplace. In addition, those countries suffer from an acute shortage of qualified management personnel during the transition to a market economy. Foreign investors in Central and Eastern Europe have introduced market-tested management skills that have trickled down to indigenous enterprises.

5. Improving the Balance of Payments
Countries in transition in Central and Eastern Europe have relied on foreign investment to increase exports and thus improve their balance of payments. Indeed, an important objective of the foreign investment regime of a country in transition should be to encourage investment in export-oriented enterprises.

As further discussed below, both the general and specific objectives of a foreign investment code described above are applicable to Cuba and should be included among the goals of that country's foreign investment legislation during its transition.

RECOMMENDED ELEMENTS OF A CUBAN FOREIGN INVESTMENT CODE
1. Introduction
The concepts discussed in previous sections can be applied to determine the type of foreign investment code that would be most beneficial to Cuba during its free-market transition. Two important observations need to be made at the outset. First, as the experience in Eastern European countries shows, it is very difficult if not impossible to develop a suitable foreign investment code in a single try. Several attempts are often necessary, either because the starting point of the effort is an inadequate code which must be molded in incremental steps into a workable piece of legislation, or because the contents of the legislation are driven by political and economic conditions that are in a state of flux.

Second, if a choice is to be made between speed and perfection, speed should prevail. There will be a great need in Cuba for foreign investment legislation that meets the country's, as well as the investors' requirements. Under those circumstances, it will be preferable to have adequate but perhaps less than perfect legislation enacted early than to hold up passage while seeking to refine the formulation.

A third observation follows from these two. The first foreign investment code that is enacted during Cuba's transition should be kept as simple as possible in an effort to shorten the drafting period, minimize debates among the decision-makers, and avoid causing strain in the transition period government structures, which may not be capable of administering overly complex statutes.

For these reasons, the substantive provisions discussed below may not all be capable of early implementation. The highest priority provisions, and consequently those that must be included from the start in the Cuban foreign investment code are those provisions granting "national" treatment to foreign investors and allowing 100% foreign ownership of Cuban enterprises; those guaranteeing full compensation in the event of expropriation; those removing restrictions on profit repatriation; and those streamlining the regulation of foreign-owned enterprises. We discuss these most urgent items first, and then turn to less pressing provisions that should eventually be included to give effect to Cuba's foreign investment objectives.

2. Provisions to implement the fundamental pillars of foreign investment legislation
a. Introduction
Foreign investors considering going into Cuba during its transition must be reassured that no burdensome limitations, conditions, or impediments will be placed on their ability to operate in the country; that their investment will be protected against adverse actions by the state; and that they will be able to repatriate profits and move capital in and out of the country without restrictions. In short, the investment climate must be fair and favorable to the investor. This section discusses the main foreign investment code provisions that will create such a favorable investment climate in Cuba.

b. Guaranteeing National Treatment
Equal treatment of foreign investors in Cuba could be guaranteed through express declarations in the Foreign Investment Code (and perhaps the Constitution) that foreign investors enjoy the equal protection of Cuba's laws and are subject to the same treatment afforded domestic individuals and enterprises. To the extent that any distinctions need to be made between foreign and domestic business entities, such distinctions should be clearly defined and should be identified in the Foreign Investment Code, or cross-referenced there to other applicable legislation.

For domestic political reasons, it is also important to avoid creating the impression that foreign investors are being given advantages over the country's nationals. This is crucial in Cuba, where growing resentment exists over special treatment accorded to foreigners by the current Cuban Government. Continued special treatment for foreign investors may be poorly received by the Cuban people, and may serve as political ammunition for those opposed to economic reform.

c. Eliminating Restrictions on Property Ownership by Foreign Investors
Restrictions on foreign equity participation in domestic enterprises are designed to ensure direct or indirect state control over the enterprises, reduce the profits repatriated abroad, and force the transfer of business know-how and technology to the local participants in the venture. These restrictions (typically in the form of mandatory percentages of local equity participation in foreign-owned enterprises) are most often imposed in "strategic" national industries such as utilities or telecommunications companies.

These types of restrictions have been prevalent in Cuba. As noted earlier, under Law 50 majority participation by local enterprises was a requirement, or at least a practice followed in most instances. Under Law XX, it would be possible for a foreign investor to be sole owner of its enterprise. However, if the law is enacted in its current form it will be interesting to see whether such investments will actually be permitted, particularly in sensitive areas of the economy.

All equity participation restrictions should be abolished in Cuba's foreign investment legislation. Restrictions on equity participation in domestic enterprises generally deter foreign investment. Under the principle of "national treatment," foreign investors should be able to use the same forms of business organization available to nationals, without additional equity participation restrictions.

The experience of countries in transition in Eastern and central Europe, which now allow 100% foreign ownership of domestic enterprises, supports the wisdom of removing restrictions on equity participation. Several countries in Latin America, including Mexico and Venezuela, have also eliminated or relaxed restrictions on foreign equity participation, although significant restrictions remain in place in some countries.

3. Protection Against Uncompensated Expropriation of Property
a. Domestic Law Protections

Considering Cuba's history of private property takings, providing strong guarantees against uncompensated expropriation must be an essential element of its foreign investment legislation. Guarantees against uncompensated expropriation should be incorporated into the country's Constitution and restated in the Foreign Investment Code.

As important perhaps as giving express guarantees against uncompensated expropriation is setting forth a proper standard for compensation in the event of expropriation. The internationally-recognized standard is the formulation coined in 1938 by U.S. Secretary of State Cordel Hull: "prompt, adequate and effective compensation." The World Bank Guidelines incorporate this standard. Under current practice, the "prompt" element of the Hull formula means payment without delay.

The "adequate" element means that the payment should reflect the "fair market value" or "value as a going concern" of the expropriated property. The "effective" element is satisfied when the payment is made in the currency brought in by the investor, in a convertible currency (as designated by the International Monetary Fund), or in any other currency acceptable to the investor.

b. Use of Bilateral Investment Treaties

Bilateral investment treaties ("BITs") protect investors from a signatory country providing a framework in the host country for national treatment of such investors and setting up dispute settlement procedures, methods for compensation for expropriation, and guarantees of the convertibility and repatriation of profits. Given the increasing use of BITs, particularly by the United States, Cuban foreign investment legislation should authorize and call for the conclusion of such agreements.

c. Multilateral Dispute Resolution Agreements

The International Convention on the Settlement of Investment Disputes Between States and Nationals of Other States ("ICSID Convention") is a multilateral agreement intended to reduce foreign investor concerns by helping resolve investment disputes, including those relating to expropriations. Accession to the ICSID Convention allows a signatory state and a national of another signatory state to submit their investment disputes to arbitration by the International Centre for the Settlement of Investment Disputes ("ICSID"). The Convention also establishes an Additional Facility for the Administration of Conciliation, Arbitration and Fact-Finding Proceedings, which is a mechanism for settling certain disputes outside ICSID's jurisdiction under the ICSID Convention.

Cuba should become a party to the ICSID Convention so that, if Cuban government agencies or instrumentalities continue to enter into joint ventures with foreign investors, the joint venture agreements can refer contractual disputes to ICSID arbitration. Cuba's participation in the ICSID would provide further assurance to foreign investors that the country is prepared to honor its commitments to them and treat them fairly.

d. Investment Insurance: OPIC, MIGA, and Private Insurers

As an additional incentive for foreign investment, the Cuban government should assist foreign investors to obtain Overseas Private Insurance Investment Corporation ("OPIC") or Multilateral Investment Guarantee Agency ("MIGA") coverage. OPIC is a corporation owned by the United States government which offers political risk insurance, loan guarantees, and direct loans to U.S. businesses which invest in foreign countries. OPIC also offers insurance against inconvertibility, that is, "the inability of an investor to convert into dollars the local currency received as profits, earnings or return of an original investment." In order for U.S. investors to, become eligible for OPIC coverage, the host country (Cuba, in this case) needs to enter into an agreement with the United States which enables the U.S. government to authorize OPIC coverage for qualifying investments in Cuba.

MIGA is an investment guarantee agency operated under the auspices of the World Bank. MIGA offers guarantees and reinsurance to eligible investments against losses resulting from four categories of non-commercial risks: 1) the transfer risk resulting from host government restrictions on currency conversion and transfers; 2) the risk of loss resulting from legislative or administrative actions or omissions of the host government which deprive the foreign investor of ownership or control of or substantial elements of his investment; 3) the repudiation or breach of government contracts in cases where the investor has no access to a competent judicial or arbitral forum, or faces unreasonable delays in such a forum, or is unable to enforce a judicial or arbitral decision issued in his favor; and 4) the risk of armed conflict and civil disturbance. MIGA will not issue a guarantee to an eligible investor without the host government's approval of the guarantee. Cuban foreign investment legislation, therefore, should include specific provisions for the expedited approval of MIGA guarantees.

Apart from any Cuban government undertakings to assist foreign investors to secure investment guarantees, the investors may also take steps to purchase private investment insurance. Insurance from private companies, such as Lloyd's of London, offers several advantages over OPIC or MIGA investment insurance. Private insurers frequently cover existing projects, while OPIC only covers "new" projects. Private insurers may also cover a wider range of contingencies, resolve claims more quickly, and indemnify a greater amount of loss than OPIC or MIGA.

While obtaining private insurance is the responsibility of the foreign investor, Cuba should avoid adopting laws or regulations that impair the activities of in-

vestment insurers. The Cuban government should also cooperate with insurers seeking to settle claims filed by investors under their policies.

e. Guarantees Of Currency Convertibility And Profit Repatriation Rights

Free convertibility of currency and unrestricted ability to repatriate profits are aspects of a foreign investment regime that are particularly important to investors. Most Central and Eastern European countries have removed restrictions on profit repatriation from their foreign investment regimes. The World Bank Guidelines also emphasize the importance of unrestricted repatriation of profits to foreign investors. Cuba provides such rights to investors under the existing and proposed foreign investment laws. These benefits should be retained in the transition period legislation.

The scope of any future controls that might be imposed on the convertibility of currency held by foreign investors would depend on the Cuban government's macro-economic policies during the transition to a free-market economy. In the interest of fostering foreign investment, however, Cuba should refrain from imposing restrictions on the repatriation of after-tax profits by foreign investors.

f. Reduction in Pre-Approval Requirements

Government pre-approval requirements often pose a significant hurdle to foreign investment. Most Central and Eastern European countries have abolished pre-approval requirements, and have simplified the procedures necessary to set up an enterprise. Many Latin American countries have also streamlined pre-approval procedures in an effort to facilitate foreign investment. The Cuban government should follow these examples and abolish or minimize pre-approval requirements for foreign investors.

Special attention should be paid to the manner in which any pre-approvals are processed. Cuba's foreign investment legislation should establish a single government agency or institution with pre-approval authority over all foreign investment. Worldwide experience suggests, however, that concentrating pre-approval authority in one government institution leads to problems in the issuance of post-approval licenses and permits to the foreign investor by other government agencies, which often seek to reassert their authority after the pre-approval process. Future Cuban foreign investment legislation, therefore, should include provisions for the automatic issuance of certain authorizations or permits upon approval of the investor, and prohibitions against lengthy evaluations of projects by institutions that control licenses and permits.

As important as the institutional aspects of investor approvals are the procedures used in the approval process. Project-by-project screening is probably the most cumbersome form of evaluation and the one most likely to hinder foreign investment. Given the importance of stimulating the rapid entry of foreign capital into Cuba, project-by-project evaluations should be abandoned. Instead, a well-defined list of requirements for investment should be set, and if sectors of the economy are to be declared off-limits to foreign investors, those should be clearly identified in the legislation so that the identification may serve as a sufficient screen. From the standpoint of a potential investor, a "negative list" describing restricted sectors would be preferable to a "positive list" of sectors open to foreign investment.

g. One-Stop Shopping

Cuba's Foreign Investment Code should establish a central office before which foreign investors can satisfy all requirements for setting up their enterprises. As noted above, the benefits of a centralized approval system include savings in time and transaction costs for foreign investors and the elimination of investment disincentives, such as duplicative regulations and multiple regulatory entities.

The one stop-shopping concept should also be applied to unifying the foreign investment regulations. Placing all the regulations affecting foreign investment in a single code (or cross-referencing all the regulations affecting foreign investment) would eliminate duplicative or inconsistent regulatory actions. The Foreign Investment Code should also include a "residual clause" stating that, to the extent not covered by its specific provisions, a foreign investor has the same rights, and is subject to the same rules and regulations, as a domestic person or entity.

A useful tool to foreign investors would be a regularly-updated handbook published by the Cuban government which contains information about legislation, regulations and procedures relevant to foreign investment. The central office handling foreign investor applications and inquiries should be charged with the task of publishing the handbook and distributing it to prospective investors.

4. Foreign investment code provisions to meet specific economic or political objectives
a. Introduction

The provisions discussed in this subsection favor foreign investment in particular sectors of the economy by giving investors in those sectors monetary advantages in the form of reduced taxes or tariffs. These types of provisions, however, have supporters and detractors, as their success in stimulating foreign investment is far from proven. They merit examination, nonetheless, because they are tools available to the lawmakers to channel foreign investment into areas where it is most urgently needed.

b. Special Tax Preferences

Special tax preferences, which are a form of subsidy, remain the most common incentive offered to foreign investors. Tax incentives are often used as a form of "signaling," to denote a country's desire to attract foreign investment in a given sector or across the board.

Many commentators have noted that special tax incentives, standing alone, do not appear to attract foreign investment. The World Bank Guidelines recommend against special tax incentives for foreign investors. Most of the countries of Central and Eastern Europe have rescinded their special tax incentives for foreign investors after having them in place for a few years, and now treat foreign and domestic investors on equal terms. Indonesia also abolished its special tax incentives in 1985, and the subsequent large inflows of foreign capital into that country suggest that the special tax incentives were not essential to attract foreign investment.

The experiences of countries which have abolished special tax incentives suggest that such incentives should not be included in Cuba's foreign investment legislation, except possibly for investment in infrastructure, high technology, and other areas deemed crucial to the economy in the early stages of the transition. Any tax incentives given should be of only limited (three to five years) duration.

c. Tariff Reductions

In general, the use of tariffs in Cuba will probably be governed by the rules of the World Trade Organization's General Agreement on Tariffs and Trade ("GATT"), and those of regional trade agreements that Cuba may join. Beyond those, Cuba's use of tariff reductions to foster foreign investment also hinges on the transition government's broad economic and development policies.

Cuba could, for example, decide to eliminate tariffs altogether, in line with certain economic arguments sometimes made against the use of tariffs in developing countries. The elimination of tariffs may attract foreign investment, particularly in the manufacturing sector, since the entire country would, in essence, become an export-processing zone. The loss of tax revenue from the elimination of tariffs could be offset by additional foreign investment and the consequent expansion of the tax base. Repealing tariffs would also eliminate the often time-consuming collection procedures, and allow disbanding the entities charged with tariff collection.

d. Export-Processing Zones

If Cuba eliminates import and export tariffs and makes very limited use of special tax incentives to foreign investment, the establishment of export-processing zones will not provide a significant further boost to foreign investment. If tariffs are retained, on the other hand, EPZs may provide some investment incentives, and may be used to encourage investment in rural areas which would otherwise see little investment in areas such as manufacturing.

The success of EPZs in Cuba may depend to a great extent on the macro-economic policies adopted by the Cuban government. If the Cuban government imposes controls on the convertibility of foreign exchange, the establishment of EPZs offering unrestricted convertibility of foreign exchange and repatriation of profits may attract foreign investment to the EPZs in the manufacturing of products for export. Special tax incentives may also attract foreign investors to EPZs, although some data suggest otherwise.

e. Trade-Related Investment Performance Requirements

Trade-Related Investment Performance Requirements ("TRIPs") are, in essence, host government policies which guide foreign-owned firms into engaging in a particular type of activity. The two most common forms of TRIPs are export quotas and local content requirements.

Export quotas and local content requirements do not appear to discourage foreign investment in many cases when other factors, such as attractive locations, protected markets, or other incentives offset the costs of the requirements. On the other hand, the World Bank Guidelines suggest that the imposition of TRIPs deters foreign investment, and that they are becoming rare. Since Cuba probably will not have the resources to adequately implement and monitor a TRIPs program, TRIPs should not be included in Cuba's foreign investment legislation.

In addition, the United States views export controls as violating standards of free-trade and creating trade distortions. The United States also contends that export controls violate the GATT, although a GATT panel upheld the validity of specific export targets in the Canadian Foreign Investment Review Act of 1982. Given that the United States will most likely become Cuba's most important source of foreign investment during the market transition, it is critical that Cuban decision-makers not impose requirements in this area that run counter to the U.S. positions.

RELATIONSHIP BETWEEN FOREIGN INVESTMENT LEGISLATION AND OTHER TRANSITION LAWS

1. Introduction

Foreign investment in a country in transition does not occur in a vacuum but, rather, operates within a legal framework that reflects the country's stage of development and the political and economic circumstances of the transition. This section explores briefly several areas of the law that are not specifically related to foreign investment but which may impact on a foreign investor's ability to operate in the country or otherwise affect his decision whether to invest.

The discussion that follows must by necessity be summary and is not intended to examine all the issues that are raised in each area of the law that is examined.

2. Laws that may encourage foreign investment
a. Business Organization Laws

Applying the principle of national treatment discussed earlier, foreign investors should be able to conduct operations in Cuba using the same types of business organization available to Cuban nationals. This principle has been taken to heart in Central and Eastern European countries, which allow foreign investors to use all form of business organization recognized by local law (e.g., corporations, limited liability companies, partnerships, etc.). The types of business organization available to foreign investors in Cuba should be those recognized by the new Companies Law that Cuba needs to enact early during its transition to a market economy. Corporate laws should authorize at a minimum those forms of business organization with which foreign investors are most familiar. Cuba could adopt as a model, for example, the business organizations forms accepted by most Latin American countries, and in doing so it would reduce transaction costs for investors interested in doing business in the island.

b. Privatization Laws

Foreign investors going into Cuba will in many cases want to participate in the privatization of state-owned enterprises. Privatization is an extremely complex process, which, in the case of Cuba, will be closely tied to the program Cuba develops for resolving the outstanding property expropriations claims.

There are advantages to conveying state-owned enterprises to foreign investors as part of the privatization process. Foreign investors bring with them capital resources, management skills, business know-how, and improved technology, plus the ability to incorporate local enterprises into the global networks of production and commerce. Allowing foreign investors to participate in the privatization of state-owned enterprises also enables the country to earn much needed foreign exchange, an important consideration for what will certainly be a cash-strapped Cuba. Encouraging the participation by foreign investors, therefore, should be an important goal of the Cuban privatization program.

Foreign investors are mostly interested in acquiring medium and large enterprises being privatized. The opportunities for investment in such enterprises, however, may be limited by the potential restitution of some properties to their former owners which might reduce the number of enterprises eligible for privatization.

The Cuban government could also elect to limit foreign investor participation in the privatization of certain state-owned assets, particularly those in "strategic" sectors of the economy. The original Polish privatization statute, for example, limited the extent of foreign owned stock in privatized companies to 10%. However, since revamping the country's infrastructure is an urgent goal during the transition period, Cuba should not restrict foreign participation in privatized enterprises, particularly those in strategic sectors.

The opportunities for foreign participation in the privatization of state-owned enterprises may be limited as a practical matter by the deterioration or obsolescence of the assets of those enterprises. Foreign investors may prefer to invest in new ventures rather than in dilapidated state-owned enterprises.

Whatever the extent of foreign investor involvement in the privatization of state-owned assets, the Cuban government should ensure that investors face as little uncertainty as possible if they choose to become involved in the privatization process. This means that programmatic issues concerning the title to state-owned assets should be settled very early in the privatization process. In addition, the approval process for the sale of state-owned assets to foreign investors should be made as simple as possible. (In the early days of privatization in Poland, for example, the sale of a state-owned enterprise often required approval by the Workers' Council after consent by a general assembly of workers, and also by the Ministry of Ownership Transformation; not surprisingly, these cumbersome approval requirements discouraged foreign investors.) Cuba should set up a privatization agency that provides a "one-stop shopping" for privatizations. The existence of such an agency would facilitate foreign participation in the privatization process.

c. Intellectual Property Rights Protection

Cuba's ability to provide effective protection to foreign investors' intellectual property rights will be a crucial factor in the country's ability to attract many types of foreign investment to the island. In addition, Cuba may will need effective laws to protect the rights to its own technological achievements, particularly in biotechnology and related fields.

The Cuban government should therefore strive to provide legal protections for intellectual property rights which meet the prevailing standards in other countries. The United States, in particular, is aggressive in demanding the protection of intellectual property rights owned by its enterprises and individuals, and often takes action against foreign governments seen as tolerating the infringement of U.S.-owned intellectual property rights.

There is no comprehensive, internationally-recognized set of standards for the protection of intellectual property rights which could serve as a model for Cuba. However, the Uruguay Round of the GATT contains an Agreement on Trade-Related Aspects of Intellectual Property Rights (hereinafter "TRAIPs Agreement," not to be confused with Trade Related Investment Performance Requirements discussed earlier), which contains provisions "for the establishment of standards to protect a full range of intellectual property rights, and for the enforcement of those standards both internally and at the border." The TRAIPs Agreement establishes minimum standards for the protection of intellectual property for patents, trademarks, and copyrights, although several important aspects of intellectual property are not addressed. Cuban intellectual property law should at a minimum seek to meet the standards of the TRAIPs Agreement.

The protection of confidential information, trade secrets, and know-how against disclosure or misuse by employees is another important aspect of intellectual property rights protection which is usually addressed by employment contracts and domestic tort laws. Cuba's tort laws should include provisions allowing employers—including foreign investors—to terminate current employees and sue former ones who divulge confidential information, trade secrets, or know-how to competitors, irrespective of whether such rights are included in the employment agreement. In addition, government sanctions should be established against employees who wrongfully divulge confidential information, trade secrets, or know-how. The sanctions could include, for example, withholding unemployment compensation and other benefits.

d. Tax Laws

A country's attractiveness to foreign investors depends in large part on its system of taxation. During its market transition, Cuba may opt to pursue tax reforms that specifically benefit foreign investors. See Section IV.C.2 above. In any case, Cuba should implement changes to its tax laws that benefit foreign investors indirectly by establishing an equitable and predictable system for all taxpayers. Indeed, experience with tax reform in developing countries shows that a healthy tax system is a pre-requisite to foreign investment, irrespective of whether preferential tax treatment is accorded to foreign investors.

A comparison between the experience of Bolivia in the 80s with that of present-day Russia is instructive in this regard. Tax reform in Bolivia in 1986 succeeded in bringing inflation down from an annual rate of 12,000 percent to 14 percent in the space of two years. The reform also sufficiently stabilized the tax environment to reverse the effects of a fiscal crisis occasioned by a world recession in the early 1980s that had all but cut off the flow of foreign investment. In contrast, Russia has created a patchwork quilt of tax laws and has implement piece-meal tax reforms, leading to an overall climate of regulatory uncertainty that deters foreign direct investment.

To be supportive of foreign investment, Cuba's tax system should be simple, uniform, centralized, and well-administered. Good administration is key: in the early stages of its transition to a free-market economy Cuba, like many developing countries, will likely face the problem of poor tax administration, which may effectively negate the benefits of even the most enlightened tax code. Likely lapses in administration should be compensated by devising a tax system that features a simple rate structure and few, broad categories of taxes that apply equally to foreign and domestic businesses. Cuban tax legislators would be well advised to use tax exemptions and targeted tax incentives gingerly, and to resist populist pressures to implement redistributive measures such as steeply progressive rates. Close attention should be paid to improving collection techniques and properly screening personnel in order to minimize the possibility of corruption by tax collectors and other officials.

It is equally important that the tax system be centralized. During their market transitions some countries, notably Russia and China, devolved taxing power from the central authority to the local governments. Though perhaps ultimately desirable, early tax decentralization has led in those countries to competing tax initiatives by central and local governments, resulting in an increased overall burden on the taxpayer.

In addressing the specific tax concerns of foreign investors, elimination of double taxation should be a top priority. Most countries follow the "territorial method" of taxation and levy taxes on all income earned in the country, whether by a citizen or a foreigner. Some countries, however, tax their residents on their world-wide income (using a "residence-based method"), and several countries combine the two methods. Double taxation results when an investor's home country and the host country follow different methods, so that the profits generated by the investment are taxed by the host country under the territorial method, and by the home country under the residence-based method.

The two devices most commonly used to alleviate the double-taxation problem faced by foreign investors are double-taxation treaties and foreign tax credits. Treaties for the avoidance of double taxation (i.e., bilateral agreements setting the order of taxation) are favored by those countries that follow the territorial principle (e.g., most countries in Western Europe), while foreign tax credits are used by those countries that tax their residents on their world-wide income (e.g., United States, China and Russia) as a way to offset the amount of foreign tax already paid. Cuba should use both treaties and foreign tax credit statutes to assist investors from countries using both systems.

Finally, Cuba should pursue a tax reform program that emphasizes consistency and advance planning. No changes should be introduced without affording those affected advance notice and opportunity for comment, and grandfathering provisions should be used where appropriate. There should also be no sudden reversals of those reforms already in place - a practice aptly termed "deform" in which, for example, present-day Russia and Colombia in the 1970s have engaged. Together with sensitivity to the tax pressures faced by foreign investors at home, consistency and ample advance notice would create a predictable tax environment that will encourage foreign investment in Cuba.

OTHER LAWS HAVING POTENTIAL EFFECTS ON FOREIGN INVESTMENT

1. Introduction
In addition to those laws that should be expected to have a positive effect on foreign investment, there are other laws that are not directly related to foreign investment, but which may indirectly affect foreign investment by improving the economic climate or, alternatively, by imposing requirements that raise costs or make the investment process more difficult. This section surveys five such types of laws.

2. Economic Restructuring Laws
Economic restructuring legislation will need to be enacted early in Cuba's transition to carry out the transformation from a centrally-planned economy to a free-market one. Some of that legislation may serve to unleash market forces and thereby foster foreign investment.

An example of economic restructuring legislation that would have beneficial impact on foreign investment would be price de-control measures. Elimination of government controls on prices is one of the basic requirements for the establishment of a free-market economy, and one that has been accomplished in most countries making the transition from socialism in Central and Eastern Europe.

A detailed discussion of economic restructuring laws is outside the scope of this paper, however, such laws provide an essential backdrop to any efforts to foster foreign investment in Cuba during its free-market transition.

3. Worker Benefits and Foreign Labor Restrictions

Labor laws and regulations, and the costs they impose on employers, are an important factor of the investment climate. In enacting new labor laws and regulations, the Cuban Government must make a trade-off between providing worker benefits and social safety nets to promote social stability, and cutting operational costs to employers so as to promote foreign investment. It seems likely that the extensive social safety net now in place in Cuba will be preserved to some extent during the country's transition to a market economy. This prospect is reinforced by the experience of most Central and Eastern European countries, which have chosen, or been forced, to preserve their well-developed social safety nets.

If Cuba retains a significant social safety net it should takes steps to clearly define foreign employers' liabilities and responsibilities towards the labor force. These steps should include provisions requiring communicating to foreign investors all social safety net laws to which they may be subject.

The Cuban government may also come under pressure to impose restrictions on the private enterprises' ability to hire foreign employees. Such restrictions could include the need to obtain work permits and the placement of limits on the number of foreign employees allowed at an enterprise. Restrictions on foreign employees, such as work permits, are in use in many countries.

In developing the transition period labor laws, provisions which require local labor participation (i.e. mandating the hiring of local management personnel) should give way to allowing investors freedom in

their employment decisions, because provisions regulating foreign investors' hiring practices will probably deter some types of investment, particularly those calling for workers with skills in short supply in the country.

4. Immigration Laws and Restrictions

As Cuba's transition progresses and the country's political and economic situation settles, foreign investors will probably seek to visit the island in increasing numbers. The Cuban government should take steps to facilitate temporary visits and the long-term or permanent migration of foreign investors.

One important issue which needs to be resolved in developing an immigration regime for foreign investors is the immigration treatment of Cuban expatriates who wish to invest in Cuba. Should they be considered "foreign" investors and be eligible for any special benefits given to such investors? On the one hand, the definition of who is a foreign citizen should be as broad and inclusive as possible to maximize the inflow of foreign-based capital. On the other hand, granting Cuban expatriates privileges unavailable to resident nationals could lead to resentment from people on the island. This is an extremely sensitive political issue that is part of the broader question of the citizenship status and rights of those Cuban nationals who have moved abroad and acquired foreign citizenship.

One component of the immigration treatment of foreign investors is the visa structure for business travelers. A business visa structure during Cuba's market transition will probably follow one of four typical patterns:

- No visa requirement for short-term business trips. A visa would be required only if the trip was to extend beyond the designated period. Several countries, such as Chile and Czechoslovakia, have implemented this type of visa structure.

- No visa requirements for business travel, unless the foreign national will be employed during the trip. Several Western European countries have a visa structure along these lines.

- A visa structure similar to that of the United States, under which there would be several categories of business visas corresponding to the nature of employment performed in the host country and the duration of the stay.

- A requirement that all business visitors obtain a visa, with different eligibility criteria depending on the purposes and intended length of stay.

In developing its business visa structure, the Cuban government should keep in mind several important considerations regarding foreign investors:

- First, and probably most importantly, foreign investors should have the ability to employ foreign personnel, particularly for key positions. The Cuban government should therefore refrain from unduly limiting the number of foreign personnel a company can bring into the country, or imposing unreasonable time limits on their visas. As noted earlier, there will be an acute shortage of skilled management personnel in Cuba during the transition to a market economy, so a large number of foreign managers will be necessary to operate foreign investors' enterprises until the local population acquires the requisite management and other business skills.

- Second, the Cuban business visitor visa structure should not establish special visa categories for particular classes of foreign investors. An example of this type of visa is the "alien entrepreneur" visa program in the United States, which reserves a certain number of immigrant visas for investors "who establish new commercial enterprises in the United States, invest at least $1,000,000 . . . and employ at least ten Americans." This type of special incentive is warranted only if a restrictive business visa structure is in place, which should not be the case in Cuba during the transition to a market economy; both large and small investors should be allowed free and easy access to the island.

Finally, the business visa structure during the transition period should be kept simple. Keeping the business visa structure simple would reduce time and transaction costs for foreign investors, and thus encourage foreign investment. In addition, a simple business visa structure would reduce the cost and complexity of administering the program, another important consideration given Cuba's lack of resources.

5. Environmental Laws

During the early phase of its transition to a market economy, Cuba may refrain from imposing major new environmental requirements or assessing liabilities for past environmental damage. Significant environmental legislation may not be put in place until several years after the transition to a market economy, when the economy has stabilized and recovery is on its way. Given the extent to which environmental degradation has already occurred in Cuba, however, the enactment of wide-ranging environmental legislation is likely to be inevitable. In addition, Cuba's growing tourism industry will require a high level of environmental quality control (i.e. clean beaches, unpolluted coastal waters, etc.), and therefore increased environmental regulation.

The need to comply with Cuba's environmental laws will be a factor that sophisticated foreign investors will include in their investment decision. Pre-investment planning often includes examining existing and imminent environmental laws to find ways of structuring the investment so that compliance with the laws is achieved while minimizing its impact on the cost of the projects. Adequate environmental compliance plans help prevent environmental disasters, allow proposed projects to proceed successfully through the pre-approval review process, and, in the event of a legal challenge, help convince the decision-maker that the project meets environmental standards.

Additional environmental compliance issues will be faced by foreign investors who become involved in the privatization of state enterprises. The main questions in those cases will have to do with the extent to which an investor acquiring a state enterprise will assume liability for environmental damage or hazards created by the enterprise while in the hands of the state.

In Czechoslovakia, for example, uncertainty over responsibility for environmental liabilities incurred in the past by state enterprises raised concerns with foreign investors that participated in the country's privatization program. The Czech government has tried to deal with this issue by promising investors limited indemnification for environmental liabilities which have not been identified at the time a venture is negotiated. Cuba will need to develop clear rules for determining the extent to which investors acquiring privatized enterprises are subject to liability for past environmental damage.

6. Alternative Dispute Resolution

The existence of effective dispute resolution mechanisms is an important factor in a foreign investment decision, since the expectation of prompt and fair resolution of disputes bears on the safety of an investment. An effective judicial system in Cuba would probably go a long way towards assuring an investor that his investment is secure. However, the Cuban judicial system will probably be overloaded and have little experience in adjudicating international business disputes during the country's transition to a market economy. Thus, foreign investors will likely favor contractually-agreed arbitration to resolve disputes that arise from doing business in Cuba.

Arbitration is increasingly used to settle international investment disputes. In the Western Hemisphere, three treaties establish substantive law and procedures for international arbitration: the United Nations Convention on the Recognition and Enforcement of Foreign Arbitral Awards ("U.N. Convention"), the Inter-American Convention on International Commercial Arbitration ("Inter-American Convention"), and the ICSID Convention, examined earlier in this paper. The Inter-American Convention essentially replicates the U. N. Convention, with the major difference being that the Inter-American Convention provides for a mechanism to administer international commercial arbitrations in the Western Hemisphere and, in addition, provides for rules of procedure. The ICSID Convention, as mentioned earlier, only applies to disputes between investors and the host state.

Cuba's accession to one or all three international arbitration conventions (which are not mutually exclusive) would set up a viable dispute resolution mechanism to handle foreign investors' claims during Cuba's transition to a market economy. Such a mechanism would be particularly well-suited to the transition period, given that the Cuban judiciary system will then be ill-equipped to deal with foreign investors' disputes.

CONCLUSIONS

Cuba has introduced a number of economic reforms in the last few years, and is likely to implement additional measures to create a favorable environment for foreign investment. Cuba has also sought to make attractive opportunities available to foreign investors, and has succeeded in bringing in investments in certain areas of its economy, notably tourism. A new foreign investment code, providing for additional liberalization of the investment rules, may soon be enacted.

Despite these advances, foreign investment in Cuba remains a difficult, high risk proposition. Unless and until there is a significant relaxation of the economic controls and investment restrictions that are now in place, it is unlikely that there will be a sufficient influx of foreign investment to turn the economy around. Accordingly, Cuba's political leaders during the transition should place a high priority on creating a foreign investment structure—in the form of a modern Foreign Investment Code, related laws, and appropriate administrative mechanisms—that make the decision of a prospective foreign investor to go into Cuba easy to reach and just as simple to carry out.

ECONOMIC FACTORS IN SELECTING
AN APPROACH TO CONFISCATION CLAIMS IN CUBA[1]

Rolando H. Castañeda and George Plinio Montalván[2]

"Explicit legal treatment of the rights of former owners not only strengthens the credibility of a country's commitment to the rights of private property, but also prevents the legal confusion over ownership that could arise if the issue were left to be settle later in courts. However, redress should be provided to former owners in a way that does not slow the privatization process: compensation should **not** take the form of giving the original owners the rights to the property itself, but rather the right to compensation by the state. New owners cannot get on with running businesses if they face the possibility of claims for restitution by former owners."

— Stanley Fisher, "Privatization in Eastern European Transformation," in *The Emergence of Market Economies in Eastern Europe*, Christopher Clague and Gordon C. Rausser, eds. (1992), p 230-231.

INTRODUCTION

Economic stabilization, law and order, food, medicines, the establishment of workable institutions and organizations for policy implementation, the establishment of clear, secure and marketable property rights, national reconciliation and social peace will be critical to Cuba's reconstruction and transition to a truly open economic and political system, and for that country to rejoin the international financial community.

While there is almost general agreement on the need to privatize state-owned enterprises and attract foreign investment to Cuba as rapidly as possible, there must first be a determination regarding the issue of property rights. Changes in property rights must be entrusted to institutions that themselves neither exercise property rights nor enforce them. Moreover, unless clear and transparent "rules of the game" are set and implemented, the amount and quality of investment taking place will be less than what is needed to put Cuba on a sustainable and high growth rate.

Privatization has proceeded at a disappointingly slow pace in some Eastern Europe countries, in part due to delays in resolving the property rights issue. Travieso-Díaz has pointed out that based on the widely differing experiences in Czechoslovakia, Hungary and Poland,

"whatever process is followed . . . must provide an unequivocal adjudication of property rights so that no legal obstacles to the privatization of enterprises are interposed by the existence of unresolved property claims against them."[3]

---

1. This paper is based on a previous paper by the authors, "Transition in Cuba: A Comprehensive Stabilization Proposal and Some Key Issues," in George P. Montalván (ed.), *Cuba In Transition*, Volume 3 (Washington, D.C.: ASCE, 1994), pp. 11-72.

2. The views expressed herein are those of the authors and in no way represent the official views of the Inter-American Development Bank.

3. Matías Travieso-Díaz and Stephan M. Bleisteiner, "Some Lessons for Cuba from the Legal Changes in Eastern Europe," April 1993, p. 19.

In this paper we explore some basic issues. We do not intend to be exhaustive, but only illustrative of the complexity of the issues. We hope we can learn from the experiences of former socialist countries, so as to increase our understanding of these issues and avoid recommending policies that would lead to costly mistakes.

Following this introduction, we present rough estimates of the breadth and depth of property confiscations in Cuba and the complications created by the foreign investment since 1990 and by the cooperativization of agricultural state enterprises in 1993. The next section includes a presentation of the Eastern European, Nicaraguan and Chilean experiences and some of their lessons for Cuba. Also some considerations will be made regarding restitution. This is followed by presents an overall appraisal of the potential package of measures that might be adopted and will conclude with some specific recommendations to tackle compensations for property confiscations and tort claims.

IDEAS CONCERNING THE MAGNITUDE OF THE PROPERTY RIGHTS ISSUE

A. U.S. Claims

The *casus belli* for the U.S. embargo on Cuba was the nationalization or confiscation of property owned by U.S. citizens and corporations in 1960. Following enactment by Congress of the Cuban Claims Act of 1964, the Foreign Claims Settlement Commission (FCSC) adjudicated close to 9,000 claims by U.S. citizens and firms, and certified awards in 5,911 cases totalling approximately $1.8 billion, of which $1.6 billion were corporate claims (see Table 1). The FCSC ruled that *simple* interest of 6 percent per annum should be charged from the date of the actual loss to the date of settlement, bringing the total value of U.S. claims to approximately US$5.5 billion at the end of 1994.[4]

From our examination of several of these claims, at least some of the FCSC's awards are open to question. In the early 1970's, the Internal Revenue Service established a program under which taxpayers were entitled to deduct from their income taxes losses sustained from confiscations by the government of Cuba. If claims awarded were inflated to a value of twice the actual loss, at a marginal tax rate of 52 percent the tax benefit would roughly compensate entirely for the loss.

As a matter of interest, official U.S. Government statistics place the total value of U.S. investment in Cuba at US$956 million.[5] While this figure may represent book value of investment, the significant discrepancy between this figure and the total of corporate awards serves to highlight the need for careful review of the FCSC's awards.

B. Claims by Cuban Nationals

Alonso and Lago[6] estimated the value of claims by Cuban expatriates to be approximately US$6.9 billion at 1957 values which, according to their calculations, was equivalent to US$20.02 billion in mid-1993. This does not include damages from human rights violations for which they indicate there is no data. They do, however, state that "compensation for these human rights claims should be paid."

The IRS program mentioned in the preceding section was extended specifically to Cuban nationals at the time of confiscation losses and were now U.S. taxpayers. Unfortunately the authors have not been able to obtain any information regarding the total amount accepted by the IRS as loss deductions.

In 1994, a group of Cuban-Americans sent a document to Secretary of State Warren Christopher requesting that the Department's Office of International Claims and Investment Disputes (OICAID) take up their claims even though they were not U.S. citizens at the time of confiscation. In doing so, they

---

4. See FCSC Decision CU-0249, American Cast Iron Pipe Company, for the FCSC ruling of simple interest at 6 percent per annum.

5. *Survey of Current Business*, August 1961, Table 3, p. 22, 23.

6. José F. Alonso and Armando M. Lago, "A First Approximation of the Foreign Assistance Requirements of a Democratic Cuba," in George P. Montalván (ed.), *Cuba In Transition*, Vol. 3, op. cit., pp. 202-204.

Table 1. U.S. Corporate Claims Against Cuba: Awards Exceeding US$20 Million at Time of Loss

Corporate Claimant	Decision	Award US$million
Cuban Electric Company	CU-4122	267.6
International Telephone & Telegraph ITT as Trustee	CU-5013	130.7
North American Sugar Industries Cuban-American Mercantile Corp. West India Company	CU-3578	109.0
Moa Bay Mining Company	CU-6049	88.3
United Fruit Sugar Company	CU-3824	85.1
West Indies Sugar Company	CU-5969	84.9
American Sugar Company	CU-3969	81.0
Standard Oil Company	CU-3838	71.6
Bangor Punta Corporation Baragua Industrial Corporation Florida Industrial Corp. of NY Macareno Industrial Corp. of NY	CU-6034	53.4
Francisco Sugar Company	CU-6066	52.6
Texaco, Inc.	CU-4546	50.1
Manatí Sugar Company	CU-6020	48.6
Nicaro Nickel Company	CU-6247	33.0
Coca-Cola Company	CU-6818	27.5
Lone Star Cement Company	CU-6217	24.9
New Tuinucú Sugar Company, Inc.	CU-6817	23.3
Other Corporate Claimants (approx. 882)		335.2
Individual and Other Claimants (5,013)		221.0
Total Amount Awarded		1,799.5

Source: United States Foreign Claims Settlement Commission, 1972.

cited precedents such as the Bernstein case (210 F.2d 375, 1954) and the "Second Italian Claims Program."[7] This was reflected in the initial provisions of the "Helms-Burton" bill considered by Congress in 1995.

C. Other Claims

Spain is the other country whose citizens sustained losses due to confiscation after January 1959, and Alonso and Lago indicate that the value of Spanish claims was US$350 million. A compensation agreement was reached between the two governments, al-

---

7. See Alberto Díaz-Masvidal, "Scope, Nature and Implications of Contract Assignments on Cuban Natural Resources," in George P. Montalván (ed.), *Cuba In Transition*, Volume 3, pp. 55-60.

though the government of Cuba has not been able to comply with the agreed amortization schedule.

D. Foreign Investment 1990 to Present— Implications re Property Rights

According to the Cuban Chamber of Commerce, as of July 1994 there were 146 joint ventures operating in four main sectors: industry, tourism, mining/oil and telecommunications. Several of these companies, however, have two or more separate joint ventures in Cuba. Carlos Lage declared that as of November 1994, there were 105 joint ventures with different companies. Most of the joint ventures are with Canadian, Mexican and European companies, particularly Spanish, French and Italian. Also, there were approximately 400 companies with representatives and/or offices in Cuba, among them *Bayer, Castrol, Hoechst, Pegaso, Sandoz* and *Total* as of November 1994.

All investment in Cuba is in the form of joint ventures with the Cuban government or with a Cuban state company. The Cuban side contributes the fixed assets and the foreign partner the working capital, the technical expertise and access to external markets. Sometimes the foreign partner merely supplies management. According to Lage the estimated accumulated foreign investment at the end of 1994 would have reached US$1,500 million.

In mid-June 1994, during a state visit to Cuba by former Mexican President Carlos Salinas de Gortari, the most important individual agreement for the purchase of 49 percent of EmtelCuba by Grupo Domos was announced, for a total of US$1.5 billion. This amount includes a direct payment of about US$500 million for its share in the company, US$200 million in the form of a swap of Cuba's outstanding debt with Mexico, and the remaining US$800 million to be invested over a 7-year period, with the Cuban government contributing half that amount. As part of the deal, EmtelCuba received a 55-year monopoly concession on local and long-distance service as well as data and image transmission. Officials of Grupo Domos indicated that the contract had been structured such that it would be

"... viable financially, politically and legally."

E. The Cooperativization of State Farms— Implications re Property Rights

In 1993 most of state-owned farms were transformed into basic units for cooperative production (UBPC) (Decree-Law No. 142 of September 15, 1993). UBPC can lease land and animals from the state for an indefinite period of time and retain part of their profits for reinvestment purposes. UBPCs organize themselves and select their own leadership. UBPC start the demise of state and collective farms, can lay off inefficient workers and cut back excess personnel. According to preliminary figures, with the establishment of the UBPC, the state sector's share of total agriculture felt from 75 percent to 34 percent while its share of cultivated land felt from 80 percent to 25 percent.

This is a striking and significant change in land tenancy in Cuba, because the UBPC are de facto "owners" of the farms. These "stakeholders" have existing ownership rights, in the sense of being able to exercise control over assets effectively. Moreover, it is likely that these stakeholders will take both economic and political action to defend their rights. Unless these stakeholders are somehow appeased, bribed or disenfranchised, the privatization of UBPC's cannot proceed or there will be "pseudo-privatization" (the transfer or "give-away" of public assets to private owners without an exchange of financial resources, skills and technological expertise).

SOME CRITERIA FOR AN APPROACH TO CONFISCATION CLAIMS

Obviously, the property rights issue is primarily a political issue, not a technical or economic one. In the final analysis, any solution should have the support of the majority of the Cuban people in order for the solutions to be enforceable, the outcome peaceful and also to encourage the proper and speedy reconstruction of the Cuban economy.

Privatization of state property and attraction of foreign investment are central tasks in the transition from socialist economies to market economies. It is now widely accepted that the transformation from a socialist economy to a market economy and the urgently- needed improvements in enterprise efficiency are unlikely to occur without extensive and fast privatization. In a socialist state, no one has the incentive to "mind the shop" of public property. Hence, privatization must be accomplished in a speedy and comprehensive manner based on the principle that "any productive activity that the government can do, the private sector can do as well or better."

Swift creation of a legal framework that defines property rights clearly facilitates public understanding of privatization, stimulates broad-based ownership, prevents abuse of power, and speeds up privatization and foreign investment. Ronald Coase (1960) and Olivier Williamson (1985) argued that once property rights are well-defined, individuals have very strong incentives and face reduced risks to work for efficient outcomes, but these outcomes will be independent of the allocation of those property rights.

Privatization improves allocative and productive efficiency based on individual freedoms and on private rights. Privatization has had, in general, eight objectives:

1. swift transfer of property and management from the public sector to private individuals to increase the economic and political power of the private sector and reduce the economic and political power and the size of the state;

2. to eradicate fiscal financing of state enterprises (soft budget and loans constraints will be replaced with hard budget and loans constraints);

3. promote the building and operating of competitive structures and environments whenever possible;

4. to improve the quality of public services (i.e., telecommunications, electricity, railways, highways, and ports), that are required for the modernization process of the economy;

5. maximize income proceeds;

6. select the "right" buyers;

7. safeguard employment; and

8. obtain investment guarantees.

Some of these goals are not necessarily independent of each other nor mutually compatible.

A. Other Experiences

From the very inception of transition policies, the clear delineation of private property rights and the fast reestablishment of private property from the inherited all-but-exclusive state ownership have been core tenets in the political debates of how best to forge ahead.

A sociopolitical consensus on restituting property that was earlier confiscated, as one notable wrong to be righted, first emerged in Czechoslovakia after the "velvet revolution" as early as October, 1990. Generally speaking, the Eastern European and Baltic countries, as well as Nicaragua, made a strong commitment to undo injustices of the past. The privatization programs of these countries address the issue of restitution of property based on their specific economic, political and social conditions, setting different time limits for claims and offering different remedies according to their reality (restitution, compensation or other). In some countries the relevant legislative work is still incomplete. As indicated in Tables 2 and 3, restitution is now on the policy and privatization agenda in these countries, at least for some classes of assets and is being resolved in different ways in each country. Certainly, the measures embraced are anything but uniform.

In Russia and in other successor states of the Soviet Union (Armenia, Azerbaijan, Belarus, Georgia, Kazakstan, Kyrgystan, Moldova, Tajikistan, Turkmenistan, Ukraine and Uzbekistan) the possibility of doing justice after 75 years was considered unfeasible because of difficulties in identifying rightful former owners or their rightful heirs and, hence, the issue of restitution of or compensation for property (except in Kyrgystan) was thus never formally placed on the agenda.[8]

---

8. A Land Fund covering up to 25 percent of arable land is to be created, for redistribution of land or compensation for nationalization in past decades. Criteria for eligibility are still under discussion (European Bank, *Transition Report 1995*, p. 33-64).

At the start it is necessary to decide how far back a country should redress injustice and what types of grievances should be considered. Evidently, violations of personal rights and freedoms in general and unjust and illegal confiscations of property in particular did not start with the communist takeover and did not necessarily end after the communist governments were established. Arbitrary and capricious violations of basic rights and freedoms, confiscations of different types of property, pensions and the fruits of labor have been a endless practice during the communist governments. Some of the people whose properties were confiscated received at least partial compensation. Some properties were obtained initially through misconduct or wrongdoing. Some of the properties were abandoned or the owners were out of the countries with no intention of returning. There were title and tax disputes at the time of the confiscations. Another critical issue is defining citizenship for the purpose of restitution laws. Most countries have defined that only those individuals who were citizens of the country and who had lived there permanently when the law came into effect are eligible for restitution, especially for agricultural and forestry lands. Also, most countries do not espouse claims against foreign governments brought by persons who were not their own citizens at the time of the confiscation.

Table 2. Main Characteristics of Restitution and Compensation Measures in Selected Eastern European and Baltic Countries

ELIGIBILITY AND FORMS OF COMPENSATION	Bulgaria	Hungary	Poland	Latvia	Former East Germany
Restitution to:					
Resident citizens	YES	NO	YES	YES	YES
Individuals, including foreigners	NO	NO	YES	YES	YES
Resident institutions	YES	YES	YES	NO	YES
Compensation to:					
Resident citizens	YES	YES	YES	YES	YES
Individuals, including foreigners	YES	YES	YES	YES	YES
Resident institutions	YES	NO	YES	NO	YES
Forms of Compensation:					
Allocation of a similar asset	YES	NO	YES	NO	NO
Cash payment	YES	NO	NO	YES	YES
Tradable vouchers, life annuities, securities, pensions supplements, etc.	YES	YES	NO	YES	NO
Non-tradable privatization vouchers	NO	NO	NO	YES	NO

Source: Economic Commission for Europe, *Economic Survey of Europe in 1992-1993*, p. 197.

Table 3. Restitution and Compensation Measures in Eastern Europe and the Baltic Countries

Country	Property Restitution and Compensation
Albania	According to two laws passed in 1993, former owners and their heirs can claim compensation or restitution for earlier government expropriation of non-agricultural land. For property that has been privatized, the law prescribes co-ownership between new and former owners.
Bulgaria	Significant restitution has taken place, following the Law on Ownership Restoration (1992) and the Compensation Law (1993). Few land titles have been issued, partly because the new owner must pay a high fee for the issue of the title deed, but 60 percent of agricultural land has been handed back to the original owners through "final land decisions" recognized as ownership documents and accepted as collateral. Recent legislation that favors cooperatives restrict the ability to sell restituted land under certain circumstances. Approximately 25,000 privately owned and managed small and medium-sized businesses were created in 1992 through restitution of urban business properties.
Croatia	No law on restitution has yet been sent to parliament, although a law is under preparation.
Czech Republic	A Restitution Law was adopted in October 1990. About 30,000 industrial and administrative buildings, forests and agricultural (nationalized between 1948-55) and 70,000 commercial and residential entities (nationalized during 1955-59) have been handed back to the original owners. The value of assets returned has been estimated in the range of CZK 70-120 billion.
Estonia	More than 200,000 claims for restitution of homes, farms and businesses had been submitted by the April 1993 deadline. By February 1994 approximately half of these had been validated. However, the need to carry out land surveys as well as legal problems have slowed the process.
FYR Macedonia	A draft law of restitution is in preparation and has received a first reading in parliament.
Hungary	About 1.2 million Hungarians have been granted "compensation coupons" as restitution, mainly for nationalization of property. The coupons carry a total nominal value of Ft 300 billion and are traded in the Budapest Stock Market. Coupons have in practice been usable mainly towards the purchase of land, apartments, and shares in state-owned companies. By the end of 1994 about 2 million hectares of land had been sold to 0.5 million people for compensation coupons. A further round of compensation was initiated in 1994 and land auctions for 185,000 hectares were to be completed with coupon participation in 1995.
Latvia	By the end of 1994, some 231,000 restitution claims for land in towns and cities had been submitted. Of these 13 percent had been settled. Claims for the restitution of urban land can be submitted during a period of 10 years. In order to avoid uncertainties for new owners of privatized property, the government issues guarantees to the new owners, which basically provide for the security of ownership of the privatized land and compensation for the claimants in case their claims are accepted.

Table 3. **Restitution and Compensation Measures in Eastern Europe and the Baltic Countries**

Country	Property Restitution and Compensation
Lithuania	The deadline for restitution applications by former owners of nationalized land was March 1994. Restitution has been granted in 86,000 cases, based on 500,000 applications. Property restitution has been impeded by administrative and legal difficulties and full resolution is likely to take many years. Uncertainty surrounding the legal ownership of properties, which may yet to be returned to the original owners, continues to complicate a number of privatization cases.
Poland	Under current law, restitution claims may only be enforced if the original nationalization law provided for compensation and none was paid. While several thousand restitution claims have been filed, compensation has been awarded to individuals in only a few cases, although a significant amount of property has been returned to the Church.
Romania	A new land on property restitution, passed by both houses of parliament in June 1995, was overruled by Romania's constitutional court in July 1995. This law would have granted restitution rights to former owners of around 250,000 residential properties that had been confiscated by the state in the post-war period.
Slovak Republic	A Restitution Law was adopted in October 1990. About 30,000 industrial and administrative buildings, forests and agricultural (nationalized between 1948-55) and 70,000 commercial and residential entities (nationalized during 1955-59) have been handed back to the original owners. A further law of restitution covering former church property was adopted in the Slovak Republic in October 1993. A restitution fund was established in 1993 to provide financial compensation to those whose claims could not met by the return of property. The fund receives 3 percent of each privatized company and currently has stakes in some 500 companies with a market value of over SK 2 billion. Revenues from sales of shares and dividends are used to meet claims.
Slovenia	Under the 1993 Law of Denationalization, land and buildings can be returned to former owners. A compensation fund is being recapitalized with shares in privatized companies.

The new commitment to democratic values and respect for the rule of law in Nicaragua and in the Eastern European and Baltic countries argues in favor of restitution or compensation for moral and ethical reasons. But, it has been argued that restitution or compensation also belong to the fundamentals, not only as a matter of justice, but also as a technical precondition for individual, collective and social stability, domestic capital formation and the influx of foreign capital. However, there are numerous legal, moral, economic, and technical objections that seriously call into question its feasibility.

Secure, clear and marketable property rights are key to the private sector's ability to respond to the changing economic environment. Privatization sales cannot start as long as the ownership of a given asset is under dispute. Few people are willing to invest, given the threat that the assets might be claimed by a former owner. The greater the risks they perceive, the less they will be willing to bid for the assets. What makes matters worse is that some of those willing to invest may lack access to credit, since the absence of a title makes it impossible for banks and other financial intermediaries to accept the assets as collateral.

Also, demarcated and unambiguous adjudication of property rights and an environment conductive to enforce them in law are a necessary prelude to the establishment of a market economy and for attracting foreign investment. However, the settlement of property rights is an issue of political economy (or normative economics) *par excellence* rather than exclusively a technical one.

While restitution may be justified on moral and ethical grounds, it implicitly favors people who used to posses physical assets over those who used to possess financial assets, rights, valid contracts or human capital and it is quite complicated to implement. Especially problematic in this context has been the question of agricultural land ownership. Yet rapid progress is urgent, for without it there will be no stimulus to increase output generation from the farm sector. Similar issues arise in connection with non-agricultural land and housing.

Some countries, such as Germany and Bulgaria, use extensive in-kind restitution as an integral part of their privatization programs. Others such as Hungary have chosen a moderate financial compensation over a direct return of physical assets in order that restitutions, which have become a transformation trap or long detour in Germany, do not muddle and delay the transformation of these societies into market entities in general and the privatization process in particular.

In Germany, where large parts of all land and buildings are subject to restitution claims, the issue of restitution has tended to obscure fundamental property rights, slow the process of privatization and give disincentives to potential investors. As a result, the Treuhandanstalt, the German privatization agency, was authorized to use financial compensation instead of in-kind restitution when it deemed this solution to be indicated by overriding public interest. In Bulgaria, Estonia, Latvia and Lithuania there is a clear danger that restitution questions will further delay privatization and foreign investment. In Hungary, where the government decided to compensate rather than to restitute, the problem has been solved by offering compensation in the form of property vouchers that can only be used for certain purposes such as buying stocks or acquiring land, apartments, or commercial properties.

In general, most of the Eastern European and Baltic countries have favored less extensive restitution or financial compensation than Germany or Bulgaria.

In Chile, the military government reduced the total number of enterprises under state control from 529 in 1973 to 47 in 1983. It began through the restitution of the seized enterprises to their original owners. The process was conducted quite rapidly; by the end of 1974, 202 had already been returned, and by 1978 only 2 had not been returned. Likewise, the government decided to regularized the situation of seized farms, to terminate the agrarian reform program, under which approximately 52 percent of agricultural land had been expropriated, and to privatize the legally expropriated land under state ownership. This process was practically completed by 1979. Of the expropriated land, 30 percent had been returned to the original owners; 44 percent allotted or sold to private owners, mainly individual families and cooperatives; and 18 percent transferred to nonprofit institutions. Of the land returned, the former owners had to renounce any legal action they may have been entitled to against the state. The shares of some enterprises were also used as payment to settle legal actions taken against the state by former farm owners who used when their land was expropriated in the agrarian land reform of the early 1970's.

In Nicaragua, about 200,000 petitions regarding the violation of property rights encompassing about 1.7 million hectares of a total of 5.7 million hectares of cultivated land and for a substantial number of houses and urban lots were presented to the Attorney General between 1990 and 1993. The agrarian reform affected about 36 percent of the total land of the country. The lack of clear ownership has encouraged land invasions and violent confrontations that have been met with a weak response from law enforcement agencies. It can take the government up to 90 days to carry out evictions, by which time the intruders have caused severe damage to property. The uncertainty created by these unresolved property conflicts and resulting climate of violence arguably constitutes the single most important obstacle to increased private investment and productivity in agriculture, and in turn negatively affects the rest of the economy. The Nicaraguan government devised a compensation scheme based on cadastral value for those whose property was unjustly expropriated or confiscated but who cannot recover the property. Transfers based on the agrarian reform laws have in general been considered legal. The compensation will be in bonds with a 20-year maturity at an annual interest rate of 3 percent (indexed to the US dollar exchange rate) that can either be kept to maturity or used to buy public assets. In general, the cadastre value of the property is less, and sometimes substantially less, than their market value.

In most countries budget deficits appear to determine the lack of feasibility of direct, prompt, adequate and effective cash or other monetary compensation. The only feasible compensation is a present good-faith gesture, together with future rights and obligations that stimulate the economic growth of the country and create future ability to pay. In some countries the government has limited restitution by imposing a strict deadline for filing claims and by restricting the amount of restitution.

In Germany, Czechoslovakia, and Hungary the restitution claims numbered in millions, most of which have not been settled. In Nicaragua the restitution/compensation issue has polarized society, created frictions between the Nicaraguan and the US governments, divided the Sandinistas and "it is the core issue holding this country back."[9] These difficulties have raised the political stakes for governments and caused logjams in administration and in the courts. Also, the expectation of engineering quick changes in property rights were frustrated in a matter of a few months.

Lawmakers in these countries have also learned that there is no way to regulate the entire process simply by passing one or two legislative acts. Indeed, implementations problems always led to modifications to the basic principles. In short, a comprehensive and just codification of restitution procedures and legal institutions for orderly adjudications of conflicting

claims proved to be a daunting task, even in the relatively more developed countries of Eastern Europe and the Baltic countries. There have been many complex and dynamic changes, refinements and amendments. In some countries restitutions and compensations, or even privatizations, were formally suspended because of underlying tensions. The changes that have occurred over the past six years taken together have fallen short even of "the most realistic expectations."

It has been this potential problem that has been slowing down the process of privatization notably in Germany. Radical policy measures were adopted in early 1991 that sought to replace the right to restitution with a right to compensation, guaranteed by the German government, in cases where the contested property could be put into productive use by a potential buyer making a commitment to invest in the asset that was the object of contention.

B. Implementation Problems: Some Lessons for Cuba

One of the fundamental implementation problems that arises with restitution can be summarized as follows. Even if the former rightful owners or their rightful heirs can be clearly identified, which is usually a very complex and demanding task, where justice lies is by no means self-evident if, after so many years, restitution of property requires an immediate declaration that all confiscations are declared null and void. This creates dislocation and pain from the revocation of the usufruct of property that was entrusted to others, or of clear property rights that were acquired by others according to existing law. At least in some countries, there have been significant investments by management and/or workers who had some authority over the usufruct of assets. Moreover, the essence of the confiscated property rights can no longer be separated from presently existing property rights, however inadequately they may have been defined and monitored under central planning. Thus

9. An unidentified diplomat in Nicaragua, quoted in "Americans' land claims unsettling for Nicaragua," *The Washington Post*, December 21, 1994, p. A-28.

resorting to restitution generates enormous difficulties.

One of the greatest problems facing any but the narrowest form of *restitutio in integrum*—for example, the return of confiscated paintings or sculptures now in museums or book manuscripts or collections in libraries to original owners—is that the legal professionals and infrastructure in the transformation economies, already inadequate at the inception of the process, is likely to get hopelessly entangled in an endless tide of grievances, claims and litigation for years to come. Forging ahead with divestment in the absence of clear titles will likely embroil the divestment agency with crippling long-term claims and litigation.

C. Physical Assets and Human Capital

"In general, favoring people who used to own real estate over those who used to own financial assets or human capital should be avoided."

— Gerd Schwartz, "Privatization in Eastern European Countries," in *Transition to Market*, Vito Tanzi, ed., (Washington, D.C.: International Monetary Fund, 1993) p. 244.

We take the position that *claims against the Cuban state should not be limited to property claims, but should include all manner of torts*—involuntary or uncompensated work, unjust imprisonment, loss of life or limb, loss of loved ones, physical or psychological abuse and harassment by agents of the state, discontinuance of pension payments, etc.[10] The people of Cuba, *especially those currently residing in that country*, have suffered incalculable losses. We see no legal, moral or ethical basis for assigning priority to settling claims against physical property over those claiming civil damages such as those suggested above.

According to Section 503(b) of Title V of the International Claims Settlement Act of 1949,[11] claims of U.S. nationals were allowed "for disability or death resulting from actions taken by or under the authority of the government of Cuba..." This included pecuniary losses and damages (e.g., loss of support, medical and funeral expenses, or other expenses.[12]

In at least one case, that of Jenny M. Fuller, et. al. (Decision CU-6199), the FCSC made an award based on what it considered to be wrongful death, because it felt that Cuban authorities had discriminated against two U.S. citizens in executing them although they had admitted guilt to armed uprising. Loss of pension benefits were also allowed by the FCSC.

D. Restitution: A Long Detour or a Transformation Trap?

"Wherever a country has adopted property restitution legislation, several consequences quickly resulted: 1) a dramatic economic decline; 2) an increase in the number of property disputes between former owners and -or their heirs- and the property possessors; 3) the abandonment of property maintenance caused by trial delays; 4) a decline in the flow of foreign investment toward areas where property disputes might affect their business; and 5) an increase in tensions between the local and exile communities."

— Juan C. Consuegra-Barquín, "Cuba's Residential Property Ownership Dilemma: A Human Rights Issue Under International Law," in *Rutgers Law Review*, Winter 1994, p. 923.

---

10. To use some well-known examples, poet Jorge Valls could make a claim for damages resulting from 22 years of unjust imprisonment; the mother of student leader Pedro Luis Boitel could likewise claim damages resulting from the wrongful death of her son while unjustly incarcerated; human rights activist and poet María Elena Cruz Varela could bring suit against the government for assault and unjust incarceration. Well-documented examples of state-sponsored mistreatment and torture are detailed in Charles J. Brown and Armando M. Lago, *The Politics of Psychiatry in Revolutionary Cuba* (New Jersey: Transaction Press, 1991). It is interesting to note that Article 26 of the 1976 Cuban Constitution provides that "any person suffering damages or loss income or value unduly caused by public officials or government agents during the performance of their duties has the right to claim and obtain the corresponding reparation or indemnification as provided by law."

11. Title V was added by Public Law 88-666 (78 Stat. 1110), approved October 16, 1964.

12. Edward D. Re, "The Foreign Claims Settlement Commission and the Cuban Claims Program," in *The International Lawyer*, Vol. 1, No. 1 (October 1966).

In the case of Cuba, various arguments have been advanced in favor of the return of confiscated property to former owners.[13] These arguments fall into the following categories:

- Property rights were protected against confiscation by the Cuban Constitution of 1940; they should therefore be returned to their rightful owners.

- Since the government of Cuba does not have (and will not soon have) the means to compensate promptly, adequately and fairly, restitution is the best (only) workable alternative.

- Restitution is the best way to implement rapid privatization and encourage recapitalization of the economy; there would be output and employment-related benefits.

- In the case of corporate claims, former owners have the managerial talent necessary for rapid development of the enterprise.

- Other formerly socialist countries (Eastern Europe, Nicaragua) have implemented restitution policies.

Fortunately, most Cuban expatriate groups have recognized that restitution of dwellings or residential property is not advisable. The discussion can then be restricted to non-residential property.

First, restitution would not be accomplished quickly, and thus there would be legal encumbrances on a significant amount of non-residential property. Lawyers representing claimants are being disingenuous in arguing that restitution could be accomplished quickly.[14] In the 35 years that have transpired since the confiscations, there have been significant transformations of the assets, property markers have been removed, records (including mortgages and other liens on properties claimed) have been lost, witnesses have passed away, etc. Ruling out restitution simply means that any litigation would be limited to challenges concerning the validity and quantification of the value of losses, and the compensation, if any. By ruling out restitution, a future government of Cuba could proceed immediately to privatize all small and medium-size businesses that do not require a significant regulatory framework, corporatize large enterprises and take steps to improve their financial footing prior to privatization.[15]

As pointed out by Gerd Schwartz in a recent book published by the IMF containing lessons from the privatization process in Eastern Europe,

> "Generous restitution programs are likely to result in a flood of claims that will strain administrative capacities and impede the clarification of property rights. Direct financial compensation will add further adverse pressure on state budgets."[16]

---

13. An interesting paper in support of restitution is Robert E. Freer, Jr., "The Significance of Restitution in the Economic Recovery of Cuba," paper prepared for the Cuban American National Foundation's Blue Ribbon Committee on the Economic Reconstruction of Cuba, May 25, 1993. The author indicates that he represents certified claimants who seek the return of their property. The National Association of Sugar Mill Owners of Cuba (Asociación Nacional de Hacendados de Cuba, Inc.) is also very active in this regard. A.R.M. Ritter, while acknowledging that it has "only a limited role to play," does not rule out restitution; see "Financial Aspects of Normalizing Cuba's International Relations: The Debt and Compensation Issues," *Cuba In Transition*, Florida International University, 1993.

14. Freer recognizes that a process of restitution "will, to some degree, inhibit the rapid privatization of property. Forcing claims into the courts could well cause a lengthy lag between the claim and the actual vindication of title." Freer, *op. cit.*, p. 12.

15. "In general, accumulated experience suggest that while small firms in the manufacturing sector can be sold early on and rapidly, the divesture of large monopolies, banks, insurance companies and public utilities that wield monopoly power is substantially more complicated. In particular, in most cases, it is desirable to define a clear regulatory framework before firms are put in the block." (Edwards, 1995, p. 175).

16. Gerd Schwartz, "Privatization in Eastern European Countries," in *Transition to Market*, Vito Tanzi, ed., (Washington, D.C.: International Monetary Fund, 1993) p. 244.

The issue of modifications to property making restitution impractical is not trivial.[17] As a result of modifications, some former owners would receive nothing while others could receive more than they lost. In the case of small business owners (there were 855 corporate awards totalling US$123.3 million), the likelihood of physical disappearance and/or substantial modification is extremely high.

Secondly, restitution would lock the country back into the pre-1959 pattern of distribution of wealth and production structure; it would not be supported by the majority of the people of Cuba. If we were to take only the fifteen largest U.S. claims (totalling US$1.2 billion, which is equivalent to 67 percent of total U.S. claims), we would find that U.S. nationals owned:

- 90 percent of all electricity generated on the island (Cuban Electric Co.)

- The entire telephone system (ITT)

- Most of the mining industry (Moa Bay Mining Co. & Nicaro Nickel Co.)

- Significant tracts of some of the best land in Cuba (between 1.5 and 2 million acres)[18]

Returning these properties, *ipso facto*, to U.S. ownership, even if it were feasible to do so, would be tantamount to insisting that nationalistic feelings in Cuba due to foreign ownership of the country's principal assets never had a basis in fact. Moreover, it would tend to lock the country back into a sugar-dominated structure of production, precisely at a time when an unintended benefit of Cuba's economic collapse is having the opportunity to diversify away from this declining industry. In the case of public utilities, the value of a concession to provide electric power or telephone service to a country of 11 million is significantly greater than for a country of 6.5 million, which Cuba was in 1959.[19] We consider that Cuba must have a very competitive, dynamic and export-oriented economy at the time of NAFTA and the WTO and such monopolistic concessions would be incompatible with this objective.

Thirdly, the output and employment benefits that have been estimated by some researchers[20] are based largely on unrealistically positive assumptions regarding its feasibility and insufficient consideration of the benefits of alternatives to restitution.

E. Privatization and Compensation

Large enterprises can be privatized by two modes: (i) the free distribution of assets to the public at large and (ii) following a case-by case commercial approach with four main variants: (a) sale of a controlling percentage of share to a private company; (b) initial public offering of shares on a stock exchange, either domestic or international; (c) employee or management buyout; and (d) liquidation of the enterprise and sale of its assets. In the free distribution of assets, while managers are liberated from government supervision, they are not put under the control of the new owners. Effective controls can be imposed gradually, no matter how fast the formal rights are distributed. Under the second mode, when a state enterprise is sold to new owners, corporate governance is immediately established, the necessary adjustments begin to follow and additional financing is often forthcoming. However, the mode proceeds case by case, it take a long time to privatize a majority of state firms. Therefore the dilemma is to choose between a wide and shallow privatization or a deep and narrow one.

---

17. See Jorge A. Sanguinetty, "Some Issues About Expropriation Claims In Cuba," ASCE *Newsletter*, Spring Issue, May 1993, p. 10, 11.

18. North American Sugar Industries alone owned a tract of land of approximately 42 miles by 30 miles (3,300 square kilometers) and three sugar mills, including two of Cuba's largest.

19. In June 1994, Grupo Domos, a Mexican enterprise, purchased 49% of EmtelCuba for US$1.5 billion. See Ted Bardacke, "Mexican firm breaks new ground in Cuban telecom field," *Development Business*, July 31, 1994. Compare that figure, which represents half of a broken-down telephone system, to the FCSC award of US$130.7 million in the ITT case for the entire telephone system of Cuba in 1960, which functioned adequately.

20. See, for example, José F. Alonso, "An Economic Exercise in Restitution," July 8, 1994, mimeo.

As pointed out above, to be fair to all parties any consideration of compensation for property loss in Cuba must be matched by arrangements to compensate for tort claims.

One essential question to be answered is whether attempting to arrange some form of non-cash compensation for tort claims will be more conducive to reconciliation than adopting a no-compensation policy. For example, in Romania it was felt that like many of its citizens, the country was suffering from post-traumatic stress syndrome, for which it had to undergo a difficult process of critical self-examination, healing, and reconstruction. Under a victim compensation law, more than 100,000 Rumanians have claimed compensation which, aside from cash, has been granted in the form of benefits such as free public transportation and preservation of job seniority.[21]

A commitment to compensate those whose assets were earlier confiscated is easier. It encompasses *a tabula rasa* approach, that is, mandates forging restitution and limiting to compensation the claims of economic agents whose property had earlier been confiscated. Swift economic progress in this environment is a distinctive possibility. Of course, compensation presents some complexities too. It could put pressure on current or future government budgets and assessing the property of claims would still have to be tackled. Ascertaining values of confiscated property is a hazardous undertaking under the best of circumstances. This is even true when the object of assessment is being narrowed down to real estate, plant and equipment. Some of them have changed to such an extent in the intervening years that fair compensation is fundamentally an impractical choice, some of them are in a physically dilapidated shape, and it is unfair to ignore many other assets such as goodwill, technologies, contracts, rights, licenses and patents, financial instruments, market position and human capital. Aside from generating much work for accounting firms and lawyers, at the great expense, in the end, to the taxpayer in the countries in transfor-

mation, such cumbersome, costly evaluations are in any case rather meaningless in the disorderly, highly inflationary and increasingly competitive environment of the countries going through the transformation. There is also the problem of the introduction of modern tax systems and accounting procedures.

Any attempt to ask a new Cuban government to compensate former rightful owners in cash or cash equivalent out of general revenues must be considered dangerous, given the already exceedingly weak fiscal base of the economy. Perhaps a commitment in principle to compensate former rightful owners from the proceeds of the sale of capital assets, including the transfer of shares in state firms to be privatized if so desired, or providing future rights and preferences would go a long way to see justice done without disrupting the transformation process.

There are two U.S. laws related to compensation for U.S. claims that are critical to Cuba's reconstruction. One bans aid to countries that confiscated property owned by U.S. citizens without equitable compensation and the other requires the U.S. to vote against aid by multilateral lending institutions to such countries. Hence, U.S. laws require resolution of U.S. citizens' confiscation claims before foreign aid can resume.

Bilateral negotiations are desirable to resolve U.S. claims. We would argue that by the act of filing claims before the FCSC, U.S. citizens and corporations formally requested the U.S. government to demand compensation, and the U.S. government did so by first placing and then maintaining an embargo on trade with Cuba.

Furthermore, the U.S. government paid at least partial compensation to claimants through the tax system. As mentioned in preceding sections of this paper, in the early 1970's, the Internal Revenue Service implemented a program allowing individual and corporate *taxpayers* (i.e., including Cuban expatriates who were taxpayers and suffered losses) to take feder-

---

21. See Geneva Initiative on Psychiatry, *Psychiatry Under Tyranny: An Assessment of the Political Abuse of Romanian Psychiatry During the Ceausescu Years*, Amsterdam, 1992, p. 14.

al income tax deductions for losses of property confiscated by the government of Cuba (see Appendix). Those who filed tax returns claiming deductions for losses also transferred their claims to the U.S. government. Groups of Cuban-Americans have also formally requested the Secretary of State to take up their cases.

Therefore, all U.S. claimants (citizen and non-citizen taxpayers) made their claims subject to international negotiation and, if the doctrine of espousal is invoked (as it should be), must abide by the settlement made by the U.S. government. Rather than negotiating with each claimant, the government of Cuba should indicate its readiness to negotiate this matter bilaterally with the U.S. government.

The purpose of massive privatization is to provide Cuba a realistic change for a fresh start as a market economy and representative democracy because Cuba faces a solvency problem and not a liquidity problem. Only interest payments on foreign loans could swallow about half of Cuba's export earnings. All compensation claims for confiscations of property and other torts must be reduced or postponed, and emergency and development economic assistance must be provided expeditiously in order that comprehensive and difficult transformation reforms are implemented and have time to take hold.

An analogy to U.S. bankruptcy proceedings is pertinent here. When an enterprise works its way through a Chapter 11 bankruptcy in the United States, three things normally happen. First, creditors are forced to refrain of pressing their claims. This breathing space, or financial standstill, provides the debtor the chance to get back on its feet. Second, the debtor may be allowed to borrow fresh funds on a privileged basis to replenish its working capital and the new creditors have higher priority than the old ones. Third, the old creditors are usually compelled to cut a deal with the debtor, in which they cancel or restructure part of the debt or convert part of it to equity, to allow the debtor to emerge from bankruptcy with an opportunity for continued operations. This is the type of scenario that will have to take place in relation to Cuba's serious financial obligations if the country is to get back on its feet.

However, an important issue to be considered is the negative impact a no-compensation policy might have on the government's credibility in reestablishing private property rights. It is also felt that future investment will be discouraged unless there is some form of official recognition of past losses, for which special consideration might be given during the process of privatization.

In a previous paper, we suggested the corporatization of certain large military bases in Cuba and their conversion to free trade zones, with labor being provided by the deactivated military. In a NAFTA and WTO world, free trade zones may be less attractive possibilities. Nevertheless, as an example of one possible means of compensation, a scheme might be built into the corporatization of military bases, converting them into poles for industrial development, and compensating with shares in these corporations.

In this regard, the government of Cuba could negotiate the earlier termination of U.S. rights to Guantánamo Bay, with its airport, port, structures and other facilities covering 117 Km^2 and occupying one of the three best Cuban ports, establish the Guantánamo Development Corporation, and use shares or profits from that corporation to compensate the government of the United States for U.S. claims.

Obviously, there is no reasonable way for a future government of Cuba to justify compensating the U.S. and not its own citizens. Compensation of Cuban and other claimants who did not receive tax benefits from the U.S. could take the form of issuance of shares or discount coupons to be used to purchase shares in selected corporations.

CONCLUSIONS AND RECOMMENDATIONS

The government of Cuba should take the following steps:

1. Reaffirm at the outset that all non-residential property in Cuba belongs to the state.

2. Declare its recognition that confiscations of properties that took place after January 1, 1959 were illegal, except properties initially obtained through misconduct or wrongdoing, and its intention to negotiate settlement of the claims.

3. Declare its willingness to enter into negotiations with the Government of the United States for direct bilateral settlement of the debt owed for properties of U.S. citizens confiscated after January 1, 1959. This debt includes (a) claims presented to the U.S. Foreign Claims Settlement Commission and found to merit awards, and (b) assets claimed as losses to the Internal Revenue Service by U.S. citizens and former Cuban nationals.

Lifting of the U.S. embargo is a necessary though not sufficient condition for Cuba to have the ability to service its obligations, apply for debt rescheduling and debt relief, and have access to fresh credit. In our view, as a result of the combination of the Foreign Assistance Act of 1961 and the Cuban Democracy Act of 1992, only a transition government of Cuba, committed to holding free and fair elections, will be able to negotiate the issue of U.S. claims with the government of the United States in order to resolve this matter.

Since the lifting of the U.S. embargo is a priority, Cuba must indicate its agreement to enter into formal bilateral (government-to-government) good-faith negotiations regarding U.S. claims, but the embargo must be lifted prior to concluding the negotiations.

Some have indicated disingenuously that lifting the embargo prior to settling all claims would "compromise the entire U.S. Cuba claims issue" and that the United States "would lose any leverage it may otherwise have had with regard to the prompt resolution of the U.S. Cuba claims matter."[22] This argument seems to us absurd, since Cuba's development hopes and ability to compensate are inextricably tied to its relations with the United States. The challenge for both the U.S. and Cuba will be to build a relationship based on mutual respect and trust.

4. Establish the Guantánamo Development Corporation (GDC), as a Cuban corporation, on the property to be vacated by the U.S. Naval Base on the basis of an agreement as part of Point (3), as an industrial development zone. The government of Cuba would retain a minimum of 25 percent of its shares, the remainder to be distributed by the government of the United States as further compensation for losses sustained by its citizens and former Cuban nationals who claimed losses to the Internal Revenue Service. Suitable agreement should be reached to safeguard the value of the GDC's shares in order for compensation to be meaningful.

5. Establish a semi-autonomous agency such as the CACUCOCO[23] to examine all other claims not included in Point (4) above, and to make a determination regarding the amount of the loss in each case.

6. Select major military bases with good infrastructure (especially port access) and establish one other industrial development corporations modelled after the GDC. Shares in these corporations would be used to compensate claims awarded by the CACUCOCO.

7. *Implement a privatization program for the non-residential properties specified in Point 1 above, providing for swift distribution of small and medium state enterprises and giving priority to Cuban residents.*[24] Privatization should be carried out with absolute transparency and without any suspicion of impropriety. This will provide robust political foundations to the economic transformation.

8. Adopt a modern foreign investment law, join the Multilateral Investment Guarantee Agency (MIGA), and invite and sign agreements with the Overseas Private Investment Corporation (OPIC) and other similar European organizations to

---

22. Ralph J. Galliano, "The Resolution of U.S. Cuba Claims: Toward a Democratic, Free Market, Post-Castro Cuba," Washington, D.C., the Selous Foundation, May 20, 1993, p. 5, 6.

23. Cámara Cubana de Compensación Constitucional. See Emilio Cueto, "La Cacucoco: Fantasía en MI Sostenido," *La Crónica* (Mexico, D.F.), 15 September 1994, p. 11-12.

24. See Castañeda and Montalván, *op. cit.*, pp. 68-70.

begin financing and insuring investments in order to reduce the country risk of investing in Cuba. Cuba should also sign the International Convention for the Settlement of Investment Disputes (ICSD) and enter negotiations with the aim of securing bilateral investment agreements to avoid double taxation in order that foreign investors can receive credit for the taxes they pay in Cuba from taxes payable in their country of origin.

COMMENTS ON

"Economic Factors in Selecting an Approach to Expropriation Claims in Cuba" by Rolando Castañeda and George Plinio Montalván

Ralph J. Galliano

It is important to draw a distinction between the terms "expropriated property" *and* "confiscated property" inasmuch as "expropriated property" implies compensation in return for the taking of property while "confiscated property" explicitly infers there has been no compensation forthcoming. Given the authors' selected title, the opportunity to develop what would otherwise be the heart-and-soul of this paper, "the economic value of confiscated property in Cuba," is seriously lacking. Moreover, the authors' reference to "property rights" as a political issue *not* an economic one, in fact, counters the titled intent of the paper. Consequently, this paper is better titled, "Selecting an Approach to Confiscated Property in Cuba."

The paper is rather unclear when it comes to distinguishing between the rights of *certified U.S. claimants* (see p.1) and *claims by Cuban nationals.* According to the authors, "Another critical issue is defining citizenship for the purpose of restitution laws. Most countries have defined that only those individuals who were citizens of the country and who had lived there permanently when the law came into effect are eligible for restitution." First of all, this paper needs to clarify and separate the rights of certified U.S. claimants from the rights of any other claimants. While a table of countries is presented, the authors fail to explain how those countries have defined citizenship with respect to the issue of restitution and the actual economic impact of that country's deci-

sion. The authors seem to be struggling with the concept of "restitution" which is the simple idea of returning to people property that was illegally taken— that means *confiscated*—a right that fully belongs to the original property owner.

The authors' paper opens with a quotation by Professor Stanley Fisher which states in part, "Compensation should *not* take the form of giving the original owners the rights to the property itself, but rather the right to compensation by the State." (emphasis added). Herein lies the inherent problem with regard to this paper whereby reliance is placed on the rights of the *state* rather than on the rights of the *individual* to resolve the issue of confiscated property.

At one point the authors concede that restitution may be justified and they cite the economic success of Chile where "It began through restitution..." presenting the strongest possible case in favor of restitution in Cuba. However, the authors tend to shun restitution as a viable solution and rely upon the consideration of the perceived benefits of the alternatives to restitution instead.

Throughout their paper, the authors put forth a series of obstacles to the settlement of property claims including: 1) the rights of the state over the rights of the individual; 2) damages from human rights violations which would render compensation untenable by its sheer magnitude; 3) usufruct of property, although, it does not apply especially if force was used to take the property or to cause the property owners to flee for their lives; 4) expand the claims against Cuba so as not to be limited to property but to "include all manner of torts" in effect attempting to render the claims process untenable; and finally, 5) not holding a future Cuban government (read post-Castro) responsible for the confiscations.

It is astounding that the authors then should suggest that the act of compensation by Cuba actually has been fulfilled through the U.S. placement of the embargo upon Cuba for its confiscation of U.S. owned property in the first instance.

The authors' conclusions and recommendations appear faulty and unworkable insofar as they call for lifting the embargo prior to the conclusion of bilateral negotiations on claims settlement. Nicaragua serves as an example where the U.S. embargo was lifted following the declaration of free and fair elections but before the property claims issue was fully resolved. Today, Nicaragua's economy languishes and the property claims linger. The authors' call for international organization financing prior to the settlement of claims is tantamount to a raid on the U.S. Treasury as well as a raid on international treasuries for the financing and revitalization of state socialism in Cuba.

RESTITUTION VS. INDEMNIFICATION: THEIR EFFECTS ON THE PACE OF PRIVATIZATION

Luis Locay and Cigdem Ural

All former communist countries undergoing transitions to market economies have faced the difficult question of whether or not to compensate those whose property had been confiscated by the previous, now deposed, regime. If a country determines that it will give compensation, it must then decide who will be eligible, how much compensation will be given, and what form it will take. In this paper we focus only on the issue of whether compensation should be in the form of restitution—the returning of property to the previous owners—or whether it should be some form of indemnification—the term we will use to designate compensation in the form of some asset (usually financial) other than the actual confiscated property.

While economists may be divided as to whether compensation of some form may increase efficiency, they are nearly unanimously in favor of indemnification over restitution. The argument is a simple one. Transition economies need to privatize quickly. Under a policy of restitution, title to property is not clear until claims are settled. Privatization must therefore wait for the resolution of property claims. Under indemnification the resolution of claims can proceed independently of the process of privatization.

Most transition economies seem to have ignored this advice. Countries that made up the former Soviet Union have not given any form of compensation—perhaps not surprising given the long time period since confiscation. The countries of Eastern Europe, however, have compensated previous owners, and the

preferred method—with the notable exception of Hungary—has been restitution (Travieso-Díaz 1995, Castañeda and Montalván 1995). We can imagine two possibilities why actual practice has deviated so much from what has been recommended. One possibility is that non-efficiency considerations are dominant. As economists, we do not know how much we can say about such considerations. In any case, we have so far not heard non-efficiency explanations we find convincing. A second possibility is that economists have overlooked ways in which restitution may actually enhance efficiency. The purpose of this paper is to put forth just such an argument.

The traditional argument against restitution ignores the fact that privatization takes place within a political context. Privatization creates not only winners, but also losers. The losers will be those who run state enterprises, their political bosses, and perhaps part of the work force. Some of these are politically well connected persons who are likely to lobby to delay or sabotage privatization, or to skew the process in their favor at the expense of efficiency. They are a powerful special interest group whose interests are the opposite of successful privatization. Restitution creates an opposing special interest group—the previous owners—whose interests are in speeding up privatization, since they will be its primary beneficiaries. In serving as a countervailing force against those who would work to delay privatization, it seems plausible that they can offset the delays caused by the settling of claims under restitution.

It may at first seem that testing such a hypothesis is straightforward. One need only compare how the pace and success of privatization has varied across countries using the two methods of compensation. We do not know if the necessary data exist. So far we have not found them, but our research is still in its preliminary stages. Even if such data exist, however, there are remaining difficulties. Among them is that the differences across countries that lead them to adopt different compensation strategies are also likely to affect the pace of privatization.[1] To correct for such "selection bias" we need some sort of model of the political process as concerns the method of compensation used. Such a model can also be an alternative, indirect, way of testing the hypothesis that we have put forth. If it is successful in explaining features of the privatization process, including perhaps which countries have chosen which method, we would gain confidence in the hypothesis.

In this paper we provide a very simple, "bare bones" model of the political process concerning compensation and privatization in a previously centrally planned economy. The political process will have two levels. One level is that of general rules of the game, such as whether restitution or indemnification should be used. It seems to us that if the work of social scientists can have any influence, it is at that level. Once the rules are set, however, we view political decisions as being completely endogenous, and our role becomes descriptive and explanatory.

In section one we present our model of privatization with indemnification as the method of compensation. The model is based on the work of Becker (1985) on political influence. We stress that the work here is very preliminary. Section two introduces restitution and analyzes how it affects the pace of privatization. In section three we look at the political equilibrium under restitution, and analyze how the pace of privatization depends on the fraction of the economy that is in private hands before the transition. We suggest that the larger is the private economy at the beginning, the more likely indemnification will be chosen as the method of compensation. We discuss some standard extensions in section 4, and how we believe they will affect our results. We briefly discuss in section five two alternative explanations for why countries may choose restitution. We conclude with a proposal for how to utilize the pressure group benefits of restitution in a system of indemnification.

1. A SIMPLE MODEL OF POLITICAL INFLUENCE IN THE PRIVATIZATION PROCESS IN THE ABSENCE OF RESTITUTION

Imagine an economy which has just had a political transition and wishes to privatize that portion of its economy which is owned by the government. We assume that when a government owned firm is privatized its productivity automatically rises. Those who previously ran that government firm, which we will refer to as managers, lose whatever surplus they were receiving prior to privatization. The longer it takes to privatize, T, the more the managers gain. They can lobby to delay privatization, but lobbying is costly to them. The surplus going to the managers of any one government enterprise, S_m, is given by the following:

$$S_m = m(T) - \varepsilon_m , \qquad (1)$$

where ε_m is the amount of lobbying done per state enterprise, and $m(T)$ is the surplus derived by the managers from the state enterprise between now and T. It is easy to show that $m'(T)>0$ and that $m''(T)<0$.[2]

If capital markets work well, the buyers of state enterprises will not receive any windfalls.[3] Who then re-

---

1. Several other potential problems come to mind. Variables other than the method of compensation used may affect the pace of privatization. The sample sizes are small. We have some first hand accounts which even question whether what in some countries is call privatization is really that at all.

2. If π_m is the instantaneous profit, or surplus, accruing to those who run the state firm, then $m(T)=\int_0^T e^{-rt}\pi_m dt$, where r is the rate of discount.

3. In section four we consider some of the implications of imperfect capital markets.

ceives the gains from privatization? We assume the beneficiaries are identical worker/consumers who experience a rise in their real wages.[4] The surplus of each of these worker/consumers is given by:

$$S_w = w(T) - \varepsilon_w ,\qquad (2)$$

where ε_w is the lobbying done by the typical worker/consumer. Since worker/consumers gain from privatization, $w(T)$ is a decreasing function of T ($w'(T)<0$), and it is easy to show that $w(T)$ is convex ($w''(T)>0$).[5]

Let θ be the fraction of firms that are privately owned prior to privatization. Historically θ has been a small number. If we normalize both the number of firms and the number of worker/consumers to one, the aggregate lobbying to delay privatization is $E_m = (1-\theta)\varepsilon_m$, and aggregate lobbying to speed it up is $E_w = \varepsilon_w$. The time until privatization, T, is determined by an influence function, I, as

$$T = I(E_m, E_w; X) ,\qquad (3)$$

where $I_m>0$ and $I_w<0$. The variable x represents the institutional framework. It is reasonable to assume that $I_{mm}<0$ and $I_{ww}>0$. The former guarantees that the second order conditions for the maximization problem of the manager of a state enterprise (see below) are satisfied. The latter is actually required by the second order conditions for the maximization problem of a worker/consumer (see below). Since we have no strong prior on the interaction of E_m and E_w in I, we will make the simplest assumption, which is that they are independent, i.e. $I_{mw}=0$.

We are ready to state the maximization problem of the managers and of worker/consumers. For each state enterprise the managers choose ε_m so as to maximize S_m subject to the influence function and to the level of lobbying by worker/consumers. The first order condition for this problem is:

$$(1-\theta)m'(T)I_m - 1 = 0 ,\qquad (4)$$

The solution of (4) is the reaction function $E_m = R_m(E_w,\theta;x)$, which relates the level of lobbying by worker/consumers to the lobbying done by the managers of the state enterprise. Differentiating (4) we can also obtain:

$$R_{mE_M}(E_w,\theta;x) = \frac{(1-q)^2 m''(T)I_m I_w}{m''(T)(I_m)^2 + m'(T)I_{mm}} > 0, \quad (5)$$

where R_{mE} is the partial derivative of R_m with respect to E_w. The function R_m is shown in figure 1. As can be seen, $R_m(E_w,\theta;x)$ is upward sloping with respect to E_w, so that the more lobbying that is done by worker/consumers, the more that is done by the managers.

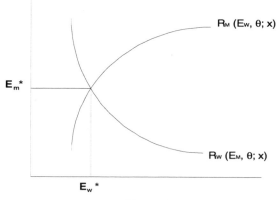

Figure 1

The reaction function for worker/consumers, $R_w(E_m,\theta;x)$ can be similarly derived. The first order condition for the worker/consumers is

$$w'(T)I_w - 1 = 0 \qquad (6)$$

Differentiating (6) one obtains:

$$R_{mEm}(E_m,\theta;x) = \frac{w''(T)I_w I_m}{w''(T)(I_w)^2 + w'(T)I_{ww}} < 0. \quad (7)$$

---

4. In reality, of course, workers (and consumers) are not identical. Some are likely to be made worse off by privatization and these would lobby for its delay.

5. Let W_b and W_a be the wage before and after privatization, respectively. Then $w(T)=\int_o T e^{-rt}(W_b-W_a)\,dt + \int_o e^{-rt}W_a dt$.

The reaction function $R_w(E_m,\theta;x)$, which is downward sloping with respect to E_m, is also depicted in figure 1.[6]

The intersection of the two reaction functions in figure 1 determines the equilibrium amount of lobbying for each group, E_m^* and E_w^*, which in turn determine how long the privatization process will take, $T = I(E_m^*, E_w^*; x)$.

The only exogenous variable we have in the model is θ, the fraction of firms that are in private hands at the beginning of the transition. We can now explore how this variable affects the pace of privatization. An increase in θ will shift down the reaction function R_m and shift the reaction function R_w to the right. That is, for any level of lobbying by worker/consumers, managers will lobby less, and for any level of lobbying by managers, worker/consumers will lobby more. This is depicted in figure 2. As can be seen, the equilibrium level of lobbying by worker/consumers, E_w^*, must increase. As shown, the equilibrium level of lobbying by managers, E_m^*, declines, but this is not necessarily so. The increase in lobbying by worker/consumers induces managers to lobby more, perhaps even to the point of compensating for the direct effect of θ. It seems reasonable to expect, however, that even if E_m^* rises, it does not rise so much that it compensates for the increase in E_w^* in the influence function, thereby increasing the time it takes to privatize. Surprisingly, despite the strong assumptions we have made, we have not yet been able to rule this possibility out. If one assumes the following specific influence function which satisfies all the conditions we have imposed:

$$I(E_m, E_w; x) = I_o + \alpha \ln(1+E_m) - \beta \ln(1+E_w), \qquad (8)$$

where I_0, α, and β are non-negative constants, it can be shown that time to privatize, T, declines as θ rises. This is reasonable because the special interest wishing to delay privatization, the managers, is smaller the greater is θ.

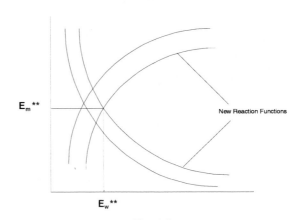

Figure 2

2. THE EFFECT OF RESTITUTION

We now assume that restitution is the form of compensation used and consider how the previous equilibrium is altered. Restitution creates a special interest group, the previous owners, whose aggregate lobbying, E_p, is directed at speeding up privatization. For now we treat E_p as exogenous.

The influence function, which relates lobbying to the time it takes to privatize, is now modified as follows:

$$T = I(E_m, E_w, E_p; x) + \tau, \qquad (9)$$

where τ is additional time involved in resolving property claims. We assume that the function $I(E_m, E_w, E_p; x)$ takes on the same values as before with $E_p = 0$. We also assume that $I_p < 0$, $I_{pp} > 0$, and $I_{pm} = I_{pw} = 0$.

Treating E_p as exogenous, we can compute the effect of an increase on E_m, E_w, and on T. The comparative statics are too messy to reproduce here, but we can show that an increase in E_p will lead to an increase in lobbying by both managers and worker/consumers. The effects of an increase in E_p on E_m and E_w are shown by shifts in the reaction functions in figure 3. Besides the indirect effect on T through E_m and E_w, E_p directly acts to reduce T. The net effect of an increase in E_p is to *decrease* T. Analytically, the effect

---

6. The denominator in (7) is negative by the second order conditions for the worker/consumers problem.

on T of changing from indemnification and restitution is like increasing in E_p from an initial value of zero, and adding τ. The effect on T of lobbying by the previous owners may or may not exceed the additional delays in privatization imposed by having to settle property claims.

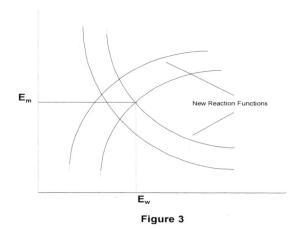

Figure 3

3. LOBBYING EQUILIBRIUM UNDER RESTITUTION

So far we have treated E_p as exogenous, which was fine for the comparative statics exercise of the previous section. Now we allow lobbying by the previous owners to be determined like that of managers and worker/consumers. Using notation analogous to that used above, the surplus of the previous owners, S_p, is given by:

$$S_p = p(T) - \varepsilon_p , \qquad (10)$$

where $p'(T) < 0$ and $p''(T) > 0$.[7] Aggregate lobbying by previous owners is given by $E_p = (1-\theta)\varepsilon_p$. The first order condition for a maximum for each previous owner is

$$p'(T)I_p - 1 = 0. \qquad (11)$$

The solutions to (4), (6), and (11) are three reaction functions, $R_m(E_w, E_p, \theta; x)$, $R_w(E_m, E_p, \theta; x)$, and $R_p(E_m, E_w, \theta; x)$. The solution to these reaction func-

tions would determine the equilibrium levels of lobbying, $(E_m{}^*, E_w{}^*, E_p{}^*)$. We do not yet have general comparative static results for changes in θ, nor even for the specific influence function in (8), suitably extended to include lobbying by the previous owners. We have done a few simulations for specific parameters for the influence function (8). A typical result is that under both restitution and indemnification the time until privatization is complete, T, declines with the fraction of firms. T declines more rapidly, however, with indemnification. If this results holds up more generally, a prediction of the model would be that the larger the relative size of the private sector at the beginning of the transition, the less are the gains in speeding up the privatization process by restitution. Since the speed of privatization is likely to be an important concern in choosing the method of compensation, we would then expect that the larger the private sector, the less likely a country would choose restitution as a means of compensation.

4. SOME GENERALIZATIONS

We have purposefully constructed a highly simplified model. Consequently, several extensions come readily to mind. One of these is the notion that the effectiveness of special interest groups may be inversely related to their size, because larger groups find it more difficult to organize. This could be modelled here by including θ directly into the influence function, allowing its value to affect the weights given to lobbying by managers and previous owners. It is not clear, however, that this is appropriate in our context. Managers and previous owners are lobbying to delay or speed up privatization of specific firms. They may not want to organize to affect the process in general.[8]

The relative size of the private sector, θ, may affect the pace of privatization directly if it takes longer to privatize a larger government owned sector. It is not evident, however, that this would affect the weights given to lobbying by the various interest groups in the influence function. Consequently, this should

---

7. If the instantaneous profit rate for the previous owner is π_p, then $p(T) = \int_T \int e^{-rt}\pi_p dt$.

8. This reasoning calls into question whether aggregate lobbying, or lobbying per firm, should be the arguments of the influence function.

not affect the decision of whether to use restitution or indemnification. By this reasoning, the time added to the privatization process for settling claims under restitution, τ, could also be made a function of θ. τ would be a decreasing function of θ, so T would decline more rapidly with increasing θ under restitution, than if τ was constant. This may seem to have the potential of reversing the simulation results discussed above, but we believe the basic outcome—that indemnification is more desirable the larger the initial size of the private sector—will remain unchanged, at least for some simple, but reasonable, functional forms for τ.

We have also assumed that the gains and losses to the various groups from privatizing do not directly depend on θ. This is unlikely to be the case, because the value of θ will affect the equilibrium wages and profit prior to the transition, and therefore affect the magnitude of the changes brought about by privatization. Specifically, we expect that the larger is θ, the less is the gain to worker/consumers from privatization, and the less the loss to managers. Both groups have less incentives for lobbying. Presumably this would give greater weight to previous owners. The owners of private firms at the beginning of the transition, however, could now be hurt by privatization, and they would have an incentive to lobby to delay it. While not denying that these direct effects of θ on the surpluses of the various groups, it is our belief that these are of secondary importance.

5. ALTERNATIVE EXPLANATIONS

It is sometimes suggested that a reason why restitution may be used by transition economies is that it places less financial burden on already strapped government budgets. While it is true, of course, that restitution saves the government indemnification outlays, it also denies in revenue from privatization. In principle one should be able to design restitution and indemnification programs that have the same impact on a government's budget. We do not see this as a viable explanation.

An alternative explanation has to do with the possibility that capital markets in a transition economy may be highly imperfect.[9] With well functioning capital markets, it should not matter from the point of view of efficiency, whether government firms are auctioned off or returned to previous owners. They will end up in the hands of those who value them most in either case. This will not necessarily happen if capital markets are highly imperfect. The best people to run the firms, for example, may not be able to obtain financing to purchase them, and so there will be an efficiency loss. Under these circumstance returning property to previous owners may result in a better assignment of ownership and control than would be achieved through the market. If this explanation is correct, we should see considerable restrictions on the return of property. For example, previous owners may be required to run the firms returned to them, or make a minimum level of investment.[10] Previous owners who for health reasons or obsolescence of knowledge of their industry could not run their previous firms, would not have them returned to them. Heirs would presumably not have claims to property, unless there was some presumption that they would make good owners. We do not know to what extent these types of restrictions have been present in transition economies using restitution.

A related argument involves the resulting distribution of wealth if capital markets are highly imperfect. It may be that those who end up purchasing government owned firms make windfall gains purely because of their superior access to financing. These windfall gains may accrue primarily to foreigners. Restitution, to the extent it involves nationals, would avoid this. A problem with this explanation is that when government assets are sold off, only the windfall gains, and not the entire value of the properties, go to the purchasers. With restitution, the entire value normally goes to the recipient. In the case of Cuba most of the recipients of restituted property would be expatriates, whose wealth levels on average far ex-

---

9. This alternative explanation was made to us by John Devereux.

10. In the case of expatriates these would normally involve returning to the country.

ceeds those of residents of the island. Restitution would seem to further skew the distribution wealth.

6. CONCLUSION

We have argued that restitution of property in a transition economy may enhance efficiency by creating a special interest—the previous owners—who have an incentive in speeding up the privatization process. This group serves to balance the pressures exerted by the losers from privatization to delay the process. Furthermore, we have taken the first steps in constructing a model that could help explain what countries choose what method of compensation, and that would eventually allow us test our hypothesis indirectly. An implication we hope to eventually develop, and which we have given some suggestive arguments for, is that an economy is more likely to choose resti-

tution the smaller is its private sector prior to the transition.

We would like to close with a suggestion. One way of incorporating the desirable feature of restitution in a program of indemnification would be as follows: indemnify owners, but do not begin settling a claim until the property involved has been privatized. Privatization need not wait until claims are settled, but yet the previous owners have an incentive to speed up the process. For the latter effect to work as with restitution, the amount of indemnification would have to correspond to the selling price of the property involved. This has the potentially useful result of bringing into the privatization process private information previous owners may have about the strength of their claims.

REFERENCES

Becker, Gary. "Public Policies, Pressure Groups, and Dead Weight Costs," *Journal of Public Economics* 28, (1985), pp. 329-347.

Castañeda, Rolando H. and George Plinio Montalván. "Economic Factors in Selecting an Ap-

proach to Expropriation Claims in Cuba," working paper.

Travieso-Díaz, Matías. "Some Legal and Practical Issues in the Resolution of Cuban Nationals' Expropriation Claims Against Cuba," *Journal of International Business Law*, 16 (2), (1995).

COMMENTS ON

"Restitution vs. Indemnification: Their Effects on the Pace of Privatization" by Luis Locay and Cigdem Ural

Roger R. Betancourt

The problem the authors choose to solve is the seeming paradox that economists recommend some form of indemnification and oppose restitution but practitioners in transition settings have usually chosen restitution rather than indemnification. In laying out the problem, the authors set up a bit of a straw man by arguing that there are only two reasons for divergence between practice and prescription: non-efficiency issues, about which they claim economists have nothing to say, and efficiency issues, which are the basis for their argument. The latter centers on arguing that restitution can enhance efficiency by speeding the privatization process.

Before looking at the authors' argument in detail, it must be emphasized that they are already ignoring a very simple answer to their paradox. All indemnification schemes require establishing the value of the asset . Indeed, in an earlier analysis of this issue at ASCE's first meeting ("The New Institutional Economics and the Study of the Cuban Economy"), I wrote: "The key issue in this approach (indemnification) is, of course, to establish the value of the asset" (p.22) and proceeded to discuss the difficulties associated with various alternatives. If one cannot solve this problem in practice as opposed to in theory, no indemnification scheme is viable; hence, there is no paradox to be explained.

My argument above questions the validity of their motivation for the paper. Nonetheless, it says nothing about the merits of their specific argument on

how restitution speeds up privatization. The authors present an ingenious model of interacting players (workers/consumers) and managers, and show how the equilibrium outcome of each pursuing their rent seeking activities optimally is one where an increase in the fraction of firms that are privately owned prior to the transition leads to a faster privatization. They assume that this corresponds to a situation with indemnification without explicitly addressing the issue of asset valuation in practice. Implicitly, it assumes that indemnification is merely a transfer of the potential profits of the enterprise from the old managers to the worker/ consumers at the time of privatization. Hence, managers want to delay and workers want to speed up privatization.

In this setting the authors introduce restitution. We now have three players instead of two but the basic outcome is the same as in the previous model. The authors discuss potential enhancements of their model and alternative explanations but again do not address the practical issue of valuation directly.

Their concluding suggestion is quite interesting but perhaps not for the reason they think. They argue that under indemnification their analysis suggests that indemnified owners should not be allowed to settle their claims until their property is privatized. Their rationale is that this gives the previous owners an incentive to speed up the process. They argue that for this to work the amount of indemnification would have to correspond to the selling price of the property. Voila, they have found one possible way of solving the asset valuation problem in practice. Of course, safeguards would be needed to prevent artificial manipulation of the prices of the privatized property. Exploring the benefits of this alternative could very well be the most valuable contribution of the paper.

THE ETHICAL FOUNDATIONS OF
PRIVATE PROPERTY: THE CUBAN CASE

Alberto Martínez Piedra

"Justice is destroyed in twofold fashion by the false prudence of the sage and by the violent act of the man who possesses power."

— St. Thomas, *On the Book of Job* (8,I)

The thirty six years of Castro's omnipotent rule seem to be coming to an end. After more than a quarter of a century of oppression and tyranny, it is to be hoped that the expectations of the Cuban people, that a new dawn of political and economic freedoms is near at hand, finally will become a reality. But, these expectations must not be frustrated by uncompromising positions concerning the way the post Castro government should deal with some of the most pressing economic problems that the island will have to face after the fall of Marxism-Leninism. Perhaps, one of the most sensitive ones is the issue of compensation for the unlawful confiscations of private properties which took place in 1959 and the years that followed. An ethical and just solution must be found to this serious problem in order to avoid further divisions and antagonisms which could endanger the country's future peace and stability, so much in need by the Cuban people.

Legitimate and honest differences of opinion, concerning the crucial issue of compensation should not only be welcomed but also encouraged. Plurality of ideas within a true democratic system, where the fundamental rights and duties of the human person are respected, are symptomatic of a healthy and free society. All Cubans affected by Castro's illegitimate take over of rightfully owned properties during the early years of the revolution, have the right and duty to express their opinions in a matter of such importance for the future credibility of Cuba as a law abiding country.

But, it cannot be overlooked that the entire question of how the post Castro government is going to deal with this delicate problem is of interest not only to all Cubans inside and outside the island but also to all countries that respect the right to private property and the basic principles of a free economic order. The respect for private property is at the core of any free society. By not recognizing the injustice of forced expropriations without due compensation, you are *de facto* making a sham of the right of private property. Who can guarantee that future expropriations will not take place? What confidence, if any, will the people have in a system that ignores the trampled rights of those who have been unjustly expropriated? Any discussion of human rights becomes purely academic if the most elemental natural right of private property is ignored and not a word of protest is uttered against the unlawful and unethical actions of the past. The term democracy becomes meaningless and it would be ludicrous to talk about political and economic freedom.

Thus, the economic and political consequences of whatever action the new government will take concerning the touchy problem of compensation must be weighed very carefully. The recognition of the right to private property, past and present, must be given the highest priority. Otherwise, how can people believe in the sincerity of the new government if it does not recognize publicly the unlawful seizure of private property together with all the other abuses and injustices of Castro's Marxist regime?

In this paper we will limit ourselves to an analysis of the ethical foundations of private property, emphasizing the traditional view that to own private property is not only a natural right of all free men and women but also that this inalienable right is closely connected with the *bonum commune* (the common good).[1] First we will discuss briefly the concept of property in accordance with the main currents of western thought that have prevailed through history. Second, we will comment on the basic forms of justice. For that, it will be necessary to relate the three basic types of justice with the three fundamental structures of community life. Third, we will mention the idea of the *bonum commune*, its distinctive attribute and the role and limitations of the public authorities as administrators of the common good. Fourth, attention will be given to the fact that justice requires some type of recompense and/or restitution to all those affected adversely by unlawful and unjust government expropriations if order and respect for the natural rights of men and women are to be maintained in a free society. Finally, it will be stressed that, as a result of Cuba's tragic and costly experiment with socialism, something more than justice will be needed to reestablish peace and order.

THE PRINCIPLE OF PRIVATE PROPERTY

Ideas on property are all important in any serious discussion of economic matters.[2] It is the cornerstone of a free economic order and anathema to those who identify property as the primary cause of alienation. Defenders of economic liberalism have always maintained that the right to private property is not only man's inalienable right but it is one of the major factors that contributes to production and efficiency.[3] On the other hand, socialists have challenged this position, claiming that in primitive societies communal property was the norm and that labour alone has the right to the product of human endeavour.

Limitations on the right of private property have been stressed throughout the entire course of history. Considerations of an ethical and a legal nature have placed restrictions on the absolute right of private property, subordinating it to a higher value: the common good. It has often been argued that the best guarantee against too much concentration of power is to give every man and woman the opportunity to own private property Greed and too much concentration of economic power in the hands of the privileged few have been considered detrimental to society. Observations such as these have been made not only by the socialists and other social reformers but also by liberal scholars, including such a prominent classical economist as Adam Smith as will be shown later.

1. The Concept Of Property Prior to the Age of Liberalism

Was there a "Golden Age" where mankind was thought to have owned everything in common? Is the right to property derived from human nature or is it the result of a social contract? Different scholars have presented different views concerning this academic debate. Plato in the *Republic*, said quite clearly that, in the ideal State, the guardians or administrators should own things in common, including wives

---

1. For an interesting analysis of the different approaches to private property see: *Marxism, Communism and Western Society*, A Comparative Encyclopedia, Edited by C.D. Kerning, (Herder and Herder, Volume VII, Principle-Socialist Patriotism, pp.68-90.

2. For the purpose of this paper the terms economic liberalism, capitalism and the free enterprise system will be used interchangeably.

3. Ludwig von Mises, the late Dean of the Austrian school ef economics establishes a direct link between private property and civilization. He says: "All civilizations have up to now been based on private ownership of the means of production. In the past, civilization and private property have been linked together. Those who maintain that economics is an experimental science and nevertheless recommend public control of the means of production, lamentably contradict themselves. If historical experience could teach us anything, it would be that private property is inextricably linked with civilization. There is no experience to the effect that socialism could provide a standard of living as high as that provided by capitalism". See Von Mises, Ludwig, *Human Action, A Treatise on Economics*, (Chicago: Contemporary Books Inc.,Third revised edition published by Henry Regnery Company in 1966, by arrangement with Yale University Press, p.264).

and children.[4] As the economist Edmund Whittaker comments: "Obviously, Plato's arguments were political, not economic. Private property was to be forbidden to public officials in order that corruption and dissention might be minimized. In his more practical *Laws*, Plato abandoned the communism of the *Republic*, substituting a form of peasant proprietorship"[5].

Aristotle rejected Plato's views on property and categorically stressed that it was more in accordance with man's nature to own property. In his *Politics*, he says the following: "Moreover, there is an immense amount of pleasure to be derived from the sense of private ownership. It is surely no accident that every man has affection for himself: nature meant this to be so. Selfishness is condemned, and justly, but selfishness is not simply to be fond of oneself, but to be *excessively* fond. So excessive fondness for money is condemned, though nearly every man is fond of everything of that kind. And a further point is that there is a very great pleasure in helping and doing favours to friends and strangers and associates; and this happens when people have property of their own"[6].

The absence of communal ownership , insists Aristotle, will not abolish the evils of society. They arise out of the depravity of human character and not as the result of private property. Although Aristotle recommends private ownership, he does suggest a spontaneous distribution of goods by custom of generosity and not by enforced regulation. No citizen should be in want of subsistence.

It has often been said that the Fathers of the Church preached communism and that private property had to be abandoned by professing Christianity. The writings of the early Fathers do not give credence to this theory. Although it is true that very often Christians disposed of their possessions in such a way that they could be distributed to the poor, it is also true that such practices were considered as counsels of perfection and not the general norm. There was no general consensus on the question of private property. For example, St. Ambrose was of the opinion that private property was unchristian whilst St. Augustine, maintained the opposite view. The late scholastic doctor Miguel Salon invoked the authority of St. Augustine in condemning the so-called "apostolics" who claimed. that those who owned property could not enter the kingdom of heaven.[7] This view of St. Augustine's on the legitimacy of property seems to be corroberated by him in his *magnum opus* the *City of God* where, when writing about marriage, he says: "Thus, unjust as it is to encroach, out of greed, on another's property, it is still more wicked to transgress, out of lust, the limits of established morals"[8].

Perhaps, it is St. Thomas Aquinas and the early scholastics who have left posterity with one of the clearest interpretation of the right of private property and its relationship with natural law. In this respect, he followed very closely the reasoning of Aristotle. He argued that property is not against natural law.[9] On the contrary,.the possession of material things is natural to man. St Thomas considered it was lawful for man to possess property for the following three reasons: 1) people take better care of what they possess for them-

---

4. Plato, *The Republic* (New York: Random House, The Modern Library, Book V, p.189).

5. Whittaker, Edmund, *A History of Economic Ideas.*(New York:Longmans Green and Co., 1940, p.181).

6. Aristotle, *The Politics* (London: Penguin Books, Revised Edition, 1981, Book II, ChapterV, 1263a40, p.115).

7. Salon, Miguel, *Commentariorum* p.389. See: Chafuen, Alejandro, *Christians for Freedom,Late-Scholastic Economics*, (San Francisco: Ignatius Press, 1986).

8. St. Augustine, *The City of God* (Image Books, New York,1958, Book XV, Chapter 16, p. 352).

9. According to St. Thomas: "The common possession of things is to be attributed to natural law, not in the sense that natural law decrees that all things are to be held in common and that there is to be no private possession; but in the sense that there is no distinction of property on grounds of natural law, but only by human agreement; and this pertains to positive law Thus. private property is not opposed to natural law, but is an addition to it, devised by the human reason". See *Summa Theologica*, II Part, Secunda Secundae, Question LXVI, Art. 2 in *Aquinas, Selected Political Writings*, Edited by A.P. D'Entreves (Oxford, England: Basil Blackwell, 1959, pp. 169-171) .

selves than what belongs to all, 2) they will work harder on their own account than on account of others and 3) the social order will be better preserved with individual ownership and there will be less occasion for quarreling about the use of things owned in common.[10]

2. The Age of Liberalism

One of the most ardent defenders of private property in the modern age was John Locke. He argued that property was a natural right. Private property, according to him, was established by natural law. It was not the result of man's consent. Locke explicitly states that: "God gave the world to men in common; but since he gave it to them for their benefit, and the greatest convenience of life they were capable to draw from it, it cannot be supposed he meant it should always remain common and uncultivated. He gave it to the use of the industrious and rational, (and *labour* was to be *his title* to it;) not to the fancy or covetousness of the quarrelsome and contentious."[11]

Thus Locke seems to imply that it is labour which establishes man's right to own property. He claims that: "Whatsoever then he removes out of the state that nature had provided, and left it in, he has mixed his *labour* with, and joined to it something that is his own, and thereby makes it his *property*. It being by him removed from the common state nature hath placed it in, it hath by this *labour* something annexed to it, that excludes the common right of other men: for this *labour* being the unquestionable property of the labourer, no man but he can have a right to what that is once joined to, at least where there is enough, and as good, left in common for others."[12]

To Locke's credit it must be stated that when he wrote his essay on property, there still existed great tracts of land that still lay waste and were available to future settlers. He had particularly in mind the American continent. Furthermore, his so-called theory of labour should not be interpreted in the Marxian sense because for him labour was very broadly defined.[13]

It is important to stress Locke's basic argument that property is a natural right. It preceded the social contract that was later entered into with the purpose of protecting the rights of private property. He insisted that no authority had the right to abrogate the right of private property without violating the social contract. In fact, Locke went as far as to say that such an unlawful action would justify a revolt and give ground for the deposition of the sovereign.

Adam Smith, as many economists within the British Classical School of Economics, had a liberal vision of the good free society. He defended freedom and justice but, as Edmund Whittaker states there was no consideration of property, as an institution, in his book *An Inquiry into the Nature and Causes of The Wealth of Nations* and much less a justification for it. [14] However, expanding on Locke's theory of property, Smith believed that as land became scarcer and population increased, the additional capital that belonged to others and provided assistance to labour resulted in greater payments to the owners of land and capital. As a result, the worker no longer received the entire produce of his labour. Both land and capital had become valuable capital and had a right to receive their corresponding share.

Smith was a firm believer in private property. He unequivocally states in *The Wealth of Nations*: "The property which every man has in his own labour, as it is the original foundation of all other property, so it

---

10. Ibid.,p.167-169. For an excellent review of the scholastic's contribution to economic analysis see, Schumpeter, Joseph, *A History of Economic Analysis* (New York: Oxford University Press, Chapter 2, pp.73-142).

11. Locke, John, *Second Treatise of Government* (Indianapolis, Indiana: Hacket Publishing Company, Chapter V, On Property, pp. 21-22).

12. Ibid. p. 19.

13. See: Vaugn, Karen Iversen, *John Locke, Economist and Social Scientist* (London: The Athlone Press, 1980, pp.81-96).

14. Adam Smith, *An Inquiry into the Nature and Causes of the Wealth of Nations* (Indianapolis, Indiana: Liberty Classics, Volume II, p.201).

is the most sacred and inviolable."[15] But, he adds also that the existence of great property leads to great inequality and is not conducive to peace. Smith's argument is as follows: "For one very rich man, there must be at least five hundred poor, and the affluence of the few supposes the indigence of the many. The affluence of the rich excites the indignation of the poor, who are often both driven by want, and prompted by envy, to invade his possessions. It is only under the shelter of the civil magistrate that the owner of the valuable property, which is acquired by the labour of many years, or perhaps of many successive generations, can sleep a single night in security. He is at all times surrounded by unknown enemies, whom, though he never provoked, he can never appease, and from whose injustice he can be protected only by the powerful arm of the civil magistrate continually held up to chastise him."[16]

Smith repeatedly criticizes "the wretched spirit of greed and monopoly". Such a spirit of greed, he claimed, was not in accordance with his theory of classical economic liberalism which was concerned with equal freedoms and rights of all men and not only of the few and privileged businessmen who monopolized all the wealth and power. Greed made a mockery of the kind of self interest that he assumed in his theory; a self interest that was subject to a legal and moral code of justice to others.

The wretched spirit of greed and monopoly, insisted Smith, conspired against the public interest. He feared that the power of civil government would fall easily into the hands of the greedy rich and powerful who would use such power to foster their own interests to the detriment of the poor. Although in theory, civil government is instituted for the security of property, in reality it is prone to defend the rich against the poor or those who have some property against those who have none at all."[17] It is precisely to avoid such a danger that Smith recommends that in order "to make sure that every individual feel himself perfectly secure in the possession of every right which belongs to him, it is not only necessary that the judicial system should be separated from the executive power, but that it should be rendered as much as possible independent of that power."[18]

However, in spite of the above reservations, Smith was convinced that the businessman, though led by his self interest and aiming only at his own profit, would also serve the best interests of the community. He believed that the "guiding hand" of the liberal institutions and the market mechanism, in conformity with the "natural" moral law, made it possible for the capitalist to invest his capital in the most productive manner so that it would increase the wealth of the nation. Behind all of Smith's reasoning there was always the "invisible hand" of Providence at work. His deistic background is quite evident in all of his writings but especially in his brilliant work, *The Theory of Moral Sentiments* where he emphasizes the stoic concept of natural harmony. For Smith the selfish rich "are led by an invisible hand to help the poor and the interests of society at large."[19] His reliance on the "invisible hand" apparently made him forget the fallen nature of man and his "natural" inclination towards evil.

15. Ibid. p.138.

16. Ibid. p.710.

17. Ibid. p.715.

18. Ibid. p.723.

19. Adam Smith opined that the selfish rich are led by an invisible hand to help the poor and serve the interest of society at large. For example, according to him: "The rich only select from the heap what is most precious and agreable. They consume little more than the poor, and in spite of their natural selfishness and rapacity, though they mean only their own conveniency, though the sole end which they propose from the labours of all the thousands whom they employ, be the gratification of their own vain and insatiable desires, they divide with the poor the produce of all their improvements. They are led by an invisible hand to make nearly the same distribution of the necessities of life, which would have been made, had the earth been divided into equal portions among all its inhabitants, and thus without intending it, without knowing it advance the interest of the society, and afford means to the multiplication of the species". Smith, Adam, *The Theory of Moral Sentiments* (Indianapolis, Indiana: Liberty Classics, 1976, p.184-185).

3. The Socialist Reaction

Socialist scholars have always maintained that private property played—if at all—an insignificant role in primitive society. This position is contrary to most western research which has assumed that, even in the most primitive societies, there always existed a well developed awareness of individuality and of the need for private ownership.

Socialists, under any of its various interpretations, have always tended to deny that the right of private property is an inalienable right that is derived from natural law. They consider private property as an abnormal departure from its original state of collective ownership. The early history of modern socialism has hardly deviated from this position.

Socialism launched its attack on capitalism primarily as a result of the early abuses.of the industrial revolution But, it is important to remember that modern socialism had its roots in that very same liberalism which served as the basis for the rise of industrial capitalism. As Eric Roll, the prominent economic historian, has said; "the philosophy of natural law, and the utilitarianism which was one of its expressions, could bear a radical as well as a conservative interpretation".[20] Marxism and the capitalism of the early industrial age are, respectively, prime examples of the radical and "conservative" interpretations of the natural law philosophy of the Enlightment.

In the process of sweeping away with traditional institutions, capitalism had given rise to a wave of rising expectation which were not fully realized. The new ideal age did not materialize, at least for the majority of the poor of the XIXth century. This, "could not prevent the revolutionary fervour from persisting and turning against the new social order, if that order was found deficient in the light of the promises made."[21] Private property became the "whipping post" of the new and often violent social revolutionary movements.

One of the most influential and pernicious writers of the new secular intellectuals of the Age of the Enlightment was Jean Jacques Rousseau. He popularized the idea that man became increasingly corrupted as society evolved from its primitive state of nature to higher stages of civilization and culture. In a large measure, he was responsible not only for the French revolution but also for the criticism that later developed of the capitalist system.

Commenting of the ideas of Rousseau, the prominent British historian Paul Johnson correctly claims that: "The evil of competition, as he saw it, which destroys man's inborn communal sense and encourages all his most evil traits, including his desire to exploit others, led Rousseau to distrust private property, as the source of social crime."[22] Rousseau identifies property and the competition to acquire it as the primary cause of alienation. Karl Marx could not have said it better. In fact, Rousseau's views on property and competition, together with his related idea of cultural evolution, helped develop socialist thought and, in particular, Marxian theory.[23]

For Rousseau "the idea of property depends on many prior ideas which could only be acquired successively, and cannot have been formed all at once in the human mind."[24] He believed that the social contract was simply a trick of the propertied classes to retain possession of what they had seized. He refused to accept the fact that possession originated in occupation or in acquisition. Neither occupation nor acquisition provided sufficient evidence to justify the right to ownership.

Rousseau's views gave ample ground for the establishment of a totalitarian state. He justifies absolute

---

20. Roll, Eric, *A History of Economic Thought* (London: Faber & Faber Ltd. 1954, p.233).

21. Ibid. p.233.

22. Johnson, Paul, *Intellectuals* (New York: Harper & Row, 1988, p.4).

23. As Whittaker correctly states: "Rousseau's ideas had great influence and undoubtedly were one of the sources of inspiration of socialist writings on the subject of property." Whittaker, op.cit.,p. 202.

24. Rousseau, Jean Jacques, *The Social Contract* (New York: Alfred A. Knopf, Revised edition, 1973, p.84).

power in the name of virtue, equality and freedom.[25] Under Rousseau's social contract, the individual not only becomes totally subordinated to the state but it is the duty of the state to reshape the minds of the citizens. As professor Nisbet says: "What Rousseau calls freedom is at bottom no more than the freedom to do that which the state in its omniscience determines. Freedom for Rousseau is the synchronization of all the social existence to the will of the state, the replacement of cultural diversity by a mechanical egalitarianism."[26]

Among the British reformers of the late XVIIIth century, William Godwin was one of the most influential. He, like some of his contemporaries, maintained that property represented exploitation. The names of William Thompson, John Gray and J.F. Bay can also be mentioned. To a greater or lesser degree, all of them believed that it was unjust for land to be in private hands and that the worker did not receive the entire product of his labour. Bray, for example stated that : "Priority of possession gives no title whatever; nor can any duration of enjoyment establish a right, where no right did originally exist". It is labour alone that gives the right to ownership.

In France the so-called Utopian socialists of the late XVIIIth and early XIXth centuries claimed to be pioneers in socialist thought but, in reality had relative influence in European society.[27] Schumpeter calls some of their "utopist" ideas unalloyed nonsense and hardly any of them can be taken quite seriously.[28]

It was P.J Proudhon who, to the question he poses in his well known book *Qu'est-ce que la propriete?* answers "*la propriete c'est le vol.*" Although Proudhon accepted the view that labour was the only source of wealth and constituted the only title to ownership, he did not attack private property as such. He believed that everyone should be permitted to enjoy the fruits of his labour. He objected to the abuse of property, what was called *droit d'aubaine* or the power to demand what was considered an unearned income. As Schumpeter says: "his big idea was gratuitous credit rather than abolition of private property."[29]

Karl Marx was the first to use the term utopian in a disparaging manner when referring to his socialist forerunners. The history of property, according to Marx and Engels, rests on well defined laws that depend on the evolution of the means and relations of production. For Marx the important thing was to make socialist thought "scientific" and not "utopian". He believed in action. All necessary steps had to be taken in order to bring to reality the ideal socialist world.

Without going into an anlysis of Marx's theory on capitalism, it suffices to say that for him and his followers private property was the root of all evil. It was the "original sin" of Marxist theory. According to Engels: "Production at all former stages of society was essentially collective and, likewise, consumption took place by the direct distribution of the products within larger or smaller communistic communi-

---

25. Nisbet, Robert, *The Social Philosophers* (New York: Washington Square Press Publications, 1982, p.44). Johnson, commenting on Rousseau's totalitarian ideas says: "In a number of ways the State Rousseau planned for Corsica anticipated the one the Pot Pot regime actually tried to create in Cambodia, and this is not entirely surprising since the Paris educated leaders of the regime had all absorbed Rousseau's ideas". Johnson, op.cit. p. 25.

26. Nisbet, op.cit. p. 41.

27. Schumpeter insists that the socialism of that period was non-Marxist and associanist because they adopted "the principle of running production by workmens' associations-of social reconstruction through producers' co-operatives". Schumpeter, op.cit.,p. 454. Louis Blanc, according to Schumpeter, is an exception. Among the better known utopian socialists are Charles Fourier(1772-1837) and Henri Comte de Saint Simon (1760-1825).

28. Schumpeter, op.cit. p. 455.

29. Ibid. p. 456.

ties."[30] Society began to decay as soon as private property became institutionalized.[31]

Private property, insisted Marx, is the cause of the inequality that exists among men. It is only through the destruction of private property that man's alienation will be eradicate and with it the existing inequalities that have brought so much misery to the labouring poor.

Capital is a collective product. It is not a personal but a social power, claimed Marx and Engels.. They considered modern bourgeois private property as "...the final and most complete expression of the system of producing and appropriating products that is based on class antagonisms, on the exploitation of the many by the few". Hence, they concluded, "the theory of the Communists may be summed up in the single sentence: Abolition of private property."[32] Lenin and Stalin did not deviate from these ideas and their destruction of private property in Russia was complete.[33]

Contrary to Marx's and Engels' expectations, both in theory and in practice, their views concerning private property have not withstood the judgement of history. With the elimination of private property, alienations and antinomies did not cease to exist in countries that were submitted to communism or other collectivist policies. If anything, they became more acute.

Past and present events have demonstrated the close relationship that exists between the right to own property and the permanence of freedom and justice. In fact, justice requires that the right to own property be respected. Freedom cannot long endure once the right to private property is abolished. Eastern Europe under communist domination and the former Soviet Union are sufficient proof of this truth.

THE BASIC FORMS OF JUSTICE

What is justice? Since early antiquity until the present day, justice has been defined in different ways but, perhaps, the most adequate definition is the one that simply states that it is the virtue which enables man to give to each person what is his due. As St. Thomas in his brilliant and practical manner has stated: "Justice is a habit (habitus), whereby a man renders to each one his due with constant and perpetual will."[34]

Thus, justice can be defined as the virtue which enables man to give to each one what is his due. But, the act of justice is preceded by the act whereby something becomes man's due. Justice comes second. Right comes before justice. No obligation to do justice exists unless it has as its presupposition the idea of the due, the right, the *suum*. How does man come to have his due? Do men and women whose properties have been confiscated without compensation have the right—the *suum*—to be re-instated in their possession or compensated for their losses?

---

30. Engels, *The Origins of the Family, Private Property and the State* in E.Burns (ed.), *Handbook of Marxism* (New York,1935, p.323). See also, Academia de Ciencias de la Unión Soviética, *Manual de Economía Política* (Mexico: Editorial Grijalbo, S.A.. Seguinda Edicion, 1957, pp. 1-8).

31. Ibid. p.330.

32. Marx and Engels, *The Communist Manifesto*, edited by Samuel H. Beer, (Arlington Heights, Illinois: Harlan DavidsonInc. 1955, p. 24).

33. After the uprising and slaughter of the Kronstadt rebellion and with the ravages of famine and disillusionment spreading throughout Russia, Lenin was ready to make concessions in order to salvage his regime. In 1921, he announced a new economic policy, better known as NEP, which restored private enterprise in agriculture and in small business. However, the government kept control of big industry, communications, banking and foreign trade. The "reforms" did not affect the total monopoly of political power. Nevertheless, as a result of the limited but resuscitated capitalism, agriculture recovered and by 1928 general living standards were back at their 1913-1914 levels. Stalin, after the banishnent of Trotsky in 1928, decided to put an end to NEP and all economic life reverted to state monopoly. See: Lyons, Eugene, *Workers' Paradise Lost* (New York: Paperback Library Inc. 1967. pp.57-58). The Russian experience with NEP should serve as a warning to all those who believe in the so-called "reforms" of marxist dictatorships. As long as total political power remains in the hands of the authorities, the "reforms" are used as a mere "facade" in order to salvage a bankrupt regime. Once the regime recovers, the "reforms' are quickly eliminated.

34. St. Thomas, *Summa Theologica*, II, II, 58, 1.

The traditional doctrine of justice is not only concerned with the declaration of human rights but also with the proclamation and establishment of the obligation to respect the inalienable rights of man. One of these rights is the right of every man and woman to possess private property. Can it be concluded that any violation of these rights is a violation against justice?[35]

There are three fundamental structures of communal life: *ordo partium ad partes*, (the relations of individuals to one another), *ordo totius ad partes* (the relations of the social whole to the individuals) and *ordo partium ad totum* (the relations of the individual to the social whole). They correspond to three basic types of justice: *iustitia commutativa*.(orders the relationship between individuals)) *iustitia distributiva* (orders the relationship between the community and the individuals) and *iustitia legalis, iustitia generalis* (orders the members' relations to the social whole).[36]

The question that needs to be raised is, when does justice prevail in a given nation? The proper answer can be reduced to the following; justice will prevail when the three basic relationships mentioned above are disposed in their proper order. As the late German philosopher Joseph Pieper states: "The hallmark of all three fundamental forms of justice is some kind of *indebtedness* different in character in each case. The obligation to pay the tax collector is different in kind from that of settling my book dealer's account. And the legal protection the state owes the individual is due to me, in principle, in quite different fashion than my neighbor owes me the return of a loan."[37]

In each of these three fundamental forms of justice a different subject is involved. It would be wrong to suggest that it is justice that orders the relations between two individuals. Men and women, the individual persons, are the ones who realize all three kinds of justice. But, the individual person is implicated in three different ways. As Pieper says: "The individual as associate of other individuals sustains commutative justice, whereas the subject of legal justice is, to be sure, once again the individual but now as the associate of the species, as it were, as a member of the community, as a 'subject.' So too, the 'social whole' cannot in any concrete sense make distributive justice a reality; again it is rather the individual man—if not the king, then the dictator, the chief of state, the civil servant or even, in a consistent democracy, the individual, insofar as he has a determining role in administering the common good."[38]

It is important to stress that the individual and the social whole cannot be represented as sharply distinctive realities because the individual who confronts the social whole is also included in it as a member. Individual persons have a reality of their own and cannot be reduced to the reality of the social whole. Neither the acts of the individuals are necessarily the acts of the whole nor the functioning of the whole necessarily identical with the functioning of the individual member. These distinctions are important to keep in mind if a sound judgement is to be reached on the question of collective guilt.[39]

A firm defender of individualism would claim that reality is composed of only individuals. Therefore, he would admit only one type of justice-commutative justice. For him the social whole is not a reality of a special order. It is simply composed of many individuals. The collectivist interpretation of justice, on the other hand, does not accept the fact that individuals are capable of entering into relationships in their own right. They do not accept private relations between individuals. According to this view: "Man's life has a totally public character because the individual is ade-

---

35. For the explanation of the fundamental structures of communal life and their coresponding types of justice, we have relied heavily on the late German philosopher Joseph Pieper and, in particular, on his book on the virtue of justice. See: Pieper,Joseph, *Justice*, (New York: Pantheon Books, 1955).

36. Ibid.,p.50.

37. Ibid, pp.50-51.

38. Ibid. p. 51.

39. Ibid. p. 52-53.

quately defined only through his membership in the social whole which is the only reality."[40]

One of the great dangers of the collectivist interpretation of justice is that all relations between individuals can be considered as "official". All human relations are reduced to the fulfillment of functions and can be terminated abruptly if they do not conform to the whims of the State. The abuses of such a collectivist interpretation of justice are so well known that there is no need to enumerate them. Cuba can offer ample examples of how a person can easily find himself no longer associated with his "friend" "spouse" or "parents" but with an anonymous co-worker who is simply a state functionary working for the "common cause". As Pieper comments: "Needless to say that from this point of view the concept of commutative justice becomes meaningless; as, equally, the concept of distributive justice, which proclaims that an individual has rights not only in his relations with other individuals but with the social whole as well. And even the seemingly unaffected concept of *iustitia legalis*, which formulates the individual's obligation toward the functions of the state, has in the last analysis become unthinkable. The notion of justice has ceased to be applicable in any sense whatsoever."[41]

Any state, which denies the existence of any of these three fundamental and independent structures of communal life and, thus, any of the three basic forms of justice, threatens justice itself. For real justice to prevail, the threefold structure of communal life must be accepted. Otherwise, it will be very difficult, if not impossible, to do justice to the reality contained in the complex relationships between the individual and society. Justice must prevail in its threefold form if the road to totalitarianism is to be avoided.[42] Did the Castro government with its policy of mass confiscations violate any or all of these three basic forms of justice or, on the contrary, can they be justified in terms of the common good?

PRIVATE PROPERTY, JUSTICE AND THE COMMON GOOD

Is there, under the guise of "legality" or of any other interpretation of either *iustitia distributiva* or *iustitia generalis*, a justification for the forced expropriations without any type of compensation that took place in Cuba and other countries around the globe as a result of communist takeovers? If not, is there an obligation on the part of post-communist regimes to re-instate a person in the possession or dominion of those properties that were illegally confiscated during the early years of the revolution? If so, how is the reinstatement or compensation going to take place after the fall of communism?

There is no doubt that the right to property forms part of *iustitia commutativa*. It obliges man to respect the possessions of others and forbids him from appropriating goods that are not his. If a man appropriates something that is not his, he has transgressed a fundamental structure of communal life, the relations between one individual and another individual and, thus, violates *iustitia commutativa*. But, is the state entitled to expropriate privately owned properties under the banner of *iustitia distributiva*?

The state incorporates and administers the *bonum commune*. It is vested with authority and has the power to maintain the common good in its fullest sense. Given the relationship which is characteristic of *iustitia distributiva* and the priority of the common good, nothing is due to the individual which is exclusively his. This is due to the fact that distributive justice is of a higher order that commutative jus-

---

40. Ibid. p.53.

41. Ibid. p.54.

42. Ibid. pp.54-55.

tice.[43] For example, in an emergency, public authority may have the legitimate right to deprive an individual of his freedom as in the case of a criminal action or of any other activity which endangers the social whole. The public authority, as administrator of the common good can also take measures that affect the individual's property under certain conditions.[44] The important thing to keep in mind is that "...in his relationship with public authority, a *suum* belongs to a private person in a fashion quite different from that applying to his relations to another private person. It is this peculiar structure in the actual fabric of communal life that we bring to light when we get to the roots of the distinction between commutative justice and distributive justice."[45] A private person's relationship with the public authority is not the same as his relationship with another private person. The former relationship falls under *iustitia distributiva* whilst the latter under *iustitia commutativa*. But, how can the authorities have the power to, for example, expropriate private property if, at the same time, the inalienability of the individual's rights vis-a-vis the state are to be fostered and maintained?

It cannot be stressed too strongly that the individual has inalienable rights that the State cannot suppress. As a part of the social whole, the individual has the right to expect justice from the public authorities and this applies not only to the distribution of goods but also to the sharing of burdens. There are definite limitations on the state's authority which the public authorities cannot overlook. In the last instance, the power of the state can only be wielded if the common good demands it.

But, what happens when a government passes laws that are unjust in the name of the common good? Communist regimes and totalitarian systems in general have the habit of dictating laws that run counter to the most basic inalienable rights of man, including the right to private property. The people in Cuba and and other countries have suffered the consequences of such nefarious legislation.

When a government dictates decrees confiscating private property without due compensation, is there a violation of justice or can those decrees be justified in the name of *iustitia distributiva* or *iustitia legalis*? Can drastic measures be taken by the authorities against any individual or group simply because they belon to a particular race, religion or social class that needs to

---

43. According to St. Thomas: "The scope of justice, as we have said, is to regulate men in their relations with others. Here there are two cases to be considered. Either when the reference is to others considered individually. Or when the reference is to others considered as a community: to the extent, that is, to which one who is a subject of a certain community is subject also to all the persons who go to form it. Justice, as such, enters in both cases. For it is evident that all those who make up the community, have to it the same relationship as that of parts to a whole. Now the part, as such, belongs to the whole: consequently any partial interest is subordinate to the good of the whole. From this point of view, whatever is good and virtuous, whether in respect of a man to himself or with respect to the relationship between men, can have reference to the common well-being which is the object of justice. In this sense all virtues may come within the province of justice, in so far as it orders men to the common welfare". St, Thomas, *Summa Theologica*, II, Secunda Secundae, Question 58, Art. 7, p.165.

44. The German philosopher-economist Anton Rauscher, when discussing the right of the state to expropriate, mentions the following conditions: "First, the measure must be limited and may not serve as a pretext to nationalize or 'socialize' important industries and in this way to eliminate ownership of the means of production or practically to abrogate the free power of disposal through an excess of state control and planning. Second, it must be a question of a measure that is urgently required by the common good. The burden of proof here lies with the state, and not with the citizen, that it 'is the only means to remedy an injustice and to ensure the coordinated use of the same forces to the benefit of the economic life of the nation, so that the normal and peaceful development of that economic life may open the gates to material prosperity for all' (Pius XII, Catholic Mind 45 1947:710). Third, there exists the duty of making appropriate recompense to the owner. We are familiar with expropriation measures, especially in the sphere of landed property, when an imperative need of the state or of the community exists. In a constitutionally governed state, the citizen has the possibility of lodging an appeal and of having examined whether the reasons advanced are really convincing or not. This is a protection against a too facile appeal to the 'common good'". See Rauscher, Anton, "Private Property, Its Importance for Personal Freedom and Social Order", *Ordo Socialis* (Koln, Deutschland: Vereinung zur Forderung der christlichen Sozialwissenschaften, pp. 45-46).

45. Pieper, op.cit. p.71.

be eliminated? To whom must the plaintiff appeal in order to find justice if justice has been violated?

The argument could be held that, because the right to property must be distinguished from its use, the proper use of possessions does not fall exclusively under *iustitia commutativa*—which obliges man to respect the possessions of others and forbids him from appropriating goods that are not his—but also under other virtues and duties that are not enforced by the courts of justice.[46] This means that the right to property and its use are not subject to the same limits.

As indicated earlier, the common good may require under certain circumstances the establishment of certain limitations to the right of private property. The authorities correctly may appeal to *iustitia distributiva* in order to justify such an action. They may even try to use such an argument in order to justify expropriations without compensation when privately owned properties are mis-used or not used at all. However, such an argument is not valid. The misuse or non use of private ownership does not give ground to illegal government takeovers and the destruction or forfeiture of the right itself.

St Thomas in his *Summa* unequivocally states that man has a natural right to own private property. Man's rational nature permits him to use his intelligence to provide for the future, something that he could not do if he did not possess material goods as his own. In addition, in accordance with his social

nature, it would be very difficult for man to maintain a family if he did not have stable property.[47] This is the position that has been maintained by the Roman Pontiffs in all official documents of the Catholic Church.[48] They all agree that the right to private property is one of the inalienable rights of man and the public authorities have the duty to protect it from unjust expropriations that run counter to the common good. Consequently, there is no doubt that the mass confiscations that occurred in Cuba after 1959 constituted a direct violation of *iustitia commutativa*. But, neither can they be justified under the banner of a false interpretation of *iustitia distributiva*.

It is erroneous to even imply that the mass confiscations were done in accordance with the precepts of *iustitia distributiva* in order to bring about a more equalitarian and "just" society. The end does not justify the means; means which were blatantly unjust and violated the inalienable right that every citizen has to own private property. Thus, the public authorities cannot appeal to distributive justice in order to try to justify the systematic destruction of private property.

Society, explains St. Thomas, through positive law or *ius gentium* (the common rights of all peoples, or customs derived from natural law) can determine the different systems for distributing material goods. But this must be done always in accordance with the more basic right (natural law, different from positive law) that cannot be violated. Positive laws enacted by

---

46. Aristotle, a believer in the right to own property, also said that: "Each man has his own possessions, part of which he makes available for his friends' use, part of which he uses in common with others. For example in Sparta they use each others' slaves practically as if they were their own, and horses and dogs too; and if they need food on a journey, they get it in the country as they go. Clearly then it is better for property to remain in private hands; but we should make the use of it communal. It is a particular duty of a lawgiver to see that citizens are disposed to do this". Aristotle, *The Politics*, Book II, v, 1263a30. St. Thomas, a firm defender of private property, distinguishes between the use (*usus*) and the management and administration of goods (*potestas procurandi et dispensandi*). With respect to the use of goods (consumption), man should not consider them as his own but as common. He should share them readily with others when they are in need. However, it should be pointed out that when St. Thomas is speaking of the *usus communis* he means that noone should use goods without consideration of the needs of others, especially of those who are in a distressed state. At the time St. Thomas was writing, almsgiving was of great social importance. Charity played a very significant role which went well beyond justice.

47. See: St. Thomas Aquinas, *Summa Theologica*, Quaestio LXVI, Art. 1 and Art. 2.

48. All papal documents and encyclicals from *Rerum Novarum* of Leo XIII to *Centesimus Anno* of John Paul II have maintained always that the right of possession is inviolable. For example Leo XIII stated that: " every man has by nature the right to possess property of his own. This is one of the *chief points of distinction* between man and the animal creation". (*Rerum Novarum* #5). John Paul II strogly reaffirms the natural character of the right to private property and adds: "This right, which is fundamental for the autonomy and development of the person, has always been defended by the Church up to our own day". (*Centesimus Anno* #30).

governments that run counter to natural law cannot be considered ethically valid even if it is claimed that they have as their objective the common good of society. It is preposterous even to think that natural law can be bypassed in the name of a badly interpreted *iustitia distributiva*.

Once it is recognized that the massive confiscations of private property, brought about by the socialist policies of the Castro government, were unequivocally illegal and unethical, the question still remains as to how *restitutio* is going to take place. In other words, how can man's *suum* be recognized and justice restored?.

THE RIGHT TO RESTITUTION OR COMPENSATION: AN ABSOLUTE OR A RELATIVE RIGHT?

It cannot be denied that the entire question of *restitutio* becomes rather complicated in the case of government confiscations of privately owned properties, especially if many years have elapsed since the time of their occurrence. This in no way means that there is no obligation on the part of the "debtor"—the social whole—to recognize the injustice committed and that there is no longer need for *restitutio*. It simply means that the obligation due to an individual in his relation to the social whole is "in principle different from his due as creditor towards debtor in a situation of commutative justice."[49]

In cases of forced expropriations or outright confiscations by the public authorities, the individual is confronted by the social whole (.i.e.,the government). It is no longer a relation of individuals with one another. The two participants are not equal not only because the social whole represents many individuals but also because, as mentioned earlier, it is of a higher order than the good of the individual.[50] But, the fact that the social whole is of a higher order does not make an unjust act just. The injustice this time is suffered by the individual whose properties have been unjustly confiscated as a result of an abuse of power by the public authorities.

In cases such as these (i.e., those that took place in Cuba and other totalitarian regimes), it is the individual who claims his due from the social whole. Hence the claim, as expressed in *iustitia distributiva* is directed at a government that, supposedly, is representing the social whole. The authorities cannot hide under the mantle of an abstract collective guilt and claim that they are not responsible for the confiscations that took place in the past. As Pieper correctly states: "Man, as administrator of the common weal, is brought to account and is obliged to give the individual members of the whole their due. The ideal image of distributive justice , however, does not authorize individuals to determine and assert on their own initiative what is due to them on the part of the social whole. But though they are not so authorized, this does not mean that such a premise would be impossible and intrinsically counter to justice."[51]

When the public authorities are the perpetrators of blatant injustices, the norm "Thou shall be just" is applicable not to the claimant but to the government who is the one who has to grant the due. In accordance with *iustitia distributiva*, the claim or appeal would have to be directed to whoever represents the total whole. However, it is quite evident that, for all practical purposes, this is impossible under totalitarian regimes such as the one existing in Cuba. Under such circumstances, all appeals would have to be postponed until a new democratic government is installed. The claims will then have to be made to the newly appointed authorities.

It is important to re-emphasize that the obligation due to the individual in his relation to the social whole differs from his *suum* as creditor towards another individual debtor under commutative justice. Under commutative justice, the creditor has the right to receive the equivalent of the loss suffered. In the case of *iustitia distributiva*, the individual is not an

---

49. Pieper. op.cit. p.64-65.

50. Pieper, op.cit. p.63.

51. Ibid. p.64.

independent, separate party to a contract with claims equal to those of his partner. The creditor (the person whose properties have been confiscated) will have to deal with the social whole (the new government) in order to receive his due. And, the partner with whom he has to deal under *iustitia distributiva* is of a higher rank; a rank of which he himself is a part as member of the social whole.

Under *iustitia commmutativa* what is due can easily be calculated by mutual agreement of the interested parties. The party entitled to his *suum* can and has the right to determine the price. Justice and equity will be met in the *aequitas rei ad rem*.[52] This is not the case under *iustitia distributiva*. For example, if, as the result of war, damage has been inflicted upon someone's property, the person suffering the damage cannot determine independently what is rightfully his. It will be the responsibility of the representative of the social whole to establish what is his due in accordance with the common good.

Furthermore, in the case of *iustitia commutativa* a just price can be determined simply by taking into consideration the market price of the object under consideration. This is not so under *iustitia distributiva*. According to St. Thomas, justice is determined by "whatever corresponds to the thing's proportion to the person." In other words, the person who administers the common good can take into consideration other factors besides the object of the obligation alone. In the case of war account may have to be taken of such factors as whether the damage has impoverished the person, whether or not he had already made any other great sacrifice for the social whole etc. Something similar may occur in Cuba as a result of the mass confiscation that took place under Castro. Many innocent people suffered whilst, at the same time new "rights" were created that cannot be totally ignored by the new government. Thus, the compromise that has to be effected both in distributive justice and in commutative justice has a quite

distinct character in each instance. In the first case it is a 'proportional' equality (*aequalitas proportionis*), in the other a purely numerical 'quantitative' equality (*aequalitas quantitis*). Aristotle, when explaining distributive justice says that "such justice is the mean between the two extremes of more and less of what is fair. In a word the just is the proportionate."[53]

The confiscations that took place in Cuba during the many years of the Castro dictatorship will, undoubtedly, create all sorts of conflicting claims affecting various people in many different ways. Thus, it will be necessary for the newly established authorities to take action in accordance with *iustitia distributiva*. It will no longer be a simple case of *iustitia commutativa* that can easily be solved by the individual parties. The social whole cannot avoid being involved in the many legal disputes that are going to occur in a free Cuba, as most of the properties confiscated are in government hands or, at least in theory, have been given to a new class of "owners". Consequently, any future solution of the property issue that pretends to be just will have to take into account the rights of the affected individual parties in the light of the common good and that involves directly the government who is the administrator of the *bonum commune*.

But what is the common good? How can it be defined in order for the public authorities to put it into effect?. In general terms the *bonum commune* represents "the *good* for the sake of which the community exists, and which it must attain and make a reality if it is to be said that all its potentialities have been brought to fruition".[54] A difficult task but a necessary one that those in authority must try to carry out if they want to respect the three fundamental structures of communal life and, thus, the three basic forms of justice. To deny or to ignore any of these three forms of justice will open the door to a new totalitarianism of either the left or the right.

In view of the above, it is highly probable that a strict applicability of compensatory or commutative justice

---

52. St. Thomas Aquinas, *Summa Theologica*, II, II, 61,2.

53. Aristotle, *Ethics*, op. cit. Book V, Chapter Three, p 147.

54. Pieper, op. cit. pp.87-88.

may not be possible or even advisable. This is especially true, given the confusing circumstances that will prevail in Cuba in the wake of over thirty five years of a ruthless communist dictatorship. Revolutionary actions like the ones that occurred in Cuba, create situations which lend themselves to inevitable conflicts of interests-the result of unjust acts—that are not easily solved. Nevertheless, the new government must, in justice, realize that some type of compensation is due to the possessor whose right, the *suum cuique*, (what is his due) has been violated. The dilemma is that the *suum* of the affected party must be measured in terms of the common good.

The successors of Castro should always keep in mind the following words of the previously quoted German philosopher Joseph Pieper: "...the man who does not give a person what belongs to him, withholds it or deprives him of it, is really doing harm to himself; *he* is the one who actually loses something—indeed, in the most extreme case, he even destroys himself."[55] This applies just as well to a nation that does not meet its obligations in accordance with justice and the common good. An unjust act that takes away from man what is his due is not so much the loss of some possession but rather "the implicit threat to the entire order of community life affecting every member."[56] Thus, in justice, the forced and illegal expropriation of private property requires a recognition of the wrong performed and some type of restitution or compensation for the damage inflicted upon the victimized party.

THE DEMANDS OF SOCIAL JUSTICE; THE LIMITS OF JUSTICE

It is the function of justice in general to regulate the entire economic order but, in a very special way, it is *iustitia generalis* or *iustitia legalis* the one that specifically relates the individual with the social whole and, thus, also with the common good. The more modern term, social justice, has tended to replace the more classical one that was used by the scholastic doctors.

The concept of social justice, which appeared already in the encyclical *Quadragesimo Anno* of Pope Pius XI and is insistently reiterated by his successors, cannot be totally divorced from commutative justice and distributive justice. The three of them are intimately connected because it is proper for social justice to demand from the individuals what is necessary for the common good but, at the same time, it also falls within its area of competence to strive for a less unequal distribution of wealth.[57] Do capitalism and socialism fulfill the demands of social justice?

Capitalism, particularly in its early stages, paid little attention to the obligations that social justice entails. Economic liberalism was greatly influenced by utilitarianism which was inspired by the basic postulates of philosophical liberalism. The typical bourgeois mentality of early capitalism was frequently guided by purely selfish interests that were hardly ever concerned with the well-being of others. Pure individualism was the norm and *iustitia commutativa* the only type of justice accepted. As the German professor Anton Rauscher has stated: "The right to property was understood in thoroughly individualistic terms as the right of the individual to dispose of the goods in his possession to the exclusion of a third party, with full freedom, according to his own pleasure, and without any social limits, obligations or duties."[58]

As already stated, Adam Smith saw quite clearly the dangers of this type of unrestrained capitalism but found the solution to the selfish interests of the monied classes in the "invisible hand" of God (the market) who somehow would solve the problem to the best interests of society as a whole. The market system, if left to operate freely, would be instrumental in bringing about the desired results. Social justice

---

55. Ibid. p.16.

56. Ibid. p.49.

57. Pius XI, *Divini Redemptoris*.

58. Rauscher, Anton, "Private Property, Its Importance for Personal Freedom and Social Order", *Ordo Socialis*, No.3, (Koln, Deutschland: Vereinigung zur Forderung der christlichen Sozialwissenschaften, p. 7).

would automatically follow as long as the market forces were permitted to operate freely.[59]

The free market system and the defense of the right to private property are to be lauded in capitalism. It has proven to be by far the most efficient economic system as its performance has demonstrated during the past two hundred years. To defend and foster the right to private property is not only legitimate but commendable. After all, it is an inalienable right of every man and woman to own property. But, this right belongs to every and each one, as Adam Smith himself often proclaimed. It can not be monopolized by the privileged few. The privileged few have to be genuinely concerned with the well-being of the less privileged many.

Capitalism correctly stresses the right to own private ownership but, at the same time, it should emphasize also that of its very nature private property has a social function which cannot be overlooked. John Paul II used the expression "the social mortgage of private property" in a speech he gave at Puebla, Mexico, the 29th of January of 1979. By that expression he meant the subordination of private property to the common good. But, this does not mean that the State has a *carte blanche* to do what it pleases. As indicated earlier, the State may, under certain conditions, have the right to nationalize and/or expropriate certain goods but always with the objective to better serve the common good.[60] Never to reduce the role or area of private property. It would violate the principle of subsidiarity. The State cannot convert itself in the common good.

The point that needs to be stressed is that God created the earth so that man could have dominion over it and enjoy its fruits. He gave it to the whole human race for all men to enjoy it without exceptions. This is the foundation of the universal destination of the earth's goods. Man's dominion over the earth, through his work, the use of his intelligence and exercising his freedom, has permitted him to make part of the earth his own. This is the origin of man's legitimate right to own private property but, at the same time, he has a responsibility not to hinder others from doing the same and acquiring also their own private property. In fact, man must cooperate with others so that they can all, in a spirit of solidarity, dominate the earth.[61] It is precisely this spirit of genuine solidarity (*affabilitas*) which is often missing in capitalism. Its technical dimension, as a creator of wealth, is unsurpassed but it is its human dimension that needs to be strengthened.

It is not enough for capitalism to claim that the right to private property is fundamental for the autonomy and development of man. It must not forget that the possession of material goods is not an absolute right and its limits are inscribed in its very nature as a human right. The possession of material goods cannot put the individual above the common good and disregard the obligations incurred under social justice.

It is not morally wrong to become rich; what is wrong and unjust is to use wealth exclusively in an egotistic manner, forgetting that there is a common good that cannot be ignored. This selfish attitude is what makes man fall into the iniquity of wealth (*mammona iniquietatis*) that is a grave moral evil. In other words, a Darwanian attitude based uniquely on a philosophy of the survival of the fittest or *sauve qui peut* is unacceptable.

---

59. According to Milton Friedman: "The view has been gaining widespread acceptance that corporate officials and labor leaders have a 'social responsibility' that goes beyond serving the interests of their stockholders or their members. This view shows a fundamental misconception of the character and nature of a free economy. In such an economy, there is one and only one social responsibility of business—to use its resources and engage in activities designed to increase its profits so long as it stays within the rules of the game, which is to say, engages in open and free competition, without deeption or fraud. It is the responsibility of the rest of us to establish a framework of law such that an individual in pursuing his own interest is, to quote Adam Smith again, 'led by an invisible hand to promote an end which was no part of his intention". See Friedman, Milton, *Capitalism and Freedom*, (Chicago: The University of Chicago Press, 1962, p.133).

60. See footnote #44.

61. John Paul II, *Centesimus Anno*, #31.

The late German economist Wilhelm Roepke, with his accustomed clarity, sends the defenders of the free enterprise system a warning note when he says: "We move in a world of prices, markets, competition, wage rates, rates of interest, exchange rates, and other economic magnitudes. All of this is perfectly legitimate and fruitful as long as we keep in mind that we have narrowed our angle of vision and do not forget that the market economy is the economic order proper to a definite social structure and to a definite spiritual and moral setting. If we were to neglect the market economy's characteristic of being merely a part of a spiritual and social total order, we would become guilty of an aberration which may be described as social rationalism."[62] What is ailing modern society, insists Roepke, is the lack of human warmth and natural solidarity.[63]

The damaging preponderance that capitalism often gives to the individual's interests and material profits must be counterbalanced by a set of moral standards which are necessary for the survival of the system and without which a nation will inevitably disintegrate. These include, respect for natural law, tradition, love of country and neighbour and all those things which anchor a community in the hearts of men.[64] But, for this to occur it will be necessary to instill in the minds and hearts of men and women the necessary human virtues that will induce them to respect the dignity of the human person. This way, the wealth created by the free market system will not be squandered through "loose" spending and, what is even worse, through corruptive practices that are vitiating the very foundations of a free society. It is not the technical dimension of capitalism or the free enterprise system that is at fault but, rather, the lack of a proper human dimension which places man at the centre of the universe and insists that man is the subject of economics and not merely its object.

Socialism tried to find a solution to the abuses of early capitalism and the resulting evils to society by the transferring of property from private persons to the community. This way "social justice" would be attained. Individual possessions would become the common property of all and each citizen would have the right to have his equal share of whatever the authorities were able to distribute.

Such an objective proved to be not only futile, as past experience has shown, but also unjust. It robs the lawful possessor of what is rightfully his, causes total confusion in the community and deprives the worker of the liberty of disposing of his legitimately earned income in whatever way he deems more appropriate for his future well-being.

But, what is even worse is that the elimination of private property violates the right of every man to possess property of his own. It is the common opinion of mankind that the foundations of the division of property are in conformity with human nature. In fact, the principle of private property is not only in conformity with human nature but also has the sanction of Divine Law. Civil laws only confirm and enforce what is in accordance with natural law. Socialism rejects both natural and divine law.

The irony of socialism and, in particular, communism is that it used indiscriminate and totalitarian methods that violate individual's rights in order to bring about a more "just" society. Socialism as well as most if not all "isms" forget that the State can only wield its power if the common good demands it. Otherwise it is pure tyranny disguised under the cloak of "freedom" and "justice."

The collectivist and materialistic ideologies of socialism are a corruption of Christianity and all major religions. They substitute coercion for the freedom of men to share freely the superabundance of their rightfully acquired goods. The utopian aspect of socialism is precisely this willingness to do coercively what Christianity preaches through justice and charity. The reform of society has to come first and fore-

---

62. Roepke, Wilhelm, *A Humane Economy,*(Chicago: Henry Regnery Company, 1960, p. 93).

63. Ibid. p. 7.

64. Ibid. p. 149.

most through a personal conversion. Not from above, through dictatorial decrees that totally disregard the rights of men.

True justice will only prevail when the three fundamental and independent structures of communal life and, thus, the three basic forms of justice are accepted and put into practice. Perhaps, the type of justice that the post-Castro era will need the most is *iustitia generalis* which goes beyond the limits of justice.

Cubans in and out of Cuba must realize that the island's present situation is such that full compensation, restitution and satisfaction for past unjust actions may not be possible. The fact that some debts may not be able to be paid will have to be accepted as a lesser evil if peace and harmony are to prevail. To maintain order and peaceful coexistence in a free Cuba something more than a strict application of justice will probably have to be required.

Hopefully, Cubans, unjustly deprived of their possessions, will come to the realization that love—in this particular case love of neighbour and country—is the greatest of all virtues. A society where man's dues are determined exclusively by pure calculations can very easily become inhuman, one of the main characteristics of the former Soviet Union and other communist dominated nations. A new spirit of *affabilitas* and understanding must permeate all sectors of Cuban society. But, this virtue, which St. Thomas relates to justice, is neither due nor can it be rightfully claimed and demanded. It cannot be forced upon people. It has to flow spontaneously from creditors, debtors and all Cubans of good will in order to reach a peaceful and equitable solution to the many problems that a free Cuba will have to face. Without this new spirit of solidarity which goes beyond the limits of justice, it will be very difficult for men and women to live together at peace and in harmony with each other.

Cubans must accept the fact that, given prevailing conditions, it will be very difficult if not impossible to restore a proper balance, through restitutions and/or compensations, for past unjust expropriations. Certain debts may not be able to be paid pack. Thus, for the benefit of the *bonum commune*, solidarity must become the guiding principle of the new Cuba if the island's communal life is to remain human. As, St Thomas, the greatest of all the scholastic doctors once said: "Charity without justice is the mother of dissolution", but "justice without charity is cruelty."

CONCLUSIONS

It is a well known historical fact that among the first measures taken in 1959 by the newly established communist regime in Cuba was the elimination of private property. At the beginning, it was done in a sophisticated way; gradually and legally. Nevertheless, it was done systematically and according to Marxist-Leninist principles or, better still, following consciously or unconsciously, Gramschi's more "democratic" approach so as to make the Cuban people and the world at large believe that the government was not communist but merely pursuing "social justice". Unfortunately, many well intentioned people, but not well versed in communist tactics, did not come to realize the true colours of Castro and his planned objective to communize Cuba until it was too late. By then, private property, for all practical purposes, was non existent and the possibility of effective resistance to the government's arbitrary measures almost if not totally nil.

The flagrant injustice of Castro's actions cannot be denied. His predetermined decision to expropriate private property without compensation was a direct violation of the virtue of justice. No excuse can be found for the numerous government decrees that were approved by his cabinet in an indiscriminate way and without due respect for natural law and the most elementary concept of justice. Not only were there systematic violations of *iustitia commutativa* but also the sham that was made of both *iustitia distributiva* and *iustitia generalis*. The State has never the right to perform unjust acts under the pretext of the "common good." Under no circumstance can it violate natural law and the basic rights of the human person, including the right to own private property, as the Castro regime has done for many years. Once these fundamental truths are accepted, the only question that remains is as as to how the new government can deal with the delicate problem of *restitutio* created by a "legal" system of forced expropriations without compensation imposed unjustly by force on the will of the people and with a total disregard of natural law and the basic rights of man.

Most Cubans would tend to agree that, as a first step, the new government should recognize publicly the injustice of the confiscations enforced by Castro. But, how can this injustice be remedied after so many years have elapsed since the fateful take over of power by Castro's communist regime?. Here is precisely where the issue becomes extremely touchy and open to debate. A plurality of arguments seems to prevail with respect to how to deal with the problem, not only among the Cuban community in exile but particularly if the opinions of the Cubans residing on the island are also taken into account. The arguments run from total to partial compensation, not to mention other possible alternatives.

No one can deny the legitimate right of every Cuban to express his or her opinions and ideas on such an important subject that has so many implications for the future stability of the country. But care must be taken not to use those rights to foster personal or group interests that run counter to the common good and which will only contribute to further bitter conflicts and antagonisms within an already divided country. The only way to resolve this controversial problem is to recognize fully the notion of justice and its limits and how they can be applied in Cuba at the end of Castro's dictatorship.

Very few would deny that, if justice is to be carried out, restitution and/or compensation for past debts must be fulfilled. Once it is recognized officially that the massive destruction of private property, brought about by the socialist policies of Castro, were unequivocally unethical, the question still remains as to how to restore a just "equilibrium" between the affected parties to a society where a healthy equilibrium no longer exists. The unjustly expropriated have a perfectly legitimate right to claim restitution or compensation for their confiscated properties, but at the same time the "new" users of these same govern-

ment confiscated properties may not want to give up their "newly acquired rights"

Although it is true that man's communal life cannot be attained fully through *iustitia commutativa*, it is also true that it is its foundation. It is the corner stone of all social relations, "which even the higher forms of mutual agreements the irreducible core of social relations finds expression."[65] And this will continue to be true in the post-Castro era. Furthermore, the act of justice *iustitia commutativa* which orders the association of individuals with one another is *restitutio*, recompense, restoration. St. Thomas quite explicitly said that the recognition of the *suum* is correctly called "re-storation, re-stitution, re-compense, re-instatement to an original right."[66]

But, the world cannot be kept in order through strict justice alone. Conditions may be so that the proper balance between the creditor and the debtor cannot take place. The fact has to be accepted that the balance may not be totally restored through restitution and the paying of debts and dues. In fact, it is highly probable that some debts will never be paid.

The new government which will have to carry out the policy of *restitutio* will have to keep in mind the demands of the common good and act accordingly: a common good which represents the good for the sake of which the community exists and which must attain and make a reality if it is to be said that all its potentialities are fulfilled. A difficult task but one which the newly established authorities must carry out if the three basic types of justice are to be respected and the well-being of all Cubans protected.

Very often, and in the light of the common good, man will be willing to give up voluntarily something that rightfully belongs to him. He will be disposed to yield a right or part of a right to which he is entitled but that no one can compel him to do so. If justice and peace are to prevail in any given country, man should keep in mind that a spirit of solidarity should guide his actions and that he should try to place the

---

65. Pieper, ibid. p. 59.
66. Ibid. p. 60.

common good above his own selfish interest. St. Thomas maintained that something more than justice is required, something over and above strict justice if communal life is to remain human. He calls this "something," liberality (*affabilitas*), kindness. By this he means friendly relations in men's everyday associations. But St. Thomas quickly adds that this virtue is neither due to another person nor can it be rightfully claimed and demanded.

It may be suggested that in the present world such an attitude is totally unrealistic if not utopian. Perhaps this is true but the reason for the lack of the virtue of *affabilitas* is due in large part to the fact that the men and women of the last decade of the XXth century have become so influenced by the prevailing atmosphere that they do not want to accept the fact that it is precisely the present day atmosphere which is "unrealistic". They simply reject the traditional doctrine of justice and charity and prefer to fall prey to the whims of whatever is in vogue, to passing dictatorships, with their false promises of earthly paradises, or to egotistic doctrines which have as their only objective man's material welfare.

Hopefully, Cuba will one day enter a new historical stage in which both political and economic freedoms will prevail. The free market system with its reliance and respect for private property seems to be the heir apparent to the disastrous collectivist policies of the Castro era. But Cubans should not fall into the error of believing that the market economy regulated by honest competition represents a cosmos in equilibrium, a natural order, that only needs to be defended from forces exogenous to the system.

It is naive to believe that the system is miraculously regulated by an invisible hand which the deist philosophers would call divine reason. The market economy is not totally autonomous. There are limits to economic freedom; limits that are not determined by the free play of the market forces. And these limits must be determined by a set of ethical norms which will serve as guidelines to man's economic activity. If man does not accept the reality of such ethical standards, the state will have to come in and impose by force what free men are not willing to accept voluntarily. This would be the first step toward a renewed type of totalitarianism of either the left or the right.

The successors of Castro must not rely on a rationalist philosophy, on which the free market system is largely based, which does not admit the need for a solid institutional and ethical framework without which the system would ultimately founder.[67] It did not believe that unrestrained self interest would ultimately and inevitably lead to all sorts of abuses and flagrant injustices; that pressure groups and powerful economic interests would use their influence to carry out their own personal goals to the detriment of society as a whole and, ironically, this would be done under the banner of a free economic order.

The new authorities must keep in mind that competition not subject to moral criteria can easily degenerate into monopoly and all sorts of corruptive practices. The wretched spirit of greed and monopoly (the phrase used by Adam Smith) has to be curtailed either voluntarily or by some external force. For the benefit of mankind, it is to be hoped that it will be done voluntarily. Economic liberalism, quoting again from Smith, is concerned with equal freedoms and rights for all men and not only for the few and privileged who can monopolize all the wealth and power. As an economy based on competition can undermine moral standards, it requires strong moral reserves coming from outside its particular subject matter.

For peace and harmony to prevail, the new Cuban authorities, must give the acquisition of wealth top priority in order to alleviate the suffering and scarcities of the average Cuban. The free market system is perfectly suited to reach such a goal. But the wealth created by the efficiency of the market system must not be permitted to be squandered by corruption and monopolistic practices which favour the rich and powerful to the detriment of the less fortunate sectors of society. It is not a question of coercion. It is simply

---

67. For an excellent presentation of the ethical foundations of capitalism see: Novak, Michael. *The Catholic Ethic and the Spirit of Capitalism* (New York, The Free Press, 1993).

the realization that all Cubans, rich and poor, have the right to enjoy the benefits of an economic system that has proven to be the most productive in the world. A new spirit of solidarity and cooperation must permeate all sectors of Cuban society for the benefit of the entire country. The Cuban people cannot permit that the coming freedom, acquired at such a high cost, will be dissipated in internal conflicts and antagonism that will only contribute to retard the road to peace and prosperity.

Justice must be carried out. Past abuses were too many and too great. The need for *restitutio* cannot be ignored by any government that considers itself democratic, if Cuba is to be respected as a law abiding country within the concert of civilized nations. How this is to be done is a question that the experts, in view of past experiences in Germany and eastern Europe, have to determine after careful study but always taking account the common good of the country. Honest differences may and will exist and have to be respected but whatever has to be done has to be carried out in a spirit of solidarity and never in a vengeful manner. It is a difficult task but, as mentioned earlier, one that has to be done with justice and charity but never in a spirit of reprisal. As Abraham Lincoln once said: "With malice toward none; with charity for all."[68]

Cuba must recover from the nightmare of communism but let the Cubans beware of falling into the temptation of building a totally materialistic society which weighs well-being exclusively in terms of wealth and power. There are other values besides wealth—spiritual, cultural etc.—without which man ceases to be human and simply becomes a brute being. In fact, wealth is the result of the search for excellence and the development of human virtue. It is to be hoped that all Cubans will remember the words of the Greek philosopher Socrates when, prior to his death, he said to his judges: "...I spend my whole life in going about and persuading you all to give your first and greatest care to the improvement of your souls, and not till you have done that to think of your bodies or your wealth. And I tell you that wealth does not bring excellence, but that wealth, and every other good thing which men have, whether in public or in private, comes from excellence"[69]

The new Cuba must be built upon the conviction that changes in the political and economic structures of the country—no matter how efficient and good they may be—are not sufficient to bring about the peace with justice that all Cubans so earnestly desire. First and foremost, it is the hearts and minds of all Cubans, both in and out of Cuba, that have to change so that the new Cuba will rise from the ashes of communism with a renewed spirit of solidarity that will place the common good above the tyranny of collectivism and/or the covetous interests of an unrestrained individualism.

---

68. Lincoln, Abraham, Second Inaugural Address, March 4, 1865.

69. Plato, *Euthyphro, Apology, Crito;Phaedo The Death Scene*, (Indianapolis: The Bobbs-Merrill Company, 1975, Inc., p. 36

CUBA'S ENVIRONMENTAL LAW

B. Ralph Barba and Amparo E. Avella

Environmental considerations were largely ignored in Cuba for almost 200 years. Only in the last decade, with the enactment of Law 33 on January 10, 1981, have environmental laws and regulations begun to play a very small role in guiding the development of natural resources exploitation and the ecology of the island.

Law 33 is a very short document of only 25 pages. It supposedly covers all the regulations from the "principles of the Cuban Communist Party concerning the environment," to the protection and use of Cuban national resources. Law 33 has a good dosage of political "garbage," including a section that compares the "wise use of natural resources by communist countries versus the indiscriminate use of natural resources by the capitalistic world."

BACKGROUND

As a guide for drafting Law 33, the Cuban Government claims they relied on legislation enacted by some former socialist countries such as the German Democratic Republic, Bulgaria, Hungary and Russia. In addition, they claim to have examined laws and regulations from Colombia, Mexico, Sweden and Venezuela together with materials from the United Nations Program for the Environment, even though it is known that some countries like Mexico had practically no environmental laws at that time. It is also common knowledge that the ecological situation of Russia is a complete disaster; therefore, that country's environmental laws were very lax or were never applied.

The "Comisión Nacional de Protección del Medio Ambiente y Conservación de los Recursos Naturales (COMARNA)" was responsible for developing Law 33 and its regulations, but the Academy of Sciences of Cuba was in charge of defining the technical terminology included in the Law.

Thus, the Law on Environmental Protection and the Rational Use of Natural Resources (Law 33) was passed in order to "establish the basic principles to conserve, protect, improve and transform the environment and the rational use of natural resources, in accordance with integral development policies" of the Cuban government, and "with the objective of the best utilization of the national productive potential".

Law 33 requires the application of these objectives to all investment projects and to regional planning. Environmental assessment measures carried out and approved by governmental institutions must be included in all projects.

Law 33 is divided into four main chapters. Chapter one covers the main concepts of the Law. Chapter two covers specific areas of the Law and the fundamentals for the use, protection and rehabilitation of water, soil, mineral resources, etc. Chapter three covers the organization of the government entity responsible for the Law: the Comisión Nacional de Protección del Medio Ambiente y Conservación de los Recursos Naturales. The last chapter, chapter four, is an attempt to legislate a system of fines for violating the Law including a mechanism to insure that they are obeyed.

KEY PROVISIONS OF LAW 33

Key provisions of the Law 33 can be summarized as follows:

Chapter I: General Provisions

This chapter, which consists of 21 Articles, includes the goals of the Law, the adopted definitions of terms used in the Law, and the obligations of all national or foreign investors regarding the treatment and final disposal of generated waste.

Article 17 establishes the regulations to produce, store, transport, use, generate and dispose of hydrocarbons, chemicals, biological and radioactive substances, waste, and other materials. Other Articles establish the duties of governmental institutions and enterprises concerning environmental protection services.

Chapter II: Specific Areas of Environmental Protection and the Use of Natural Resources

This section of the Law has nine sections. Key provisions of each of the nine Sections of the Law are:

Section I. Water. This Section establishes the definition of territorial waters: underground, aboveground, thermal and medicinal waters. It also deals with planning for the use and development of fisheries resources in rivers, lakes and lagoons; establishes the need for rational use of water and the utilization of treatment water technologies in all new projects; the prohibition of water discharges before treatment and the prohibition to locate any project in areas designated as source aquifers.

Section II. Soils. Article 42 establishes that all persons dedicated to mining activity, road construction and/or another economic activity affecting the soils must adopt the necessary programs to replace or rehabilitate the construction site. The cost of rehabilitating the site must be included as part of the investment.

In order to prevent soil contamination, the following is prohibited:

- Disposal and/or underground injection or storage of contaminants without a permit.

- Use of contaminated water for irrigation.

- Use of chemical products in the agricultural industry without a permit.

Section III. Mineral Resources. This Section deals with the preservation of mining resources and establishes rules to promote the controlled development of mining areas. Prior to any mining investment, a favorable environmental assessment is required on each site.

Section IV. Marine Resources. This Section applies to coastal areas, estuaries, beaches, dunes, barriers, coral reefs, fish and wildlife, and regulates the dumping of all types of materials into marine waters. It prevents and/or restricts the dumping of materials adversely affecting human life, the marine ecosystems, or the economy.

Along with the goals to preserve the marine resources, the following is prohibited:

- Unauthorized use of mangrove forests in coastal zone.

- Exploitation of marine sand without a permit.

- Dumping of any kind of shipping waste, petroleum products, industrial waste and/or municipal waste.

- Unauthorized construction of any building or structures in coastal zones.

The Law also established some protected areas in order to protect marine resources.

Section V. Flora and Fauna. This Section seeks to preserve endangered and threatened species. It establishes the National System of Protected Areas and procedures to exploit the forests. It outlines the considerations to maintain, preserve and manage the forests and wildlife.

Section VI. Atmosphere. The major provisions of this Section are intended to set goals for cleaner air and the establishment of permits for industrial emissions levels. It also outlines the responsibilities of all national or foreign investors to limit the levels of contaminant emissions. In the case of new industrial projects, approval of construction in a proposed location depends on standards related to human settlement, climatic conditions and topographic relief.

Section VII. Agricultural Resources. Law 33 defines agricultural resources as follows: all classes of crops, different types of cattle and all installations dedicated to protect, develop and the reproduction of cattle. For export and import purposes, a sanitary certification is required.

Section VIII. Human Settlements. Article 105 establishes regulations related to the location of industries near human settlements, including the requirement of a buffer zone around industrial developments. The collection, transportation, disposal and recycling of urban waste must be done with adequate technology.

Section IX. Landscape and Tourism Resources. The Law prohibits the construction of any type of development in coastal zones without authorization. The zones dedicated to foreign tourism have a special administrative status issued by the Council of Ministers. Tourist developments located in areas within the National System of Protected Areas have special regulations.

Chapter III: The System of Environmental Protection and the Use of Natural Resources

Law 33 created the "National System of Environmental Protection and the Rational Use of Natural Resources." The functions of the National System are:

- Coordination and control of the established policies for protection of the environment and the rational use of natural resources.

- Creation of rules and regulations to protect the environment.

- Elaboration and control of environmental contingency plans.

Chapter IV: Violations of Standards and Provisions

Actions and/or omissions which violate standards and provisions for environmental protection and the use of natural resources established by the Law will be subject to penalties through different procedures established by the Council of Ministers.

COMMENTS CONCERNING THE CUBAN ENVIRONMENTAL LAW

The main problem of Law 33 is the lack of consideration for the environment. Article 2 establishes that the "environment is a system integrated by biotic, abiotic and socioeconomic elements, which is in interrelationship with the humans," But the Law does not include any parameters to measure or quantify any of these indicated factors.

Environment means many different things to different people. To some, it means a pleasant suburban neighborhood, quiet campus, woodlands, scenes with fresh, clean air and pristine waters, threatened species, etc. Actually, the environment is a combination of all of these concepts and includes not only the areas of air, water, plants and animals, but also other natural and human-modified features which constitute the totality of our surroundings.

Thus, transportation systems, land-use characteristics, community structures, and economic stability all have one thing in common with carbon monoxide levels, dissolved solids in water, contamination by hydrocarbons products and lead in blood: they are all part of the environment. The environment must also include aesthetic, historical, cultural, economic and social aspects.

Law 33 seems more like political propaganda, or a glossary of terminology, than a Law. It reads like a document not intended to be taken seriously by anyone reading it. Who the Cuban authorities pretend to mislead with this simplistic document is not clear. It cannot be aimed at foreign companies because it pales in comparison to existing international laws. It does not make much sense for internal use either because the Cuban Government is responsible for all the industries and is therefore the principal, if not the only, polluter and consumer of natural resources.

Let us give a specific example of the crudity of Law 33. Chapter II, Section I, Article 29 states: "Residual substances created as a result of economic and social activities need to receive proper treatment before being dumped in the environment in order to protect surface and groundwater." What is the meaning of proper treatment? Where is it defined?

Article 29 is so vague and imprecise it makes no sense and could never be implemented legally. For example: What are residual substances? Industrial wastes? Agricultural wastes? or Household Wastes? Assuming it were the latter, how should household wastes be treated? Incineration? Landfill? Recycling? What constitutes surface and groundwater that needs to be protected? There is no provision in the law defining fresh water and brackish water or establishing the salinity of the water, as determined by the Total Dissolved Solids concentration. What are the levels of contamination established by the Law? Or more important, what are contaminants? Are naturally-occurring minerals such as zinc, copper, chromium and lead classified as contaminants? It is known that lead, arsenic and cadmium, to name a few, are hazardous to human health in large quantities, but those values need to be quantified and some parameters need to be established.

Since Law 33 is so vague and no parameters have been specified, foreign investors could be forced, at the convenience of Cuban authorities, to do extensive clean-up costing million of dollars.

Chapter IV covers the fines to be imposed for violating the Law in only two pages. Article 127 indicates that violating the Law could result in fines and restitution of damages caused to the environment. Article 128 assigns to the Council of Ministers the responsibility for imposing the fines and restituting damages. Article 129 defines two types of fines:

- Personal fines, which will be collected from the individual's pay check at a rate of one- fifth (1/5) of the salary.

- Institutional fines, which will be collected at once.

Once again, this portion of the Law could be very damaging to foreign companies investing in Cuba. If a Cuban working for a foreign enterprise (let us say a hotel in Varadero) is found guilty of contaminating the environment, he could be fined at the rate of one-fifth of his monthly salary, which is approxi-

mately 20 pesos a month. At 20 pesos a month, it will take several lifetimes to collect the expenses to remediate a contaminated site. However, "institutional fines" are to be paid at once. Therefore, it is very possible that the foreign enterprise employing the Cuban national could be found responsible for the contamination and ordered to pay the clean-up costs immediately.

Under Law 33, environmental regulations do not have a major effect on the economy of Cuba. In practice, environmental regulations are seldom applied and a majority of decisions are being taken without any consideration of environmental effects.

An environmental impact study is the logical first step before any construction because it represents an opportunity to consider the positive and negative effects of human actions. The Cuban government requires foreign investors in the mining industry to submit a report on the environmental consequences of the proposed mining activities. However, the Cuban environmental regulations never took into consideration this analytical process for the most important projects developed by the present government.

The common theme of all environmental considerations is that good environmental quality is beneficial for the economy in the long run. Unfortunately, the current economic problems in Cuba forced the government philosophy that "any environmental problem occurring today will be corrected tomorrow." In others words, the Cuban government is presently giving priority to the economy and not the environment.

Another reason Law 33 is not being applied is because the Cuban population has not yet developed an "environmental awareness" and the realization of the dependence of human beings and the long-term viability of the environment for sustaining life. Similarly, the Cuban government does not have the "new ethic" regarding the conservation of natural resources that is present in most countries.

Finally, the areas most likely to affect the environment in the future are the new revisions to the Cuban foreign investment law, the size of foreign participation, and the contracting of Cuban workers (see Cuba News April 1995).

In spite of the business world's increasing recognition that sustainable development and production can, indeed, be good for business, efforts to reduce waste, recycle waste materials, control pollution, and conserve resources have been overlooked in order to maintain low production cost. Serious environmental problems that have surfaced since the collapse of the totalitarian regimes of eastern Europe are vivid examples. The disclosure of environmental problems of this region and of the former Soviet Republics has revealed the extreme environmental degradation brought about by the use of improper technology.

Cuba is not an exception. Recently, the President of the Cuban Council of Ministers, Lionel Soto, declared in an interview that Russia has a debt with Cuba as a result of natural resources exploitation and environmental contamination created by the Russians. According to Mr. Soto, the amount of the debt is between 20 and 25 millions dollars. This statement by a high-level Cuban official confirms that the Cuban Government plans to use the environment and Law 33 as political tools for its own convenience and for its own benefit.

THE SPECIAL PERIOD AND THE ENVIRONMENT

Sergio Díaz-Briquets and Jorge F. Pérez-López

The dissolution of the socialist community has had severe repercussions on the Cuban economy. Prior to these momentous changes, the former Soviet Union and the socialist nations of Eastern Europe were Cuba's economic lifeline. In 1989, the most recent year for which official data are available, the former Soviet Union and the socialist countries of Eastern Europe bought about 85 percent of Cuba's exports and provided a like share of imports; these nations were also the source of the bulk of Cuba's external financing for economic development.

Over the two-year period 1989-90, the former socialist countries severed trade and financial relationships with Cuba, forcing severe adjustments on the island. The set of emergency measures implemented by the Cuban government—beginning in September 1990—aimed at preventing the total economic collapse of the regime, have been referred to by the leadership as the "special period in peacetime," highlighting that the situation being addressed was the equivalent of wartime conditions, although no open military conflict was present. Austerity measures adopted by the Cuban leadership during the special period—rationing consumption, increasing domestic food production, stimulating exports that generate hard currency flows, attracting foreign investment—have been aimed at operating the economy with much reduced levels of imports and external financial resources.

The economic crisis that has swept Cuba in the 1990s, coinciding with the special period in peacetime, has affected every facet of Cuban life. Analysts have focused a great deal of attention on the effects of

the crisis on overall levels of economic activity, on population standards of living, or on the performance of specific sectors of the economy (such as sugar cane agriculture, electricity, or transportation). Relatively unstudied, however, are the effects of the economic crisis associated with the special period on other aspects of Cuban life, such as the environment.

This paper presents a preliminary analysis of the effects on the Cuban environmental situation of special period policies and outcomes. The analysis is broad, extending beyond the agricultural sector—on which there already has been some published work—and examining special period-environment interactions across the economy at large, including industry, mining, tourism, nutrition, public health, etc. The paper is divided in three sections. The first one gives some necessary background on the state of the environment in Cuba in the late 1980s, that is, prior to the start of the economic crisis associated with the special period. The second section examines aspects of special period policies and outcomes that have had a positive impact on the environment. The third section does the same with regard to those whose impact on the environment has been negative. The paper concludes with a tentative assessment of the overall effect of the special period on the Cuban environmental situation.

THE CUBAN ENVIRONMENTAL SITUATION BEFORE THE SPECIAL PERIOD

In a self-congratulatory document presented to the June 1992 Earth Summit in Rio de Janeiro, which emphasized the Cuban socialist government's commitment to the preservation of the environment and natural resources, President Castro nevertheless made brief reference to some pressing environmental problems. He highlighted the following (Castro, 1992:46):

- pollution of bays;

- soil erosion and degradation, particularly in mining areas;

- pollution of surface waters from the waste of the sugar industry; and

- erosion of beaches and coastal areas and salinization of low-laying coastal lands.

Many of these environmental stresses were inherited from the past, but some arose or were intensified by sectoral development strategies pursued by the revolutionary government. Urban pollution, for instance, could be partly traced to Cuba's extreme reliance on inefficient and highly contaminating Soviet and Eastern European-built vehicles and factories. In the agricultural sector, a practice that resulted in much environmental damage was the promotion of Soviet-style, large-scale state farm production model based on widespread mechanization, heavy chemical inputs (e.g., fertilizers and herbicides), and extensive irrigation (Pérez-López, 1991b; Solares, 1994). The effect of large scale mechanization on the compaction of soils has been reported as severe (Sáez, 1994). The pollution of streams and coastal areas by organic waste discharges from the sugar industry was a major concern for years. By the late 1980s, when sugar production was at its peak, the problem was considered so serious that to lower discharge rates, measures were instituted in more than 90 mills to fertilize sugar cane fields with organic waste (Clark, 1989).

Some of Cuba's bays became severely polluted because of human, industrial, and agricultural discharges, but also by the runoffs associated with the deforestation resulting from strip mining (e.g, in Moa). By the late 1970s, the United Nations Development Program was providing financial and technical assistance to the Cuban government to arrest the growing contamination of Havana harbor (Menéndez, 1979). High levels of industrial and agricultural pollution were also in evidence in the bays of Nipe, Chaparra,

and Puerto Padre (Dávalos, 1984). By 1990, Cienfuegos bay was added to the list, partly because of the very inefficient use of existing industrial pollution control systems (Schlachter, 1990).

Many instances of soil salinization and erosion can be blamed on waterlogging caused by poor irrigation and drainage practices, by excessive water extraction rates from coastal aquifers, and hare-brained schemes that led to the damming of low water volume streams and rivers that dried out during the dry season months (Díaz-Briquets and Pérez-López, 1993). It is estimated that one million hectares, or about 14 percent of the country's agricultural surface have excessive salt deposits. Of these, about 600,000 hectares are deemed to have light to modest salinization levels and the rest heavy salinization ("Estudio," 1991). The regions with the heaviest levels of salinization are in Guantánamo and the Cauto valley.

The Cuban non-sugar industrial sector is also a heavy polluter, discharging polluting agents into the atmosphere, the sea, or other ecological systems. According to Oro (1992:47-56), among the chief pollutants in the non-sugar industrial sector were:

- the cement industry, a heavy generator of dust and smoke;

- the chemical and metallurgical industries, producers of acid steams, smoke and soot;

- the steel and non-ferrous alloy industries, also heavy producers of smoke and soot;

- the sugar cane derivative industry, consisting of plants producing torula yeast, bagasse boards, paper, etc., and generating a variety of air pollutants and solid wastes; and

- the mining industry, especially the nickel industry, which launches extremely heavy amounts of dust into the atmosphere and releases by-products into streams and the sea.

POSITIVE SPECIAL PERIOD-ENVIRONMENT INTERACTIONS

The special period has had some positive effects on the Cuban environmental situation. As President

Castro stated in the mentioned document presented to the June 1992 Earth Summit,

> [The special period] is a period of readjustment ... requiring maximum economizing and austerity in economic and social policies, along with many creative initiatives, a large number of which have come directly from the people. Many of the steps taken as a result of the special period fit in with the strategic lines prepared by the Revolution. Some of them have helped accelerate the policies put into effect by the country in defense of the environment (Castro, 1992:49).

The sector of the economy in which the special period-environment interactions have been positive that has received the greatest attention is agriculture (Carney, 1993). The special period has also positively affected the environmental situation in other economic sectors, such as industry and transportation, and has had some positive (as well as some negative) effects on public health.

Economic growth and environmental degradation: Environmental degradation in all societies occurs due to two primary reasons: (1) population growth, urbanization, and industrialization place increasing pressure on the environment; and (2) society fails to incorporate the true cost of environmental resources in its production and consumption decisions (Pearce and Warford, 1993; Espino, 1992:327).

To the extent that overall economic activity in Cuba has declined during the special period, so has the degradation of the environment associated with the emission of greenhouse gases from burning fossil fuels, the generation of industrial pollutants, the contamination of water by runoffs of chemical fertilizers and pesticides, etc. The contraction in economic activity no doubt has had some positive impact on the environmental situation in Cuba, particularly since such contraction in economic activity has been very sharp. According to available statistics, Cuba's gross domestic product (GDP) fell from 19.3 billion pesos in 1989 to 10.0 billion pesos in 1993, or by more than 48 percent. Over the same period, GDP per capita fell from 1,828 pesos to 909 pesos, or by more than 50 percent (Pérez-López, 1995:11). The economy probably contracted again in 1994, although the Economic Commission for Latin America and the Caribbean (ECLAC) has reported that a growth rate of 0.7 percent was achieved in that year (ECLAC, 1995:1).

Perhaps the most tangible aspect of special period adjustment policies has been the sharp reduction in Cuba's ability to import. Between 1989 and 1993, Cuban imports fell from 8.1 billion pesos to 2.0 billion pesos, or by 75 percent (Pérez-López, 1995:11). Such a sharp reduction in imports affected all categories of imported goods: oil and oil products, food, machinery and equipment, spare parts, chemicals, raw materials, etc. Although Cuba has not published foreign trade statistics by commodity since 1989, a reconstruction of such statistics carried out by the Central Intelligence Agency based on partner country statistics (Table 1) confirms that reductions in imports over the period 1989-93 affected all import categories. Particularly relevant for purposes of this paper were the reductions in imports of fuels (76 percent), chemicals (72 percent), transportation equipment (86 percent), and consumer goods (82 percent). According to Cuban official Carlos Lage, in 1993, Cuba imported 5.7 million tons of oil and oil products (Carlos Lage, 1993:4) and domestic crude production reached 1.1 million tons, for a total apparent supply of 6.8 million tons, compared to the approximately 11 million tons per annum that Cuba consumed during 1984-88 (Pérez-López, 1991a:224).)

Agriculture: At the end of 1989, the Cuban state owned more than 90 percent of the nation's land, most of it in the form of state farms (AEC, 1989:185). Agricultural machinery (equipped with internal combustion engines), chemical fertilizers, herbicides, and pesticides were extensively used. In sugar cane agriculture, for example, most planting, cultivating, and harvesting activities were carried out using machinery; in the late 1980s, over 65 percent of sugar cane cutting and 98 percent of sugar cane loading and transportation activities were mechanized (Pérez-López, 1991:68). Sugar cane agriculture also demanded high levels of productive inputs such as fertilizers and herbicides (Alvarez and Peña Castellanos, 1995:10). Burning of oil products in agricultural machinery contributed to air pollution, while

Table 1. Composition of Cuban Imports, 1989-93 (in million pesos)

	1989	1990	1991	1992	1993	% Change 93/89
Food	1011	840	720	450	470	-53
Raw Materials	307	240	140	40	35	-89
Fuels	2598	1950	1240	835	620	-76
Chemicals	530	390	270	170	150	-72
Semifinished goods	838	700	425	195	180	-79
Machinery	1922	1790	615	350	235	-88
Transportation equipment	609	590	170	125	80	-86
Consumer goods	277	225	90	50	50	-82
Other	32	20	20	20	20	-38
TOTAL IMPORTS	8124	6745	3690	2235	1840	-77

Source: CIA 1994.

use of fertilizers, herbicides, and pesticides did the same for soil and water resources.

According to official statistics, the agricultural sector consumed nearly 468,000 metric tons of oil and oil products in 1988, roughly 4 percent of the 11.1 million tons of such products consumed nationally (CEE, 1989). Imports of fertilizers and of herbicides and pesticides amounted to 158 million and 80 million pesos, respectively, in 1989 (AEC, 1989:283), roughly 3 percent of overall imports in that year. The overall import coefficient for fertilizers used in Cuba was 94 percent and for herbicides 97 percent (Rosset and Benjamin, 1994:18). By comparison, in 1992 Cuban fuel imports reached only 6 million metric tons, fertilizer imports 300,000 metric tons (compared to 1.3 million tons in 1989), and pesticides less than 30 million pesos (Lage, 1992).

These sharp reductions in imports of fuels, fertilizers, and pesticides during the special period forced changes in agricultural techniques that, although disastrous in terms of agricultural output, have had positive environmental consequences. By November 1991, about 12 percent of Cuba's stock of agricultural tractors was idle because of lack of fuel, and 100,000 oxen had been trained for duty in animal traction (Roca, 1994:105). In 1992, Cuba applied chemical fertilizers to 817,000 hectares of sugar cane, compared to 2,625,000 hectares in 1989; for herbicides application, the corresponding areas were 1.7 million hectares in 1992 compared to 2.2 million hectares in 1989 (Alvarez and Peña Castellanos, 1995:29).

Recent literature on Cuban agriculture (e.g., Dlott et.al. 1993; Gersper et.al., 1993; Vandermeer et.al., 1993; Rosset and Benjamin, 1994a and 1994b) posits that, as a result of the special period exigencies and reductions in imports, Cuba has adopted an environmentally-friendly "alternative model" of agricultural development that de-emphasizes mechanization (and therefore pollutants associated with internal combustion engines) and the use of chemical fertilizers and herbicides. This model was recently described as a "National Experiment in Sustainability" (National Public Radio, 1995). What these observers have failed to note is that the productivity decline associated with this model—a model reminiscent of agricultural practices in Cuba four decades ago—is inconsistent with the demand for agricultural products of a population of eleven million in the 1990s, as opposed to 6 million in the 1950s.

Industry: Reductions in imports of fuels, raw materials, machinery, and spare parts have reduced industrial activity and therefore air, soil, and water pollution associated with such activity. Since most industrial plants are located in medium to large urban areas, the principal beneficiaries of reduced pollution levels have been the cities. In 1988, the industrial sector used 6.6 million metric tons of oil products, or nearly 60 percent of overall consumption (CEE, 1989). According to estimates, up to 80 percent of industrial facilities in the island were idle at the end of 1993 due to a dearth of fuel, raw materials, and spare parts (Mesa-Lago 1994:11). This means that most industrial plants were not operating boilers that generate greenhouse gases.

The electricity generation industry, in particular, has been heavy hit by the special period fuel and spare part shortages. In 1988, the Cuban electricity system had a generation capacity of 3.853 megawatts and generated 14.453 gigawatt hours of electricity; 99.5 percent of the electricity was produced by thermo-electric plants fueled by residual fuel oil and crude oil (Pérez-López, 1991:240). Electricity generation used up 3.3 million metric tons of liquid fuels, or half of the total amount of oil and oil products consumed by the industrial sector (CEE, 1989).

Data are not available on electricity generation during the special period, but fragmentary information suggests that the reduction in electricity production has been significant. In the 1990s, Cuba has instituted a system of rotating blackouts throughout the island. In the summer of 1993, electricity outages stretched for 12-16 hours, with some cities in the interior of the nation facing up to 20 hours of power outages per day. Such power outages not only inconvenienced consumers, but they also shut down factories and affected other public services (Whitefield, 1993).

Air pollution from the country's several cement plants, a major source of contaminants prior to the special period (Norniella, 1985), must have declined considerably as well, due to lowered production after

1989 because of fuel shortages. By the beginning of the special period there was mounting concern about the adverse environmental impact of the cement plants, since they could no longer be fitted with imported pollution abatement equipment (Palazuelos Barrios, 1990a and 1990b).

Transportation: In 1988, the transportation sector accounted for 11.9 percent of total energy consumption (CEE, 1989). In August 1990, Cuba instituted mandatory energy conservation measures to address a 2-million ton oil shortfall in energy imports, which included reductions of gasoline deliveries to the state sector of 50 percent and to the private sector of 30 percent (Whitefield, 1990). Subsequent reductions in gasoline allocations have essentially eliminated private transportation via automobiles.

Public transportation, particularly in the capital city of La Habana, deteriorated severely, with the number of buses reportedly declining from 1,200 to about 500 in May 1993 because of the lack of spare parts and fuel ("Crítica," 1993). Buses outside of the capital at the end of 1992 were running less than 20 percent of the routes they covered three years earlier (Farah, 1992). The reduction in public transportation had a significant positive impact on air pollution. Referring to the Hungarian buses that were extensively used in Cuba, Castro said:

> The Hungarian buses travel six kilometers on a gallon of fuel. They fill the city with smog. They poison everybody. We could get together some data. We could get statistics on the number of people killed by Hungarian buses ("Castro Discusses," 1990:15).

To address the transportation needs of the population, over 1.2 million bicycles have been imported from the People's Republic of China and at least 5 bicycle assembly plants set up on the island (Hockstader, 1993). In the city of La Habana alone, it has been estimated that in 1992 there were 500,000 bicycles in operation, serving a population of 2.1 million inhabitants (Carranza Valdés, 1990:151). Because of the drastic decline in the number of internal combustion vehicles in circulation and lower levels of industrial air contamination, the streets of La Habana have become, in the words of one observer, "almost smog free" (National Public Radio, 1995).

Public Health: Special period policies have had some unintended positive effects on public health. For example, with regard to the widespread use of bicycles to provide means of transportation for the population, Castro has said:

> To make cuts in transportation usage, a solution was introduced which is innovative because of its mass scale: the use of bicycles. Hundreds of thousands of bicycles were imported, several factories were modified to manufacture bicycles and almost a half a million bicycles have been distributed to workers and students. The proliferation of cyclists of all ages is perfectly compatible with the policies promoted for several years to guarantee health for all, including exercise programs for senior citizens. In this way, the current shortages of fuel, although they negatively affect daily life, also have a positive effect on the environment (Castro, 1992:49).

Other "ecologically valuable" outcomes of the special period, according to Castro, are "the intensified use of herbal medicine, the promotion of local fruit and vegetable gardens (even in residential areas in yards and terraces), the gradual utilization of animal traction in agriculture, the development of composting, and much more" (Castro, 1992:49-50).

As the average daily intake of calories, proteins, and other nutrients has declined, the composition of the Cuban diet has changed. Cubans, accustomed to a diet high in fats and carbohydrates, have not only seen their food intake decline drastically, but have been forced to attempt to supplement their limited diets with domestically-grown fruits and vegetables, many of which are produced in home gardens. While this shift away from fatty foods may be beneficial, the weight of the evidence seems to point out to a decline in health standards as a consequence of the severe deterioration in food intake (see below).

Another positive effect of the special period is that it has reduced waste, as recycling has been stepped up. Cubans have become extremely frugal, and people look for all sorts of left overs to make gadgets to make a living or to use at home. To the extent that recycling contributes to the reduction of waste, it makes a positive environmental contribution by limiting the need for dumps. Recycling has also helped alleviate La Habana's sanitation crisis. The amount of city waste has also declined as people use their meager food leftovers to feed animals (e.g., pigs) in their yards.

NEGATIVE SPECIAL PERIOD-ENVIRONMENT INTERACTIONS

The economic crisis associated with the special period presents serious challenges to Cuba's environmental situation and prospects. As two analysts have pointed out,

> Cuba's severe economic crisis has forced its government to cut back drastically on its budget for environmental research in its various aspects. Cuba's vast scientific collections are at risk of swift destruction, for lack of funds for preservation and maintenance. Scientific training has also been curtailed. Many scientists are shifting to other professional work as a result of these paralyzing circumstances.

> The same economic crisis, moreover, tempts the Cuban government to search for petroleum and mining resources, or to develop tourist facilities, on a scale and at a speed which also increase the likelihood of environmental damage, especially to Cuba's smaller cays and its marine resources (Cole and Domínguez, 1995:4-5).

This section of the paper examines environmental challenges presented by the special period, in particular with regard to the agriculture, industry, mining, tourism, and public health sectors.

Agriculture: While the environmental effects of Cuba's strategy to overcome the economic crisis appear to be largely benign on the agricultural sector, several developments merit continued attention. Cuba has launched an all-out effort to substitute chemical pesticides with biological agents (Shishkoff, 1993). While these initiatives appear at this time to be meritorious from an environmental point of view, they may carry long-term dangers not readily appreciated because they are being implemented on a wide scale without prior adequate experimental study. Of note are some biotechnology products used as substitutes for imported pesticides.

Shortages of commercial fuels for home cooking (electricity, kerosene, gas) during the special period have brought about increased demand for firewood and charcoal, and placed additional pressure on already sparse Cuban forest resources (Espino, 1992:331). The increased demand for firewood has brought about the indiscriminate cutting of trees and bushes, adding to Cuba's already serious problem of soil erosion.

Particularly damaging has been the cutting down of mangroves to produce charcoal (Solano, 1995). The problem is reported to be most acute in the Zapata swamp where military brigades are harvesting soplillo tree stands in selected areas to supply the city of La Habana with charcoal. The government claims, however, that the areas chosen for logging are carefully selected to protect the swamp's unique natural habitat (National Public Radio, 1995).

Industry: The overall reduction in imported fuels, machinery, and raw materials during the special period has brought about a slow down in industrial activity and pollution. Government policies to overcome the crisis nevertheless have put additional pressure on the environment.

To ease the bottleneck caused by shortages in imported fuels, Cuba has gone all out to increase domestic production and use of crude oil. The drive to increase crude production has meant that drilling and production has been permitted in certain areas that were formerly considered environmentally fragile, for example in coastal areas. Cuba has also approved joint ventures with foreign firms to explore offshore, potentially affecting the ocean environment and risking the possibility of an offshore oil spill.

Because of the financial pinch, Cuba has bought cheap oil in the world market to fire its power plants; this low-quality oil generates dense clouds of pollution that embrace La Habana and other areas near the power plants (McGeary and Booth, 1993:44). Domestically-produced crude oil, used extensively in power plants, is of very low quality and has a very high sulphur content, thus generating a great deal of air pollution.

Special period financial strains have stopped Cuba's efforts to build a nuclear electricity generation plant, a source of electricity that would be more environmentally friendly in terms of carbon dioxide emissions, although it would raise other environmental concerns associated with nuclear radiation.

Mining: Joint ventures with foreign investors to exploit Cuba's mineral resources negotiated during the special period are placing severe pressures on the environment. Foreign firms have expanded operations in nickel-producing plants in the Eastern part of the island. A joint venture with Canada's Sherritt, Inc. operates the aging nickel ore processing plant at Moa Bay, in Eastern Cuba. The plant produces a mixed sulfide containing nickel, cobalt, and traces of other metals. According to a Canadian journalist,

> Because of leaky equipment and other factors, the sulphur compounds used in the process pollute the air and water, producing what residents say is acid rain. Heavy erosion from surface mining is also filling Moa Bay with earth (Knox, 1995).

Residents of Moa told the same journalist that they took it for granted that "one of the reasons a foreign mining company would be interested in operating in Cuba was that environmental standards would be lower" (Knox, 1995).

The "Pedro Soto Alba" nickel plant, the subject of the Sherritt, Inc. joint venture, reportedly produces 12,000 cubic meters of liquid wastes per day. These wastes, which are disposed of in the sea, carry a wide range of light and heavy metals, such as sulfates and great amounts of sulfuric acid. According to a Cuban journalist

> Every day, 72 tons of aluminum, 48 tons of chrome, 15 tons of magnesium, and 30 tons of the dangerous sulfuric acid get dumped into the sea. This harms the marine flora and fauna and in the long term, could cause irreversible damage ("Nickel Plant," 1994).

Further, some environmentalists have expressed concern that coral reefs from Moa Bay are being dredged so that the calcium carbonate they contain can be used to neutralize the sulfuric acid in waste materials (Oro, 1992:82). A spokesperson for Sherritt, Inc. has admitted that materials of coral reef origin are being used for this purpose, from "coral mud that has long decayed by natural methods...we don't do anything to wreck reefs" (Knox, 1995).

Strip mining of the nickel ores has been an environmental concern for years, as remediation and reforestation have not kept pace with mining activity. This is a major source of environmental damage at Moa Bay, according to Sherritt, Inc. Chairman Ian Delany (Knox, 1995). New plants are on the drawing board. Other joint ventures to exploit copper, gold, and silver deposits also raise environmental concerns.

Tourism: One of the leading sectors in Cuba's adjustment policies during the special period is international tourism. The Cuban leadership has identified the international tourism industry as one that can contribute significantly to the country's hard currency balances and has aggressively sought foreign capital to develop additional tourist facilities, particularly seashore resorts.

The Cuban government claims to be sensitive to the fact that growth in the tourist industry depends not only on the availability of more and better facilities, but also on the implementation of cautious development plans to preserve the country's natural tourist attractions. However, in expanding its tourism infrastructure—hotels, recreation facilities, roads, airports, etc.—Cuba has often emphasized speed and low cost to the detriment of the environment. To allow access by tourists to beaches in the numerous small keys that surround the island, particularly on its northern coast, Cuban tourism authorities have constructed causeways bridging barrier islands to the mainland and to one another called "pedraplenes." These "pedraplenes" block the movement of water in the intracoastal waters, exacerbating contamination and destroying coastal and marine habitats (Espino, 1992:335). Examples of "pedraplenes" deemed to have caused substantial harm to the environment and fishing resources include the one joining the islands of Turiguanó and Cayo Coco and others in Caibarién and the northern region of Ciego de Avila province (Solano, 1995).

Foreign observers note that while the Cuban government "talks a good line," in practice it is willing to sacrifice the environment in the name of economic survival (National Public Radio, 1995). The growth in tourism, and in particular the development of the country's pristine outer keys and islets, has alarmed the conservation community. Some in this community note that while the country was sheltered from market forces (due to Soviet subsidies), it did not have to face the same tough growth/ environmental tradeoffs other island countries in the Caribbean did. As a result, Cuba remains as one of the world's "richest storehouses of unique animals" (Dewar, 1993), with some experts estimating that about 40 percent of Cuba's species still remain to be discovered (National Public Radio, 1995). Continued efforts to develop the international tourism industry can only exacerbate pressures on natural resources, and lead to the decimation of rare species.

Transportation: Cuba's transportation stock is getting older and, because of poor maintenance and lack of spare parts, can only be more polluting and environmentally unfriendly. As long as the economic crisis continues, Cuba will not be able to modernize its fleet of cars, trucks, and buses (other than for those few vehicles serving the tourist industry). The occasional used buses donated to Cuba by Canada, Spain, and other countries as a rule have been retired after years of service, tend to be obsolete, and do not have the latest environmental control technology.

Public Health: The special period has had considerable negative impacts on the health of Cubans and on the vaunted public health system. Some of these problems have been caused in part by some of the measures introduced to cope with the deteriorated economic conditions. There are reports, for example, of a major increase in the number of deaths and injuries associated with the manifold increase in bicycle ridership. As in every other sector of the economy, poor maintenance and lack of spare parts has taken a toll, with insufficient fuel available to pump and distribute underground water and water from aboveground reservoirs. The dearth of foreign exchange may have also interfered with the country's ability to purify its potable water supply.

Several urban health problems can be attributed to the practice of raising chickens and pigs at home. Because fuel and imported spare parts are lacking, many sanitation trucks in the city have been taken out of service. Garbage collection schedules are irregular and often carried out with animal powered vehicles. The incidence of gastrointestinal ailments is certain to have risen as the availability of running water for distribution has declined and become more erratic.

With the shift of urban workers to agricultural pursuits, in some rural areas the public health situation may have worsened as well. In agricultural areas receiving large contingents of urban-origin workers, the sanitary infrastructures is likely to be insufficient to accommodate the needs of a larger population.

In 1993, Cuba reported the outbreak of a mysterious disease that blinded people. There has been considerable speculation about what the cause of the disease might have been. A team of physicians from the Pan American Health Organization (PAHO) found that 50,000 of the 11 million inhabitants were suffering from such maladies as optic neuropathy (visual loss), deafness, sensory neuropathy (loss of sensation in the hands and feet) and a spinal cord disorder that impaired walking and bladder control (Stix, 1995:32). The PAHO team concluded that a spare diet, along with great physical exertion because of the lack of transportation, had caused severe thiamine deficiency and the outbreak of neuropathy, which was curbed through the distribution of B vitamins to the population (Stix, 1995:32).

According to health specialists, the scarcity of certain medications and foodstuffs has contributed to a modest increase in the incidence of low birth weight among Cuban infants that occurred in 1992 and to a suspected rise in the infant mortality rate (French, 1993). Data from a recent report indicate that the percent of low birth-weight babies rose from 7.6 percent in 1990 to 9 percent in 1993, while the percent of under weight women entering pregnancy increased from 8.7 to 10 percent between 1990 and 1993. There have also been reports of significant increases in mortality among residents of nursing homes in 1993 (Johnson, 1993). The gravity of the dietary changes are summarized in the same report: between 1989 and 1993 the daily per capita nutrient intake has declined by 40 percent in proteins, 64 in

fats, 67 percent in Vitamin A, 62 percent in vitamins C, 22 percent in iron, and 19 percent in calcium ("U.S. Blockade Causes," 1995:4).

Cuba's advanced system of health care delivery, one of the most trumpeted accomplishments of the revolutionary government, has not been spared by the economic crisis and the end of subsidies from the former Soviet Union and the socialist countries. According to an analyst who visited Cuba in the autumn of 1992, the country's health care system was already "disintegrating" (Barrett, 1993:1). This analyst observed a shortage of imported medical products such as over-the-counter and prescription medications, anesthetics, suture, surgical gloves, X-ray plates, diagnostic kits, etc.; also in short supply in the autumn of 1992 were soap, detergents, other personal hygiene items, chlorine to treat the public water supply, and pesticides to control insects.

More recent evidence suggests that the situation continues to be critical, with basic supplies, from antibiotics to sterilizing detergents, hard to find (Stix, 1995:32). As noted in a report to the United Nations by Roberto Robaina, Cuba's Foreign Minister, "it has been impossible to procure the necessary resources to maintain the levels of performance of medical services, availability of medicines, and nutrition achieved by Cuba in past decades" ("U.S. Blockade Causes," 1995:4)

CONCLUDING REMARKS

The special period has had a profound effect on Cuba's environmental situation. It has, on the one hand, arrested a secular process of environmental deterioration in the agricultural sector that was vastly aggravated by the uncritical adoption, since the 1960s, of the large-scale, input-intensive farm model imported from the Soviet Union. This agricultural development model, predicated on the heavy use of chemical inputs, mechanization, and irrigation, contributed to the deterioration of Cuba's soils and the contamination of its waters.

The collapse of the economy has also served to reduce industrial pollution. The adoption of a Soviet-inspired model of industrial development was environmentally damaging, since ecological safeguards and associated technologies were not a priority. Cuba's industrial infrastructure, including its oil refineries and cement plants, is inefficient and a major source of air and water pollutants. Another important pollution source is the technologically-backward national fleet of cars, trucks, and buses, mostly imported from the former Soviet Union and the Eastern European countries.

On the other hand, many of the economic emergency measures introduced during the special period convey grave threats to the environment. Particularly alarming are those associated with the development of the mining and tourist industry. The Castro government, in its zeal to promote the development of the latter sector, appears to be repeating the same mistakes responsible for the ecological deterioration of most insular Caribbean countries.

What is undeniable is that, with the decline in imports, particularly fuel, and the general economic collapse, agricultural and industrial pollution has declined, but at a substantial economic cost. The economic/environmental interactions are complex. For example, the reduction in the volume of imported fuels has stimulated the use of firewood and charcoal as cooking fuels, with adverse implications for forest resources and soil erosion. The long-term environmental effects of these developments remain to be seen.

Cuba's economic and political future is as uncertain as its environmental future. Economic recovery is likely to exacerbate the same environmental pressures alleviated under the special period. Cuba's environmental tomorrow will depend on the development model the country pursues in years to come, and on the extent to which this model takes into account economic/ environmental tradeoffs regarding production and consumption decisions.

REFERENCES

Alvarez, José, and Lázaro Peña Castellanos. 1995. *Preliminary Study of the Sugar Industries in Cuba and Florida Within the Context of the World Sugar Market.* International Working Paper Series IW95-6. Gainesville: Institute of Food and Agricultural Sciences, University of Florida.

Anuario estadístico de Cuba (AEC). 1989. La Habana: Comité Estatal de Estadísticas.

Barrett, Kathleen. 1993. *The Collapse of the Soviet Union and the Eastern Bloc: Effects on Cuban Health Care.* Cuban Briefing Paper No. 2. Washington: Center for Latin American Studies, Georgetown University.

Barrio Menéndez, Emilio del. 1979. "Comenzó a materializarse proyecto para investigar y controlar la contaminación marina en Cuba," *Granma* (28 November) 1.

"Carlos Lage Comments on Economy." 1992. Havana Radio Rebelde Network (7 November), as reproduced in *FBIS-LAT-92-219* (12 November 1993) 2-14.

"Carlos Lage Interview on Economic Situation." 1993. Havana Radio Rebelde Network (3 November), as reproduced in *FBIS-LAT-93-216A* (10 November 1993) 2-15.

Carney, Judith A. 1993. (editor) "Low-Input Sustainable Agriculture in Cuba," special issue, *Agriculture and Human Values,* 10:3.

Carranza Valdés, Julio. 1992. "Cuba: Los retos de la economía." *Cuadernos de Nuestra América* 9:19 (July-December) 131-158.

Castro, Fidel. 1993. *Tomorrow is Too Late.* Melbourne: Ocean Press.

"Castro Discusses Revolution, USSR, Nicaragua." 1990. Havana Domestic Radio and Television

Services (7 March), as reproduced in *FBIS-LAT-90-046* (8 March) 1-17.

Central Intelligence Agency (CIA). 1994. *Cuba: Handbook of Trade Statistics, 1994.* ALA 94-10011. Washington.

Clark, Ismael. 1989. "Problemas ambientales en Cuba y en el mundo." *Granma* (5 June) 4.

Cole, Sally, and Jorge I. Domínguez. 1995. "U.S.-Cuban Environmental Cooperation: Shared Interests, Problems, and Opportunities." In *The Environment in U.S.-Cuban Relations: Opportunities for Cooperation,* pp. 1-8. Washington: Inter-American Dialogue.

Compendio estadístico de energía (CEE). 1989. La Habana: Comité Estatal de Estadísticas.

"Crítica la situación del transporte público en Cuba." 1993. *Diario las Américas* (8 May) 7A.

Dávalos, Fernando. 1984. "En tres años la bahía de Nipe será esteril, si no se detiene la contaminación," *Granma* (11 September) 3.

Dewar, Heather. 1993. "Unlocking the Mysteries of Cuba's Rare Species," *The Miami Herald,* (26 October) 1A.

Díaz-Briquets, Sergio, and Jorge Pérez-López. 1993. "Water, Development, and Environment in Cuba: A First Look." In *Cuba in Transition, Volume 3—Papers and Proceedings of the Third Annual Meeting of the Association for the Study of the Cuban Economy,* pp. 123-138. Miami: Florida International University.

Dlott, Jeff, Ivette Perfecto, Peter Rosset, Larry Burkham, Julio Monterrey, and John Vandermeer. 1993. "Management of Insect Pests and Weeds." *Agriculture and Human Values* 10:3 (Summer) 9-15.

Economic Commission for Latin America and the Caribbean. 1995. "Cuba: Evolución Económica durante 1994," LC/MEX/R.524, Mexico, 23 May.

Espino, María Dolores. 1992. "Environmental Deterioration and Protection in Socialist Cuba." In *Cuba in Transition, Volume 2—Papers and Proceedings of the Second Annual Meeting of the Association for the Study of the Cuban Economy,* pp. 327-342. Miami: Florida International University.

"Estudio para utilizar suelos con salinidad." 1991. *Trabajadores* (15 July) 12.

Farah, Douglas. 1992. "Cubans Are Feeling Unempowered." *The Washington Post* (21 December) A15.

French, Howard. 1993. "Cuba's Ills Encroach on Health." *The New York Times* (16 July) A3.

Gersper, Paul L., Carmen S. Rodríguez-Barbosa, and Laura F. Orlando. 1993. "Soil Conservation in Cuba: A Key to the New Model for Agriculture." *Agriculture and Human Values* 10:3 (Summer) 16-23.

Inter-American Dialogue. 1995. *The Environment in U.S.-Cuban Relations: Opportunities for Cooperation,* Washington.

Johnson, Tim. 1993. "Crisis cubana cobra alto precio a ancianos." *El Nuevo Herald* (12 July) 1A, 5A.

Knox, Paul. 1995. "Sherritt Breathes Life Into Cuba Mine," *The Globe and Mail* (31 July).

McGeary, Johanna, and Cathy Booth. 1993. "Cuba Alone." *Time* (6 December) 42-54.

Mesa-Lago, Carmelo. 1994. *Are Economic Reforms Propelling Cuba to the Market?* Coral Gables: North-South Center, University of Miami.

National Public Radio. 1995. Broadcast of "All Things Considered," (30 May).

"Nickel Plant Said to Pollute Sea with Metals, Acids." 1994. Havana Prensa Latina (9 December), as reproduced in *FBIS-LAT-94-238* (12 December) 15.

Norniella, José M. 1982. "Contará la fábrica de cemento de Nuevitas para 1985, con tres electrofiltros que evitarán el escape de polvo a la atmosfera," *Granma* (27 October) 3.

Oro, José R. 1992. *The Poisoning of Paradise: The Environmental Crisis in Cuba.* Miami: The Endowment for Cuban American Studies.

Palazuelos Barrios, Raúl. 1990a. "Cuatro hitos de una rehabilitación industrial," *Granma* (12 April) 1-2.

Palazuelos Barrios, Raúl. 1990b. "Avanza rehabilitación de la primera línea de la René Arcay," *Granma* (22 August) 2.

Pearce, David W. and Jeremy J. Wardford. 1993. *World Without End: Economics, Environment, and Sustainable Development*, Oxford University Press (for The World Bank).

Pérez-López, Jorge F. 1991a. "Cuba's Transition to Market-Based Energy Prices." In *Cuba in Transition, Volume 1—Papers and Proceedings of the Third Annual Meeting of the Association for the Study of the Cuban Economy*, pp. 221-241. Miami: Florida International University.

_____. 1991b. The Economics of Cuban Sugar. Pittsburgh: University of Pittsburgh Press.

_____. 1995. "Castro Tries Survival Strategy." Transition 6:3 (March) 11-14.

Roca, Sergio. 1994. "Reflections on Economic Policy: Cuba's Food Program." In *Cuba at a Crossroads: Politics and Economics After the Fourth Party Congress*, pp. 94-117. Gainesville: University Press of Florida.

Rosset, Peter, and Medea Benjamin. 1994a. "Cuba's Nationwide Conversion to Organic Agriculture." *Capitalism, Nature, Socialism* 5:3 (September) 79-97.

_____. 1994b. *The Greening of the Revolution: Cuba's Experiment with Organic Agriculture.* Melbourne: Ocean Press.

Sáez, Héctor R. 1994. "The Environmental Consequences of Agricultural Development in Cuba," paper presented to the XVIII International Congress of the Latin American Studies Association, 10-12 March.

Schlachter, Alexis. 1990. "Analizán contaminación marina en zonas de Cuba," *Granma* (22 June) 2.

Solano, Rafael. 1995. "Catástrofe del ecosistema cubano." *El Nuevo Herald* (22 April) 15A.

Solares, Andrés J. 1994. "Situación del medio ambiente en Cuba, in Colegio de Ingenieros Agrónomos y Azucareros, *Desarrollo Agrícola en Cuba*, Vol. II, Miami.

Stix, Gary. 1995. "Ban That Embargo." *Scientific American* 272:3 (March) 32-34.

"U.S. Blockade Causes Significant Economic Losses in 1994. 1995. *FBIS-LAT-95-141*, 3-4.

Vandermeer, John, Judith Carney, Paul Gesper, Ivette Perfecto, and Peter Rosset. 1993. "Cuba and the Dilemma of Modern Agriculture." *Agriculture and Human Values* 10:3 (Summer) 3-8.

Whitefield, Mimi. 1990. "Cuba admite problemas con petróleo." *El Nuevo Herald* (20 June) 1A, 5A.

_____. 1993. "Blackouts Increase Miseries for Cubans." *The Miami Herald* (11 August) 6A.

MORE ON THE STATISTICAL COMPARISON OF CUBAN SOCIOECONOMIC DEVELOPMENT

Jorge Luis Romeu[1]

To the many generations of Cubans, who created our Nation

PROBLEM STATEMENT

A nation's socioeconomic development, as its human rights situation, is a multidimensional problem. This occurs because many factors (e.g. health, education, communication facilities, individual consumption) have to be taken into consideration, thus defining a p-dimensional vector: $X=(X_1,...,X_p)$. Comparing socioeconomic data thus becomes a difficult problem. First, very seldom if ever, we find that the socioeconomic situation of a given country (say X), completely dominates that of another (say Y), i.e. $X_i > Y_i$, $I = 1,...,p$. Hence, assessments and comparisons are only possible through a process of dimension reduction, i.e. through the evaluation of a function:

$$f(X) = \sum \alpha_i g_i(X_i) + \alpha_o g_o(X_1,...,X_p)$$

where the α_i's are weights and the g_i's are (possibly non-linear) functions with g_o to collect all possible interactions.

A serious drawback occurs because of the arbitrary way these weights and functions are defined. For, the socioeconomic factors (X_i, $I = 1,...,p$), their weights (α_i, $I = 1,...,p$) and the specific functional forms (linear, non linear, increasing, decreasing) of the g_i's, are often selected to reflect the analyst philosophies and not by scientific criteria. This is often why, and based on the same data, conflicting results are obtained by analysts that hold conflicting political philosophies (and Cuba is a blatant example).

Statistical Problems

In addition to the above described human bias, there are several, non trivial statistical design problems that also affect the analyses. For, a country's population is heterogeneous and its subpopulations are affected differently by different socioeconomic policies. Therefore, by analyzing the effects of selected variables in specific subpopulations that are particularly affected by them (say health care advances in historically marginalized minority groups or censorship techniques in intellectual milieus), the analyst can distortion the comparison results. For example, one would be forced to trade-off given percentages of decrease in rural infant mortality vis-a-vis a decrease in freedom of speech, locomotion and thought among the intellectuals and middle classes.

To circumvent bias in variable and weigh selection of the dimension reduction process, some analysts have suggested using index numbers. For example, one

1. Many friends and colleagues have contributed to our research in various ways throughout time. In particular we acknowledge our discussant, Dr. A. Lago, President of ASCE; Mr. J. F. Alonso, also of ASCE, who facilitated us some data; Dr. C. Mesa-Lago, of U. Pittsburgh; Mr. S. Lippe, of Radio Marti; Dr. J. Clark, of Miami Dade CC.; Messrs. T. Bonn and L. Styles, of SUNY-Cortland, who facilitated or provided us with useful comments, bibliographic notes and encouragement. Finally, we acknowledge our ASA Human Rights Committee colleagues, Profs. D. Banks, T. Jabine, D. Samuelson and H. Spirer, who have for years collaborated with us or encouraged us in this project.

could use the Consumer Price Index (Connover and Inman, 1982) to compare two nations. But this would imply accepting as the standard the free-enterprise, consumer-oriented philosophy. Any other weighting system (index) would, in the same manner, imply spousing some other economic philosophy. Such choice biases the process of comparing nations with different socioeconomic systems. In addition, indices such as Paasche, Laspeyres, etc., which are based on market consumption and price fluctuations, are worthless in countries (say, like Cuba) where both, prices and (rationed) consumption, are strictly regulated by the government and the black market cannot be monitored.

To make things worse, there are important data collection problems that arise when analyzing and comparing socioeconomic data from different countries. Some problems found by this researcher, when using the U.N. Yearbooks and Cuban Censuses as sources include: *(i)* different definitions for the same variables (does secondary education include normal or vocational schools?); *(ii)* different units (gross national product, given in domestic currencies); *(iii)* different time periods (results given per year vs. per five years); *(iv)* overlapping periods (data collected from January to January vs. from June to June); *(v)* vanishing/appearing series (cost of living indices); *(vi)* changing bases (index numbers); *(vii)* changing definitions within a series (the value of the monetary unit in which (say exports) are reported, fluctuates from year to year); and *(viii)* biased, incomplete or revised data, are just a few problems.

Finally, there are important effects from certain concomitant variables that are commonly left out of the analysis of socioeconomic data. And these can seriously affect the problem at hand. They include: *(i)* the status of any pre-existing infrastructure (for it is not the same to increase literacy by 20 % when the starting level was 10 %, than when it was 75 %); *(ii)* the (S-curve) growth effect (for there is a steeper rate of growth in the middle of any process, when conditions have been established and needs have been discovered, than at its start or end); *(iii)* the saturation effect (for there are just so much, say miles of road that should be constructed); and *(iv)* policy

trade-offs to be made (20 kilometers more of roads vs. a day care center) in the face of contention for limited resources.

Precisely due to all the above problems, statistics can contribute greatly to the socioeconomic analysis methodology in at least three different ways. First, by raising awareness among both, analysts and the public, to the complexities in such types of comparisons. Then, by providing a scientific framework (statistical thinking and philosophy) where such analyses may be performed in a more unbiased fashion. Finally, by incorporating three of the best statistical tools: *(i)* case/control methodology, *(ii)* longitudinal studies and *(iii)* the use of (historical information as) concomitant variables.

In the present paper we introduce methodology for socioeconomic data analysis that addresses the above discussed concerns and problems. We do so via the examination of a specific example: that of Cuba. We claim that our analysis methodology is of general use and may be easily adapted to other cases. And in order to apply it to the Cuban case, we next give some necessary background information.

Information Use, Abuse, Misuse ...
Throughout the last 36 years, the Cuban government and many of its sympathizers have (and this has also been singled out before, e.g. Eberstadt (1986) and Díaz-Briquets (1986)) actively portrayed a pre-1959 Cuba far worse than it actually was. As a result, the undeniable (differential) increments that (say in education and health) Cuba has achieved, have been unduly magnified, in a similar way as it occurs when a bar chart is sliced or the scatter plot's axes are distorted. Such misuse of statistics is not exclusive of governments nor of politics, but does lie at the core of the socioeconomic comparison problem.

For example, the Cuban government statistics always ignore how, in the 1953 census (taken only five years before Castro came to power) there were almost 6000 physicians in Cuba (a ratio of one physician for every 1000 inhabitants). And how nation-wide and inexpensive medical cooperatives (models for current American HMO's) covered a big segment of the Cuban population. Both of these indicators were (at the time and even today) among the highest in Latin America, with Chile, Uruguay and Argentina. Also, how Cuban industrial output in 1953-1957 grew 24 %, or 4.8 % annually (Mesa-Lago 1981, p. 57). In 1951-1958 there was a surplus trade balance of 420 million dollars (p. 63). And the housing gap was being reduced, in the period of 1945-57 at a rate of 7 % annually (p.70).

Another example is provided in Castro's 1953 speech "La Historia me Absolverá." There, Castro stated that there were 700,000 unemployed in Cuba, when the 1953 Census gave only 173,811 unemployed and a total of 266,572, at all other levels of underemployment. Also, the Cuban government reminds us that the 1961 literacy campaign taught "one million Cubans" to read and write. But it does not say that there were over four million adults already literate, nor that Cuba's literacy rate was 73 %, among the highest in Latin America at the time.

Also, comparisons are taken out of context. For example, current Cuban achievements in health and education are either compared with levels of 36 years ago or with poorly chosen countries (controls) such as Guatemala or Nicaragua. Finally, growth rates of the variables under comparison are seldom analyzed.

Paper's Objectives

We aim to show (i) that pre-Castro's Cuba was hardly the backward country some like to imagine -but one that had laid the socioeconomic infrastructure for Cuba's current achievements. (ii) That the "differential increment" (used in this paper as the difference between the levels attained by Cuba and other comparable sister countries in Latin America) in health and education, are not as wide as they are usually assessed. For, these last 30 years have been of large socioeconomic development everywhere, particularly in Latin America. (iii) We will establish some of these "differential increments" by comparing Cuban growth rates with those of the other three control countries. (iv) We will discuss the social costs incurred in obtaining these differential increments and show how they are higher than usually depicted. Finally, (v) in the process of establishing the above objectives, we will demonstrate our methodology of analysis.

We will compare socioeconomic data from two, adjacent, 30-year periods (before and during Castro) obtained from Cuba and from three other countries used as "controls". In the next section we first compare and discuss data from the 1930's to the 1950's, then overview some of Cuba's political, economic and social problems in the 1959-1990 period and compare Cuba's growth rate with that of the other three countries (controls), during this latter period. Finally we summarize our results and give some general conclusions.

DATA ANALYSIS

We now present socioeconomic data from Cuba (used as case) and three other comparison countries (used as controls): Chile, Costa Rica used as and Mexico. These four Latin American countries have a common historical, economic and social background. Chile is by far the closest match. Even though it is larger in territory, Chile has vast, thinly inhabited (desert and frigid) regions. Its population is comparable to that of pre/post revolutionary Cuba, as is the racial composition. Chile's levels of education and other socioeconomic variables are also close. Mexico is larger, while Costa Rica is smaller, than Cuba in area and population. But the Mexican economic system has some similarities with that of post-revolutionary Cuba. And both colonial histories have many common points (it is said that Spain trained its Mexican Viceroys as Cuban Governor Generals). And Costa Rica, even though it is smaller than Cuba in size and population, has also attained high socioeconomic standards. Mexico had for many years a state-oriented economy and quite singular political party system. Costa Rica, in turn, has had a long-standing pluralistic one. And Chile has experimented, both, pluralistic and authoritarian regimes in the recent past. Cuba has had a hard line Marxist dictatorship and a complete state-oriented economy for the past thirty six years (political systems determine the socioeconomic development).

Therefore, in the same spirit of using two siblings or twins to examine the effects of a treatment versus a control, we are taking these three comparison or control countries. Through them, we examine the effect of Cuba's socioeconomic system. Additional discussion about the reasons for the selection of these specific countries to be used as comparison controls, of these socioeconomic indicators as variables and of this case/control methodology, can be found in Romeu (1993 and 1994). This paper continues the research started there and in Romeu et al. (1992).

The 1930 to 1959 Period

In Table 1, we present data from *The Statesman Yearbook* (1929). The selected variables provide a snapshot of several economic, political and social conditions in these four countries, during the mid 1920's.

Table 1. Socioeconomic Indicators; Mid-1920's.

Variables	Cuba	Chile	Costa Rica	Mexico
1	3.57	3.75	0.45	14.9
2	31.05	4.9	20.5	19.7
3	0.139	0.133	0.098	0.084
4	$2.05_{e\text{-}3}$	$2.88_{e\text{-}3}$	$3.57_{e\text{-}3}$	n/a
5	1.337	0.511	0.919	0.375
6	$2.34_{e\text{-}2}$	$4.66_{e\text{-}2}$	$0.56_{e\text{-}2}$	n/a
7	$6.84_{e\text{-}2}$	$1.87_{e\text{-}2}$	$1.79_{e\text{-}2}$	$2.43_{e\text{-}2}$
8	4.84	0.185	0.060	0.059
9	$2.21_{e\text{-}2}$	$2.60_{e\text{-}2}$	$7.18_{e\text{-}2}$	$0.44._{e\text{-}2}$

These variables are: total population (1), in millions; and population density (2), per square kilometer; primary students (3), teachers (4); and cattle (5), in per capita; miles of paved roads (6), rail roads (7), and telegraphs (8), per square km.; and number of post offices (9), also per capita.

Notice the large similarities between Chile and Cuba. Mexico and Costa Rica are, in this epoch, further behind in socioeconomic development. They will be used to compare development growth level at later dates. In particular, notice how Chile and Cuba, with similar population sizes, also had similar coefficients for primary teachers and students and for post offices. These signal out similar levels of education and social interaction. A snapshot description as that of Table 1 is insufficient to characterize a socioeco-

nomic process. We need the time series development data for the case (Cuba), as well as for the *controls* (Chile, Costa Rica and Mexico).

This is shown in Table 2, taken at three times: circa 1938, 1948 and 1958, respectively. The variables selected are: population density (1); infant mortality (2); energy (3); primary students (4) per capita; and number of radio receivers (5) per thousand inhabitants. They reflect health, education and nutrition conditions, and are taken from the corresponding U.N. Yearbooks.

Table 2. Pre-1959 Longitudinal Comparison

Variables	Chile	Costa Rica	Cuba	Mexico
1-c.38	6.41	11.29	38.1	9.51
1-c.48	7.7	15.23	45.9	12.61
1-c.58	9.84	21.1	56.5	16.43
2-c.38	235.7	123.1	83.0	128.0
2-c.48	160.4	93.3	n/a	99.7
2-c.58	126.8	89.0	34.7	80.8
3-c.38	0.67	0.17	0.34	0.44
3-c.48	0.76	0.22	0.47	0.61
3-c.58	0.80	0.26	0.93	0.75
4-c.48	$13.1_{e\text{-}2}$	$14.4_{e\text{-}2}$	$10.7_{e\text{-}2}$	$11.6_{e\text{-}2}$
4-c.58	$13.8_{e\text{-}2}$	$15.6_{e\text{-}2}$	$10.8_{e\text{-}2}$	$14.7_{e\text{-}2}$
5-c.38	$3.1_{e\text{-}2}$	n/a	$3.4_{e\text{-}2}$	$1.9_{e\text{-}2}$
5-c.48	$9.6_{e\text{-}2}$	$2.9_{e\text{-}2}$	$10.9_{e\text{-}2}$	$3.0_{e\text{-}2}$
5-c.58	$8.9_{e\text{-}2}$	$7.0_{e\text{-}2}$	$17.0_{e\text{-}2}$	$7.7_{e\text{-}2}$

Notice, for example, how Mexico doubled its population in the 30 years elapsed, while the other three increased it only by half. On the other hand, Cuba halved its infant mortality rate, from a 1938 level comparable to that of 1958 for the three controls (showing how Cuba was historically ahead of most Latin American countries in health care). In levels of energy, pre-revolutionary Cuba came from behind with respect to both, Mexico and Chile, and surpassed them by almost tripling its energy consumption in these 30 years. In (primary) education Mexico made the most significant gains while the others remained at constant levels (Cuba lagging somewhat behind). In number of radios (which reflect consumerism as well as level of information and standard of living) Cuba was by far the country with the highest levels. Finally, it is worth noticing how, in 1950, the illiteracy rates were: Costa Rica (20.6 %); Chile (19.8 %); Cuba (22.1 %) and Mexico (43.2 %).

Cuban Model Implementation Cost Trade-Offs

We now analyze and compare Cuban data before and after 1959. They illustrate some often overlooked social costs associated with the implementation of the current Cuban socioeconomic model.

Results from the 1953, 1971 and 1980 censuses yield that there were, respectively, 8.8 %, 87 % and 93 % of government employees in the work force. Private workers reported in 1962 were 740,000 but only 175,000 in 1978 (while the population grew from 6 to 8 million (M) inhabitants). In the area of housing, the 1980 Census reports that 21 % of the units that existed in that year were built between 1946 and 1958 (when population was 6 M). It also reports that 22 % of the units were built in a comparable period of 1959 to 1970 (when technology was far more advanced and population was 8 M). In the 1953 Census, there were 1.2 M. housing units for 5.9 M people. In the 1980 census there were 2.3 M units reported for 9.7 M people. The growth in housing units has not kept pace with population growth; the housing problem remains on top of

Cuba's priority list as attested by the fact that the "extended" family nucleus, defined in the 1980 census as "couples with their children and other relatives" (in-laws, grand children, cousins, nephews, grand parents) constituted 32.5 % of the units. During this period, private construction was banned and only the government built new housing units. The 1953 Census reports 72 % of whites, 11 % black and 15 % mixed race. In 1980 the corresponding census results are 66 %, 12 % and 21 %.

In the realm of public education, in 1953 there were 73 % of 14 year old or above who could read and write. This figure went up to about 95 % after mas-

sive literacy campaigns in the early 60's. The University of Havana (the largest of pre-revolutionary Cuba's three public universities) had 25,000 students and 2,500 professors in 1956; it decreased to 20,500 students and 1990 professors in 1962 (and lower yet in 1965) due to massive, politically-motivated, faculty and student purges in the early 1960's (e.g. this researcher was expelled from the University of Havana in 1965, along with hundreds of others, and then sent for two years to the UMAP Labor Camps, with thousands of others). After 1970 large increases in an extremely docile student population have been achieved (e.g. 256 thousand, third cycle students in 1986). In the editorial field, for example, over ten thousand titles were published between 1975 and 1985. But, of these, only 7 dealt with religion or theology, in a country that, in 1956, had 80 % self-avowed Catholics and 8 % Protestants (Romeu et al, 1992).

Internal migration is constrained because the government controls both housing and ration cards. The 1980 Census reports a general growth, among the 14 provincial capitals, of 17 % (the smallest of which is Matanzas with 14.5 %). However, Havana shows only 7.7 % growth, half as much as that of any other large city. Emigration is also severely controlled by the government. In spite of this, 10 % of Cuba's population has gone into exile since 1960. Most recently, over 120,000 left during the 1980 Mariel Boatlift and 35,000 during the 1994 Raft Exodus. Among these exiles there are tens of thousands of university professionals, administrators and technicians, forever lost to contributing toward Cuba's advance.

Finally, tens of thousands of Cuban men and women have been incarcerated and several thousand have been executed by the government or have perished trying to leave Cuba in rafts. They suffered such fate as a result of the Castro regime's ban on (i) peaceful political activism, (ii) free enterprise, and (iii) free emigration.

On the other hand, in the area of health care (Alonso and Lago, 1994) Cuba went from a life expectancy of 64 years (1960) to 74.2 (1984); from an infant mortality rate of 34.7 per 1000 (1959) to 10.2 (1992);

from 0.93 physicians (1959) to 4.33 (1992); from 0.74 nurses (1959) to 6.83 (1992); from 4.22 hospital beds (1959) to 6.1 (1992), all per 1000 inhabitants. All private health cooperatives and clinics were taken over by the state and half of the 1959 health professionals went into exile.

Finally (Excelsior, 1994), the Cuban Gross Internal Product per capita has continually declined (after having increased steadily from 1980 to 1986). Recent figures show these decrease as: 1,116 (1988) to 1050 (1989), to 1000 (1990), and to 879 (1991) M pesos.

However, these statistics cannot be assessed in isolation. In the next section they are compared with similar ones obtained from the three controls, during these same years.

Comparing the 1959-1990 Period

Most indicators for the 1928-1958 period show how Cuba was a rapidly developing nation. For example, standard of living and health indicators such as cars, radios, TV, roads and life expectancy, were going up, while negative indicators such as infant mortality were going down. In addition, Cuban indicators were significantly better than those of the three other comparison or control countries. It could be reasonably be expected that such situation would continue under any other government. And it would be interesting to compare Cuban long term forecasts based on the 30-year period growth of 1928-1958, with the Cuban achievements of the 1990's. The difference between the two results could be attributed to the effects of the Marxist Cuban regime on Cuba's socioeconomic development.

However, this is a highly controversial approach and we will not pursue it further. Instead, we will use the levels of the three above selected comparison countries, used as *controls*, whose 1928-1958 growth rates were at par or below those of Cuba, for the same period. And we will use them to assess the present Cuban achievements with what they could presumably have been, using the old development model. The difference would, then, provide the *differential increments* we are looking for.

Therefore, paralleling the above section, we present (in Table 3) a longitudinal study and (in Table 4) a final snapshot of the socioeconomic conditions of the four countries under comparison.

In Table 3 we present population density (1); infant mortality (2); female life expectancy (3); energy consumption (4) and primary students (5) per capita, and radio receivers, per thousands. They are taken at several points in time in the past twenty years.

Table 3. **Post-1959 Longitudinal Comparison**

Variables	Chile	Costa Rica	Cuba	Mexico
1-1970	13.2	34.1	73.3	24.9
1-1980	14.9	44.0	86.3	36.5
1-1990	17.7	58.7	92.6	43.7
2-1980	47	30	22	58
2-1990	18	16	15	41
3-1980	70.6	73.1	74.8	68.4
3-1990	75.1	77.7	77.0	72.1
4-1970	86	67	74	66
4-1980	135	145	150	155
4-1986	170	193	200	221
5-1975	22.4_e-2	18.3_e-2	19.2-2	19.0_e-2
5-1980	19.7_e-2	15.5_e-2	14.8_e-2	20.4_e-2
5-1989	15.1_e-2	14.1_e-2	8.3_e-2	16.8_e-2
6-1975	164	77	194	111
6-1985	330	246	326	189
6-1990	340	259	343	242

In Table 3, we see how Cuba and Chile have contained their population growth, an indicator of social advance, as opposed to Mexico (who has only slowed it). Next, we see how Chile and Costa Rica have gone from a level of infant mortality much higher than Cuba, to one comparable to it. Mexico still laggs behind in this indicator, having also made big advances. In life expectancy, however, all three control countries have attained much larger levels, particularly Costa Rica has matched those of Cuba. These two health indicators signal out how there have also been strong improvements throughout Latin America. Also, they show how these other countries have achieved a larger growth rate. It is then possible to conjecture whether Cuba's large advances in health care would have been obtained anyway, especially when Cuba already had, in the mid 1950's, high health standards and a long health care tradition.

In energy consumption (indicator of industrial development and of standard of living) Costa Rica has maintained a growth level similar to that of Cuba. Mexico has had a larger growth rate, but it is known how Mexico has had an industrial awakening in the last fifteen years. Chile has had a smaller growth rate than Cuba. Primary students have decreased as a percentage of the general population. But this has been a world phenomenon as a whole. Higher and technical education continue to be Cuba's showcase. But the three controls are rapidly closing the gap. Finally, number of radio receivers is similar in Cuba and Chile. Costa Rica and Mexico are lagging behind, but have made big increases (having started from lower levels). Table 3 allows us to compare, not only the *level* attained by each country, but also its growth rate. Mexico is still the one with the highest population growth and lower socioeconomic indices, among these four. But the gap (from 1930) has shrunk. Chile, Costa Rica and Cuba, starting from different levels (Cuba generally ahead), have practically closed the gap.

Table 4 shows the 1990 (U.N. Yearbook) statistics on selected socioeconomic variables. Notice how close indicators from Cuba, Chile and Costa Rica now are. Mexico has closed the gap, too. This shows that significant socioeconomic advances have been achieved by all countries in the entire region, during the last thirty years, independent of the type of socioeconomic system that prevails in each country.

From Table 4 we notice how Chile and Costa Rica have also reduced their illiteracy rate to single digits. Mexico has reduced it from 44 % to 17 %, which denotes a significant effort. With regard to intake of calories and proteins (nutrition indicators) Cuba is still about 10 % above the three comparison or control countries in the former and about the same in the latter. However (Gordon 1983) the high stan-

Table 4. Socioeconomic Indicators c. 1990

Variables	Chile	Costa Rica	Cuba	Mexico
Illiteracy	8.9	7.4	3.8	17.0
Infant Mort	17.1	13.9	11.1	43.0
EMaleLife	68.1	72.4	72.6	62.1
EFemLife	75.1	77.0	76.1	66.0
Calories	2480	2711	3153	2986
Proteins	69.6	64	71.6	81.5
Cement	2115	n/a	3696	24683
Energy	1270	602	1461	1788
Phones	8.3	14.9	5.8	11.8
TV Sets	201	136	203	127
Radios	340	259	343	242
Newspapers	47	6	15	216
Students-1	1991	422	885	14508
Students-2	742	123	1073	6704
Population	13.1	3.0	10.6	86.2

dards of nutrition of pre-revolutionary Cuba are well known, so this is no surprise: Cuba had an original headstart. In energy consumption, basis of an industrial policy, Cuba fares between Mexico and Chile (Costa Rica, mainly agricultural and rural, sags way behind). Finally in consumer indicators (phones, TV, radios). Cuban levels of yester years have been surpassed or attained by the control countries. Given Cuba's higher levels in the 1950's, we conclude that a higher growth rate was achieved by the three control nations, with regards to standards of living.

CONCLUSIONS

In the previous sections we proposed four objectives. We now review them under the light of the data presented in Table 1 through Table 4. We have analyzed them using the proposed methodology (case/control, time series and concomitant information). Providing the necessary caveats (regarding variable and weight selection) we conclude the following:

Tables 1 and 2 show how Cuba was, before 1959, a rapidly (but unevenly) developing country. Especially so in the areas of health, education and individual consumption. Cuba's main problem during the 1950's was, precisely, how to extend these rapid development gains to all social/geographical sections of the country.

Table 3 shows how the past 30 years have been ones of intense development, not only in Cuba but in all Latin America. And how the three countries selected as control have also grown, from levels usually *below* those of Cuba, to levels either *close* to that of Cuba or *higher*. The **differential increments**, or differences between these levels, can then be estimated from Table 4.

For example, we now calculate the differential increment with respect to Costa Rica, for the variable *infant mortality*. This **differential** is of 2.8 (per 000's). And with respect to illiteracy, it is of 3.6 %. These values are obtained assuming that Cuba would have attained, at least, the illiteracy rate of Costa Rica (7.4 %) under the pre-revolutionary model, instead of its own 3.8 %.

This premise is based on the fact that, with the previous model, Cuba was always at par or above Costa Rica in educational indicators. Therefore, any difference between the two may be attributed to the effect of the current Cuban socioeconomic development model and would constitute an estimate of the **differential** for the variable *eradication of illiteracy*. All other differentials are obtained in a similar way.

Another approach to obtaining estimates of the **differential increments** of a given variable, consists of using the growth rates of the three control countries and applying them to the Cuban data, for forecasting. Then, the difference between the levels forecasted in this way and the actual Cuban levels would provide an estimate of such *differential*.

For illustration, we present, in Table 5, the indices of total production of electricity for 1970-1986, taken from the *Statistical Abstract of Latin America*. The year 1975 corresponds to 100 %. We have included the slope and Index of Fit (IOF) of a simple linear regression obtained from these data. First, they were obtained separately for each country and then for the combined three controls. The average values per year are also given. The combined regression corresponds to all of the (3x4=12) control countries' data points.

We take the slope from the combined regression (8.1) as the estimate of the general group growth in the variable electric energy. We then compare it with the (growth) slope for Cuba alone (7.7). Using the slope of the combined data, for the Cuban electric growth data, one can obtain a higher index for the 1985 index of production of electricity. However, notice that a confidence interval for the *combined* slope will include the individual Cuba slope. Therefore, we can say that the Cuban growth in production of electricity, during this time, in not significantly different than the growth of the combined three control countries, none of which has followed the Cuban socioeconomic development model. Even more, if we take Chile out of this comparison, Cuba's growth would be significantly smaller.

This supports our statement that growth, in general, has been such that other countries with different socioeconomic systems have caught up with Cuba's rates of growth. This result questions the statements of some, in the sense that the only way to obtain Cuba's achievements in health and education was through the pains suffered during the revolution.

Table 5.   Index of Total Electricity Production: 1975=100 %

Countries	1970	1975	1980	1985	Slope	IOF
Chile	86	100	135	161	5.2	97
Costa Rica	67	100	202	185	901	81
Cuba	74	100	150	185	7.7	98
Mexico	66	100	155	216	10.1	98
Average	73	100	164	187	8.1	97

At present, this research is at the stage of obtaining such *differential increment* estimates for a number of variables from the data base. Toward this and other related objectives, a proposal to NEH has been written and submitted and is pending evaluation.

Finally, some social costs of implementing the Post 1959 Cuban socioeconomic model have also been discussed. Whether the differential increments obtained by Cuba, in health care and education, justify or not such costs depends on each analyst's philosophy and ideology. Statistics does its job by signaling out this crucial fact in an unambiguous way.

REFERENCES

Alonso, J. F. and A. Lago. "A First Approximation Design of the Social Safety Net of a Democratic Cuba." *Cuba in Transition Volume 4* (Washington, 1994).

Connover, W. and R. Inman. *Introduction to Business Statistics.* Wiley, 1982.

Cuban Census of 1953, 1971 and 1980.

Díaz-Briquets, S. "How to Figure Out Cuba: Development Ideology and Mortality." *Caribbean Review* (Spring 1986).

Eberstadt, N. "Literacy and Health: The Cuban Model." *Caribbean Review,* Vol. 5 (Spring 1986}.

Excelsior Newspaper (Mexico City). May 6, 1994; Economic Section.

Gordon, A. "The Nutriture of Cubans: Historical Perspective and Nutritional Analysis." *Cuban Studies/Estudios Cubanos,* Vol. 13, No. 2 (Summer 1983).

Mesa-Lago, C. *Cuba in the 1970's.* University of New Mexico Press, 1987.

Mesa-Lago, C. *The Economy of Socialist Cuba: A Two-Decade Appraisal.* University of New Mexico Press, 1981.

Mesa-Lago, C., ed. *Revolutionary Change in Cuba.* University of Pittsburgh Press. 1971.

Romeu, J. L., Samuelson, D. and H. Spirer, "An Assessment of the Human Rights Situation in Cuba."" *Proceedings of the 1992 Social Statistics* (ASA).

Romeu, J. L. "Statistical Thinking Can Enhance Cuban Human Rights Assessments." *Proceedings of the 1993 Social Statistics* (ASA).

Romeu, J. L. "A Statistical Comparison of Cuban Socioeconomic Development." *Proceedings of the 1994 Social Statistics* (ASA).

The Statesman Yearbook. 1929.

Statistical Abstract of Latin America. Vol. 28.

U.N. Yearbook. Vols. 1948 to 1993.

COSTO SOCIOLÓGICO Y PSICOLÓGICO
DE LOS LOGROS DE LA REVOLUCIÓN CUBANA

Maida Donate Armada

Según el diccionario *logro* es la acción de alcanzar, conseguir algo. La idea de *logro* siempre expresa sentido positivo y se relaciona con desarrollo y evolución. Cuando afirmamos que hemos logrado algo establecemos una comparación con un determinado punto de partida, el resultado de esa comparación debe ser positivo para que se pueda considerar *logro*.

A medida que crece el consenso nacional e internacional sobre la necesidad del cambio político y económico en Cuba, el gobierno cubano y diferentes políticos e intelectuales no cubanos intentan justificar la lentitud de las medidas económicas y el no realizar cambios políticos, con el pretexto de salvaguardar los *logros* de la revolución, en particular el desarrollo alcanzado en la educación y la salud.

Mucho se ha hablado de los *logros* sociales de lag revolución cubana, pero poco se ha dicho del punto de partida socioeconómico que permitió al gobierno liderado por Fidel Castro desarrollar tales acciones sociales.

En este trabajo analizo cuatro de los llamados *logros* de la revolución: la educación, la salud, el pleno empleo y la liberación de la mujer. Estos temas han estado presentes desde el primer momento en el discurso socio-político cubano y en los últimos treinta seis años han alcanzado determinado desarrollo a nivel internacional.

En función de organizar las ideas me he planteado las siguientes preguntas. En materia de educación, salud, empleo y situación de la mujer en Cuba:

- ¿Qué recursos encontró en 1959 y qué tiempo demoró el gobierno revolucionario para activar esos recursos y poner en marcha las nuevas acciones sociales?

- ¿Cuáles han sido los principales resultados alcanzados por esas acciones hasta el presente?

- ¿Cuál es el balance sociológico y psicológico de las acciones sociales y políticas ejecutadas?

Para el análisis utilizo datos de diferentes investigaciones realizadas por mi en Cuba entre 1970 y 1993, y lo complemento con bibliografía sobre Cuba escrita por especialistas residentes en el extranjero.

EDUCACION

Históricamente la educación en Cuba ha tenido un desarrollo acelerado. Entre mayo de 1902 y enero de 1959 se alcanzaron en este campo, resultados importantes y significativos que fueron la base de los cambios posteriores:

El 80,0% de la población mayor de 6 años de edad estaba escolarizada. El 20,0% que no lo estaba, se concentraba en las zonas rurales.

- En 1953, el 57.0% de la población total de Cuba era urbana y el 43,0% rural.

- La constitución reconocía la enseñanza laica y obligatoria hasta el sexto grado, para los niños de 6 a 14 años. La escuela pública era gratuita. En la escuela primaria, además de las asignaturas generales, se impartía educación física, música y artes manuales por maestros debidamente preparados.

- Se había logrado sentar las bases para la enseñanza técnica especializada, que se encontraba en proceso de expansión y desarrollo.

- Existían tres universidades oficiales: la hoy bicentenaria Universidad de La Habana y otras dos nuevas, la Universidad de Oriente y la Universidad de Las Villas. Se estudiaban las carreras tradicionales de Ciencias, Humanidades, Derecho, Medicina, Farmacia, Odontología, Arquitectura, Ingeniería Eléctrica y Civil, Agricultura, Pedagogía, Contador Público, Agronomía, Veterinaria y otras.

En la Universidad de Oriente y en la Universidad de Las Villas, se cursaban otros estudios de mayor actualización: Economía, Química Industrial, Ingeniería Mecánica, Minería, etcétera.

- En el contexto del sistema, con sus tipos y niveles de educación, florecía paralelamente la escuela privada.

- El sistema de formación de maestros estaba organizado en las Escuelas Normales para Maestros, en correspondencia con la división política administrativa del país. La totalidad de los maestros estaban titulados y organizados en Colegios que los representaban como grupo social activo en la vida pública de la nación.

- La manera de acceder a una plaza de maestro en la enseñanza pública, era a través de oposiciones que estaban reglamentadas. En el escalafón para acceder a las aulas, se contemplaba al maestro rural y la atención a las zonas rurales.

- Los maestros y pedagogos cubanos eran uno de los sectores sociales más activos políticamente. Jugaron un papel trascendente en la huelga general de 1935 y estuvieron presentes como fuerza cívica influyente en los momentos históricos en que había que defender los derechos civiles y constitucionales de los cubanos. Enseñaban a pensar.

Si tenemos en cuenta que estamos hablando de una república que sólo tenía cincuenta y nueve años de vida socio-política independiente, y algo menos de seis millones de habitantes, se puede concluir que la situación de la educación en Cuba al momento del arribo al poder de la revolución, distaba mucho de ser caótica ni similar a la situación de otros países de América Latina.

De haber habido otra situación en la educación, no le hubiera sido posible al gobierno revolucionario realizar las primeras acciones de las que tanto se ufana en este campo.

Por ejemplo, las 10.000 nuevas aulas rurales que se crearon con la Ley 561 de setiembre de 1959, fueron ocupadas por maestros normalistas graduados y jóvenes graduados de bachillerato o próximos a concluir estos estudios que habían sido formados antes de enero de 1959.

La creación de esas aulas formaba parte del conjunto de acciones que el magisterio cubano estaba haciendo desde hacía mucho tiempo. No constituyó parte esencial del programa político de Fidel Castro. Fue una acción política que utilizó el terreno abonado por los maestros y pedagogos cubanos, para buscar un efectivismo populista.

La Ley de Nacionalización General de la Enseñanza de 6 de junio de 1961, sólo abolió el derecho a la enseñanza privada, y en consecuencia, la posibilidad de otras maneras de enfocar el proceso educativo. La enseñanza laica, gratuita y como derecho de los cubanos estaba recogida en la Constitución de 1940.

Las dos medidas más trascendentes en las tres últimas décadas en la educación en Cuba: la campaña de alfabetización en 1961 y la reforma universitaria en 1963, se llevaron a cabo con un determinado saldo social positivo, pese a la irracionalidad de los ajustes que exigía Castro, por la profesionalidad de una buena parte del magisterio cubano formado en las décadas anteriores a la revolución.

La campaña de alfabetización se pudo plantear a dos años escasos del triunfo de la revolución, porque la población cubana estaba esencialmente escolarizada. En las estadísticas de la campaña no se ha hecho propaganda a la distribución de los alfabetizados según edad, porque una gran parte de los analfabetos eran personas mayores de 50 años. Para hacer más efectistas los datos, la tasa de analfabetismo a la que se hace referencia corresponde al total de población cubana mayor de 10 años, pero se reporta como referida al total de personas entre 10 y 49 años, según las definiciones internacionales.

La Reforma Universitaria de 1963 amplió el espectro de las ingenierías y sentó las bases para controlar el desarrollo del pensamiento filosófico, político y humanístico en las universidades. Las ciencias sociales y las humanidades, muy poco tiempo después, dejaron de jugar el papel activo que siempre habían jugado en el paisaje intelectual cubano. Se terminó con la autonomía universitaria.

Hay otras cuestiones relacionadas con la educación: los planes de becas, la reestructuración del plan de formación de maestros, las escuelas de enseñanza especial -música, artes plásticas, deportes-, la universalización de la enseñanza universitaria en 1970, el plan estudio-trabajo, que se incluyen en el acápite de los *logros en la educación*, que sólo se mencionan y no se profundizan en el discurso socio-político del gobierno cubano y sus simpatizantes, porque los resultados no son de exhibición y en la práctica han tenido un impacto muy fuerte en la desestabilización de la psicología social cotidiana de los cubanos.

El plan nacional de becas comenzó en 1962 después de terminar la campaña de alfabetización. El antecedente directo de ese plan lo encontramos en 1959 en las escuelas para los niños y las jóvenes campesinas que vivían en la Sierra Maestra y se trajeron a estudiar a la ciudad de La Habana. Al poco tiempo se comprobó el populismo de aquella falacia y la irracionalidad de aquella idea.

Al finalizar la campaña de alfabetización se reestructuró el plan de formación de maestros, bajo la dirección de Elena Gil surgieron las escuelas pedagógicas *"Antón Makarenko."* El enfoque filosófico que debían aprender las nuevas generaciones de maestros cubanos era: el mejor sistema de educación es el que se basa en el quebranto de la voluntad del educando, porque el sacrificio, como estilo de vida, es el recuerdo vívido de la verdadera condición humana y el único objetivo del ser social.

Los adolescentes y jóvenes que deseaban estudiar magisterio, debían probar su vocación para el sacrificio y estudiar los tres primeros años de la carrera en condiciones de campamento guerrillero en *Minas del Frío*, zona situada en las montañas de la Sierra Maestra en la región oriental del país. Después, pasar dos en *Topes de Collantes*, en el edificio que en su día fue sanatorio antituberculoso, en medio de la cordillera del Escambray en la región central. Sólo a los que habían pasado satisfactoriamente esos cinco años de privaciones materiales y de lejanía de la familia, se les permitía continuar un año más en *Tarará*, zona residencial de playa al este de La Habana, hasta graduarse. Si por voluntad propia, los alumnos de las escuelas makarenko interrumpían el ciclo una vez admitidos y matriculados, se les consideraba desertores, se dejaba constancia de ello en el expediente escolar y se les tenía en cuenta a la hora de solicitar otros estudios.

Para distinguir a los que eran o habían sido alumnos de ese plan del resto de los maestros que no se habían formado en la "fragua del sacrificio", los estudiantes y graduados de las escuelas makarenko tenían la obligación de ir de uniforme todo el tiempo. La mayoría absoluta de los estudiantes eran del sexo femenino.

Casi desde el principio la revolución abolió la enseñanza de la música, las artes manuales y la educación física en las escuelas primarias. Más tarde, se exigió a los maestros de enseñanza general que dieran clases de educación física. La enseñanza de la música y las artes manuales no se ha sistematizado aun. El sistema no prevé esos conocimientos como parte de la educación general.

Se trata de suplir esta deficiencia con las escuelas de enseñanza especial que libran convocatorias de matrícula muy selectiva. Según las especialidades se determinan las edades de acceso. El profetizar si un niño de siete u ocho años será un eminente músico, bailarín, pintor, etcétera, lo hace un tribunal de profesionales del ramo, ante el cual desfilan durante unos pocos días, aquellos niños cuyos padres se hayan enterado de la convocatoria. Otra limitación para acceder a esas escuelas, es que todas están concentradas en la capital y en algunas de las principales ciudades del país.

La enseñanza de idioma extranjero no se contempla hasta el séptimo grado y en las escuelas de idiomas no se admiten menores de 15 años.

En 1970 no se hicieron los tan anunciados diez millones de toneladas de azúcar. Aquel evidente fracaso económico y político, afectó de manera particular al sistema de educación cubano.

La más dramática de las afectaciones fue el desmantelamiento de la enseñanza politécnica en todo el país. A los estudiantes de las escuelas y de los institutos tecnológicos los movilizaron a cortar caña. En un curso de nueve meses lectivos estaban hasta cuatro cortando caña sin asistir a clases. En julio de 1969 se dio inicio oficial a la zafra de los diez millones, los centros de enseñanza tecnológica cerraron y sus estudiantes estuvieron en los campos de caña los dieciocho meses que duró aquella locura.

Llegó el tiempo de la institucionalización de la revolución, pero, como los *dirigentes* del staff no cumplían los requisitos de instrucción que se estaban planteando para ocupar los cargos de dirección, la solución fue una amnistía de cinco años para que todo aquel que no fuera universitario lograra un título. Bajo el amparo de la Ley de Universalización de la Enseñanza de 1970, la universidad graduó en los cursos para trabajadores a los funcionarios y *dirigentes* de cualquier nivel de dirección, para que las "nuevas medidas de orden" no los afectaran en su status social.

La participación sistemática en jornadas de trabajo voluntario en labores agrícolas que se exige a los cubanos, en especial a los jóvenes, y de manera notable a los capitalinos, son el complemento de la filosofía de la expiación permanente por el hecho ...*de consumir sin gastar esfuerzo físico, lo que otros producen.*(sic)

La idea del plan estudio-trabajo tuvo su génesis en las movilizaciones para la recogida de café en 1960, a las que siguió la institucionalización de la escuela al campo: todos los estudiantes de la enseñanza media, preuniversitaria y técnica-profesional especializada, junto a sus profesores tenían -tienen- que ir cada curso escolar durante un período de tiempo, a trabajar al campo y vivir en campamentos en condiciones de ruralidad.

A principio de los años setenta, la primera ola de la explosión demográfica de los sesenta arribó a la enseñanza secundaria básica, las escuelas que existían no alcanzaban. Por otra parte, las empresas agrícolas justificaban la falta de productividad y eficiencia con la escasez de mano de obra. Coyuntura que aprovechó el gobierno de Fidel Castro para dar otro enfoque al sistema de becas: de la escuela al campo se pasó a las escuelas en el campo. Se construyeron las escuelas en zonas rurales apartadas de los pueblos y principales centros urbanos. Los alumnos de secundaria básica y preuniversitario trabajaban en labores agrícolas o de otra naturaleza en la sesión contraria a la de clases.

En Cuba el acceso a la instrucción no ha significado acceso a la información. El sistema de educación cubano no entrena al educando en la búsqueda de información ni lo adiestra en cómo orientarse para acceder a fuentes de información más variadas y complejas. El fracaso de la revolución en el terreno de la educación se hace manifiesto en la relación instrucción-información.

SALUD

El sistema de salud cubano es reconocido internacionalmente como un sistema de cobertura nacional, integral en el alcance de los servicios, universalmente accesible, evaluado y con participación comunitaria en la movilización de los programas de salud.

Analizando los antecedentes de este resultado en el campo de la salud hallamos que en 1953 los indicadores de salud de Cuba eran de los mejores en América Latina, y la escuela de medicina cubana formaba profesionales de indiscutible calificación, informados y actualizados en los adelantos científicos de su época. La enseñanza de la medicina en Cuba siempre se ha guiado -en la revolución también- por la enseñanza de la medicina en Estados Unidos y Canadá.

En los años 60, cuando emigró gran parte de los médicos cubanos, aquellos que se quedaron en la Isla y habían estudiado medicina antes del triunfo de la revolución, fueron quienes instrumentaron el sistema de salud actual y han sido los profesores de las posteriores generaciones de médicos cubanos. La carrera de medicina no se estudió en los países ex socialistas, los estudios de post grado en el extranjero y los proyectos de investigación médica, se han estado concertando a través de los organismos internacionales, en instituciones de países desarrollados -Francia, Inglaterra, Estados Unidos, Canadá, Suecia.

La enseñanza de la medicina en Cuba mantuvo un alto nivel de calificación hasta que se planteó, en los primeros años de la década de los ochenta, la masificación de la formación de médicos. Fidel Castro tuvo la idea de "exportar" médicos cubanos a países que contrataban y pagaban en dólares los servicios de los especialistas. Justificó esa idea con la idea del médico de la familia, el resultado final ha sido un descenso sensible en la calidad de la formación profesional de los médicos cubanos.

Todos los niveles del sistema nacional de salud cubano no han tenido igual desarrollo. El personal médico -general y especialista- puede calificarse de muy bueno. El personal de enfermería de regular, porque en la selección y el proceso de formación de este personal, no se ha seguido el mismo rigor que en la selección y la formación del personal facultativo.

El personal paramédico puede evaluarse de bueno, por lo general, son graduados de la enseñanza preuniversitaria que quisieron estudiar medicina y por alguna razón no lo pudieron hacer, entonces se vincularon a la salud pública como técnicos en rayos X, laboratoristas, etcétera.

Algo muy diferente sucede con el personal dedicado a los servicios infraestructurales de las instituciones hospitalarias. Se les paga salarios muy bajos, tienen que realizar su trabajo en condiciones muy difíciles, no tienen estabilidad laboral -como promedio están entre uno y tres meses en el puesto de trabajo-, comienzan a trabajar en salud pública como última alternativa, para después trasladarse a otro centro de trabajo. Son los que deben garantizar las condiciones de higiene y limpieza, pero ni ellos ni sus supervisores tienen la suficiente conciencia que de ellos depende, en gran medida, la no proliferación de las infecciones cruzadas que ponen en peligro la vida de los pacientes, tras las más espectaculares actuaciones médicas.

En el panorama de las estadísticas cubanas, las de salud pública son las más confiables y susceptibles de ser comparadas internacionalmente. No por ello dejan de ser manipuladas para resaltar lo que conviene al gobierno cubano.

La *mortalidad infantil*, sin dudas, es la más baja de América Latina -lo era desde 1953- pero hay algunas decisiones a la hora de recoger los datos que ayudan a redondear el número que se exhibe. Por ejemplo, el concepto de nacidos vivos se mueve a discreción del equipo médico: si se sabe que un niño morirá después de nacido, se informa como muerte fetal, aunque técnicamente sea un nacido vivo ...*porque Fidel Castro ha dicho que la tasa de mortalidad infantil tiene que seguir bajando...*

En 1990 el informe anual del Ministerio de Salud Pública, en el capítulo de mortalidad, las *muertes violentas*, aparecen como tercera y única causa de muerte que aumenta la tasa. Bajo este concepto se agrupan los accidentes -de tráfico y otros-, los suicidios, las lesiones autoinflingidas y los homicidios.

Las muertes por accidentes a partir de 1989 han tenido un ascenso consecuencia de la brusca introducción de la bicicleta como medio de transporte cotidiano.

En la década de los setenta, la muerte por suicidio y lesiones autoinfligidas duplicó la tasa. Aunque ha bajado ligeramente, no ha vuelto a presentar los valores anteriores a ese año. Este indicador sí se ha modificado respecto a América Latina, Cuba ha pasado a ser uno de los países del mundo, donde más muertes por suicidio hay. En particular, en el grupo de edad 15-49 años.

El aumento de la demanda del servicio de psiquiatría, del consumo de psicofármacos, del alcoholismo y de las muertes por homicidios, se han declarado datos de *"alta sensibilidad política, utilizables por el enemigo imperialista."*

EMPLEO

En 1958, en Cuba había un 12.5% de desempleo, que representaba alrededor de 700.000 personas sin trabajo. En 1970 las estadísticas censales informan un

1.3% de desempleo. Una reducción tan dramática merece algunas reflexiones.

La creación de puestos de trabajo para eliminar el desempleo fue una medida política que transcendió, irresponsablemente, las posibilidades reales de la economía del país. Muy poco tiempo después, esa solución mágica -la más mágica de todas las adoptadas durante la etapa de la revolución-, se convirtió en un boomerang contra los trabajadores, al erigirse el estado como único y absoluto empleador.

En la trayectoria hacia el *pleno empleo*, desde el punto de vista sociológico, encontramos dos momentos significativos que giran alrededor de la zafra de los diez millones de toneladas de azúcar: primero, las medidas que anunció Castro en el discurso del 13 de marzo de 1968, conocidas como la *ofensiva revolucionaria*, convirtieron en delito punible cualquier vestigio de actividad laboral privada; segundo, en 1969, la *Ley 1231 contra la vagancia*, instituyó el *estado pre-delictivo de vagancia* y estableció cuatro tipos de medidas para sancionar a los varones que estando en edad laboral no establecieran vínculo laboral con el estado, por demás, único empleador posible. Previamente, en 1966, se desarticularon los sindicatos.

La fuerza laboral cubana en 1970, había perdido cualquier posibilidad de actuar. Los mecanismos de control laboral se acabaron de perfilar en el *Código del trabajo* de 1980 -este documento merece ser estudiado en sí mismo, como ejemplo de legislación limitante de los derechos de los trabajadores. Años más tarde, cuando las crisis económicas y la insatisfacción de la población han ido en aumento, se ha denominado este control total sobre los trabajadores *paternalismo de estado*, en un intento de presentar como protección lo que en realidad es represión.

En la práctica el problema del empleo no se ha resuelto. Cada cierto tiempo el gobierno tiene que dar respuesta a situaciones críticas de sobre empleo. El remedio más utilizado ha sido mandar a estudiar a los trabajadores que sobraban en los centros de trabajo. En la mayoría de los casos, los que sobraban oficialmente eran los que de alguna manera entorpecían -o presumiblemente entorpecerían- alguna medida que se quería implantar, como sucedió en el caso de los contables en 1963, cuando la lucha contra el burocratismo, y como está sucediendo ahora en los años 90.

En Cuba, invariablemente, la racionalización de la fuerza de trabajo -variante del despido con prestaciones-, ha respondido más a razones políticas que económicas.

El gobierno cubano se vanagloria de no privar a los trabajadores de sus salarios, aunque cierren los centros de trabajo o se limiten las actividades laborales que venían desempeñando. A los trabajadores cubanos no se les priva del salario porque a nivel de toda la sociedad se deprimen las condiciones de vida, y el trabajo no es medio de satisfacción de las necesidades individuales y familiares.

SITUACION DE LA MUJER

El tema de la mujer como sujeto de derecho ha sido planteado como uno de los *logros* importantes de la revolución cubana.

El análisis retrospectivo de tal afirmación muestra que, desde época tan temprana como 1920, la mujer cubana ha estado en la palestra pública luchando por sus derechos.

Antes de la Constitución de 1940, legislativamente se reconoció a las mujeres el derecho al voto, ocupar cargos públicos, el acceso a la enseñanza universitaria -incluso en carreras como medicina, no comunes en aquel tiempo entre el sexo femenino-, el divorcio era legal y se reconocían los hijos fuera de matrimonio.

En la Asamblea Constituyente de 1940, quedaron refrendados: el derecho de la mujer a igual salario por trabajo igual y el derecho a la protección de la maternidad de las trabajadoras.

Entre 1920 y 1929 se celebraron varios Congresos Nacionales Feministas, en los que participaron mujeres de todas las tendencias políticas, donde se hicieron planteamientos tan trascendentes como el derecho de la mujer a que se le reconociera su participación en la lucha política, y consecuentemente, el estatuto de presa política, si por sus actividades en este campo era objeto de privación de libertad.

Obviamente, el hecho del reconocimiento legal no implica la aplicación en la práctica de la legislación. Pero, sí es un indicador del activismo social y político del grupo para el que se legisla.

En materia legislativa muy poco ha ganado la mujer cubana con la revolución. En la práctica social la discriminación no ha dejado de estar presente.

La liberación de la mujer en Cuba se manifiesta en la incorporación a variopintas actividades extralaborales, de dudosa utilidad individual y social y no en un cambio de los roles en el seno de la familia y de la sociedad. Hecho que puede explicar algunos cambios en las estadísticas femeninas.

Las mujeres cubanas redujeron pronto el promedio de hijos durante su vida fértil. A comienzos de los años cincuenta la tasa de fecundidad ya era baja en el contexto latinoamericano. De 4.0 hijos por mujer entre 1950-1955, se ha pasado a 1.8 hijos por mujer en el período 1990-1995.

A pesar de disponer de métodos anticonceptivos variados, las estadísticas reportan un incremento de la cantidad de abortos a partir de 1975. En 1986 la relación fue de 96.6 abortos por cada 100 partos. En 1991 la relación fue de 78.4 por cada 100 partos.

El divorcio presenta un comportamiento atípico comparado con las estadísticas internacionales, la ruptura del vínculo matrimonial se produce con independencia del tiempo de duración del mismo y de la edad de los cónyuges. En 1990 hubo 37 divorcios por cada 100 matrimonios.

Comparada con América Latina, Cuba exhibe una tasa de actividad femenina -38.2- alta. Sin embargo, esta participación resulta baja en comparación con las tasas que se alcanzaron en los ex países socialistas.

La incorporación laboral de la mujer cubana ha transitado por etapas: 1960-1969, se caracterizó por la masividad de la incorporación, 1970-1974, se produjo un proceso de desincorporación laboral de la mujer, 1975-1989, las mujeres se incorporan al trabajo calificado, 1990 hasta la fecha, con el empeoramiento de las condiciones de vida, las mujeres, al igual que los hombres, se han replanteado la participación en la actividad laboral estatal.

La esperanza de vida de las cubanas ha aumentado de 61.3 años en 1950-1955, a 77.6 años en 1985-1990. Pero, la tercera causa de muerte para las mujeres en edad adulta, es la *muerte violenta* (accidentes, suicidios, lesiones autoinflingidas y homicidios). En 1988 fue la primera causa de muerte en los grupos de edades de 15 a 24 años, con el 64.2% del total de muertes por esa causa, y de 25 a 44 años, con el 72.9% del total.

CONCLUSIONES

A treinta seis años de la toma del poder por el régimen de Castro, el balance del costo sociológico y psicológico de los *logros del socialismo cubano* en la educación, la salud, el empleo y la situación de la mujer, pueden ser resumidos de la manera siguiente:

- En Cuba, la ampliación de la cobertura del sistema de educación a toda la población, no ha significado la posibilidad de acceder a fuentes más amplias de información y ha limitado el desarrollo de las capacidades potenciales de los educandos. Esta limitación se hace más evidente fuera de La Habana y de las principales capitales de provincia.

- La orientación, homogenización y control estatal centralizado de los planes de estudios, han inhibido el papel activo que tiene que jugar el maestro en el proceso educativo, de estimular en sus alumnos el pensamiento creativo, la investigación, la toma de decisión y el asumir la responsabilidad por las decisiones propias.

- El nivel educacional de la fuerza de trabajo cubana no se refleja en el desarrollo socioeconómico del país.

- Los resultados en el campo de la salud evidencian un énfasis en los aspectos curativos de la medicina más que en los preventivos. En sus decisiones el gobierno no ha considerado la influencia de las condiciones materiales de vida en la salud de la población.

- El aumento de las tasas de los accidentes y de los suicidios entre las principales causas de muerte, a partir de la década de los ochenta, es indicativo de alteraciones en la adaptación psico-social en la población cubana, particularmente en el grupo de edad 15-49 años.

- La alta demanda por la población de los servicios psiquiátricos, del consumo de psicofármacos, el incremento del alcoholismo y de la violencia, también están indicando situaciones de adaptación psico-social límites a nivel de toda la sociedad.

- En la práctica, el problema del empleo no se ha solucionado en Cuba. La imagen paternalista que proclama el gobierno cubano, encierra una acción de represión contra los trabajadores, que les inhibe la capacidad de actuar como individuos y no les deja otra opción que la de aceptar las condiciones que le impone el único empleador posible: el estado.

- El estado cubano ha mantenido los salarios a los trabajadores porque a nivel de toda la sociedad, deprime las condiciones de vida y el trabajo no es el principal medio de satisfacción de las necesidades individuales y familiares.

- En las últimas tres décadas la mujer cubana ha ganado muy poco en el terremo legislativo. En la práctica social la discriminación no ha dejado de existir.

- La liberación de la mujer en Cuba se manifiesta en la incorporación a variopintas actividades extralaborales de dudosa utilidad individual y social, y no en un cambio de los roles en el seno de la familia y de la sociedad.

- Algunos indicadores estadísticos muestran modificaciones en el comportamiento de las mujeres cubanas durante las tres últimas décadas. La tasa de divorcios, la reducción de la fecundidad, el uso del aborto como método anticonceptivo, la oscilaciones en la incorporación de la mujer a la actividad laboral y las muertes violentas como tercera causa de muerte y primera entre las mujeres de 15-49 años.

En las teorías del cambio social hay consenso en considerar que las bases esenciales para el desarrollo de un país se establecen cuando logran que la población alcance altos niveles de educación, tenga salud y empleo acorde con su calificación.

El caso Cuba pone en tela de juicio esta conclusión y nos plantea la interrogante: ¿exactamente qué *logros* se perderían y qué se podría ganar si se produjeran cambios políticos en Cuba?

REFERENCIAS

Anuario Estadístico de Cuba 1989. Comité Estatal de Estadísticas.

Barret, Kathleen. *The Impact of the Collapse of the Soviet Union and East Bloc on the Cuban Health Care System*. Thesis for Master of Arts in Latin American Studies. Washington, D.C., 1993.

Censo de Población y Viviendas 1953. Editorial Lex.

Clark, Juan. *Cuba: mito y realidad*. Saeta Ediciones, Miami-Caracas, 1992.

Cuba: Nivel educacional de la población y población en edad escolar según Censo de Población y Viviendas, 1981. Comité Estatal de Estadísticas, 1984.

Desincorporación Laboral Femenina. Encuesta Nacional. Ministerio del Trabajo de Cuba, 1974.

Díaz-Briquets, Sergio. "Collision Course: Labor Force and Educational Trends in Cuba." *Cuban Studies* 23. University of Pittsburgh Press, 1993.

Encuesta de los trabajadores rurales 1956-1957. Agrupación Católica de Cuba.

González Quiñones, Fernando. *La participación de la mujer en la fuerza de trabajo y la fecundidad en Cuba.* Tesis de doctorado. La Habana, 1986.

Informe Anual 1990. Ministerio de Salud Pública de Cuba.

Mesa-Lago, Carmelo. "Countdown in Cuba?" *Cuba in the Nineties.* Freedom House, 1991.

Mujeres Latinoamericanas en cifras. Cuba. Instituto de la Mujer y FLACSO. Madrid, 1992.

Rodríguez, J.L. y Carriazo Moreno, G. *Erradicación de la pobreza en Cuba.* Editorial de Ciencias Sociales, La Habana, 1987.

San Martín, Hernán. *La Crisis Mundial de la Salud.* 2da edición. Editorial Ciencia. Madrid, 1985.

Susser, Mervyn. *La salud y los derechos humanos: Una perspectiva epidemiológica.* Discurso inagural. Segunda Reunión Científica Nacional de Epidemiología, Rep. Dominicana, 1991.

The World's Women, 1970-1990. Trends and Statistics. United Nations. ST/ESA/STAT/SER.K/8.

CUBA'S REFUGEES: MANIFOLD MIGRATIONS

Silvia Pedraza

El vino, de plátano; y si sale agrio, ¡es nuestro vino!

— José Martí, "Nuestra América" (1891).[1]

Over thirty years of political migration brought close to a million Cuban immigrants to American soil, harboring distinct waves of immigrants as well as distinct refugee "vintages," alike only in their final rejection of Cuba. Each of the major waves of migration has been characterized by a very different social composition. To understand the changing characteristics of the exiles over time, we need to pay attention to the changing phases of the Cuban revolution. As Peter Rose (1981, p. 11) underlined, "refugees do not live in a vacuum. They are part of an intricate sociopolitical web that must be seen as the background against which any portrait of their travails must be painted and any dissection of their innermost thoughts and feelings must be pinned." This analysis focuses both on the nature of the decisions the refugees made to leave Cuba and the larger social structures that shaped the exodus. As C. Wright Mills (1961) said, so long ago, the sociological imagination lies at the intersection of personal troubles and historical issues.

Including those who were born here, the total number of Cubans in the United States as of 1990 was approximately 1,042,433, 73 percent of which were immigrants.[2] The 1990 census data gives us, for the first time, the opportunity to look at the social and demographic characteristics of the distinct waves of the Cuban exodus.[3] The various waves of Cuban migration brought very different sets of social resources with them—such as their social class, race, education, family, institutional knowledge, and values. Over the course of more than 30 years of exodus, they also arrived in the U. S. at times when the social context that greeted them presented them with vastly different amounts of opportunity—such as economic growth or recession, government policy programs, a warm welcome or cold reception. Hence, Cuban immigrants from the various waves of migration have undergone rather different processes of incorporation into American society, as will be seen in their contrasting social outcomes. As a result, to portray Cubans in the United States by figures that describe them as a whole (e.g., by their overall education or poverty level) masks the vastly different social realities which they represent. Those many social realities are the result of their manifold migrations.

---

1. The wine is from plaintain; and if it proves sour, it is our wine! José Martí, "Our America" (1891). Translated by Juan de Onís (1954).

2. Data for this article is from the U.S. 1990 census of the United States, 5 percent sample, Public Use Microdata Sample, weighted. The author wished to gratefully acknowledge the assistance of Lisa J. Neidert, University of Michigan, Population Studies Center, and Rubén G. Rumbaut, Michigan State University, Department of Sociology, in helping her obtain the 1990 census data for this article.

3. Close to 20 percent of Cuban immigrants arrived after the 1980 Census.

REFUGEES AS A SOCIAL TYPE

As E. F. Kunz explained, a refugee "is a distinct social type." The essential difference between refugees and voluntary migrants lies in their motivations:

> It is the reluctance to uproot oneself, and the absence of positive original motivations to settle elsewhere, which characterizes all refugee decisions and distinguishes the refugee from the voluntary migrants (1973, p. 130).

Hence, the key idea necessary to understand the refugee in flight is that of the "push" (cf. Lee 1966). While ordinary immigrants are more likely to be "pulled" by the attraction of the opportunity to fashion a better life, as Barry Stein (1981, p. 322) succinctly expressed it, "the refugee is not pulled out; he is pushed out. Given the choice, he would stay." Political exile is the last step of a process of profound political disaffection that, as Kunz (1973) stressed, is often accompanied by the refugees' fear for their safety given their interpretation of events and self- perceived danger.

To explain the enormous variance among refugees' experiences, Kunz spoke of "vintages," or refugee groups that are distinct in "character, background, and avowed political faith" (1973, p. 137). When dramatic changes in the society take place gradually, individuals react differently. Some oppose changes that others support, some call for compromises that to others smell of collaboration:

> As the political situation ripens for each, they will leave the country as distinct 'vintages' each usually convinced of the moral and political rightness of his actions and implicitly or openly blaming those who departed earlier or stayed on (1973, p. 137).

"Vintages" (defined by attitudes) may or may not be the same as waves (defined by timing). The Cuban political exodus holds both distinct waves of migration and "vintages."

THE FIRST WAVE: CUBA'S ELITE

Nelson Amaro and Alejandro Portes (1972) portrayed the different phases of the Cuban political immigration as changing over time with the exiles' principal motivation for their decision to leave. With the unfolding of the Cuban revolution, over the years "those who wait" gave way to "those who escape," and they to "those who search." Bringing the analysis up to date, I have added "those who hope" and "those who despair." Overall, the Cuban migration is characterized by an inverse relation between date of departure and social class of the immigrants.

Typical of the first phase of the immigration were "those who wait." The Cuban exodus began with the triumph of the Cuban revolution in 1959 over the tyranny of Fulgencio Batista with the exit of the *Batistianos*. But at this time the majority of Cubans shared in the euphoria of the revolution's hard-won success. It was only when the revolution entered a more radical phase that the exodus of political immigrants really took force.

In this first wave, those who left were Cuba's elite. These upper and upper-middle classes were not tied to Batista's government but were bound to a political and economic structure that, Amaro and Portes underlined, was completely interpenetrated by the demands and initiative of American capital:

> These executive and owners of firms, big merchants, sugar mill owners, manufacturers, cattlemen, representatives of foreign companies and established professionals, were those most acquainted with the United States' political and economic guardianship of Cuba, under which they had created or maintained their position, and thus were the least given to believe that the American government would permit the consolidation of a socialist regime in the island (1972, p. 10).

Hence, amidst the economic and diplomatic war that ensued between Cuba and the U.S. (cf. Schreiber 1973), they decided to leave. The refugees of this first wave came to the United States driven by Cuba's overturning of the old order through revolutionary measures such as the nationalization of American industry and agrarian reform laws, as well as by the United States' severance of diplomatic and economic ties with Cuba, all of which entailed serious personal losses. Maximiliano Pons[4] came to the U. S. in 1960 after Castro nationalized the American company he was working for. The son of Spanish immigrants, Catalan traders from Barcelona, like many of his social class Maximiliano was educated in the United States:

> I finally broke with my father when I went to college. I elected to go to Yale and not to Salamanca, where my father wanted me to go. I wanted to be an American very badly. I became an American aspirant. The United States had just emerged victorious from World War II. I was away at Yale then. Four years later I returned to Cuba, went to work for a leading American company, bought a house in the Marianao suburbs—the whole thing. Fidel turned me back into a Cuban (Llanes 1982, pp. 53-54).

"Those who wait" characterizes those first refugees that came imagining that exile would be temporary, waiting for the inevitable American reaction and help to overthrow Cuba's new government. In this first stage the exile's political activity was intensely militant, supporting military counterrevolution against Cuba. Of these, the exiles' invasion of Bay of Pigs in April 1961 was the largest and most tragic. This first phase of the Cuban exile ended with the fiasco of the Freedom Fighters' attempt to liberate Cuba from Castro's hold. In *Playa Girón* the 2506 Brigade fought against the Cuban rebel army, waiting for the air cover the United States had promised. They waited in vain (see Thomas 1977).

"Those who escape" constituted the second phase that was set on by the growing political turmoil when the Catholic church was silenced after denouncing the communist direction the revolution was taking (cf. Alfonso 1984); the electoral system collapsed when the jubilant crowds chanted around Castro "*¿Elecciones para qué?*" ("What do we need elections

for?"); and Castro announced that he had always been a Marxist-Leninist and would be so until the day he died (cf. Thomas 1977). The exodus doubled. As Amaro and Portes noted, the inverse relationship between date of emigration and social class in Cuba began to show. Still largely a middle-class exodus, now it was more middle than upper: middle merchants and middle management, landlords, middle-level professionals, and a considerable number of skilled unionized workers, who wanted to escape an intolerable new order.

The immigrants of the first two phases were not so much "pulled" by the attractiveness of the new society as "pushed" by the internal political process of the old. When the private universities and schools began to close in 1961, fear that the children would be educated by the state became prevalent. Miranda Martín, the daughter of a doctor that had initially sympathized with the revolution, remembered:

> We became aware gradually of the shift in Fidel's policies to the left, but *papi* didn't want to leave Havana ... My mother, on the other hand, was panicked. What will they do to the children in school? Will they force them to go to communist schools? Finally in August we left (Llanes 1982, pp. 23-24).

Over 14,000 children came alone through Operation Peter Pan, sent by their frightened parents (Walsh 1971). "What began as a trickle," wrote Richard Fagen et al. (1968, p. 62), "was, by the middle of 1962, a small flood." Data from the 1990 census show that of the 757,187 Cubans in the United States who immigrated after the revolution, 25 percent arrived during the first wave, 1960-1964[5] (see Table1). At this time the Cuban Refugee Program was initiated that assisted most of the refugees in Miami.

---

4. Based on the collected life stories of hundreds of Cubans, José Llanes (1982) drew 58 composite characters whose human dramas were representative of immigrants from the various waves of immigrants. Names are fictitious.

5. The U.S. census precoded the variable on year of immigration by intervals: before 1950, 1950-59, 1960-64, 1965-69, 1970-74, 1975-79, 1980-81, 1982-84, 1985-86, 1987-1990, and born in the U.S. Hence, while technically the Cuban exodus that belongs to the revolution should begin with the year 1959, when the revolution triumphed, it is not possible to disaggregate the data in that way. Fortunately, this precoding does not do too much violence to the data because, as Fagen et al. (1968) pointed out, it was really the nationalization of American industries in October 1960 that turned the emigration from a trickle into a flood. Likewise, the migration from Mariel is pretty well approximated by the years 1980-81, although technically it took place in 1980.

The higher class origin of these Cuban refugees has been well documented. This initial exodus over represented the professional, managerial, and middle classes, 31 percent, as well as the clerical and sales workers, 33 percent. Likewise, the educational level of these refugees was remarkably high (Fagen et al. 1968, Table 7.1).

With breathtaking speed, in a couple of years the Cuban revolution had moved through distinct phases. Nelson Amaro (1977) captured the progressive stages as: first, democracy; then, humanism; followed by nationalism; thereafter, socialism; culminating in Marxism-Leninism. The United States' punitive policy—cutting the sugar quota, instituting a trade embargo, and backing the exiles' invasion of Cuba— no doubt aided the rapidity of this transition. Amidst this swift progression of stages, some refugees dissented at one point, some at others. To Castro, they were all the same: *gusanos*, or counterrevolutionary "worms."

Casal (1979) observed that although the "highly belligerent" counterrevolutionary movements of the first two phases never actively engaged all exiles, they did draw on the financial or moral support of most exiles who hoped for Castro's overthrow and for their own return to Cuba. Unable to reach their goal, the Cuban communities became disenchanted with such activities and withdrew their support. As Kunz (1973, p. 133) specified, when refugees realize "that the doors are closed behind" them, they begin to take the steps that change them from temporary refugees into exiles.

Kunz (1981, pp. 45-46) also distinguished various refugee types according to their ideological- national orientation while in exile. Kunz's labels for the various ways in which one can be an exile constitute an effort to delineate the types: the *Restoration Activists*, the *Passive Hurt*, the *Integration Realists*, the *Eager Assimilationists*, the *Revolutionary Activists*, and the *Founders of Utopias*. *Revolutionary Activists* single-mindedly "subjugate matters of family and chances of long term resettlement" to the purposes they set out to achieve, while *Eager Assimilationists* may engage in a "hyperactive search for assimilation and the achievement of material success" as a way to forget

their guilt and their past. Still, it is important to realize, as Kunz proposed, that while these "solutions" to the problem of exile may be found side by side, most individuals "pass through these role-phases from their day of flight, progressing and regressing" throughout their exile careers (Kunz 1981, p. 46), passages that may well be facilitated by specific events.

The very life of Lourdes Casal attests to various exile role passages and to diametrically opposed ways of shouldering the felt sense of historic responsibility which exile can entail. In her attempt to express her strong identification with Cuba and to solve her personal problem of exile, Lourdes Casal lived through many exile lives. Casal was a formidable woman: a Black Cuban from the middle class, in the early seventies she was the founder of the magazine *Areíto* and the Antonio Maceo Brigade, for Cuban-Americans open to or in sympathy with the revolution. Yet at the beginning of the revolution, in the late fifties and early sixties, she had been an active member of groups, such as the *Juventud Universitaria Católica* (Catholic University Students) and the *Directorio Revolucionario Estudiantil* (Students' Revolutionary Directorate), that fought against Batista's dictatorship but also actively opposed the communist direction in which the revolution was then headed. As a result of her travels to Africa and her return to Cuba, as well as the social movements then rippling through the United States, she underwent a profound personal change and, in the early seventies, became an active supporter of the Cuban revolution. When she learned that she had little time left to live, she chose to return and, in 1981, died in Cuba, where she is buried (see Institute of Cuban Studies 1982). As Peter Rose (1981, p. 11) highlighted, few social scientists have turned their attention to the sociology of exile, and even those few "rarely have delved into the social and psychological ramifications of those affected" by refugee migration and resettlement.

After the October Missile Crisis in 1962, the flights ceased, forcing the migration rate to slow down. The U.S. provided direct transportation only for over 1,000 Cuban exiles that had been imprisoned in

Cuba as a result of the Bay of Pigs fiasco and their relatives. The Cuban government exchanged the prisoners for vital needs: medicine, medical and surgical equipment, food, and money.

During this period, Cubans arrived that had either previously stayed in other countries, or had escaped Cuba illegally in boats and rafts to the shores of Key West. Francisco Mateo crossed the 90 miles between Cuba and Key West on a small rowboat:

> Some of the people who left from Mariel (in 1980) took twenty hours to cross the distance in a motorboat. We took twenty days in 1962, my family and me, in a boat with three oars and holes....You tell me how eight people could leave on an eight-foot rowboat and expect to get anywhere. Across the Miami Causeway maybe, but not those stinking, treacherous ninety miles. God was with us. There is no other answer (Llanes 1982, p. 19).

During this phase of the exodus, close to half of the arrivals were blue-collar workers, skilled and unskilled, and a large proportion were agricultural workers and fishermen (Casal 1979, Table 1). Cuba introduced food rationing and compulsory military service at this time, further spurring the exodus.

THE SECOND WAVE: CUBA'S PETITE BOURGEOISE

In the Fall of 1965 a chaotic period ensued when hundreds of boats left from Miami for the Cuban port of Camarioca, where they picked up thousands of relatives to come to the United States. "Those who search" characterized this next major wave of the Cuban migration. In response to President Lyndon Johnson's "open door" policy that welcomed refugees from communism, the Cuban exodus was organized and concerted. For eight years, the United States and Cuban governments administered an orderly air bridge as the *Vuelos de la Libertad,* or Freedom Flights, daily brought Cubans from Varadero to Miami that the Cuban Refugee Program swiftly processed and resettled, dispersing them throughout the United States.

Kunz (1973) distinguished anticipatory refugee movements from acute ones. The joint policy of the Unites States and Cuban governments turned this

Table 1. Number of Cubans in the U.S., by Year of Immigration, 1990

Year of Immigration	Number of Cubans	%	% that Immigrated from 1960-1990
Born in U.S.	285,244	27.4	—
1987-90	33,837	3.3	4.9
1985-86	16,963	1.6	2.4
1982-84	23,163	2.2	3.4
1980-81	125,313	12.0	18.2
1975-79	33,256	3.2	4.8
1970-74	109,731	10.5	15.9
1965-69	173,287	16.6	25.1
1960-64	174,275	16.7	25.3
1950-59	50,956	4.9	--
Before 1950	16,406	1.6	--
Total	1,042,433	100.0	(689,825) 100.0

Source: U.S. 1990 Census, Public Use Microdata Sample, 5 percent, weighted.

initially acute exodus into a coordinated and orderly anticipatory refugee movement. Though for quite different reasons, the U. S. and Cuban governments have often "cooperated with the enemy," as Jorge Domínguez (1991) stressed. When the refugee airlift closed, thousands of flights had brought more than a quarter of a million persons. As Table 1 shows, 41 percent of Cubans who immigrated to the United States after the revolution came over during the years of the airbridge: 1965-1974.

Throughout this period, the Memorandum of Understanding regulated the immigrants' departure, giving the immediate family of exiles already living in the United States priority (Thomas 1967). Both countries compiled their "master lists" -- one composed in the U. S. of those who claimed their relatives in Cuba, and one composed in Cuba of those who requested departure. Jointly, both governments decided who would emigrate and the migration proceeded through family networks. Cuba barred from exit young men of military service age, as well as professionals, technical, and skilled workers whose exit would cause a serious disturbance in production or delivering social services, such as doctors (Clark 1975).

With this phase of the migration, the exodus of the upper and upper-middle classes largely came to an end. This wave of immigration was largely working class and "petite bourgeoisie": employees, independent craftsmen, small merchants, skilled and semi-skilled workers. Amaro and Portes judged (1972, p. 13) that over time the political exile increasingly became an economic exile as "those who search" searched for greater economic opportunities than were provided in a socialist society that instituted a new ethic of sacrificing individual consumption to achieve collective goals.

Without doubt, these were some of the leanest and most idealistic years of the Cuban revolution. To spread access to a basic education and health care, young, educated Cubans went to live in the countryside, working in literacy campaigns to educate the poor, illiterate peasants, and in public health campaigns to provide basic health care. At the same time, the impact of the hemispheric trade embargo imposed by the Organization of American States in 1964 resulted in a spare parts crisis and other profound economic dislocations (Schreiber 1973); the exodus drained technical and administrative skills; and Cuba failed in her attempts to cease being a sugar monoculture, industrialize, and diversify. In Amaro and Portes' view, increasingly the immigration ceased to be a political act and became an economic act. Yet their distinction missed the reality that while life in Cuba grew harsh for all, it turned particularly bitter for those who had announced their dissent by declaring their intention to leave. Those who applied to leave lost their jobs, were ostracized as enemies, and were forced to do hard labor in agriculture. Antonio Chacón applied to leave Cuba in 1962, but was unable to leave until 1966, by which time he was suffering from malnutrition, diabetes, and high blood pressure:

> We had applied for an exit permit. This meant that I would lose my job at the newspaper. We had planned for a few months of unemployment. It was unavoidable... Then, slam...The door closed and I was inside. Unemployed. We finally left in 1966. Can you imagine that? Four years knocking around doing "volunteer work" on weekends in order to get the food allowance. We lost our belongings. Everything we owned was sold or traded for food. We ended up living with my friend Jacobo, who took us in at great risk. I lost eighty pounds in those four years (Llanes 1982, pp. 93-94).

The social transformations the Cuban revolution effected—political *and* economic—were so pervasive that they always "pushed" Cubans. America, in facilitating the migration, always "pulled" them. Moreover, the Cuban migration is unique in the extent to which both the United States and Cuban governments organized, concerted, and facilitated the exodus (Tabori 1972). Together, I argued, they set in motion a system of political migration that for many years proved beneficial to both. The loss of the educated, professional middle classes indeed proved erosive to the Cuban revolution, but it also served the positive function of externalizing dissent. At the same time, in the United States the arrival of so many refugees who "voted with their feet" also served to provide the legitimacy necessary for foreign policy actions during the tense years of the Cold War (Pedraza-Bailey 1985).

Now the Cuban community in the United States became increasingly heterogeneous, varying widely in their social class origin. The former social distinctions were perpetrated and reenacted in exile, often with little bearing to their life in America. Those who had belonged to the five most exclusive yacht and country clubs in Havana founded another in Miami, with nostalgia dubbed "The Big Five." Cubans of working-class origin remain outsiders to these attempts to recreate a golden past that seems to ever grow only more golden.

When the migration began in the early 1960s, 31 percent of the Cubans who arrived in the Unites States were professionals or managers. By 1970, only 12 percent were professionals or managers. More than half the arrivals, 57 percent, were blue-collar, service, or agricultural workers (Aguirre 1976, Table 2). While Cuban exiles are clearly heterogeneous, their celebrated "success story" obscures it. It particularly serves to obscure the many Cuban poor. Still,

Table 2.   Number of Cubans in the U.S., by Race, and by Year of Immigration, 1990

Year of *Immigration*	Race				Total	
	White	Black	Other Race	Asian	Number	Percent
1987-90	84 .0	2 .6	13 .0	0 .4	33,838	100.0
1985-86	85 .8	3 .3	10 .9	—	16,963	100.0
1982-84	76 .8	5 .6	17 .0	0 .6	23,163	100.0
1980-81	77 .3	6 .0	16 .3	0 .4	125,313	100.0
1975-79	74 .8	5 .6	18 .5	1 .1	33,256	100.0
1970-74	84 .1	1 .7	13 .9	0 .3	109,731	100.0
1965-69	82 .4	1 .5	15 .6	0 .5	173,288	100.0
1960-64	90 .7	1 .9	7 .3	0 .1	174,275	100.0
Total	83 .5	2 .9	13 .3	0 .3	689,825	100.0

Source: U.S. 1990 Census, Public Use Microdata Sample, 5 percent, weighted.

the Cuban poor have always been evident in many neighborhoods of *la Southwestcera*, as Miami's Southwest is affectionately called. But not only are they hidden from the view of Americans, Cubans also tend to hide them from themselves (cf. Domínguez 1975). Casal (1979, p. 116) emphasized the costs of the "success story": it prevents Cubans from getting "a clear picture" of their true situation; it desensitizes them and others to the hidden costs of "success;" and it isolates Cubans from other American minorities.

Cuban immigrants that arrived after the airbridge ended consisted of refugees that had first lived in Spain. Portes, Clark, and Bach (1977) found that these émigrés represented Cuba's "middling service sectors:" cooks, gardeners, domestics, street vendors, shoe shiners, barbers, hairdressers, taxi drivers, small retail merchants. They had left Cuba during the period when Castro launched a new "revolutionary offensive" in Cuba, confiscating over 55,000 small businesses that were still privately owned (Mesa-Lago 1978), "pushing" out the little entrepreneur and his employees. By and large, the refugees of this "vintage" believed in the promises of the revolution until the Cuban government labelled them *parásitos*, or "parasites," and took over their small businesses.

With the economic transition to socialism effected, in the seventies the Cuban government cast the shape of the political system: the new Cuban Communist Party held its First Congress; a new Constitution was declared; and Fidel Castro formally became President. In many ways, the old idealism and romanticism of the 1960s gave way to what Mesa-Lago (1978) called pragmatism. The failure of the mobilization of hundreds of thousands of Cubans all over the island to make the national goal of cutting 10 million tons of sugar in 1970 issued this new phase. Cuba reintroduced material incentives and wage differentials to promote greater economic growth; other mass organizations, such as the *Poder Popular*, or Organs of Peoples Power, took form. With this institutionalization, Cuba increasingly took on the features of Eastern European communism (cf. Roca 1977).

For the vast majority of Cubans in the United States, throughout these years the issue continued to be life in America. Yet that very stability, and cultural impact on the young who lived face to face with the social movements of "the sixties" in America, gave birth to an increased ideological pluralism, denser than that which had always existed though obscured by the uniform rejection of Cuba. As Casal (1979, p. 128) observed, "the Cuban community is not monolithic now (if it ever was)."

Among other splits, such as social class and waves of migration, the Cuban community is certainly cleft by age, by generations. Typically, immigrants experience a pronounced generation gap when parents raised in the Old World confront their children raised in the New. But this gap reflects more than that; it is the difference between political generations that result from sharing a common location in a historical social process that subjected them to specific experiences during their youth — a stratification of experience that shapes a frame of reference for the future (Mannheim 1952). Among Cuban exiles, the gap between the political generations which came of age during certain critical periods of Cuban history (cf. Zeitlin 1966), and that which came of age, American, under the impact of the Civil Rights and anti-Vietnam War movements, is often a chasm.

It was 55 progressive young people that, in December 1977, first broke through 19 years of hostility, abuse, and isolation. Grouped as the Antonio Maceo Brigade, their visit throughout the island left behind a profound mark. Cuba filmed it: *55 Hermanos* (55 Brothers and Sisters) captured their search for cultural identity; for some, for political identity. Widely shown in Cuba, it proved heartrending: evidence of the suffering that exile had brought both those who left and who were left behind.In 1978, a Dialogue took place between the Cuban government and representatives of the Cuban community in exile as a result of which the Cuban government agreed to the release of political prisoners; to promote the reunification of families rent apart by the exodus; and to allow Cubans in the United States to visit their family and their homeland.

All at once, the counterrevolutionaries, *gusanos* of yesterday, respectfully became "members of the Cuban community abroad," the release of political prisoners began, and the return visits of Cuban exiles commenced. The Cuban community split into the opposing camps of those who supported and opposed the Dialogue; those who returned and refused to visit Cuba. Still, since that day, hundreds of thousands of Cubans have returned to Cuba every year -- seeking the family they loved and the vestiges of the life they once led.

THE THIRD WAVE: CUBA'S *MARIELITOS*
Since the flow of Cuban refugees had halted for many years, few expected the chaotic flotilla exodus

in 1980. Initiated in April by those who asked for political asylum at the Peruvian Embassy, within days it grew massive. When this acute refugee exodus ceased the following Fall, it had brought over 125,000 more Cubans to America, approximately 18 percent of all Cuban immigrants (see Table 1). This wave lacked order and process. From Miami, thousands of boats manned by relatives sped across the 90 miles of sea to Cuba's Mariel Harbor. At times they succeeded in bringing their families, other times they brought whomever angry officials put on the boats. Towards the end, this included Cuba's social undesirables: those who had been in prisons (whether they had committed real crimes or had only succeeded in challenging the state), mental patients, and homosexuals.

In Cuba, these "antisocial elements", this *escoria*, or "scum," as the government called them, represented a large public slap in the face: no longer the immigrants of the transition from capitalism to communism, but the children of communism itself. In America they arrived in the throes of President Jimmy Carter's ambivalent government policy that both welcomed them "with open hearts and open arms" and sought to delimit the flow.

In the United States, after twenty years of celebrating the achievements of Cuban exiles, the press contributed to their damaging portrayal. It focused on the criminals, the homosexuals, the many Blacks: categories of people to whom Americans accord too little respect. Who were the *Marielitos*? Were they "scum"?

To dispel the more damaging and inaccurate portrayals, Robert Bach (1980; Bach *et al.* 1981/82) studied their characteristics, sampling the *Marielitos* soon after their arrival, while they were still in the processing centers and the refugee camps. Among the most salient was their youth (most were young men single or without their families) and the visibly higher proportion of Blacks than ever (Bach *et al.* 1981/82, pp. 33-35). Their former occupations showed that most were from the mainstream of the Cuban economy, hardly scum. Also salient was their overwhelmingly working class origins — close to 71 percent were blue-collar workers. Mechanics, heavy equipment and factory machine operatives, carpenters, masons, and bus, taxi, and truck drivers led the list of occupations (Bach *et al.* 1981/82, p. 34). These characteristics, stressed Fernández (1982), suggested new generational strains may have developed from the more limited economic and political opportunities available to the young when the older generation of Cubans who made the revolution held the key posts, as well as the burden of military service in Cuba and overseas shouldered by the young (cf. Díaz-Briquets 1983). "Those who hope" might well characterize this wave.

In the United Sates, the press focused inordinately on the criminal element. Indeed, there were many who had been in prison. According to the the Immigration and Naturalization Service, of the 124,789 Mariel refugees around 19 percent, or 23,970, admitted they had been in jail in Cuba. Of those who had been in prison, 5,486 were political prisoners, while 70 percent of those who had been in prison had been jailed for minor crimes or for acts, such as vagrancy or participation in the extensive black market that were crimes in Cuba but not in the United States. The Cuban *Ley de la Peligrosidad* (Law of Dangerous Behavior) made some forms of dissent "anti-social" behavior, controlled by prison terms, such as participating in the black market (buying or selling clothes and food); dodging military service or desertion; refusing to work for the state, particularly in the cane fields; and trying to escape Cuba illegally (Bach *et al.* 1981/82, p. 46). Of those who had been in jail, the immigration service considered only 7 percent to be serious criminals — less than 2 percent of all the *Marielitos* (Montgomery 1981).

Given their youth, the *Marielitos* clearly constituted a different political generation, one whose coming of age was long after the early revolutionary struggle and sharp social cleavages that demanded enormous sacrifices but also affirmed the loyalty of many. Roughly half of the Mariel immigrants came of age during the late 1960s or the 1970s, when problems of freedom of expression became particularly acute for artists and intellectuals, such as the incident sparked by Heberto Padilla's poem expressing the marginality of those who were *"Fuera del Juego"* ("Out of the Game"). Moreover, deviance, particu-

larly homosexuality, was scorned and dealt with by prison sentence. Comparisons with the years of Batista could no longer serve to promote the consent of a generation that scarcely could remember them.

The *Marielitos*, therefore, were a significantly different "vintage" — one whose lived experience (*experiencia vivencial,* as we say in Spanish) contrasts sharply with other "vintages." In particular, at the two poles of twenty years of emigration, stand two "vintages" that at best can hardly comprehend one another and at worst may be, as Kunz noted (1973), hostile. Over time the dramatic changes the Cuban revolution effected progressed through distinct stages, and these stages interacted with the social characteristics of those affected to produce markedly different processes of political disaffection.

To put it simply, let me give two stark examples. A typical 1960 émigré was an executive, older, male, and White that would likely have become disaffected by the nationalization of American industry in the early years of the revolution. But a typical 1980 émigré was a bus driver, young, male, and Black that would scarcely have minded that nationalization. Instead, he might have spent many years believing in the professed goals of the revolution, until a bout of prison terms for his participation in the extensive black market of the 1970s promoted his disaffection. Mariano Medina was a Black Cuban and former Army officer that fought in Angola. He spoke of the distance that separated him from the earlier exiles:

> I can now see that they feel no ill will toward me and may even want to help me, but they can't help me come to grips with the twenty years I've spent in Cuba. They don't understand how I feel... (Llanes 1982, p. 170).

Despite the willing help of many in the Cuban community, many others exhibited a defensive prejudice against the newcomers, who might tarnish their reputation. The first and latest waves of Cuban refugees in the United States live side by side but remain aloof from one another. For them, as Kunz (1973, p. 137) pointed out, the date of departure from Cuba "signifies the bona fide" of their "political credo." Thus, they tend to blame each other for having left too soon or stayed too late. And the Cuba they long for is not quite the same Cuba.

Oscar Handlin (1973) wrote of the immigrants from Europe at the turn of the century, those who came to fashion America. He caught the sadness, despair, and nostalgia of every person that has been uprooted:

> Yesterday, by its distance, acquires a happy glow. The peasants look back ... and their fancy rejoices in the better days that have passed, when they were on the land and the land was fertile, and they were young and strong, and virtues were fresh. ... Alas, those days are gone, that they believed existed, and now there is only the bitter present (Handlin 1973, p. 98).

Cuban immigrants in America for many years missed Cuba so. But one night in Key West, while speaking with four refugees from Mariel, the difference struck me. While fishing, they listened on the radio to a baseball game being played right then in their hometown in Cuba. The early refugees' nostalgia attached them to the Cuba they knew—*la Cuba de ayer*, before the revolution. The Mariel refugees' longing was for *la Cuba de hoy*, of the revolution.

THE FOURTH WAVE: CUBA'S *BALSEROS*

The Mariel exodus proved so traumatic, both for the United States and Cuba, that immediately thereafter the doors to further migration closed. However, in the mid 1980s both governments signed a new Migration Agreement that provided for the immigration to the U. S. of up to 20,000 Cubans and up to 3,000 political prisoners a year, as well as for the deportation of excludable *Marielitos* back to Cuba. However, in actual practice only around 2,000 visas were being given a year.

Cuba's economic crisis reached new depths when communism collapsed in Eastern Europe, particularly in the Soviet Union, on whom Cuba had been enormously dependent for trade and economic subsidies. The impact of these losses has been devastating: a decline in the national product of one half, and in investment by two-thirds from 1989-1993 (Mesa-Lago, 1994). As a result, Cuban industry has been paralyzed, public transport hardly operates, the sugar harvest was abysmally low, and electricity has become sporadic, with Havana suffering blackouts dur-

ing which people rely on candles, if candles can be found. As Mesa-Lago explained, "because of the eroding value of the peso, health care, education, pensions and other free services -- which used to be the pride of the revolution -- are rapidly deteriorating." The economic crisis is so severe that in the Fall of 1990 Castro himself declared it "a special period in a time of peace." Such a *período especial* was to have been temporary, but coupled with the United States' tightening of the embargo (the Torricelli Law) in 1992, the end of the crisis is not in sight.

Cuba has attempted to forestall the worst of it by opening the economy to trade, investment, and tourism, and by reintroducing the use of U. S. dollars, measures which, Castro himself emphasized, were not intended to reintroduce capitalism but to "save socialism." But these policies have not succeeded in turning the economy around. Abject need and hunger have now become the reality of Cubans' lives during this "special period."

At the same time, the dissident movement has grown and developed into a social movement. Despite different political thrusts (e.g., democratic socialist, environmentalist, Christian democrat), all dissidents in Cuba have increasingly called for a new democratic opening, a liberalization of the political structures that Castro adamantly refuses (See Hidalgo 1994). Hence, both economic and political want now drive the new Cuban emigration, together with the ever present desire for the reunification of families still rent apart.

The new Cuban exodus has taken several forms (cf. Rodríguez-Chavez 1993), with illegal emigration being the major one. Cubans have become so desperate that they leave on *balsas*—rafts, tires, or other makeshift vessels—risking death due to starvation, dehydration, drowning, or sharks. The *balseros*, as they are called, risk the arduous crossing now so regularly that from 1991 on *Los Hermanos al Rescate* (Brothers to the Rescue) constantly patrol the sea in helicopters searching for them. According to the U. S. Coast Guard, 5,791 *balseros* managed to reach safety in the United States from 1985 to 1992. As economic conditions worsened in Cuba, the numbers have risen dramatically. While in the year 1989 less than 500 *balseros* arrived, by 1991 the numbers had risen to over 2,000 and by 1993 to 3,656. In 1994, due to the crisis in August and September, over 37,000 Cubans were rescued at sea. Their gratitude to their rescuers knows no limits. Early one morning in August, Lizbet Martínez, a 12-year old girl with a long, blonde pony tail, climbed aboard a raft with her parents. She took aboard her most prized possession — her violin. When the U. S. Coast Guard rescued them, she played "The Star-Spangled Banner" on her violin for them—a plaintive melody of gratitude for those who had saved her life (Balmaseda 1994a).

When the *balseros* arrive in Florida, they are welcomed—briefly—as heroes. But so many died tragically at sea. Claudia Pérez was 15 months old when she died in her mother's arms—one hour before she was rescued. Raísa Santana died because she drank seawater, reserving the only drinking water left in their vessel for her son (*El Nuevo Herald*, 26 December 1993). "Those who despair" constitute this last wave of migration.

August 1994 comprised yet another historic turn in Cuba. On August 5th, massive riots took place in the streets of the Center of Havana, in which thousands of Cubans participated all day long, whose behavior expressed the enormous material want that shapes their lives, their disdain for the privilege reserved for Party members and foreigners, and the enormous wish for civil liberties that now also permeates Cuban society (Rivas-Porta 1994).

Shortly thereafter, Castro gave orders to the Cuban Coast Guard not to discourage the illegal emigration from Cuba's shores. Immediately, thousands of *balseros* put out to sea, in the hopes of reaching Miami. But an abrupt policy change made the Cubans unwelcome. Under orders from President Bill Clinton and Attorney General Janet Reno, the U. S. Coast Guard blocked their progress and directed them to Guantanamo (U. S. base in Cuba), where over 30,000 people lived in tents for the 9 months during which they were allowed entry to the U. S.

As a result of the crisis, a new Migration Agreement was signed in September 1994 that promised that the U. S. will now actually give at least 20,000 visas a year for Cubans to immigrate to the United States. However, in May 1995 another abrupt policy change allowed the refugees in Guantanamo to come to the U. S. at the same time that the United States signed another Migration Agreement with Cuba that stipulated that all *balseros* found at sea will actually be returned to Cuba. "Cuba bleeds," headlined Liz Balmaseda (1994b), "and the drops are called rafts." But the U. S. government now denies their claim to being refugees.

CUBANS IN THE UNITED STATES
Race

Though Cuba has always been a multi-racial society, despite their differences, prior to Mariel both major waves of Cuban immigrants were predominantly White. Yet, while throughout the decade of the sixties the occupational distribution of Cuban refugees became more representative of Cuban society, "paradoxically," said Benigno Aguirre (1976, p. 105), Cuban Blacks "participated less in it."

The 1953 Cuban Census put the proportion Black at 27 percent. In Cuba, like much of the Caribbean, social class and race overlapped in the extreme. But while the social class level of the Cuban migration dropped, for 15 years the immigrants remained overwhelmingly White. Data from the 1990 census shows that 86.3 percent of the immigrants were White Cubans, 0.2 percent were Black Cubans, 0.3 percent were Asians (no doubt *Chinos Cubanos*), and 13.2 percent designated themselves as belonging to "other race."[6] In Cuba, as in the rest of the Caribbean, this usually corresponds to Mulattoes, or *Mulaticos*, as affectionately called. Charles Wagley (1968) described the social definition of the races in the Americas. In the South of the United States a dual racial classification was used—Black *vs.* White—that was based on ancestry ("one drop of Black blood"). By contrast, throughout the Caribbean the

---

6. In recent U. S. censuses, data on race, ethnicity, and ancestry are the result of self- identification by those answering the census questions.

social definition of race was based on phenotype buttressed by social status—"money bleaches," the Brazilians say. Moreover, three different racial categories were recognized—Black *vs.* White *vs.* those who were mixed, variously referred to as *Mulatos* (Cuba), *Pardos* (Brazil), and *Trigueños* (Puerto Rico).

The differential migration of the Cuban races up to this time was quite explainable. Two different social processes, Aguirre concluded, were at work. At the outset, the revolution pulled out the power from under the upper classes, that had deliberately excluded Blacks from their midst. The immigration proceeded through the chain of extended family and friends, further selecting Whites. In addition, the migration policy of the United States and Cuba contributed to Blacks being excluded as they gave priority to close relatives of Cubans already in the United States.

Moreover, Blacks in Cuba did benefit from the revolution. Cuba never had a "separate but equal" system of legal segregation; and Cuban culture was a "creolization" of White Spanish and Black African cultural traditions. Yet prerevolutionary Cuba excluded Blacks from the pinnacles of society: yacht and country clubs, the best vacation resorts and beaches, hotels, private schools reserved for the elite.

One of the first acts of the revolution was to make these exclusive facilities public, available to all, regardless of color or wealth. In addition, the Cuban government promoted new opportunities for Blacks in employment and education. Richard Fagen *et al.* (1968, p. 120) noted that the race problem in Cuba was "a boon to Castro." The revolutionaries found it extremely useful for discrediting the old social order. With the "instant liberation" of Blacks "tens of thousands of disadvantaged Cubans were recruited into the ranks of revolutionary enthusiasts."

Indeed, as Table 2 shows, about 91 percent of the refugees who came over in the first wave, Cuba's elite, were White. But the proportion White declined quite markedly during the second wave. From 14 to 19 percent of those who immigrated from 1965-1979 considered themselves as "other." The *Marielitos* had the lowest proportion White of any wave, 77 percent, while 16 percent considered themselves "other" (most likely Mulattoes) and 6 percent considered themselves Black. By American standards, fully 22 percent were non-White.

Given the Cuban revolution's appeal to race, why such a large presence in recent years? As early as the seventies, Geoffrey Fox (1971, p. 21) remarked that "almost all those emigrating today are among the poorer classes in Cuba, the very people in whose name the revolution was made," Blacks included. To study "the defections of the sans-culottes," Fox interviewed a few working-class émigrés in Chicago and concluded that both for White and Black workers the salience of race in the revolution created strain—Whites complained of favoritism, Blacks of tokenism. Moreover, although discrimination was eliminated, racial prejudice persisted in Cuba, attitudes which Cuban Blacks might have sensed as real, denying the changes effected. As Max Weber ([1922] 1946, p. 280) pointed to so long ago, whatever their origins, ideas, once established, take on a life of their own and guide action.

Whatever role their race may have played in the decision to emigrate, Black Cubans find their steps uncertain in America. As Blacks, they are not fully accepted by Whites; while among Blacks, they are Cubans (cf. Dixon 1988).

Poverty

Looking at other indexes of structural assimilation (cf. Gordon 1964), as one might expect, these racial differences have consequences in America. The 1990 census puts the proportion of all Cubans in the U. S. whose incomes are below the officially defined poverty line as 16.5 percent—a figure that compares quite favorably to that of the total U. S. population. But when we consider Cubans by their race, we can see that while only 14 percent of White Cubans fall below the poverty line, 35 percent of Black Cubans and 23 percent of racially mixed Cubans fall below the poverty line—figures that compare most closely to the poverty rates among Black Americans and Puerto Ricans in the United States. Representations of Cubans as a homogeneous group by social and demographic profiles of the total Cuban-American population mask these dramatic differences. Table 3 shows

Table 3. Number of Cubans in the U.S., by Poverty Status, and by Year of Immigration, 1990

| Year of Immigration | Poverty Status | | Total | |
	Above *Poverty Line*	Below *Poverty Line*	Number	Percent
1987-90	61.3	38.7	33,838	100 .0
1985-86	79.4	20.6	16,963	100 .0
1982-84	83.8	16.2	23,163	100 .0
1980-81	72.1	27.9	125,313	100 .0
1975-79	71.3	28.7	33,256	100 .0
1970-74	87.7	12.3	109,731	100 .0
1965-69	88.0	12.0	173,288	100 .0
1960-64	91.5	8.5	174,275	100 .0
Total	83.5	16.5	689,825	100 .0

Source: U.S. 1990 Census, Public Use Microdata

the proportion of Cubans who are poor in 1990. Among Cuba's elite and their children who immigrated during the first wave, it is rather negligible: around 8 percent.

By and large, this first wave of Cuban migration brought enormous social resources with them — resources of social class, race, education, training, values, and expertise consonant with those of an industrial capitalist society, and the intimate knowledge of American society many had as its closest neighbors to the South. These social resources were "translated," made valuable in America by the warm welcome they received when they came to the United States—the multifaceted Cuban Refugee Program of assistance (see Pedraza-Bailey 1985). Moreover, at the time of their arrival in the 1960s and early 1970s, substantial economic opportunities existed in the U. S., particularly in Miami. Together, all of these opportunities allowed the development of a Cuban ethnic enclave in Miami (see Portes and Bach 1985; Rieff 1993; Portes and Stepick 1993) and a Cuban "success story" much loved by the American media.

By contrast, the poverty rates are much higher in the other waves of Cuban migration, from around 12 percent of those who immigrated during the air bridge (1965-1974) to 28 percent of the *Marielitos*. These immigrants brought with them far fewer social resources — of social class, race, education, prior

knowledge of American institutions and culture. They also arrived when the social context was not propitious — after the assistance provided by the Cuban Refugee Program had ended and when the U. S. was in a serious recession. Among the *balseros* who arrived most recently, 1987-1990, the proportion poor rises to a dramatic 39 percent. It is unlikely that this is solely due to the recency of their arrival. Time, of course, will tell.

Gender

That immigration has a decided impact on the labor force participation of women is a recurrent finding of immigration research (Pedraza 1991). It is also a central issue in studies of Cuban immigrants (Pérez 1988; 1986). In contrast to the extremely low rates of labor force participation of women in Cuba prior to the revolution, when most women did not work outside the home, Cuban women who immigrated to the U. S. after the revolution have extremely high rates of labor force participation. Yolanda Prieto's (1987) study of Cuban women in New Jersey, a more working-class community than Miami, concluded that the major determinant of the massive entrance of these women into the labor force was their social class: these women were middle class either in their origin or, if working-class, in their aspirations. Achieving the upward mobility of the Cuban family in the U. S. made women's work necessary and broke with the traditional Cuban notion that a woman's place is in the home, justifying the massive entrance of women into the labor force.

Indeed, Cuban women overwhelmingly saw work as the opportunity to help the family, rather than as an opportunity for self-actualization. Thus, Myra Max Ferree (1979) wrote that Cuban women were an example of employment without liberation. Cubans had apparently stretched the traditional view of women existing for the family to include employment as part of that role, while implying no necessary change in values. However, Lisandro Pérez (1988) argued that generational differences should be taken into account. The first generation reared in the traditional culture might well view employment as instrumental, but the second generation, more American, might hold a different set of attitudes. Pérez (1986) also showed that Cubans' relatively high family income is partly due to the high proportion of dual-income families, underscoring the central role of women's work in the Cuban "success story."

Occupations and Education

Among Cuban immigrants, educational and occupational attainment also vary by waves. Data from the 1990 census show that fully 25 percent of Cubans who immigrated during the first wave had graduated from college, while only 7 percent of the *Marielitos* had the same level of education.

Table 4 shows their occupations. Over a third of the immigrants who came over in the first wave, both men and women, work as managers and professionals, and another very sizeable proportion work in white-collar jobs in sales, technical, and administrative support. Among the *Marielitos*, the most common occupations were operators, fabricators, and laborers. Next come precision, production, craft, and repair workers for the men (nearly a quarter); and sales, technical, and administrative support for the women (over a third).

The occupational insertion of the immigrants from the second wave also shows the uniqueness of the first. Among those who immigrated on the heels of the revolutionary transformation of Cuba, over a third of the immigrants today—as well as then—

hold managerial and professional occupations, while among those who immigrated during the period of the air bridge, the proportion of professionals and managers is half that.

POLITICAL REFUGEES OR ECONOMIC IMMIGRANTS?

Differences abound, yet the questions the recent refugees posed were the same that for over thirty years have framed the debate over the meaning of the Cuban migration. Interpretations of the meaning of the exodus once again polarized into two positions: at one pole, the immigrants were said to be a manifestation of the loss of legitimacy of the Cuban revolution, discrediting it; at the other pole, the immigrants were said to be propelled by the scarcity of consumer goods, merely embarrassing it (see Fernàndez 1982). Hence, at one pole the immigrants were seen as political refugees; at the other, as economic immigrants. Over a million persons for a third of a century: Are they political or economic immigrants?

As Figure 1 makes clear, two different axes determine the definition. First, the motivation of the immigrants serves to define them as political or economic immigrants — a sociological distinction. Since all societies are simultaneously and inextricably political and economic, in our perceptions, political and economic conditions are entangled. In a society in transition, political disaffection easily results when government policies to change the basic economic allocation dislocate people: they lose their economic, social, and ideological "place." Even in a stable society, lack of economic opportunities easily results in lack of trust for public leaders. In this sense, Cuba's refugees are, and have always been, both political and economic. But when people grow politically disaffected, when they lose faith and trust in their government and its cause, they can no longer be disposed of as simply economic immigrants. Cuba's refugees are, and have always been, fundamentally political.

Second, the governments that regulate their exit and arrival define immigrants as political or economic immigrants—a legal distinction (see Pedraza-Bailey 1985). At one end, in the United States, Haitian refugees have consistently encountered a hostile recep-

Table 4. Number of Cubans in the U.S., by Occupational Attainment, Year of Immigration, and by Sex, 1990

Year of Immigration	Occupational Attainment						Total	
	Managerial, Professional	Technical, Sales, Admin. Support	Services	Precision Production, Craft, Repair	Operators, Fabricators, Laborers	Farming, Forestry, Fisheries	Number	Percent
Men								
1982-90	10.8	16.2	19.2	20.2	29.5	4.1	23,688	100.0
1980-81	8.9	18.7	15.6	23.0	30.2	3.6	57,206	100.0
1965-71	19.3	25.1	11.7	21.2	21.1	1.6	109,119	100.0
1960-64	37.8	27.8	7.3	13.7	12.3	1.1	58,100	100.0
Total	20.4	23.4	12.3	19.8	21.9	2.2	248,113	100.0
Women								
1982-90	10.0	32.6	23.8	6.9	26.7	—	19,056	100.0
1980-81	9.6	36.1	25.5	5.3	23.2	0.3	27,413	100.0
1965-79	17.2	42.8	16.5	4.1	19.2	0.2	102,425	100.0
1960-64	33.9	41.6	11.6	3.5	9.2	0.3	57,556	100.0
Total	20.2	40.7	17.0	4.3	17.6	0.2	206,450	100.0

Source: U.S. 1990 Census, Public Use Microdata Sample, 5 percent, unweighted.

Figure 1. Typology of Migration

Psychology and Motivation for Migration	Legal and Political Status	
	Conferred	Not Conferred
Economic	Legal immigrants (e.g., Koreans, Indians)	Undocumented labor (e.g., Mexicans)
Political	Legal refugees (e.g., Salvadorans, Guatemalans)	Undocumented refugees (e.g., Salvadorans, Guatemalans

tion: the refusal to grant them amnesty, their interdiction at sea, and their deportation back to Haiti despite the political violence that reigned there. Haitians who were refused asylum can be seen as undocumented refugees. Until now, Cubans had always been recognized and welcomed as refugees. But during this last crisis, for the first time they were defined as aliens attempting to enter the United States by illegal means. With the end of the Cold War and under the resurgence of nativistic attitudes across the land, Cubans have now become undocumented refugees.

At the other end, in Cuba, over the course of time, all who left were labeled traitors and counter- revolutionaries, whether they were supporters of the *ancien régime* of Batista or, like Hùber Matos, had fought against Batista in the hills of the Sierra Maestra, side by side with Fidel Castro for a nationalist and social-democratic revolution they felt Castro's espousal of communism had betrayed (cf. Zolberg et al. 1989).

A society where the only choice possible is to "love it or leave it" provides too few choices. A truly democratic society is defined not only by its party structure, constitution, delegation of authority, or electoral representation, but principally by its capacity to tolerate and incorporate dissent. The Cuban exodus, now over a third of a century old, has been driven not only by the trauma of revolutionary change in Cuba, and by the economic hardships caused both by the inefficiencies of the new economic system as well as by the isolation of the trade embargo, but also by Cuba's incapacity to tolerate dissent. The Cuban revolution's only solution to dissent has been to externalize it. Cuba has yet to provide political channels to express and incorporate the other dissenting voices.

CONCLUSION

Over the time span of the exodus, over a third of a century, Cubans in the United States have been undergoing a profound attitudinal transition: from refugees to immigrants to ethnics. The first part of this transition in attitudes "from refugees to immigrants" has, under the impact of constant new immigration and the centrality of Cuba in the lives of the immigrants, been slow to take place (cf. Rieff 1993). But to the degree that Cubans have ceased to look backwards (like Lot's wife) to Cuba as the only source for the meaning of their existence and identity, to the degree that they have started to look forward and to carve their future in this country as Cuban Ameri-

cans, to that degree it has been achieved (cf. Portes 1984).

The second part of this transition in attitudes, "from immigrants to ethnics" is more inexorable because it corresponds to the demographic transition presently underway. Although quite young still, a second generation born in this country is now in our midst that was raised under American institutions and socialized in American schools, the great transmitters of tradition, culture, and values. Although these young Cubans' assimilation may have been delayed by their growing up in the Cuban enclave in Miami, like any people, they are the soil in which they rooted and grew. Moreover, they lack the felt sense of a Cuba they did not know.

In "The Agony of Exile," Rubén G. Rumbaut (1991) underscored that the meaning of exile is different across generations. To the parents' generation, who made the decision to leave, exile represents a profound loss and a profound commitment, both. And it entails a worldview that will be defended. By contrast, to their children's generation, exile is an inherited circumstance. Typically, they are in solidarity with the family's predicament, but do not need to protect their parents' worldview. Their focus is on the future in the new society.

In between these two lies the "1.5 generation"— those who left at the dawn of their adolescence and, like Robert Park's (1928) "marginal man," are forever caught between two worlds, the land of their birth and the land that tended them. As one of them, it is my hope that the second generation that has now rooted in the United States will not be so American that they will lose touch with their history and culture, with their *Cubanía*. But as a sociologist I have to recognize that such may well be the price to be paid for shedding the pain of exile.

REFERENCES

Aguirre, Benigno E. 1976. "The Differential Migration of Cuban Social Races." *Latin American Research Review* 11: 103-24.

Alfonso, Pablo M. 1984. *Cuba, Castro, y los Católicos.* Miami, Florida: Ediciones Hispamerican Books.

Amaro, Nelson, and Alejandro Portes. 1972. "Una Sociología del Exilio: Situación de los Grupos Cubanos en los Estados Unidos." *Aportes* 23: 6-24.

Amaro Victoria, Nelson. 1977. "Mass and Class in the Origins of the Cuban Revolution." Pp. 221-51 in *Cuban Communism*, edited by Irving Louis Horowitz. New Brunswick, New Jersey: Transaction.

Bach, Robert L., Jennifer B. Bach, and Timothy Triplett. l981/l982. "The Flotilla 'Entrants': Latest and Most Controversial." *Cuban Studies* 11/12: 29-48.

_____. 1980. "The New Cuban Immigrants: Their Background and Prospects." *Monthly Labor Review* 103: 39-46.

Balmaseda, Liz. 1994a. "Balserita Violinista Toca pero También Escribe como los Angeles." *El Nuevo Herald*, 19 Octubre.

_____. 1994b. "Cuba Bleeds, and the Drops are Called Rafts." *The Miami Herald*, 17 August.

Casal, Lourdes. 1979. "Cubans in the United States: their Impact on U.S.-Cuban Relations." Pp. 109-36 in *Revolutionary Cuba in the World Arena*, edited by Martin Weinstein. Philadelphia: Ishi.

"Cifra Anual de Balseros Cubanos Marcó Récord." 1993. *El Nuevo Herald*, 26 Diciembre.

Clark, Juan M. 1975. "The Exodus from Revolutionary Cuba (1959-1974): A Sociological Analysis." Ph.D. dissertation, University of Florida.

Díaz-Briquets, Sergio. 1983. "Demographic and Related Determinants of Recent Cuban Emigration." *International Migration Review* 17: 95-119.

Dixon, Heriberto. 1988. "Black Cubans in the United States: A Case of Conflicts between Race and Ethnicity." Paper presented at the Annual Meeting of the American Studies Association, Miami, Florida, October 27-30.

Domínguez, Jorge I. 1991. "Cooperating with the Enemy? U. S. Immigration Policies toward Cuba." Harvard University, Center for International Affairs.

_____. 1975. "La Tradición Liberal y la Emigración Cubana. *Areíto* 1: 4-5.

Fagen, Richard R., Richard A. Brody, and Thomas J. O'Leary. 1968. *Cubans in Exile: Disaffection and the Revolution.* Palo Alto, California: Stanford University Press.

Feagin, Joe R. 1978. *Racial and Ethnic Relations.* Englewood Cliffs, N. J.: Prentice Hall.

Fernàndez, Gastón. 1982. "The Freedom Flotilla: A Legitimacy Crisis of Cuban Socialism?" *Journal of Interamerican Studies and World Affairs* 24: 183-209.

Ferree, Myra Max. 1979. "Employment without Liberation: Cuban Women in the United States." *Social Science Quarterly* 60: 35-50.

Fox, Geoffrey E. 1971. "Cuban Workers in Exile." *Trans-Action* 8: 21-30.

Gordon, Milton M. 1964. *Assimilation in American Life.* New York: Oxford University Press.

Handlin, Oscar. [1951] 1973. *The Uprooted.* Boston: Little, Brown.

Hidalgo, Ariel. 1994. *Disidencia.* Miami: Ediciones Universal.

Institute of Cuban Studies. 1982. *Itinerario Ideológico: Antología de Lourdes Casal.* Miami, Fl.: Ediciones Diáspora.

Kunz, E. F. 1981. "Exile and Resettlement: Refugee Theory." *International Migration Review* 15: 42-51.

_____. 1973. "The Refugee in Flight: Kinetic Models and Forms of Displacement." *International Migration Review* 7: 125-46.

Lee, Everett S. 1966. "A Theory of Migration." *Demography* 3: 47-57.

Llanes, José. 1982. *Cuban-Americans: Masters of Survival.* Cambridge, Mass.: ABT.

Mannheim, Karl. 1952. *Essays in the Sociology of Knowledge.* New York: Oxford University Press.

Martí, José. 1891. "Nuestra América." *Revista Ilustrada de Nueva York*, 1ro. de Enero.

Mesa-Lago, Carmelo. 1994. "Will Cuba's Economic Reforms Work?" *The Miami Herald*, 2 January.

_____. 1978. *Cuba in the 1970s: Pragmatism and Institutionalization.* Albuquerque: University of New Mexico Press.

Mills, C. Wright. 1961. *The Sociological Imagination.* New York: Grove Press.

Montgomery, Paul L. 1981. "For Cuban Refugees, Promise of U. S. Fades." *The New York Times*, 19 April.

Onís, Juan de. 1954. *The America of José Martí.* New York: Minerva Press.

Park, Robert Ezra. 1928. "Human Migration and the Marginal Man." *American Journal of Sociology* 33: 881-93.

Pedraza, Silvia. 1991. "Women and Migration: The Social Consequences of Gender." *Annual Review of Sociology* 17: 303-25.

Pedraza-Bailey, Silvia. 1985. *Political and Economic Migrants in America: Cubans and Mexicans.* Austin: University of Texas Press.

Pérez, Lisandro. 1988. "Cuban Women in the U. S. Labor Force: A Comment." *Cuban Studies* 18: 159-64.

_____. 1986. "Immigrant Economic Adjustment and Family Organization: The Cuban Success Story Reexamined." *International Migration Review* 20: 4-20.

Portes, Alejandro, and Alex Stepick. 1993. *City on the Edge: The Transformation of Miami.* Berkeley: University of California Press.

_____, and Robert L. Bach. 1985. *Latin Journey: Cuban and Mexican Immigrants in the United States.* University of California Press.

_____. 1984. "The Rise of Ethnicity: Determinants of Ethnic Perceptions among Cuban Exiles in the United States." *American Sociological Review* 49: 383-97.

_____, Juan M. Clark, and Robert L. Bach. 1977. "The New Wave: A Statistical Profile of Recent Cuban Exiles to the United States." *Cuban Studies* 7: 1-32.

Prieto, Yolanda. 1987. "Cuban Women in the U. S. Labor Force: Perspectives on the Nature of the Change." *Cuban Studies* 17: 73-94.

Rieff, David. 1993. *The Exile: Cuba in the Heart of Miami.* New York: Simon & Schuster.

Rivas-Porta, Guillermo. 1994. "El Pueblo Cubano: Protagonista, Víctima, y Espectador." *Desafíos* 1 (Agosto/Septiembre): 4-5.

Roca, Sergio. 1977. "Cuban Economic Policy in the 1970s: The Trodden Paths." Pp. 83-118 in *Cuban Communism*, edited by Irving Louis Horowitz. New Brunswick, N. J.: Transaction.

Rodríguez-Chavez, Ernesto. 1993. "Tendencias Actuales del Flujo Migratorio Cubano." *Cuadernos de Nuestra América* 10: 114-37.

Rose, Peter I. 1981. "Some Thoughts about Refugees and the Descendants of Theseus." *International Migration Review* 15: 8-15.

Rumbaut, Rubén G. 1991. "The Agony of Exile: A Study of the Migration and Adaptation of Indochinese Refugee Adults and Children." Pp. 53-91 in *Refugee Children: Theory, Research, and Practice*, edited by Frederick L. Ahearn, Jr., and

Jean Athey. Baltimore: Johns Hopkins University Press.

Schreiber, Anna P. 1973. "Economic Coercion as an Instrument of Foreign Policy: U. S. Economic Measures against Cuba and the Dominican Republic." *World Politics* 25: 387-413.

Stein, Barry N. 1981. "The Refugee Experience: Defining the Parameters of a Field of Study." *International Migration Review* 15: 320-30.

Tabori, Paul. 1972. *The Anatomy of Exile*. London: Harrap.

Thomas, Hugh. 1977. *The Cuban Revolution*. New York: Harper & Row.

Thomas, John F. 1967. "Cuban Refugees in the United States." *International Migration Review* 2: 46-57.

Wagley, Charles. 1968. "The Concept of Social Race in the Americas." Pp. 155-174 in *The Latin American Tradition*, edited by Charles Wagley. New York: Columbia University Press.

Walsh, Bryan O. 1971. "Cuban Refugee Children." *Journal of Inter-American Studies and World Affairs* 13: 378-415.

Weber, Max. [1922] 1946. "The Social Psychology of World Religions." Pp. 267-301 in *From Max Weber: Essays in Sociology*, edited by H. H. Gerth and C. Wright Mills. New York: Oxford University Press.

Zeitlin, Maurice. 1966. "Political Generations in the Cuban Working Class." *American Journal of Sociology* 71: 493-508.

Zolberg, Aristide R., Astri Suhrke, and Sergio Aguayo. 1989. *Escape From Violence: Conflict and the Refugee Crisis in the Developing World*. New York: Oxford University Press.

PHILOSOPHICAL INQUIRY
AND THE CRISIS OF CUBAN PUBLIC LIFE

Roberto J. Vichot

From a historical perspective, the crisis of Cuban public life is rooted in Cuba's colonial experience. It was then that the seed of an incompatible relationship between Cuba's economic and political institutions was planted. The genesis of this crisis is the nature of the social stratification created by Spanish colonialism. It engendered a form of social stratification which interrupted the development of democratic political culture and a social sense of national character. The peculiar social stratification system undermined the development of a national political culture capable of adjusting the country to the economic growth it experienced after its independence. The social stratification permeated public life with a limiting instrumentalist sense of action.

The thesis of the essay is that exacerbated by the incompatibility between economic and civic life, the U.S. Intervention (1898-1902) steered the fledgling Cuban republic into a course of political development which fomented and aggravated the crisis incipient in the society since its colonial period. The U.S. intervention vested the society with a shroud of modernity which merely served to cover up the country's beleaguered political culture. Relying on Max Weber's typology of political legitimation and social organizations, this essay presents the crisis of Cuban public life in terms of the evolution of Cuba's political and economic institutions. In the first part of this essay I rely on Weber's theory of legitimation

and outline the historical evolution of this crisis during Cuba's colonial period and then during its period of constitutional republicanism. On the second part of the essay I begin by identifying the main philosophical lines of interpretation which have been used to explain this crisis and conclude with the philosophical implications of the crisis.[1]

THE CRISIS OF CUBAN PUBLIC LIFE: A WEBERIAN INTERPRETATION

Weber's theory of legitimization.

Cuba presents a relationship between legitimacy and economics which is different from that of traditional societies such as Japan's and the other Pacific economies. Pacific market economies develop in societies which partake of a traditionalist type of legitimacy. However, unlike Japanese, South Korean, Taiwanese and Singapore economies, which are compatible with a traditionalistic type of political legitimacy, the Cuban economy is faced with a political culture which is the off-shoot of Spanish colonialism. Cuba's colonial experience eliminated most remnants of traditionalism in Cuban society, creating a legitimation vacuum which is at the root of Cuba's political culture. In comparison to the path followed by traditional societies, Cuba's economic forces and its socio-political structures were also set apart by the discrepancies which surfaced during the Republic between legal structures and bureaucratic management.

---

1. Thanks to Professors Benigno E. Aguirre and Michael A. Weinstein for their commentaries and editorial suggestions.

Weber argues that public life is a consequence of the secularization of traditional society. He defines public life as a political association in which rules become a formal principle of social organization. According to Weber, there are three different ideal-type of organizational structures around which all organizational structures of decision-making associations are organized; these are the traditionalistic, the charismatic and the legal-rational. The traditionalistic and the charismatic structures rely on habitual orientation and revelation, respectively, as the justification of the rules. Modern society begins only when legalism becomes the principle of decision-making and rational and secular principles of organization become the bases of association. Weber calls legalist organizational structure "bureaucratic management." Weber also argues that bureaucratic-management is the foundation of public life.[2] For Weber, public life is a form of bureaucratic management in which decision-making associations are organized on the principle of legal action.

Weber further maintains that historically bureaucratic management is not the rule but the exception, with its beginnings dating to the early Middle Ages.[3] He identifies two factors which he says are essential to the sustained development and stability of public life: one is a market economy, the other is the spirit of Protestantism. Weber writes that while there is no necessary relationship between economic organization and administrative structures, "without a money economy the bureaucratic structure can hardly avoid undergoing substantial internal changes, or indeed, turning into another type of structure," something other than public life.[4] To support his argument Weber cites examples of Egyptian, Chinese and Roman antiquity, as well as Medieval Europe.[5]

The importance of a money—as a opposed to a subsistence—economy is that it promotes the protection of private economic structures such as property rights, debt payments, contracts, etc. Under such circumstances, public officials are embedded in offices which discharge functions that by their very nature imply a *position or space* distinct, independent or autonomous from that which may be described and prescribed as personal or private. Public officials are staff and function by providing continuous administration without which organized domination and state power does not exist. Based on this argument, Weber concludes that even though "the full development of a money economy is not an indispensable condition for bureaucratization, bureaucracy as a permanent structure is knit to the one presupposition of a constant income for maintaining it."[6] A money economy conditions the organization of human life into two distinct spheres—public and private. Without a private sphere there is at best a political domain but there is properly speaking no public sphere.

Weber's theory of legitimation holds that wherever economically and socially comparable levels of rational organization do not coexist, an autocratic government will be established based on charismatic leadership. The advantage of charismatic leadership is that, due to its personal or vital basis of authority, it functions independently of rational organizational structures. In situations where the powers of tradition have dissipated and rational social order do not or cannot take its place, devotion to individual action becomes a source of regularity and stability. Of course, the disadvantage of charismatic leadership is that it has no other source of legitimacy than the proven personal strengths of the leader. Intrinsic to it is a disregard of all permanent or institutionalized

---

2. *Max Weber: Essays in Sociology*, translated, edited and with an introduction by C. Wright Mills and H. H. Gerth (New York: Oxford University Press, 1973), p. 196.

3. Ibid.

4. Ibid., p. 205.

5. Ibid., pp. 204-209.

6. Ibid., p. 208.

structures of legitimacy, undermining a social order which is the opposite of the economic order.[7]

Cuba's period of colonialism disassociated the country's market forces, or economic organizations, from most forms of socially structured bureaucratic organizations. Hispanic colonialism created a discrepancy between the bureaucratic-management apparatus, the *apparatus* of domination, and the rational legal structures of the Cuban nation. In this context, Cuba's colonial experience undermined most remnants of traditional and modern political institutions, while creating a legitimation vacuum for Cuba's political culture. This discrepancy continued during Cuba's period of republican governance. This is what I term the genesis of the crisis of Cuban public life, a crisis rooted in the dissociation of market growth and Cuba's bureaucratic managerial patterns during its republican form of government. To document this thesis I will now present an outline of the political and economic conditions engendered by Cuba's Spanish colonial legacy.

The colonial sources of the crisis of Cuban public life

This crisis of Cuba's public life is the product of three particular factors engendered by Cuba's Spanish colonial history. These factors are a) the obfuscation of the national political culture as a socially binding sense of "national" character, b) a lack of general experience in the practice of democracy, and c) a reliance on the family structure as a basis of political-economic power. I will briefly discuss the importance of these three factors which have contributed to limiting the function of political legitimacy in Cuban society.

1) Colonialism and the obfuscation of Cuban political culture and national identity. This first factor refers to the difficultly of identifying the origins of Cuban culture. Commenting on the history of Latin American subnational groups living in the U.S., Earl Shorris writes that any "history of Latinos stumbles from the start, for there is no single line to trace back to its ultimate origins."[8] This is particularly true of Cuba. While Amerindian civilizations remained at the center of many Central and South American societies, the near extermination of Indians from most of the Caribbean and the introduction of African slaves in their place substantially decreased the possibility of finding an original ethnic source of Cuban culture. The problem was further complicated by the practices of African-slave trade which, in the words of Melville J. Herskovits, prevented the recreation of tribal customs in the New World.[9] Under these conditions the Spanish Crown's heavy-handed domination of the people—both slaves and the general population—was the principal source of social order.

The single most important effect of Spain's colonial racial policies in Cuba was to minimize the effectiveness of the single most common cultural vehicle for the development of modern political institutions, nationalism. Enrique José Varona maintains that the social forces of Spanish colonialism so stratified the society that they obstructed the emergence of a collective soul, a nation. Varona writes: "When the conquest sets two or more completely dissimilar races in one another's presence, and obliges them to occupy the same territory, the society is divided into layers, into strata which mix with difficulty, and which more or less take on the organization of closed castes."[10] Instead of a national consciousness, he writes, what emerged was a form of social conscious-

---

7. Weber, pp. 248-250.

8. Earl Shorris, *Latinos: A Biography of the People* (New York: W. W. Norton & Co., 1993), p. 15.

9. See Melville J. Herskovits, *The Myth of the Negro Past* (Boston: Beacon Press, 1958), p. 39.

10. Enrique José Varona, *De la colonia a la república: Selección de trabajos políticos, ordenado por su autor*, Biblioteca de la Cultura Cubana, vol. 2, "El fracaso colonial de España: período revolucionario" (La Habana: Sociedad Editorial Cuba Contemporanea, 1919), p. 120. The Spanish text reads: "Cuando la conquista pone en presencia dos o más razas completamente disímiles, y las obliga a ocupar el mismo territorio, la sociedad se divide en capas, en estratos superpuestos que se mezclan dificilmente, y que toman más o menos la orginazación de castas cerradas."

ness founded upon an individual's ethnic or racial consciousness. Ethnicity and not nationality became the identifying element in society.[11] Those who fought and died together for national independence did so bound together by a shared desire to over-throw a master.

Varona argues that in modern history there is no so-ciological equivalent to the social stratification en-gendered by the colonization of Spanish-America. The Spaniards did not contemplate educational re-forms nor efforts at culturally improving the higher social classes and developing the people's social ener-gy. Likewise, Leví Marrero argues that the process of land appropriation and "latifundio" which took place during the initial years of colonization in Cuba has no equal in America.[12] The Spaniards sought nothing but domination.

Varona characterizes Spanish colonialism as abnor-mal and suggests that this abnormality marked the inception of Latin American colonial societies, spe-cially when compared to the effect of England's colo-nialism. In English America, he writes, the spirit of local autonomy was born robust and remained vital. In Spanish America it was hardly born at all and grew feebly.[13] The political benefits derived by the people of the U.S. not only from the form of their colonial governments but also from the practices of Congre-gationalism and other forms of Protestantism[14], in-cluded along with their experience of democratic governance and local self-rule, the possibilities of a variety of public associations.

Marrero corroborates but also qualifies Varona's ar-gument about the role of race as a condition which hindered the development of Cuban nationalism. Marrero, along with Varona, credits Felix Varela y Morales with the pedagogical and philosophical revo-lution which made possible Cuba's first intellectual nationalist movement, and which included liberal in-tellectuals like José Antonio Saco, José de la Luz y Caballero, and Domingo del Monte.[15] In this initial phase, the concept of "Cuban nationality" emerged as a critical concept used by liberal intellectuals, par-ticularly Saco, to argue against Cuba's annexation to the United States in the 1840s. However, as Marrero notes, Saco's defense of Cuban nationalism was very much a product of his times, identifying "cuban na-tionalism" with "cuban white race."[16] Marrero goes on to argue that nationalism in Cuba was hostage to the inability of its proponents to discern the impor-tance of the role of the slaves in the culture. Conse-quently, while nationalism functioned as an effective source of insurrectional force against Spanish colo-nialism, Cuban nationalism, as Gordon K. Lewis ar-gues, "divided into various and sometimes contradic-tory elements." One tendency was anti-Spanish but pro-American, another was "autonomist" but re-formist, while yet another was autonomist and "in-surrectionist."[17]

According to Marrero, the pattern of development of Cuban nationalism changed with the beginning of new navigational routes that reinforced a type of commercial regionalism which had already been de-veloping within Cuba. This development gave impe-tus to the drive for the war of independence in the

---

11. Idem., "El fracaso colonial de España: período revolucionario," p. 120.

12. Leví Marrero, *Cuba, Economía y Sociedad*, vol. 15 (Rio Piedras, Puerto Rico: Editorial San Juan, 1972), p. 1.

13. Enrique José Varona, *De la colonia a la república: Selección de trabajos políticos, ordenado por su autor*, Biblioteca de la Cultura Cu-bana, vol. 2, "El fracaso colonial de España: período colonial" (La Habana: Sociedad Editorial Cuba Contemporanea, 1919), p. 98.

14. While Protestantism promoted self-rule and democratic institutional experiences in the U.S., in Cuba Protestantism was sparsely present in the XVI and XVII century, but did not establish itself among Cubans until after the 1902; see José Antonio Ramose, *Panora-ma del protestantismo en Cuba*, prólogo del Dr. Justo L. González: San José, Costa Rica: Editorial Caribe, 1986, p. 20, 159.

15. Leví Marrero, *Cuba, Economía y Sociedad*, vol 15. p. 42.

16. Ibid., p. 166.

17. Gordon K. Lewis, *Main Currents in Caribbean Thought: The Historical Evolution of Caribbean Society in its Ideological Aspects, 1490-1900* (Baltimore: The Johns Hopkins University Press, 1983),p. 286.

country's Western regions, where the social, economic and military importance of race had been recognized. In the Epilogue to his fifteen-volume work on Cuba, Marrero concludes that while Varona's pessimistic interpretation of Cuba's Independence war was profound it was also incomplete because Cuba's war for independence, the War of 1868, the Great War, as Marrero calls it, gave Cuba a new form of self-identification. The war forged the earlier sixteenth-century concept of Cuban nationalism, the "criollo," into that of the "mambí," which applied to any black or white person who fought in the Independence Army. In this sense, the War of Independence gave Cuba a new form of nationalist consciousness.

2) Colonialism and democratic institutions in Cuba.
While nationalism managed to function as an effective source of insurrectional force against colonialism, Cuba's Spanish colonial legacy had a more detrimental effect on Cuba's democratic experience. With varying degrees of success, the spirit of constitutional democracy helped mold European nationalisms into the framework of modern political institutions. However, in countries stripped of the more traditional social framework of liberal constitutional democracy, nationalist ideologies became an accomplice to democratic despotism and populism. Thus, in Luis Aguilar León's words, nationalism limited Cuba's political development. According to Aguilar, while Cuba's historical nationalism is in appearance similar to Europe's, it is in fact its opposite because it weakens and spoils the Cuban historical social fabric and does not make the past a unifying force. Consequently, while it is true that, as Marrero argue, the War of Independence provided Cubans with the seed of a multi-racial national identity, in Cuba patriotism lacked the democratic experience necessary to prevent it from turning into a source of discord, psychological complexes, and resentments.[18] Nowhere is this more evident than in the Law of the Fifty Per-

cent, which in the 1930s, in order to provide employment for Cuban nationals, stripped of employment non-Cuban nationals who were already employed; many immigrants, most of them Spaniards who were also parents of Cuban-born children, were left without income and forced to leave the country.[19]

Beginning with Varela, Saco, and Varona and continuing up to Marrero, Cuban scholars have emphasized how Spain did not bother to transfer its political institutions to the New World and how instead it imposed an "external" form of social organization, based on an outmoded form of estate and caste hierarchies, which functioned at a rudimentary level. Spain did transplant its demagogic scholasticism, empty theology, chaotic jurisprudence, and an empirically blind medical science to the New World.

A bifurcation was created in Cuba between internal or "satellite" and external or "metropolis" oriented structures of domination. Periods of civil liberties were short-lived. For instance, from 1811 to 1814, under the impetus of the ratification of the American constitution and the Bill of Rights, a certain degree of freedom of the press briefly reached Cuba and works like Jean Jacques Rousseau's, *The Social Contract* were published. But these instances were sporadic, quickly ending at the hands of censors who feared tolerance of dissent.[20] Varona comments on how this lack of democratic experience meant that after gaining their independence, young new states like Cuba would be almost in a state of atrophy, not having had the experience and opportunity of exercising the vital functions and organs of communal life. Having known only social isolation and submission, societies like Cuba went about building their institutions by "blind routine." They could neither imitate nor invent.[21]

3) Colonialism and Cuba's subsistence economy. Along with these cultural and democracy-related problems,

---

18. Luis Aguilar León, *Pasado y Ambiente en el proceso Cubano* (Habana: Ediciones Insula, 1957), pp. 25-27.

19. Rafael Esténger, *Sincera historia de Cuba: 1492-1973* (Medellín, Colombia: Editorial Bedout, S.A., 1974), pp. 281-282.

20. Marrero, *Cuba, Economía y Sociedad*, vol. 15, pp. 24-27.

21. Varona, "El fracaso colonial de España: período colonial," p.102.

issues related to Cuba's colonial subsistence economy are also relevant to my argument. Throughout its colonial history, Cuba lacked adequate political institutions to support the development of a market economy. By the middle of the nineteenth century, explains Marrero, Cuba's economy, already thwarted by Spain's earlier commercial policies favoring other colonies like Mexico and Peru (under the assumption that there existed vast amounts of gold and other precious metals reserves in these countries) was characterized by large sugar plantations and a preponderance of commercial coffee and tobacco agriculture. Habana was the exception, benefitting from its strategic geographic location as passage-port. This agricultural type of economy, as Weber suggests, is consistent with traditional family and aristocratic structures, which oftentimes develop into a patriarchal type of political system, as was the case in Cuba.[22] However, patriarchal political structures disassociate rational legal structures and bureaucratic management organizations, depriving the society of the two-dimensional organizational structure which supports market economies like the one introduced in Cuba at the end of nineteenth century by the U.S. intervention (1898-1902).

The crisis of Cuba's constitutional republic

By stabilizing and nourishing Cuba's market forces, the U.S. intervention did change the course of Cuba's economic and political history, fomenting the public crisis incipient in Cuba's colonial past. The fledgling Cuban republic was launched on an economic course of development without a complementary form of public life. The old colonial institutional political framework, more in tune with the social dynamics of a subsistence than a market economy, failed to provide Cuba with political structures which would be compatible with a demand economy and financial capitalism.

The Constitution of 1902, with its guarantee of U.S. intervention, while giving stability to Cuba's economic and political system, did not promote the so-

cialization process necessary to make a constitutional democracy work in Cuba. It was foreign investment from abroad, mostly from the U.S, and military intervention by the U.S., often at the request of Cuban officials, what prevented anarchy and kept order in the country, while political corruption and social disregard for the law and the Constitution ran unabated. As evidenced in Varona, Aguilar, and Marrero's comments, as well as those of other writers, the intervention and presence by the U.S. stabilized and sustained the political life of the country, which would have otherwise probably continued to drift politically.

In the aftermath of the U.S. intervention, the realization of republicanism, a political system in which citizens exercise power through elected representatives, the ideal of Cuban political society, was suppressed. Throughout their history Cubans had hoped for the arrival of the day when their dream of political autonomy and self-determination would become a reality. Now this dream would be postponed. The 1902 constitution, negotiated between the U.S. and non-elected Cuban representatives, would delay this process. In the absence of the type of ratification-convention debate which provided the U.S. Constitution with a social foundation unlike that of any other country, Cuba's 1902 Constitution aborted the "public dialogue" that would have engaged the people in a process of historical knowledge and education which would have better prepared them for the type of organizational responsibilities they were about to assume as citizens of the new republican form of government. The necessity and importance of this dialogue was neglected in the commotion and justified concerns of most Cubans over the U.S.'s role in Cuba's future, specially as defined by the Platt Amendment. This state of affairs changed in 1933, when, in the words of Rafael Esténger, "the economic crisis, interlaced with the constitutional reform which had paralyzed the free play of democracy, placed the country's great majorities against the [government's] dictatorship."[23] By then, however, politi-

---

22. Marrero, *Cuba, Economía y Sociedad*, vol. 15, pp. 259-264.

23. Rafael Esténger, *Sincera Historia de Cuba: 1492-1973*, p. 274.

cal instrumentalism, manifested in factionalism, fragmentation, and corruption in Cuban politics, had already taken a heavy toll on the society, making apathy and martyrdom staple values of Cuban political culture.

The Constitution of 1940, which was drafted through a constitutional assembly in which a majority of the country's principal factions participated, and which instituted many provisions which had been sources of conflict in earlier administrations—such as a one-term limit on the Presidency, the limitation of the Executive's power (with a semi-parliamentary structure), and the protection of individual liberties, to name a few—was immediately undermined by groups of armed thugs, corrupt administrators and, most importantly, the people's mob-level of political participation and their fanatical devotion to a few leaders.[24] The Constitutional gains of 1940 thus failed to achieve the level of legitimacy and public order required by Cuba's market economy.

Even more detrimental was the paradoxical effect of the U.S. 1902 intervention. It contributed to the development of a market-type economy in Cuba by supporting its infrastructure, including bridges and roads, water and sewage treatment systems and certain types of legal and educational improvements.[25] These developments instilled among the populace a premature sense of confidence in economic progress, public life and stability. These collective erroneous perceptions were reinforced by a set of demographic changes which began to evolve through the Presidential administrations of Tomas Estrada Palma (1902-1909), Mario García Menocal (1909-1913), José Miguel Gómez (1913-1920), and Alfredo Zayas Alonso (1920-1924).[26] During these years, the development of a market economy in Cuba gave impetus

to the perception that the society was on a sure path towards modernity. Thus, by the 1950s trends of socioeconomic characteristics common of developed industrialized nations, such as declining birthrate, rise in the number of women in the workforce, rise in the rate of divorces, a very high average standard of living, especially in comparison to other Latin American countries, and a large population density in urban areas lent a quasi-modern quality to Cuban social life and encouraged the belief that Cuba was a modern developed society[27].

Summary. The poverty of Cuba's nationalism, its deprived legacy of democratic experience, and its subsistence economy, conspired to frame the colonial characteristics of the crisis of Cuban public life at the end of the nineteenth century. Under the new constitutional republic, Cuban continued to project its bias against rational administrative organizational life, as shown, for instance, by its weak governmental authority at its local level and its strong, centralized, executive authority. This trend is corroborated by Cuba's weak local and provincial governments, its concentration of political power at the level of the national Ministries, its Presidential (as opposed to a parliamentary) system of government, and the weak presence or lack of public, as opposed to private, associations. This pattern is still evident in Cuban society today. As Dr. Ricardo Puerta shows the Cuban government prohibits all form of associations which engage in social criticism or which monitor the security forces.[28]

ALTERNATIVE SOLUTIONS TO THE CRISIS OF CUBAN PUBLIC LIFE

A philosophical analysis of the forces that historically have permeated Cuba's politics and public life, would enlighten us about the "meaning of action," in

---

24. Ibid., pp. 288-300.

25. 24. Juan Clark, *Cuba: mito y realidad, testimonios de un pueblo,* con la colaboración de Angel de Fana, Juan Figueras, y Roberto Lozano. Miami-Caracas: Saeta Ediciones, 1990, pp.12-13; see also Charles E. Chapman, *A History of the Cuban Republic: A Study of Hispanic American Politics,* New York: Octagon Books, 1969, Ch. 5.

26. Clark, Idem., pp. 13-20.

27. Ibid., pp. 26-29.

28. Dr. Ricardo Puerta, "Sociedad civil si, pero... de que tipo?" Paper presented at the Association for the Study of the Cuban Economy Fifth Annual Meeting, Miami, August 10-12, 1995.

Weber's terms, that constitute the cultural structures of Cuban political culture and public life.[29] While a general analysis of Cuban political culture, involving a study of the relationship between institutions, social practices and ideas, is outside the scope of this essay, generally speaking, some currents of Cuban thought which illustrate important interpretations and experiences of Cuban public life are relevant to this discussion.

Prior to the late twentieth-century, Thomistic training, like that received by Varela and Varona, enabled Cuban philosophers to appreciate the importance of reflection, rigorous logical thinking and mental discipline for politics. This, in turn, led them to emphasize the political value of education and pedagogy in Cuba. Varona for instance, wrote:

> Propender a la educación política es propender a que se enriquezca la inteligencia del pueblo con los datos y nociones que le sirvan para dirigir su razon a la consecución de fines sociales. Es propender a que esté en aptitud a dirigirse a si mismo; de tal modo que al cabo las leyes que se de, para regular su actividad, no sean el resultado de impulsos inconcientes, sino la expresión clara y comprendida de los dictados de la razón colectiva.[30]

While the relationship between pedagogy and public life distinguishes much of nineteenth-century Cuban political theory, in the 1950s Cuba's historicist and instrumentalist intellectual tendencies intermingled, contending for domination. In the work of Aguilar we find a good representation of the "historicist" bent of Cuban philosophy.

Historicism. Aguilar's historicism is strongly influenced by José Ortega y Gasset's and consequently carries existentialist and phenomenological insights which are important for a philosophical inquiry into public life. This historicism has influenced philosophy throughout most of Latin America, as evidenced in the works of Leopoldo Zea, Luis Recasens Siches, and Enrique Miró Quesada. All historicist philosophy emphasizes the temporal.

Historicism, in Aguilar's term, stresses the influence of the past ("tiempos remotos") on concepts, values, and technologies.[31] Calling attention to the immanence of the past in the present, historicist philosophers underscored the effect of Cuba's colonial legacy and its cultural values on the nation's public life.

The importance of this historicist approach becomes evident in Aguilar's argument that if all that is behind us, except the emancipation struggles, is shadows and repeated theft, if our generation (growth) is imposed upon us by inheritance, then the duty of the present generation has to be to break forever with such cynical bondage.[32] To this end, he argues:

> Nos hace falta... una filosofía beligerante y escalpelo que se atreva a hendir sin misericordia, a profundizar seriamente, y a proclamar en voz alta las verdades que encuentre. Seriedad en el conocimiento y sinceridad en la expresión son los pivotes sobre los que debe girar hacia atras nuestra generación para replantar, con ánimos de solución, nuestro proceso colonial y republicano.[33]

Among the contributions of historicist thought to the analyses of Cuban public life is the emphasis it gives to the role of history and tradition in Cuban political culture. In this context, it is possible to obtain an insight about the experience of time in contemporary Cuban political culture. Shorris, describing the Cuban-exile culture states that unlike other immigrants, Cubans do not seek to escape the past or the future; rather, they seek to rehabilitate the past, from whence there derives an aggressiveness, a sense of hard work, a take-charge sort of attitude within the community. The objective of this aggressiveness

---

29. Max Weber, "Basic Sociological Terms," in *Understanding and Social Inquiry*, Fred R. Dallmayr and Thomas McCarthy, eds. (Notre Dame, IN: University of Notre Dame Press, 1977). p. 38.

30. Varona, "El fracaso colonial de España," p. 93.

31. Ibid., p. 16.

32. Ibid., p. 30.

33. Ibid., p. 30-31.

appears to be to overcome the experience of nostalgia; aggressiveness increases the time devoted to action and allows one to transform the phenomenon of lived time (nostalgia) into the phenomenon of "control."[34]

Instrumentalism. This reduction of existential time to chronological or measured time and the use of action to transform time into a cause-and-effect phenomenon, is neither uniquely nor primordially historicist. Nor is it unique to the Cuban exiles; it is a type of instrumentalism common in Cuban political culture. By instrumentalism I do not mean here the type of "pragmatist" epistemology associated with Dewey's experimentalist theory of knowledge. Instrumentalism, as used here, refers to the effort of asserting human mastery over nature, which, as Michael Weinstein argues, has its origins in the evolutionary philosophies of history of Comte, Marx, and Spencer.[35]

In Cuba, as in Mexico, to some extent, instrumentalism is rooted in the desire to come to terms with the country's colonial legacy of a sense of social, political and historical orphanage. By reducing the experience of lived time to action, instrumentalism endeavors to lengthen the duration of the consciousness of the "present" moment. It is a way to endure the dreadfulness of the presence of a dubious past. The Cuban predisposition towards action, essential to the characterization of Cubans as hard-working, aggressive, self-confident, and impetuous people, reflects this meaning and is consistent with Weber's use of the term.

Social action, according to Weber, is the purposive orientation of the actions of an individual to the action of other individuals. In so far as social action is based on the expectation that others will act with a view towards rules which have been established rationally, the action is instrumental.[36] These expectations are used as "conditions" or "means" for the attainment of the actor's own rationally-pursued and calculated ends. When the purposive orientation of actions consists of maxims regarded by the actor as in some way obligatory or exemplary for him, the action is normative or value-rational.[37]

Cuban society displays an instrumentalist social orientation, not in the sense that it is a society void of all sense of fundamental values, but in the sense that it is a society bereft of traditional values. In this context, individuals' behavior is instrumentalist in that it is constituted through the effort to control the effect of change and of the discrepant structures of social action upon the self. This is done through the attempt to prevent history from having an effect on and overtaking the actor. Such attempts succeed when the actor's efforts at manipulating change effectively overtake experience. In this purely instrumentalist mode of existence both the object and the subject, history and the agent, are dissolved. Existence and experience become one and the same. Consequently, maxims of obligatory or exemplary action cease to be regarded by the actor as in some general way relevant to him; the norm loses its independent normative character. This instrumentalism significantly divests social action and social life of normative meaning. When action is simply a means to an end, not only life but all that is part of that life, including other human lives, lose intrinsic value. Instead of being regarded as ends-in-themselves, the contents of experience are regarded as means to an end.

This social process is evident in Cuban public life both in Miami and Cuba in the aftermath of the Cuban socialist revolution. Capitalist and socialist instrumentalism in Miami and Cuba function by helping Cubans to develop a substitute form of social-

---

34. Shorris, *Latinos*, Ch.5.

35. Michael A. Weinstein, *The Polarity of Mexican Thought: Instrumentalism and Finalism* (University Park, PA: The Pennsylvania State University Press, 1976), p. 4.

36. Max Weber, "Types of Social Action and Groups," Appendix 1, *Economy and Society: An Outline of Interpretive Sociology*, ed. by Guenther Roth and Claus Wittich (N.Y.: Bedminster Press, 1968), p. 1376-1379.

37. Ibid., "Basic Sociological Terms," Chapter 1, vol. 1, p. 25.

identity in terms of consumerism and collective identity, respectively. Consumerism and collective identity rely on action to transcend time, transforming the self into a function of change.

Time is a function of duration and is part of every experience. It distinguishes between the beginning and the end of an experience, and the end of one experience and the beginning of another, making people aware of the finitude or enclosure of experience, and its openness to infinity. This distinction discloses time as a form of interdependence which extends to the individual's relationship with the environment, other persons, and cultural objects. Everyday life reflects this interdependence as a collective product which "is unified by a transpersonal meaning linking human beings to a past that happened before they became aware and to a future that will occur after they die."[38]

The lack of an adequate sense of cultural time jeopardizes one's appreciation of experience's temporal quality and its function in human action. Existence is experienced as a transitory process, void of an existential sense of finitude and infinity, and totally open to human manipulation. A society's sense of cultural time can be undermined by different forces and events. Cuba's is undermined by its colonial legacy and the effects of the U.S.'s Intervention, giving rise to capitalist instrumentalist consumerism and comfort in Miami and socialist collective-identity in Cuba.

Capitalist Instrumentalism. Deprived of a strong sense of cultural traditionalism and Protestant individualism, and bereft from Cuba's socio-political environment where the family institution was the basis of social integration and economic mobility, the process of adaptation and acculturation of Cubans in Miami is framed by business and capitalistic endeavors which have culminated in what Alejandro Portes and Alex Stepick identify as the "enclave," a distinctive economic formation, characterized by the special concentration of immigrant-controlled enterprises which serve their own ethnic population.[39] In this context, not even the family institution is spared from this process of economic adjustment, in which it is transformed into another instrument of the labor market, a process documented by Lisandro Perez.[40]

Engaged in economic activity strictly as a secular or materialistic endeavor, Cuban instrumentalism in Miami transforms capitalism into a ceaseless drive for consumerism and comfort. Consumerism involves a very basic type of activity, namely the satisfaction of wants. Since consumption is a type of activity which is easy to mimic, it helps to make an individual feel socially greater than others by virtue of his/her ability to dispose or purchase resources.

Comfort is the bourgeoisie's trademark solution to the problem of finitude and unhappy consciousness. It is prevalent among those who seek in it a means to circumvent a past riveted with betrayed promises, syphoned hopes, and unfulfilled dreams. Comfort is a feeling of relief or consolation for those who succeed in their efforts to possess and keep material goods. Comfort is a sense of relative security from physical perils which is established by the control over material conditions.

Like consumerism, comfort relies on action to transcend time, transforming the self into a function of change. Both reduce action to a means to action and hereby avoid the experience of finitude. Both are instrumentalist alternatives which help one to cope with the problem of social identity and its effect on the individual's ability to overcome anxiety and dread.

However, while consumerism remedies this problem through a continuous consummation of experience, comfort does it by engaging people in action that

---

38. Michael Weinstein, *Meaning and Appreciation: Time and Modern Political Life* (West Lafayette, IN: The Purdue University Press, 1978), pp. 11-12.

39. For a discussion of the importance of the entrepreneurial character of the Cuban exile community see, Alejandro Portes and Alex Stepick, *City on the Edge: The Transformation of Miami* (California: University of California Press, 1993).

40. Lisandro Pérez, "Immigrant Economic Adjustment and Family Organization," *International Migration Review* 20 (1986): 4-20.

preempts its own consummation. Comfort mitigates the effects of time on experience by repressing the inevitable end which comes from the consummation of an experience; consumerism does it by exacerbating it through a myriad of new experiences. Comfort satisfies this function of mitigating the effects of time on expereince by engaging people in wealth accumulation for the sake of wealth accumulation; consumerism does it by engaging people in consumption for the sake of consumption. Comfort relies on insatiable acquisitiveness, acedia, and greed as its motivational incentives; consumerism relies on conspicuous consumption and the erotization of commodities. These differences notwithstanding, consumerism and comfort help Cubans in a market economy to cope with temporality through the power to dispose of resources to transform experience into a totalizing form of activity.

Socialist Instrumentalism. In Cuba, socialism represents an effort to transform instrumentalism into a form of collective identity. In contemporary socialist thought this effort to distance meaning from time, reflection from action, is expressed in the works of Armando Hart Dávalos, Cuban Minister of Culture and member of the Political Bureau of Cuba's Communist Party. The saliency of Marx's "ideological" interpretation of philosophy—to displace philosophy to a secondary, epiphenomenal level, to emphasize action over theory, economics over politics—concurs with the fundamental principle of Cuban culture: the reduction of time to action as an effective outlet from the dreadfulness of historical rootlessness.

Hart consistently argues for this reduction by identifying politics with culture. Political culture, he argues, is a material instrument of cultural identity; democracy is the effort to place these instruments "in the hands" of the people.[41] According to this line of argument, whatever the people do to further their

cultural identity is democratically sound and politically correct. Once politics is reduced to culture, it is dissolved into "collective identity." Identifying politics as a collective identity dissolves politics into a kind of cultural conformism. National identity is reduced to cultural identity by transforming whatever is collectively done into a socially binding reality.

It follows from this that collective action is always right because it is sanctioned by culture. The people's cultural identity is always right; it is never illegitimate or wrong. When everything that is cultural is legitimate because everything that is legitimate is action-based, and where nothing is illegitimate because there is nothing which is not action-based, public life becomes unnecessary. Moreover, since a non-collective identity cannot exist, there are no dissidents in Cuba, only anti-social deviants. From this perspective, political dissidents are non-entities because only the people's identity is culturally binding and only what is culturally binding is democratic. (Rafael Saumell's essay, "El otro testimonio, literatura carcelaria en Cuba," confirms how repressive techniques and propaganda campaigns are used in Cuba to silence dissident behavior or reduce it to a non-individualist politics.)[42]

In Cuba there is only the "politics" of collective identity, which is no democracy at all, since all democracy engages individuals and groups in dialogue. Hart and the Cuban leadership support this view of public identity by claiming that there is no system of domination in Cuba. They claim that there is no difference in Cuba between societal legal norms, or what Hart calls "culture," and the apparatus of bureaucratic management, or what Hart calls politics.

From a Weberian perspective, Cuba's social system constitutes an example of the "iron cage," that is, of a society in which the state is the *principal* source of social "integration." Cuba's socialist leadership reduces

---

41. Armando Hart Dávalos, "Segunda Conferencia Mundial Sobre Politicas Culturales de UNESCO," La Habana, 1982, in *Pensamiento y Política Cultural Cubanas: Antología,* vol. 3 (Habana: Editorial Pueblo y Educación, 1986: 146-159; see also his essay, "La educación estética:" 92-113.

42. Rafael Saumell, "El otro testimonio: literatura carcelaria en Cuba," paper presented at the Association for the Study of the Cuban Economy Fifth Annual Meeting, Miami, FL, August 10-12, 1995.

politics to culture in order to deny culture and values their critical function, which if politically affirmed, would give rise to legal structures that would involve the state in a critical social integration function. This one-dimensional character of social integration is criticized by Herbert Marcuse, who argues that the reduction of culture and aesthetic qualities to political functions strips culture of the critical function of limiting state power.[43]

Critique of Cuban Instrumentalism. Unfortunately, neither public nor private moral roots grow deep when the standards of individual action are constituted instrumentally, by the ability to transform successfully one instance of action into another. This engenders a morality in which the ends justify the means and the essence of moral integrity is action. Instrumentalism may or may not successfully sustain the life of a given individual at a given time but it reduces public life to a mode of action. In this environment public life is reduced to a means of action to more action, and distinctions between public and private life eroded.

Cuban instrumentalism in Miami and Cuba effaces not only time and history but most objects of human action, including self, other human beings, and the environment. Capitalist and socialist Cuban instrumentalism are a reduction of politics to action and are contrary to the very conditions of public life. What delimits public and private morality for most Cubans is the fact that in private life an individual, the proprietor, sets limits to action. In the public realm everyone is allowed to dispense with existence as a means to action. Public morality in Cuban society is reduced to what seventeenth- and eighteenth-century Liberal political theory terms a "state of nature:" a place where every individual struggles for position to impose control over the rest of society. To this the end, public action is transformed into a struggle for domination, into an instrument or tech-

nique, in Ortega's sense, of personal control.[44] This is true of capitalist and socialist Cuban instrumentalism.

CONCLUSION

Philosophy and the Future of Cuba. To overcome Cuba's legitimation crisis, Cubans must go beyond traditional historicism and socialist\capitalist instrumentalism, and engage in philosophical inquiry. Philosophy is important to public life because it is its first constitutive element. Public life has a social and individual dimension but it is distinguished from these in that, to use John Dewey's terms, it results when persons make an effort to regulate the consequences of actions in which they are not directly engaged but which indirectly affect them.[45] Not being primary actors, their participation is mitigated by impersonal and abstract meanings. These meanings constitute public reality. This impersonal and abstract foundation indicates that, properly speaking, public life is neither a social structure nor an individual condition but an abstract relationship.

This abstraction is the essence of the linkage between philosophy and public life. Historical analysis reveals that the first political institutions appeared at the end of the Greek Dark ages and the beginning of the Greek Modern Age. These institutions, along with philosophy, emerged at a time of a legitimation crisis, when traditional Hellenic institutions were changing and cultural values were being challenged. Like the contemporary Cuban era, it was a period of historical orphanage, institutional collapse, cultural transition and legitimation crisis.

It is in this period that philosophy is born. When Parmenides, Anaxagoras, and Socrates offered solutions to this crisis they were accused of "blaspheming" authority and corrupting the minds of youth. For this they were sentenced to exile and death. But Greek society managed to overcome this autocratic

---

43. Herbert Marcuse, *The Aesthetic Dimension: Toward a Critique of Marxist Aesthetics* (Boston: Beacon Press, 1978); see also Herbert Marcuse, *Soviet Marxism* (New York: Vintage Press, 1961).

44. See José Ortega y Gasset, "Meditación de la técnica," (1933), rpt. in *Obras Completas,* 6ta ed., vol 5 (Madrid: Revista de Occidente, 1964).

45. John Dewey, *The Public and Its Problems* (Athens, Ohio: Swallow Press: 1985), p. 12.

"modern" historical phase, and its degeneration and fundamental change of cultural values and traditions,[46] by relying on philosophy and self-doubt to identify the meaning of public life and to reconstitute society. Great institutions of public life, the direct democracy of Athenian society, the representative democracy of British society, and the republican democracy of the U.S.—all bore the imprint of philosophical inquiry. That they do so is a tribute to the intelligence of the peoples, the convictions of their philosophers, and their shared belief that public life is not a self-sustained reality but the product of a collective effort to live and share life in common, not based upon blood ties, tradition, or customs but, in the words of José Ortega y Gasset, upon a will of mind to abandon these forms of common life and think out another form not previously existing.[47]

The importance of the "new origin" of public life underlies the fact that the foundation of politics is not action or culture as the instrumentalists and Hart, respectively, would have us believe, but the alternative offered by philosophers and individuals who face the collapse and crisis of their cultural values and traditional institutions with an intellectual dialogue. Ortega underscores this point stating:

So the *urbs* or the *polis* starts by being an empty space, the *forum*, the *agora*, and all the rest is a means of fixing that empty space, of limiting its outlines. The polis is not primarily a collection of habitable dwellings, but a meeting place for citizens, a space set apart for public functions. The city is not built as is the cottage or the *domus*, to shelter from the weather or to propagate the species—these are personal or family concerns—but in order to discuss public affairs.[48]

Not only is public life, then, different from private life but also from traditional social or cultural life. Freedom and equality, for instance, are cultural practices which are different from other social institu-

tions. Most social institutions are engendered by beliefs, things which we do not doubt. The customs of freedom and equality are not of this type. They are the type of habits which, like ideas, we develop to sustain us at every moment; this is why they may endure times of crisis. For this reason, political philosophers, from Plato to John Dewey, emphasize the relationship between public life and education. In public life, as defined by Aristotle, individuals associate as equals under the law, free from the social inequalities of economics and tradition. Public life is a "space," which, like ideas, exists as the product of human effort and which like ideas, as Ortega never tired of reminding us, cease to exist when the effort which sustains them ceases. It is thus not due to simple coincidence but to their essential similarity that, since the Greeks, public life and philosophy have shared a coetaneous existence. Both are historical orphans.

Philosophic inquiry is important to public life because, as it has often been said, philosophy draws attention to the life of the mind and the human condition. In doing so, it draws our knowledge to the experience of time and of the effect of tradition on the human mind, experience, and cultural structures. Philosophical analysis is a precondition of public life because public reality is neither just a natural nor a social institutional condition; it is a human creation and like all human creation it is constituted through intelligence and consciousness. It is, thus, through the undoing of the reduction of experience to action in Cuban thought that the crisis of Cuban public life will overcome the autocratic, bureaucratic, charismatic system in which it is based. If we are to overcome the political conflicts of Cuban society and achieve a stable political system compatible with a market economy, it is imperative to identify the basic structures which institute the separation of its rational legal structures from its administrative bureaucracy and perpetuate the instrumentalist thinking pattern.

---

46. For a lengthier treatment of the meaning of modernity see chapter three of José Ortega y Gasset's, *The Revolt of the Masses*, authorized translation from the Spanish, 25 Anniversary ed. (1932, N.Y.: W.W. Norton & Co., 1957).

47. Ibid., p. 155.

48. Ibid., p. 151.

REFERENCES

Max Weber: Essays in Sociology, translated, edited and with an introduction by C. Wright Mills and H.H. Gerth (Ny York: Oxford University Press, 1973).

Earl Shorris, *Latinos: A biography of the People* (New York: W. Norton and Co., 1993).

Enrique José Varona, *De la colonia a la república: selección de trabajos políticos, ordenado por su autor.* Biblioteca de la Cultura Cubana, vol.2, "El fracaso colonial de España: Período revolucionario" (La Habana: Sociedad Editorial Cuba Contemporanea, 1919).

Leví Marrero, *Cuba, Economía y Sociedad,* Vol. 15, (Rio Piedras, Puerto Rico, Editorial San Juan, 1972).

José Antonio Ramose, *Panorama del protestantismo en Cuba,* San José, Costa Rica: Editorial Caribe, 1986.

Gordon K. Lewis, *Main Currents in Caribbean Thought: The Historical Evolution of Caribbean Society in its Ideological Aspects, 1490-1900,* (Baltimore, The John Hopkins University Press, 1983).

Luis Aguilar León, *Pasado y Ambiente en el Proceso Cubano,* La Habana, Ediciones Insula, 1957).

Rafael Esténger, *Sincera historia de Cuba: 1492-1873,* (Medellín, Colombia: Editorial Bedout, S.A., 1974).

Juan Clark, *Cuba: mito y realidad, testimonios de un pueblo,* (Miami- Caracas, Ediciones Saeta, 1990.

Charles E. Chapman, *A History of the Cuban Republic: A Study of Hispanic American Politics,* New York: Octagon Books, 1969.

Max Weber, "Basic Sociological Terms," in *Understanding and Social Inquiry,* Fred R. Dallmayr and Thomas McCarthy, eds. (Notre Dame, IN: University of Notre Dame Press, 1977).

Michael A. Weinstein, *The Polarity of Mexican Thought: Instrumentalism and Finalism,* (University Park, PA: The Pennsylvania State University Press, 1976).

Max Weber, "Types of Social Action and Groups," Appendix 1, *Economy and Society: An Outline of Interpretative Sociology,* ed. by Guenther Roth and Claus Wittich (N.Y.: Bedminster Press, 1968).

Michael Weinstein, *Meaning and Appreciation: Time and Modern Political Life,* (West Lafayette, IN: The Purdue University Press, 1978).

Alejandro Portes and Alex Stepik, *City on the Edge: The Transformation of Miami,* (California: University of California Press, 1993).

Lisandro Pérez, "Immigrant Economic Adjustment and Family Organization," *International Migration Review,* 20, 1986.

Armando Hart Dávalos, "Segunda Conferencia Mundial Sobre Políticas Culturales de UNESCO," La Habana, 1982, in *Pensamiento y Política Cultural Cubanas: Antología,* Vol. 3 (Habana: Editorial Pueblo y Educación, 1986).

Rafael Saumell, "El otro testimonio: literatura carcelaria en Cuba," paper presented at the Association for the Study of the Cuban Economy, Fifth Annual Meeting, University of Miami, Miami, FL, August 10-12, 1995.

Herbert Marcuse, *The Aesthetic Dimension: Toward a Critique of Marxist Aesthetics,* (Boston: Beacon Press, 1978).

Herbert Marcuse, *Soviet Marxism,* (New York: Vintage Press, 1961).

José Ortega y Gasset, "Meditación de la técnica," in *Obras Completas,* 6th Edition, Vol.5. (Madrid: Revista de Occidente, 1964).

John Dewey, *The Public and Its Problems,* (Athens, Ohio: Swallow Press, 1985).

EL OTRO TESTIMONIO: LITERATURA CARCELARIA EN CUBA

Rafael E. Saumell

Los testimonios sobre experiencia carcelaria en Cuba post-revolucionaria han sido estudiados y promovidos, fundamentalmente, por el periodismo literario. La crítica académica, sin embargo, casi no se ha ocupado de estas obras, las cuales incluyen poemarios, relatos y hasta documentales cinematográficos. Si exceptuamos *Linden Lane Magazine*, co-dirigida por los poetas Belkis Cuza Malé y Heberto Padilla, o la desaparecida *Mariel* a cargo del fallecido Reynaldo Arenas, hay muy pocos ensayos al respecto.

En los Estados Unidos textos como *Contra toda esperanza* (1985), de Armando Valladares y *Veinte años y cuarenta días* (1988) de Jorge Valls, se mencionan escasamente en los seminarios que sobre literatura testimonial se estructuran en los cursos universitarios. Incluso en los meticulosos listados bibliográficos que prepara Modern Language Association (MLA), hay una sola "entrada" a nombre de Valladares— *New Orleans Review* Summer 1985 12(2): 70-72—y ninguna concerniente a Valls.

Por el contrario, los artículos dedicados a testimonios escritos por prisioneros o ex-prisioneros de regímenes derechistas, aparecen con mucha mayor frecuencia, a pesar de que una simple lectura de los mismos demuestra que hay mayores coincidencias entre estos y sus equivalentes literarios bajo la dictadura del proletariado, de lo que tal vez presuman los habituales atrincheramientos políticos. Los testimonios sobre la cárcel en Cuba están muy hermanados con las obras de quienes sufrieron encierros y torturas bajo las tiranías que han plagado a Latinoamérica y el Caribe, en especial desde 1959 hasta la fecha.

Para demostrar la validez de cuanto digo he escogido, además de los títulos mencionados, un documental de largometraje (*Nadie escuchaba*, 1987) de los realizadores Néstor Almendros y Jorge Ulla, y la novela que inaugura la temática de la prisión en Cuba después de 1959.

ARCHIPIÉLAGOS TEXTUALES

El rasgo más sobresaliente de estas obras es que ellas son capaces de exponer los diferentes anti-discursos que genera en Cuba el régimen marxista-leninista encabezado por Fidel Castro. No hay un modelo ideológico dominante en la oposición a Castro. Por consiguiente, no estamos frente a diversas variantes de un discurso derechista y desafiante del proyecto de un estado que se autoproclama revolucionario.

Con los textos emanados desde las tiranías derechistas los testimonios de Cuba comparten el afán de cuestionar los relatos del poder. La represión y el castigo son universales, con independencia de las etiquetas filosóficas de los respectivos gobiernos, llámense como se llamen. Estos documentos tienen un profundo sentido de denuncia, una intensa ansiedad por acabar con los abusos físicos y psicológicos cometidos contra los opositores.

Esta es la perspectiva de Roberto González Echevarría en *The Voice of the Masters* (1985), un ensayo que ayuda a cuestionar las lecturas "partidistas" típicas de cierta crítica en Latinoamérica, Europa Occidental y los Estados Unidos. ¿Por qué? Porque el texto evita los esquematismos retóricos de la derecha y de la izquierda y, a la vez, porque demuestra cuánto hay de común entre ambas posturas políticas.

Al comienzo del libro González Echevarría explica su posición. Dice que autoridad y autoritarismo son conceptos esgrimidos por los estudiosos de las ciencias sociales y por los políticos para disculpar, valga la redundancia, políticas que a menudo son genocidas, y anade que el autoritarismo es una realidad política en Latinoamérica que afecta a la izquierda y a la derecha. Por otra parte observa lo siguiente: aunque los fines declarados son excluyentes, los líderes autoritarios en Latinoamérica apenas se diferencian entre sí. Se trata de varones militares que ejercen un poder absoluto.

La sociedad cubana reúne todas las características señaladas en esa cita. Castro es el máximo líder, el comandante en jefe, el lector y hermeneuta en jefe, el presidente de los Consejos de Estado y de Ministros, el secretario general del único partido tolerable. La ubicuidad de este individuo en todas las esferas de mando bastaría para demostrar que hay en la Isla un solo discurso posible y permitido. Esta es la cualidad que hace de Cuba un modelo totalitario y convencional pero a la vez distinto. Está a la izquierda de los Estados Unidos, pero no en relación con la extinguida Unión Soviética, Corea del Norte y la Republica Popular China.

Debido a ello, la represión en la Isla ha sido medida con un doble patrón. Los prisioneros en Cuba no lo son por causas políticas, sino contrarrevolucionarias; ellos no son exponentes de la lucha de clases, sino lacayos al servicio de Norteamérica. Cuando se denuncian los abusos cometidos contra ellos, la izquierda clásica los justifica porque se trata de un caso de auto-defensa del estado revolucionario frente a los provocadores financiados por Washington. El "otro" en tanto que categoría de un anti-discurso legítimamente alterno y endógeno no es admitido en el caso de Cuba. No se le reconoce autenticidad a la resistencia opuesta al relato castrista aunque ésta no sea pro-imperialista.

Castro no puede ser medido con el rasero de Pinochet, digamos, dado el origen de sus respectivos mandatos y de las formas socio-económicas imperantes en Chile y en Cuba. No obstante, ambos caudillos se cruzan en el punto convergente de los totalita-rismos: la persecución, el arresto, el exilio y el asesinato de los opositores.

Michel Foucault define al fascismo y al stalinismo como "formas patológicas" o "enfermedades del poder." En uno y otro lado el estado es una institución de mando supremo que se asigna deberes "pastorales": preservar a la sociedad de sus enemigos internos y externos—marxismo o reacción capitalista—; mantener la independencia de la patria amenazada; asegurar la "pureza" de las leyendas patrióticas y defender la "soberanía nacional."

Para Castro y para Pinochet se hace necesario erradicar los anti-discursos que puedan corromper el proyecto nacional. Para ellos es imprescindible combatir el "diversionismo ideológico" porque se debe fomentar la unidad nacional y evitar el contagio de ideas enemigas.

La nación oficiosa, la que produce los testimonios sobre la cárcel, se territorializa en las prisiones superpobladas, en las emigraciones masivas, en las salas de torturas y en los apéndices del discurso jurídico que establece y clasifica los delitos y las penas. El Código Penal vigente en Cuba determina y sanciona con privación de libertad de uno a ocho años, mediante el artículo 103 o de la "Propaganda enemiga," a los autores o divulgadores de textos que emplacen a la autoridad marxista-leninista.

A pesar de lo anterior, se producen situaciones políticas lamentables en materia de solidaridad. Cada bando, es decir la izquierda y la derecha, ha establecido barreras de sensibilidad selectiva, que han colocado a las víctimas de los totalitarismos en compartimentos incomunicantes. Este atrincheramiento de las simpatías ha contribuído a otorgarles cierta impunidad a los responsables de crímenes incalificables. La izquierda y la derecha se han comportado con una tozudez y con un oportunismo de la peor ralea.

Es significativo que *Nadie escuchaba* sea el título de un documental cinematográfico sobre la experiencia carcelaria en Cuba. Almendros comenta que "se han hecho películas contra las dictaduras de derecha pero contra Castro no. Su régimen ha tenido ese beneficio siempre, aunque algún día habrá películas estoy seguro, cuando esté muerto." Esto se debe a que "nadie escuchaba" los alegatos bien fundamentados contra las ejecuciones sumarias, los tratos crueles, inhumanos y degradantes ocurridos en Cuba. Almendros da varias explicaciones a ese silencio: el temor que sienten muchas personas por los dictadores, incluidas las víctimas, y la visión ingenua de quienes visitan a la Isla en plan de turismo revolucionario, con la disposición de entender a los "camaradas" cubanos a todo precio, con tal de no "hacerle el juego a la reacción."

Añádase a lo dicho, la costumbre invariable de los gobernantes acusados, que radica en negar toda evidencia, tal y como hacen hoy quienes afirman la inexistencia del holocausto, o quienes han acusado de revisionistas de derecha a quienes han denunciado las matanzas bajo Stalin. Castro, apelando a la misma estrategia, ha tratado de desacreditar a sus impugnadores con la respuesta siguiente: nunca se ha sancionado a nadie por el hecho de haber sido disidente, y ha jurado que jamás se ha dado un solo caso de maltrato físico o de tortura en los treinta y cuatro años que él lleva en el poder.

Nadie escuchaba demuestra que la resistencia a Castro siempre ha sido pluralista. Jorge Valls, uno de los testimoniantes, es el primero en informar cuán compleja, rica, tensa y abundante es la anti-discursividad presente en el presidio, donde hay trozkistas, marxistas-leninistas, maoístas, democristianos, liberales, social-demócratas, fascistas, anarquistas y extremistas de todos los colores. Valls va más lejos y agrega que la libertad de expresión en Cuba se halla en la cárcel, primero porque allí nadie teme caer preso y, segundo, porque morir es muy fácil y muy natural en semejante sitio.

Aryeh Nyer, uno de los directores de "Americas Watch" ha escrito que una de las dificultades del caso cubano, en materia de derechos humanos, ha consistido en que algunos exilados cubanos han estado afiliados a causas de la extrema derecha, mientras que la mayoría de los activistas por los derechos humanos tiene una definida militancia de izquierda. Al parecer para recibir solidaridad ante las torturas y las vejaciones se requiere no sólo ser víctima, sino padecer a determinados verdugos. *Nadie escuchaba* cuestiona la visión excluyente de la izquierda y de la derecha.

Veinte años y cuarenta días es precisamente el testimonio que Nyer y Americas Watch necesitaron para probar que la oposición a Castro no ha estado vinculado siempre a causas de extrema derecha. No todos los presos políticos cubanos son peones de la CIA. Valls escribió su testimonio para confirmar la veracidad de los informes de "Americas Watch," que durante años no ha podido investigar sobre el terreno la violación de derechos humanos en Cuba. Valls fue un prisionero de consciencia según la categoría creada por "Amnistía Internacional." Fue un "preso plantado," que pasó la mayor parte de sus veinte años en la cárcel en calzoncillos y en camiseta, participando en huelgas de hambre aniquiladoras, sin poder ver a sus familiares por años, sin poder recibir una sola carta de ellos, golpeado, maltratado. Valls, como J.F. Manzano en el siglo XIX escribió con fines políticos, amparado por instituciones, sin intenciones literarias.

El testimonio no es, por supuesto, un modelo narrativo propio de la izquierda, según lo ha admitido John Beverley, quien se ha referido a lo que él denomina "articulacion anti-socialista" del género. Comparto ese juicio a pesar de que me resulta muy vaga la idea de "articulación anti-socialista." Es una opinión que, por lo demás, aparece como nota final de su muy conocido trabajo, cuando debería ocupar el cuerpo principal de aquél. En fecha reciente la colocó en ese lugar pero entre paréntesis. Incluso ha citado el testimonio de Armando Valladares usando el título de la versión inglesa, *Against all Hope* sin explicar por qué. ¿Acaso porque asocia el testimonio de Valladares con el idioma de un centro de poder?

En *Contra toda esperanza* Valladares reproduce estas palabras de Castro: "En 25 años de revolución, a pesar de las dificultades y los peligros por los que hemos atravesado, jamás se ha cometido un crimen." Esto es exactamente lo que Valladares trata de desmentir. Por eso me resisto a aceptar la idea de "articulación anti-socialista," porque me parece una operación de sometimiento de los textos por el crítico. El criterio de "articulación" no es negativo, si se trata de una línea de crítica posmoderna del marxismo, en aras de una izquierda democrática que rechaza el modelo socialista entendido y aplicado por Castro.

El testimonio de Valladares no puede ser tratado como periferia de lo testimonial, o periferia de la periferia, por favorecer una sola tendencia, la del tipo de izquierda que promueve Beverley. En el libro de Valladares un preso es golpeado salvajemente por haber escrito el apellido Martí sobre la pared de su calabozo. El régimen intenta borrar, mediante la golpiza más brutal, toda lectura martiana que no respalde la recepción marxista-leninista, diría mejor castrista, del poeta de *Ismaelillo* y del ensayista de *Nuestra América.*

La novela *Perromundo* inaugura el tema de la cárcel en la narrativa post-revolucionaria de Cuba. Para Seymour Menton, una de las virtudes de la obra consiste en que no destila "anticomunismo dogmático." Montaner la escribió bajo el clima experimental propiciado por el "boom." Mediante el uso de diversos pronombres y formas de escritura el autor propone distintas maneras de representación del referente. No hay una sola alusión directa a Cuba, porque el texto elude cualquier fatalismo, sea insular, topográfico, ideológico o literario.

Su personaje principal debe tomar una decisión: aceptar o no el ingreso al plan de reeducación, resistir o no los infinitos y brutales mecanismos de manipulación de la subjetividad, aplicados por el poder. Obviamente éste no es un problema típico de Cuba. La literatura existencialista de Francia, por ejemplo, se ha ocupado del tema de la elección y de la responsabilidad de elegir entre los prisioneros. El personaje del cuento *Le Mur* de Jean Paul Sartre, debe delatar o no a sus compañeros de la resistencia.

En *Perromundo* el prisionero se niega a convertirse, quiere ser coherente con los principios que lo llevaron a la cárcel. Los problemas relacionados con la conversión, que como ha demostrado González Echevarría es un asunto frecuente en la literatura cubana de los últimos tres decenios, tiene en *Perromundo* un caso ejemplar.

Las opciones son extremas, internalizar o no al victimario.

Ariel Dorfman ha estudiado esta problemática desde la izquierda en su "Código político y código literario." De la misma forma, el narrador de *El nombre de la rosa* de Umberto Eco medita sobre la morbosa relación de dominio y subyugación entre el preso y el carcelero. Los estados neo-fascistas y neo-stalinistas cuando no aniquilan físicamente a sus oponentes, acuden a la práctica del desequilibrio mental de estos, para imponerles la reeducación forzosa. Los testimonios sobre la cárcel contienen numerosos relatos donde los torturadores fracturan la resistencia de las víctimas. El carcelero puede disciplinarlas pero nunca reeducarlas. Puede obligarlas a emitir señales de docilidad y de obediencia, puede incluso conseguir un flujo de simpatía y de comprensión por parte de los torturados.

No obstante, la existencia de una literatura carcelaria prueba entre otras cosas que la prisión y los abusos físicos y psicológicos fracasan. No consiguen eliminar la gestación de un anti-discurso vigoroso, a pesar de todas las estrategias de dominación y silenciamiento. En las cárceles de Cuba ha nacido ya esa narrativa—y esa lírica—fundacional que ha dado al trasto con los patrones de la modernidad.

Desde los calabozos y desde las celdas comienzan a salir los testimonios no institucionalizados, verdaderamente periféricos, de la literatura cubana, aquellos que inauguran una forma de relación alterna, por tanto tiempo escamoteada, asediada o preterida por el Estado y sus epígonos, dentro y fuera de la Isla, dentro y fuera de las academias. Es hora ya de iniciar los estudios sobre esta forma de alteridad en Cuba, de conocer un archipiélago textual penitente y, sin embargo, resistente.

THE TRANSFORMATION OF THE STATE EXTENSIVE GROWTH MODEL IN CUBA'S SUGARCANE AGRICULTURE

Lázaro Peña Castellanos and José Alvarez[1]

During the decade of the 1980s, activities in Cuba's agricultural sector were conducted under a state extensive growth model. Sugarcane agriculture was no exception. At the end of the decade, however, there were signs of the exhaustion of such model, which was transformed into one based on a new form of production called the Basic Unit of Cooperative Production (Unidad Básica de Producción Cooperativa, UBPC).

The objectives of this paper are to describe and analyze the main characteristics of (a) the state extensive growth model applied to the Cuban sugarcane sector until the end of the 1980s and the reasons for its failure; (b) the status of the sector during the 1990-93 period; and (c) the changes taking place at present in this sector and the potential for their success.

SUGARCANE AGRICULTURE DURING THE PERIOD 1980-89[2]

The State Extensive Growth Model[3]

The decade of the 1980s was a period of expansion and development for the Cuban sugarcane sector. In fact, the indicators of area under cultivation and harvested area, and the corresponding volumes of production and value, show considerable growth when compared with previous decades (CEE, Anuario Estadístico de Cuba). They are also, on the average, the highest of Cuba's sugarcane agricultural history.

The expansion of sugarcane agriculture during this period had two basic features: an extensive growth model and a form of organization and management essentially under state control: the state farm. Hence the name "state extensive growth model."

The basic characteristics of the state extensive growth model applied to sugarcane agriculture in state farms were: (a) expansion of agricultural areas; (b) high capital investment; and (c) high use of productive inputs.

Expansion of Agricultural Areas: Forty-three percent of the total 4.4 million hectares under cultivation in the country are devoted to sugarcane. No other crop has such an extensive area in Cuba.

At the beginning of the 1980s, the area devoted to sugarcane was more than 1.6 million hectares (ha). About 250,000 ha were added during that period to reach 1.9 million ha in 1990 (Table 1).

1. This paper is a summary of one of the sections in Alvarez and Peña (1995). The authors would like to acknowledge the financial support of the John D. and Catherine T. MacArthur Foundation. Thanks to Pedro Pablo Acosta, Armando Alvarez Dozáguez, Jorge F. Pérez-López, Ricardo A. Puerta, Alberto Ribalta and Federico Sulroca for the information and useful reviews provided at different stages of this manuscript. All usual caveats apply.

2. In general, the statistics presented in this paper cover the 1980-93 period. For previous years, consult Alvarez (1992). For a throrough description and analysis of Cuba's sugar industry from 1959-1987, the interested reader is referred to Pérez-López (1991).

3. Interestingly enough, sugarcane is still paid by weight and not by sucrose content in Cuba.

Table 1. Main indicators of Cuba's sugar agroindustry, 1969-90

Year	Sugar Product	Cane Product	Yield 96	Agric. Yield	Area with Cane	Harv. Area	Total Plant.	Spring Plant.	Cold Plant.
	Million m t	Million m t	Percent	1000 mt/ha		————1000 ha————			
1969	4.46	40.3	11.02	43.8	1544	950	286	227	58
1970	8.54	79.5	10.71	55.5	1635	1469	128	70	58
1971	5.92	51.4	11.49	41.4	1446	1259	252	123	130
1972	4.32	43.4	9.96	37.2	1395	1199	355	188	167
1973	5.16	48.1	10.87	44.7	1430	1079	408	277	131
1974	5.82	50.3	11.73	45.3	1457	1110	389	255	134
1975	6.20	52.3	12.21	44.1	1516	1188	421	288	134
1976	6.04	53.7	11.63	43.7	1542	1231	420	266	154
1977	6.37	60.3	11.34	52.7	1640	1145	408	213	196
1978	7.22	69.6	10.76	55.9	1650	1245	313	200	114
1979	7.84	77.2	10.74	54.9	1696	1320	344	232	112
1980	6.52	63.9	10.78	44.2	1669	1400	406	275	131
1981	7.20	66.5	11.08	53.0	1735	1216	543	424	120
1982	8.03	73.0	11.17	53.4	1763	1335	348	215	127
1983	6.95	69.6	10.35	55.0	1754	1207	238	136	101
1984	8.03	77.3	10.47	55.8	1760	1358	290	174	116
1985	7.82	67.3	11.99	49.0	1770	1355	342	224	117
1986	7.09	68.4	10.62	50.1	1774	1336	355	213	142
1987	6.95	70.7	10.64	48.0	1789	1366	397	239	158
1988	7.42	67.5	10.85	51.7	1759	1305	339	201	136
1989	8.12	73.9	10.83	54.5	1797	1355	360	236	124
1990	8.04	74.4	10.65	52.0	1774	1427	289	182	108

Source: Compiled by Sulroca (1994) with MINAZ data.

This continued increase in sugarcane agricultural area was tied to two factors: (a) the projected increases in production levels, and (b) the still low agricultural yields. On the average, sugarcane agricultural production showed a positive growth during the decade of the 1980s when compared with the two previous decades. Its annual indicator, however, was rather unstable (Table 1).

This unstable behavior of sugarcane production was due, to a certain extent, to both epidemiological and climatic factors. In 1979, for example, rust severely affected the B-4362 sugarcane variety which, at that time, was planted in more than one-fourth of the cane area (Nova González, 1990, pp. 262-301). During 1980, it became necessary to replant the affected areas and substitute the Barbados variety for others more resistant to rust, which affected the 1979-80 and 1980-81 harvests (Table 1).

Climatological problems had also negative impacts on sugarcane production. Out-of-season rains (related to the so-called Niño phenomenon) in 1983, and hurricane Kate in 1985, had negative impacts on the harvests from 1982-83 through 1984-85, leaving losses of about two million metric tons of sugar (Table 1). This was followed by two years (1986 and 1987) of intense dry weather with annual levels of rainfall of 970 and 1,215 mm, respectively, well below the country's historical mean of 1,375 mm (Rodríguez Hernández, 1989, p. 24).

Despite these problems, sugarcane production averaged 71 million metric tons during the decade of the 1980s. This was 28% above the average annual production for the 1970s and 54% above the results of the 1960s.

During the 1980s, there was also a favorable balance concerning average sugarcane yields, although these continued to fall well below the agricultural potential of the country. Furthermore, and as explained below, the gaps between potential and actual yields were different at the provincial level.

Based on edaphic, climatic, and other limiting factors, a research project on potential agricultural cane yields was initiated at the national level in 1986. The results, also evaluated at the provincial level during the 1977-89 period, showed that, while the minimum average yield potential of the country was 77.28 mt/ha, only 57.5 mt/ha were being achieved, or about 67% (Sulroca, 1990, p. 17). A close look at both participation (cane sent to the mill), and average performance by province during the 1981-89 period (Anuario MINAZ, 1990, p. 2), shows the following results:

a. Only one province (Habana) of the seven provinces whose share ranged from 8% to 13% during the 1980s, maintained yield levels above 69 mt/ha. This province, however, barely reached 77% of its average potential yield during the study period. Matanzas only achieved yields around 59 mt/ha—a performance well below its minimum potential. The remaining of this elite group of provinces (Villa Clara, Ciego de Avila, Camagüey, Las Tunas, and Holguín), did not achieve 75% of their minimum yield potential. The cases of Ciego de Avila and Camagüey (provinces with a low population density in rural areas), and Las Tunas, are critical since they have the highest average participation in the harvests and, at the same time, high minimum yield potentials. In these provinces, however, actual yields achieved during the past decade only represented 56 to 61% of their minimum potential.

b. Average yields in the provinces of Cienfuegos, Sancti Spíritus, Santiago de Cuba, and Granma, with sugarcane shares between 4 and 7%, were always below 57 mt/ha, and around 48 mt/ha in the case of Sancti Spíritus.

c. Pinar del Río and Guantánamo, provinces with average sugarcane shares below 3%, showed different performances. Pinar del Río ranked as a medium-yield province (58.6 mt/ha) with a minimum average potential of 71.4 mt/ha. Guantánamo, on the other and with a high minimum yield potential (above 77.3 mt/ha) only achieved levels below 46.6 mt/ha, which represented 40% below its minimum potential.

When average agricultural yields for the 1981-85 (53.24 mt/ha) and 1986-90 (51.26 mt/ha) periods are compared, the drop of about 1.90 mt/ha becomes obvious. (A simple linear regression analysis shows average yields decreasing by 0.243 mt/ha from 1981 through 1990.) Therefore, average agricultural yields were not only relatively low but also showed a decreasing tendency during the 1980s. However, as already pointed out, the volumes of cane milled during this period were increasing at a rate of 0.292 mt, as shown by a simple linear regression model. This was only possible by increasing cane area and, above all, harvested area. In other words, the increase in volumes of sugarcane milled during the 1980s were the result of extensive plantings.

Other experiments conducted in Cuba between 1970 and 1985 give credibility to the possibility of achieving average yield levels above 67.2 mt/ha. All the experiments confirmed that, through the implementation of intensive cultural practices, and an efficient system of organization and management, it was feasible to achieve average country yields above 67.2 mt/ha (Alvarez Dozáguez, 1993, p. 5).

High Capital Investment: Forster (1989) has explained the reasons behind the high capital investments in Cuba in the following manner:

> Faced with a rural labor shortage, it is not surprising that Cuban planners—like their counterparts in much of the developing world—became increasingly enamored with capital-intensive agriculture. With their emphasis on irrigation, mechanization, and the use of "up-to-day" technology, the Cubans have also concluded that capital inputs can best be introduced on large-scale units which allegedly afford economies of scale (p. 251).

During the period 1981-90, total investments in the agricultural sector reached 7.9 billion pesos—4.2 billion during 1981-85 and 3.7 billion during the remaining years (CEE, Anuario Estadístico de Cuba, 1989, p. 133). Such investments represented 20.3% of total investment in the country during this nine-year period.

The investment level in the sugarcane agricultural sector during 1981-90 reached US$2.4 billion (US$1.3 billion during 1981-85 and US$1.1 billion during 1986-90). That figure accounted for 30% of total investments in the agricultural sector during the ten-year period. In relation to the 1976-80 period, during which investments in the agricultural sugarcane sector reached 987 million pesos, the increase in 1981-85 was 30%.

The continuing investment growth pattern is also observed in the last four years at the end of the 1980 decade for which data are available. In fact, average annual investment per year for the period 1981-85 was 264.5 million pesos, and 271.8 million pesos for each of the remaining four years (CEE, Anuario Estadístico de Cuba, various issues; Anuario Estadístico MINAZ, 1990, pp. 156, 247-255).

Although the investment flows for the sugarcane agricultural sector during the decade of the 1980s were high, the efficiency of the investment process was insufficient, as shown by the following facts. First, despite the increase in investment, the value of gross production did not increase. The annual average of the value variation of sugarcane production/investment indicator (dvp/inv) for the years 1980-89 was

only 0.05 pesos. In other words, for every peso invested in the sugarcane agricultural sector during that period, the value of production only grew an average of 5 centavos (Alvarez and Peña Castellanos, 1995, p. 9).

Second, when this indicator is analyzed for variations in milled cane at the mills (dcm/inv), the average results, measured in kg/peso invested, also show similar results. The annual mean value for this indicator is 7.02 kg per peso invested during the years 1981-89, with a correlation coefficient between the two variables of 0.019 (Alvarez and Peña Castellanos, 1995, p. 9).

In other words, the investment flows into the sugarcane agricultural sector did not have a relevant positive impact on the increases in production values or on the cane volumes for the industry. The three processes lacked the necessary integration.

In summary, the absence of the necessary integrity in the behavior of the three parameters, the maintained increases in investment levels, and the low global efficiency of the investment process, were clear indications at the end of the decade of the 1980s of the exhaustion of the state extensive growth model being applied to sugarcane agriculture.

High Use of Productive Inputs: There were absolute increases in fertilizer levels for sugarcane production, and in the indexes relative to the input of these nutrients during the 1980s (Table 2).

There was a strong statistical correlation between area benefitting with balanced or nitrogenous fertilizers and volumes of sugarcane production. In the case of nitrogen, the correlation coefficient was 0.84, while it was 0.46 for balanced fertilizers. Correlation coefficients between areas benefitted with nitrogenous or balanced fertilization and agricultural yields were 0.64 and 0.57, respectively. As explained in a later section, the decrease in the availability of fertilizers since 1991 was one of the main reasons for the fast decreases in both cane volumes and yields after that year.

The situation with herbicides was similar to the fertilizer case. There were increases in both the sugar-

Table 2.   Main fertilizer indicators in Cuba's sugarcane agriculture, 1975 and 1984-89

Indicator	Unit	Year						
		1975	1984	1985	1986	1987	1988	1989
Area fertilized (a)								
Nitrogenous	mill. ha	0.6	1.2	1.2	1.2	1.1	1.1	1.2
product	000 tons	108.7	235.4	259.8	229.9	217.8	214.3	253.6
index	kg/ha	178.0	193.0	206.0	186.0	190.0	203.0	218.0
Balanced (b)	mill. ha	1.2	1.3	1.2	1.3	1.3	1.1	1.2
product	000 tons	417.9	640.6	308.5	592.2	562.4	532.8	535.6
index	kg/ha	341.0	495.0	493.0	455.0	438.0	467.0	460.0
Total cost	mill. pesos	NA	78.1	77.2	78.7	69.8	65.4	78.8
Nitrogenous	mill. pesos	NA	31.7	31.9	29.2	24.1	27.3	33.0
Balanced	mill. pesos	NA	46.4	45.3	49.5	45.7	38.1	45.8

a) Includes only the first application b) Basic elements include nitrogen, phosphorous, and potassium.

Sources: CEE, Anuario Estadístico de Cuba, (1989, p.190); MINAZ data

Table 3.   Sugarcane agriculture area treated with herbicides (first application) in Cuba , 1975, 1980, 1988, and 1989 (1000 ha)

Year				
1975	1980	1985	1988	1989
990.9	1231.3	1090.2	1117.9	1274.1

cane area receiving herbicides and the number of applications during the 1980s (Table 3).

Sugarcane Agricultural Production Costs

Cuban sugarcane agriculture experienced rising levels of production costs during the 1980s (Table 4). Cost break-downs by item for all the provinces and the country are not available. Such break-down, however, was available for 1988 for the province of Villa Clara, one of the main sugarcane-producing areas.   .

As shown below in Table 5, the high hidden cost of the "other" category had a tremendous impact on the level of total costs (23% of total costs), which is intimately related to the problems of efficiency and organization at the firm level.

Integrated Care to Sugarcane: Important Deficiencies

There are many conflicting views on the role of the following elements in determining agricultural and industrial yields (Dirección de Agrotécnica MINAZ): (a) the timing of the harvest; (b) the management of the sugarcane plant; (c) the planting and replacement of sugarcane fields; and (d) the integrated control of weeds.

The Timing of the Harvest: Timing of the harvest is defined as the time period between the beginning and the end of the sugarcane harvest for industrial purposes. These two dates are the subject of intense debates because of their impact on agricultural and industrial yields.

The historical evidence shows that, concerning industrial yields, no date in the month of November is advisable for starting the grinding season. The reason is that, in November and still in December, the residual humidity in the soil has a negative impact on the sucrose concentration of the sugarcane, translating into low industrial yields (Table 6).It is obvious that a harvest lasting approximately 150 real days (which reflect Cuba's climatic conditions and milling capaci-

Table 4. Cost indicators in Cuba's sugarcane agriculture and sugar domestic prices, 1982-90.

Year	Cost/ton cane (Pesos)	Indust. yield (%)	Agric. cost/ton sugar (Pesos)	Price/ton sugar (Pesos)
1982	13.67	11.17	122.19	138.89
1983	14.23	10.35	137.23	138.89
1984	13.91	10.47	132.63	161.83
1985	17.27	11.99	143.78	161.83
1986	15.50	10.62	145.67	161.83
1987	16.24	10.64	152.35	161.83
1988	14.41	10.85	132.53	161.83
1989	15.46	10.83	142.44	161.83
1990	15.89	10.65	148.90	161.83

Souces: Calculated by the authors from Anuario Estadístico MINAZ (1990).

Table 5. Sugarcane agricultural production costs for the province of Villa Clara, by item 1988

Item	Cost/ metric ton (Pesos)
Fertilization	1.40
Transportation	2.18
Machinery and equipment	2.64
Irrigation	0.46
Depreciation	2.11
Salaries and social security	3.30
Other	3.61
Total	15.70

Source: Bazán Reyes and Rivero González (1985, p.5).

ty) should not start before the 15th of December. (The previous statement assumes an adequate and effective organization of harvest activities under a criterion of industrial yield maximization.) When there are doubts with regards to the pace, organization, and effectiveness of harvest activities, the tendency to an early start becomes strong due to the danger of prolonging the harvest until May, or even June,

Table 6. Comparison of average industrial sugar yields during early and late harvests, 1976-80 through 1986-89 (percent)

Date	Time period			
	1976-80	1981-85	1986-89	1976-89
1-10 December	8.45	8.58	8.30	8.45
20-30 April	11.37	11.07	10.81	11.10

Source: Rodríguez Hernández (1989, p.13)

which are the months with the highest rainfall in Cuba.

A harvest extended into the rainy season also brings about a drastic reduction in industrial yields due to the following factors: (a) disruption in harvest activities, especially in mechanical cutting (during the 1980 decade, mechanical harvesting reached more than 70% of the harvest); and (b) lower polarization in the cane (decreasing pol in cane forces a higher harvest per ton of sugar). Nevertheless, every single Cuban sugar campaign from 1976 through 1989 (and also later), has started extremely early and finished extremely late (Alvarez and Peña Castellanos, 1995, p. 15).

The beginning of the harvest is, therefore, a factor that affects industrial yields. However, the ending time is even more relevant for efficient sugar production. Extending the Cuban sugarcane harvests beyond April 30th (that is, into the months of May, June, and July), has been the result of three factors: (a) insufficient flow of cane to the mills (subutilization of industrial capacity); (b) insufficient cane quality (low pol content); and (c) the need to grind more cane than that committed to fulfill a determined plan when actual industrial yields have been below expected yields.

Rainfall is an exogenous and imponderable factor that affects the utilization of milling capacity. Out-of-season rains, during the dry period between February and March, cause severe damage to plantations and result in an extended harvest beyond the month of April. In addition, problems related to organization and efficiency in harvests tasks, both manual and mechanical, have also played very important roles.

The most relevant deficiencies with manual cut have been the relative scarcity of a labor force and the level of productivity of the labor force employed. Mechanical harvesting did not achieve the required levels of productivity during the last decade either. For example, on average, the real time lost in milling due to machinery and equipment break-downs fluctuated between 2.5% and 3.5% during 1981-90.

The Quality of Cane: Of special importance in the Cuban case is the quality of cane delivered to the mills since this can become the unchaining factor in a progressive process of cane depopulation. In fact, an extended harvest—due to low industrial yields—extends the cutting to sugarcane areas unscheduled for harvesting under the sugar production plan. Tardy harvesting also brings about disruption of the growing and maturing months for sugarcane and, therefore, has a negative impact on agricultural yields and availability of cane of adequate maturity for the following harvest.

Finally, the early harvest of cane of insufficient quality affects industrial yields of the following harvest (during the period January-April) and leads to other extensions of harvests. Such a cycle of early and late harvesting has a cumulative effect and leads, in the medium-term, to the depopulation of sugarcane areas.

Management of the Sugarcane Plant: This concept includes a group of basic rules that govern the relationship between "balance area" (area planted with cane on December 31) devoted to sugarcane agriculture with an adequate and efficient organization of planting activities and the integrated care of weeds that the crop requires. In general, according to MINAZ (1990, p. 216), a sound management strategy for the cane plant must fulfill the following requirements: (a) depending on the type of cane, the age of all sugarcane harvested must fall between 12 and 22 months; (b) cold cane (early cold cane planted between July and September, or late cold cane planted between October and December), must be harvested at age 16 to 18 months, and at age 15 to 19 months only in exceptional cases; (c) the spring canes left (long cycle) ought to be harvested at age 18 to 20 months, and exceptionally at 24 months; (d) the cane stubbles (canes with three of more cuttings) should be harvested at 12 to 15 months of age; and (e) the spring canes (canes planted between the months of January and June) that had been planted between the months of May and June, must always be harvested in the following harvest (left cane, or caña quedada).

An optimal management program also presupposes that the harvested area will never be above 75% of the "balance area." When this rule is not followed, sugarcane harvested in subsequent seasons shows a decrease in agricultural yields. Furthermore, when the area harvested is beyond 85% of the area with available cane, there is a cumulative tendency to depopulation of cane areas as a result of the continuing weakening of the cane plant.

The percentage relationship between harvested area and area with available cane shows some fluctuations during the period 1970-90 (Alvarez and Peña Castellanos, 1994, p. 85). Between 1971 and 1980 (1970-71 through 1979-80 harvests), this indicator had an average of 79%, which means that, in order to ensure the volumes of cane necessary for the harvest, it was necessary to cut, in some years, extensive areas with stubbles with one to two harvests, canes with less than 12 months of growth, and cold and spring canes of only 14 or 15 months of age. Such a management plan can be extremely damaging because the reiteration of early cuttings in areas of short cycles can become a degrading factor of the cane plant. Such is the case of the so-called "spring cane of the year," of only 10 to 11 months of age, considered a cane of bad quality (MINAZ, 1990, p. 216).

In 1981-85 (1980-81 through 1984-85 harvests) this indicator decreased below 75%. This was due, in part, to the intensive planting plan carried out during this period to replace the stubble affected with rust. However, between 1985 and 1989, the indicator increased again to reach 76%, and continued its increasing trend until reaching 79% during the 1990-92 period.

The influence that the harvesting of areas with plantings of different ages and cycles exerts on sugarcane yields can be seen from a summary of the results of a study conducted in 148 sugar agroindustrial complexes (Complejos Agro-Industriales, CAI) during the 1977-86 harvests (Table 7). It is obvious that the lowest agricultural yields were obtained from spring canes and stubbles with less than two cuts, while those from winter and long-cycle canes rendered the highest agricultural yields. In addition, when the comparison is made between cold canes (early cold canes are harvested between 14 and 18 months of age) and long-cycle canes (harvested between 20 and 22 months of age) the latter produced the best results.

Planting and Replacement of Fields: The planting and replacement of sugarcane fields have an enormous influence on the behavior of agricultural yields. Planting constitutes a very complex activity that requires a sophisticated and efficient organization to concatenate links such as the selection and treatment of seed, adequate land preparation, and the quality of the planting and replanting activities.

Table 7. Comparison between the best and worst triennium of 148 sugar agro-industrial complexes in the harvests between 1977 and 1986

Indicator	Unit	Worst triennium	Best triennium
Area harvested	1000 ha	1332.45	1261.90
Production	1000 ton	654.32	711.02
Yield	mt/ha	49.14	56.45
soca[a]	mt/ha	47.71	52.58
stubble[b]	mt/ha	43.68	48.30
spring	mt/ha	39.90	43.76
cold	mt/ha	66.70	72.32
long cycle[c]			
spring	mt/ha	77.62	82.91
stubble	mt/ha	62.41	72.24

Source: Acosta Pérez (1987, p.14)
a. *Stubbles with 1-2 harvests, cut with less than 12 months of growth*
b. Older stubbles
c. Plant cane. In a long harvesting cycle, the cane has between 20 and 22 months of growth.

Planting is also a very costly endeavor. For example, during the second half of the 1980s, planting costs were estimated to be between 596 and 969 pesos per hectare (Fernández Carrasco, 1990, p. 8). Obviously, such a high planting cost (in relation to total variable costs) emphasizes the need to follow economic criteria concerning planting and stubble management and replacement.

There exists an ongoing debate in Cuba concerning the programming of planting activities. In fact, the optimal planting time depends on the specific conditions of the soil type, rainfall patterns, and the availability of labor (MINAZ, 1990, p. 27). It is a known fact that, in Cuba, and because of the biological characteristics of the crop and the country's climatological conditions, the planting of early cold cane renders higher yields (considered twice as high by many cane specialists) and lower levels of losses, than spring cane. It has been estimated that about 20% of the area planted in the spring is lost (Alvarez Dozáguez, 1993, p. 6). Spring plantings in the country, however, have been historically higher than early cold plantings (Table 1). The main reasons have been organizational difficulties in mobilizing the labor force during the months of August and September, and the difficulties of ensuring an adequate preservation of the soils prepared since April, before the May rainfalls, until the beginning of the so-called cold plantings.

The preservation of the soils, even including their improvement, can be achieved through an agricultural technology of short-cycle crop rotations, the use of pre-emergence herbicides, or a combination of both.

The implementation of a short-cycle crop rotation in extensive planted areas demands, of course, a complex and efficient organizational system in the agricultural sector. Until the end of the 1980s, the method of soil preservation for the early cold plantings implemented mostly in the country was agrochemical: that is, through the use of pre-emergence herbicides.

The possibilities for mobilizing the necessary labor force to fulfill cold planting goals depend on the system of organization and management of the sugarcane agricultural activity, the degree of the real bond of the workers to the land, and the efficiency of the system of incentives applied.

Plantings not only impact on yields because of their quality and timing. A very important aspect of the relation planting-agricultural yields, is its stubble replacement capacity. Stubbles with three or more cuttings is one of the factors that increases crop costs the most. This is due to the careful attention that they demand (number of cultural activities, fertilization regimes, intensive irrigation tasks, etc.) and to the decreasing tendency of agricultural yields year after year. As a matter of fact, the stubbles are the canes with highest costs (Acosta Pérez, 1987, p. 7) and lowest agricultural yields (Table 7).

A study of 87 sugar CAIs during the 1978-87 harvests showed that sugarcane fields were not replaced according to a criterion based on optimization of agricultural and industrial yields (Fernández Carrasco,

1990, p. 8). The amount of planting necessary for stubble replacement depends on a number of factors. They include, among others, the physiological status of the cane plant, the decreasing tendency of agricultural yields due to number of cuttings and cane age, the limiting agro-technical characteristics of the soil, and the economic thresholds of costs and returns (Fernández Carrasco, 1990, p. 8).

The Cuban sugarcane experience has shown that the age of cane should not exceed 7.5 years (five or six cuttings), under optimal crop care conditions (Fernández Carrasco, 1990, p. 8). Therefore, a realistic stubble replacement policy that considers the current conditions of the cane population is forced to consider shorter periods and, therefore, higher costs.

Using data in various issues of the CEE Anuario Estadístico and Anuario MINAZ, Alvarez and Peña Castellanos (1995, pp. 86-88) compared areas harvested whose canes must be replaced and the annual average rate of plantings intended for field replacements (to arrive at this indicator one has to subtract from total annual plantings in new areas the total losses experienced in this activity), based on a number of assumptions. They are: under normal management replacement conditions (seven years of age with six cuttings), and, for conditions of six, five, four, and three years of age with five, four, three, and two cuttings, respectively.

In general, Alvarez and Peña Castellanos (1995, pp. 86-88) have shown that the harvested area that requires replacement grows more rapidly than the average plantings intended to replace plantations in all the cases. In some instances, it is obvious that the rate of plantings can not provide the necessities of plantation replacement, which severely affects the levels of existing cane populations and, therefore, the agricultural yields of the crop. In fact, specialists consider the current stubble replacement program in Cuba to be insufficient (Alvarez Dozáguez, 1993, p. 6).

The Integrated Control of Weeds: The implication of the depopulation of cane areas is, without a doubt, the unrestrained growth of weeds. Table 8 shows some data on the behavior of the items included in the indicator "cultural care to the crop" during the

1980s. The data show a considerable increase of the areas benefitted with activities included in crop care. It is estimated, however, that unrestrained weed proliferation is responsible for agricultural yield losses in sugarcane that are above 40% (Alvarez Dozáguez, 1993). A theoretical-empirical study has shown that weeds not controlled in time (between 30 and 120 days after planting or harvesting) lower agricultural yields between 37% and 66% (Alvarez Dozáguez and Acosta Pérez, 1985, p. 1).

Table 8. Cultural care practices to the sugarcane crop and benefited areas in Cuba, 1981-85 and 1986-90

Item	Period 1981 - 85	Period 1985 - 90
	million ha	
Fertilization		
Balanced	6.747	6.355
Nitrogenous	6.975	6.811
Herbicide application	8.671	10.545
Total cultivation	17.361	17.700
Hand weeding	13.258	17.454

Source: Anuario, MINAZ (1990, pp.140-144).

The situation concerning the integrated weed control program in the first years of the decade of the 1990s has not improved. In fact, in 1992, the area benefitted from crop care activities during the first semester of the year was only of 2.55 million hectares, or less than half the average of the last years of the 1980s (Alvarez Dozáguez, 1993).

SUGARCANE AGRICULTURE DURING THE 1990-93 PERIOD

All main indicators of sugarcane agriculture and industry have been deteriorating rapidly in the last few years. In fact, the demise of socialism in the Eastern European countries and the former Soviet Union, and of the Council for Mutual Economic Assistance (CMEA), represented the elimination of the main framework within which Cuba's economic relations were taking place. At the end of the 1980s, Cuba was conducting around 81% of its external commercial relations with the member countries of CMEA. This group of countries was importing the bulk of Cuba's total exports (63% of sugar, 73% of nickel, 95% of citrus), and was the origin of around 85% of Cuba's total imports that included 63% of food, 86% of raw materials, 98% of fuels and lubricants, 80% of machinery and equipment, and 57% of chemical products (Alvarez González and Fernández Mayo, 1992, pp. 4-5). Furthermore, the trade relations between Cuba and the CMEA took place under conditions favorable to Cuba. For example, it has been estimated that, during the 1981-90 period, Cuba had earnings from sugar exports about 50% higher than would have been obtained at world market prices (Alvarez González and Fernández Mayo, 1992, p. 4).

The direct impact that the demise of socialism in the above-mentioned countries and the CMEA had on the Cuban economy becomes more obvious when comparing Cuban imports statistics for 1989 and 1992. In 1989 Cuban imports reached over 8 billion pesos, while in 1992 the figure was 2 billion pesos, for a decrease in value of more than 70% in only three years (Alvarez González and Fernández Mayo, 1992, p. 8).

A reduction of such magnitude necessarily and severely affects the economic and social activity of the country. In the case of sugarcane agriculture, the inputs and equipments experiencing the most severe restrictions due to the fall in imports are: potassium chloride, ammonia, herbicides, potassium sulfate, ammonium sulfate, triple superphosphate, urea, cane loaders, irrigation motors, agricultural tools, towing equipment, tractors (crawler and with rubber tires), etc., in addition to fuel and lubricants, spare parts, and many others that also impact on the whole economy.

Sugarcane and sugar production have fallen drastically from 1989 through 1995. Although such decreases have been the result of several factors, the most severe problem that Cuban sugarcane agriculture is facing today is the depopulation of cane areas. In only five years, sugarcane areas diminished by 10% and harvested areas by 15%. This depopulation is not only obvious from a diminishing number of available areas. The sharp decrease in agricultural yields under conditions of decreasing harvested areas (30% in only three years), is a clear sign of the decreasing and weakening of existing plantations (Alvarez and Peña Castellanos, 1995, p. 29). In that regard, it is conservatively estimated that, at present, 30% of the areas under cultivation are depopulated (Alvarez Dozáguez, 1993, p. 6).

The depopulation of sugarcane areas is the main reason for the decrease in cane volumes delivered to the industry. In fact, between 1990 and 1993, cane harvested decreased by almost 50%, or from 75 to 42 million metric tons. The weakening of the plantations also surfaced in the quality of the sugarcane harvested. Data on industrial yields show a 1% decrease between 1988 and 1993, which translates into considerable losses in pol levels (Alvarez and Peña Castellanos, 1995, p. 29).

Two main reasons account for the situation just described: (a) the deficient integrated care to the crop explained above, which is inherent to the state extensive growth model and to the forms of organization and management that were in place in the Cuban sugarcane agriculture for more than twenty years; and (b) the impact that the demise of the socialist system in Eastern European countries and the former Soviet Union had on the Cuban economy.

NEW FORM OF ORGANIZATION AND MANAGEMENT IN SUGARCANE AGRICULTURE: THE BASIC UNIT OF COOPERATIVE PRODUCTION (UBPC)

Law-Decree No. 142 of 20 September 1993 dictated the established of UBPCs for the fulfillment of the following goals: (a) to achieve a closer relationship between man and working place; (b) to channel the cooperative efforts of the workers and their families in the improvement of the living conditions of the collective, including self-sufficiency; (c) to closely and rigorously relate the workers' earnings to the production achieved; and (d) to develop the autonomy of management of the collective on their resources with the objective of achieving self-sufficiency in

the productive process (MINAZ, 1993b, p. 3). Related to Law-Decree 142, the Sugar Ministry enacted its Resolution No. 160-93 eight days later, which contained the "General By-Laws of the Basic Units of Cooperative Production in Care of MINAZ" (MINAZ, 1993b, p. 6).

Under Articles 1, 2, and 3 of the By-Laws, the UBPCs are: (a) part of the production system of a CAI, constituting one of its primary links; (b) directly related to the CAI without intermediate organizations; (c) the owners of the production and of the basic means they purchase on credit; (d) allowed to sell their production to the CAI and to have management autonomy over their productive and monetary resources; and (e) fundamentally established with the sugarcane farmers that are related through work to the lands intended for their creation and that voluntarily express their wish to belong to this new form of sugarcane organization (MINAZ, 1993b, pp. 9-10).

Concerning the economic framework of the sugarcane UBPCs, and the remuneration to the collective and to the individual worker, the By-Laws expressed the following in Chapter IV (Economic Framework):

a. The first priority commitment of the UBPC is to work for the development and increase of sugarcane production with a higher sucrose content.[4] The UBPC can affect the areas devoted to sugarcane only when exceptional circumstances so dictate and with prior approval of the MINAZ Territorial Delegate.

b. In all UBPCs, once the economic cycle is finished, and with prior estimation of total revenues, payments will be made for assets acquired at the time of its establishment, fulfillment of the responsibilities acquired by receiving loans, taxes, and other expenditures generated during the productive process. Once the remaining total balance is determined, up to 50% of such balance can be distributed among the members, and the rest must go into a reserve fund for its utilization in the following areas: contingencies, acqui-

---

4. Interestingly enough, sugarcane is still paid by weight and not by sucrose content in Cuba.

sition of basic and rotational means, house buildings, construction of productive and social installations, incentives, and others, with prior approval of the General Membership Assembly.

c. The remuneration received by each member depends on the quantity and quality of the work performed and on the economic result of the UBPC. To that effect, each member receives a periodic cash advance equivalent to the fulfillment of the work norms. At the end of the economic year, he/she receives part of the profits, which are distributed according to the work performed.

d. The hiring of seasonal workers by the UBPC, with the funds it autonomously administers, is allowed (MINAZ, 1993b, pp. 20-21).

The Board of Directors of each UBPC is composed of nine members: the Manager, the Chiefs of Economics, Production, Services, Machinery, Parcels, and the Principal Engineer, and two other UBPC members.

The similarities between the Agricultural Production Cooperatives (CPA) and the UBPC are obvious. The economic frameworks, as well as the means of collective and individual remunerations, are very similar. The only exception, of course, is land ownership in legal terms: the CPA is the owner of its land while the UBPC receives the land in usufruct from the state for an indefinite period of time.

In fact, the UBPCs are based on the experiences of the CPAs, whose economic performance was, in general, much better than the state farms throughout the decade of the 1980s. Alvarez and Puerta (1994) have shown that non-state farmers (CPAs plus independent farmers), even with a dramatic disparity in their access to inputs when compared to state farms, "have performed better than state farms in each of the last

twenty-one seasons (zafras) for which data are available" (p. 1667).[5]

Once the establishment of the UBPCs in sugarcane agriculture was approved, an accelerated process of change took place in the sector. By the end of 1993, less than three months later, practically all state lands devoted to sugarcane production were reorganized under this new form of management and direction, and more than 98% of the cane agricultural workers became cooperative members (Table 9).

The conversion of state farms into UBPC not only was a structural change but also meant a transformation of land distribution from the standpoints of growing, producing, and managing the cane. According to MINAZ (1994), at the beginning of 1993, there were approximately 734 sugarcane farms with a gross cane area of 1.3 million ha and a net area of 1.2 million ha. Under such circumstances, the average agricultural area per farm was 1825 ha, 1665 of which were specifically devoted to sugarcane. By December 1993, 1.2 million ha of the total state agricultural area, approximately 93%, was shifted to UBPCs, with 1556 such units already established. This translated into an average agricultural area of about 799 ha per UBPC (a reduction of 56% in relation to the area under control by the state farm), of which, and on the average, 710 were devoted to sugarcane.

By the end of 1993, the land distribution in the UBPCs was as follows (Table 9):

<540 ha	15%
Between 541 and 810 ha	37%
Between 811 and 1080 ha	22%
Between 1081 and 1350 ha	11%
>1350 ha	15%

The UBPCs have an average of 11.42 ha per worker, while the remaining state farms in sugarcane have almost 30 ha/worker.

---

5. Based on prior observations by Fry (1988), and his own analysis, Pérez-López (1991, pp. 31-32) argues that yield differences are much less significant when the data are examined at the provincial level. Alvarez and Puerta (1994), however, have stated that "although his analysis of the three zafras in the provinces of La Habana, Matanzas, and Villa Clara (where yields tend to be the highest and where nonstate farmers tend to be concentrated) seem to support that assertion, nonstate yields in those provinces are still higher than state yields on the average and much higher in the remaining 10 provinces" (p. 1674).

Table 9. Selected indicators of Cuba's Basic Units of Cooperative Production (UBPC) in sugarcane, by province, December 1993.

Province	No.	Range of size (ha)					Agric Area (1000 ha)	Number of Workers
		<540	541-810	811-1080	1081-1350	>1350		
Pinar del Rio	47	10	24	12	1	-	37.8	3709
Habana	48	3	7	9	7	22	86.4	6989
Matanzas	107	6	22	23	20	36	141.7	9500
Villa Clara	235	53	120	50	6	6	229.5	18599
Cienfuegos	158	34	104	18	1	1	137.7	8325
Sancti Spiritus	103	21	24	16	14	28	128.2	9196
Ciego de Avila	104	-	4	35	25	40	176.8	13507
Camaguey	193	8	51	61	32	41	230.8	17138
Las Tunas	201	29	89	48	25	10	205.2	19189
Holguín	117	5	9	30	23	50	201.1	18493
Granma	128	29	68	19	8	4	120.1	16915
Stgo. de Cuba	86	27	42	11	6	-	70.0	12138
Guantánamo	29	1	12	13	3	1	41.8	4480
Nation	1556	226	576	345	171	238	1806.3	158171
CPA	386							
State farms	11						31.1	1047

Source: MINAZ (1994)

It is still early for evaluating the effectiveness of the UBPCs. Nevertheless, it is important to keep in mind that they developed at a particularly critical moment for both the sugarcane sector and the Cuban economy as a whole. For that reason, spectacular results in the short-run should not be expected.

There exists, at present time, an internal debate in Cuba about the UBPCs, their structure and economic and productive performance, their degree of autonomy, their incentive mechanisms, their relationship with the CAI, and many others. For example, the debate includes the pricing mechanism that will be applied to sugarcane production during the next harvests to stimulate agricultural yields. In reality, a proposal has been put forward to apply a system sim-ilar to the one in the CPAs, based on a differential price system according to yields (MINAZ, 1994).

The most contentious debate relates to the degree of autonomy of the UBPC from the CAI, and the relationship of the UBPCs with suppliers and with other coops and state enterprises. There is a general consensus among UBPC, CAI, and MINAZ, of the need to improve the mechanisms of autonomous management in the UBPCs, such that these could exert, in practice, a greater control of their resources according to their collective interest and in correspondence with the objectives for which they were established: the sustained development of sugarcane agriculture (MINAZ, 1994).

The process of the establishment of the UBPCs is still in its infancy, and it is possible that their development will be slow and long.[6] But the UBPCs are already a transcendental fact. The UBPCs are a new modality of organization and management in both sugarcane agriculture and Cuban agriculture in general, implemented within an extremely complex economic framework, both in terms of the global potential of the country's economy and the external context within which it has to function. In that regard, the UBPCs are a necessary alternative to the new conditions facing the Cuban economy but they are also an irreversible alternative.

SUMMARY AND CONCLUSIONS

During the 1980s, Cuba's sugarcane agriculture developed following a state extensive growth model characterized by the utilization of extensive agricultural areas, heavy use of productive inputs, high capital investments, and increasing costs. However, during that period, agricultural yields were far below the country's potential, which unveiled the existence of relevant deficiencies in the integrated care to the crop that the model could not overcome.

The specific forms of organization and management of the sugarcane agricultural activities have an extraordinary importance in ensuring cane volumes sent to the mill, in the behavior of agricultural and industrial yields, and in the general efficiency of the agro-industrial activity. In that regard, the performance of the state extensive growth model was less than satisfactory.

The newly-created UBPCs, although still in their infancy, may help in solving, or at least mitigating, the problems that the state extensive growth model could not resolve. At the same time, the prohibition of foreign investment in the sugar sector has been lifted by the Cuban government. Perhaps these two policy changes will bring about some needed relief to Cuba's sugarcane and sugar industries.

The process of recovery, however, appears to be a very difficult one. In early April 1995, Vice President Carlos Lage announced that Cuba had acquired credits to partially finance (mainly input purchases) the 1995-96 zafra. The loans are to be paid with sugar. According to him, interest rates were very high and repayment conditions were very hard for the country. For those reasons, "the 1995-96 zafra will be one of high risk" since the country needs to produce the sugar to repay the loans. If not, "we would be facing an even bigger problem that the one we have today."

REFERENCES

Acosta Pérez, Pedro P. "Combinación entre la lluvia, su distribución y organización, y el manejo de cepas en la agricultura cubana." Havana: Agrotechnical Direction, Sugar Ministry, 1987.

Alvarez, José. "Cuba's sugar industry in the 1990s: Potential exports to the U.S. and world markets," *Cuba in Transition—Volume* 2 (1992): 133-151.

Alvarez, José, and Lázaro Peña Castellanos. "Preliminary study of the sugar industries in Cuba and Florida within the context of the world sugar market," International Working Paper IW95-6, Food and Resource Economics Department, In-

6. However, since the very beginning (and a very important signal), they have been guided by the concept of economic efficiency in most activities. The authors were able to confirm it during their visit to one sugarcane UBPC in the municipality of Bauta, Havana province, in the summer of 1994. Economic efficiency criteria guided the cooperative members at the time of (a) selecting machinery, equipment, and personnel from the previous state farm; (b) making decisions about input purchases; (c) performing different cultural practices; (d) restructuring the bureaucratic apparatus of the coop; and in many other instances.

stitute of Food and Agricultural Sciences, University of Florida, March, 1995.

Alvarez, José, and Ricardo A. Puerta. "State intervention in Cuban agriculture: Impact on organization and performance," *World Development*, 22:11 (1994): 1-13.

Alvarez Dozáguez, Armando. "Caña de azúcar: La materia prima más deficitaria hoy en la patria de Alvaro Reynoso." Documento ATAC. Havana: Cuba's Association of Sugarcane Technologists, 1993.

Alvarez Dozáguez, Armando, and Pedro Pablo Acosta Pérez. "Resultado del control de hierba en CAI Pablo Noriega en los años 1977-1984." Documento MINAZ. Havana: Sugar Ministry, 1985.

Alvarez González, Elena, and María Antonia Fernández Mayo. "Dependencia externa de la economía cubana." Documento INIE. Havana: Institute of Economic Research, National Planning Board, 1992.

Bazán Reyes, Adriana, and Oscar Rivero González. "El perfeccionamiento estructural y el funcionamiento de las brigadas permanentes de producción." Villa Clara: Department of Industrial Engineering and Economics, Central University of Las Villas, 1985.

Comité Estatal de Estadísticas (CEE). *Anuario estadístico de Cuba*. Annual issues. Havana: Editorial Estadística.

Dirección de Agrotécnica MINAZ. "Cartas tecnológicas—manual de procedimiento." Havana: Sugar Ministry, 1983, 1985.

Fernández Carrasco, Miguel. "¿Ciclo largo o corto de cosecha?" *Tribuna del Economista,* (March 1990).

Forster, Nancy. "Cuban agricultural productivity," in I.L. Horowitz (Ed.), *Cuban Communism.* New Brunswick, NJ: Transaction Publishers, 1989, pp. 235-255.

Fry, James. "Cuba's sugar statistics: How reliable are they?," *Cuba Business* (London), 2:2 (April 1988): 8-10.

MINAZ. *Anuario Estadístico MINAZ.* Annual issues. Havana: Sugar Ministry.

MINAZ. "Consideraciones generales sobre el sistema de estimulación por los resultados finales de la producción para las granjas cañeras." Documento MINAZ. Havana: Sugar Ministry, 1993a.

MINAZ. "Documentos en torno al perfeccionamiento de las UBPC, Diciembre 1993-Junio 1994." Documentos MINAZ. Havana: Sugar Ministry, 1994, various issues.

MINAZ. "Documentos sobre la creación y perfeccionamiento de las unidades básicas de producción cooperativa." Documentos MINAZ. Havana: Sugar Ministry, 1993b.

MINAZ. "Manual técnico para el cultivo y cosecha de la caña de azúcar." Havana: Sugar Ministry, 1990.

Nova González, Armando. "Importancia de la economía agrícola en Cuba: La agroindustria azucarera." Documento INIE. Havana: Institute of Economic Research, National Planning Board, 1990.

Pérez-López, Jorge F. *The Economics of Cuban Sugar.* Pittsburgh, PA: University of Pittsburgh Press, 1991.

Rodríguez Hernández, Julio L. "Breve análisis sobre la problemática de las zafras azucareras en Cuba." Documento MINAZ. Havana: Sugar Ministry, 1989.

Sulroca, Federico. "La agricultura cañera y su papel en la eficiencia agroindustrial azucarera en Cuba." Paper presented at the Provincial Encounter of the ATAC, Havana, November 1990.

Sulroca, Federico. Statistics provided with MINAZ data, 1994.

CUBA AND THE INTERNATIONAL SUGAR MARKET

Oscar A. Echevarría

The purpose of this paper is to review the evolution after 1959 of sugar production both in Cuba and among major world producers and to assess the role which sugar could play in the Cuban economy when the political circumstances allow for a return to a market economy and access to the U.S. market. Given the difficulties of obtaining first hand reliable information about Cuban costs and production conditions, the paper has relied fundamentally on published data as well as other documents prepared on the subject all of which have been properly quoted or referred in the text and the bibliography.

The author would like to express his recognition to Ralph Kazi, former Statistician and Secretary of the Board of Czarnikow-Rionda, for his support in providing excellent sources and documents that were needed and were used in preparing this paper and for the cooperation of his former student and colleague, Economist María Inés Fernández, whose devotion in flushing out our vision on the subject deserve the consideration of co-author of this document.

HISTORICAL BACKGROUND

Since colonial times, sugarcane production has played a leading role in the Cuban economy. While a colony, sugarcane and tobacco were preferred over other crops for different reasons. Fruits and vegetables as well as fish and meat were not suitable to the long trip back to Europe and local tubers, such as yucca (yucca), did not have a market. Spain had forbidden the planting of cotton, wheat and rice. On the other hand the flatness of the land and the possibility of farming most of the year made sugar cane one of the most beneficial crops, on an island where 52% of the land was arable.

Sugarcane has also some advantages over tobacco. While sugarcane is homogeneous crop whose quality is not greatly affected by the micro-climate, this is not the case of tobacco culture where a special knowledge and expertise is also required. Increasing tobacco production requires very intensive manual care, fertilizers, herbicides and fungicides, inputs that tend to increase production costs. In the case of sugarcane, no such intensive cultivations is needed.

At the beginning of this century, the United States was the largest consumer of Cuban sugar. The topography of the island and its proximity to the U.S. market resulted in low transportation cost both by rail and roads and short shipping time to U.S. ports. Inasmuch as local consumption was relatively small, because the population of the island was not large, almost all the production was exportable. In turn the United States exported to Cuba all the products that it needed. For this reason, the prosperity or recession of the economy in Cuba depended on the fluctuation of the prices of sugar in U.S. and international markets, which was a factor outside of the control of the country.

For most of this century, Cuba has been either the largest or among the largest sugar producers in the world. In the 1920's, it was the world leading producer. In the years just preceding the 1959 Revolution, Cuba's exports of around 5 million tons annually provided almost one-third of global sugar exports. This important participation in the world market, as well as its capacity to increase supply by 2 to 3 million MT in a given year, made Cuba also the dominant factor in policing the International Sugar Agreement and gave the island a major role in the International Sugar Council in London whose purpose was to maintain an orderly market.

After the Second World War and until 1958, Cuba consolidated its commanding role in the international sugar market. During those years, Cuba was not only among the three largest producers, but was by far the largest exporter.

Cuba succeeded in maintaining its dominant role due to two majors factors:

1. Cuba has a very well organized sugar industry and was able to produce sugar at competitive prices, due to:

   • outstanding natural conditions of soil and climate;

   • a well organized agricultural sector; and

   • excellent industrial capacity.

2. Cuba also enjoyed a privileged situation due to its share of the U.S. sugar market. The U.S. quota system allowed Cuba to export over 50% of its production to the United States at the highly protected prices of the U.S. market.

The implicit subsidy to the Cuban economy that resulted from the U.S. quota allowed Cuba to have available a substantial stand-by reserve of almost a million tons of raw sugar and a capacity to extend the crop season and harvest for almost an additional million tons, when needed. This reserve — amounting to almost 20% of what at the time was the volume of the international sugar market — allowed Cuba to be a market leader that was very efficient and effective in controlling price and thus the cornerstone of the International Sugar Agreement.

SOCIALIST CUBA AND SUGAR PRODUCTION

Changes in Trade Patterns

At the time of the 1959 Revolution, the United States bought annually nearly 3 million tons, or 60% of Cuba's annual sugar exports (Buzzanell and Alonso, 1989). This commercial relationship collapsed in 1960 when Cuba nationalized U.S. oil refineries and other businesses. The United States suspended Cuba's sugar quota and embargoed all trade. Cuba was able to maintain a fairly high, but not efficient, level of sugar production due to the subsidy paid by the Soviet Union. Cuban sugar was sold to the Soviet Bloc (Soviet Union and other socialist countries in Eastern Europe) and China at prices that were far above the world market.

The 1960's were characterized by uneven performance in production because of the exodus of many experienced managers and skilled field and factory workers, and the transformation of production to a Socialist model. By 1965, two-thirds of Cuba's sugar exports were shipped to Socialist markets. Trade ties were solidified with these countries through a series of agreements, including access to the Socialist world's Council for Mutual Economic Assistance (COMECON) (Buzzanell and Alonso, 1989). Cuba sold one-third of its export to the free market to receive hard currency from non- socialist countries, such as Canada and Japan.

During the 1970's, Cuba's regime expanded sugar production, beginning the decade with the "long harvest" of 217 days in 1969/1970, during which the nation's physical and human resources were focused on producing a 10 million ton sugar crop. But this effort produced a sharp fall in production the next three years. Production bounced back toward the end of the 1970's due to the expansion in area harvested and improved sugar yields.

In the late 1980's, between 50% and 60% of Cuban exports went to the Soviet Union, by then the world's leading importer. During most of the 1980's, Cuba has been hard pressed to meet its commitments to COMECON countries and to produce enough sugar to sell for hard currency. In 1987 and 1988, the situation got worse, as poor crops and exports over commitments led Cuba to mortgage its sugar export future: Cuba promised part of its 1989 crop as collateral to repay over 1 million tons of sugar borrowed from a major international trade house Sucre et Denre (Sucden) to fulfill export commitments to the Soviet Union.

Between 1970 and 1990, Cuba's sugarcane agriculture switched from manual labor to machinery: 67% of the area was harvested by machine combines in 1988/1989, compared with 45% in 1980 and 25% in 1975 (Buzzanell and Alonso 1989).

After the fall of the communism of the Soviet Union, Cuba's production collapsed as well and now Cuba is not even among the ten largest producers of sugar and ranks only as the fourth exporter, with half the export volume of Australia. New efficient sugar exporting countries have appeared (Thailand, Brazil, Guatemala, Australia and Colombia) so that if Cuba were to apply appropriate cost and price methods, it might be that it is lagging far behind those countries in terms of profitability.

Changes in Sugar Production and Exports

Changes in Cuban sugar production and exports are presented in Table 1 and Figure 1. Sugar production between 1950 and 1955 averaged 6.3 million tons per annum and exports averaged 5.7 million tons per annum, with a maximum of 8.4 and 7.2 million tons respectively in the year 1990. The figure shows the strong correlation between production and exports as well as the fact that consumption is a low percentage

of production. Large production increases were recorded in 1961 and 1970. After 1973, there was a steady increase in production through 1990. After 1990, production collapsed to almost 4 million tons, a level similar to that recorded in the worst production years of the period, 1963 and 1973.

Figure 2, based on Table 2, plots critical production factors such as area, sugarcane yield, sugarcane milled, and production. It is interesting to notice that after 1968, the amount of sugarcane milled in many years was lower than the amount of sugarcane produced, which could indicate increasing problems with industrial plants as well as the harvesting process.

The Sugar World Market
Major Producers and Consumers

Major world sugar producers by region are presented in Table 3 and Figure 3. The top twelve producing countries accounted for 65% of world production in 1995 (Table 4). Meanwhile, the 10 major consumers totalled 56% of world consumption (Table 5). In comparing production data for 1986 and 1959 we see countries with a very high rate of increase (such as Thailand, China, France and Pakistan, where pro-

Figure 1. Cuba: Sugar Production and Exports (thousands of metric tons)

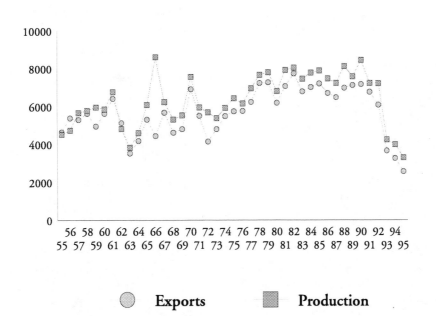

○ Exports   ▧ Production

Figure 2. Cuba: Sugarcane Area, Production and Yield

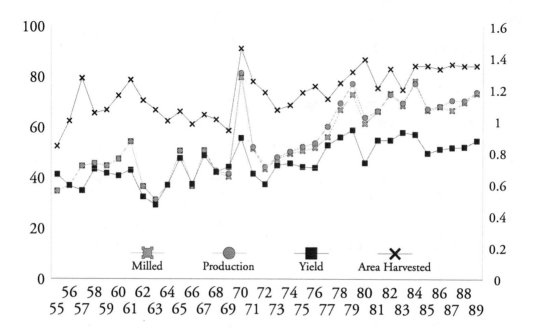

duction has increased by over 300%), while in Cuba production grew by only 23%. In fact, after 1959, Cuba had the lowest increase among major producers and was the only country among them with an increase lower than the world average. In the decade between 1986 and 1995, production increased at significant rates in countries such as India, Thailand, and Pakistan, while Communist countries such as Cuba and Ukraine had poor performances during that period.

While world production increased in the last decade by 18%, consumption increased by 14%, as consumption fell sharply in Russia and grew at a slow rate in Germany, Japan and the United Kingdom.

Major Exporters and Importers

The ten top sugar exporters are presented in Table 6. They accounted for 70% of total export volume in 1995, while the ten major importers (Table 7) represented 49% of total volume in the same year. In the decade between 1986 and 1995, world exports decreased by 1%, with Cuba and the Ukraine shouldering the bulk of the decrease, in line with decreases in production. World imports increased by 1.3%,

mainly due to increases in imports by China partially offset by decreases in India and the United States. Imports by Japan and Canada—Cuba's main non-Communist markets—were reduced by 2-3%. Sources do not explain this contradiction between increases in world imports and decreases in world exports.

CAN THE CUBAN SUGAR INDUSTRY REVIVE?

Cuba's sugar industry has received two major jolts:

1. The loss of the privileged markets of the former Soviet Union and the countries of COMECON, which paid very high prices for Cuban sugar— up to four times the world market price—as the United States had done in the past.

2. A decrease in export volume both due to production difficulties and to the reduction in the size of the markets of its customers.

Because of this, the Cuban government has been hoping to receive foreign capital in order to help reactivate the economy. The Cuban government is willing to accept loans that have seniority in collec-

Figure 3. World Sugar Production, 1995

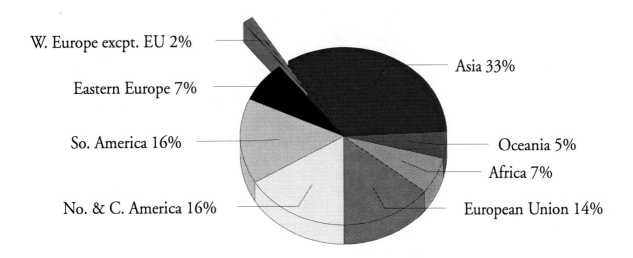

W. Europe excpt. EU 2%

Eastern Europe 7%

So. America 16%

No. & C. America 16%

Asia 33%

Oceania 5%

Africa 7%

European Union 14%

Source: F.O. Licht's Int'l Sugar and Sweetner Report, 1995

tion, secured by sugar produced until repayment is completed. The Cuban sugar industry not only needs new capital influx but also management and technical expertise to meet competitive challenges in the markets of potential customers.

The interest of the international community in investing in Cuba is demonstrated by an offer of financing from the Netherlands International Group (ING), which provided a credit of $30 million, to be paid back with sugar, a method usually called a red-clause loan. According to ING, Cuban production could go back in five years to the 8.5 million ton per annum level. This is considered too optimistic not only because, from the production side, it would require the industry to produce 35% over the average of the last years in a very short period, but also because it would be difficult to place the increased production of sugar in the world market without bringing about a substantial reduction in price levels.

Many of Cuba's former communist markets—such as East Germany, Hungary, Poland, and the former Soviet Union, with exception of Russia—do not need to acquire raw sugar in the international market, as they now have sufficient production themselves. Additionally, Cuba's traditional non-Commu-

nist markets since 1959—Japan and Canada—have ceased to grow ("Cuba Struggles" 1995).

If Cuba is not able to rely on preferential treatment by its trading partners, in order increase production and sell its output it will have to compete efficiently for market share. While there are no available or accurate data on Cuba's cost of production to enable one to compare them with those of the major present exporters, we can extrapolate the results by looking at the past as a proxy. It is obvious that there are now new major exporters that were able to achieve that position in a free market and therefore have demonstrated their ability to compete on prices, reliability, timely delivery, etc.

There is no assurance that Cuba could reach such level of efficiency simply on the basis of its climate and soil condition. Therefore, it is an open issue whether Cuba can regain a predominant position in the sugar export market without the advantages it had in selling 60% of its production at a preferential price to the United States and later doing the same at even higher prices during the communist era when preferential trade agreements prevailed.

CONCLUSIONS

It is not evident that Cuba could recover its leading role in the sugar international market under the

367

present circumstances, even if a dramatic change were to take place in the economic and/or political conditions of the island. To better its position in the sugar market, Cuba will require to steadily improve its agriculture and industrial efficiency by going back to rational, market-oriented production and will need a considerable infusion of capital invested both in the sugar mills as well as in the cane fields and transportation infrastructure.

Also, one must recognize that a change in the political system in Cuba, and the subsequent opening of the U.S. market, will not contribute to regaining Cuba's premier role in that market. The rationale behind such statement is the following:

- The U.S. import quota has dwindled from 9.4 million tons in 1959 to the neighborhood of 1 million tons in 1995.

- The United States will not abandon its current suppliers of sugar just to accommodate Cuba.

- There is a high probability that eventually the U.S. quota system will go through dramatic changes in light of the new farm bill reforms now being discussed in Congress.

Thus, although the change in the political system would certainly facilitate improvements in the sugar industry, it will not mean a miracle turn-around whereby Cuba will again enjoy a privileged position in the U.S. sugar market as a factor to regain a commanding role in the World Market.

At present, we ignore Cuban cost of production, but having lost its privileged markets that provided it with a substantial subsidy, and having to compete with new countries (such as Brazil, Colombia and Australia) that have established their predominance in a free market environment, without any benefits or privileged associations, it will very difficult for Cuba to regain in the short run its leading position in the international sugar market.

BIBLIOGRAPHY

Alvarez Díaz, José, Alberto Arredondo, Raúl Shelton, José Vizcaino. *Cuba: Geopolítica y Pensamiento Económico*. Miami: Duplex, 1964

Buzzanell, Peter, and José Alonso. "Cuba's Sugar Economy: Recent Performance and Challenges for the 1990s. "In *USDA Sugar and Sweetener Yearbook* (Washington: U.S. Government Printing Office, June 1989).

Carreño, Pablo A. *The Cost of Reconstructing the Sugar Industry in Cuba*. 1994.

"Can Foreign Capital and Restored Markets Markets in Russia and China Revive the Cuban Sugar Industry." *F.O. Licht's International Sugar and Sweetener Report* (April 13, 1995).

"Cuba Struggles to Revive Sugar Sector." *F.O. Licht's International Sugar and Sweetener Report* (March 17, 1995).

Grupo Cubano de Investigaciones Económicas. *Un Estudio Sobre Cuba*. Coral Gables: University of Miami, 1963.

"Third Estimate of the World Sugar Balance, 1994/95." *F.O. Licht's International Sugar and Sweetener Report* (June 21, 1995).

"World Sugar Balance," *F.O. Licht's International Sugar and Sweetener Report* (1995).

Table 1. Cuba: Sugar Production and Exports (thousands of metric tons)

Year	Production	Exports	% Exp.
1955	4,528.00	4,644.00	102.56%
1956	4,740.00	5,394.00	113.80%
1957	5,672.00	5,307.00	93.56%
1958	5,784.00	5,632.00	97.37%
1959	5,964.00	4,952.00	83.03%
1960	5,862.00	5,635.00	96.13%
1961	6,767.00	6,414.00	94.78%
1962	4,815.00	5,131.00	106.56%
1963	3,821.00	3,521.00	92.15%
1964	4,590.00	4,176.00	90.98%
1965	6,082.00	5,316.00	87.41%
1966	4,867.00	4,435.00	91.12%
1967	6,236.00	5,683.00	91.13%
1968	5,315.20	4,613.00	86.79%
1969	5,534.18	4,798.82	86.71%
1970	7,558.56	6,906.29	91.37%
1971	5,950.03	5,510.86	92.62%
1972	5,687.80	4,139.56	72.78%
1973	5,382.55	4,797.38	89.13%
1974	5,925.85	5,491.25	92.67%
1975	6,427.38	5,743.71	89.36%
1976	6,150.80	5,763.65	93.71%
1977	6,953.28	6,238.16	89.72%
1978	7,661.55	7,231.22	94.38%
1979	7,799.97	7,269.43	93.20%
1980	6,805.24	6,191.07	90.98%
1981	7,925.63	7,071.45	89.22%
1982	8,039.48	7,734.28	96.20%
1983	7,460.23	6,792.09	91.04%
1984	7,783.41	7,016.51	90.15%
1985	7,889.24	7,209.01	91.38%
1986	7,467.42	6,702.59	89.76%
1987	7,231.77	6,482.14	89.63%
1988	8,119.05	6,978.22	85.95%
1989	7,579.01	7,123.31	93.99%
1990	8,444.70	7,171.76	84.93%
1991	7,233.39	6,767.46	93.56%
1992	7,218.80	6,084.88	84.29%
1993	4,245.72	3,661.96	86.25%
1994	3,994.00	3,264.00	81.72%
1995	3,300.00	2,568.00	77.82%
Annual Average	6,263.71	5,696.64	90.95%

Table 2.   Cuba: Sugarcane Area, Yield and Production

Crop Year	Area Harvested (MM Ha.)	Yield (M tons/ Ha.)	Production (MM tons)	Milled for Sugar (MM tons)
1955	0.84	41.4	34.8	34.8
1956	1.00	37.0	37.0	37.0
1957	1.27	35.0	44.7	44.7
1958	1.05	43.5	45.7	45.7
1959	1.07	41.9	44.8	44.8
1960	1.16	40.9	47.5	47.5
1961	1.26	43.1	54.3	54.3
1962	1.13	32.5	36.7	36.7
1963	1.07	29.3	31.4	31.4
1964	1.00	37.2	37.2	37.2
1965	1.06	47.8	50.7	50.7
1966	0.98	37.6	36.8	36.8
1967	1.04	48.9	50.9	50.9
1968	1.01	42.4	42.8	42.3
1969	0.94	44.4	41.7	40.5
1970	1.46	55.8	81.5	79.8
1971	1.25	41.7	52.2	51.5
1972	1.18	37.5	44.3	43.5
1973	1.07	45.0	48.2	47.5
1974	1.10	45.8	50.4	49.6
1975	1.18	44.4	52.4	50.8
1976	1.22	44.1	53.8	52.0
1977	1.14	53.0	60.4	56.2
1978	1.24	56.1	69.6	67.0
1979	1.31	59.0	77.3	73.0
1980	1.39	46.0	64.0	61.6
1981	1.21	55.0	66.6	66.4
1982	1.33	55.0	73.1	73.5
1983	1.20	58.1	69.7	68.7
1984	1.35	57.3	77.4	78.4
1985	1.35	49.9	67.4	66.8
1986	1.33	51.5	68.5	68.3
1987	1.36	52.1	70.8	66.9
1988	1.35	52.4	70.7	70.0
1989	1.35	54.8	74.0	73.5

Source: Buzzanell and Alonso, June 1989.

Table 3.   World Sugar Production 1986-1995 (thousands of metric tons)

Region	1995	1994	1993	1992	1991	1990	1989	1988	1987	1986
European Union	16,598	18,401	18,032	16,757	17,988	16,906	16,231	15,588	16,580	16,344
West Europe (excepted European Union)	2,125	2,481	2,728	3,164	3,043	2,456	2,213	2,799	2,419	2,485
Total West Europe	18,722	20,882	20,759	19,920	21,031	19,362	18,444	18,387	18,998	18,829
East Europe	8,613	10,774	9,922	10,597	13,547	13,259	12,384	13,350	12,667	12,224
North & Central America	18,941	18,385	19,541	20,739	21,452	20,861	21,102	21,296	20,541	20,137
South America	18,241	16,146	16,627	15,262	14,401	13,281	12,502	13,833	14,353	12,353
Africa	7,612	7,078	6,649	7,815	8,064	7,989	7,884	7,965	7,968	7,683
Asia	38,258	32,059	34,212	38,554	33,060	30,252	27,877	25,956	25,793	23,666
Oceania	5,695	5,591	4,876	3,937	4,171	4,111	4,410	3,900	3,882	3,687
World	116,082	110,914	112,585	116,824	115,725	109,115	104,602	104,685	104,202	98,578

Source: F.O. Licht's International Sugar and Swetener Report, 1995.

Table 4.   Largest Sugar Producers (thousands of metric tons)

Country	1995	1994	1993	1992	1991	1990	1989	1988	1987	1986
India	15,774	10,601	11,554	14,595	13,064	11,947	9,524	9,898	9,224	7,624
Brazil	12,236	10,534	11,104	9,510	8,952	8,000	7,460	8,900	9,265	7,371
U.S.A.	7,413	6,802	7,106	6,379	6,265	6,008	6,098	6,678	6,027	5,455
China	6,304	6,515	8,402	8,578	6,880	5,669	5,357	4,706	5,730	5,550
Thailand	5,461	4,009	3,792	5,106	4,055	3,506	4,052	2,704	2,637	2,586
Australia	5,161	5,067	4,375	3,419	3,708	3,706	3,942	3,397	3,444	3,291
France	4,370	4,725	4,723	4,412	4,736	4,198	4,372	3,973	3,734	4,324
Mexico	4,355	3,859	4,430	3,577	3,943	3,408	3,699	3,852	3,986	4,031
Germany	3,981	4,742	4,398	4,250	4,673	4,005	3,512	3,759	4,256	4,228
Ukraine	3,804	4,022	3,758	4,178	5,856	5,390	4,811	5,207	4,673	4,348
Cuba	3,300	3,994	4,365	7,104	7,729	8,156	8,188	7,548	7,219	7,347
Pakistan	3,263	3,261	2,604	2,528	2,100	2,017	2,011	1,936	1,398	1,213
Total 12 major producers	75,422	68,130	70,610	73,635	71,960	66,009	63,024	62,557	61,594	57,366
World	116,082	110,914	112,585	116,824	115,725	109,115	104,602	104,685	104,202	98,578
% 12 major producers	64.97%	61.43%	62.72%	63.03%	62.18%	60.50%	60.25%	59.76%	59.11%	58.19%

Source: F. O. Licht's International Sugar and Sweetener Report, 1995

Table 5.   Largest Sugar Consumers (thousands of metric tons)

Country	1995	1994	1993	1992	1991	1990	1989	1988	1987	1986
India	13,940	12,928	13,025	12,316	11,496	11,037	10,791	10,231	9,401	8,928
U.S.A.	8,395	8,377	8,219	7,993	7,926	7,747	7,458	7,418	7,288	7,186
Brazil	8,060	7,766	7,459	7,400	6,924	7,281	6,799	6,582	7,126	6,379
China	7,950	7,800	7,717	7,550	7,450	7,050	6,502	7,572	7,578	6,867
Russia	5,200	5,650	5,600	5,678	6,661	7,476	7,296	7,302	6,920	6,362
Mexico	4,501	4,445	4,434	4,414	4,566	3,990	3,972	3,716	3,517	3,638
Germany	2,979	2,946	2,944	2,923	2,911	3,086	3,075	3,078	3,050	3,030
Indonesia	2,955	2,737	2,615	2,582	2,581	2,527	2,465	2,393	2,213	2,013
Pakistan	2,937	2,794	2,693	2,559	2,348	2,211	2,266	1,981	2,148	1,743
Japan	2,703	2,634	2,572	2,793	2,816	2,775	2,873	2,817	2,707	2,755
U.K.	2,390	2,438	2,409	2,470	2,522	2,533	2,458	2,510	2,461	2,436
France	2,278	2,197	2,231	2,141	2,043	2,024	2,053	2,138	2,218	2,012
10 Largest Consumers	64,286	62,712	61,918	60,820	60,244	59,738	58,008	57,739	56,627	53,350
World	114,609	113,021	111,500	111,045	110,314	109,431	106,960	107,168	105,922	100,457
% 10 largest consumers	56.09%	55.49%	55.53%	54.77%	54.61%	54.59%	54.23%	53.88%	53.46%	53.11%

Source: F.O. Licht's International Sugar and Swetener Report, 1995.

Table 6.   Largest Sugar Exporters (thousands of metric tons)

Country	1995	1994	1993	1992	1991	1990	1989	1988	1987	1986
Brazil	4,238	3,727	2,837	1,771	1,409	1,421	1,359	2,054	2,012	2,606
Australia	3,997	3,992	3,591	2,324	2,662	3,182	2,991	2,855	2,785	2,707
Thailand	3,503	3,036	2,464	3,270	3,195	2,783	2,872	2,218	1,910	1,930
France	2,816	2,952	2,785	2,706	2,741	2,718	3,021	2,560	1,893	2,792
Cuba	2,568	3,264	3,968	6,439	6,596	7,026	7,517	6,387	6,973	6,947
Ukraine	1,750	1,550	1,780	1,800	3,588	4,187	4,431	3,500	3,633	3,500
Germany	1,493	1,904	1,431	1,423	2,138	1,298	1,317	1,283	1,682	1,499
Belgium	1,213	1,297	870	959	1,010	597	552	614	630	695
Colombia	781	624	676	427	290	407	334	117	182	199
Guatemala	748	860	605	725	618	492	465	369	274	433
10 Largest Exporters	23,107	23,205	21,006	21,842	24,247	24,112	24,858	21,956	21,974	23,307
World	33,043	33,584	32,535	32,561	34,847	34,675	35,115	32,481	33,421	33,430
% 10 largest exporters	69.93%	69.10%	64.56%	67.08%	69.58%	69.54%	70.79%	67.60%	65.75%	69.72%

Source: F.O. Licht's International Sugar and Sweetener Report. 1

Table 7. Largest Sugar Importers (thousands of metric tons)

Country	1995	1994	1993	1992	1991	1990	1989	1988	1987	1986
Russia	3,100	3,350	4,350	3,901	4,100	4,550	4,250	3,502	3,452	3,292
China	2,900	1,331	561	1,193	1,075	1,116	2,890	2,883	1,523	1,255
Japan	1,826	1,706	1,730	1,845	1,733	1,760	1,879	1,801	1,762	1,862
U.S.A.	1,767	1,766	1,859	2,105	2,509	2,102	1,804	1,183	1,625	2,047
U.K.	1,418	1,348	1,354	1,427	1,412	1,368	1,435	1,412	1,406	1,216
South Korea	1,183	1,272	1,197	1,183	1,159	1,112	1,111	1,151	1,021	978
Canada	1,115	1,155	1,107	1,000	1,009	865	712	967	1,182	1,148
India	1,079	1,383	0	0	0	275	0	152	1,072	1,980
Malaysia	929	956	873	842	901	754	795	752	672	645
Algeria	857	905	882	832	889	901	828	786	818	746
10 Largest Importers	16,173	15,171	13,913	14,326	14,786	14,802	15,704	14,589	14,532	15,169
World	32,862	32,209	31,526	31,774	33,955	34,666	35,226	32,546	32,374	32,442
% 10 largest importers	49.21%	47.10%	44.13%	45.09%	43.55%	42.70%	44.58%	44.83%	44.89%	46.76%

Source: F. O. Licht's International Sugar and Sweetener Report. 1995

CUBAN CITRUS PRODUCTION
IN A POST-TRANSITION ECONOMY

Joseph M. Perry and Louis A. Woods

When the transition from a centrally-planned economy to a market system finally occurs in Cuba, a number of important industries whose growth has been slowed or depressed will face conditions more favorable to expansion. Once the U.S. embargo is lifted, institutional change occurs, and foreign capital flows into the reviving system, market alignments for major export crops may be altered. The Cuban citrus industry provides a prime example. Expanded significantly as a part of the agricultural diversification program of the Castro regime, the citrus sector has suffered a slowdown in recent years. It should have the capacity, after transition, to supply at least 2 percent of the world output of citrus products. Although this market share is not a dominant one, it still places Cuba in the top dozen citrus producing countries around the world (Perry, Woods and Steagall, 1993 and 1994).

Given the emerging effects of NAFTA on the Mexican economy, the development of workable regional trade blocs in this hemisphere, and the continuing inefficiency of many smaller citrus producers in the Caribbean, the re-emergence of Cuba as a major player in hemispheric citrus markets would suggest changes in market shares and export earnings for some countries (Woods, 1987; Woods and Perry, 1991). It is possible that the market position of citrus producers in the United States could be affected, if only marginally. This paper briefly delineates the world citrus market, and examines production and marketing conditions in selected major producing nations. It describes the Cuban citrus industry, within the limits of available information, and concludes with observations about the potential impact of expanded participation by Cuba in hemispheric citrus markets.

THE WORLD CITRUS MARKET

Citrus fruits originated in the Orient. They were introduced commercially to other nations when European trade began to expand after the Middle Ages. Ultimately, citrus plantings were made all around the Mediterranean, in those countries having an appropriate climate. When the New World was opened up by Spanish and Portuguese exploration, citrus cultivation followed. Plantings were made in most of the circum-Caribbean countries, including the Spanish territory that was later to become the State of Florida.

During the seventeenth and eighteenth centuries, the mercantilistic thinking of the time emphasized cash crops that could contribute to a colonizing country's self-sufficiency and could help to generate a favorable balance of trade. As a result, crops such as sugar, coffee, indigo, and tobacco were emphasized and supported. Citrus remained a minor item of commerce, primarily in the so-called "triangular trade" patterns around the Atlantic Ocean (Blouet and Blouet, 1993, pp. 136-137; Callender, 1965, pp. 50-54, 85-121; Nova González, 1994, p. 1).

Larger-scale commercial production of citrus and trade in both fresh and processed fruit began during the nineteenth century. As common sense suggests, a burgeoning world market for an agricultural commodity requires adequate production technology, efficient transportation, well-developed financial institutions and instruments, an international economy stable enough to support continued exchange, and markets large and affluent enough to absorb the product. This complex of requirements took shape as the nineteenth century wore on.

Today, citrus fruits are grown and traded around the world. Table 1 presents basic estimates for world production of citrus during the 1992-1993 season, generated by the Food and Agriculture Organization of the United Nations (FAO). Total world citrus output was estimated at 75.6 million metric tons, the highest level to date. As the data indicate, oranges dominated the world production of citrus fruits, accounting for 73.2 percent of total production volume in 1992-1993. Tangerines made up 11.0 percent of the total, lemons 9.1 percent, and grapefruit 6.6 percent.

FAO estimates are periodically revised, as better market information is acquired, so that annual comparability is not always assured. Nevertheless, the following FAO estimates for world citrus output suggest a growth trend over the recent past:

Crop Season	Output in *000 Tons*
1992/1993	75,607
1991/1992	70,519
1990/1991	66,185
1989/1990	68,343
1988/1989	64,483
1987/1988	60,714

Since the average annual world output for 1978-1980 was 53.465 million metric tons, the output level shown for 1992/1993 suggests an average annual growth rate for citrus output of 2.7 percent, computed over a thirteen year period (FAO, Commodity Review and Outlook, various issues).

Much of the world output of citrus is destined for domestic consumption in the producing countries. Nevertheless, international trade in citrus fruit and products has become substantial. FAO estimates in

Table 2 show the levels of citrus fruit exports for 1991, 1992, and 1993. Slightly different figures are presented in the 1993-1994 FAO *Commodity Review and Outlook*. Total world citrus exports for 1991/1992 are estimated at 7.8 million metric tons, and for 1992/1993 at 7.6 million metric tons. In spite of these differences, it is clear that approximately ten percent of the annual world output is exported in the form of fresh fruit. Substantial amounts of the annual output are also processed, and exported as concentrate, segments, frozen concentrated orange juice (FCOJ), and similar products.

It is worth pointing out that the level of citrus production in a given country exerts a two-dimensional impact on trade in that commodity. The higher the level of citrus output relative to domestic consumption, generally the smaller the reliance on imported citrus products (apart from distributional effects, when consumers prefer a type of citrus or citrus product that is not produced domestically). And the higher the level of output relative to domestic production, the greater the probability that there will be a surplus for export.

The share of major producing countries in world citrus output has shifted in recent years, responding to significant changes in the international political and economic environment, as well as to resource limitations in specific countries. Table 3 compares the ranking of leading citrus-producing countries for three recent time periods. The countries are ranked by the volume of citrus output, measured in metric tons.

Note that Brazil and the United States have been the two primary world producers over the past decade, although Brazil assumed first ranking only recently. China, however, has moved up rapidly to a position that now challenges Spain and Mexico. Israel has dropped in the rankings since the 1970's, while Cuba has finally achieved a position among the top twelve citrus producers with the 1992-1993 crop. These rankings suggest a market that is not only open to entry, but that permits fairly rapid changes in market shares among competing producers.

Table 1. World Production of Citrus Fruits—Major Producing Countries, 1992-1993 Season (000 Metric Tons)

Country or Area	Total Citrus Production	Oranges	Tangerines	Lemons	Grapefruit
World	75,607	55,379	8,322	6,880	5,026
Developing Countries	46,488	36,737	3,641	4,224	1,885
Developed Countries	29,119	18,642	4,680	2,656	3,141
Brazil	16,062	14,974		803	
United States	12,976	9,249	352	834	2,541
China	6,103	5,350	260		340
Spain	5,290	3,002	1,521	737	
Mexico	4,026	2,852		845	
Italy	3,524	2,218	515	785	
Japan	2,180	194	1,986		
Argentina	1,620	650		560	180
Greece	1,316	1,061		169	
Morocco	1,151	831	316		
Israel	894	377	116		383
Cuba	777	428			307
Australia	620	509			
Uruguay	246	135			

Note: Normal crop year is October-September. For southern hemisphere countries, data refer to crops harvested in 1993.

Source: FAO (1994a).

PROFILES OF CITRUS PRODUCTION IN MAJOR PRODUCING COUNTRIES

A brief review of the production characteristics of selected citrus-producing countries and regions will emphasize some of the factors leading to dominance or change. Note that the coverage below is not comprehensive or exhaustive, but should provide a representative sample of production arrangements and institutions.

The United States: Citrus plantings in the United States date from the earliest Spanish explorations and settlements. By the time William Bartram made his famous trips through the Southeast, both cultivated and wild groves of citrus could be found along the major Florida waterways and in the settled areas. Today, citrus production is concentrated in the states of

Table 2. Annual World Exports of Citrus Fruit, 1991-1993, Metric Tons

Category	1991	1992	1993
Oranges, Tangerines, Mandarins	5,521,003	5,864,228	6,356,218
Lemons and Limes	1,020,404	1,089,440	1,133,507
Other Citrus Fruit	1,100,363	994,422	1,008,237
Total of the Above	7,643,761	7,950,082	8,499,955

Source: FAO (1994b).

Florida, California, Texas, and Arizona. Florida dominates the industry, with 71 percent of the annual orange output and 69 percent of the grapefruit output (1989 percentages). California produces 27 percent of the oranges, while Texas accounts for 19

Table 3. The World's Major Citrus-Producing Countries

Rank	Ranked by 1985-1987 Average Production Levels	Ranked by Production for 1989-1990 Crop Season	Ranked by Production for 1992-1993 Crop Season
1	Brazil	Brazil	Brazil
2	United States	United States	United States
3	Spain	Spain	China
4	Japan	China	Spain
5	Italy	Italy	Mexico
6	Mexico	Mexico	Italy
7	Egypt	Japan	Japan
8	Morocco	Egypt	Argentina
9	Israel	Argentina	Morocco
10	Argentina	Turkey	Israel
11	Turkey		Greece
12	Greece		Cuba
13	South Africa		Australia

Sources: FAO (1994a); Ward and Kilmer (1989); and Behr and Bedigian (1991).

percent of the grapefruit. Lemons are a California and Arizona specialty (Ward and Kilmer, 1989, p. 7).

The U. S. citrus industry is characterized as "self-regulated with little government involvement in the daily marketing transactions" (Ward and Kilmer, 1989, p. 150). Citrus production is highly competitive, with more than 20,000 producers serving the market. They may sell their output directly, on the spot or by contract, or they may operate through a cooperative. As in a number of other countries, processing is more concentrated. The top 5 Florida processors, for example, controlled 50 percent of production in 1989, qualifying this stratum of the market as oligopolistic.

Governmental policies to protect the domestic citrus industry are of long standing. In 1790, for example, the first national tariff act was amended to include import duties on plums, prunes, oranges, and lem-

ons. In 1922, California lemon interests exerted enough political pressure to raise import duties on competing fruit. In 1929, the Federal government provided aid to the State of Florida in its fight against the Mediterranean fruit fly. And during both the Hoover Administration and the succeeding Roosevelt Administration, Federal aid to the industry was extensive (Benedict, 1953, pp. 45, 204, 260-265).

The citrus industry was a prominent player in early New Deal attempts to revive the economy. Under the Agricultural Adjustment Act of 1933, for example, agreements among citrus owners were aimed at coordinating shipments so as to stabilize the national industry. National coordination proved unworkable, soon devolving into regional programs. Marketing orders, both Federal and state, have been fairly common since the 1930's. Between December 1993 and June 1955, for example, 14 major Federal marketing orders or licenses were issued, variously affecting citrus activities in Florida, California, Arizona, and Texas (Benedict and Stine, 1956, pp. 381-394). The Florida Department of Citrus is sanctioned by a marketing order. The Florida Citrus Commission thus can exert its influence to control citrus grades and standards, and to provide support for market development (Ward and Kilmer, 1989, pp. 150-151).

The success of the U. S citrus industry rests upon a number of favorable characteristics: the availability of regionally limited but spatially adequate land for citrus plantings; competitive conditions at the producing level, contributing to more efficient production; access to the latest technology; access to adequate financing; access to markets; and a favorable governmental climate in which to operate.

Brazil: The Brazilian citrus industry expanded rapidly in recent years, bringing Brazil to the top position among citrus producers world-wide. The industry is competitive at the production level, with at least 5,000 grower-owned groves. The situation at the processing level is quite different, suffering from substantial governmental control through taxes, subsidies, licensing procedures, and credit programs. Processing qualifies as an oligopolistic market organization. The government also issues export licenses, and influences export prices through the Foreign Trade Department of the Bank of Brazil (Ward and Kilmer, 1989, pp. 152-154).

The production of citrus juice concentrates has assumed increasing economic importance since 1965. The industry is concentrated in and around São Paulo, and was originally financed by domestic capital. Recent inflows of foreign capital have supported its continued expansion. Seven of the eight major producers of concentrate were located in the São Paulo area in 1978. Three of those firms controlled over two-thirds of concentrate output. The concentrate industry absorbed about two-thirds of national orange production in 1976, and planned to export ninety percent of its output (Dickenson, 1978, p. 71).

The Florida citrus industry experienced severe freezes in 1981, 1982, 1983, and 1985, substantially reducing field production capacity. Brazilian citrus products filled the gap. By 1983, Brazil's annual output of oranges equaled that of the United States. In subsequent years, Brazilian production became dominant in the world market. Today, Brazil and the United States normally supply over 50 percent of the world's annual commercial supply of oranges. They also supply a high percentage of the world's processed citrus juices (Ward and Kilmer, 1989, pp. 130, 144, 147).

In spite of hyperinflation and other recent economic and political problems, Brazil has maintained its leading position as an exporter of coffee, orange juice, soybean oil, and soybean meal. It has also enjoyed a large positive balance of trade with the United States. In 1990, Brazil also benefited from the Florida crop freeze, which held the price of FCOJ above production costs (USDOC, ITA, 1992, p. 5).

Brazil's recent rise to citrus dominance is documented in Table 4. Since the 1979-1980 growing season, both orange and FCOJ output have doubled, while exports of FCOJ have more than doubled. It is clear that extensive governmental control of the processing and marketing levels of the industry have not eliminated the advantages Brazil enjoys: extensive landholdings, some of them well suited to citrus culture; a large and relatively low-paid labor force; adequate

access to both domestic and foreign financing of the industry; a growing market for the primary product; and access to the latest production technology.

Mexico: The Mexican citrus industry offers a major success story. Beginning commercial production in the late nineteenth century, Mexican citrus growers gradually expanded acreage under cultivation to 915,000 acres in 1990. In terms of physical volume of output, Mexico ranked sixth among world producers from 1985 to 1991, and moved up to fifth place during the 1992/1993 crop season (see Table 2). It is anticipated that the trade-enhancing effects of NAFTA, the availability of suitable citrus land, abundant supplies of relatively cheap labor, and access to current technology will spur additional growth in the industry (Perry, Woods and Steagall, 1993 and 1994; Behr and Bedigian, 1991, pp. 1-2, 14).

Citrus plantations are located throughout Mexico, where land availability and climate support production. The highest concentration of groves is found in the river basins in the eastern part of the country. The state of Veracruz typically produces about 35 percent of annual citrus output. Other important citrus centers are found in San Luís Potosí, Tamaulipas, and Nuevo León (Behr and Bedigian, 1991, p. 2).

The productivity of the citrus industry has been limited in part by the system of land tenure in Mexico. Ejidatarios control some of the smaller, poorly maintained groves, with little opportunity for improvement. Private grove owners normally have larger, more productive holdings, but even these are limited in size by government regulations. It is not unusual to see members of an extended family pooling their ownership rights to obtain larger contiguous parcels of land. Until very recently, foreign ownership of Mexican assets was also severely limited, discouraging the flow of venture capital into many agricultural pursuits (Behr and Bedigian, 1991, pp. 5-7).

The number of processing plants in Mexico has risen from 9 in 1981 to 22 in 1991. Increasing amounts of frozen concentrated orange juice are being produced, but the plants still reportedly have unused capacity,

Table 4. **Brazilian Production and Utilization of Oranges and FCOJ, 1979-1980 to 1994-1995**

Season	Orange Production and Utilization, São Paulo Millions of 90-pound Boxes			Brazilian FCOJ Production and Utilization Millions 42° Brix Gallons		
	Fresh	Processed	Total	Production	Domestic Consumption	Exports
1979-1980	31	124	155	150.0	3.8	132.1
1980-1981	32	138	170	170.0	4.1	171.4
1981-1982	25	155	180	207.6	4.5	204.8
1982-1983	34	161	195	195.8	4.5	174.8
1983-1984	35	165	200	214.1	3.4	231.4
1984-1985	20	185	205	270.3	5.2	263.8
1985-1986	19	220	239	301.7	6.9	242.0
1986-1987	50	170	220	207.9	6.9	241.0
1987-1988	40	180	220	244.8	6.9	254.5
1988-1989	35	175	210	245.8	6.9	243.8
1989-1990	40	255	295	362.0	6.9	330.7
1990-1991	40	202	242	297.6	6.9	280.0
1991-1992	38	212	250	327.2	6.2	341.0
1992-1993	40	274	314	394.8	6.2	375.8
1993-1994	55	247	302	358.6	6.2	351.7
1994-1995	55	245	300	353.4	6.9	353.4

Note: Fresh orange figures include fresh orange exports. 1994-1995 level is forecast.

Source: Agricultural Officer, Sao Paulo, as reported in Behr, *The 1994-1995 Situation and Outlook for the Brazilian Citrus Industry.*

being able to process 20 to 30 million boxes per season (Behr and Bedigian, 1991, pp. 9-10).

Table 5 delineates the growth of the Mexican citrus industry from 1980 to 1990. Total citrus output increased by about a million metric tons over the decade, with the strongest increases in oranges and tangerines. The average level of output during the 1970-1980 period was slightly less than 2 million metric tons, which confirms an earlier beginning for the growth trend.

In spite of the constraints placed upon the Mexican citrus industry by landholding patterns and government policies, it has grown and, certainly compared with the industries of many other citrus-producing countries, has prospered. The market-expanding effects of NAFTA have yet to be realized.

China: English-language source materials concerning the citrus industry of the People's Republic of China are scarce. Standard Chinese histories and economic geography texts emphasize other major cash and export crops, and refer to citrus production in a peripheral manner, if at all. Some aggregate information has been provided in recent years by the Chinese State Statistical Bureau, but no details are readily available to permit disaggregation into citrus types or varieties.

Some fragmentary data suggest regional specialization of the industry. In 1985, citrus production was reported for 16 separate provinces in China. Six provinces accounted for about 90 percent of output:

Table 5.   Citrus Production in Mexico, 1980/1981 to 1990/1991, 000 Metric Tons

Year	Oranges	Grapefruit	Tangerines	Other*	Total
1980-81	1,600	163	120	530	2,413
1981-82	1,650	115	130	632	2,527
1982-83	1,380	100	110	623	2,213
1983-84	1,220	85	110	603	2,018
1984-85	865	55	60	603	1,583
1985-86	1,410	82	123	509	2,124
1986-87	1,683	91	131	609	2,514
1987-88	1,942	105	151	681	2,879
1988-89	2,268	75	157	689	3,189
1989-90	2,200	100	169	709	3,178
1990-91	2,400	118	198	713	3,429

*Includes lemons and limes. 1990-1991 figures are forecast.

Source: USDA, FAS, AAO, Mexico City, cited in Behr and Bedigian (1991).

Sichuan, Guangdong, Zhejiang, Hunan, Guangxi, and Fujian. Sichuan province ranked first, with 574,729 metric tons. Estimated export figures for 1993 show 103,491 tons of oranges, 250 tons of lemons and limes, and 7,541 tons of other citrus fruit (PRC, 1990, p. 147; FAO, 1994b, Tables 54-56). The salutary effects of Nixon-administration diplomacy are in evidence here, as the opening of mainland China to other world markets stimulated much diversification and increasing interest in export markets.

SMALL CITRUS-PRODUCING COUNTRIES IN THE CARIBBEAN BASIN

A number of small nations in and around the Caribbean (in addition to Cuba) produce citrus fruit for the world market. The list of such island nations includes the Bahamas, Barbados, Dominica, the Dominican Republic, Jamaica, Martinique, Saint Lucia, St. Vincent, and Trinidad and Tobago. On the periphery of the Caribbean, Belize and Guyana are also citrus producers. Many of these nations are members of CARICOM, and most of them are accorded preferential access to the U. S. market by the Caribbean Basin Initiative, to Canada through Caribcan, and to European markets through the Lomé IV agreement.

The Caribbean Basin Initiative (CBI) and Caribcan: The CBI began operation on January 1, 1984, with an anticipated 12-year initial life span. Its basic purpose was "to promote private sector-led economic growth, stability, and diversification in the CBI region . . . through the provision of duty-free access to the large and lucrative U. S. market" (USDOC, ITA, 1988: Woods, 1987). CBI represented the response of the U. S. government to deteriorating economic conditions in the Caribbean Basin, recently worsened by the effects of the 1981-1982 recession.

Reconsideration of CBI by Congress led to passage of the Caribbean Basin Economic Recovery Expansion Act of 1990 (CBERA). This revision of the 1983 legislation made CBI a permanent program of the U. S. Government, with no termination date; it also targeted some developing countries (Belize and the Eastern Caribbean islands) for special efforts to encourage wider use of CBI preferences (USDOC, ITA, 1990). Currently, 23 countries qualify under CBI for exemptions from U. S. customs duties, Belize among them. Four other countries are eligible, but have chosen not to participate at this time. Panama was suspended from the program in April, 1988, and was reinstated on March 17, 1990.

CBI does not provide blanket access to U.S. markets. The law specifically excludes a variety of items from duty-free entry, including most textiles and apparel, canned tuna, petroleum and petroleum products, most footwear and gloves, some leather goods, and watches and watch parts originating in communist countries. In addition, any goods entering the United States from CBI countries must meet all relevant laws and regulations for consumer safety and protection. Two specific screening requirements are that the imported goods must show at least 35 percent value added by the producing country (prohibiting a simple "pass-through"), and that goods produced from materials originating outside the CBI must show a "substantial transformation" in the CBI manufacturing process (USDOC, ITA, 1990, pp. 7-10).

Caribcan is a similar preferential access program, covering most of the same Caribbean countries, established and maintained by the Canadian government. Many of the same provisions are found in Caribcan, including restrictions on the domestic content of Caribbean exports entering Canada.

The Caribbean Basin Initiative has generated uneven results. As the figures in Table 6 show, exports to countries covered under the latest version of the legislation (CBERA 1990) have just about doubled since 1984. In contrast, imports actually dropped from 1984 to 1986 (in spite of a strong dollar that peaked in 1985), and then recovered through 1993. According to these figures, the CBERA countries still suffer an aggregate balance of trade deficit with the United States.

Not insensitive to this imbalance, policy-makers in Washington have attempted to encourage the development of non-traditional exports, including citrus fruit and citrus products. Some success has been observed. In 1993, for example, frozen concentrated orange juice exports valued at US$12.9 million (c.i.f.) entered the United States from CBERA countries. Leading items that have benefited from CBERA since 1984 include beef, pineapples, frozen concentrated orange juice, tobacco leaf, and rum. As a result of U.S. lending, 17 export-enhancing projects received $103 million in financing in 1993, among them fruit processing and juice processing facilities.

Table 6. U. S. Exports to and Imports from CBERA Countries, Selected Years, US$000

Year	Value of Exports	Value of Imports
1984	5,952,884.00	8,649,235.00
1986	6,064,644.00	6,064,745.00
1988	7,421,840.00	6,061,054.00
1990	9,307,140.00	7,525,208.00
1992	10,901,693.00	9,425,616.00
1993	11,941,917.00	10,094,033.00

Source: U.S. International Trade Commission, *Impact of the Caribbean Basin Economic Recovery Act.* National Trade Data Bank (NTDB), ITEM TC LCARIB, April 7, 1995, Tables B-3 and B-4.

The countries that have benefitted include the Dominican Republic, Dominica, and Belize (USITC, 1995, Chapter 3, Table 3-2).

The Lomé Convention: The Lomé Convention was signed in Lomé, Togo, in 1975, by representatives of the European Economic Community (EEC) and some 50 low-income countries in Africa, the Caribbean, and Oceania (ACP). It replaced and broadened a prior preferential treaty between France, Belgium, and 18 former African colonies. Following the provisions established by the General Agreement on Tariffs and Trade (GATT), the EEC provided indirect aid to the low-income countries through lower tariffs for specified trade commodities. It has been renewed three times. In its latest negotiated version, Lomé IV currently provides free entry into EEC countries for manufactured goods and some agricultural products from the more than 60 ACP members, and the entry of primary commodities at stable prices. The EEC also provides development assistance and food aid to ACP countries (Grennes, 1984, pp. 202-214; USDOC, ITA, 1994, Appendix C).

The export data in Table 7 confirm that citrus exports from major Caribbean countries have increased over the past decade, perhaps five-fold, while the dollar value of these exports has trebled. Although citrus exports do not constitute a large percentage of the value of exports from these countries, citrus never-

Table 7.   Citrus Fruit Exports from Selected Caribbean Countries, 1980 and 1991-1993

Country	Total Citrus Fruit Exports in Metric Tons				Value of Exports, 1980, US$000	Value of Exports, 1993, US$000
	1980	1991	1992	1993		
Bahamas	0	2,226	696	1,970	0	745
Barbados	0	4	3	1	0	1
Dominica	1,040	2,344	1,780	1,880	249	790
Dominican Republic	191	10,336	9,300	9,750	28	2144
Grenada	0	66	60	60	0	30
Guadeloupe	17	0	1	0	15	0
Jamaica	3,188	9,999	11,106	12,073	1818	3585
Martinique	1	72	11	3	1	4
Saint Lucia	31	46	48	49	13	45
St. Vincent	0	200	202	170	0	40
Trinidad and Tobago	479	57	62	122	208	52
All Countries Listed Above	4,947	25,350	23,269	26,078	$2,332	$7,409

Note: Some of the figures for later years are estimated or forecast by the FAO, and may be revised as better information becomes available. Zero entries indicate either no production, negligible commercial production, or unrecorded production.

Source: FAO, Trade Yearbook, 1981 and 1993.

theless is an effective producer of foreign exchange. The economies of these countries are best described as fragile, with limited land resources and opportunities for diversification. Some of them have developed petroleum resources (Aruba, the Bahamas, the Netherlands Antilles, Trinidad and Tobago) to compensate for the debilitating effects of sugar quotas. Tourism has also become an effective generator of foreign exchange, creating dual monetary systems in some areas (Perry, Woods, and Steagall, 1994).

World Bank analysts conclude that the future of preferential trade agreements, such as those in the Caribbean, is uncertain. Sugar preferences will probably continue for the immediate future, they argue. However, a "banana shock" is quite possible, since the banana market is more vulnerable (The World Bank, 1993, *passim*).

THE CUBAN CITRUS INDUSTRY

The first plantings of citrus trees in Cuba were accomplished in the early 16th century. Strong commercial development of citrus waited until the beginning of the 19th century, long after the mercantilistic

drive for trade surpluses emphasized the production of sugarcane, tobacco, and coffee. Expansion continued over the decades, emphasizing grapefruit. By the end of the Second World War, Cuba had over 3,200 acres of citrus plantings, concentrated in the provinces of La Habana, Pinar del Río, and Oriente.

At the time of the Cuban Revolution, in 1959, the island economy had approximately 30,000 acres of citrus plantings, which produced about 60,000 metric tons of fruit per year. This output equaled 1.5 million 90-pound boxes. About 3,000 metric tons were exported mainly to the United States. The U. S. market was closed to Cuban citrus exports by 1961 (Nova González, 1994; pp. 1-3; Behr and Albrigo, 1991, p. 2).

The drive to diversify the Cuban economy, reducing its dependence upon export crops such as sugar, included significant expansion of citrus plantings, the encouragement of domestic citrus consumption, and the support of better agricultural practices. New annual plantings of citrus gradually increased after 1959 (when 40,928 acres were planted) and 1974 (when 84,407 acres were planted). During the 1980's, 10,000 to 18,000 acres per year were routinely planted to citrus, much of it replacing or supplementing less productive plots (Nova González, 1994, pp. 3-5, Table 6).

By 1990, Cuba had 355,700 acres in citrus, 281,600 acres of which were bearing (79.2 percent of the total). The remaining 74,100 acres, about 21 percent of the total, were devoted to non-bearing uses such as roads and schools. The plantings are concentrated in the central and western portions of the island, with the largest individual groves situated in Jagüey Grande, Matanzas Province, and on Isle of Youth (Behr and Albrigo, 1991, pp. 1-3, Figure 2).

In order to compensate for the vagaries of the weather, irrigation systems were installed to service most of the plantings. By 1989, approximately 81 percent of the acreage was served by some kind of irrigation system, portable, semi-static, or permanent. In addition, dams were built to provide a reliable water supply in areas where underground water supplies are undependable. (Nova González, 1994, pp. 10-11). Álvarez lists 19 dams built from 1966 to 1989, whose primary or partial purpose was for citrus cultivation. Another six new or expanded dams were reported to be under construction in 1989 for the same purposes. Government data indicated that the physical area of citrus plantings irrigated in 1989 was 164,500 hectares. (Álvarez, 1994, pp. 39-47).

The organization of the citrus industry leaves no doubt that it is part of a centrally-planned economy. Thirteen government "enterprises" are responsible for about 90 percent of citrus output. The enterprises are, in turn, subject to control by the Junta Central de Planificación (JUCEPLAN). Private interests control the remaining 10 percent of output. In 1990, 20 packinghouses packaged fresh fruit for the market. Three new processing plants came on line from 1975 to 1990, supplementing an older and probably obsolescent plant. Hard data are lacking, but it appeared that only about 200,000 tons of citrus were being processed in 1990. The fresh market still was dominant (Behr and Albrigo, 1991, pp. 4-8).

From 1959 to 1990, Cuban citrus production increased about fourteen-fold (Nova González, 1994, pp. 6-7). Reliable, consistent, and comparable data tracking this growth are difficult to access. The general expansionary trend may be documented by linking three partially overlapping sets of estimates. Table 8 reports the levels of citrus production in Cuba that Pérez-López computes for the 1965-1982 period. Table 9 shows the levels of citrus output for Cuba reported by CUBAFRUTAS for the period from 1984 to 1990. Finally, Table 10 presents the estimates prepared by the Food and Agriculture Organization of the United Nations for Cuban citrus output, from the 1987-1988 through the 1992-1993 growing season.

A clear expansionary trend emerges from these figures, even allowing for data defects. Citrus output apparently peaked in 1989-1991, and has declined since that time, as the constricting effects of the U.S. embargo have been felt in the lack of fuel, fertilizer, tools, replacement parts, and new equipment. The Cuban government established a goal of 1.6 million tons of citrus output by 1995. Conditions in Russia and Eastern Europe, combined with the U. S. embargo, have rendered that goal impossible of realization in the immediate future (Behr and Albrigo, 1991, pp. 5-7).

Outside investment has been a key factor in the growth of the Cuban citrus industry. In 1981, the communist nations, members of the Council for Mutual Economic Assistance (CMEA), pledged $350 million in investment funds for Cuban citrus. Some of these funds were used to provide irrigation equipment and to improve cultural practices. With the breakup of the Communist Bloc, and the resulting decline in both export markets and foreign support, Cuba has successfully moved to encourage investment flows from other nations.

The AFL-CIO reports that foreign investment has been used to support several citrus operations in Cuba. Israel has invested US$22 million in a large plantation in Jagüey Grande, with a size variously reported at 96,000 to 115,000 acres. The investment began in the 1960's, stopped when diplomatic relations worsened, then resumed in 1990. The grove uses Is-

Table 8.   Citrus Production in Cuba, 1965-1982 (metric tons)

Year	Oranges	Grapefruit	Lemons	Tangerines	Total
1965	85,880.6	10,541.7	9,377.5	4,306.7	110,106.5
1966	117,615.3	12,504.8	7,257.8	12,718.0	150,095.9
1967	109,790.9	13,197.9	8,127.6	4,316.2	135,432.6
1968	120,365.4	14,690.5	11,715.7	11,662.8	158,434.4
1969	108,142.8	12,579.8	12,348.2	11,360.6	144,431.4
1970	122,278.5	16,859.1	8,046.3	9,184.6	156,368.5
1971	84,842.6	14,266.6	11,348.4	8,115.0	118,572.6
1972	110,449.6	19,459.1	11,914.7	10,875.9	152,699.3
1973	117,047.7	25,475.2	15,504.6	9,891.7	167,919.2
1974	109,381.1	30,685.6	16,630.5	11,651.6	168,348.8
1975	126,519.4	25,128.1	14,028.6	10,154.7	175,830.8
1976	123,987.7	33,797.3	14,633.6	17,792.1	190,210.7
1977	131,748.9	11,389.7	13,899.7	12,817.6	169,855.9
1978	141,418.3	14,251.8	12,068.9	22,661.7	190,400.7
1979	136,093.9	12,990.6	15,014.9	20,665.7	184,765.1
1980	193,716.2	19,483.8	21,537.6	25,980.0	260,717.6
1981	250,617.5	53,703.3	35,070.5	33,833.1	373,224.4
1982	347,065.4	46,869.1	47,826.2	20,055.7	461,816.4

Source: Pérez-López (1987, Table A-2).

Table 9.   Citrus Production in Cuba, 1984-1990 (000 Metric Tons)

Year	Oranges	Grapefruit	Tangerines	Other*	Total
1984	371	155	20	53	599
1985	408	237	32	70	747
1986	441	250	25	64	780
1987	496	285	25	80	886
1988	508	385	26	62	981
1989	474	264	17	69	824
1990	604	332	15	66	1017

*Includes mostly limes.

Source: CUBAFRUTAS, as cited in Behr and Albrigo (1991).

raeli and Brazilian irrigation technology, and is under the management of GBM and Union Nacional de Cítricos. Greek funds support 25,000 hectares of plantations producing oranges and grapefruits for export to countries such as France and the Netherlands. A related processing plant in Ciego de Ávila Province

Table 10. Citrus Production in Cuba: Total, Oranges, and Grapefruit 1987/1988 to 1992/1993 (000 Metric Tons)

Period	Total Citrus	Oranges	Grapefruit
1992/1993	777	428	307
1991/1992	823	493	271
1990/1991	1,013	600	332
1989/1990	1,020	520	400
1988/1989	993	520	385
1987/1988	881	n/a	285

Source: FAO (1994a).

is intended to produce concentrate for export to Great Britain. The Greek investment is in conjunction with Lola Fruits and the Corporación Nacional de Cítricos. Chilean investors are involved in a partnership on the Isle of Pines, involving 11,000 hectares, to produce fruit for export to Europe and the newly independent Russian states. The partnership has been in effect for about four years. It is also reported that the Cuban government is contracting to use the marketing expertise of other governments, such as Chile to market its citrus products (AFL-CIO, 1995, p. 1; Behr and Albrigo, 1991, pp. 3, 9-10).

Interestingly, Israeli investments in Cuba and other Latin American countries come at a time when the country's own citrus industry has suffered a period of understandable decline. Citrus acreage in Israel reached a peak of 113,000 acres in 1966, and gradually declined thereafter to its current level of about 75,000 acres. Undependable water supplies, high production costs, and the lack of suitable additional citrus acreage drove the Israelis to the rational decision of downsizing. Israel still produces about a million tons of citrus per year, and exports significant amounts of fresh fruit to Europe. Their investors are now increasingly seeking foreign opportunities (Behr, 1992, pp. 2-5).

The planned growth of the Cuban citrus industry has thus achieved only conditional success. Acreage and

output increased dramatically over three decades, only to be contained by international market changes, foreign political upheavals, and a tightened embargo. In addition, the agricultural diversification movement that stimulated citrus expansion never generated reliable and substantial alternative sources of foreign exchange. In their best year, citrus exports accounted for only 3.1 percent of the value of all Cuban exports. Cuba remains primarily dependent on its sugar industry—which is now in a state of decline (Nova González, 1994, p. 9; and Álvarez, 1992, Addendum).

CUBA'S TRANSITION AND POST-TRANSITION CHANGES

The method and timing of the Cuban transition are now and will continue to be the subjects of hot debate. What is virtually certain is that there will be significant alterations in the governmental structure, the legal system, the complex of domestic financial institutions, the structure of landholding, the types of business organizations, and the occupational structure of the labor force. The movement toward a market system may be gradual, given the thirty years of central economic control and the lack of legal small-scale private enterprise in the country. Discussions of the timing among Cuban analysts often produce the consensus view of a transition that will last two decades.

Regardless of the timing, the transition will be supported by large inflows of capital from foreign countries. With the U. S. embargo just a memory, with U. S. tourists and U. S. investors able once more to exercise their interests, and with formal governmental approval of such interchange, financial pressures on the system may speed up the transition. It can be expected that the key industries generating foreign exchange will be quickly refurbished and expanded: sugar, tobacco, and tourism. Similarly, the expanded citrus industry should receive the resources it needs to move back to full production (Perry, Woods, and Steagall, 1993 and 1994).

How the newly revived Cuban economy will affect its potential competitors in this hemisphere depends to a high degree on the trade alignments and agreements in force. CBI, Lomé, and Caribcan were discussed above. The newest addition to the concerns of developing nations is the North American Free Trade Agreement (NAFTA), which links Canada, the United States, and Mexico in a grouping that will move toward a free trade area over the next 10 years.

Bernal (1994) argues that NAFTA will affect Caribbean countries adversely (and Mexico positively) if it is not expanded to include them. "NAFTA's most detrimental effects on the Caribbean will come through inevitable trade diversion, investment diversion, relocation of productive capacity, and contraction of economic activity as products and services that once were supplied by the Caribbean to the United States are now exported from Mexico" (p. 23). The clear implication is that Mexico stands to gain much more in the future from the full implementation of NAFTA, and that the process is one of economic transmission. Barton concurs with Bernal, arguing for strong negotiations to maintain and increase preferential access to U. S. markets (Barton, 1992).

Bernal points out that 50 to 70 percent of the exports of individual CBI countries go to the three NAFTA countries. NAFTA therefore could result in trade diversion for these countries, rather than trade creation. Using the apparel industry as an example, he projects the impacts of NAFTA after 10 years, as follows:

- **Trade Diversion:** The advantage enjoyed by CBI apparel producers is lessened as Mexican apparel faces a duty-free market. The World Bank estimates that 36 percent of CBI exports to the United States are subject to displacement. For St. Lucia, the figure may be as high as 79 percent.

- **Investment Diversion:** Declining trade prospects in Caribbean countries will cause investors to shift their funds to Mexico.

- **Relocation of Production Capacity:** Firms may move entire plants from the CBI countries to Mexico, to take advantage of the more favorable trade conditions.

- **Contraction of Economic Activity:** The losses noted above could lead to a contraction of economic activity, or at least to a slowdown.

- **Job Losses:** Jobs would be lost as a result of relocation of productive capacity and contraction of economic activity.

It is likely that a revived Cuba would return to a position of favor relative to the United States, with renewed and expanded trade ties. Given that relationship and the potential market strength of the Cuban economy, some of the same trade-diverting effects on Cuba's Caribbean neighbors might be expected after the transition. The combined effects of the two phenomena on the Caribbean could be substantial indeed.

As indicated above, much depends on the kinds of regional trade arrangements that are in force. Hallett and Primo Braga argue that regional integration arrangements (RIAs) have not materially hindered the growth of overall international integration in the past. They have doubts about the future, however, based partly on the limited ability of GATT to discipline cheaters. RIAs, in contrast, may establish a credible commitment mechanism, although they probably will not contribute to a better GATT. The authors conclude that the best alternative for developing countries is still a multilateral trading system, with the ability to identify larger trading partners who may take advantage of them. The burgeoning World Trade Organization (WTO), they point out, may be able to restrain large RIAs (Hallett and Primo Braga, 1994, pp. 29-31).

SUMMARY AND CONCLUSIONS

The world citrus market is a highly-developed, competitive, and growing market, dominated by a dozen or so major producers. Over the past two decades, the list of major producers has changed, as countries such as Israel have downsized citrus operations, and countries such as the People's Republic of China and Cuba have risen in importance. The latest available figures indicate that Cuba is the twelfth largest producer of citrus products, based upon volume of output.

A combination of factors appears to be present in those countries that are most successful in citrus production: appropriate climate, adequate amounts of suitable land, access to modern technology, a plentiful supply of labor, adequate financing, and access to markets. Some countries, such as Brazil and Mexico, have become major producers of citrus products in spite of some internal or governmental factors tending to reduce productivity in the industry. Market concentration at the processing level also appears not to be a major hindrance to effective operation of the industry. In a free market setting, Cuba should possess and be able to exploit all of the desirable characteristics noted above.

The government of Cuba has expanded citrus plantings from about 30,000 acres in 1959 to over 355,000 acres today. Foreign funds have helped with parts of the expansion. Output apparently peaked between 1989 and 1991 at around one million metric tons per year. Since then, annual output has dropped by perhaps 20 percent, most probably because of the constricting effects of the U. S. embargo and the reduction in Soviet subsidization.

Once the transition occurs, market changes and an inflow of funds will permit the Cuban citrus industry to operate at its most efficient level. A projected output level of 1.6 million tons per year, the original target for crop year 1995, appears to be a reasonable post-transition, short-term target.

The impact of the revived Cuban citrus industry on other citrus-producing countries in the western hemisphere will depend critically upon the trade alignments that exist and the trade alignments that Cuba can negotiate. It is likely that Cuba will be able to return to the favored trading position it occupied relative to the United States before 1959. That being so, access to U.S. markets by Cuban citrus producers should be assured.

Given the putative level of output of Cuban citrus after the transition, which will be a relatively small percentage of world and U.S. output, a major and damaging impact on the U.S. citrus industry appears unlikely, although fresh fruit sales could be affected. In other words, the Cuban citrus industry by itself does not appear to be a significant threat, especially if domestic consumption of citrus products in Cuba remains high.

It is more likely that other, smaller, and less efficient Caribbean producers of citrus will be affected adversely by renewed Cuban competition. The damage will not be created by citrus alone, however, but by a revived complex of major Cuban industries. Post-transition Cuba should enjoy a strong sugar industry, expanded tobacco sales, and a tourism industry of major proportions—in addition to efficient citrus production. Since most of Cuba's Caribbean neighbors are engaged in producing essentially the same export products, Cuba will clearly cut into their markets.

Many Caribbean countries have been encouraged by preferential access programs such as CBI, Caribcan, and Lomé, to expand citrus production. This has given them an additional option for the generation of foreign exchange, during a period when sugar quotas have fallen and the competition for tourists has increased. As Cuba revives, it has the potential to attract tourists who normally would visit other Caribbean locations. And a revived Cuban sugar industry threatens those countries that have enjoyed the absence of Cuba in the U. S. sugar quota system.

If the Cuban citrus industry revives along with other segments of the Cuban economy, post-transition Cuba will have the potential to reduce or, in some cases, eliminate one of the most recent options developed by its neighbors to generate foreign exchange. From that point of view, Cuban citrus will be a threat to at least a dozen Caribbean nations.

These possibilities will certainly be taken into account by Caribbean trade negotiators as the transition occurs. The recent inability of CARICOM nations to impress on the U. S. government the threat to them posed by NAFTA is not a favorable omen.

REFERENCES

AFL-CIO. Instituto Americano para el Desarrollo del Sindicalismo Libre (1995). *Inversionistas Extranjeros: Lubricando la Maquinaria Gubernamental Cubana.* Washington, D. C.: AFL-CIO, Instituto Americano para el Desarrollo del Sindicalismo Libre.

Alvarez, José. (1994) *Cuba's Infrastructure Profile.* International Working Paper Series No. IW94-4. Gainesville: University of Florida, Institute of Food and Agricultural Sciences, Food and Resource Economics Department, International Agricultural Trade and Development Center.

Barton, Winston E. (1992) "NAFTA and the Commonwealth Caribbean Economic Community: The Economics of Absorption." Paper presented at the Caribbean Studies Conference, Kingston, Jamaica.

Behr, Robert M. (1992) *Israel's Citrus Industry.* Florida Department of Citrus, Working Paper Series. Gainesville, Florida: Florida Department of Citrus.

Behr, Robert M., and Gene Albrigo (1991). *Cuba's Citrus Industry.* Florida Department of Citrus, Working Paper Series. Gainesville, Florida: Florida Department of Citrus.

Behr, Robert M., and Karen Bedigian (1991). *Mexico's Citrus Industry.* Florida Department of Citrus, Working Paper Series. Gainesville, Florida: Florida Department of Citrus.

Benedict, Murray R. (1955). *Can We Solve the Farm Problem? An Analysis of Federal Aid to Agriculture.* New York: The Twentieth Century Fund.

Benedict, Murray R. (1953). *Farm Policies of the United States, 1790-1950: A Study of their Origin and Development.* New York: The Twentieth Century Fund.

Benedict, Murray R., and Oscar C. Stine (1956). *The Agricultural Commodity Programs: Two Decades of Experience.* New York: The Twentieth Century Fund.

Blouet, Brian W., and Olwyn M. Blouet (1993). *Latin America and the Caribbean: A Systematic and Regional Survey.* Second edition. New York: John Wiley and Sons.

Callender, Guy Stevens, editor (1965). *Selections from the Economic History of the United States, 1765-1860.* New York: Augustus M. Kelley.

De Blij, H. J., and Peter O. Muller (1991). *Geography: Regions and Concepts.* Sixth edition. New York: John Wiley and Sons, Inc.

Dickenson, John P. (1978). *Brazil.* Studies in Industrial Geography. Boulder, Colorado: Westview Press.

Fairchild, Gary F. (1985). *The Caribbean Basin Initiative and the Florida Citrus Industry.* Florida Department of Citrus, Working Paper Series. Gainesville, Florida: Florida Department of Citrus.

Food and Agriculture Organization of the United Nations (1994a). *Commodity Review and Outlook, 1993-1994.* Rome: Food and Agriculture Organization of the United Nations.

Food and Agriculture Organization of the United Nations (1994b). *FAO Yearbook: Trade, 1993.* Volume 47. Rome: Food and Agriculture Organization of the United Nations.

Grennes, Thomas (1984). *International Economics.* Englewood Cliffs, N. J.: Prentice-Hall, Inc.

Hallett, Andrew Hughes, and Carlos A. Primo Braga (1994). *The New Regionalism and the Threat of Protectionism.* World Bank Policy Research Working Paper 1349. Washington: The World Bank.

Hopkins, James T. (1960). *Fifty Years of Citrus: The Florida Citrus Exchange, 1909-1959.* Gainesville: University of Florida Press.

Inter-American Development Bank (1990). *Economic and Social Progress in Latin America: 1990 Re-*

port. Washington: Inter-American Development Bank.

Inter-American Development Bank (1992). *Economic and Social Progress in Latin America: 1992 Report.* Washington: Inter-American Development Bank.

Inter-American Development Bank (1993). *Economic and Social Progress in Latin America: 1993 Report.* Washington: Inter-American Development Bank.

Langley, Lester D. (1989). *The United States and the Caribbean in the Twentieth Century.* Fourth edition. Athens, Georgia: The University of Georgia Press.

Moberg, Mark (1992). *Citrus, Strategy, and Class: The Politics of Development in Southern Belize.* Iowa City: University of Iowa Press.

Nova González, Armando (1994). *The Cuban Citrus Industry: Historical Development Through 1990.* International Working Paper Series No. IW94-9. Gainesville: University of Florida, Institute of Food and Agricultural Sciences, Food and Resource Economics Department, International Agricultural Trade and Development Center.

People's Republic of China. State Statistical Bureau (1990). *China Statistical Abstract: 1990.* New York: Praeger.

People's Republic of China. State Statistical Bureau (1986). *Statistical Yearbook of China 1986.* New York: Oxford University Press.

Pérez, Louis A., Jr. (1990). *Cuba and the United States: Ties of Singular Intimacy.* Athens, Georgia: The University of Georgia Press.

Pérez-López, Jorge F. (1995). *Cuba's Second Economy: From Behind the Scene to Center Stage.* New Brunswick: Transaction Publishers.

Pérez-López, Jorge F. (1987). *Measuring Cuban Economic Performance.* Austin: University of Texas Press.

Pérez-López, Jorge F. (1991). *The Economics of Cuban Sugar.* Pittsburgh: University of Pittsburgh Press.

Perry, Joseph M, Louis A. Woods, and Jeffrey W. Steagall (1994). "Dual Monetary Systems in the Western Hemisphere and the Cuban Transition." In *Cuba in Transition: Volume 4,* Papers and Proceedings of the Fourth Annual Meetings of the Association for the Study of the Cuban Economy. Washington, D.C.: Association for the Study of the Cuban Economy.

Perry, Joseph M, Louis A. Woods, and Jeffrey W. Steagall (1993a). "Hemispheric Trade Alignments and the Trade Options for Post-Transition Cuba." In *Cuba in Transition: Volume 3,* Papers and Proceedings of the Third Annual Meetings of the Association for the Study of the Cuban Economy. Miami: Florida International University.

Perry, Joseph M, Louis A. Woods, and Jeffrey W. Steagall (1993b). "Regional Trade Alignments and the Role of Cuba: The 'Transition' and After." Paper presented at the 63rd Annual Conference of the Southern Economic Association, New Orleans, La., November 21-23, 1993.

Smith, J. Russell, and M. Ogden Phillips (1946). *Industrial and Commercial Geography.* Third edition. New York: Henry Holt and Company.

U.S. Department of Agriculture (1977). *Agricultural Statistics: 1977.* Washington: U.S. Government Printing Office.

U.S. Department of Agriculture (1986). *Agricultural Statistics: 1986.* Washington: U.S. Government Printing Office.

U.S. Department of Agriculture. National Agricultural Statistics Service (1993). *Agricultural Statistics: 1993.* Washington: U.S. Government Printing Office.

U. S. Department of Commerce (1991). *1990 Caribbean Basin Investment Survey.* Washington: U.S. Government Printing Office.

U. S. Department of Commerce. Bureau of the Census (1994). *Statistical Abstract of the United States: 1994*. Washington: U.S. Government Printing Office.

U.S. Department of Commerce. International Trade Administration (1992). *Foreign Economic Trends and Their Implications for the United States: Brazil*. Washington: U.S. Government Printing Office.

U.S. Department of Commerce. International Trade Administration (1994). *Guide to the Caribbean Basin Initiative*. Washington: U.S. Government Printing Office.

U.S. Department of Commerce. International Trade Administration (1988). *1989 Guidebook: Caribbean Basin Initiative*. Washington: U.S. Government Printing Office.

U.S. Department of Commerce. International Trade Administration (1990). *1991 Guidebook: Caribbean Basin Initiative*. Washington: U.S. Government Printing Office.

Ward, Ronald W., and Richard L. Kilmer (1989). *The Citrus Industry: A Domestic and International Perspective*. Ames, Iowa: Iowa State University Press.

Weeks, Jerry Woods (1977). *Florida Gold: The Emergence of the Florida Citrus Industry, 1865-1895*. Doctoral Dissertation, University of North Carolina-Chapel Hill. Ann Arbor: University Microfilms International.

Woods, Louis A. (1987). "The Caribbean Basin Initiative and Its Impact on Belize." Paper presented at the annual meetings of the American Popular Culture Association, Montreal, March, 1987.

Woods, Louis A., and Joseph M. Perry (1991). "Regional Integration, Foreign Trade, and Economic Development: CARICOM and Belize." In *Fourth Annual Studies on Belize Conference*, SPEAReports 7 (Belmopan: Cubola Productions). Revised version of paper presented at Fourth Annual Studies on Belize Conference, Belize City, October 25-27, 1990.

The World Bank (1988). *Caribbean Countries: Economic Situation, Regional Issues, and Capital Flows*. Washington: The World Bank.

The World Bank. (1993). *Caribbean Region: Current Economic Situation, Regional Issues, and Capital Flows, 1992*. Washington: The World Bank.

Worrell, DeLisle (1987). *Small Island Economies: Structure and Performance in the English-Speaking Caribbean Since 1970*. New York: Praeger Publishers.

Woytinsky, W. S., and E. S. Woytinsky (1955). *World Commerce and Governments: Trends and Outlook*. New York: The Twentieth Century Fund.

Zimbalist, Andrew, and Claes Brundenius (1989). *The Cuban Economy: Measurement and Analysis of Socialist Performance*. Baltimore: The Johns Hopkins Press.

THE ECONOMIC DIMENSION OF EIA IN THE TRANSITION FROM A CENTRALLY PLANNED ECONOMY TO A TRULY PARTICIPATIVE MARKET BASED ECONOMIC SYSTEM

René Costales[1]

One way in which an economist familiar with cost-benefit analysis (CBA) may look at environmental impact assessment (EIA) is that EIA is a CBA requiring a large amount of information rigorously collected and analyzed by a group of scientists of various disciplines. One can appreciate that the development of EIA has served to advance the systematic description and quantification of environmental effects in a way which can only serve to improve the quality of CBA undertaken. One can also appreciate that EIA constitutes a process, formalized through environmental legislation, regulations and procedures, which in turn reinforces the community participation required for informed decision-makers seeking the common good. While CBA within EIA is a key generator of information to the decision-makers, recognition should also be given that the EIA process is both a planning tool and an execution monitoring tool. Thus, the role of CBA is not as an intermediate step, but rather as an integrated parallel process. Hence, the CBA should follow up, quantify and evaluate the dynamic iterations created by the exhaustive search of alternatives, by the efficient inclusion of environmental protection and mitigation measures and by the explicit valuation of preference and choice articulated by community, society and their representatives acting in the best interest of present and future generations.

VALUE OF CONSIDERING ENVIRONMENTAL EFFECTS EARLY ON IN THE PROJECT CYCLE

The main purpose of the economic analysis of a project is to ascertain whether the project can be expected to create more net benefits than any other, mutually exclusive option, including the option of not doing it. Consideration of alternative options, therefore, is a key feature in proper project analysis. Often, important choices about alternative project options are made early on in the project cycle. These options may differ considerably in their general economic contribution, and they may also differ greatly concerning their environmental impact. Therefore, including environmental effects in the early economic analyses, however approximately, should improve the quality of future decisionmaking.

The CBA process—defining objectives, searching for alternatives, costing out the resources involved, specifying the effects of each option involved and comparing all the costs and benefits—normally requires considerable efforts. In the case of Cuba, we are faced with two joint families of economic valuation problems: the "environmental" ones and those problems associated with the incipient transition from a centrally planned economy to a truly participative market based economic system.

---

1. The views presented in this paper are those of the author and not necessarily those of his employer.

In principle, economic analyses are to take into account *all* costs and benefits of a project. With regard to environmental impacts, however, there have been two basic problems even in developed countries. First, environmental impacts are often difficult to measure in physical terms. Second, even when impacts can be measured in physical terms, valuation in monetary terms can be difficult. In spite of such difficulties, a greater effort needs to be made everywhere to 'internalizes' as many environmental costs and benefits as possible by measuring them in money terms and integrating these values in the economic appraisal. The measurement in money terms are made even more difficult in countries undergoing market reforms.

The environmental valuation problems can be summarized as follows:

VALUE OF ENVIRONMENTAL ASSETS

While man-made and human capital may be valued with relative ease by observing existing market systems, where available; the existence value of clean water and air, tropical forests, wetlands, coral reefs and other environmental assets and their functions is much more difficult since not even market prices can reflect their full contribution to other economic activity and to human welfare. In particular, the market price of water does not reflect the various services it provides nor do market values can accurately reflect what happens when irreversible loss or damage of natural resources occurs as environmental degradation exceeds a critical threshold level. Complexity of environmental valuation also arises due to the multiple functions of being a source of raw materials and energy, being a sink for assimilating man-made wastes and providing other services such as recreational/tourism services, storage of genetic diversity and scientific and educational benefits.

The following classification is useful:

* *Direct use* values are derived from the economic uses made of the natural system's resources and services. Examples of these are outputs such as timber, game and recreation from forests or fish and scuba tourism from coral reefs.

* *Indirect use* values are the indirect support and protection provided to economic activities and property by the resource system's natural functions or environmental services. Examples of these are watershed protection and soil erosion prevention provided by forests, and beach sand and mooring facilities protection provided by coral reefs.

* *Non-use* values lie in the special attributes of the natural system as a whole, its cultural and heritage uniqueness; it includes both existence and option values. Existence values reflect public goods which can be enjoyed by more than one consumer without decreasing the amounts enjoyed by others such as clean air, beaches and forests. The existence value is the utility that consumers derive from just knowing the public good exists. A way of measuring that utility would be to measure the willingness to pay or the contingent value assigned if the public good were to disappear. Option values reflect what current generations wish to bequeath for future generations to inherit. They imply both an ethical commitment to sustainabilty for the children of our children and in a shorter time-frame the maintenance of options to solve current problems. Examples of option values have been developed for forests relating to biodiversity and the search for cures of cancer and AIDS - "if forest were to disappear then the options to find such cures will vanish" or "as long as the forest is protected there is the option to find the cure".

Direct Effects Valued on Conventional Markets

Some methods are directly based on market prices or productivity. This is possible where a change in environmental quality affects actual production or productive capability.

Change-in-Productivity. Development projects can affect production and productivity positively or negatively. The incremental output can be valued by using standard economic prices where available.

Loss-of-Earnings. Environmental impacts can significantly affect human health. In theory, the value of health impacts should be determined by the willingness to pay of individuals to maintain their health. In practice, one uses earnings lost upon early death, disease or job absence. This approach is used in highway and industrial safety, and in air pollution studies.

The "implicit value of human life" approach is rejected by many as dehumanizing since human life can be said to have infinite value. However, society, government regulations, insurance companies and judicial courts implicitly and explicitly place finite values on human life and health. This is a necessity reflecting limited resources to be allocated for health expenditures. The relatively high level of health expenditures in Cuba would indicate a high implicit value of human life and health. However, one can also discern a political motivation and its attendant benefits behind it.

Preventive Expenditures. Individuals and governments invest in prevention measures to avoid or reduce unwanted environmental effects. Environmental damages, are often difficult to assess, but historical information on preventive measures and their costs may be interpreted as a minimum value for the expected benefits that the preventive measures seek. If it is found, for example, that there is a historical pattern of under investment in Cuba for natural disaster planning and prevention; then, it can be inferred that the benefits expected from such preventive measures have been very low. This conclusion would in turn imply that the loss of human life would be assigned a relatively low value. While this possible conclusion may appear to conflict with the high political priority for health expenditures, it can be observed that the level of damages or loss of lives caused by natural disasters cannot be easily attributed to government inaction and thus the political cost may be easily explained away.

Potential Expenditure
Valued on Conventional Markets

Replacement Cost. Simply, the costs that would have to be incurred in order to replace a damaged asset. The estimate is not a measure of benefit of avoiding damage since the damage costs may be higher or lower than the replacement cost.

Valuation Using Implicit (or Surrogate) Markets

Sometimes one must use market information indirectly. Approaches to be considered are the travel cost method, the property value approach, the wage differential approach, and uses of marketed goods as surrogates for non-marketed goods. Each technique has its particular advantages and disadvantages, as well as requirements for data and resources. One must determine which techniques might be applicable to a particular situation.

Travel Cost. This approach measures the travel cost (and time involved) which reflects the willingness of consumers or users can serve to measure the benefits produced by recreation sites (parks, lakes, forests, wilderness). It can also be used to value "travel time" in projects dealing with fuelwood and water collection.

Property Value. This valuation method is based on the general land value approach and can determine the implicit prices of certain land areas. The property value approach can help analyze willingness to pay for properties with different pollution levels and infer the implicit cost of pollution. The method compares prices of houses in affected areas with equal size and similar neighborhood characteristics elsewhere in the same metropolitan area.

Valuation Using Constructed Markets

Contingent Valuation. When society's preferences as revealed in market prices are not available, the contingent valuation method tries to obtain information on individual preferences by posing direct questions about willingness to pay. It basically asks people what they are willing to pay for a benefit, and/or what they are willing to accept by way of alternate compensation to tolerate an environmental cost. This process may be achieved through a direct questionnaire/survey. Willingness to pay is difficult to measure and depends on the income level of the sample subjects, and involves problems of designing, implementing and interpreting questionnaires. While its applicability may be limited, there is now considerable experience in evaluating the quality of supply of potable water and electricity services.

Artificial Market. Such markets can be constructed for experimental purposes, to determine consumer willingness to pay for a good or service. For example, a home water purification kit might be marketed at various price levels, or access to a game reserve may be offered on the basis of different admission fees, thereby facilitating the estimation of values placed by individuals on water purity or on recreation facilities.

THE DISCOUNT RATE

Discounting is the process by which costs and benefits occurring in different time periods may be compared. The discount rate to be used has been a general problem in cost-benefit analysis, but it is particularly important with regard to environmental issues, since some of the associated costs and benefits are very long-term or irreversible in nature. In standard analysis, past costs and benefits are treated as "sunk" and are ignored in decisions about the present and future. Future costs and benefits are discounted to their equivalent present value and then compared. In theory, in a perfect market, the interest rate reflects both the subjective rate of time preference (of private individuals) and the rate of productivity of capital.

Higher discount rates may discriminate against future generations. This is because projects with social costs occurring in the long term and net social benefits occurring in the near term, will be favored by higher discount rates.

It is often argued that discount rates should be lowered to reflect long-term environmental concerns and issues of intergenerational equity. However, this would have the drawback that not only would ecologically sound activities pass the cost-benefit test more frequently, but also a larger number of projects would generally pass the test and the resulting increase in investment would lead to additional environmental stress.

Many environmentalists believe that a zero discount rate should be employed to protect future generations. However, employing a zero discount rate is inequitable, since it would imply a policy of total current sacrifice, which runs counter to the proposed aim of eliminating discrimination between time periods—especially when the present contains widespread poverty.

In the case of projects leading to irreversible damage (e.g., destruction of natural habitats, etc.), the benefits of preservation may be incorporated into standard cost-benefit methodology using the Krutilla-Fisher approach. Benefits of preservation will grow over time as the supply of scarce environmental resources decreases, demand (fueled by population growth) increases, and possibly, existence value increases. The Krutilla-Fisher approach incorporates these increasing benefits of preservation by including preservation benefits foregone within project costs. The benefits are shown to increase through time by the use of a rate of annual growth. While this approach has the same effect on the overall CBA as lowering discount rates, it avoids the problem of distorted resource allocation caused by arbitrarily manipulating discount rates.

CONCLUSIONS

In order to achieve economically sustainable management of natural resources and environmental protection, one must effectively incorporate environmental concerns into decision making through the EIA process.

This presentation has reviewed concepts and techniques for economic valuation of environmental impacts within EIA procedures. The process of internalizing these environmental externalities can be facilitated by making rough qualitative assessments early on in the project evaluation cycle—the advantages of which would include:

* early exclusion of alternatives that are not sound from an environmental point of view;

* more effective in-depth consideration of those alternatives that are preferable from the environmental viewpoint; and

* better opportunities for redesigning projects and policies to achieve sustainable development goals.

In order to fully reflect society's values and preferences about environmental values, non-market methods of estimation can be used and will enhance community participation through well designed and administered questionnaires and surveys. Research and training about EIA and embedded economic analysis methods is needed in Cuba. As developing countries learn to successfully apply EIA methodologies the goals of sustainable development will become more attainable.

THE PROCESS OF ENVIRONMENTAL IMPACT ASSESSMENT IN CUBA

Amparo E. Avella

For many countries, the past several years have been characterized by passage of environmental legislation. New terminology has arisen in conjunction with the process of complying with the requirements of those laws. Three of the most significant new terms are environmental diagnosis, environmental assessment, and environmental impact.

Environmental impact means environmental change, positive or negative, from a desirability standpoint. The words environmental effects or consequences have generally the same meaning of impact. An impact can be defined as any change in the physical-chemical, biological, cultural, and/or socioeconomic environmental factors, that can be attributed to human activities.

The environmental impact assessment (EIA) was developed as a consequence of increased public awareness of the harmful biophysical and socioeconomic effects of development. Public concern for environmental quality and "quality of life" were important political factors in the late 1960s and early 1970s in many countries. EIA is defined as a systematic examination of the environmental consequences of projects, policies, and programs. Its main objective is to provide decision-makers with an account of the implications of alternative courses of action, before a decision is made.

In order to perform EIAs it is necessary to develop a complete understanding, and clear definition, of the proposed action:

- What is to be done?

- Where?

- What kinds of materials, labor and resources are involved?

- Are there different ways to accomplish the original purpose?

Additionally, it is necessary to gain complete understanding of the affected environment.

- What is the nature of the biophysical and socioeconomic characteristic that may be changed by the actions?

- How widely might some effects be felt?

- What is the affected area? A mile? A region?

The necessity for preparing an EIA varies with individual projects, proposed actions, environmental conditions, and the enacted legislation. In the United States, the National Environmental Policy Act requires an EIA for major projects that have federal relevance. Other nations have enacted legislation requiring environmental assessment of all projects that may affect the environmental quality of an specific site and its surrounding area. For example, in Mexico, the list of projects that should be evaluated consists of federal projects and all projects located in urban areas and that may affect environmental quality.

Good professional practice requires EIAs even if the law or existing regulations do not. In contrast with many countries, where the EIA is prepared by environmental consulting firms, in the United State the federal agencies that are proposing the actions are responsible for preparing the Environmental Impact Statement. In others countries, the private investor is required to submit a report on environmental changes expected and the measures to mitigate effects on the environment. The report is prepared by a consulting firm. In my personal opinion, this option is preferred.

The minimum requirements for an environmental impact assessment are as follows:

- Conditions of the environment prior to the actions

- Geographical location of the actions

- Time period for the projected actions

- Factors affected

- Identification of impacts by factors

- Qualitative and quantitative measurements of the impacts

- Identification of secondary impacts

- Mitigation measures

- Public notice and consultation with the affected community

- Monitoring of effects.

Different methods for EIAs have been developed. The functions associated with EIAs are many: to identify, to predict, and to evaluate. There are five main activities involved in EIA:

- identification of impacts;

- measurement of impacts;

- interpretation of the significance of impacts;

- communication of the results;

- identification of monitoring schemes.

The style of analysis adopted for EIA varies from country to country, but common features are:

- A two-stage approach defining environmental effects during the construction stage (short term) and during the working life of the project (long term).

- An assessment of the effects on local employment, services, and living standards as well as the more directly visible effects on the physical environment, such as noise, air pollution, visual intrusion, land degradation, and water contamination.

According with the explanation presented above, what is the situation regarding EIAs in Cuba? Cuban Law 33, enacted in 1981, requires an environmental site assessment of all investment projects. However, today the following environmental problems surpass those existing in 1959: soil erosion, soil salinization, water pollution, deforestation, extinction or severe reduction of native species, and the erosion of the beaches.

Cuban tourism development is based on natural resources, especially beaches. Although Cuba has a great quantity of natural resources, tourism development has been concentrated on only a few coast line areas, and the level of development of the industry has been relatively low. The irrational building process of hotels, roads, and houses on sand dunes is the principal cause of soil erosion. Construction on the sand dunes and marine pollution are the main problems at Varadero Beach. Because of this, Cuban authorities responsible for urban planning restricted new development in Varadero Beach, an area that remains 50 percent undeveloped. However, Cuban authorities plan to diversify tourism into other areas, such as Trinidad, the north coast of Holguín Province, several districts outside of Havana, and the keys north of Ciego de Avila and Camagüey.

Cuba has a variety of environmental problems caused by development decisions made without regard for future consequences, or in others words, without an environmental assessment. The environmental impacts of tourism were recognized in the Manila Declaration on World Tourism. The following example shows the need to pay closer attention to wise resource management in Cuba, particularly with respect to the beaches.

In order to make the keys located in the north and on the south side of the main island accessible to tourists, the Cuban government, and specifically Fidel

Castro, established a program to join these keys with a series of stone roads named "pedraplenes" (which means "stone and earth embankment"), blocking substantial sea water and the normal currents between the coastline and the keys. This action has resulted in irreparable damage and disturbance to the native flora and fauna. Sea life has been drastically reduced in all these areas, with an accompanying decrease in the fishing resources. The results were predictable before construction of the "pedraplenes": entire marine areas have been reduced to salty lagoons, with low oxygen levels and little life.

This keys are areas with high environmental fragility. When their carrying capacity and saturation levels are exceeded, there will be a number of negative effects. In this case, rather than choosing to avoid the predicted environmental problems, it was more important for the Cuban government to offer international tourists a unique attraction, with rare ecosystem, on scarce land, in a place where it is also difficult to provide fresh water, electricity and other infrastructure requirements.

It is known that one of the reason tourism is so important economically is that it is labor intensive. Tourism offers a promising source of new jobs in Cuba, demanding large number of highly skilled workers, and well-trained and educated managers. However, the classic role of tourism as a great economic contributor to the growth of domestic industries such as agriculture, and food processing, is not totally realized in Cuba right now. The impact of tourism on the local economy, and the benefits from tourism, are usually in areas such as employment, income generation, and diversification of the economic base. However all of these positive impacts do not occur in Cuba.

Often one of the negative environmental impacts of tourism is the appearance of social pathology, including prostitution and robbery. Sometimes, these are responses to direct tourist demands, but in Cuba these phenomena result from the total absence of social and material satisfaction for the Cuban people.

The return of prostitution associated with tourism is one the most disturbing recent developments in Cuba. This is mainly due to the desperate economic condition of the Cuban people, and is a consequence of the social and economic policies of the Cuban government. The cost of enjoying one night with a young Cuban girl is equivalent to one pair of jeans, two bars of soap, or ten to twenty dollars. This is equivalent to more than a month's salary for a Cuban worker. It is viewed as a necessary means of economic survival by many Cubans who see that foreign tourists eat while they are hungry.

There is also a secondary negative environmental impact on education stemming from foreign tourism that is also alarming. Many young Cubans do not want to study at the universities. They prefer go to work in hotels, restaurants, and bars linked with foreign tourism, because they can receive dollars, worth much more in terms of what goods and services can be acquired than the wages they could earn in pesos with university degrees.

The present negative social impacts for the Cuban people are likely to increase, with more tourist dollars resulting in more prostitution and other undesirable social effects. Biophysical and social impacts from tourism development are likely to continue at an accelerated pace. More irreversible impacts are almost certain to occur.

In conclusion, all of these problems are consequence of the incomplete character of Law 33, because the process of the EIA cannot be considered in isolation from other aspect of the planning process. Two factors, not included in this law are of particular significance: the relationship between EIA and decision-making and public participation. In practice, it is not always possible to separate the technical and the political components because they are very closely interrelated.

ASPECTOS ESENCIALES SOBRE LA MITIGACIÓN DE LOS DESASTRES NATURALES EN CUBA

José Carlos Lezcano

Para que la acción de un evento natural sea considerada como un desastre mayor, la Oficina del Coordinador de las Naciones Unidas para el Socorro en Casos de Desastres (UNDRO), considera una situación que implique, al menos 10 pérdidas de vidas humanas y/o un millón de dólares estadounidenses (Zupka, 1988). Segun este criterio, Cuba es blanco anualmente de dos o tres desastres de mayor categoría, que por lo general superan ampliamente los requisitos oficialmente estipulados.

Varios fenómenos naturales se consideran potencialmente devastadores:

- Terremotos

- Erupciones volcánicas

- Huracanes

- Lluvias torrenciales (a las que se asocian eventos de acción consecutiva, como los deslizamientos de lodo o las inundaciones, estas últimas pueden ser por invasión marina, precipitación o ambas).

Existen otros acontecimientos cuyos efectos cobran fuerza a más largo plazo, pero en muchas ocasiones, representan pérdidas aun mayores y más difíciles de cuantificar, tal es el caso de las sequías.

El hombre es cada vez más vulnerable a los eventos naturales, debido a los siguientes factores:

- Acelerado crecimiento y concentración de la población sobre las áreas urbanas, principalmente en países del tercer mundo.

- Degradación del medio ambiente.

- Ausencia de políticas efectivas para la mitigación de los desastres naturales.

- Falta de un ordenamiento territorial en forma planificada.

- Infraestructura industrial y civil en áreas de riesgo

El archipiélago cubano se integra a la faja de los trópicos estacionalmente húmedos, con una longitud en su perímetro costero que supera los 6,000 kilómetros y un territorio donde no existe actividad volcánica, mientras los movimientos sísmicos se limitan a la región oriental, pero presentando índices de peligro despreciables, comparados con huracanes, inundaciones o prolongadas sequías.

Los desastres naturales además de causar numerosas víctimas humanas y estados de trauma en los sobrevivientes, imponen descomunales pérdidas económicas que, anualmente a nivel mundial, pueden oscilar entre 10 y 20 mil millones de dólares estadounidenses, y en el año 2,000 probablemente sobrepasen los 50 mil millones de dólares. Por tanto, los efectos de los fenómenos naturales además de su enfoque humanitario y social, adquieren cada vez más una connotación profundamente económica. En el caso de muchos países en desarrollo, provocan reducciones estrepitosas del producto nacional bruto, echando por tierra todos los planes económicos a corto y mediano plazo, e impidiendo un progreso estable. Por lo general, los gobiernos de estos países se concentran más en las medidas de socorro y olvidan la etapa de preparación previa, la más importante. En el caso de Cuba, resultan incomparablemente superiores las pérdidas asociadas a los efectos producidos por lo fenómenos naturales, que cualquier error vinculado a una incorrecta evaluación o interpretación del impacto ambiental. Esta situación, en última instancia, tiende a exacerbar el problema, por la evidente relación que une a estos elementos secuenciales, pero ambos requieren de un tratamiento totalmente separado y asumen señales diferentes.

ELEMENTOS GENERALES DE LA PREVENCION Y LA PLANIFICACION DE LOS DESASTRES NATURALES

Los desastres naturales no pueden considerarse como factores aislados o lejanos a la política económica de cualquier país. Los efectos directos que originan sobre las propiedades e ingresos de la población, los efectos indirectos derivados de una disminución en los ingresos y la reducción de la producción causada por ellos, así como los efectos secundarios pueden ir apareciendo poco tiempo después de la catástrofe. Entre estos efectos figuran: la disminución de las reservas monetarias, repuntes inflacionarios y aumentos de los gastos públicos. Para los países en desarrollo es vital la comprensión de estos aspectos, pues están más expuestos a los riesgos, ya que sus asentamientos humanos y actividades económicas se concentran en zonas peligrosas con economías poco diversificadas y recursos monetarios muy escasos para enfrentar acontecimientos de tal envergadura; por tal motivo, las medidas de prevención y planificación, basadas en principios de costo/beneficio, adquieren mayor relevancia.

En el proceso de mitigación de los desastres naturales, es esencial la combinación de la prevención (actividades de evaluación técnica, como: programas a largo plazo, medidas y normas constructivas, estudios aplicados, información, etc.) y la planificación (planeamiento logístico, planes de emergencia, legislación, medidas financieras, pronósticos, evaluación, etc.). La gravedad de los efectos causados por estos acontecimientos, cuya duración e intensidad varía considerablemente, será distinta según el grado en el cual, el hombre haya creado un medio susceptible de ser dañado y en la mayoría de las ocasiones, esta situación puede determinar el número de víctimas y pérdidas materiales, que cobrará el fenómeno (UNDRO, 1991).

La planificación para casos de desastres, comienza por la identificación y comprensión del peligro natural, que se entiende como la probabilidad de que se produzca, dentro de un período y zona determinada, un evento potencialmente dañino. El análisis debe continuar con el cálculo y evaluación de la vulnerabilidad, que no es más que el grado de pérdida de un elemento o un conjunto de elementos en riesgo (población, edificaciones, servicios, etc.) y finalmente obtener el riesgo propiamente dicho, o sea, el número previsto de muertos, lesionados, daños a la propiedad y perturbación de las actividades económicas. Resulta imprescindible comprender debidamente la posible naturaleza de diferentes escenarios en los desastres, como única vía para delinear planes logísticos efectivos.

SITUACION DE CUBA ANTE LOS DESASTRES NATURALES

Existen varios conceptos que pretenden poner fronteras a la zona costera. Algunos autores, básicamente en áreas continentales, establecen su límite en unos 60 km. tierra adentro, otros prefieren utilizar el borde de la intrusión salina y en algunos casos se escoge una determinada curva de nivel topográfico, generalmente la de 5.0 metros. Para Cuba, se puede afirmar que la población asentada entre el nivel cero y la isolínea topográfica de 5.0 metros, supera el millón de habitantes, o sea, entre el 9 y el 10% del total de la población, constituyendo la primera línea de peligro, ante la mayoría de los eventos naturales que afectan la Isla (Lezcano et al, 1993), aunque el resto de la superficie también es azotada con relativa frecuencia.

La población cubana resulta especialmente vulnerable a la acción de fenómenos meteorológicos (ciclones tropicales y extra-tropicales, frentes fríos, lluvias torrenciales, etc.), los que ocasionan anualmente decenas de millones de pesos en pérdidas materiales, y en lo que va de siglo han cobrado la vida de miles de seres humanos. Solamente el tristemente célebre huracán de Santa Cruz del Sur, el 9 de noviembre de 1932, dejó más de 2,000 víctimas fatales, arrasando para siempre con este pueblo costero, el que posteriormente debió ser relocalizado. Con gran fuerza también penetraron en la Isla, afectando directamente a la capital, los huracanes de octubre de 1926 y 1944, provocando cuantiosas pérdidas.

El huracán Kate, un ciclón de moderada intensidad y poca lluvia, que afectó la Isla los días 18 y 19 de noviembre de 1985, perjudicando a más de 20,000 viviendas, de las cuales 1,365 fueron pérdidas totales, unas 2,400 instalaciones agropecuarias quedaron dañadas, así como más de 400 industrias de todo tipo, 70,500 caballerías de caña y decenas de miles de caballerías en cítricos, cultivos varios y plátanos. Se evacuaron 80,000 habitantes (más de un 25% en exceso), 16,000 vehículos participaron directamente en la evacuación y se reportó un muerto y un desaparecido. Estas cifras suman varios cientos de millones de pesos o dólares. En términos de desastres, cualquier moneda brinda sólo una pálida idea de lo ocurrido y no reflejan toda la magnitud del asunto. Las inundaciones costeras que afectan la costa norte de la región occidental, específicamente la zona del malecón habanero, tienen mayor frecuencia y los daños materiales suelen ser extraordinarios, basta recordar una de las más recientes y probablemente la mayor de los últimos 100 años, ocurrida en febrero de 1992, cuando el agua del mar rebasó ampliamente los límites de la Calle Línea, paralizando a un 30% de la ciudad por más de una semana.

Las sequías también han afectado a Cuba con bastante intensidad, como en el período 1983-1986 en que la media nacional de precipitación acumulada quedó siempre por debajo del 85 % con respecto a los promedios históricos, límite a partir del cual se considera afectación por sequía (Rego y Cioffi, 1977), aunque hubo cortos períodos de lluvias torrenciales en algunos meses, como en junio de 1986, concentradas en las provincias orientales.

Más fresco aún en la memoria, están las intensas lluvias provocadas por el huracán Allison, el primero de la temporada de 1995, ocasionando la pérdida de

una vida humana y 32 derrumbes en la capital, aunque mucho peor, fueron los torrenciales aguaceros de la segunda quincena de ese mismo mes de junio sobre las provincias del centro y occidente, reportándose tres muertos, unas 700 viviendas desplomadas, cerca de 7,000 con daños de diferente consideración y más de 8,000 personas evacuadas. Por supuesto, la agricultura sufrió serios daños, fundamentalmente en el arroz y el tabaco; también se afectó la ganadería y gran parte de la vía férrea central quedó fuera de servicio. Todavía en agosto de 1995 se estaban evaluando estos daños.

La problemática de los desastres naturales reviste para Cuba una importancia extraordinaria, dada su ubicación geográfica, la crítica situación económica que enfrenta y la política de constante agresión a sus ecosistemas, la que aumentó dramáticamente en las últimas tres décadas, incrementando la vulnerabilidad de la población y la economía. Otro problema es la ausencia de un sistema efectivo de prevención y planificación ante estos eventos, lo que se traduce en acciones de socorro sumamente inefectivas, costosas y basadas más en el conocimiento empírico, que en un delineamiento técnico.

En 1966 la Ley 1194 institucionalizó la Defensa Civil como órgano, adscrito al Ministerio de las Fuerzas Armadas, encargado de la protección de la población y la economía en situaciones de desastres) ya sea por fenómenos naturales, accidentes de grandes proporciones, epidemias o guerras, mediante trabajos de salvamento y reparación urgente de averías. En 1976 el país también institucionalizó sus órganos de gobierno a través de una nueva división político-administrativa y con el objetivo de mejorar el sistema de medidas de protección, entró en vigor la ley 1316 del perfeccionamiento orgánico de la estructura de la Defensa Civil. En la actualidad, la planificación de las medidas de protección para casos de huracanes e intensas lluvias es parte esencial de las actividades de este organismo.

El Plan contra huracanes se define a nivel territorial mediante los llamados Comités de Defensa de la Revolución (CDR), sus zonas de defensa, el municipio, la provincia y la nación. A nivel ramal el

Plan incluye: talleres y establecimientos pequeños, empresas, direcciones del poder popular y los organismos de la administración central del estado.

En la práctica toda esta división es puramente formal y la toma de decisiones se subordina casi siempre a elementos de causa y efecto, surgidos durante el período de acción del fenómeno y donde la jerarquía a nivel provincial o nacional ejecuta las medidas, mientras los niveles menores (CDR, zonas de defensa y municipio) transcurren por una etapa contemplativa o de pura recepción, con un papel poco activo, nebuloso y casi siempre espontáneo. El problema parte del hecho que no están estructurados o peor aún, que no se han elaborado los análisis de peligro, vulnerabilidad y riesgo a las diferentes escalas territoriales y no hacen caso a los criterios que recomienda la UNDRO, por lo que en los casos de amenaza de fenómenos naturales se hace sentir la ausencia de un sistema interactivo, que incluya toda una base cartográfica de fácil acceso, con la definición de estos factores bien calculada sobre la base de experiencias anteriores y no expresada únicamente en función de analogías.

Las fases que se establecen ante la amenaza de un ciclón tropical (informativa, alerta, emergencia y recuperativa), permiten activar una serie de medidas para enfrentar el evento, pero por si solas, no pueden mitigar sus daños, porque no están respaldadas por un sistema moderno de prevención y planificación previa, ni por una educación sistemática y consciente de la población, lo que tiende a generar gastos excesivos en sobre-evacuaciones, transporte y apoyo en general.

El Instituto de Meteorología, actualmente adscrito al Ministerio de Ciencia, Tecnología y Medio Ambiente, es la entidad encargada de la vigilancia y predicción de los fenómenos meteorológicos que afectan a la Isla y sus mares adyacentes, jugando un rol de suma importancia en caso de amenaza ciclónica, pues de la efectividad de sus predicciones depende estrechamente la preparación y las medidas que deberán ponerse en práctica para enfrentar los distintos eventos. Pero sucede que sus posibilidades de respuesta ante las amenazas son con frecuencia lentas e inexactas en muchas ocasiones, entre otras causas, por el pobre estado de su anticuada tecnología de apoyo (radares, estaciones meteorológicas de superficie e instrumentación para la recepción de imágenes de satélite, etc.), así como por una estructura operativa deficiente y costosa, que demuestra sus abundantes limitaciones cuando la situación es más comprometida para el país, pues los eslabones del sistema de coordinación, con los diferentes mandos de la Defensa Civil, se rompen fácilmente y el resultado es un desastre natural, con efectos agigantados.

Hasta finales de los años ochenta, el país contaba con un subsidio impresionante de la antigua Unión Soviética, lo que le permitía movilizar todos los recursos posibles para enfrentar un desastre, pero esta movilización no se sustentaba en una relación de costo-beneficio, enmascarando la inefectividad del sistema para enfrentar estos casos. Ahora bien, ni aún contando con los resultados detallados de estudios de planificación y prevención a cualquier escala y para cada tipo de fenómeno, con una entidad de predicción meteorológica completamente equipada y las arcas repletas de dinero, el problema se resolvería, pues el principal enemigo de un esquema eficaz para la mitigación de los desastres naturales o de cualquier tipo en Cuba, es la centralización estatal y la relación social de propiedad.

Esto se distingue fácilmente cuando se activan las distintas fases ante la amenaza de un ciclón tropical. Por ejemplo, la masa ganadera debe ser situada con suficiente antelación en lugares seguros, previamente estudiados, según la magnitud del evento que se pronostica, pero sucede que ni los administradores de las granjas estatales, ni ningún asalariado, siente estímulo, ni necesidad, de poner a salvo a las reses, las que con frecuencia ven como un elemento ajeno a su contexto, aunque les sirva como medio diario de labor. En muchos casos prefieren que estos animales se ahoguen, pues podrían servir, como la fuente ilícita de la proteína que no consumen sus hijos. Esta situación es aún más lamentable cuando se trata de extensiones de cultivo, donde se pierden miles de caballerías de plátano, caña, tabaco y cítricos, por no hacer funcionar correctamente los planes operativos requeridos antes, durante y después del fenómeno.

De forma similar, actúa el administrador de cualquier empresa, quien en la mayoría de los casos, prefiere culpar a un fenómeno natural por el bajo resultado en la producción, exagerando los daños materiales que supuestamente se generaron o el tiempo perdido debido a esta causa. Por supuesto, detrás de esta consideración fatalista, casi siempre se oculta el estado de negligencia perpetuo de la mayor parte de los trabajadores en cada lugar, por lo que probablemente, no es tomada ni una sola medida de prevención. En este sentido, estos administradores no hacen más que seguir la vocación casi enfermiza de la dirección del gobierno, de culpar a las "irregularidades del clima" y al embargo norteamericano, por todos los males económicos del país, sirviendo como excusas favoritas para justificar la debacle del régimen.

De acuerdo a las actuales condiciones que vive la nación, la vulnerabilidad se ha incrementado exponencialmente para más de un 80% de la población, entre otras causas, porque como ahora no puede contarse con los recursos mínimos indispensables en las operaciones de socorro, se aleja aún más la ejecución del sistema estructurado de planificación y prevención, y se hace prácticamente imposible la rehabilitación de los asentamientos afectados.

Existe un aspecto que por su importancia merece destacarse, se trata de la aceleración de los efectos de un evento natural, como consecuencia de las profundas transformaciones que han sufrido numerosos ecosistemas, algunos de ellos muy sensibles y cuyos daños ya tienen carácter irreversible. Tal es el caso del sur de la provincia Habana, donde fue construido un dique paralelo y próximo a la costa, con más de 51 kilómetros de longitud, extendido desde Majana hasta las inmediaciones de Surgidero de Batabanó, supuestamente para disminuir los contenidos de salinidad en la cuenca sur y favorecer la recarga del manto freático. Los estudios de factibilidad e impacto ambiental, demostraban que la obra era un soberano disparate, pero de poco sirvieron las opiniones de decenas de especialistas en diversas ramas y los análisis efectuados por mas de dos años. En realidad, la decisión de diseñar y construir el bautizado "Dique-Sur", como en infinidad de otras obras, había sido tomada con antelación por el máximo líder y cualquier estudio representaba un esfuerzo formal, que en última instancia, sólo sirvió para agrandar una enorme carpeta muy bien decorada, que hoy "duerme" en las gavetas de los profesionales más consagrados y de algunos funcionarios.

El "Dique-Sur" ciertamente disminuyó la instrucción salina en la cuenca costera, pero en su lugar, aumentó la contaminación química y orgánica, haciendo detonar diversos tipos de enfermedades de transmisión hídrica, diseminando las plagas a niveles sin precedentes, agrietando los pisos de las casas, destruyendo decenas de kilómetros cuadrados de mangle por sobre-saturación acuosa y llevando las inundaciones a lugares donde antes no se recordaban. Lógicamente, la agricultura, que según la idea original sería la principal beneficiaria, siguió su estrepitosa caída, pues ningún sistema de riego, fertilizante o dique millonario puede detener su colapso.

A pesar de estas calamidades, lo peor está por venir, pues el paso de un ciclón tropical por el sur de la provincia Habana, donde por si fuera poco, se registra una de las más elevadas frecuencias del Caribe, provocaría inundaciones entre 20 y 30% superiores en magnitud a las conocidas en toda la región, arrasando potencialmente con Surgidero de Batabanó, Güanímar y Cajío, entre otros, pues el agua de mar que se vincula a la marea de la tormenta, no podría evacuarse en condiciones normales, ya que el dique interrumpe su proceso natural de compensación y la disminución del manglar impide transformar el oleaje, por tanto, los planos inundables podrían alcanzar 10 kilómetros tierra adentro, sin tomar en cuenta la precipitación pluvial, que suele alcanzar niveles extraordinarios al paso de estos huracanes, con la seguridad que serían superados en destrucción, casos como los huracanes de 1926 y 1944, poniendo en máximo riesgo a más de 10,000 personas, en unos 1,840 Km2 (Lezcano, 1993).

Desdichadamente el "Dique-Sur" es sólo un ejemplo del número de transformaciones graves y arbitrarias del medio natural, a lo largo y ancho de la Isla, que incluyen pedraplenes, presas, pozos para la extracción de hidrocarburos y tala indiscriminada, con cientos de casos debidamente registrados.

Otro factor que incrementa la vulnerabilidad, es el alto grado de deterioro que presentan las viviendas. Según cifras oficiales, solamente en la capital, casi el 50% de las 556,000 que constituyen el conjunto habitacional, presentan un estado que se evalúa de regular a malo y para otras 88,000 viviendas no hay soluciones. El pasado año, sin haber sido afectado por un acontecimiento natural de significación, se produjeron 614 derrumbes, demoliéndose otras 375 viviendas mientras que decenas de miles fueron apuntaladas.

Los sistemas de drenajes, cuya función es decisiva en períodos de intensas lluvias, dada su posibilidad de evacuar grandes volúmenes de agua, presentan una situación crítica en todas las urbes del país. En la Ciudad de la Habana, están "estranguladas" las principales líneas de escurrimiento, lo que favorece las inundaciones por desbordamiento de los ríos, agravado por el estrechamiento de sus secciones transversales, edificaciones cercanas, vertimiento incontrolado de desechos sólidos y la tala indiscriminada de sus márgenes, con áreas inundables que llegan a las 6,000 hectáreas, cerca del 10% de la superficie total de la provincia (García et al, 1991).

Actualmente, sólo el 50% de la población capitalina es servida por alcantarillado, cuya estructura principal fue proyectada y ejecutada en el siglo XIX, con una capacidad máxima original para dar servicio a 400,000 personas y no a las más de un millón que hoy sobrecargan sus mermadas posibilidades. El 90% de esta red no funciona o lo hace pobremente, por esa razón las inundaciones multiplican sus estragos, alcanzando lugares sin precedentes. Todo el perímetro del malecón se ha visto seriamente afectado por invasiones extraordinarias del agua de mar, y a pesar que la magnitud de los eventos meteorológicos y la posición del legendario muro, han sido esgrimidos públicamente como únicas causas del desastre originado, es bueno señalar, que verdaderamente, la pésima situación de la red de drenaje y la ineficiencia en el sistema de protección de las vidas y recursos materiales, jugaron el papel protagónico por los efectos del fenómeno.

LINEAMIENTOS PARA LA MITIGACION DE LOS DESASTRES NATURALES EN LA CUBA POST-CASTRO

El futuro gobierno democrático deberá colocar, entre sus muchas prioridades, el problema de la mitigación de los desastres naturales, planteándose las premisas siguientes:

- Los desastres naturales, tienen alcance global, afectando a todos los sectores de una nación, incluyendo la economía, la sociedad y el medio ambiente, por lo que sólo podrán mitigarse mediante un esquema efectivo de planificación y prevención previa, como parte integral del proceso de desarrollo, e instrumentado hacia la protección de vidas y recursos materiales.

- Cualquier costo en las inversiones con miras a fomentar programas de planificación y prevención, siempre serán menores que el costo económico y social de las catástrofes, cuya connotación es hoy mucho más grave que hace 40 o 50 años.

- Difícilmente los países en desarrollo pueden afrontar y superar, un desastre natural de gran magnitud, sin la cooperación internacional.

En medio de la profunda crisis que se vive actualmente en Cuba, existen varios elementos que pudieran contribuir positivamente para enfrentar esta problemática, con garantía de éxito:

- Un número considerable de profesionales de alto nivel en todas las ramas del conocimiento científico, pero específicamente, en cada una de las disciplinas que convergen en el proceso de mitigación de los desastres naturales.

- Disponibilidad de series de observaciones suficientemente extensas sobre fenómenos meteorológicos peligrosos y las principales variables que describen su comportamiento, con gran cantidad de estudios, análisis y resultados a todas las escalas geográficas.

- Experiencia acumulada, aunque en cierta forma dispersa, sobre las acciones de socorro y salvamento.

La estrategia de enfrentamiento contra los desastres naturales, reviste características muy específicas en cada nación, dependiendo de su posición geográfica, economía, población, tradición y elementos socio-culturales, entre otros. Para Cuba, resulta, esencial incluir una serie de objetivos de carácter prioritario. Cuba necesita: 1) Profundizar en los estudios aplicados y en los resultados ya obtenidos en materia de fenómenos naturales peligrosos, con vistas a completar y actualizar los elementos de impacto que pueden converger en el futuro; 2) Implementar un sistema de organización integral entre las instituciones del estado y las futuras ramas del sector privado, que de forma ágil y efectiva permitan afrontar la acción de un evento natural; 3) Modernizar y definir la estructura para la ejecución de los programas y proyectos, determinando el marco legal, financiero y administrativo por el cual transitan las fases de prevención, emergencia y rehabilitación, y finalmente 4) Monitorear y evaluar cada uno de los programas, en sus distintas etapas.

CONCLUSIONES Y RECOMENDACIONES

La situación actual de Cuba para enfrentar los desastres naturales es crítica y bajo las condiciones de centralización estatal, continuará empeorando, por tanto:

- Puede esperarse una mayor frecuencia de desastres naturales de mayor categoría en los próximos años, no por incremento en la incidencia de los fenómenos, más bien por aumento exponencial en la vulnerabilidad de la población y la economía.

- El país está totalmente indefenso a los efectos colaterales de cualquier evento, incluyendo la posibilidad latente de que se desaten epidemias incontrolables.

- La ayuda internacional de emergencia será imprescindible para enfrentar las catástrofes, pero en modo alguno podrá sustituir el papel de las instituciones estatales, básicamente en cuanto a la planificación y prevención previa.

Resulta impostergable diseñar, estructurar y poner en práctica un sistema integral de análisis de riesgo ante los fenómenos naturales, que incluya todas las escalas posibles y permita adoptar las medidas que se requiere para cada grado de peligro, priorizando las regiones más amenazadas en la actualidad.

Es necesario reestructurar todo el sistema de la Defensa Civil, despojándolo de todos los vicios ideológicos y limitaciones burocráticas que limitan el cumplimiento de sus objetivos, y poner a disposición de las instituciones científicas encargadas del estudio, monitoreo y pronóstico de los fenómenos naturales la base tecnológica necesaria para enfrentarlos con éxito.

Se debe solicitar a los Ministerios de la futura República la inclusión de los análisis de riesgos naturales en todos los programas y proyectos, como medio primario para el aseguramiento de la población y las inversiones, y finalmente asumir la planificación física como una respuesta válida para la mitigación de los desastres naturales, enfocada dentro de planes de reordenamiento territorial, que requieran la identificación a plazo mediano de los riesgos a que están sometidas las distintas regiones del país y una definición práctica sobre las normas constructivas.

REFERENCIAS

García, Araceli, Rosa Olivárez y Jorge C. Diez. *Esquema del Plan Director al año 2010 para la Ciudad De La Habana.* La Habana: Dirección Nacional de Planificación Física, 1991.

Lezcano, José Carlos. "SOS de la naturaleza en Cuba." *Boletín No. 66 del Colegio Nacional de Ingenieros Agrónomos y Azucareros Cubanos.* Miami, Florida (1994), pp. 5-7.

Lezcano, José Carlos, Ada L. Pérez, Reynaldo Casals y Alejandro Peñate. "Aspectos esenciales del mapa de riesgo por penetraciones del mar en las costas cubanas," *Geodinámica Ambiental y Riesgos Naturales: IV Encuentro de Geógrafos de América Latina.* Tomo I. Mérida, Venezuela: 1993, pp. 391-397.

United Nations Disaster Relief Organization (UNDRO). *Mitigating Natural Disasters: Phenomena, Effects and Options: Manual for Policy Makers and Planners.* New York: United Nations, 1991.

Rego, J. y D. Cioffi. *La Sequía, un aspecto importante del Clima de Cuba.* La Habana: Instituto de Meterología, Academia de Ciencias de Cuba, 1977.

Zupka, Dusan. "Actividades de prevención y planificación previa a los desastres naturales y sus impactos económicos." *Informe Final del Encuentro Regional sobre Desastres Naturales y Planificación de Asentamientos Humanos.* Quito, Ecuador, 1988. pp. 50-54

A ROAD MAP FOR RESTRUCTURING FUTURE U.S. RELATIONS WITH CUBA

C. Richard Nelson

EXECUTIVE SUMMARY

The summary of this policy paper provides guidelines for U.S. government officials and Congress for dealing effectively with the range of topics that will need to be addressed once decisions are made to restore normal relations with a Cuba whose leaders are committed to establishing a fully democratic system of government. The process of restoring normal relations will be lengthy and difficult because of the many contentious issues to be resolved.

Several assumptions must be stated at the outset. First, the recommendations included herein apply only after a decision is made to restore normal relations and do not address current U.S. policy. The Cuban Democracy Act of 1992 (Pub. L. No. 102-484) clearly states U.S. law and the conditions required for normalization, namely Cuba's pledge to hold free, fair and internationally observed elections and adhere to accepted standards of human and civil rights. This act, therefore, is the point of departure for any process of restructuring relations. In the event that the Cuban Liberty and Democratic Solidarity (LIBERTAD) Act becomes law, it will supersede the Cuban Democracy Act in certain respects and increase the restrictions on current bilateral relations. Nevertheless, the potential for passage of this legislation does not alter the recommendations of this paper, except to the extent that the bill, in its final form, could specify additional requirements and linkages during a Cuban transition.

Second, the paper assumes a cooperative government in Cuba but does not suggest a particular scenario for political change. Although the specific sequence and pace of restoring normal relations depend on the nature of that change and the political composition of the Cuban government, as well as the political circumstances then existing in the United States, this paper only prescribes basic principles and general steps for U.S. policy. The process will most likely be gradual, with some issues resolved before others. A logical first step would be an agreed framework that addresses the more contentious issues like claims, migration and trade, but this does not preclude simultaneous work on other topics. Indeed, it may be preferable to handle "smaller" issues like communications and travel before resolving the larger ones, but again, this decision depends on political factors beyond our power to foresee. The purpose here simply is to suggest *how* to deal with each issue on its own. The order of presentation of the issues does not imply a proposed sequence of policy-making.

Finally, this paper assumes that U.S. policies during the Cuban transition will be predicated on the basic principle of full respect for the sovereignty of Cuba and the right of the Cuban people to freely choose their form of government and leaders.

This paper is based on (1) analysis of the laws, regulations and policies that govern bilateral relations at the present time; (2) extensive interviews with current and former U.S. government officials, members of Congress, business leaders, academics and prominent members of international organizations; and (3) ideas and recommendations developed by members of the working group, individually and collectively.

MAJOR RECOMMENDATIONS

1. Once a decision has been reached to embark on a program for restoring normal relations with Cuba, the president should appoint a senior coordinator in Washington to oversee the implementation process, including the management of aid and assistance programs, liaison work with multinational organizations and the establishment of contacts with Cuban officials. Meanwhile, the head of the U.S. Interests Section in Havana should be appointed chargé d'saffaires while the president begins the process of appointing an ambassador.

2. The first priority for the senior coordinator should be the drafting of a framework agreement that outlines a process and a timetable for addressing the outstanding bilateral issues. The coordinator should draft the agreement in close consultation with the U.S. Congress and Cuban officials.

3. The Department of State should negotiate an agreement with the Cuban government to establish as soon as possible a mechanism for dealing with U.S. citizen confiscation claims against Cuba. This agreement should set forth a process that expeditiously frees up as much property as possible from claims; for example, the process could move quickly on the certified claims while simultaneously devising a mechanism to settle the remaining claims in a just and equitable manner. The Department of State should not espouse additional claims unless Congress passes legislation to do so. The public release of this agreement will clarify a program for dealing with claims that will undoubtedly require more time to settle in practice. Meanwhile, claimholders will be reassured that a fair process of settlement is underway and that they need not attempt to bring pressure to impede or postpone other aspects of the normalization process.

4. The U.S. government should encourage prompt Cuban accession into international organizations like the International Monetary Fund and the World Bank once Cuba satisfies readmission requirements, while supporting the lifting of the Cuban government's suspension in the Organization of American States. Congress should resist pressures to link the demands of sectors in the United States with U.S. financial commitments to the organizations and their programs for rebuilding Cuba

5. Restoring normal relations will require immediate lifting of the trade embargo and other economic sanctions. The U.S. government should also encourage a process which facilitates the granting of Most Favored Nation status to Cuba. The Export-Import Bank and the Overseas Private Investment Corporation should take the lead in expanding incentive programs for U.S.-based trade and investment, assuming that Cuba has embarked on a plan for resolving its outstanding debt and meets other normal requirements by these institutions.

6. Unilateral U.S. restrictions on travel, port entry and access, and mail services should be lifted quickly. The need for continuation of Radio and TV Martí will have to be examined, but these programs should proceed as long as the U.S. government determines that they could play a constructive role during a Cuban transition.

7. The departments of State and Justice should move towards implementing, to the extent circumstances permit, a normal immigration policy that treats Cubans like other immigrants. In implementing such a policy, the United States should give due regard to the protection of political refugees and take steps to permit the reunification of families with members both in Cuba and the United States.

8. The National Security Council and the Department of Defense should examine plans for the future of Guantánamo Naval Base within the overall context of U.S. base policy and security relations in the hemisphere. It may be useful to propose future creative uses of the base if and when full sovereignty over its territory is returned to Cuba.

9. U.S. aid and assistance programs for Cuba should be carefully targeted and monitored. As-

suming that the conditions in the U.S. Congress will not favor large appropriations of bilateral aid, the U.S. government's role should focus mainly on stimulating and coordinating efforts among private and international donors. To that effect, the United States should request that the World Bank constitute at the earliest possible time a consultative group on Cuba. Finally, all aid programs should be designed to have limited duration and encourage the processes of political reform, economic self-reliance, domestic and foreign investment, and positive trade relation-

ships. Emergency aid should continue to be available to Cuba as long as conditions on the island require it, especially if a future transition turns chaotic.

More extensive recommendations for each issue are included in the Atlantic Council's policy paper[1]. The steps it describes should contribute to a smoother process of restructuring relations as well as stimulate the efforts of Cuba to establish itself as a democratic state and a responsible participant in regional and global affairs.

---

1. Atlantic Council of the United States. *A Road Map for Restructuring U.S. Relations with Cuba: A Policy Paper.* Washington D.C.: Atlantic Council of the United States. 1995.

POTENTIAL IMPACT OF THE
HELMS/BURTON ACT ON CASTRO'S REGIME

Ernesto F. Betancourt

This is a policy paper, not a research paper. It analyzes the current Cuban situation from an operational perspective, including possible outcomes and policy suggestions as to how the Helms/Burton Act can be modified to encourage change inside the Cuba. The paper is based on a systematic review of discrete events in the context of previous patterns of behavior and some motivational assumptions. Underlying the analysis is the model of revolutionary propensity developed in my book *Revolutionary Strategy*.[1]

The possibility of a conventional revolutionary process leading to a change of government in Cuba is a most unlikely outcome. The reasons why were discussed in the paper I presented at the 1992 ASCE meeting.[2] Despite the deterioration in the situation since then, it seems unlikely that a conventional revolutionary process could develop against the Castro regime. But although it may not be subject to the conventional revolutionary threat, Castro's regime is not going anywhere either, it merely survives. However, even if outwardly the Castro government conveys an image of stability, the regime's abysmal failure is eroding its base of support. And, for the first time since coming to power, Castro is merely reacting, within a rapidly narrowing political and economic space.

This paper is predicated on the assumption that this impasse is likely to end through other outcomes. The current propaganda offensive to get the U.S. Embargo lifted and rely on foreign investment and tourism as props for the Cuban economy is bound to fail. As is the other goal of Castro's diplomatic offensive of having access to the International Monetary Fund (IMF), The World Bank and the Inter-American Development Bank (IDB) over U.S. objections. It is also predicated on the assumption that Castro is psychologically unfit to lead a transition to democracy. In the short or medium term, therefore, the most likely outcome in Cuba seems to be a coup d'etat or, if Castro manages to prolong his rule for too long, total regime collapse and widespread chaos and anarchy.

The regime's survival is due mostly to the effectiveness of Castro's repression in discouraging the emergence of an opposition leadership and the articulation of opposition movements or, if you may, a civil society. It is due also to the policies pursued by the U.S. and the Cuban opposition in exile, which unwittingly reinforce Castro's charisma and, by threatening basic interests of his followers, help Castro rally them around him. A systematic review of recent events reveals that on all scores, repression, Castro's weakening charismatic hold and cohesion of regime

---

1. Ernesto F. Betancourt. *Revolutionary Strategy: A Handbook for Practitioners.* New Brunswick, New Jersey: Transaction Publishers, 1991.

2. Ernesto F. Betancourt. "Revolutionary Propensity, Possible Outcomes and the Political Climate for Cuba's National Reconstruction." In *Cuba in Transition. Vol. 2,* Miami: Florida International University, 1993.

forces, there is a trend that may be converging at a point that, with proper external encouragement, could trigger a significant change in the internal political equilibrium. And, when real change comes in Cuba, it is likely to be swift, as it happened during the collapse of the Soviet Bloc.

The choices made by the Cuban people so far could be grouped as follows:

a. supporting the regime, with diverse degrees of commitment, from the most violent activism of the Rapid Reaction Brigades to mere survival and the opportunistic corruption of some managers of joint-ventures;

b. anomie, a loss of purpose in life that leads to a passive attitude of resignation, manifested in the highest suicide rate in the Americas, eight of every ten pregnancies ending in abortion, more than a hundred youngsters contaminating themselves with the AIDS virus as a way to live better for a shorter period of time and people taking refuge in the consolation of religion;

c. exile, by legal means, desertion or rafting;

d. dissidence, centered initially on human rights issues and extending now to independent associations of economists, journalists and lawyers, which so far have been peaceful and, realizing their vulnerability, have made extraordinary efforts to stay within the revolution's laws in order to survive; and,

e. open defiance, which has been manifested in tearing Party membership cards, an increasing crime wave and in occasional outbursts of protests against excessive repression, as it happened in Cojímar and Regla in 1993 and in downtown Havana last August 1994.

The deterioration of the quality of life in Cuba as a result of the disintegration of the Soviet Union, the ideological collapse of Marxism-Leninism as a workable political and economic system and the end of the heroic phase of "internationalism," which was a heavy brew for Cuban nationalistic pride, have led to the practical collapse of the social contract between ruler and ruled in the island. Castro's charisma has

been weakened and he is making piecemeal concessions to citizens who are asserting more and more control over their own lives once they realize the regime is increasingly incapable of meeting their most basic material and spiritual needs. Contempt for authorities and defiance of revolutionary laws are more evident everyday, while people increasingly turn to religion to satisfy their spiritual needs.

Events in the last five years reveal a slow but significant shift in behavior from a) towards e), while c) has become a moot option for most disaffected Cubans as a result of the recent immigration agreement between Cuba and the U.S., despite the increased number of visas offered for legal migration. Meanwhile, the regime seems unwilling to make the basic changes required to cope effectively with popular dissatisfaction. The so-called opening amounts to token changes while insisting on preserving Castro's rule, the single party system and apartheid capitalism, in which foreigners are the only ones allowed to create enterprises.

In view of the narrowness of the concessions made so far, it is not too farfetched to say that it is inevitable that sooner or later popular pressure will force a more significant outcome, whether Castro agrees or not. The question then is: will the present disaster end in an apocalyptic catastrophe or is a peaceful evolutionary outcome possible? It is evident that for all parties involved, except Castro and some groups in the exile community, the most desirable outcome is the evolutionary. In that case, which policies would be required from the U.S. to contribute to that most desirable outcome?

In this paper we will consider four possible outcomes: Castro's opening, a popular explosion, a U.S. intervention and a coup d'etat. To keep the paper short, no discussion is made of the future regime resulting from these outcomes. For a discussion in depth about the desired regime, the reader is referred to the author's paper entitled "Governance and Post-

Castro's Cuba"[3] which was presented at ASCE's 1994 meeting.

THE SO-CALLED CASTRO OPENING

To define that desirable outcome we should use a standard that is in line with contemporary trends in the world and, in particular, the Western Hemisphere. There are some self-appointed mediators, or "Dialogueros" as they are called in Miami, who are willing to settle for any token economic or political Castro initiative as proof that there is an opening. But fake solutions won't work. The problem is too profound to be solved by halfway measures. Furthermore, it would be dishonest to settle for standards for the Cuban people that are lower than those demanded for the rest of mankind. Therefore, with full awareness of the difficulty of attaining them, the standards guiding this analysis include:

a. a fully independent and sovereign Cuban society that satisfies the nationalist aspirations for which the Cuban people has been striving for two centuries;

b. a society in which power is vested in the rulers by the people, in free and open elections, and guarantees to all its citizens social and political freedoms consistent with internationally established standards; and,

c. the introduction of a modern market-based economic system capable of restoring the material well-being Cuba had attained before Castro's regime and then allows the island to grow beyond that by integrating its economy into world markets in the next century.

We should now consider the recent evolution of the Cuban situation in relation to these three dimensions. Afterwards, there will be a brief discussion of other possible outcomes, in particular the possibility of a coup d'etat. Then, in the light of the evolving situation, we will consider the impact the Helms/ Burton legislation may have on encouraging or discouraging such an outcome. It is recognized that an effective U.S. policy in that respect may well be a necessary but not sufficient condition for a coup to take place. Recent history shows that, except in the case of Romania, the armed forces do not overthrow Communist regimes.

Nationalism

It would be the ultimate Castro betrayal if his regime were to end in a situation that finds Cuba's sovereignty weakened to a point lower than when he came to power. His rise to national leadership and international acclaim was based to a great extent on his becoming the embodiment of Cuban nationalist sentiment. The failure of the regime and the disaster it has entailed for the Cuban people in no way reduce the nationalist cravings Castro so effectively mobilized in support of his leadership role. In fact, in the form of fears of a return to American domination, it is one of the emotional forces he still uses to rally his followers around him, in particular, within the Cuban armed forces.

True, a fully sovereign Cuba requires acceptance by political forces in the U.S. of what The Atlantic Council of the United States wisely states in the Executive Summary of its recently released report on *A Road Map for Restructuring Future U.S. Relations with Cuba*,[4]

"Finally, this paper assumes that U.S. policies during the Cuban transition will be predicated on the basic principle of full respect for the sovereignty of Cuba and the right of the Cuban people to freely choose their form of government and leaders."

For this to work, though, it would also be necessary for Cuban exiles and Cuban Americans who are prone to use their influence within the U.S. political system as a means to reach power in Cuba to modify their behavior. They could make a greater contribution to a free Cuba if they were to accept that change

---

3. Ernesto F. Betancourt. "Governance and Post-Castro Cuba," in *Cuba in Transition. Vol. 4.* Washington D.C.: Association for the Study of the Cuban Economy (ASCE), 1994.

4. Atlantic Council of the United States. *A Road Map for Restructuring Future U.S. Relations with Cuba.* Washington, D. C. : Atlantic Council of the United States, 1995.

has to come from within Cuba and help dispel the suspicions of those within the regime who feel threatened by the possibility that the end of Castro will bring the imposition by the U.S. of a particular group in power.

But Cuba's nationalism should not be perceived as exclusively an anti-U.S. issue. As the recent incident involving a former Ministry of Interior (MININT) Lt. Colonel, Nildo Labrada, reveals, nationalist feelings are reacting in other directions as a result of Castro's creating a capitalist apartheid for foreign investors. In an anecdotal reflection of underlying nationalist feelings within Cuban society, after throwing out of the porch of his house his uniforms, medals and books on Marxism, the Colonel asked for Castro's resignation for giving up Cuba's wealth to foreign investors—in particular Spanish—and making Cubans work as slaves for them. He also mentioned the death of thousands of Cubans in Angola and Ethiopia, where he served, pointing to a latent anti-Soviet theme.

Needless to say, Lt. Col. Labrada was arrested and taken to an insane asylum. But, more than craziness, his outburst reflects repressed feelings within regime ranks. It is worth pointing out that the Colonel did not talk about lack of food or transportation or the quality of housing and health services. His complaint reflects a reaction to Castro's betrayal of the heightened nationalism he himself instilled in Cubans.

Russian leaders may also generate a nationalist reaction against them if they continue looking at Cuba as a pawn in their efforts to restore the international strategic role they lost. In Cuba that is a geo-political absurdity. It must be remembered that Russia did not invest any blood to gain its Cuban foothold, it was merely Castro's betrayal of the revolution that opened the door for them. They have no historical, religious, racial, cultural, systemic or economic grounds on which to base hegemonic pretensions over Cuba.

As the recent research effort by Nestor Sánchez for the Pentagon reveals, Russia's strategic interests in a presence in Cuba are predicated on the use of the island as an electronic monitoring base against the

U.S.—but with the consent of the Pentagon since it is used to verify compliance with strategic agreements—and a warm water port in the middle Atlantic for its fleet. And, economically, in preserving a formerly captive market for the shoddy products of its obsolete enterprises. A more insurmountable obstacle to that relationship is the Russian pretense that Cuba pay its foreign debt to the former Soviet Union. They don't seem to realize that rather than a one-way flow of subsidies, there was also a flow in the other direction in loss of lives and opportunity costs incurred while Cuba contributed to Soviet imperial dreams, particularly in Africa and Latin America. Not even the Castro brothers accept Russian debt claims.

In summary, as the experience described by the Russian participants in the Pentagon study quoted above shows, despite the appearance in principle of convergent interests derived from their former association, cooperation between the two countries is difficult to attain in practice. The truth is that Russia has a shallow base indeed on which to maintain any hegemonic influence over Cuba. And, as the Helms/Burton Act shows, such attempts could hinder rather than help their primary interests in developing a good relationship with the U.S.

Spanish leaders, from the left, like Felipe González, and the right, like Manuel Fraga Iribarne, whether they realize it or not, are interfering in Cuba's political affairs. It does not matter if they are acting in response to an understandable desire to renew Spain's influence in a country with which it shares many bonds or historic resentments against the U.S. resulting from the final demise of their empire. They must realize that Cuban memories of the colonial era are very negative and the name of Governor Valeriano Weyler evokes the same reaction in Cuba that the name of Heinrich Himmler evokes in Europe. For Spaniards to come to Cuba to acquire control of Cuban assets from Castro at bargain prices and for their tourists to prostitute Cuban women is awakening the worst memories of Cuba's experience as a Spanish colony.

Spain should heed the advice of its former Ambassador to Havana, Juan Antonio Gil, published in the

April 23, 1995 issue of the Madrid newspaper *El País*. In his article, Ambassador Gil explains that Spain tried to help Cuba open up politically and economically motivated by a sense of solidarity with the Cuban people, but in November, 1994 a high ranking Spanish official was told by Vice-President Carlos Lage that the purpose of any changes was not to reform the regime but to consolidate Castro's stay in power. The unwillingness of the González Government to face this reality is what led Ambassador Gil to resign and he adds:

> "Castro is convinced he can continue counting with the full support of the Spanish Government, no matter what, ignoring the serious harm such behavior could do to the image, prestige and interests of Spain in Cuba since such support—no longer justified by the initial noble purpose which determined and legitimized it—could be perceived by the Cuban people as connivance with the tyranny that oppresses them."

Finally, some Europeans and Latin American leaders use Cuba, and the tragedy endured by its people, as a proxy to vent their disguised or open anti-Americanism, failing to distinguish between helping Castro and helping the Cuban people. These mediators should get their facts straight. Castro's hold over Cuban public opinion is declining. His betrayal of Cuban nationalist aspirations for the sake of his own ambition for a place in history is becoming more evident to Cubans. The totalitarian nature of his regime cannot be brushed aside lightly with token reforms. And, it is the failure of his absurd economic policies, and not the U.S. embargo, that has deprived Cubans of the previously attained levels of material well-being.

The attitude of the Europeans, in particular, is reflected in the report issued on June 23, 1995 to the European Parliament and the Council promoting relations with Cuba. It is not a matter of questioning the provision of humanitarian aid, in fact they should be encouraged to provide as much as possible. While extremely critical of the U.S. embargo, the report is frankly dishonest in its coverage of events on the Cuban side.

The report omits events such as the Cojímar and Regla incidents in 1993 or the Malecón riots in 1994, not to mention the massacre of the 13th of March tugboat on July 13, 1994, when 41 persons, including 20 children, were drowned by Cuban fireboats with people being hosed out of the deck of the tugboat, which was eventually rammed and sunk. It accepts as evidence of a political opening regime staged events with so-called moderate exiles who are nothing but Castro sympathizers in disguise or the setting up of a fake opposition with leaders de facto selected by Castro, instead of making a general opening and letting the people select who they want to follow.

It glosses over the limitations of the purported economic reform, while supporting access of the regime to international financing agencies ignoring the "governance" requirements which are increasingly being applied to the rest of the world by the OECD or the respect for human rights required by the European Community statutes. Finally, it encourages the naive notion of Cuban officials that they can enter the IMF, the IDB and the World Bank over the opposition of the U.S.

Political Situation

It is assumed that a satisfactory democratic political system would involve as a minimum respect for human rights and basic freedoms as established in the Universal Declaration of Human Rights, guaranteed by the rule of law under an independent judiciary and the installation of a representative government that allows a pluralized party system to articulate the demands and aspirations of a vigorous and active civil society.

Ever since the beginning of the revolution a dual government has existed. For purposes of simplicity we will label one the "caudillo" and the other the "institutional" governance systems. The caudillo system reflects Castro's way of ruling. The institutional system was sponsored by the Soviets through his brother Raúl, who is a much better administrator but lacks Fidel's charisma. Needless to say that the Soviets were advocating institutions that failed miserably in the Soviet Bloc. Despite Soviet support, however, over the years Raúl was rebuked by Fidel in his institutional efforts one time after another. At those times, the brothers argued violently and in some occasions Raúl even threatened to resign. But in the end he submitted to his brother's decisions. Caudillismo always prevailed.

However, we should not ignore the fact that the only effective institution emerging from the Cuban Revolution is the Cuban Armed Forces under MINFAR. The MINFAR has been Raul's bailiwick from the beginning and at least this writer is not aware of any instance in which he was overruled by Fidel in the military sphere. It must also be kept in mind that, in the military sphere, Soviet influence was overwhelming. It was essential for regime survival in its defiance of the U.S. When Raúl has dallied into the political or economic sphere, however, on his own or in most instances with Soviet support and encouragement, the results up to now have been negative. And it is reasonable to assume that now, when there is no Soviet Union anymore, he is even less likely to prevail. In the early years of the revolution, it was Raúl who pressed for his former comrades of the old Communist Party to organize the party of the revolutionary government. To Raúl's embarrassment, this ended in plots, with Soviet support, to seize power from Fidel and led to several notorious trials. But by 1968, Castro was forced to bend to Soviet dictated changes in the internal leadership and support the invasion of Czechoslovakia, as well as to start a modest effort at institutionalization.

After the failure of the 10 million ton sugar harvest in 1970, Castro's caudillista style was seriously questioned and the Soviets imposed the sovietization of Cuban political institutions and governmental entities as a condition for entry to the COMECON. By the time of the First Party Congress, in 1975, institutionalization appeared to have gained the upper hand. Not only the Party but the Constitution and the Government organization were drawn following Soviet models.

One interesting aspect of this institutionalization was that the judiciary branch was subordinated to the executive. This was part of a process of judicial reform advocated by former President Dorticós under the banner of "socialist legality." Later on, Dorticós killed himself, according to some versions, in despair over Fidel's brutal reaction to a court's decision he

did not like. This was known as the Solidarity trial, in which the judge and the defense lawyers were thrown in prison, the defendants were tried again and found guilty. The fact is that "socialist legality" has assured Fidel—as was made evident at the Ochoa trial in 1989—that there is not going to be any rule of law in Cuba to interfere with the whims of the caudillo about the life, freedom or property of any citizen.

It was at that time that some of the Castrologists in American academe started talking about institutionalization of the revolution. It dressed the Revolution with respectability and conveyed the image of consolidation. Following Max Weber's theories, the logic was that charisma was being bureaucratized and as a consequence legitimacy was attained. But institutionalization is impossible without the rule of law.

In reality, the caudillo system was far from abandoned. At this time, and parallel to institutionalized authority along functional or sectorial lines, Castro established a caudillo delegated direct line of authority. It included the Coordination and Support Group attached to his office and delegated power along geographical lines to the Provincial Party Secretaries, making them directly answerable to him, with authority in their respective territories to override any ministerial decisions. In fact, the Provincial Party Secretaries are the ones who give the yearly reports to the Assembly of Popular Power during the budget discussion. The Party Secretaries were even given authority over the Territorial Troops Militia created in 1980 as a military alternative in case the institutionalist and their Soviet sponsors got ideas detrimental to Fidel's interests.

In 1980, the Mariel exodus revealed the profound unhappiness within the population because of economic hardships. The Soviets, through their man in Havana, Humberto Pérez, the head of JUCEPLAN—who also had Raúl's full support—promoted a moderate economic opening through the Free Farmers' Markets. Fidel continued handling directly his pet projects in cattle raising, chicken, biotechnology, etc. through the Coordination and Support Group. Any conflict in priority use of resources was settled in favor of Fidel's pet projects.

In 1986, Fidel launched the "Rectification of Errors" phase. The Free Markets were dismantled and Pérez was fired. In essence, the opening was threatening Fidel's political interests by creating a new moneyed class free of his control that was resented by Party cadres. The sacking of Humberto Pérez took place despite Soviet subsidies of more than 5 billion dollars a year. Raúl gave haven to Pérez at MINFAR for a while and eventually he was transferred out of the centers of power into some obscure job.

With the emergence of *Glasnost* and *Perestroika*, Raúl, the inveterate institutionalist, endorsed the reform ideas of his new Soviet mentors. Carlos Aldana, one of Raúl closest collaborators and head of the Department of Revolutionary Orientation—the Party Secretariat unit responsible for ideological and media guidance and control—was thrown into the ring as the advocate of those ideas during the preparatory period previous to the Fourth Party Congress in 1991. Meanwhile, the advocate of caudillo rule expressed openly his reservations about Gorbachev's ideas predicting, quite correctly, that they were going to end in the disintegration of the Soviet Union. Despite a humiliating acknowledgment of his mistake and the wisdom of Fidel, Aldana was also sacked on charges of corruption, whether trumped or real we do not know.

The advocates of institutionalism suffered a mortal setback with the collapse of the Soviet Union in 1991. Since then there is no longer any Soviet subsidy or strategic umbrella to give leverage to Raul's institutionalists. By the time the 1992 Constitutional reforms were enacted, Fidel was back in full caudillo control. The much heralded political reforms were scuttled. Instead, the power to impose emergency rule was added to his many powers, a provision nonexistent in the previous Constitution. This power allows him legally to suspend the Assembly of Popular Power and rule personally as Chairman of the Council of State in case of emergency. That would be a very convenient power to have were a collective will to emerge among groups within the Cuban nomenklatura to challenge Fidel's authority.

As the aggregate impact of the collapse of the Soviet metropolis hit the regime in all its dimensions, Fidel

Castro invoked a plan devised for a military crisis during which Cuba could be isolated, it is called the Special Period in Times of Peace. The last part of the title reflects the fact that there is no war. It is a Khmer Rouge type of mobilization of the population away from the cities and into the countryside with a return to a primitive survival level of living. For obvious reasons, the regime has been hesitant in implementing these measures to their fullest.

Fidel is waiting for the proper opportunity to justify its implementation. That opportunity may well present itself with the 1996 sugar harvest for which they need an additional 300 thousand workers to do manually what the tractors and harvesting machines cannot do for lack of oil and spare parts and there are between 500 and 800 thousand redundant urban workers in non-producing factories throughout the island.

Meanwhile, Raúl and his institutionalists have discovered that the kind of institutions they were advocating, in particular for managing the economy, were an international failure and started experimenting on how to apply their military managerial skills to productive activities. This was politically urgent in particular because the collapse of internationalism and Soviet subsidies had made budget retrenchment inevitable and blocked military careers. MINFAR expanded its economic role, which included a study group directly under Raúl's office and the Military Industrial Enterprises (EMI), with the Gaviota tourist enterprise, agricultural producing activities and the new free peasant markets.

These additional economic undertakings provided an employment outlet, with access to pay in dollars, to redundant military officers. The Youth Working Army (EJT), formed by draftees, provides the labor force for many of these activities. As reports coming from Cuba reveal, such activities are corrupting military cadres and could make the armed forces the source of resentment from Party cadres not allowed to enjoy such privileged status, not to mention average citizens.

Fidel's caudillo political system prevails at present but hidden behind the draping of Raul's institutionalization. Lifting the embargo has become a rallying cry for the regime. Fidel has mobilized his friends and sympathizers in the media and in the international left to convey the image that the transition in Cuba has to be made under Fidel's tutelage. This message has been raised by Nobel Prize winner Gabriel García Márquez and many others to the level of a dogma. Under this scheme, a token opening to the "moderates" in exile, who are really pro-Castro groups or people who have no political base of their own and are willing to play the role of Castro's loyal opposition, justifies lifting the embargo. It is revealing that the real dissidents inside Cuba, Arcos, Payá, Sánchez, etc., who are advocating peaceful changes within the system, continue to be persecuted and harassed under this purported political opening of the regime. The fact that the "moderates" in exile do not condition their participation in Fidel-sponsored forays to an opening for the internal dissidents, raises serious questions as to the legitimacy of their claimed moderation.

An excellent summary of the workings of Cuba's political system has been made by Dr. C. Miriam Gras Mediaceja, a Cuban researcher with the Political Science Group at the School of Philosophy and History of Havana University. In a courageous paper entitled, *El Sistema de Gobierno Cubano: Control vs Autonomía,* Dr. Gras describes how Cuba is ruled through a top-down political system under which there are no autonomous institutions. In her paper, Dr. Gras documents thoroughly the caudillo nature of the Cuban political system and how it was reinforced by the Leninist concept of the party as the vanguard of proletariat rule. She considers that such a top-down approach is no longer consistent with the needs of contemporary Cuba, suggesting that the ability to disagree and organize dissent has to be introduced into the system, as well as to vest in the people control over elected and administrative officials, rather than the other way around as at present.

In what is perhaps the most shattering revelation in the paper, Dr. Gras describes in Footnote 19 how decisions made at the top are merely legitimized by the masses under the guise of participation:

"An example of the legitimizing role was made evident in the process of discussion and approval of the 1976 Constitution. Although 6 million Cubans discussed the draft project and 16,000 made proposals for change, when the initial draft is compared with the final version, we can see that the final version only incorporates minor editorial changes. Changes of substance were made in only 4 or 5 paragraphs."

Needless to say that, as the previous quote from the article by Spain's former Ambassador indicates, the intention of Fidel Castro and his immediate collaborators is to preserve top-down rule, while popular participation is merely a ruse to legitimize the decisions made at the top. Caudillismo rather than institutionalization prevails in today's Cuba. The political opening offered so far fails to meet the most elementary standards for democratization stated above. The slogan synthesizing the present political opening seems to be: Manipulation, Yes! Democratization, No!

Economic Situation

It is assumed that in economic matters, the opening would involve a process similar to what is called structural adjustment, except that in Cuba's case it would involve also a significant systemic adjustment. This requires the shift to a market ruled economy in which the state plays a subsidiary role, with the private sector taking the lead in finance, infrastructure, production, services and distribution. Under these reforms, the state retains responsibility for creating the proper macroeconomic environment for attaining growth with monetary stability and for regulating the economy to prevent abuses from private monopolies. The state must also retain responsibility for protecting the rights of citizens as consumers, investors and workers, as well as, of society as a whole, from environmental deterioration. Under a market system, the state may also support private sector efforts in diverse degrees but it is expected to do so without distorting the market.

Since there are many papers at this meeting dealing with various aspects of Cuba's economy and, in particular, our colleague Carlos N. Quijano[5] has prepared a chart comparing the economic opening in Viet Nam with the one in Cuba, it is not necessary to delve at length on how the Cuban reforms fail to meet the above criteria. Instead, these comments will be focused on the potential political impact of the measures taken under the banner of the economic opening.

The economic reforms introduced in the last two years have generated their own problems and are bringing Cuba into another crisis. Two of the reformers, Messrs Julio Carranza and Pedro Monreal,[6] from the Havana based Center for the Study of the Americas, recently presented their views on the future of economic reforms in Cuba at a meeting in Washington, D.C. They are not dissidents. On the contrary, they openly state that the goal of the reforms they advocate is to preserve the regime's socialist orientation and Fidel's rule.

According to Carranza and Monreal,[7] while limited success has been attained in reducing excess liquidity in the economy, a huge budget deficit continues as a result to a great extent of 1.2 million workers being paid while 70 percent of the enterprises are unable to produce for lack of energy, transportation, raw materials and spare parts. In considering these facts, one must take into account that this is only redundant labor in the productive sector. In addition there are bloated payrolls for education (414,000) and health (277,000), social services which Castro insists must be provided totally free, not to mention the military and police. In total, Cuba's public sector employment, outside state productive enterprises, exceeds one million workers. Cuba's GDP has been reduced by half since the Soviet collapse started in 1990 and

there is no way the paralyzed Cuban economy can sustain such a heavy public sector burden.

Under questioning at the workshop of April 10, 1995, Monreal and Carranza acknowledged that the government intends to dismiss 500 thousand workers and send them Cambodia-like to work in the countryside or as independent workers in the cities. Afterwards, the head of the unions raised the number to 600 to 800 thousand. An EFE dispatch from Havana on July 11, 1995 reported that 300 thousand workers will be mobilized to try to save next year's sugar crop, essential to regime survival after the disastrous 3.3 millon tons crop harvested in 1995.

At the same time, Castro is hesitating in dismissing the redundant workers. He seems to fear another social explosion similar to what happened last August with the rafter exodus. More so now that the emigration door has been closed as a result of the Alarcón/Tarnoff agreement of May 2, 1995. An agreement, incidentally, which Castro is likely to honor in the breach, once he realizes that in exchange there will be no lessening of his external financial constraints. Therefore, he will lack the financial means to avoid possible internal social turmoil generated by the reforms. As Castro warned last year at the May session of the legislature, this time the reforms "have to be right or we are going to face a disaster."

But even the lower number of dismissals, between 300 and 500 thousand will leave between 900 and 700 thousand subsidized workers on the government payroll. To get an idea of the dimension of Castro's dilemma, this would be equal to the Federal Government subsidizing 24 million idle workers, planning to fire 6 to 10 million of them, thus leaving between

5. Carlos N. Quijano, "Vietnam and Cuba: I- Institutional and Legal Reforms, II- Structural Policies, III- Macro-Economic Policies." A Presentation to the Fifth Annual Meeting of the Association for the Study of the Cuban Economy (ASCE), Miami, August 10-12, 1995.

6. Julio Carranza Valdés, Pedro Monreal González and Luis Gutiérrez Urdaneta, "Cuba: Restructuring of the Economy (A Proposal for Discussion)." Paper presented at the Shaw, Pittman Potts & Trowbridge Workshop on The Future of Cuba's Economic Reforms, Washington D.C., April 10, 1995.

7. Julio Carranza Valdés, Luis Gutiérrez Urdaneta and Pedro Monreal González. *Cuba: La Restructuración de la Economía*. La Habana: Editorial de Ciencias Sociales, 1995.

18 and 14 million in the payroll. Not even a thousand days of Newt Gingrich could deal with that!

Castro's hope is that foreign investment, particularly in tourism, and independent work will absorb the remaining redundant workers. As anybody familiar with foreign investment knows it is usually capital intensive. The amounts of foreign investment flowing to Cuba are too tiny to make a dent on those huge numbers of redundant workers. According to an Ana Radelat dispatch in the June 23, 1995 issue of *El Nuevo Herald*, at a recent meeting in New York, Cuban officials acknowledged that there was a slowdown in foreign investor interest caused not only by the threat of the Helms/Burton legislation but also by Cuba's delay in enacting the long-promised new law regulating foreign investment. That same day, at the State Department briefing, the issue of the U.S. Treasury enforcing the embargo against the Canadian nickel company Sherritt joint ventures with Cuba under the Torricelli legislation made it clear that Cuba's efforts to attract foreign investment face an uphill battle.

The arrest of Robert Vesco and the summary dismissal of Abraham Maciques, the head of the Cubanacán tourism conglomerate, who was very popular with foreign investors, should discourage investors further. According to a July 14, 1995 story by Pablo Alfonso, the special reporter for Cuba of *El Nuevo Herald*, the explanation circulating in Havana was that Maciques had agreed to put US$30 millions into the AIDS drug plant promoted by Donald Nixon. Anybody familiar with Vesco's history would not be surprised that he could not sit idly by while all these deals with foreign investors were being cooked. And Vesco, who served Fidel in operations to violate the embargo and even drug transactions, is not reluctant to engage in corruption.

Therefore, it would not be surprising if there is a link between the Vesco arrest and the *Granma*, the party organ, report on July 13 on corruption. In a three page spread, it reported that, at a three day meeting with 350 Cuban managers of joint-ventures, Castro had denounced widespread corruption caused by "foreign investors and tourists." Audits will be made of all joint-ventures. Castro raised the issue again in

his 26th of July speech and linked capitalism—in the form of foreign investors—to corruption in contrast with their experience when they were dealing with Soviet enterprises. The resulting repressive climate is not likely to improve Cuba's 167th standing in the worldwide ranking on investment climate issued by *Euromoney* recently.

No mention was made of what was going to de done to tourists, but the mere announcement could chill Cuba's attraction as a tourist destination. Travel agents better start issuing warnings to travellers to Cuba because, if past experience is to be taken into account, sooner or later there are going to be arrests of tourists who engage in what the regime will define as not permissible activities, prostitution being the most likely target.

At this time, foreign investors and tourists could discover that there is no rule of law in Cuba. The bad image of Vesco has prevented his arrest in early June and the fact that he has been denied any legal protection or the services of an independent legal counsel to receive the attention it deserves. This lack of legal rights may further discourage potential investors. As commented above, investors seem to be losing interest in Cuba. On June 30, 1995, *The Financial Times* reported that the price for Cuban debt paper, which was 9.5 U.S. cents to the dollar in June, 1993 and had climbed to 28 U.S. cents to the dollar in January, 1994, had fallen to 14.5 U.S. cents to the dollar by June, 1995. Cuban debt paper is used in swap deals by foreign investors, and the decline in price indicates lack of demand. The three page treatment given to corruption in *Granma*, the Party organ, signals a mayor event and probably a trial. Therefore, the price of Cuban debt paper may fall even further.

The other outlet Castro hopes will absorb redundant workers is no more promising. After profound deliberations among the ministers responsible for the economic opening, new measures were announced on June 15, 1995 on independent work. Nineteen activities were added to the 140 already allowed. But the nature of the categories of work sounds more like a joke than a serious effort to solve a massive employment problem: "dog hairdressers," "doll repairing," "sewer cleaners," "piñata building," etc.

Professional workers, such as engineers, doctors, architects, lawyers and teachers, who are forbidden to collect dollars for their professional services, were authorized to earn dollars, but not in their professional capacity. They can moonlight as taxi drivers, bartenders, waiters, and in some very sad cases even as prostitutes. The "paladares" restaurants were authorized also, provided they limit themselves to no more than twelve chairs. In both cases, this merely legalizes what people are already doing. These measures, in addition to the restricted nature of the free markets for agriculture and industrial products, are insufficient to create a market economy and much less to start up the Cuban economy.

The partial liberalization of dollar transactions and the creation of parallel agricultural and industrial markets, where prices are higher, has led to a modest improvement in food supply but, as was to be expected, at prohibitive prices for the majority of Cubans. Supply of industrial goods, which are heavily dependent on imports of raw materials, has not improved however. But, as a result of the reforms, the egalitarian basis of Cuban society, alleged to be one of the attainments of the Revolution, has been shattered.

A dual economy divides Cubans into a minority of "winners" with access to dollars and an 80 to 90 percent majority of "losers" who don't have that access. Since the losers include retirees, many in the military and police, as well as doctors, teachers and engineers who are unable to trade in dollars, this breach in the revolutionary social contract is raising tensions within Cuban society. This could explode into internal strife.

True, there has always been a privileged revolutionary elite around Castro, the people call them "Mayimbes," which means vultures. But they were few, basking under the aura of Castro's charisma, and in relative isolation from the majority of the population, while the egalitarian policies promoted by the revolution allowed for an equitable distribution of whatever goods were available, and that was substantially more than has been available recently. Now, however, the "winners" are mingled with the population and "losers" among Party cadres resent them because they not only enjoy comforts not available to

the "losers", but many are openly against Castro and the revolution.

According to the two reformers mentioned above, Carranza and Monreal, another undesirable consequence of free agricultural markets is that there has been a massive transfer of income from the cities to the countryside and that transfer has been heavily concentrated in some individuals, what the Cubans call "macetas." In their opinion, the Government made a mistake in not confiscating the savings of the "macetas" through a currency exchange or in accordance to the draconian decree 149 issued in May, 1994.

But now these "liberalizing reformers," are not only advocating that the confiscation take place but also that measures be taken to ensure there is no "excessive accumulation of surpluses" under the private enterprises schemes they are proposing. We can see that the idea behind the reform is to encourage people to produce more while limiting the financial benefits they could derive from their efforts in accordance to some bureaucrat's or, more likely, Castro's notion of what is "excessive accumulation." Current reforms in Cuba are predicated on a misguided notion of how the profit motive works. If this is what the "reformers" advocate, one wonders what is the position of the "hardliners."

Under the proposed scheme for economic reform, therefore, most Cubans are doomed to work for a debased pay from the Government in Cuban pesos worth two or three US cents as indentured workers for foreign investors who in turn pay their salaries to the Government in dollars or for a shrinking state payroll that does not provide them with a minimum purchasing power. The rationing card, which provides access to goods at lower prices, is fulfilled less and less. Cubans are also offered an extremely restricted space for independent self-employment but with access to dollars. Professional work is not adequately rewarded and university registration is declining.

In summary, the measures taken so far have shattered the egalitarian goals of the revolution by creating a dollar earning privileged class, while preventing real expansion of production. As a result, the regime is caught in an explosive dilemma, to liberalize allows enemies of the regime, along with some corrupt members of the nomenklatura allied to foreign investors under apartheid capitalism, to enjoy privileges and a consumption pattern not available to most loyal Party cadres and the average citizen. That may well be the reason for Fidel's recent attack on corruption. Reports reaching Washington at the time of this writing, attribute to "hardliner" José Machado Ventura, who is head of the Party Organization Department responsible for Party cadres, exerting pressure on Castro to crack down on corruption. As it happened in 1986, Fidel may be cracking on corrupt behavior to placate the diehard "Patria o Muerte" cadres left out of the dollar market. This may be a move to avoid the "disaster" that concerns Castro.

OHER POSSIBLE OUTCOMES

The previous section makes clear that the "Castro opening" outcome is unlikely to provide a long term solution to the Cuban crisis, since the policies followed by Castro will only prolong the present regime and drag the Cuban people through a long agony. Therefore, we shall consider some of the other possible outcomes:

a. A popular explosion leading to the disintegration of the regime, which could become the final option for the Cuban people if the present drift continues.

b. An intervention by the U.S. in response to a deliberate Castro provocation or chaos in the island.

c. A coup d'etat by elements within the regime's armed forces in the wake of Castro's death or to prevent the disintegration of the regime.

The feasibility of each option will be considered briefly. For a more elaborate discussion of the internal political climates resulting from each outcome

the reader is referred to the previous paper presented to the ASCE meeting in 1992.[8]

A Popular Explosion

This would be the most violent of the outcomes, which would result from a massive shift in population behavior from choice a) to support the regime to choice e) open defiance. In other words, this would mean that the revolutionary propensity bottled-up by Castro's repression reached a point that exceeded the repressive capacity of the state, changing dramatically the internal equilibrium of forces, with the likely outcome of a disintegration of the regime and the armed forces, as well as a total breakdown of law and order.

The more Castro delays his departure or setting the machinery for an orderly transfer of power, the more likely that the armed forces will become discredited as it happened to the army under Batista in Cuba in 1958 or to the Guardia Nacional under Somoza in Nicaragua in 1979. This possibility increases to the extent the armed forces become associated with repression, which so far has not happened in Cuba.

The increased disaffection of the population has led to the creation of the special coordinated repressive units, the SUVP, and the Rapid Reaction Brigades. Sometime in the future it is not impossible to visualize a situation of significant disturbances. According to a paper prepared by Humberto León, a researcher at the North South Center of the University of Miami, for the Néstor Sánchez study commissioned by the Pentagon,[9] Government measures to cope with such a situation were revised under prodding from the military after the Cojímar and Regla riots in 1993 and were reflected in the less provocative handling of the Malecón riots in August, 1994, although it must be pointed out that no such restraint is reflected in the handling of the tugboat incident the previous month. If more widespread open resistance were to occur in the future, there are two choices for the armed forces, to repress brutally in a bloodbath or to refuse to do so and rebel instead. The future

---

8. Betancourt, "Revolutionary Propensity," *op. cit.*

9. Humberto León. "The Impact of the Economic Crisis on the Cuban Revolutionary Armed Forces (FAR)." In International Research 2000 Inc., *The Military and Transition in Cuba.* Bethesda, MD: International Research 2000 INC., March 17, 1995.

context for the reconstruction of Cuba will be decided at that crucial moment. That is why it is so important and urgent for those who may face such a dilemma to have a clear alternative reassuring them that they will be accepted by the exile community and the U.S.

Popular explosions usually lead to fragmentation of authority and chaos. The divisions of the exile community and the dissident movement within the island is a good indication of how difficult it will be to articulate a transition government under this outcome. The more violent the outcome, the less likely that there will be a central authority having legitimacy, international recognition, control of repressive capacity and enough political cohesion to take the decisions required to bring an orderly transition and create a climate conducive to reconstruction. On the other hand, this outcome could trigger either a U.S. intervention or a coup d'etat.

An Intervention by the U.S.

This outcome could result either from chaos inside Cuba or from a deliberate provocation by Castro. It would be a historical disaster for both countries. At the time of the Bay of Pigs, the wisest decision made by President Kennedy, after making the great mistake of buying the plan presented to him for the operation, was to refuse to be dragged into an intervention. There are many who do not share this viewpoint and argue that merely an air strike would have been enough. However, the death and destruction an intervention would have brought to Cuba would have been very high, since resistance would have been intense even from revolutionaries critical of Castro. And, by crushing the high Cuban nationalist expectations prevailing at the time, it would have generated a wave of resentment that would still be haunting us.

Fortunately, there is only a remote possibility this could happen. The U.S. military leaders who considered this was an option right after the Gulf War seem to have lost the upper hand in the Clinton Administration and the present Pentagon position seems to be one of adamant opposition to such an outcome. There are influential groups in the exile community who downplay the nationalist feelings aroused by

Castro as a temporary thing that is being discredited by the failure of the regime and continue to hope for an intervention as the final outcome. At present, this position has lost any credibility except in Castro's propaganda, but could gain acceptance if there is chaos and bloodshed in Cuba or Castro decides to end his regime, once he becomes convinced there is no hope for him, with a final provocation against his hated enemy the U.S.

A Coup d'Etat

This outcome could occur as the result of the actions of a lone assassin escaping Castro's extraordinary security or due to natural death or as a result of self-interest within the military once they perceive Castro's unwillingness to yield constitutes a long run threat that could lead to regime disintegration.

Were such an event to result from Castro's death, it would lead initially to a transition long planned by Castro himself, since for quite some time Raúl has been the designated heir. The change in the Constitution allowing the Chairman of the Council of State to declare a state of emergency and assume even more powers than at present could be useful to Raúl were he to move from the number two spot he has now in all the positions occupied by his brother to the number one spot in the regime hierarchy.

However, Raúl lacks Fidel's charisma and would be forced to rule in some collegiate form. Once the opening starts, he will be less likely than Fidel to have enough control to provide a stable climate for the transition, although as was discussed above he has been an advocate of some form of liberalization. Challenges to the new order would come from dissidents, labor unions, displaced party leaders and the many officers within MINFAR and MININT who have contempt for Raúl.

Despite the measures taken by Castro to make a coup very difficult, such as rotation of commanders, severe intelligence monitoring within the armed forces, limited distribution of ammunition to units and even separate armies leading to a dispersion of control of troops, the overall deterioration of the internal situation does not permit this outcome to be ruled out completely.

For this to occur, it would be necessary for a consensus to develop among military commanders, and perhaps some political leaders, that Castro's continuation in power is a bigger threat to the interests of the armed forces than his removal from power. Perhaps an event that gets out of control and forces the army to make a hard choice, such as having to repress a popular demonstration protesting increased police abuses or a protest by workers forced to move to the countryside to work in the sugar crop may be the trigger event for the coup.

Contrary to the view that has been projected of monolithic support from the armed forces, there is growing evidence that the armed forces are asserting an independent position within the regime in the face of a decline in Castro's charismatic appeal and in their growing concern that increasing popular dissatisfaction could face them with the prospect of having to repress a revolt.

This progressive weakening of Castro's hold over the military is described in detail in the excellent and insightful paper by Humberto León in the Sánchez report commissioned by the Pentagon. One central factor in León's observation of the current situation is that:

> Today in Cuba a very significant change is taking place within the political class, and even inside the inner circle, in the growing perception of Fidel Castro as an obstacle to reform, as someone who is constantly curtailing diverse projects and initiatives dealing with economic reforms.[10]

According to León, the deteriorating situation has led to Raúl taking the initiative in the advocacy of reform leading to a transition. "Raúl Castro also emphasized, together with his reformist approach, two things: the notion and authority of the "Commander-in Chief" and that he was acting in full accordance with his brother." However, as we have seen under the section on political reform, over the years Fidel has in the end overruled all of his brother's efforts at institutionalization. And that was at a time when Raúl's efforts were undertaken with the support of a Soviet Union that provided several billion dollars a year of economic assistance and the strategic umbrella.

In the presence of a failure of the foreign investment and limited independent work reform to improve the economic situation and of the effort to repeal or soften the U.S. embargo, stop the Helms/Burton Act and gain access to international lending institutions, it is quite likely that Fidel will again stop Raúl on his tracks. In fact, this may already be taking place in the move against corruption and in the delay in enacting the revised investment law. The recent departure of one of the leading reform advocates, Osvaldo Martínez, as Minister of Economics and Planning only four months after taking the job and the laughable nature of the jobs made available for independent work may be additional indications that Fidel, the caudillo, is reasserting himself and rebuking his brother, the institutionalist, efforts to promote an albeit limited reform.

The question arises then, how will the armed forces react to this last assertion of caudillo rule over institutional rule? It is at this point that we must take into account that there are divergent generational interests and historical experiences within the armed forces. A former Cuban army officer groups them as follows:

a. the "old guard" from the insurrectionary period who fought mostly under Raúl and who were provided afterwards with formal military training, including in many cases at the Frunze and Voroshilov Soviet military academies. This group includes most, if not all, of the General rank officers. They enjoy the privileges and living conditions of the nomenklatura. They are also very conscious that their fate is closely linked to the fate of the Castro brothers and are unlikely to move against them unless they are faced with regime disintegration, in which case they may react in response to their individual interests. Their behavior at the Ochoa trial is significant. Forty seven general rank officers signed his death sen-

---

10. Humberto León., *Op. Cit.*, p. III - 6 - 19

tence, although twenty some felt the need to express on the record their admiration for General Ochoa explaining that their support of the sentence was predicated on the seriousness of the accusations made;

b. the next group includes the bulk of the Colonel, Lieutenant Colonel and Major rank officers in the FAR. They do not come from the ranks of the guerrilla war against Batista and do not have bonds with the Castro brothers as close as those of the first group. A substantial number are professional soldiers trained in the Soviet Union and were involved in "internationalist" missions overseas, particularly in Ethiopia and Angola. Despite having access to some extra compensation and benefits, this group does not enjoy the privileged status and consumption of the "old guard" and their families share with the population many of the hardships of current life in Cuba. Nevertheless, nationalism and the fear of their fate, not to mention the effectiveness of the security apparatus, have so far deterred this group from challenging the present leadership;

c. the next group is constituted by younger officers who have even less of a historical linkage to the leadership and the old guard. They came into the armed forces at the tail-end of the "internationalist" phase and did not share the glorious years of revolutionary successes and massive Soviet economic support. In general, they share the shortcomings of daily life with the rest of the population despite the fact that they get some extra benefits in kind as part of their remuneration. As is the case with the other groups, besides the effective security apparatus, their behavior is influenced by nationalists feelings and the fears of what may happen to them in a post-Castro period.

At present, the high profile of exile leaders projecting themselves as "protagonists" in a post-Castro government, with their image within Cuba of being intent on a policy of restoration of the past and revenge, is the greatest asset Castro has to discourage this outcome. Castro continues playing this theme in his domestic propaganda along with the threat of a U.S. invasion. Unfortunately, that is the biggest flaw in the present U.S. policy towards Cuba. The Clinton Administration early in its tenure issued low profile statements that may have been intended to reassure potential plotters inside the regime indicating implicitly that, were they to move, we would accept and support them.

However, under the most recent reorientation of Administration policy, the central objective is perceived to be to avoid any crisis in Cuba between now and November, 1996, while at the same time reiterating support of Torricelli's Cuban Democracy Act. Politically, this is a logical attitude, particularly in view of the impact such a crisis may have on the mood of U.S. public opinion on the immigration issue. According to Cuban sources, Castro is claimed to be willing to go along to help reelect Clinton. The argument being that, in a second term, Clinton is likely to lift the U.S. embargo and normalize relations with Cuba. But Castro may heed the advice of Andrei V. Kortunov, a member of the Russian Academy of Sciences Institute of the USA and Canada Studies, who states in his paper in Sánchez report for the Pentagon, that:

> "Only a strong and forceful President with an unquestionable conservative record could reverse long-standing U.S. policy towards Cuba. Bill Clinton does not qualify."[11]

The Administration, in the voice of Richard Nuccio, White House Cuba Advisor, has in fact endorsed Castro's tentative selection of Gutiérrez Menoyo as the chosen leader of a fake political opposition, tacitly accepting Castro's move as a legitimate step towards a political opening. This undermines the position of potential plotters. It also ignores the fact that a real opening requires that this right be granted on an unrestricted basis to other dissident groups inside

---

11. Andrei V. Kortunov, " The Role of External Factors in the Cuban Transition." In International Research 2000 Inc., *The Military and Transition in Cuba.* Bethesda, MD: International Research 2000 Inc., March 17, 1995., p. III - 13 - 3.

the island or exiled opposition groups. Otherwise, Castro is selecting his political opposition.

Another worrisome action is the cancellation at the request of the State Department of a Voice of America editorial on the sinking of the tugboat 13th of March on July 13, a massacre that has become a rallying point for anti-Castro sentiment in exile as well as in the island. Does this means human rights violations are to be down-played for the sake of improved diplomatic relations?

Mr. Nuccio is also promoting openly Track II of the Torricelli legislation by which measures will be taken aimed at undermining in the long run the closed nature of the regime by helping development of a civil society. The problem with this approach is that it underestimates Castro's political savvy. Castro's 26th of July speech reveals he is aware of the danger this implies to the regime. All indications are that the regime is about to crack down on Track II activities.

The Clinton Administration has been hesitant and contradictory in its actions—as has been the trademark of its foreign policy—with respect to the leadership of the Cuban American and exile communities. It provided a high profile support for the most conservative elements in the exile community when it wanted their endorsement of the immigration measures against the rafters last year. It has shifted more recently to a deliberate policy of down-playing this conservative Miami leadership. This is one of the most positive developments in U.S. policy in terms of the coup d'etat outcome. However, as is usual with this Administration, the message is contradictory, because these same groups are still allowed full control of Radio and TV Martí broadcasts to Cuba. We are exposed to the spectacle of the Chairman of a Presidential Advisory Commission leading pickets in front of the White House. The net result of these contradictions is far from reassuring to potential plotters inside the regime. On the contrary, a hesitant policy enhances Castro's hold over regime cadres. After all, should these men move against Castro, they would be risking their lives against immense odds. It is unlikely that they will take such a risk in the presence of less than a clear cut U.S. policy, particularly in terms of the position towards people in

the exile community whom they perceive as a threat to them.

There is nothing the U.S. can do to reduce the impact of Castro's effective repressive apparatus on the behavior of potential plotters. However, U.S. policy can be aimed at reassuring their nationalist concerns, at dispelling their fears about our power being used to impose on Cuba a leadership that may threaten their lives and positions and to assure them that, should they move, we are prepared to provide the assistance necessary for a successful transition government. Were the U.S. to make its position on these points explicit, the possibility of a coup as a solution in Cuba will be enhanced substantially.

IMPACT OF THE HELMS/BURTON ACT

As can be seen from the previous section, there is a growing potential for the coup outcome, although far from a certainty. In that context, these comments address the Helms/Burton Act from the perspective of what should be our policy towards Cuba. The legislation has the potential to become an excellent instrument to encourage the end of Castro's regime. But, in its present form, it could help prolong his rule.

Since the 1962 missile crisis, our Cuba policy has not pursued as a goal the removal of Castro. Despite Cuban claims to the contrary, once the goal of removing Castro was abandoned as a result of the Kennedy/Khrushchev exchange of letters in 1962, the aim of the embargo was containment and raising the cost to Castro and the Soviets for their anti-U.S. actions. That is, until the Torricelli legislation, which was itself contradictory in that, although it made the goal of Castro's removal explicit, it offered no incentives whatsoever to the only ones who could act against Castro.

Our policy towards Cuba seems to have been responsive to seeking a combination of goals: to satisfy visceral negative feelings among conservatives towards Castro, which lead to a punitive stance; to leftover Cold War syndromes, which are no longer relevant and are easily challenged by Castro's friends here and abroad; or, to ambitions for power of influential Cuban exiles which do nothing more than provide Castro with a strong argument to rally his cadres around him. But, with some changes, the proposed Act may serve a policy whose goal is to offer encouragement to those within Cuba who may be considering a move against Castro, since for the first time it limits exclusions from an acceptable transition government to Fidel and his brother Raúl.

The Act needs to address the fact that the most advantageous outcome for the U.S. is for change to come from within Cuba. In line with the above discussion, the coup d'etat is the most favorable outcome for both Cuba and the United States. Up to now U.S. policy has not been designed to encourage those around Castro to make a move against him. To the contrary, our policy and behavior have pushed people inside the regime to rally around Castro. That is against our national interest and that of the Cuban people. However, the essence of this paper is predicated on the opinion that, with changes to reduce some negative unintended consequences, the Act could encourage the desired behavior within Cuba. As has been said before, this would be a necessary but not sufficient condition for a coup to take place.

To that effect, we should make it clear to the Cuban people and potential plotters that, first, although as long as Castro is in power there will be no relief from the present policy, as soon as there is a transition government, there will be a substantial alleviation of their present predicament and, second, to state explicitly and categorically that the policy of the U.S. Government is not to impose any person or group to rule Cuba, that we respect the right of Cubans to choose their rulers in internationally supervised elections.

Having set the context within which to consider the impact of the Helms/Burton Act, some reservations will be presented from the perspective of whether it facilitates or discourages the coup d'etat outcome. The Act may be seen from other perspectives and the evaluations in those cases may be quite different from the points raised here. There is no pretense either that these are the only considerations to take into account. Also, since Robert Freer has presented an excellent brief on legal aspects of the Act, this paper will not address legal issues, for which, anyway, the author is not professionally qualified.

The comments are based on the text already approved by the House International Relations Committee and of the one under consideration in the Senate Western Hemisphere and Peace Corps Affairs SubCommittee. Issues about which comments are made will be in italics and the comment will follow.

- *Radio and TV Martí* are mentioned in both versions incorrectly. The point to be made is that Castro is jamming the signals and in doing so is denying Cubans access to other informational sources as provided in the Universal Declaration of Human Rights. At the same time, one must recognize that the present fight over the USIA Inspector General report on these stations is not helping their credibility. These would be critical instruments of our foreign policy if we are to encourage confidence among potential plotters.

- *Purposes* in both versions are adequate in terms of the objective of offering encouragement to potential plotters.

- *United States national* definition in both versions would be detrimental to encouraging change inside Cuba. In fact, aware of the benefit to him of the proposed wording, Castro has been holding sessions throughout the island to raise fears among people that their houses and land may be subject to reclamation from those Cubans who have become American citizens after their properties were seized. Without denying the legitimacy of the desire of former owners to regain their holdings, not only for economic reasons but in many cases for sentimental reasons involving childhood and family memories, the question that should be put to them is: if your offering to renounce to your claim could encourage the end of the Castro regime, would you insist in getting it back? Perhaps Cubans have changed a lot, but the history of the last decades shows that the much maligned Cuban-American and exile community has been capable of reacting with great generosity and willingness to forgive whenever faced with a crisis. It is quite likely that many of them will be willing to do so this time and renounce to their claims. This action could show the world that most of them are not the vengeful and greedy people frequently portrayed in the liberal media. In fact, during the discussion on property rights in another panel, one of our colleagues, the University of Michigan's Dr.Silvia Pedraza, made statements indicating exactly such a generous position.

- *Requesting United Nations endorsement of an embargo against Cuba* would be the final tightening of the noose around Castro's neck. If the rest of the world were to be consistent, it would recognize that Castro is no better than Hussein, Cedras or the Apartheid regime in South Africa. However, we must face the facts, at the United Nations there has been an overwhelming vote opposing the U.S. embargo. There does not seem to be any change in the mood of international opinion in respect to the Castro regime to encourage us to think that we can win on this issue. If we are rejected in that body, which is highly likely, we will be delivering a diplomatic victory to Castro. From the perspective of a potential plotter, should that happen it will reinforce Castro's charismatic image.

- *Enforcing the embargo* is an issue about which we must develop an eclectic approach. On the one hand, whether right or wrong, most affected governments consider some aspects of the U.S. embargo an infringement of their sovereignty, while stating that this does not mean an endorsement of the present Cuban regime. On the other hand, the U.S. has a sovereign right to take whatever measures it deems necessary to deal with a hostile power. Other governments are equally free to agree or disagree with us and make a choice. But they certainly have no right to ask us, as so many are doing, that we make painless to them dealings with a sworn enemy of the U.S. Robert E. Freer's[12] paper shows, at least to the satisfaction of this layman, that the Helms/Burton Act is consistent with international law. Rather than take a confrontational position, since politics is the art of the possible, it would be advisable for us to review the enforcement provisions to ensure that, first, they can be enforced effectively, and, second, that we avoid any unnecessary irritant to other governments or contravening our international commitments under trade agreements. If we are found at fault in international fora or our policies are not enforceable, we may end by giving a boost to Castro's image and discourage potential plotters.

- *Indirect financing* is an issue in which considerations similar to those made above in relation to trade would apply, although they don't seem to raise the same questions of contravening international agreements.

- *Cuban membership in international financial institutions* is an issue that is worth our attention because it is one of the main thrusts of the Castro diplomatic offensive. Castro has discovered that at present financing through these agencies is a bigger source of funds than through direct U.S. assistance and also is a requirement for access to commercial banks and settlement of foreign debt since Cuba is in default in its debt with the Paris Club. The Commission message to the European Union commented above clearly supports that Castro offensive. In Washington, Castro representatives and his friends, in particular the Inter-American Dialogue, are actively trying to find out how that could be accomplished even over the opposition of the U.S. A possibility they have been told time and time again is quite unlikely to obtain. Should Castro succeed, it would be a great diplomatic victory with significant economic consequences. Therefore, it would help consolidate Castro and discourage potential plotters.

- *Cuban membership in the OAS* has to be seen in the same context as the previous issue not be-

---

12. Robeert E. Freer, "The Helms and Burton's Bills: Myth and Reality." Paper presented at the Fifth Annual Meeting of the Association for the Study of the Cuban Economy (ASCE), Miami, August 10-12, 1995.

cause the OAS has direct economic benefits to offer, but because that membership is required to access the Inter-American Development Bank. And, at present, IDB is the largest source of international agency funds in the Hemisphere.

- *Support for a free and independent Cuba* is a key section of the legislation in terms of its potential impact on the dynamics of the internal situation in Cuba. Of the two Section 201 versions, the Senate version seems to be the most effective from the perspective under discussion. In this respect, care is necessary to allow for nationalist feelings among potential plotters which Castro may exploit to his advantage. The briefer Senate text seems to be more adequate for that purpose than the one coming out of the House, which could be construed as an attempt at legislating from Washington about Cuban internal matters.

- *Assistance for the Cuban people* should be revised carefully asking the question: are we providing adequate incentives for potential plotters to act now? Are we putting obstacles for these people, once they take power, to be able to bring immediate economic improvement to the population? Both versions reflect a sincere effort to give positive answers to these questions. The only caveat is that it would be advisable to revise carefully—in more detail than is possible in this paper—the difference in conditionality between the transition and the democratically elected governments. The desire to ensure that we are not helping a new dictatorship should be balanced with the need to avoid tying the hands of the Executive Branch in its dealings with a transition government in such a way that the ability of that government to manage an orderly transition, which is quite an undertaking by itself, is not placed in jeopardy.

- *Protection against confiscatory takings* raises issues in two directions commented previously. One in the definition of U.S. nationals extending to those who acquired their citizenship after the property was seized. As Freer's paper explains, this extension is consistent with existing U.S. law in the case of "trafficking" in confiscated property. Furthermore, the cases of enterprises or na-

tionals of other countries acquiring those confiscated properties do not necessarily affect the internal situation in a way Castro can exploit politically. After all, he is contradicting his proclaimed nationalism by giving up Cuban assets to foreigners at bargain prices. Besides, those whose properties were confiscated should be entitled to some compensation in case restitution to them is not feasible for considerations of social peace or other reasons. Therefore, for them to make claims against these new foreign investors will not be easy to exploit by Castro and is legal. The only aspect to take into account, then, is the feasibility of implementation so as not to generate our diplomatic isolation in a way that would benefit Castro or appear inept if the measures are not feasible to implement.

- *Exclusion of certain aliens* is included only in the House version and it seems that in line with criteria used above it would entail the imposition of control on visas and entry to the United States in a manner that will be more detrimental to the U.S. image than to Castro, particularly when extended to the relatives of those investing in Cuba. In that respect, therefore, it would have a negative impact on the possibility of encouraging potential plotters to move against Castro.

- *Invasion of executive powers,* according to the comments made by Dr. Pamela Falk, both committees have been willing to introduce wording that allows for executive discretion on the grounds of national interest. This attitude could enhance the bipartisan nature of the legislation and present Castro with a united U.S.

Finally, despite these caveats, on a personal basis, I restate my conviction that the embargo should be maintained and tightened, while making efforts to reduce unnecessary irritants to our allies, to avoid advocating measures impossible to implement, or discouraging potential plotters inside the regime. From my perspective, to lift the embargo at this time will give Castro a huge propaganda victory, unduly reward greedy speculators and discourage potential plotters. That is against U.S. national interests and would be a disservice to the Cuban people.

HELMS-BURTON MYTHS & REALITY

Robert E. Freer, Jr.

Early in 1995, Senator Helms, Chairman of the Senate Foreign Relations Committee, introduced in the Senate, along with a bipartisan coalition of more than twenty co-sponsors, the Cuban Liberty and Democratic Solidarity (Libertad) Act of 1995. Dan Burton, Chairman of the Western Hemisphere Subcommittee of the House's International Relations Committee, along with an even broader bipartisan coalition, introduced a similar provision in the House. Though as introduced, the measures were, with one important difference, mostly reintroductions in one omnibus package of bills which had been introduced in the prior Congress, the presence of a Republican majority in both Houses of Congress has assured a more serious consideration of the proposals.

While the reaction at times has been so loud on both sides as to drown out rational consideration, the adherents of the bill have not turned a deaf ear to well reasoned objection, have made many improvements to the bill and, in my view, have responded to almost all of the well reasoned objection.

As I write, in August 1995, the bill is poised for consideration on the House floor after the August recess, at which time I believe it will pass with a substantial majority. Its consideration in the Senate will follow soon thereafter. Having responded to most of the legitimate criticisms, the bill is faced with continued opposition by those who have traditionally been against the embargo and is supported by those who traditionally have believed that an effective embargo is the only cornerstone upon which any principled agreement can be reached with Cuba.

The debate over the past months has been waged, as was the battle over the Cuba Democracy Act, not just on policy grounds, but against charges that the bill violates international law and will have dire consequences for the U.S. if enacted. What follows is recitation of most of the "myths" spun by its opposition and a discussion of the reality of the bill as of its passage out of the House International Relations Committee (Draft date July 12) and as introduced by Senator Helms on July 31 as an amendment to S.908, the Foreign Relations Revitalization Act.

Before moving to the body of the paper, let me add a thought about international law. First, international law is *not* yet equal to our domestic criminal or civil law in that if you deviate from an accepted norm you are not dragged to international jail or, except in rare circumstances, before an international court to pay damages. International law is a developing body of law composed of specific agreements between and among states, international organizations and custom accepted over the years. Its vitality depends on the will of nations and as such there is, as a practical matter, give and take in its application. And there are holes in its coverage, which over time are filled first by one state, then others follow.

As a world leader and an international commercial transaction powerhouse, the U.S. has both a responsibility to initiate advances in international law on the one hand and to be careful not to "break the crockery" on the other. In this regard, it is clear that under the domestic law of almost all of our principle trading partners, if a man steals from another and a third party knowingly and intentionally takes advantage of that theft to receive or beneficially use the fruits of the theft, that person would be as guilty of that theft as the original perpetrator. The user would also be, under the law of most of our trading partners, subject to civil remedies in their own courts for his "conversion" or "trespass" upon the property of the other.

Title III of Helms-Burton adopts this principle, a principle already available under the common law for our own citizens, as a part of our federal statutory law, and in the case of the wholesale theft of our citizens' property by Cuba, says to international traffickers in this stolen property:

> "Don't do it. It is morally wrong and if you do, nevertheless, then don't try to do business in the United States. We don't want you here and if you come, then expect to rectify the wrong you committed before we will allow you the benefits of our market."

In taking this position, the sponsors of Helms-Burton have filled an important missing piece in international commercial law. The Cuban Government opposes this bill because Title III is the single element of the bill it fears most. Stripped of its false rhetoric about Americans coming back to reclaim their houses, it realizes that it is the element that will succeed in denying it access to the tainted dollars of those propping up its regime at the expense of its own people and our citizens' property rights. This measure needs to be adopted, and I for one would welcome similar legislation around the globe. If this were to occur, international business and people everywhere would have little cause to fear unlawful confiscation of their property.

The importance of the adoption of this right into our statutory law will, I believe, ultimately transcend the downfall of the Cuban Government that it will help bring about. In saying this however, I remind you of my second admonition regarding "care for the crockery." As the legal analysis that follows will indicate, it has long been held by our courts and the courts of our principle trading partners that a country is free to determine property issues within the country that concern only its own citizens.

Though the right of action in Helms-Burton has been greatly restricted and will not have a particularly significant impact on the administration of our courts, by allowing individuals who were not citizens of the U.S. at the time their loss occurred to take advantage of this privilege, it deviates from the norm. Those who favor this extension suggest that the action created is not a remedy for the "theft" that occurred when they weren't citizens years ago, but rather for the "trafficking" that is occurring now when they are citizens and entitled to equal access to our courts. I am sympathetic to this plea, but have not been able to sufficiently separate the Cuban right to determine the ultimate property rights issue as to its own citizens from the "trafficking" issue presented to our courts. At the very least it "cracks" the crockery. Given the restrictions in the statutory proposal as it now exists, I question as a matter of policy whether it is worth the potential disadvantage to all of us, including Cuban Americans, in our world-wide trading arrangements, should this notion of a remedy for post-confiscation nationals gain wider acceptance.

MYTH: LIBERTAD DETRIMENTALLY AFFECTS THE INTERESTS OF REGISTERED CLAIMANTS

Reality

- Nothing in Helms-Dole requires or authorizes the President to espouse the claims of naturalized citizens in any settlement with Cuba. Rather, the Helms-Dole amendment specifically states that the U.S. *only* has espousal responsibility for the existing certified claimants and that only they shall have an interest in any such settlement.

- Post-confiscation nationals (naturalized citizens) are entitled only to a limited right of civil action to sue in U.S. courts those who can be found in the United States who traffic in their commercial property after having been given adequate notice to stop and where the amount in controversy is $50,000 or more.

- The opening of a nation's courts to private judicial remedies against a person over whom it exercises domestic jurisdiction does not constitute "state espousal" of a claim.

- It is a well-established principle that nations may prescribe rules of law regarding activities which have a substantial effect on that nation, even if those activities are outside a nation's borders.

Discussion

The terms of *Libertad* are specific: no provision of the Act will be construed to create new espousal rights for post-confiscation nationals. In addition, traditional jurisdictional requirements, combined with a variety of additional protective measures, required under Title III, will severely limit the number of such actions. Consequently, the interests of certified claimants in a lump sum agreement will be enhanced by inhibiting third party traffickers from dealing in confiscated property of U.S. claimants, and by creating a setoff for sums received in actions against traffickers. The provisions in the bill addressing the Exclusivity of Foreign Claims Settlement Procedure clearly state that no one but certified claimants shall have an interest in any settlement.[1] According to section 303(c)(1):

> "nothing in this Act shall be construed to require or otherwise authorize the claims of Cuban nationals who became United States citizens after their property was confiscated to be included in the claims certified to the Secretary of State by the Foreign Claims Settlement Commission for purposes of future negotiation and espousal."

Further, the provisions for reopening the Commission's determination of ownership of Cuban claims emphasize that such a determination may only be used for evidentiary purposes in an action against third party traffickers by post-confiscation nationals.[2]

The bill and its proposed amendments also limit post-confiscation nationals' right of civil action. Post-confiscation nationals may sue traffickers in U.S. courts only after traffickers have been presented with adequate notice and where the amount in controversy is at least $50,000.[3]

Further, the bill contains an election of remedies provision. Under this provision, a U.S. national who brings a claim under Title III is precluded from bringing another claim under the common law, Federal law, or state law.[4] Similarly, the bill prevents the double compensation of certified claimants by setting off any trafficking action recovery against any future interest in a lump sum agreement.[5]

In addition, the Helms-Dole proposed amendments incorporate and amend the service provisions of the Foreign Sovereign Immunities Act[6] by explicitly stating that no default judgments will be entered against Cuba, its agencies, or instrumentalities, unless a Cuban government, which we recognize, is given the opportunity to cure, or be heard, and the plaintiff has proven his case to the satisfaction of the court.[7]

Most important, Title III's provision for a private right of action does nothing to dilute the claims of certified claimants. Title III does nothing to eliminate or even limit traditional minimum contacts requirement for personal jurisdiction.[8] Relatively few actions will be brought under Title III, as both parties must be sufficiently present in the U.S. to sustain the jurisdiction of the courts. Private judicial remedies, where the plaintiff retains the traditional personal jurisdictional burdens, do not constitute state

---

1. H.R. 927, 104th Cong., 1st Sess. § 304 (1995) (amending Title V of the International Claims Settlement Act of 1949 (22 U.S.C. § 1643 et seq.)).

2. *Id.* at § 303(a)(2).

3. Section 2303(b) Helms-Dole amendment to S.908 provides the amount in controversy requirement to ensure that judicial resources are directed only towards matters of significant economic interest. S. 908, 104th Cong., 1st Sess. § 2303(b) (1995).

4. H.R. 927, 104th Cong., 1st Sess. § 302(e) (1995); S. 908, 104th Cong., 1st Sess. § 2302(e)(1) (1995).

5. S. 908 at § 2302(e)(1).

6. 28 U.S.C. § 1608.

7. *Supra* note 3, at § 2302(c).

8. International Shoe Co. v. Washington, 326 U.S. 310 (1945).

espousal of claims and do not interfere with any future lump sum agreement.

MYTH: LIBERTAD'S PROPERTY SETTLEMENT REQUIREMENTS WILL DELAY PRIVATIZATION AND HINDER THE ABILITY OF THE U.S. TO ASSIST A POST-CASTRO CUBA

Reality

- The property settlement requirements are consistent with international law and U.S. foreign policy, and will facilitate, not hinder, Cuba's economic progress.

Discussion

Libertad requires a post-Cuban Government to settle the outstanding claims of U.S. nationals to qualify as a transition government eligible for U.S. assistance.[9] The U.S. has the sovereign prerogative to create such conditions for the normalization of relations, and has taken such action with its embargo on all Cuban trade pending equitable compensation to citizens who have had property illegally confiscated by the government of Cuba after January 1, 1959.[10] Although the Act requires settlement of Cuban American claims as a prerequisite to normalization and the provision of aid that will flow thereafter, it does not assert rules which govern a sovereign state with regard to the settlement of property claims by its own citizens. As a result, the structure of a system and the nature of the remedies provided to its own nationals remain the decision of the Cuban people. Thus, protest against the bill based upon an expressed concern about foreign tribunals ruling on local property disputes are unsubstantiated.[11]

Libertad's requirement for restitution is fully consistent with international standards, where we are talking about prerequisites for aid. Further, as to certified claimants, it is a well established matter of international law that states who confiscate the property of foreign nationals are obligated to pay compensation.[12]

Cuba's political and economic progress will depend on the efficient resolution of property claims, as the transformation to a market economy requires effective solutions to property questions.[13] A transition government will have the opportunity to provide either restitution or compensation, in order to meet

---

9. *Id.* at § 206(5)(G) requires that a transition government make [] public commitments to and make[] demonstrable progress in—. . . (G) taking appropriate steps to return to United States citizens (and entities which are 50 percent or more beneficially owned by United States citizens) property taken by the Cuban government from such citizens and entities on or after January 1, 1959, or to provide equitable compensation to such citizens and entities for such property . . .

10. Prohibitions Against Furnishing Assistance, 22 U.S.C.A. § 2370 (1979).

11. Nestor E. Baguer, "Bill Grants U.S. Undue Powers Over Cuban Affairs," *The Miami Herald*, 15A (June 7, 1995).

12. Ian Brownlie, *Principles of Public International Law* 532-35 (1990).

13. As a strictly personal note, the solutions to Cuba's problems do not rest solely in their hands. Our government's behavior towards both Cubans and its own citizens has historically not been entirely blameless. While it is unconstitutional to take the property of a citizen, our government has heretofore succeeded in taking property value indirectly through regulations, which if done directly would have resulted in successful litigation and compensation. Quite possibly, the most directly relevant instance of such a taking by the United States government is suggested by the following comment of the United States Department of Agriculture (U.S.D.A.) in the GAO Report on the Sugar Program: "The report's discussion of effects of the program on sugar users does not mention its impact on U.S. Refiners. Ten U.S. refineries, representing 35 percent of U.S. cane sugar refining capacity, have closed since the implementation of the current sugar program in 1982. While not all of this decline in industrial activity can be attributed to the sugar program [no other cause cited], the program's limitation on imports of raw cane sugar is a major contributing factor." Report to the Hon. Charles E. Shumer, House of Representatives, *Sugar Program Changing Domestic and International Conditions Require Program Changes* (April 1993).

It is significant that in its report, the USDA omits the fact that the very regulation that it attributes as a major contributing factor to the destruction of a substantial number of privately owned industrial facilities in the United States was later found to be a violation of the United States trade obligations by a GATT dispute resolution determination that was accepted by the United States.

The fundamental reality is that the problems of the Cubans and the U.S. domestic sugar refineries have been caused, in part, by our government's regulation of the access to the United States market for foreign raw cane sugar. The United States government needs to do a better job of complying with its own obligations to its citizens while it seeks adherence by Cuba to similar obligations both to its own citizens and ours.

Opposition to the sweetener provisions of NAFTA by those who benefit from the sugar quotas suggests that restoration of U.S. market access for Cuban sugar will face strong opposition. The sugar program responds to certain domestic economic interests rather than to actions of the Government of Cuba. Reforms by or changes in the Government of Cuba will not moderate this opposition.

the property settlement requirements. A lack of available assets may force a transition government to provide restitution.[14] Settlement in the form of restitution should provide economic benefits to the Cuban people.[15] Consequently, a system of restitution can facilitate the privatization process, as evidenced by the experiences of Eastern European nations.[16]

Libertad provides that humanitarian assistance be offered to a transition government, and that the United States support Cuban membership in the international financial institutions("IFIs") once a democratically elected Cuban government is in power.[17] The assertion that the Act is too restrictive in terms of impeding Cuban access to IFIs is erroneous. It is unlikely that a transition government would be eligible for aid from the IFIs given that the standards established for eligibility by IFIs are very similar to the conditions set out in the Act itself,[18] and the delay between application and admission would most likely be longer than the existence of the transition government itself.[19]

MYTH: THE CUBAN GOVERNMENT'S CONFISCATIONS ARE NOT VIOLATIONS OF INTERNATIONAL LAW
Reality
- The Cuban Government's confiscations violated customary international law as prompt, adequate, and effective compensation has never been provided to U.S. property owners.

Discussion
Libertad recognizes international law's prohibition of confiscation and holds the Cuban Government liable under this basic principle.[20] Under traditional principles of sovereignty, the Cuban Government's expropriations would have been legal if justified by a public purpose and by the payment of prompt, adequate, and effective compensation to the private owner. Under customary international law, an expropriating state acts in clear violation of customary international law if it fails to provide prompt, adequate, and effective compensation to the private owner. An expropriation is also illegal if it "includes interference with the assets of international organizations and taking contrary to promises amounting to estoppels."[21] Further, illegal expropriations include:

---

14. *See* Barbara Ehrich Locke, Holland & Knight, "Resolution of U.S. Claims Against Cuba: Comparative Models," presented at The Evolving Cuban Marketplace: What Every U.S. Company Needs to Know (May 5, 1994) (discussing Cuba's effective default on its 1986 settlement agreement with Spain); *see also Final Report of the Cuban Claims Program*, Foreign Claims Settlement Commission of the United States, 414 (1972) (estimating value of U.S. claims).

15. While I am not proposing such a limited use of restitution, a restitution process which returns the top ten U.S. claims, even assuming no new investment by the returning property owners, will increase the ability of the Cuban economy to absorb the net possible non-inflationary imports by over a billion dollars in the first five years. José F. Alonso, "An Economic Exercise in Restitution" (July 8, 1994), *construed in* Robert E. Freer, "Restitution's Role in the Recovery of the Cuban Economy" (July 1994).

16. For a survey on restitution schemes and their productive results, see Nicolás Gutiérrez, "Righting Old Wrongs: A Survey of Restitution Schemes for Possible Application to Democratic Cuba," Cuban-American Bar Association Cuban Law Project, Property Rights Symposium (November 5, 1993).

17. H.R. 927 § 202(e)(1); s. 381 § 202(E)(1).

18. Ernesto F. Betancourt, "Governance and Post-Castro's Cuba,"in *Cuba in Transition-Volume 4* (Washington: Association for the Study of the Cuban Economy, 1994).

19. Carlos N. Quijano, "The Role of International Organizations in Cuba's Early Transition," *statement at* the Cuban Transition Workshop (January 27, 1994).

20. *Supra* note 1, at § 301. Statement of Policy.

21. Ian Brownlie, *Principles of Public International Law* 538 (1990).

"seizures which are a part of crimes against humanity or genocide, involve breaches of international agreements, are measures of unlawful retaliation or reprisal against another state, are discriminatory, being aimed at persons of particular racial groups or nationals of particular states, or concern property owned by a foreign state and dedicated to official state purposes."[22]

These latter conditions for illegality are sometimes characterized as factors distinguishing nationalizations from expropriations of particular items of private property.[23]

Unlike the murky distinctions between nationalizations and individual expropriations, the general rule of compensation is well established and is directly applicable to the Cuban Government's confiscations. Under U.S. law, the compensation rule gained formal recognition as the "Hull formula," when U.S. Secretary of State, Cordell Hull, outlined the requirements of prompt, adequate, and effective compensation to the Mexican Government during a 1939 dispute over Mexico's nationalization of foreign-owned oil fields.[24] The compensation rule is underpinned by a cornerstone of international law, the international minimum standard,[25] and sometimes substantiated by principles of acquired rights,[26] unjust enrichment, and human rights.[27]

That the Cuban government's expropriation of the property of U.S. nationals is a violation of international law under the compensation rule is virtually undisputed. More than three decades have passed since the Cuban Government regime began its socialist program of widespread confiscations, yet neither compensation nor the assurance of compensation to private owners is imminent.

Moreover, some observers charge that Cuban confiscations have been discriminatory,[28] thus inherently violative of basic norms of international law. These commentators claim that the confiscation of the property of U.S. nationals was motivated by retaliatory intent against the U.S. government for its poli-

---

22. *Id.* at 538.

23. Some scholars distinguish between these two cases for purposes of compensation analysis. Under this analysis, where the expropriation of particular items of property is concerned, only a duty to pay compensation for direct losses is involved. Where a nationalization, or the expropriation of a major industry or resource is concerned, liability for consequential loss—otherwise known as *lucrum cessans*—is implicated. In addition, some scholars argue that only the former case creates valid title; however, scholarship is mixed on this point. *Id.* at 538-39.

24. Patrick M. Norton, "A Law of the Future or a Law of the Past? Modern Tribunals and the International Law of Expropriation," 85 *American Journal of International Law* 474, 475 (1991), *citing* G. Hackworth, *Digest of International Law* 655-65 (1942) (reproducing the diplomatic correspondence).

25. The doctrine of an international minimum standard dictates the supremacy of a moral standard of the treatment of aliens over national standards. Although the global community has not reached consensus on the debate, the international minimum standard has gained increasing support throughout the twentieth century, including the support of a majority of states at the Hague Codification Conference and United Nations affirmation through the General Assembly's 1962 Declaration on Permanent Sovereignty over National Resources. *Supra* note 21, at 524-25, 539-41.

   The U.S.-Mexico General Claims Commission ratified the standard in the 1926 *Neer Claim* case: ". . . the propriety of governmental acts should be put to the test of international standards. . . the treatment of an alien, in order to constitute an international delinquency should amount to an outrage, to bad faith, to willful neglect of duty, or to an insufficiency of governmental action so far short of international standards that every reasonable and impartial man would recognize its insufficiency. *Supra* note 21, at 525. More recently, the international minimum standard and compensation rule was ratified by President Nixon in a policy statement. "Statement of Policy by the President of the United States Concerning the International Minimum Standard," 8 *Weekly Compilation of Presidential Documents* 1334 (1972).

26. The principle of "acquired" or "vested" rights appears in some judicial and academic discussions of property rights, particularly in the context of state successions.

27. Some human rights treaties refer to the individual right to not be arbitrarily deprived of property. *See, e.g.,* Universal Declaration of Human Rights, Art. 17, G.A. Res. 217 A (III), Dec. 10, 1948; American Convention on Human Rights, Art. 21, OEA/Ser.L/V/II.23 (1978).

28. Some of these observers note that the Cuban Government's confiscations violated Cuba's 1940 Constitution.

cies toward Cuba[29] and by distrust of individuals who left post-revolution Cuba.[30]

Although the discrimination allegations are more controversial and may be more difficult to firmly substantiate, the Cuban Government's retaliation and suppression of counter-revolutionary elements provide some basis for illegality. More important, Cuba's consistent violation of the compensation rule provides ample support for a U.S. nationals' claim of an international law violation. Thus, Title III is well supported by international law and U.S. practice.

MYTH: TITLE III IS UNFAIR TO TRAFFICKERS

Reality

- The right of action applies, potentially, only to those who "knowingly and intentionally" use, benefit from, or gain an interest in, property wrongfully confiscated from American nationals as of six months after the provision's date of enactment. Potential liability does not attach for past activities, as the right of action does not apply retroactively.

- The provision allows a six month grace period, plus notice, so that those who have put themselves at risk can avoid liability if they so choose.

- The underlying concept of the right of action provision is similar to that for actions against those who deal in (i.e., "fence") stolen property.

- The Helms-Dole provision sends a clear message that the United States, as a matter of domestic law, finds "trafficking" in wrongfully confiscated property unacceptable behavior and that anyone who engages in or wrongfully profits from this activity faces the prospect of either compensating the legal owner of the property or staying clear of the jurisdiction of U.S. courts.

Discussion

Third party traffickers have no claim against the Cuban government for protection of their interests in expropriated property, nor do they have any viable defense against suits by U.S. nationals. Their precarious position is due to the fact that they cannot claim to be *bona fide* purchasers. By knowingly and intentionally engaging in joint ventures involving confiscated property, third party traffickers have tainted their own legal status with Cuba's international law violations. *Libertad* is consistent with international law, which recognizes that defective title cannot properly be transferred; more specifically, international law recognizes that a property interest gained through confiscation cannot properly be trans-

---

29. One commentator argues that: "Castro's confiscations of U.S.-owned property violated international law 'because, *inter alia*, its purpose was to retaliate against United States nationals for acts of their government, and was directed against United States nationals exclusively.'" *Hearing on the Cuban Liberty and Solidarity Act of 1995*, June 14, 1995 (statement of Brice M. Clagett for the Subcommittee on Western Hemisphere Affairs of the Senate Foreign Relations Committee), *citing*, 1 *Restatement (Third) of Foreign Relations Law of the United States* 210; Banco Nacional de Cuba v. Farr, 243 F. Supp. 957 (S.D.N.Y. 1956), *aff'd*, 383 F.2d 166 (2d Cir. 1967), *cert. denied*, 390 U.S. 956 (1968); *see also* Department of State, *Foreign Relations of the United States* 777-876 (1987) (documenting discriminatory impact of Cuba's reduced participation in the U.S. sugar market); Statement by Bruce Fein, constitutional and international law expert regarding the application of developing notions of human rights law to the traditional property construct.

30. *Id.* at note 15, *citing*, International Commission of Jurists, *Cuba and the Rule of Law* 100 (1962).

ferred.[31] At least one leading international scholar calls for "an international legal duty of non-recognition of the Cuban Government's titles."[32] Additionally, foreign tribunals have held that title acquired by confiscation is invalid and cannot be transferred.[33]

Even in the absence of judicial and scholarly recognition of the invalidity of title gained by confiscation, international law provides such liability. Under the principle of *jus cogens*,[34] third parties should be liable for trafficking in confiscated property. Under this fundamental principle of international law, general principles of law recognized by virtually all nations

rise to the level of peremptory norms enforceable as international law. Thus, in theory, international law recognizes the concepts of conversion, possession of stolen property, and trespass.

U.S. law recognizes that, unless the initial title is valid, no rights can arise in favor of anyone; any agreements that arise from the initial "contract" are tainted by the prior defect.[35] Although every holder is presumed to be a holder in due course,[36] if it is established that there is a defect in title through illegality, etc., the burden shifts to the holder to demonstrate that he is a *bona fide* endorsee for value. Under the

---

31. One scholar notes: "Where the foreign State has taken property in circumstances which, for one or the other reason, are contrary to international law, the forum should treat the taking as null and void. In its courts the original owner should continue to enjoy title. . . . The chattel confiscated in a manner considered to be internationally illegal should be treated as having been stolen. The original owner, therefore, has retained his title except where a subsequent purchaser in accordance with the general law of the *lex situs* has acquired it. Where title to stolen property can be acquired at all, the purchaser will usually have to act without actual or constructive notice. If the person in possession of "hot products" knows their origin he may also become liable in damages to the true owner, not only for such a tort as conversion, but also for conspiracy committed by co-operating with others to deprive the true owner of his rights." F.A. Mann, *Further Studies in International Law* 177, 186 (1990). For further discussion of this issue in international law, Brice Clagett cites: Sir Robert Jennings and Sir Arthur Watts, *Oppenheimer's International Law* 371-75 (1992); "Nationalization and International Law: Testimony of Elihu Lauterpacht, Q.C.," 17 *International Lawyer* 97 (1983); F.A. Mann, *Studies in International Law* 373-90, 420-65 (1973); Martin Domke, "Foreign Nationalizations," 55 *American Journal of International Law* 585, 610-15 (1961); Ignaz Seidl-Hohenveldern, "Title to Confiscated Foreign Property and Public International Law," 56 *American Journal of International Law* 507, 508-09 (1962). See *Hearing on the Cuban Liberty and Solidarity Act of 1995* (June 14, 1995 (statement of Brice M. Clagett for the Subcommittee on Western Hemisphere Affairs of the Senate Foreign Relations Committee).

32. Clagett, *supra* note 31, at 20, *citing*, F.A. Mann, *Studies in International Law* 385-86 (1973): "If, then, the sacrosanctity of the foreign act of State is treated as a rule of the municipal law of the United States, Britain, and Holland, it cannot be so extended as to lead to the legalization of the international wrong. Such a consequence would be opposed to the very "comity of nations" which was invoked to justify the maxim. On the contrary, as has already been suggested, if a State commits an international wrong and the court of another State, the forum, refuses recognition to that wrong, the latter does what international law expects it to do and what it must do in order not to become an accessory to the delinquency." Mann, *supra*, at 385-86.

33. Anglo-Iranian Oil Co. v. Jaffrate (*The Rose Mary*), W.L.R. 246, 20 I.L.R. 316 (Aden Sup. Ct.) (awarding title to expropriated owner, denying validity of title through confiscation, and finding [the property] in dispute to still be the property of the plaintiffs), *cited in*, Clagett, *supra* note 31, at note 26. Clagett also cites the following decisions of French courts that awarded title to the expropriated owner: Bouniation v. Societe Optorg (1924); Banque et Societe des Petroles v. Compagnie Mexicaine (1939); Braden Copper Co. v. Le Groupement d'Importation des Metaux (1972). *See also* F.A. Mann, *Further Studies, supra* note 31, at 183-83 (providing additional international case law).

34. Article 38 of the Statute of the International Court of Justice outlines four traditional sources of international law: a) international conventions; b) customary international law; c) general principles of law "recognized by civilized nations" (*jus cogens*); and d) judicial decisions and the writings of "the most highly qualified publicists." It is a widely accepted position by publicists that these four categories operate in some form of descending order of weight. Consequently, law promoted by *jus cogens* may generally have more influence than judicial decisions or the writings of publicists.

35. *Williston on Contracts* (3rd ed. 1959) § 364A.

36. Two commentators offer the following definition: "A transferee of a "negotiable instrument" who takes his interest by "negotiation" under circumstances that qualify him as a "holder in due course" is *not* subject to conflicting claims of ownership or to most defenses which the obligor could raise against the transferor. The only defenses that may be raised against a holder in due course are the so-called "real" defenses: infancy, fraud "in factum," duress or illegality that would "render the obligation of the party a nullity." Michael Slattery and Ron Martinetti, "The Rights of "Owners" of Lost, Stolen or Destroyed Instruments Under UCC Section 3-804: Can They Be Holders In Due Course?," 98 *Commercial Law Journal* 328, 328 (1993).

U.C.C., the holder must show that he was without notice of any potential defect in title to meet this requirement.[37] In other words, the holder must meet a good faith requirement.[38]

This principle is not unique to U.S. law. For example, under British law, "every holder is *prima facie* presumed to be a holder in due course, but if in an action it is established that '. . . the acceptance, issue, or subsequent negotiation of the bill is affected with . . . illegality, the burden of proof is shifted, unless and until the holder proves that, subsequent to the alleged fraud or illegality, value has in good faith been given for the bill.'"[39] In fact, the defective title, holder in due course, and good faith principles are not unique to any legal system.[40] Indeed, the basic principle that defective title cannot be transferred to a third party who is aware of a potential defect may exist in Cuban law itself.[41]

Third party traffickers cannot claim to be good faith purchasers of interests in expropriated property. Cuba's program of expropriation has been well-publicized and the tenuous relations between the U.S. and Cuba are well-known to the international community. In addition the U.S. Department of State has since 1992 warned all diplomatic and consular posts abroad, on at least three occasions, that "Cuba may be selling or leasing to foreign investors property expropriated from U.S. nationals in order to earn dollars and investment commitments."[42] These missions then informed their host governments that U.S. expropriation claims against Cuba were unsettled.[43] Thus, foreign governments and, effectively, foreign investors, have received adequate notice that questions of defective title surrounded joint ventures involving expropriated property. The holder in due course defense, consequently, is unavailable to these third party traffickers.

MYTH: TITLE III VIOLATES CUBA'S SOVEREIGNTY AND THE ACT OF STATE DOCTRINE

Reality

The United States, like any state, has the authority to prescribe domestic law to govern conduct or effects occurring within its own territory or conduct outside the United States that has substantial impact on the United States.[44]

- Title III is consistent with current U.S. law which limits the act of state doctrine.

- The "act of state" doctrine is a judicially-created restriction that U.S. courts have imposed on themselves. The doctrine is subject to modification by statute, such as Congress's approval of the "Hickenlooper" amendments, which reversed the application of the "act of state" doctrine in cases of claims to ownership in cases of confiscations.

---

37. *See* Slattery and Martinetti, *supra* note 36, at 332.

38. "Good faith" is defined in Revised Article 3 of the U.C.C. as "honesty in fact and the observance of reasonable commercial standards of fair dealing." This standard incorporates both subjective and objective elements. Slattery and Martinetti, *supra* note 36, at 332.

39. L.P. Hitchens, "Holders for Value and Their Status," *Journal of Business Law* 571, 574 (1993), (*quoting* the Bills and Exchange Act of 1882 § 30(2)).

40. Hitchens notes that there is "universal understanding" with respect to the good faith requirement of holder in due course status. *Supra* note 39, at 575 (*quoting* Parke B. in Bailey v. Bidwell (13 M. & W. 73) (*quoted in* Smith v. Braine (1851) 16 Q.B. 244 at 251)).

41. *See* Brice Clagett, "Public International Legal Standards Applicable to Property Expropriation in Cuba" (delivered at ABA Annual Meeting, New Orleans, August 9, 1994, as part of Showcase Program, Cuba in Transition: Options for Addressing the Challenge of Expropriated Properties); Alberto Díaz-Masvidal, "Scope, Nature and Implications of Contract Assignments on Cuban Natural Resources (*Mineral and Petroleum*)," presented at the Fourth Annual Meeting of the Association for the Study of the Cuban Economy, August 11-13, 1994.

42. Message from Secretary of State Warren Christopher to all diplomatic and consular posts: "Buyer Beware: Cuba May Be Selling American Property" (September 1993) (on record with Dept. of State); *infra*, note 76.

43. Id.

44. *See* Joseph Modeste Sweeney et al., *The International Legal System* 84-108 (1988).

- Helms-Dole operates within a recognized limited general exception to the doctrine, as Congress has every right to do and has done before. In fact by further restricting the circumstances under which a default judgment can be obtained against Cuba, the bill is more conservative than existing law under other statutes.

Discussion

According to established principles of foreign relations law, "a state has jurisdiction to prescribe law with respect to . . . conduct outside its territory that has or is intended to have substantial effect within its territory."[45] The conduct of third parties who traffic in the confiscated property of U.S. nationals has substantial harmful effect within the U.S. The U.S. may therefore enact domestic laws creating a domestic remedy in domestic courts.

Not only does the U.S. have jurisdiction to prescribe domestic law to curtail and punish traffickers in confiscated property, it has the jurisdiction to enforce such law and provide a remedy in U.S. courts. The Foreign Sovereign Immunities Act of 1976[46] provides federal jurisdiction over the commercial activities of foreign states, their agencies, and instrumentalities, where there is a rational nexus to the United States.[47] Moreover, the FSIA provides that the commercial property of states "may be levied upon for the satisfaction of judgments rendered against them *in connection with* their commercial activities"[48] (emphasis added).

Title III of Helms-Burton thus derives enforcement authority from the FSIA as third party trafficking in confiscated property falls within its scope. Regardless of the controversy over the illegality of Cuban confiscations of U.S. nationals' property, third party traffickers cannot portray their own conduct as quintessential state activity.

Some critics might continue to assert that Title III nevertheless contravenes the spirit of the act of state doctrine. The act of state doctrine is, however only a judicially created instrument and is no longer a dispositive jurisdictional defense. The Hickenlooper Amendment and the FSIA have themselves limited the doctrine's influence in U.S. courts.[49]

Further, the act of state doctrine itself has been inaccurately equated with the Supreme Court's ruling in *Banco Nacional de Cuba v. Sabbatino*.[50] The act of state doctrine may be correctly understood as two strands of judicial deference, rather than one.[51] Before *Sabbatino*, there existed a tension between a conflicts-of-law approach[52] and a judicial restraint ap-

---

45. American Law Institute, *Restatement (Third) of Foreign Relations Law* § 402(c) (1987). *See, e.g.,* Handelswerkerjj G.J. Bier and Stiching Reinwater (The Reinwater Foundation) v. Mines de Potasse d'Alsace S.A., Court of Justice of the European Communities, 1976, [1977] 1 *Common Market Law Reports* 284 (concluding that Dutch court of appeal had jurisdiction over suit for pollution originating in France and causing damage in the Netherlands).

46. 28 U.S.C. § 1602 et seq.

47. The FSIA codifies the restrictive theory of sovereign immunity, whereby immunity is granted for claims arising out of quintessential government activities (*de jure imperii*) and immunity is denied for claims arising out of private activities (*de jure gestionis*). *See* Alfred Dunhill of London, Inc. v. Cuba, 425 U.S. 682 (1976) (ratifying the FSIA and the restrictive theory of sovereign immunity).

48. 28 U.S.C. § 1602.

49. *See* F. Palicio y Compañía, S.A. v. Brush, 256 F. Supp. 481 (S.D.N.Y. 1966) (ratifying the second Hickenlooper Amendment); *Dunhill, supra* note 41 (ratifying the FSIA).

50. 376 U.S. 398 (1964) (holding that the Court would not review the merits of the plaintiffs action against Cuba, despite the fact that a violation of customary international law was alleged).

51. *See generally* Anne-Marie Burley, "Law Among Liberal States: Liberal Internationalism and the Act of State Doctrine," 92 *Columbia Law Review* 1907 (1992) (utilizing the act of state doctrine as a model to apply and extend a Kantian theory of liberal internationalism).

52. The conflicts approach can be viewed as an affirmative doctrine, directing the court to apply foreign law in a transnational approach.

proach[53] as a means of applying the act of state doctrine.[54] The holding in *Sabbatino* marked the height of the judicial restraint approach. However, since this ruling, the history of the doctrine is marked mainly by efforts to undermine it. Outrage from academic and professional communities that the *Sabbatino* approach would position the U.S. in effective violation of international law provided at least part of the motivation behind the Hickenlooper Amendment and the FSIA.[55] In fact, the post-*Sabbatino* case history of courts applying the act of state doctrine suggests a trend back toward the conflicts approach.[56]

Moreover, a retrospective look at the *Sabbatino* ruling suggests that the Court's "constitutional underpinnings" analysis of the act of state doctrine "was not simply a detour around the public policy and international law exceptions, but rather a more fundamental statement that the act of state doctrine could not function as a conflicts rule on the particular facts of the case."[57] Specifically, the Court was cognizant of the fact that the normal "private law model" of individual dispute resolution was displaced by the anticipation of a negotiated lump sum settlement.[58] The Court also could not justify applying Cuban law under the conflicts approach on the basis of comity; there was no reasonable expectation of reciprocity or predictability.[59]

The act of state doctrine is consequently no longer a significant barrier to Title III or any other aspect of Helms-Burton. Although the doctrine may still exist in some form to protect quintessential sovereign acts, Helms-Burton does not violate current international or U.S. law addressing sovereign immunity.

Rather, Helms-Burton buttresses traditional principles of comity. If U.S. courts were to invoke the act of state doctrine to shield Cuba's illegal confiscations from legal redress, the U.S. would effectively position itself in the global community as an accessory to Cuba's international wrongs. Helms-Burton thus protects the United States from the potential of judicial misappropriation of the act of state doctrine.

MYTH: THE CREATION OF A CIVIL REMEDY IN U.S. COURTS AGAINST THIRD PARTY TRAFFICKERS SUBJECT TO THEIR JURISDICTION VIOLATES INTERNATIONAL LAW

Reality

- There is no rule of international law that limits a state's ability to regulate only conduct which occurs within its territory, or to establish private remedies/rights of action for those within its domestic jurisdiction.

- International law recognizes that a state has jurisdiction to prescribe rules of law with respect to conduct outside its territory that has or is intended to have substantial effect within its territory when the exercise of such jurisdiction is reasonable in all circumstances.

- Helms-Dole provides for a private remedy against those who are subject to U.S. law and a U.S. court's jurisdiction. The remedy is available to U.S. nationals, who continue to hold legal title to the property. The property may be situated outside the U.S., but the legal owner of the property is a U.S. national.

---

53. The judicial restraint approach, the approach of the *Sabbatino* Court, can be viewed as a negative doctrine, forbidding review of the validity of a foreign act.

54. *Supra* note 51, at 1928-33.

55. *Supra* note 51, at 1936-39.

56. *Supra* note 51, at 1961-85. Professor Burley conducted a study of over seventy lower court decisions to arrive at this conclusion. She also notes that a closer look at W.S. Kirkpatrick & Co. v. Republic of Cuba, 425 U.S. 682 (1976) (construing the Hickenlooper Amendment narrowly), demonstrates a tilt back toward the conflicts approach. *Supra.*

57. *Supra* note 51, at 1950.

58. *Supra* note 51, at 1950.

59. *Supra* note 51, at 1949.

- The right of action is analogous to the common law actions of trespass and conversion which, arguably, are available to U.S. claimants already. U.S. courts currently are open to handle cases of foreign nationals for actions against other foreign nationals that occurred outside the United States (e.g., Alien Tort Statute and Torture Victim Protection Act).

- Existing U.S. law offers a solid precedent for this right of action: The "Second Hickenlooper Amendment" states that "No court in the United States shall decline on the ground of the federal act of state doctrine to make a determination on the merits giving effect to the principles of international law in a case in which a claim of title or other right of property is asserted...based upon (or traced through) a confiscation or other taking..."

- The Foreign Sovereign Immunities Act (FSIA) provides that an agency or instrumentality of a foreign state is not immune from claims based "upon an act outside the territory of the United States in connection with a commercial activity of the foreign state elsewhere and that act causes a direct effect in the United States."

- New causes of action have been created in this way, ranging historically all the way from trespass and tort, through antitrust, securities and trademarks derelictions, down to strict liability for environmental offenses and discrimination.

Discussion

Helms-Burton would create a civil remedy for United States citizens to obtain compensation from third parties who choose to profit from use of property confiscated by the Cuban Government in violation of international law. The proposed remedy is an essential component of the existing lawful United States boycott of Cuba. The remedy is a logical and timely development of international law. Cuba has no lawful title to give to third parties. A third party profiting from use of the unlawfully confiscated property is committing an act that would be criminal under any other circumstances. Our allies have no justifiable interest in protecting such conduct.

Title III of Helms-Burton would provide United States citizens, whose property was unlawfully confiscated by the Cuban Government, with the ability to protect their interests pending normalization of relations between Cuba and the United States. The legislation would allow them to recover damages from predatory third parties who have wrongfully "knowingly and intentionally" derived benefit from use of the property without legal title. The Cuban Government has entered into commercial agreements with others for the purpose of exploiting these properties, confiscated without compensation, to enrich himself and to finance his government.

Present international law does not contain effective means to address unlawful confiscations of property. The United States embargo of Cuba and freezing of its assets, now more than thirty years old, has failed to force the Cuban Government to come to terms, possibly because the stakes are simply not high enough.[60]

International resolutions of such disputes are entirely consensual and may take an exceedingly long time to bring about. Recovery through espousal between governments almost always leads to a severe compromise in the compensation paid as a condition for normalization of relations.[61] Given these realities,

---

60. The only success in this areas was the United States' freezing of assets of Iran which lead to the Algiers Accords of 1981, and the Iran-United States Claims tribunal. In this instance both parties were motivated to resolve the dispute. The United States had frozen $13 billion dollars in Iran assets and it desperately wanted to recover the U.S. embassy hostages.

61. Richard Lilich & Burns Weston, *International Claims: Their Settlement by Lump Sum Agreements* (1979). Payments averaged 4.59 percent to 60.6 percent of adjudicated value and were paid without interest though the average payment was made twenty years after the original confiscation. The 1979 settlement between the United States and China, more than thirty years after the confiscation, was for 40 percent of the value of the property at the time of the taking, without interest. The 1992 settlements between the United States and Germany for acts of East Germany were for 100 percent of value at the time of the taking without interest or appreciation for the 40 years period during which the assets were used by others.

and Cuba's impoverished condition, the only current opportunities for owners of confiscated Cuban property to obtain fair compensation are to preserve their assets for eventual restitution and/or to recover from third parties who have entered into business relationships with the Cuban Government whereby they have derived ill-gotten profits.

The properties used in these unlawful transactions are, in essence stolen, and the remedies proposed, consistent with conventional legal concepts of trespass and conversion. Under international law, confiscation without compensation did not effect a transfer of title recognizable under international law.[62] As the illegality of the Cuban Government's actions are universally known, those who entered into business relations with him to exploit the property of others are not acting innocently, a concept known in commercial law as being a "holder in due course" and thus are, in effect, receivers of stolen property.[63]

Because Cuba cannot convey title to third parties, they have no legitimate defense against actions for conversion or trespass. Title III merely creates a cause of action which supplements such common law claims and provides a Federal forum where subject matter and personal jurisdiction can be found. Other nations have no legitimate interest in protecting their citizens who have committed an obvious wrong against a United States citizen. Indeed, it is in the interests of all nations to protect against this very type of illegal behavior. Helms-Burton will strengthen the rule of law and property rights in the international community.[64]

MYTH: THE PROVISIONS OF HELMS-BURTON WHICH SAFEGUARD AGAINST THE IMPORTATION INTO THE UNITED STATES OF CERTAIN CUBAN PRODUCTS, ESPECIALLY SUGAR, VIOLATE OUR OBLIGATIONS UNDER THE GATT AND NAFTA TREATIES

Reality

- The provision tightens enforcement of existing prohibitions against the importation of Cuban sugar or products containing Cuban sugar by requiring a certificate of origin that provides the Secretary of the Treasury with an additional means of ensuring compliance with existing U.S. laws and regulations.

- U.S. accession to NAFTA does not modify or alter U.S. sanctions against Cuba. The NAFTA Statement of Administrative Action clearly noted that "Article 309(3) permits the United States to ensure that Cuban products or goods made from Cuban materials are not imported into the United States from Mexico or Canada and that United States products are not exported to Cuba through those countries."

- This provision does not violate GATT or NAFTA obligations. They are mere implementations of the longstanding United States policy of prohibiting Cuba from benefiting from trade effecting the United States as long as it continues to benefit from the unlawful confiscation of the property of U.S. citizens.

- A certificate of origin requirement does not constitute a secondary embargo, is consistent with

---

62. Ignaz Seidl-Hohenveldern, "Title to Confiscated Foreign Property and International Law," 56 *American Journal of International Law* 507, 508-9 (1962); Martin Domke, "Foreign Nationalizations," 55 *American Journal of International Law* 585, 610-15; F.A. Mann, *Further Studies in International Law*, 177 (1990).

63. Mann, *supra*, note 56 at 186.

64. Some have argued that Helms-Burton will be met with mirror legislation in other countries, which will allow their citizens to bring an action against a State, County or regulatory body for a regulatory taking. As a general rule, the United States does not engage in the extra-judicial confiscation of the property of its citizens or foreign nationals. *But see supra* note 13. Lands are taken, if at all, pursuant to condemnation laws, which provide for valuation and compensation. There is presently a debate in this country regarding regulatory takings. However, the trend in this area is toward compensation, *Dolan v. City of Tigard*, 114 Sup.Ct. 2309 (1994), and indeed, legislation is pending in the Congress to address this concern with regard to all Federal regulatory takings. There is already some precedent— the Hickenlooper Amendments, for example—recognizing regulatory takings as a confiscation without compensation.

the rights of nations to determine rules of origin, and does not raise quota allocation or denial of access problems under GATT Articles XIII and XI.

Discussion

The House and Senate versions of the proposed legislation both contain provisions directed towards ensuring that no sugar or other product, which has been produced in, transported through, or is derived from products of Cuba shall be imported into the United States or dealt with by U.S. citizens abroad.[65] The drafters of the legislation have been mindful of U.S. obligations to other nations. The policy upon which the proposed legislation is based is not new, but rather a continuation of a thirty-five year effort to compel Cuba to return to U.S. citizens the property which it illegally took from them in the early 1960's and to eliminate Cuba's threat to peace and democracy in the Western Hemisphere. The policy is consistent with international law, specifically referred to by the North American Free Trade Agreement treaty (NAFTA) and violates neither it nor U.S. obligations under the General Agreement on Trade and Tariffs (GATT).[66]

International law recognizes the principle that incident to its sovereignty, a nation has the right to choose those economic principles that will govern its trade relations with another nation.[67] Indeed, secondary boycotts of other nations intended to effect foreign policy are not *per se* illegal.[68] The United Nations has in the past sanctioned boycotts against Rhodesia, South Africa, Iraq, and the former Yugoslavia.

The drafters of the legislation have been mindful of our treaty obligations. The United States accession to the NAFTA specifically addresses this issue. Article 309(3) permits the United States to ensure that Cuban products or goods made from Cuban materials are not imported into the United States from either Mexico or Canada and that United States products are not imported into Cuba. Indeed, it allows for secondary boycotts.[69]

GATT Article XI does contain a provision which generally prohibits embargoes and secondary boycotts. However, Article XXI creates an exception to this prohibition, and indeed, all of its obligations by prohibiting construction of the treaty to preclude

> "any contracting party from taking an action which it considers necessary for the protection of its essential security interests...[when] taken in time of war or other emergency of international relations, as long as their implementation is not applied"

in a manner which would constitute a means of arbitrary or unjustifiable discrimination between countries where the same conditions prevail.[70] The proposed legislation clearly is consistent with the GATT restrictions on boycotts.

The findings upon which the proposed legislation is based clearly set forth an emergency in international

---

65. H.R. 927, Section 109 and S. 908, Section 2110.

66. Memorandum to the U.S. Senate Foreign Relations Committee from the American Law Division of Congressional Research Service, July 31, 1995.

67. *Nicaragua v. U.S. Military and Paramilitary Activities in and Against Nicaragua,* 1986 I.C.J. 14 ("A State is not bound to continue trade relations longer than it sees fit to do so in the absence of a treaty commitment or other specific legal obligation.")

68. Fenton, "Transnational Boycotts," 17 *Vanderbilt Journal of Transnational Law* 205, 230 (1984) ("[T]he circumstances under which a boycott is implemented, the motivations underlying its use and the degree of severity it assumes generally determine its legal status.")

69. Article 309: Import and Export Restrictions: "3. In the event that a Party adopts or maintains a prohibition or restriction on the importation from or exportation to a non-Party of a good, nothing in this Agreement shall be construed to prevent the Party from: (a) limiting or prohibiting the importation from the territory of another Party of such good of that non-Party; or (b) requiring as a condition of export of such good of the Party to the territory of another Party, that the good not be re-exported to the non-Party, directly or indirectly, without being consumed in the territory of the other Party." Mexico's and Canada's obligations related to expropriation under article 1110 of NAFTA must also be noted.

70. GATT Article XX, XXI, para. (g)

relations. The Cuban government is an international outlaw whose conduct continues to cause palpable injury to its neighboring States.[71]

The proposed legislation's provisions which address the movement of U.S. and Cuban products are not a new concept. They represent a long and consistent U.S. policy to protect the property of its citizens from confiscation without compensation in violation of international law and to refuse to trade with nations which it views as a direct threat to international peace. This policy is more than thirty years old, predating U.S. accession to either NAFTA or GATT. Certainly, the other parties to these treaties were aware of U.S. policy regarding the embargo of Cuban products when the treaties were contemplated.

Premised upon the Trading With the Enemy Act, 50 U.S.C. App. 5(b), as amended, and the Foreign Assistance Act of 1961, 22 U.S.C. 2370 in 1985, the U.S. initiated 31 C.F.R. Sec. 515 et seq., Cuban Assets Control Regulations. These regulations, prohibit all aspects of trade involving Cuba.[72] However, they also contain identical prohibitions against trade with other countries viewed to be international outlaws.[73] This policy has been restated as recently as 1985. Section 902(c) of the *Food Security Act of 1985, Public Law* 99-198, requires that the President not allocate any of the sugar import quota to a country that is a net importer of sugar unless that country can verify to the President that any imports of sugar pro-

---

71. H.R. 927 Section 2 (13-28): Sec 2. Findings. "The Congress makes the following findings:... 13 The Cuban government engages in the illegal international narcotics trade and harbors fugitives from justice in the United States. 14. The Castro government threatens international peace and security by engaging in acts of armed subversion and terrorism such as the training and supplying of groups dedicated to international violence. 15. The Castro government has utilized from its inception and continues to utilize torture in various forms (including by psychiatry), as well as execution, exile, confiscation, political imprisonment, and other forms of terror and repression, as means of retaining power. 16. Fidel Castro has defined democratic pluralism as "pluralistic garbage" and continues to make clear that he has no intention of tolerating the democratization of Cuban society. 17. The Castro government holds innocent Cubans hostage in Cuba by no fault of the hostages themselves solely because relatives have escaped the country. 18. Although a signatory state to the 1928 Inter-American Convention on Asylum and the International Covenant on Civil and Political Rights (which protects the right to leave one's own country), Cuba nevertheless surrounds embassies in its capital by armed forces to thwart the right of its citizens to seek asylum and systematically denies that right to the Cuban people, punishing them by imprisonment for seeking to leave the country and killing them for attempting to do so (as demonstrated in the case of the confirmed murder of over 40 men, women, and children who were seeking to leave Cuba on July 13, 1994). 19. The Castro government continues to utilize blackmail, such as the immigration crisis with which it threatened the United States in the summer of 1994, and other unacceptable and illegal forms of conduct to influence the actions of sovereign states in the Western Hemisphere in violation of the Charter of the Organization of American States and other international agreements and international law. 20. The United Nations Commission on Human Rights has repeatedly reported on the unacceptable human rights situation in Cuba and has taken the extraordinary step of appointing a Special Rapporteur. 21. The Cuban government has consistently refused access to the Special Rapporteur and formally expressed its decision not to "implement so much as one comma" of the United Nations Resolution appointing the Rapporteur. 22. The United Nations General Assembly passed Resolution 1992/70 on December 4, 1994, Resolution 1993/48/142 on December 20, 1993, and Resolution 1994/49/544 on October 19, 1994, referencing the Special Rapporteur's reports to the United Nations and condemning "violations of human rights and fundamental freedoms" in Cuba. 23. Article 39 of Chapter VII of the United Nations Charter provides that the United Nations Security Council "shall determine the existence of any threat to the peace, breach of the peace, or act of aggression and shall make recommendations, or decide what measures shall be taken ..., to maintain or restore international peace and security." 24. The United Nations has determined that the massive and systematic violations of human rights may constitute a "threat to peace" under Article 39 and has imposed sanctions due to such violations of human rights in the cases of Rhodesia, South Africa, Iraq, and the former Yugoslavia. 25. In the case of Haiti, a neighbor of Cuba not as close to the United as Cuba, the United States led an effort to obtain and did obtain a United Nations Security Council embargo and blockade against that country due to the existence of a military dictatorship in power less than 3 years. 26. United Nations Security Council Resolution 940 of July 31, 1994, subsequently authorized the use of "all necessary means" to restore the "democratically elected government of Haiti," and the democratically elected government of Haiti was restored to power on October 15, 1994. 27. The Cuban people deserve to be assisted in a decisive manner to end the tyranny that has oppressed them for 36 years and the continued failure to do so constitutes ethically improper conduct by the international community. 28.For the past 36 years, the Cuban government has posed and continues to pose a national security threat to the United States."

72. 31 C.F.R. Sec. 515.204.

73. North Korea, 31 C.F.R. Sec. 500.201(d)(1); Cambodia, 31 C.F.R. Sec. 500.201(d)(2); North Vietnam, 31 C.F.R. Sec. 500.201(d)(3); South Vietnam, 31 C.F.R. Sec. 500.201(d)(4) (now being repealed.)

duced in Cuba are not reexported to the United States. It was restated again in 1991.[74]

House and Senate versions vary in terms of the specific provisions, but do no more than add to the existing enforcement apparatus. Section 109 of H.R. 927 merely provides the Secretary of the Treasury with an additional means of ensuring compliance with pre-existing U.S. laws,[75] by allowing him to require certificates of origin and providing penalties if they are fraudulent. Section 110 of S. 381 prohibits the increase of the absolute quantity of sugar imported to the U.S. above that allocated in 1995 for any country that imports sugar from Cuba. Mindful of our GATT obligations, the Senate draft emphasizes that "Nothing in this provision shall abrogate or otherwise impair U.S. obligations under GATT to allow the minimum of 1,139,195 metric tons of sugar per year to enter the United States."

MYTH: HR 927 SECTION 401 CONTAINS LANGUAGE WHICH WILL PREVENT CANADIAN AND MEXICAN BUSINESS PERSONS AND THEIR FAMILIES FROM ENTERING OUR COUNTRY IN VIOLATION OF OUR TREATY OBLIGATIONS UNDER NAFTA, AND THUS BRAND US AS AN UNRELIABLE TRADING PARTNER

Reality

- Section 401 merely excludes from this country only those senior corporate executives, controlling shareholders, or other persons who knowingly and intentionally traffic in property of United States citizens which was illegally confiscated by Cuba.

- It is narrowly tailored, authorizes exceptions where in the national interest and is permissible under language in NAFTA which creates an exception to its provisions for actions necessary to our security interests and the enforcement of the Cuban embargo.

Discussion

The sponsors of Helms-Burton seek to supplement American foreign policy as expressed in the Cuban embargo. The twin purposes of the embargo are to force Cuba to restore lands and property unlawfully confiscated from United States citizens and to compel Cuba's return to the family of nations in the Western Hemisphere as a democracy which no longer exports aggression or oppresses its population.

To support this effort, section 401 of H.R. 927 complements Title III's focus on the problem of third party traffickers in illegally confiscated property. Where Title III provides U.S. citizens with access to Federal District Courts to remedy trafficking, section 401 and its Senate equivalent require that the Secretary of State shall exclude from entry into the United States, any alien who has confiscated property, the claim of which is owned by a U.S. national, or who knowingly and intentionally traffics in confiscated property after the enactment of the legislation. Excluded aliens include corporate officers, principals, controlling shareholders and family and agents. The Secretary is authorized to make exceptions, on a case-by-case basis, when in the interest of the United States. The section is to be enforced consistent with U.S. treaty obligations. In the Senate, comparable language appears in an amendment to the Foreign Relations Revitalization Act of 1995.

Some claim that this restriction may bar Canadian and Mexican business persons from access to the United States and that this would constitute a violation of the United States' obligations under the NAFTA treaty. In fact, language in NAFTA allows for the proposed restrictions.

NAFTA does require that its participants provide entry visas to business persons for purposes of developing economic opportunities. Chapter 16 of NAFTA provides that a business person who resides in a contracting party must be afforded a temporary visa to

---

74. The Cuban Democracy Act, Pub.L.No. 102-484, Title XVII, 106 Stat. 2575 (1992).

75. Section 515.204 of title 31 C.F.R. prohibits the importation of, or dealings in, goods that are of Cuban origin. Section 902(c) of the Food Security Act of 1985 requires verification from those countries which are net importers of sugar that no sugar destined for the U.S. is of Cuban origin.

enter into the territory of another contracting party. However, this provision recognizes that other concerns may restrict or prevent entry and thus requires entry only if the person seeking a visa "otherwise qualifies for entry under applicable measures relating to public health and safety [or] national security . . . ."[76] It also allows entry to be conditioned upon the business person otherwise complying with existing immigration measures applicable to temporary entry."[77]

As we have seen elsewhere, the "national security" exception to our treaty obligations is, under international law, a valid treaty authority for our initiation of boycotts and secondary boycotts. Certainly, it is also authority to prevent the entry into the United States of persons who have violated our laws.

MYTH: TITLE III WILL COMPLICATE A FUTURE SETTLEMENT WITH CUBA OF CERTIFIED CLAIMS

Reality

* To the contrary, it is the Cuban Government's policy of selling and/or transferring confiscated properties to foreign investors that *is complicating* any attempt to return the properties to their original owners even after Castro is no longer in power.

* This consequence of Cuban Government conduct is recognized by the State Department in its periodic "Buyer Beware" cable to foreign governments: "Cuba may be offering equity in Cuban factories and other assets, including properties expropriated from U.S. nationals, in order to obtain hard currency, ... *Transfer of these properties to third parties would complicate any attempt to return them to their original owners* [emphasis added]."

* Having an added deterrent, like a private right of action, will not complicate resolution. Rather, it helps, as it will cause a would-be investor to give second thoughts about investing in Cuba in confiscated American properties or activities derived from confiscated properties.

* Just by its introduction, the Helms-Dole bill has caused foreign investors to re-assess investing in Cuba:

  * "Foreign investments in Cuba are slowing because of concerns over a bill in the U.S. Congress that would tighten the U.S. trade embargo..." [*Miami Herald,* June 23, 1995].

  * "One thing seems clear already. The chilling specter of lawyers enforcing the embargo has led more than one foreign investor to conclude that investing in Cuba nueva may not be worth the risk of having their U.S. assets attacked by companies that did business [i.e., that have claims to confiscated properties] on the island". [*National Law Journal,* July 10, 1995]

  * The right of action will help reduce the pool of certified claimants eligible for espousal by providing an offset for recoveries against third party traffickers. This will make a future settlement more likely and easier to achieve by lightening the burden on any post-Castro government, and increasing the *pro rata* share of the certified claimants whose cases remain unsettled.

Discussion

Title III provides United States citizens possessing claims for illegal confiscation of their property by Cuba in the 1960's to obtain a remedy in Federal Court from third parties who enter into business

---

76. NAFTA art. 1603(1).

77. *Id.* at Annex 1603(A)(1). For the United States, "existing immigration measures" are defined as the immigration laws contained in Section 100(a) (15)(B) of the Immigration and Nationality Act ("INA"), 1952, as amended. *Id.* at Annex 1603 (A)(3). Pursuant to the INA, an alien may be excluded from the United States if the Secretary of State believes, based on reasonable grounds, that his/her entry or proposed activity in the United States would have potentially serious adverse foreign policy consequences for the United States. INA Section 212(a)(3)(C), 8 U.S.C. Section 1182(a)(3)(C).

ventures with Cuba and take possession of or traffick in what is essentially stolen property. Obviously, these parties enter into such ventures in order to profit at the expense of our citizens. Clearly, it is appropriate, where we can, for us to protect our citizens against the consequences of such behavior. And, as is the case with all similar legislation, it is also the intent of the drafters of the legislation that Title III serve as a deterrent to this conduct. Indeed, there is some indication that the proposed legislation is already slowing investment by third parties in such projects.

Critics of Title III argue that the litigation which may result from Title III will forestall Cuba's ability to provide restitution in a timely manner. Further, claiming that Cuba's bill for its unlawful confiscations may reach 100 billion dollars at present day values with interest, they argue that the Title III litigation may deplete Cuba's minimal resources for payment through a negotiated espousal of the claims certified by the Cuban Claims Commission in the 1960's.

Nothing could be further from the truth. A lump sum settlement by espousal is unworkable now, without Title III. Cuba does not have any cash assets to make a meaningful payment. International law presently favors either full compensation or restitution. An examination of the international law standards governing compensation in cases of unlawful expropriation[78] leads to the conclusion that a future government would have serious difficulty meeting those standards monetarily[79]. Cuba's present inability to fulfill its obligations under existing agreements, such as that with Spain, is additional evidence that an adequate settlement of certified claims will have to involve restitution in a form other than money.[80]

Title III should have the effect of preserving the confiscated properties from exploitation, complex title arguments, and dissipation. For those properties for which espousal nonetheless will be considered, Title III will make a successful negotiation more likely, as it will help reduce the number of certified claimants. Its election of remedies provision requires that claimants who prevail in litigation against third party traffickers and satisfy their claim financially against solvent defendants shall be eliminated from the espousal class.[81]

---

78. Lawful expropriation must be for a public purpose, non-discriminatory, in accordance with due process of law, and on payment of compensation equal to the fair market value of the property. NAFTA, Article 1110, Expropriation and Compensation. Cuba's confiscations of the property of registered claimants were discriminatory. Law No. 851 confiscated all property owned by U.S. citizens. See Resolution No. 1, *Gaceta Oficial* (August 6, 1960), p.1.

79. There is a growing consensus that the remedy for unlawful confiscations is full compensation or restitution. See *Texas Overseas Petroleum Co. & California Asiatic Oil Co. v Libyan Arab Republic*, 17 ILM 1 (1978); *Amoco Int'l Fin. Corp.*, 15 Iran-U.S. C.T.R. 189 (1987 II). See also Norton, "A Law of the Future or a Law of the Past? Modern Tribunals and the International Law of Expropriation," 85 *American Journal of International Law* 474 at 489 (July 1991). Some of the recent settlements made by the U.S. with other countries have obtained full compensation, though the agreed upon rate varies. Registered claimants obtained 100% compensation and 89% interest in the settlement with Vietnam. See transcript of additional questions submitted for the record to Under Secretary Peter Tarnoff by Senator Helms, Senate Foreign Relations Committee, Western Hemisphere Subcommittee, May 21, 1995, question 16, p. 2. This presents a striking contrast with the settlement between the U.S. and China, which resulted in a recovery of approximately 40 cents on the dollar, and led to the case of *Shanghai Power*. See "Agreement between the Government of the United States of America and the Government of the People's Republic of China Concerning the Settlement of Claims," May 11, 1979, 18 *International Legal Materials* 551 (1979).

80. The Cuban settlement with Spain provides ample evidence of this. Although they reached an agreement in 1986 which would allow recovery of about 12 cents on the dollar to be paid over a fifteen year period, they have effectively defaulted. Barbara Ehrich Locke, Esq.: "Resolution of U.S. Claims Against Cuba, Comparative Models," p. 4. Paper presented at "The Evolving Cuban Marketplace: What Every U.S. Company Needs to Know," May 5, 1994, Washington D.C., sponsored by Holland and Knight. U.S. claims amount to $1.8 billion in 1960 dollars, $1.6 of which are corporate claims. See *Final Report of the Cuban Claims Program*, Foreign Claims Settlement Commission of the United States, 414 (1972). It is estimated that value of blocked Cuban assets in this country is no more than $149 million. Stanley J. Glod, "Potential Approaches to the Resolution of U.S. Claims," p. 3 in CTW 95.

81. H.R. 927, 104th Cong., 1st. Sess. § 302(e) (1995); S. 908, 104th Cong., 1st Sess. § 2302(1) (1995).

In any event, Title III's impact on settlement of the property issue with Cuba, by encouraging restitution, does not create a new issue. Restitution would have played a large part in the settlement of certified claims under existing United States law. The Foreign Assistance Act mandates that no government of Cuba will be eligible for U.S. aid until "such a government has taken appropriate steps according to international law standards to return to United States citizens ... or to provide equitable compensation to such citizens and entities for property taken ... by the Government of Cuba."[82]

Restitution is certainly then the only viable option for satisfaction of the certified claims. Cuban Government's transfer or waste of the illegally confiscated properties will make any restitution program more difficult. The State Department has recognized this in its "Buyer Beware" cables: "Transfer of these properties would complicate any attempts to return them to their original owners."[83]

Discouraging third parties from trafficking in these properties protects the interests of certified claimants and increases the likelihood of a settlement by preserving the possibility of restitution.

---

82. 22 U.S.C.A. 2370 (2)

83. Warren Christopher, "Buyer Beware: Cuba May be Selling American Property," Cable to all United States Diplomatic and Consular Posts, September 9, 1993; State Department Action Cable re Unilever joint venture with the Cuban Government-owned firm, Suchel, for the marketing and manufacture of Unilever products in Cuba; State Department cable re Unilever investment involving expropriated U.S. property in Cuba, Ref. (A) 94 STATE 175951; Lawrence C. Eagleburger, "Buyer Beware: Cuba May be Selling American Property," Ref. A (91 Rome 18558) January 1991. The cables' reference to "original" owners is actually inappropriate. In fact, the ultimate reality is that these "original" owners remain the *only owners* recognized by international law.

PRELIMINARY ANALYSIS OF RETIREMENT PROGRAMS FOR PERSONNEL IN THE MINISTRY OF THE ARMED FORCES AND MINISTRY OF INTERIOR OF THE REPUBLIC OF CUBA

Ricardo Donate-Armada

Law-Decrees 101 and 102 of the Republic of Cuba provide retirement, disability, and survivor pensions for the personnel of the Ministry of the Armed Forces (MINFAR) and the Ministry of Interior (MININT) of the Republic of Cuba. These two laws effective February 24, 1988 provide better pension benefits than those provided under Law 24 on Social Security that provides pension coverage for almost every other Cuban worker. The generous benefit provisions under Laws 101 and 102 combined with the size of the work force in the two Ministries (estimated at between 5% and 10% of the Cuban labor force) produce significant financial obligations that would have to be addressed during a Cuban transition to a market economy.

This paper describes the benefit provisions under both laws, pointing out the differences in the treatment of the MINFAR and the MININT employees. It also points out the differences between the pension promises for the members of this select group, and those for the great majority of the Cuban labor force. Estimates of the costs of these programs are calculated using an individual actuarial model that reflects Cuban mortality and various possible economic scenarios. Finally the paper contains a brief outline of

cost reducing alternatives to the current pension schemes for the personnel of these two Ministries during and beyond the Cuban transition to a market economy.

LAW-DECREE 101 OF SOCIAL SECURITY FOR THE REVOLUTIONARY ARMED FORCES (FAR)

Law-Decree 101 of Social Security for the Revolutionary Armed Forces (Law 101) was signed by the Cuban President, Mr. Fidel Castro Ruz on February 24, 1988.[1] Its stated purpose is the improvement of the living conditions of the military personnel and their families. It replaces Law 1322 of November 29, 1976 whose benefit provisions were found lacking according to Law 101's preface. Law 101 provides pensions to the military personnel in the event of either retirement from the military, or disability during active military duty, as well as pensions to the surviving dependents of military personnel who died during active military duty.[2] Law 101 covers not only current active military personnel and their families but also those who have retired under the previous legislation, Law 1322.[3]

The pension amounts under Law 101 are determined according to formulae that take into account final

---

1. *Gaceta Oficial de la República de Cuba* (February 24, 1988), "Decreto-Ley 101 de Seguridad Social de las Fuerzas Armadas Revolucionarias."

2. *Ibid*, Chapter I, Article 3.

3. *Ibid*, Chapter I, Article 2.

pensionable pay and the years of pensionable service. The final pensionable pay is determined as the sum of the last monthly salary, which is based on military rank and job position, and the seniority pay[4] but in the case of military personnel paid according to a civilian pay scale the final pensionable pay is equal to their last monthly slary.[5] For participants in special historical events such as the assault on the Moncada barracks or the landing of the Granma, years of pensionable service include not only service in the FAR but also the years elapsed since those events. Actual months of service are also increased by a multiplier that ranges from a factor of three (3) for those involved in the attack on the Moncada barracks and the landing of the Granma, to a factor of two (2) for jet pilots and one and a half (1.5) for pilots, seagoing personnel, Guantanamo border troops, air assault troops, paratroopers, divers, and special education instructors.[6]

Retirement pensions are called seniority pensions because they can be granted according to years of military service independent of reaching any particular age. Seniority pensions are granted after either 25 years of service, or after 20 years of service but less than 25 years of service, or at age 50 after 25 years of combined civilian and military service of which at least 12.5 years has been in military service.[7]

The monthly seniority pension is calculated as the product of the final pensionable pay and a base percentage that varies according to retirement age plus an additional accrual per year of service in excess of the years of service required for retirement. For those with at least 25 years of service and age 55 and over, the retirement pension is equal to 60% of pensionable pay plus 3% of final pensionable pay per year of

service in excess of 25 but no more than 90% of final pensionable pay.[8] The seniority pension formula for someone younger than age 55 but with more than 25 years of service is similar to the preceding formula except that the base accrual rate is 50% rather than 60% and the pension amount cannot exceed 80% of final pensionable pay. At no time the seniority pension can be less than $126 per month.[9]

For example, a member of the FAR could retire at age 45 after 25 years of service and receive a monthly pension equal to 50% of his final pensionable pay for the rest of his life. A jet pilot would be eligible to receive a similar pension while in his mid-thirties after only 12.5 years of active service, as would be the case for a seagoing sailor after 16.67 years of service. The top commanders of the FAR, Fidel Castro Ruz and Raúl Castro Ruz, whose service dates back to the Moncada assault, have accrued to this date 126 years of pensionable service (July 26, 1953 to July 26, 1995 times a factor of 3) but their pensions are capped at 90% of their final pensionable pay ($450 per month[10]) or $405 per month.

Those collecting seniority pensions are entitled to receive their pensions with no reduction while employed in the civilian sector after retirement from active military service. The only exception applies to those who have completed higher or professional education, and who are working in a position similar to the one they held while in active military duty.[11] The pension for this type of retiree is reduced by the amount that the sum of their Law 101 pension and their civilian salary exceeds their last military salary. This and other features of Law 101 can be waived or

---

4. *Ibid*, Chapter I, Article 8.

5. *Ibid*, Chapter I, Article 9.

6. *Ibid*, Chapter I, Article 13.

7. *Ibid*, Chapter II, Article 17.

8. *Ibid*, Chapter II, Article 19.

9. *Ibid*, Chapter II, Article 23.

10. *Gaceta Oficial de la República de Cuba* (June 29, 1981), "Resolución No. 769," Tercero.

11. "Decreto-Ley 101 de Seguridad Social," *op cit.*, Chapter V, Article 52.

ignored by a decision of the Minister of the FAR[12] who can also assign special pensions to those whom he deems deserving.

Law 101 also provides pensions payable to a MIN-FAR member in the event of total or partial permanent disability. The amount of the disability pension is based on final pensionable pay at the date of disability, the number of years of service, whether the disability is related to combat conditions or military service, and whether the disability is total or partial. Short term disability payments are provided under a separate set of FAR regulations.[13]

The amount of a total and permanent disability pension ranges from 75% to 90% of final pensionable pay if the disability is directly related to military activities and from 60% to 75% of final pensionable pay if the disability is not directly related to military activities.[14] Partial and permanent disability pensions range from 40% to 50% of pay for military related disabilities and from 30% and 40% of pay for non-military related disabilities. Disability coverage is normally extended to the three months after leaving military service but it is extended indefinitely for those whose disability is directly related to injuries or illnesses suffered while in active military service or during the insurrection against the Batista regime.

Law 101 also provides pensions to the surviving relatives of military personnel who died or who are declared presumed dead during their active military service, and to the surviving relatives of military pensioners. The survivor's pension is calculated as a percentage of either the applicable seniority pension or the disability pension. The continuation percentage varies from 70% for one dependent to 100% for three (3) or more dependents.[15] Dependents eligible to receive these survivors pensions are spouses, children, grandparents and grandchildren.[16]

Law 101 pensions are paid through the Population Agencies of the People's Savings Bank (Agencias de Población del Banco Popular de Ahorro) from the general funds budgeted for Social Security.[17] Law 101 does not address the issue of the contribution amounts or the method of financing the military pensions during the active military service of the MINFAR personnel. It gives the Minister of the MINFAR (currently Raúl Castro Ruz) the right to decree additional pensions, increases in pensionable service, and special payment conditions to reward members of the MINFAR who are perceived particularly deserving of special treatment due to extraordinary service or personal needs.[18]

Law 101 pensions can be suspended, modified, or terminated under a variety of circumstances. Among these, two special circumstances requiring the termination of the pension payments should be noted: permanently emigrating from Cuba, and being sentenced to a jail term for a crime against State Security.[19]

LAW-DECREE 102 OF SOCIAL SECURITY FOR THE MINISTRY OF INTERIOR

Law-Decree 102 of Social Security for the Ministry of Interior (Law 102) was also signed by President Fidel Castro Ruz on February 24, 1988. Its stated purpose is to improve the living conditions of the Ministry of Interior personnel whose Social Security coverage is deemed insufficient due to the nature of their jobs. Law 102 provides pension benefits for the "combatants" of the MININT and their dependents

---

12. *Ibid*, Disposiciones Especiales, Primera.

13. *Ibid*, Chapter III, Article 24.

14. *Ibid*, Chapter III, Article 27.

15. *Ibid*, Chapter IV, Article 41.

16. *Ibid*, Chapter III, Article 35.

17. *Ibid*, Chapter I, Article 6.

18. *Ibid*, Disposiciones Especiales, Primera/Segunda.

19. *Ibid*, Chapter VI, Article 58.

in the event of retirement, disability, or death.[20] Law 102 is very similar to Law 101 except for some key provisions that are noted in this section.

As in Law 101, pensions are provided after 25 years of service but there is a minimum retirement age of 45.[21] Seniority pensions are only provided following a decision by the MININT to retire an employee or after an employee receives approval to retire from the MININT.[22]

As is the case for those covered by Law 101, those under Law 102 have their years of service counted from either their date of joining the Ministry of Interior or from the date on which they participated in a historical event such as the assault on the Moncada barracks or the Granma landing.[23] Also as under Law 101, years of service are increased by a multiplier applied to special service periods except that there is no multiplier for pilots or seagoing personnel, and there is a multiplier of one and a half (1.5) for service in the border guards' units.[24] Final pensionable pay is determined based on the last monthly salary according to rank and seniority.[25]

Pension payments under Law 102 are made from the same source used for paying the pensions under Law 101: the Social Security budget. Law 102 does not address the issue of the type or level of contributions required to finance the pension accruals during the active service period of the MININT personnel. The Minister of Interior also has the power to provide additional pensions, to increase pensionable service, or to establish special payment conditions without regard to other provisions of Law 102.

COMPARISON OF PENSIONS PROVIDED UNDER LAW-DECREES 101 AND 102 AND THOSE PROVIDED UNDER SOCIAL SECURITY

The benefits provided under Laws 101 and 102 are more generous than those provided under Law 24 of Social Security (Law 24). This more generous treatment extends to each of Law 24's monetary benefits: retirement pensions, permanent disability pensions, and survivors' pensions. The most significant improvements over the provisions of Law 24 are discussed below.

Pensionable Pay

Pensions are calculated under Laws 101 and 102 based on final monthly salary, while under Law 24 they are calculated using the average pay of the highest five (5) years of the last ten (10) years preceding the pensionable event: retirement, disability, or death. This difference in defining the pensionable pay is not important in a constant salary environment (one in which the salary stays constant during the ten years preceding the pensionable event), but in a normal inflationary environment where salaries are expected to increase over time, having pensionable pay based on the last monthly salary provides a larger pension than when it is based on the average of the last five years.

Because of this definition of pensionable salary, pensions under Laws 101 and 102 are greater than equivalent pensions under Law 24 by a factor, roughly equal to twice the salary increase rate of the averaging period. For example, Law 101/102 pensions would be 6% greater than Law 24 pensions if one assumes a modest salary increase rate of 3%, and 49% greater if one assumes a high salary increase rate of 25%.

---

20. *Gaceta Oficial de la República de Cuba* (February 24, 1988), "Decreto-Ley 102 de Seguridad Social de las Fuerzas Armadas Revolucionarias," Chapter I, Article 2.

21. *Ibid*, Chapter III, Article 12.

22. *Ibid*, Chapter III, Article 11.

23. *Ibid*, Chapter II, Article 6.

24. *Ibid*, Chapter II, Article 8.

25. *Ibid*, Chapter I, Article 5.

In addition, pensionable salary under Law 24 is calculated using 100% of the annual salary up to $3,000 and 50% of the annual salary above that amount. Laws 101/102 recognize all pensionable salary at 100%. This means that anyone earning more than $250 per month would receive a greater pension under Laws 101/102 than under Law 24. The additional value ranges from a 5% greater pension for a captain who earns approximately $300[26] per month to 29% greater pension for the Minister of Defense who earns approximately $450 per month.[27]

Retirement Age

Law 24 sets a normal retirement age of 60 for men and 55 for women after 25 years of normal employment conditions, defined as conditions that do not lead to premature aging or deteriorating health. This is in contrast to Law 101 which does not set a normal retirement age but rather a service requirement of 25 years and Law 102 which sets a normal retirement age of 45 after 25 years of service. Because of these retirement conditions those retiring under Laws 101/102 are expected to receive pension payments during a longer period than those retiring under Law 24.

The total value of these additional payments can be determined as the increase in the annuity value of the pension due to the earlier commencement age. The magnitude of this additional annuity value depends on the interest rate used to discount the future pension payments. For illustrative interest rates of 0%, 6%, and 9%, the annuity value of the Laws 101/102 pensions is increased by 66%, 28%, and 20% respectively due to pensions being paid starting at age 45 rather than at age 60.

Minimum Pension

Laws 101/102 provide a minimum pension of $126 per month. This is about twice the minimum monthly pension of $60 provided under Law 24. The relatively high minimum pension under Laws 101/102 provides a replacement income greater than 50% for all pensioners with monthly salaries of less

than $252 per month which seems to apply to all FAR personnel below the rank of captain.[28]

Post-Retirement Employment

Laws 101/102 allow for the collection of a full pension after retirement as long as the pensioner has not received higher education and is not employed in the same kind of job performed while in active service. If both these conditions are met, the pension is reduced by the amount that the sum of the pension and the current salary exceeds the last monthly salary while on active service with the FAR or MININT. Law 24 applies the same pension reduction formula to all retirees.

The author does not have access to any documentary evidence on the application of this provision of Laws 101/102. Nevertheless, anecdotal information suggests that FAR and MININT pensioners who are retired around age 45, and who join a civilian enterprise after retirement, are collecting both their full pensions and their full civilian salaries. In a market economy this practice would lead employers to hire military pensioners over equivalently qualified civilian personnel because they have lower salary requirements. In a highly politicized non-market economy with limited desirable employment options such as Cuba today, this policy leads to the exclusion of civilian personnel from many desirable employment positions because of the established relationships among former FAR and MININT personnel, and the classification of large sectors of the Cuban civilian economy as national security sectors.

COSTS AND LIABILITIES OF PENSIONS UNDER LAW-DECREES 101/102

To accurately establish the costs and liabilities of the pension promises under Laws 101/102 one would need far greater data than what is readily available from published sources about the FAR and the MININT. This section details an estimate of the costs and liabilities for Laws 101/102 first from an individual participant perspective and then in aggregate for

---

26. Defense Intelligence Agency, *Handbook on the Cuban Armed Forces* (May 1986), p. 1-27, Table 3.

27. *Gaceta Oficial de la República de Cuba* (June 29, 1981), "Resolución No. 769," Tercero.

28. *Handbook on the Cuban Armed Forces, loc cit.*

the entire FAR and MININT. This section is divided into two parts: the first briefly describes the assumptions and methods used in determining the costs and liabilities, while the second details the results of this estimation.

Assumptions and Methods

Due to the lack of data on the demographic composition of the FAR and MININT personnel, costs and liabilities have been estimated assuming hypothetical participants under both an average salary method and an average pension method. Both methods result in ranges of possible costs, expressed in pesos and as percentage of salaries. The average pension method also provides a range of values for the pension liabilities.

Average Salary Method: Under the average salary method, costs are determined as a percentage of salary for a hypothetical participant who joined either the MININT or MINFAR at age 20 and who will retire after 25 years of service at age 45. Costs are determined under two salary scenarios: Slow Track and Fast Track. The salary under the Slow Track Scenario is assumed to remain constant throughout the entire 25 year career, while under the Fast Track Scenario, the monthly salary increases annually from $120 at hire to $450 at retirement. The Slow Track Scenario reflects the career of a noncommissioned officer who is never promoted while the Fast Track Scenario simulates the career of a noncommissioned officer who rises to minister at retirement. The Slow Track Scenario results provide a lower limit on the costs of these programs while the Fast Track Scenario results provide the upper limit.

Costs under the average salary method are determined by first calculating a pension cost as percentage of salary by dividing the present value at age 20 of a pension equal to 50% of final salary payable from age 45 by the present value of salaries from age 20 to age 45. These present values are determined using representative interest rates of 0%, 6%, and 9%. No actuarial decrements are assumed during the 25

years of active service but mortality derived from a Cuban life expectancy table[29] is assumed in the post-retirement period. The total cost of the program is then calculated by multiplying this percentage of salary by a total payroll that assumes 180,000 active participants with an average salary of $250 per month. This total cost does not reflect the accumulated cost for past pension liabilities.

Average Pension Method: Under the average pension method, the present value of future pensions is determined assuming an average monthly pension of $126 per participant. This present value is calculated assuming six different service scenarios: 25, 20, 15, 10, 5, and zero years to retirement at age 45, and three different interest rates scenarios: 0%, 6%, and 9%. As under the average salary method, no actuarial decrements are assumed while in active service and Cuban mortality is assumed after retirement at age 45. Similarly the estimates are based on the assumption of 180,000 active participants with an average salary of $250 per month.

Costs under the average pension method are determined as the sum of two components: a Normal Cost, and an Amortization Cost. The Normal Cost is determined by dividing the present value of future pensions by the total years of pensionable service (25). The Amortization Cost is determined by amortizing over the number of years to retirement the Accrued Pension Liability. The Accrued Pension Liability is determined by multiplying the Normal Cost by the number of years of past service. Costs under this method are also expressed as a percentage of total salary by dividing the sum of the Normal Cost and the Amortization Cost by the total payroll.

Estimates of the Costs and Liabilities of the Pensions under Laws 101/102

Tables 1 and 2 detail the results of applying the pension cost methodology described above. It should be emphasized that these cost estimates are very rough and that a more accurate estimate of the pension costs and liabilities would require far more detailed

---

29. Ricardo A. Donate-Armada, "Cuban Social Security: A Preliminary Actuarial Analysis of Law #24 of Social Security," in *Cuba in Transition—Volume* 4 (Washington: Association for the Study of the Cuban Economy, 1994), Table V, p. 168.

demographic information. Still, the above described methods allow for the establishment of a range of possible accrual costs for Laws 101/102 pensions.

The average salary method produces current service accrual costs that range from 637 million pesos to 32 million pesos. The most realistic interest scenario of 6% narrows this range to between 140 million pesos and 65 million pesos with a median accrual cost of 103 million pesos. This accrual cost does not reflect the additional cost of recognizing any accrued pension liabilities for past service to date.

The average pension method results in a wider range of accrual costs, principally because it includes the additional cost of amortizing the past service liabilities over the remaining years to retirement. The current service accrual costs under this scenario range from 13 million pesos to 8.5 billion pesos. It should be noted that among these scenarios the more realistic ones are those assuming 10 or 15 years to retirement and an interest rate of 6%. The accrual cost for these two scenarios range from 122 million pesos to 243 million pesos with a median accrual cost of 183 million pesos.

It is interesting to note that the results for the 20 years to retirement scenario under the average pension method are similar to those for the Slow Track Salary scenario under the average salary method. There is a similar correlation between the 15 years to retirement scenario under the average pension method and the Fast Track Salary scenario under the average salary method.

Both methods ignore the current cost of Laws 101/102 for pensions in payment. Monthly retirement pensions could range from the minimum monthly pension of $126 to 90% of the maximum pensionable salary or approximately $405 if one takes the official Minister's salary as the maximum monthly salary. The number of pensioners under both Laws 101/102 could be estimated as 20% of the number of active participants or 36,000. This would lead to total annual pension payments of between 54 million pesos and 175 million pesos with a median of 115 million pesos.

Putting together the median estimates for both actives' accrual costs and pensions in payment, the total annual costs for Laws 101/102 could be estimated to fall between 218 million pesos and 298 million pesos. The low end does not include the accrual costs for any past service liabilities.

TRANSITION ISSUES AND RECOMMENDATIONS

From the previous section it is clear that there are significant financial issues that must be faced during the transition to a market economy because of size of the pension liabilities created by Laws 101/102. The beneficiaries of these pension promises are probably the individuals most responsible for placing Cuba in its current economic distress, not to mention its political situation, but unless one could bring about a complete liquidation of existing legislation, institutions, and relevant individuals, the transition team would be faced with the challenge of reducing the MINFAR and MININT ranks in a gradual and orderly manner.

Laws 101/102 could provide a mechanism to cashier many if not all of those who would be most antagonistic to a transition to a market economy. At the same time the generous benefits regime under Laws 101/102 cannot be continued without putting serious pressures on the finances of the new government or on the health of the transition economy.

Whatever decision is reached regarding the ultimate fate of Laws 101/102, a complete actuarial study should be completed to determine the liabilities and future costs of their pension obligations. This study requires the identification of all those eligible for benefits under both laws including those in active service and those receiving pensions. For those receiving pensions an additional effort should be made to identify which portion of their pension was calculated according to the letter of the law and which portion is due to discretionary decisions by the relevant ministers or government officials.

The actuarial study should calculate each participant's accrued benefit and corresponding annuity value. The calculations for active participants can be used in the establishment of a compensation baseline for cashiering active MINFAR and MININT personnel. Annuity values for pensions in payment will be used to establish the funding requirements for the pensions in payment.

If Laws 101/102 are kept as the bases for providing pensions for military and security personnel, they should be amended to improve administration and accountability. The first step should be to separate the funding and administration of these pensions from the administration and budget of other Social Security programs. Both laws should be amended to eliminate the Ministers' discretionary powers to provide or improve benefits, and the service multipliers due to participation in historical events. They should also be amended to permit the payment of pensions to those leaving the country. Special effort should be made to revoke additional pensions granted in the past for reasons other than economic hardship.

An alternate system to Laws 101/102 would be to provide benefits in line with those provided by a revamped Social Security system. This may involve the establishment of individual retirement accounts which are funded by participant contributions at the same level as the general Social Security system, and supplemented by additional government contributions for increases in salary or rank, or performance of meritorious services. This system will provide benefits which are similar to those of the general population and it is subject to the same annual budget discipline required to establish payroll budgets. It also has the advantage of vesting the participants in pension accruals at the time they earn them.

It would be advisable also to establish a fund for paying the old pensions under Laws 101/102. At its inception, this fund could be built up from the proceeds of sale of military properties and surplus equipment. Any unfunded liability should be funded over the long-term from general revenues. It is beyond the scope of this paper to determine the specifics of establishing this fund.

CONCLUDING REMARKS

This paper provides a first estimate of the financial costs and liabilities under the special pension regime of the MINFAR and MININT personnel. Although the lack of accurate and detailed demographic data hampers the estimation of these costs, this paper provides a basis to roughly estimate the annual cost of the Laws 101/102 at around 300 million pesos assuming 180,000 active participants and 36,000 retirees. Any transition to a market economy should include placing these pensions on a sound financial footing which would include recognizing any legitimate promises made to exiting pensioners but replace the current system with one that is more financially sound.

Table 1. **Estimate of Annual Costs for Active Participants under Laws 101/102 under Average Salary Method**

			Interest Rate=0%	Interest Rate=6%	Interest Rate=9%
1.		**Costs as a Percentage of Annual Salary**			
	a.	Slow Track Salary	63%	12%	6%
	b.	Fast Track Salary	118%	26%	14%
2.		**Total Annual Salaries**			
	a.	Number of Participants	180,000	180,000	180,000
	b.	Average Monthly Salary (Pesos)	250	250	250
	c.	Total Annual Salaries (Pesos)	540,000,000	540,000,000	540,000,000
		(2.a.) x (2.b.) x 12			
3.		**Total Annual Costs (In Millions of Pesos)**			
	a.	Fast Track Salary	340	65	32
		(1.a.) x (2.c.)			
	b.	Slow Track Salary	637	140	76
		(1.b.) x (2.c.)			

Table 2. Estimate of Annual Costs for Active Participants under Laws 101/102 under Average Pension Method

		Interest Rate=0%	Interest Rate=6%	Interest Rate=9%
1	**Costs as a Percentage of Salary**			
	a. 25 Years of Service to Retirement	63%	6%	2%
	b. 20 Years of Service to Retirement	79%	12%	6%
	c. 15 Years of Service to Retirement	105%	23%	12%
	d. 10 Years of Service to Retirement	157%	45%	28%
	e. 5 Years of Service to Retirement	315%	113%	77%
	f. 0 Years of Service to Retirement	1574%	688%	519%
2	**Total Annual Salaries (Pesos)**	540,000,000	540,000,000	540,000,000
	(See Table I, 2.c.)			
3	**Total Annual Costs (Millions of Pesos)**			
	(1._) x (2.)			
	a. 25 Years of Service to Retirement	340	35	13
	b. 20 Years of Service to Retirement	425	65	30
	c. 15 Years of Service to Retirement	567	122	66
	d. 10 Years of Service to Retirement	850	243	149
	e. 5 Years of Service to Retirement	1,700	609	416
	f. 0 Years of Service to Retirement	8,502	3,716	2,802
4	**Accrued Pension Liability**			
	a. 25 Years of Service to Retirement	-	-	-
	b. 20 Years of Service to Retirement	1,700,450,237	231,744,592	99,978,933
	c. 15 Years of Service to Retirement	3,400,900,474	620,253,080	307,659,962
	d. 10 Years of Service to Retirement	5,101,350,710	1,245,057,805	710,059,482
	e. 5 Years of Service to Retirement	6,801,800,947	2,221,557,601	1,456,686,037
	f. 0 Years of Service to Retirement	8,502,251,184	3,716,181,504	2,801,615,040

ISSUES OF LEGITIMACY AND CONSTITUTIONALISM IN THE CUBAN TRANSITION

Mario Antonio Rivera

There is an unspoken assumption in much of the popular media coverage as well as academic treatment of Cuba that the Castro regime's longevity is tantamount to legitimacy, under the further assumption that his hold on power indicates a significant reservoir of majority support. This support is taken to stem from the social welfare gains putatively made during thirty-six years of Revolutionary rule. There are at least two difficulties with this position: (1) It is a facile stance with little empirical grounding, and it cannot dispose of the counter argument that longevity derived from the powers of what Castro himself has admitted is a repressive state (at least as far as freely expressed dissent is concerned) is particularly devoid of legitimacy, on both moral and politico-legal grounds; (2) There is no way to know the extent of support for or disaffection with the regime absent freedom of expression and dissent, nor to gauge independently the extent and depth of Revolutionary accomplishments, especially against the base line of pre-1959 socioeconomic indicators, and the very existence of a near-totalitarian state apparatus that is oriented toward these ends calls into question the presumption of popular support.

These and other conflictive issues over definitions of the Cuban situation amount to a struggle over the definition of Cuban national identity. National identity has long been at issue in the policy area of Cuban immigration to the United States, and it figures centrally, though largely implicitly, in assessments of the current Cuban transition and its prospects. A balanced evaluation of these questions requires analysis of the issues of regime legitimacy, including the constitutionality of post-regime transitions, and necessary developments in political and social culture in Cuba.

DEBATES OVER THE CUBAN TRANSITION

Recent studies of post-Castro transitions in Cuba have often focused on "overthrow" scenarios, or suggest elements of post-regime restructuring which depend implicitly on such scenarios. Enabling conditions range from internal insurrection and domestic solutions to United States or international military intervention and, in effect, temporary occupation.[1] The emphasis also tends to be formal/legal and institutional, rather than functional or process-oriented, in the treatment of post-regime political and economic change. While acknowledging their value, this paper avoids these lines of argument to focus principally, in broad preliminary terms, on functional prerequisites for a constitutionally legitimate and normatively defensible political transition in Cuba, in direct contrast with the "longevity is legitimacy" premise.

---

1. As plausible as any "theory" of transition from communism with applicability to Cuba, is Jorge I. Domínguez's tongue-in-cheek "poof factor" hypothesis: "The experience of communist regimes in transition is that they hold on to power for a long time, seemingly in control. Then there's some incident—a disturbance, a demonstration—and, poof, it all comes apart rather suddenly." Quoted by Ricardo Chavira, *Dallas Morning News* (September 28, 1993).

For the sake of argument, specifically argumentation over constitutional legitimacy, the relevant premises of the analysis that follows are (1) that Cuba's 1940 Constitution—never repealed—may be regarded as still having validity, if only because it was long the focus of broad national consensus, even during and after the triumph of the Revolution, whose leaders (including Castro) often spoke of its full restoration; (2) that if it were somehow restored, its most progressive and far-sighted provisions—for example those concerning labor protection and civil rights—should be retained, and for once made enforceable, since criticisms of that Constitution often centered on its non-enforceability; and (3) that, in all likelihood, the entire document, if readopted, would be modified by (or under) an interim or "plebiscitary" government, as the pertinent provisions of the 1940 Constitution provide.

It is essential that any post-Castro Cuban transition be both constitutionally-grounded and maximally participatory. In general, issues of constitutional and governmental legitimacy and (implicitly) national identity and national reconciliation need to be better addressed in transition studies. It is for this reason that con-sideration of the status of the last democratically-enacted constitutional document of Cuba's is instructive in the context of a critical analysis of regime legitimacy.

If the 1940 Constitution were to be readopted provisionally, consideration should be given to amending several sections—regarding nationality (Articles 8 to 18), public office and civil service (Art. 97-117), the representative composition of the national legislature (Art. 119 ff.), and other matters—for which original dispositions have been overtaken by events, such as demographic transitions, or developments in employment law and in labor relations. Students of Cuban politics and law often make specific recommendations of this sort, which are logical in view of all that has transpired there during the last thirty five

years. However, the intention in assuming the applicability of the 1940 constitution is neither to insist upon it specifically nor suggest that any political structure could or should be imposed from without. Rather, it is intended as a heuristic argument, so as to insist on the imperative need for legitimacy—actual and perceived—from the very outset for any transitional government in Cuba.[2]

Were one to wager, the odds are that any post-Castro transition will be punctuated by social and political violence, that domestic order will be a paramount concern, and that constitutional questions will be relegated to the end of what could be an extended transition during which there will be other pressing priorities, such as the overhaul of public sector management. However, one might hope for more sanguine prospects, at least in view of the unexpectedly rapid and relatively bloodless, albeit chaotic, transitions in the former Soviet Union and among the Central and Eastern European states. Renewed exile debates about Cuban migration and unprecedented turns in U.S. immigration policy, as well as recent legislative initiatives to strengthen the U.S. embargo, make deliberation about transition prospects all the more pressing.

PRELIMINARY QUESTIONS: CONFLICT AND CONCILIATION

An operative assumption in this paper is that the Cuban transition will be directed toward major political and economic openings, discontinuous with the Castro regime, with a movement toward a market economy (or a mixed economy relying principally on market mechanisms) and a democratic political system. Another assumption is that the transition will very likely be contentious, involving many competing groups: domestic dissident or opposition groups with a claim to involvement in anti-regime activities, exile groups with like (or differing) claims, emerging political groups (including not only political parties but also more diffuse political movements, newly estab-

---

2. It bears repeating that this article does not advocate restoration of the 1940 Constitution as a necessity for the legitimacy of a transitional political system in Cuba; nonetheless, the fact that there is continuing debate about the 1940 *magna carta* in exile circles points to fundamental questions about the legitimacy of post-1959 impositive political structures, including Castro-era constitutions. There is no reason why the 1940 charter could not serve to lend legitimacy to a participatory political transition.

lished or reestablished labor and professional groups, and the like), and remnants of the previous regime wishing to participate (typically technocrats, along with Castro-era ministerial officials, many of whom might attest to clandestine, or simply surreptitious, resistance). Such patterns have been evident in Russia and Eastern Europe. It might be anticipated, moreover, that Cuba will be no less polarized and conflict-ridden during a transition than it has been for most of this century, and indeed for most of its history.

Consequently, a central question to consider is the following: What are the functional requirements for democratic political re-structuring in Cuba, in light of (a) the simultaneous transition to a market or mixed economy, and (b) the need for arbitration, mediation, and adjudication of interests, and for collaboration, if not immediate reconciliation, among many social and political groups with divergent viewpoints and values? Secondly, what sort of process should determine the legal and political structures which will constitute a new Cuban society so as to make for a substantive, rather than simply declarative, legitimacy?

RECONSTITUTING THE PUBLIC SPACE OF CIVIL SOCIETY

Guillermo O'Donnell and Philippe Schmitter characterize a typical post-authoritarian (or post-totalitarian) transition as follows, in a manner that seems apt in the present case:

> No description of the forms that [a restoration of civil society] can take could expect to be exhaustive: it might involve the resurgence of previous political parties or the formation of new ones ... the sudden appearance of books and magazines on themes long suppressed by censorship; the conversion of older institutions such as trade unions, and universities, from agents of government control into instruments of interests, ideals, and rage against the regime; the emergence of grass-roots organizations articulating demands long repressed or ignored by authoritarian rule; [and] the expression of radical concerns by reli-

gious and spiritual groups previously noted for their prudent accommodation to the authorities.[3]

These authors add that artists, intellectuals, professionals and professional bodies (new and old), and "[h]uman rights organizations, relatives of the victims of prison, torture, and murder, and often churches are the first to speak out" during both late regime and early post-regime transitional phases, along with, ironically, many of those individuals and groups who were most privileged under the previous regime, and who reassess it in light of its passing.[4]

Domestic human rights advocacy groups, most of relatively recent origin, would include the Association of the Defenders of Political Rights, the Cuban Commission for Human Rights and National Reconciliation, the Harmony Movement, and the Cuban Committee for Human Rights—these have worked on monitoring activities at considerable risk and under ever-changing rules, often with outside organizations, such as Americas Watch and Amnesty International. Exile groups of very different political orientations would include (most prominently) the Cuban American National Foundation, along with the avowedly pro-dialogue Cambio Cubano, the recently-formed, and militant, Cuban Unity group, and the Madrid-based, social democratic Cuban Democratic Platform. Finding an Archimedean point of agreement among these groups, which are putatively united in their opposition to the regime, would be a daunting task in itself; adding to them the Catholic Church and other religious groups, organized labor (which has been relatively outspoken and factional even under Castro), military officers and bureaucrats, municipalities-in-exile, and academics and other professionals, among many participants, complicates the task of concertation exponentially.

"Concertación," or concertation in politics and public policymaking, is a fond ideal in Latin America; in Cuba's case, concertation during and beyond a dem-

---

3. Guillermo O'Donnell and Philippe C. Schmitter, *Transitions from Authoritarian Rule: Tentative Conclusions about Uncertain Democracies* (Baltimore: The Johns Hopkins University Press, 1986), p. 49.

4. *Ibid.*, p. 51.

ocratic transition may be an unlikely prospect, but also a pragmatic necessity in any attempt at fundamentally reorienting a very fractionated Cuban society and polity. All of this presupposes significant modification of the extant political culture, which has been characterized since 1959, as Aguirre argues, by the "conventionalization of collective behavior" by means of mass organizations such as the Committees for the Defense of the Revolution and the Central Organization of Cuban Trade Unions, and by the electoral mobilization afforded by the 1976 socialist constitution.[5] Horowitz characterizes Cuba's political culture, along with North Korea's, as resting on the "pseudo forms of legitimacy" of family dynasties or dictatorships, which as such are resistant to liberalization—in conventional political terms—even more than they are averse to economic liberalization.[6]

Democratic political culture requires the widespread acceptance of democratic procedural rules and of differing interests, values, and perspectives. In other words, a civic culture of republicanism, entailing political participation, liberty, freedom of expression, pluralism, and tolerance of dissent, is necessary if Cuba is to move from ritualized to democratic forms of political behavior, as well as to abandon statism and overcentralization. Historically, republicanism has meant the development of a "public sphere of influence" for citizens and for voluntary groups and associations of all kinds. Democratic theory regards this space either as a market-like political arena or as a domain for interest mediation by the state, where power is competitively structured and conflict is contained by consensus.[7] Political tradition, and particularly constitutional tradition, in pluralist systems may be seen as the aggregate outcome of continual conflict and bargaining. Even when the resolution of conflict is really only an agreement to disagree, and

to build a space for continued interest competition—a very partial and temporary accord—it is normatively significant if it forms part of a vital democratic tradition.

To accept the provisionality and even ambiguity of pluralist democracy is difficult under the best conditions, much less during the contemplated transition in Cuba, when inherent pressures toward forced consensus would be great. However, it is precisely the move from forced conformity to free participation that is necessary, as a precondition, in fact, to new political institutions. Therefore, if Cuban democracy is to be marked by pluralism and the diffusion, separation, and balancing of political power, as the 1940 constitution envisioned, and not some unitary alternative, commitment to a project of democratic nation-building—to the reconstitution of national identity—and to political education would become a fundamental requirement, as important as electoral rules and constitutional or institutional design. Revitalization of political culture—as well as of civic commitment, which those in a transitional government must above all exemplify—would be as determinative of democracy as any written constitution.

THE GOVERNMENTAL TRANSITION

It seems clear that the new Cuban government must strive for maximum efficacy throughout, in pursuit of the urgent goals of a democratic and concerted transition. Antonio Villamil, a Senior Fellow at the Florida International University Latin American and Caribbean Center, argues convincingly that a post-Castro Cuba will have to: (1) move effectively toward a free-market economy, and (2) successfully engage both international financial institutions and the United States in a partnership aimed at the accelerated reconstruction of Cuban infrastructure, harnessing of scientific and technological potential, and development of factor endowments in the cause of the

---

5. Benigno E. Aguirre, "The Conventionalization of Collective Behavior in Cuba," *American Journal of Sociology* 90 (November 1984), pp. 541-566. Aguirre speaks of the "joyful crowd," the rote celebration of "death and martyrs," the mass political gathering, and the "testimonial of solidarity", among other forced rituals.

6. Irving Louis Horowitz, "Longevity and Legitimacy in Communist States," *Studies in Comparative International Development* 27 (Spring 1992), pp. 61-75. Horowitz argues that mere longevity is not tantamount to legitimacy, as often assumed in the Cuban case.

7. Gianfranco Poggi, *The State: Its Nature, Development, and Prospects* (Stanford: Stanford University Press, 1990), pp. 136-138.

most rapid possible reconstruction.[8] It may be wise, nonetheless, to look to the Russian and Eastern European experience so as to avoid the traps of wrenching liberalization.

What are the systemic requirements of this extraordinarily difficult and dangerous time of managed change in Cuba? Matías Travieso-Díaz and Steven Escobar project a three-stage transition, during which the integral development of political, economic, and legal institutions proceeds.[9] The core of his proposal is that these developmental dimensions are necessarily interlinked. They would also need to operate in tandem with the planned as well as evolutionary development-opment of political institutions, and political and civic culture, as was suggested previously.

OPEN QUESTIONS ON GOVERNABILITY AND CONSTITUTIONALISM

One unknown is whether there would (or should) be a national referendum on the restoration of the Constitution of 1940, in its totality or in part, at least temporarily pending its amendment by a constituent assembly—which would presumably be convened and conducted under the constitution's own provisions. This presents logical and procedural quandaries that stem from the self-referential nature of constitutions and of law, and which can only be resolved by prior agreement. These rule-making questions suggest again the importance of a project of public education, since the 1940 charter will not be familiar to most Cubans born since the Revolution.

A contemporary "crisis of governability" is much discussed in the political science and public administration disciplines today, as much in Latin America as in the United States.[10] This crisis is understood to encompass all forms of contemporary government, and it is traced to a single overriding cause: the tendency of states, including democratic ones, toward over-promising and overcommitment. The Swedish economist Stefan de Vylder, in a study of Cuba, along with Chile, Nicaragua, and Peru, finds that professedly progressive policies, though aimed at combating inequality, have quite often worsened income and resource disparities and inadvertently promoted various forms of corruption. These policies betray complex, self-defeating causation: overspending based on "exaggerated optimism," which engenders shortages and deficits, a lack of financial and monetary discipline, and overvaluation and overuse of central plan-ning and control, including price controls and subsidies. There are also, incidentally, clear indications that the Cuban government has long over-promised on the issues of racial and gender equality, among other social projects, and that these should be paramount concerns for a transitional government and constituent assembly.[11]

A conundrum which would surely face a transitional government is how to balance: (a) managing the process of building democratic institutions with the goal

---

8. Antonio Villamil, "The Impact of Global Economic, Investment, and Commercial Trends on Post-Castro Cuba," *North-South* 2, no. 6 (1993), pp. 29-32.

9. Matías Travieso-Díaz and Steven R. Escobar, "Overview of Required Changes in Cuba's Laws and Legal Institutions During Its Transition to a Free-Market Democracy," in *Cuba in Transition-Volume* 4 (Washington: Association for the Study of the Cuban Economy, 1994).

10. E.g., Mauricio Merino Huerta, ed., *Cambio Político y Gobernabilidad* (Mexico: Colegio Nacional de Ciencias Políticas y Administración Pública/Consejo Nacional de Ciencia y Tecnología, 1992).

11. Stefan de Vylder, "How Progressive are Progressive Economic Policies? A Note on Latin America's 'Catch 22'," *Economic and Industrial Democracy* 12 (February 1991), pp. 19-29. On discrimination, see: (1) Jorge I. Domínguez, "Racial and Ethnic Relations in the Cuban Armed Forces: A Non-Topic," *Armed Forces and Society* 2 (Winter 1976), pp. 273-290. Domínguez found Black under-representation in the Cuban officer corps and over-representation in the ranks, due to the channeling of Blacks in particular into military service; (2) Benigno E. Aguirre, "Women in the Cuban Bureaucracies: 1968-1974," *Journal of Comparative Family Studies* 7 (Spring 1976), pp. 23-40. Aguirre found women to be underrepresented, and segregated by traditional lines of work, in the bureaucracy; and (3) Raúl J. Cañizares, "Cuban Racism, and the Myth of the Racial Paradise," *Ethnic Studies Report* 8 (July 1990), pp. 27-32. The author found a persistent history, and characteristic pattern, of racism as well as sexism in Cuba, with continuing or deepening attitudes and practices of prejudice, stereotyping, and segregation, "despite Fidel Castro's revolutionary discourse against discrimination."

of wide democratic participation; (b) deliberate planning for limited government with its own, immediate, self-limitation; and (c) providing for economic reconstruction with the decentralization of economic power (and privatization). It also must avoid the temptation, common to transitional governments, of remaining in place beyond its mandate. In other words, it has to avoid the errors of the regime it is replacing, while its incumbents must exhibit an ethic of true public commitment.[12] An obvious way to try to ensure this kind of self-abnegation is to disqualify the members of the provisional body from holding office in the subsequent government, barring unanticipated circumstances.

PUBLIC ADMINISTRATION AND POLITICAL RECONSTRUCTION

The functional requirements for a reconstituted public sector are, at minimum, two-fold. One is for the utilization of Cuba's relatively rich human resource base along with exile expertise, not only because these represent technical assets but also because professionals can play a significant role in fostering social and political integration during and after a transition. A second is for the intensive preparation of public managers, both in Cuba and abroad. These underscore the need for conciliation and political concertation at home, along with support from the United States and from international institutions.

To appreciate the attendant difficulties, one might consider just a few of the policy challenges which labor economist Jorge Pérez-López sees facing Cuba in any attempt to build institutional frameworks for the market and democracy: legal and fiscal reform, constitution-building and political reconstruction, creation of decentralized economic structures, and institution of competent, and transparent, management information and control systems. Furthermore, these

problems have to be addressed all at once, while avoiding, as Pérez-López argues, the "overzealousness" which resulted, in an analogous situation, in the destruction of those Eastern European institutions which had been engaged in similar functions, before new structures could be put in place.[13]

Even more than institutions (the legitimacy of which may well be questioned), it is the many individuals with the training, experience, and commitment necessary for effective participation in a transition who must be brought into the project of national reconstruction. Accomplishing this would require a good measure of mature and disinterested accommodation.

CONCLUSION: REGIME LEGITIMACY, U.S. POLICY, AND NATIONAL IDENTITY

There are contradictory tendencies in current U.S. policy toward Cuba that bear directly on the interrelated questions of regime legitimacy and the prospects for a Cuban transition consistent with national identity and with conciliation. One current runs in the direction of changing U.S. immigration policy emanating from the executive branch. The other, originating in the Republican-controlled Congress, aims at strengthening the U.S. trade embargo toward Cuba and conditioning full diplomatic recognition not only on tangible and specific steps toward democracy but also on the restoration of confiscated property.

The Clinton administration's decision to interdict Cuban rafters at sea and return them to Cuba amounts to a repudiation of a thirty-five year policy of recognition of Cuban claims to refuge and asylum. The unique recognition extended to Cubans in this regard, found most distinctly in the now imperiled Cuban Adjustment Act, derived from a tacit if not explicit recognition of a unique identity of interests

---

12. A question which will surely arise, for example, is what emergency powers the transitional government, as well as the succeeding government, might legitimately claim. Article 27 of the American Human Rights Convention, and the 1940 Constitution itself, provide for the declaration of national emergency by appropriate political entities, when "concurrent" conditions of "extraordinary gravity" are duly found to threaten the independence, security, or viability of the state. See Claudio Grossman, "El Régimen Hemisférico Sobre Situaciones de Emergencia," *Revista IIDH* 17 (January-June 1993).

13. Jorge F. Pérez-López, "Economic and Financial Institutions to Support the Market," in *Cuba in Transition-Volume 4* (Washington: Association for the Study of the Cuban Economy, 1994).

and values between the United States and Cuban exiles, or Cuba-in-exile. As Queiser Morales suggests, Cuban migration to the United States since 1959 has been about the search for and defense of national identity and culture in a difficult but protective host country environment.[14] The divide between Cubans in exile and Cubans on the island is cultural as much as political, turning on attitudes toward economic as well as political freedom, as well as conflicting definitions of nationalism, national iden-tity, and even social justice. National reconciliation and the perceived legitimacy of post-transition institutions will depend on mutual adjustments around these divergent conceptions of what constitutes the national good.

The Cuban Democracy Act of 1992 stipulates that U.S. sanctions on Cuba will remain in place until specific moves toward democracy bring about a calibrated adjustment. The Cuban Liberty and Democratic Solidarity (Libertad) Act—or Helms-Burton bill—which Senators Helms, Dole et al. have introduced in the Senate, goes further in strengthening international sanctions, establishes a civil right of judicial action for U.S. citizens having ownership of or interest in expropriated properties—with reference either to fair market value or amounts certified by the U.S. Foreign Claims Settlement Commission. These features of the Helms-Burton legislation, which have prompted the most vigorous resistance from the Cuban government, are a clear affirmation of the legitimacy of property claims irrespective of the passage of time.

It should be said that Cubans themselves—on the island, in the U.S., and elsewhere—rather than academicians, journalists, or other opinion-makers in the United States—should be the ones who set the terms of debate and define the pertinent criteria for political legitimacy. It is the moral province of those who have been seriously aggrieved by the Cuban regime to establish the terms for national reconciliation and restoration—certainly not the prerogative of those with a vested interest in the regime's longevity.

---

14. Waltraud Queiser Morales, "In Search of National Identity: Cuban and Puerto Rican Migration," *Revista/Review Interamericana* 4 (Winter 1980/81), pp. 567-574.

ECONOMIC EDUCATION FOR A MARKET ECONOMY: THE CUBAN CASE

Jorge A. Sanguinetty

The transformation of a centrally planned economy (CPE) into a market economy provides an excellent example of hysteresis between the trajectories corresponding to the transformation of each economic system into the other. The first process involves a transformation of a low-complexity system to one of much higher complexity. Inversely, upon establishing a centrally planned economy following Marxist-Leninist tenets, the process is characterized by a reduction of complexity in several dimensions: a) institutional, b) legal, c) economic, d) behavioral, and e) cognitive. A *Washington Post* reporter, John Pomfret (1994) captured the phenomenon of hysteresis very succinctly, "Everybody knew how to go from a free economy to a communist one, but nobody knew how to go back." Pomfret's critical variable is knowledge and it will also be the focal variable in this paper.

The reduction in institutional complexity is easily observed when the newly established economy eliminates institutions such as financial intermediation, advertising, industrial organizations and relations, legal and other services associated with a market economy, and reduces the number of enterprises in all industries (rationalization). This process of institutional reduction is accompanied by the creation of some institutions, but they do not match in complexity the old ones. For instance, the creation of a Central Planning Board and state monopolies are simple processes of concentration and centralization of old institutions. Besides, the disregard for money and profits brings about a general neglect of accounting and financial management systems in virtually all enterprises, deepening the process of institutional simplification at that level.

The simplification of the legal system starts with the elimination or significant constraining of property rights, the keystone of a market economy, followed by the elimination of all legal instruments related to contractual security, market regulations, etc. This process is accompanied by the obvious reduction and simplification in the institutions that correspond to the legal system, starting with legislative bodies, the judiciary, tribunals, the human resource endowment (judges, attorneys, etc.), the accumulated practice, libraries and archives, etc. Even though there are new additions to the legal system, they are focused in the reduction of the degrees of freedom of the individuals to conduct all sorts of businesses and activities appropriate to a civil society. This characteristic involve a process that is predominantly of simplification because it reduces the range of choice of the society at large and, therefore, the implications of having more choices.

As institutional and legal constraints increase and become more binding, economic choices are reduced for all economic agents, consumers, workers, entrepreneurs, investors, savers, etc. This process takes place directly and indirectly. Direct effects are represented by those created by the new legal and institutional constraints. Examples of direct effects could be the impossibility of buying equitable instruments, selling real estate, or getting a loan in a bank. Indirect effects are those that appear as secondary, usually unexpected consequences of the implementation of the new constraints. Among the most common are the reduction in the availability of consumer and producers goods due to decreases in production and distribution efficiency and rationing.

As individual choice is so severely constrained, individual behavior is equally constrained and a general loss of welfare can be expected at some point in the process.[1] Under these circumstances, how can a political system impose such radical changes without jeopardizing its tenure in power? The answer lies on the application of sheer physical power (military, police), social intimidation, and persuasion. The latter factor, persuasion, is a combination of educational strategies designed and applied for many audiences, at all levels of the society and covering virtually any topic, from economic to political, religious to philosophical, and scientific to artistic. Any person vaguely familiar with a CPE under a Marxist regime knows how many resources are dedicated to this effort, and how critically important this activity is considered by the authorities.

Why then has a similar effort not been made to prepare the ground for the establishment of market economies in the former members of the Soviet empire? It can be argued that this type of effort is necessary because it takes a great deal of deception (along with total control of all forms of communication) to impose a society whose ideological foundations would not stand freedom of expression, and this is true. But is also necessary to recognize that, after years of Marxist indoctrination, there is a great deal of prejudices in these societies, and they must be addressed in very specific terms. Such prejudices work against the installation of market economies and represent one of the sources of ammunition for those

who oppose the advent of a market economy and a free society.

Economists, unfortunately, have not paid too much attention to the needs for economic education in these contexts for two main reasons. First, the lack of glamour or drama in economic education. Many of the economists involved in transition economics seemed fascinated by the apparent opportunities to be influential in economies in transition as soon as the Soviet block began to unravel and there were initial movements towards liberalization. Second, the lack of understanding of how these societies were organized, from their institutional setup to the existence of mentalities and attitudes—after decades of indoctrination and lack of freedom of expression— generally incompatible with market economies and an ample spectrum of individual freedoms. Few know that in Marxist dominated societies the mere study of western economics is not allowed and to pursue it may bring severe punishment to those who dare break the rules, and many underestimate the extent of the damage done by the government control of all forms of communication and information.[2] There seem to be the pervasive notion among many economists that individuals will automatic and instantly adapt to a new set of prices and macroeconomic conditions, regardless what they know, their values, etc.

This paper is based on the assumption that, although economic behavior can be significantly influenced by all sorts of typically neoclassical variables, the cognitive endowment and values of individuals, and their nature and distribution in a society do play an important role in the workings of the society and its capabilities to evolve. This paper is an attempt to catalog what the author believes are some of the most critical issues in economic education in a previously

---

1. This is a highly controversial statement but we can assume that at least a large segment of the population will experience such a loss.

2. A dramatic example of the ensuing isolation is provided by Reid (1994, p. A26) reporting on an interview with North Korean official Kim Dal Hyun, a nephew of Kim Il Sung trained in economics. Until then he had believed that Kim Il Sung defeated Japan in World War II and liberated Korea from Japanese rule. After been asked about the role played by the U.S. in defeating Japan, Kim Dal Hyun replied "This is the first time anyone ever suggested to me that America helped defeat Japan in World War II. History shows that it was Kim Il Sung who defeated the Japanese."

Marxist-dominated environment. The paper draws significantly on the author's years of experience in Cuba, as a student of Marxist economics, as an official in the Central Planning Board, and, later, as a professor of planning in American University and an international economic advisor in Washington, D.C. The paper has three sections. The first section is a he catalog of issues *per se* with individual discussions of the nature of each topic and how to address it in an education program for a market economy. The second section provides the elements of an educational program including a view of the audiences that must be identified and targeted for in any education program of this sort. Finally, the third section presents concluding remarks.

A CATALOG OF ISSUES

The issues discussed below and the corresponding prejudices or misconceptions generally have a Marxist origin. Nevertheless, this is not always the case. Some economic misconceptions prevalent in Marxist societies are actually originated by governments or are more modern than Marx. In the Cuban case, the most important one is perhaps concerning *imperialism* and its role in determining the relative backwardness of less developed countries (LDCs), especially the U.S. imperialism. This will be discussed further below.

Surplus Value and Profit

In Marx's system, value is only generated by the worker through the application of "labor-power.[3] Surplus value is what remains of the total value generated by the work force after paying for the corresponding wages and other inputs excluding the use of capital. Marx then illegitimates the payment to the factor capital (profit) by stating that capitalists monopolize the access to the means of production according to a legal system based on private property. In this logic, it follows that surplus value is tantamount to stealing from the workers.

Though Marx's logic was not understood by most of the people living in former or current socialist countries, it still serves to feed those in charge of ideological and political propaganda. They appeal to the intuition of their audiences to expose the illegitimacy of profits as a result of the exploitation of man by man. In socialist planning, on the other hand, the concept of profit was never taken into consideration for a number of reasons. First, the Stalinist centralization of enterprises, combined with price controls and rationing, made profits virtually obsolete. There was not even a substitute term. Enterprises could always spend more than what they registered as income. It is important to keep in mind that in this system the enterprises have very little influence, if any, on prices, levels of employment or investment; they are essentially limited to implementing quantitative production targets. In other words, even when there is space for a concept of profit in a socialist economy, profits have not been important and the general public is not used to associating profits with efficiency.

The lack of importance of profits is reflected in many ways. In Cuba, for instance, accounting schools at all levels ceased to exist towards the end of the nineteen sixties. One prevalent notion in government circles was that accounting was not important since the country was already marching towards communism where money is not necessary! Yet lack of or poor accounting is not only a problem in CPEs, it is also a major obstacle in the privatization process necessary to establish a market economy. This is illustrated by Pomfret (1994, pp. A1 and A13) when reporting on a joint venture between General Motors and the Polish carmaker FSO: "Socialist accounting didn't factor in profits, and it didn't care about losses. A culture flourished, the old saw goes, in which the state pretended to pay the workers and the workers pretended to work."

In order to reestablish the legitimacy of profits is necessary to work on two fronts simultaneously. Firstly, educating the public to erase the notion that access to the means of production is a monopoly of "capitalists." This includes demonstrating the importance of small enterprises in most modern economies, and

---

3. See Heilbroner (1991, p. 158) for a simplified, but effective treatment of these concepts.

why market efficiency and financial intermediation are essential to widen the access of the general public to ownership of capital. The second front should be the public enterprises themselves before they can be privatized. It is necessary to quickly reestablish accounting systems and publicize the financial statements of these enterprises as a means to educate the workers and the general public. As relative prices and other distortions come to an end, losses will be frequent and discussions about their causes and how to transform them into profits could be used as important educational material at many levels.

Private Versus Public Property

Private property of the means of production is considered immoral by many members of Marxist societies. Private property is also perceived as predatory by large segments of the population, a perception that owners of capital refuse to accept as fact. These notions are consistent with the early Marxist concept of monopoly of access to the means of production. The feeble defense of private property against massive expropriations by the Cuban government in the early sixties lend support to this notion, as well as the lack of sufficient popular support to return expropriated holdings to their former owners in Nicaragua after the Chamorro government took over.

It is also important to realize that certain social-democratic trends in Cuban circles, inside and outside the country, show their lack of confidence in private property of capital by their continuous advocacy to the future development of a mixed economy. The most vociferous defenders of the full restoration of private property rights, however, have been those who suffer expropriations in the early sixties. Nevertheless, they have based their arguments on notions of fairness instead of on notions of economic expediency. Neglecting to accept the possibility that the restoration of private property rights in a post-Castro Cuba may depend on the will of the millions of constituents living currently in Cuba, acting in a democratic context, previous holders of properties in Cuba may be unwillingly contributing to the permanent loss of their holdings for not recognizing the ideological or educational complexities around this subject.

Yet property rights may be fully reestablished in Cuba before recognizing all of the existent claims. Regardless of the damage that this course of action can be expected to inflict upon the Cuban economy, there are additional reasons to educate the Cuban population at large about the legitimacy and the economic advantages of universal property rights. Even if a transition government decides to recognize previous claims on capital ownership and return the corresponding properties to their former owners, there is an unknown volume of state property that was never private, but a result of the government's investment plans since the early sixties. These properties can easily fall into the hands of their administrators as a result of the combined effect of (a) the workers lack of understanding of their potential role as future owners, and (b) a lack of a well-designed and implemented privatization program, as is taking place in many ex-socialist economies. Pomfret (1994, p. A13) reports that,

> "a recent study by researchers at the University of Warsaw found that at least six out of 10 managers of medium-sized to big businesses were former Communists. Hungary's privatization program effectively allowed many former Communist plant managers to buy up the firms. In the Czech Republic, two waves of a voucher privatization program will theoretically place 80 per cent of the economy in private hands by early next year. But beneath the surface, the old Communist bosses remain: the privatization has yet to be accompanied by changes within most companies."

The point here is not the former political affiliations of the new owners, but the ironic lack of equity of a privatization process that may exclude most of the non-militant population simply because the current bosses are better positioned to become the new capitalists and the lack of preparedness of the majority of the working population. This result may cast serious doubts on the legitimacy of property rights for a long time, and is not a desirable outcome of an effort to establish a market economy. To avoid this a major public education campaign should be implemented to raise the public understanding of these issues in behalf of their own private interests. It would be a gross mistake to assume that such an education is not necessary since the public is intelligent and would be able to determine where their interests lies in all conditions. This is true in the long run, but in the short run, those with more knowledge of these issues and more access to the relevant sources of information are better prepared to take advantage of the confusion of the transition—especially if it is not well planed and executed.

Trade

According to Marx, surplus value is only produced by work-power when applied in the sphere of material production. Commercial activity is a net consumer of surplus value, the argument follows, therefore it does not generate wealth. Such is the conceptual rationale for the virtual marginalization of trade activities in CPEs. Trade is seen as an activity that could be automatically performed as a necessary consequence of the socialist division of labor, but without deserving the level of attention that it enjoys in market economies.

These concepts are additionally reinforced by the Marxist labor-theory of value, the concomitant rejection of any "subjective theory of value," and the extrapolation of both concepts to a CPE.[4] In other words, in a "perfect" economy, prices are determined by the amount of "socially necessary labor," a notion founded on the philosophy of dialectic materialism that leaves no room for supply and demand, consumer preferences, or any "subjective" factor. Under these tenets, the freedom that is involved in trading is illegitimated, disregarding the need for the massive exchanges of information that take place in a market economy between producers and final buyers, including the essential intermediation of traders at different levels, covering all the spectrum from wholesale to retail commerce. All this results in the marginal position of the commercial sector in CPEs, expressed not only in terms of a reduced number of establishments, but also in their chronic lack of supplies and inventories, and their generally drab appearance.

The prejudices against commercial activity are reinforced in non-socialist economies, when there are intermediation and transportation monopolies, which traditionally affect agricultural products. Pre-Castro Cuba seemed to have been full of these cases, which notoriously included among many others the alleged monopoly of pineapple wholesale trade held by Benito Remedios, a Senator of the Republic, and controls of stands in the "Mercados Libres" or Free Markets. Latin American countries are also full of similar examples. Cargo transportation monopolies in Panama are legendary, while this and other countries still suffer from serious restrictions to free trade by the power of government-granted monopolies and protection privileges. Such restrictions are rooted in the mercantilist tradition of the rent-seeking Spanish colonial system and contribute to a culture that accepts government centralization and intervention as part of the natural economic order.

An education campaign to overcome these concepts can be easily designed on the abundant empirical evidence about the benefits of trade. This campaign, however, may be less necessary today in Cuba as even the limited and timid liberalization of "mercados agropecuarios" or agricultural markets and small family-operated restaurants ("paladares") are showing a significant impact on the population's level of consumption.[5]

MONEY, SAVINGS, INVESTMENT AND INTEREST RATES

The rate of interest is the price of an inter-temporal transaction between economic agents. As property becomes public in a CPE the state becomes the only economic agent, financial intermediation virtually disappears. All savings—with minor exemptions for consumer purposes—and all investment is done by

---

4.   We must remember that Marx wrote almost nothing on the economic theory of socialism.

5.   With the disappearance of the Soviet subsidies, the Cuban government was forced to do its own structural adjustment program, more reluctantly so as it did not count with the anesthetics that could have been provided by the International Monetary Fund and the World Bank. The work of a post-Castro transition government will be undoubtedly easier if Castro finishes fundamental macroeconomic adjustments before departing.

the government. Individual time preferences lack a vehicle of expression, which is logical in a society that does not believe in "subjective theories of value."

In a CPE, while the government seems to adopt a growth-maximizing behavior within a budget constraint dedicated to internal and international security, investment expenditure tend to be maximized too, the level of aggregate consumption receiving a residual treatment. Investment projects are chosen by haphazard methods, as profits cannot be taken into consideration, in most cases. The Cuban case is somewhat different, since economic considerations seem to be less relatively important that political ones. The Cuban government, at least until the demise of the Soviet block, seemed to have followed what can be characterized as a policy of maximizing its influence in external affairs. In both cases, however, decisions concerning investments were never made taking risk, profits, or the population's time preferences into account.

It is not possible to predict what the consequences of this lack of exposure to fundamental economic decisions have on the population. Many people may have grown used to not taking chances and live under the protective umbrella of the state paternalism. This type of attitude is frequently reported among the citizens of former socialist states, especially those that have voted the old Communist rulers back into power, with the exception of the Czech Republic.

Public education to address these issues should be well coordinated with the issues raised previously about privatization. The topics covered in this section, however, are more abstract in nature than those relative to property rights and ownership, and they will require a different approach.

Rationing and Price Flexibility

Rationing was instituted in Cuba in March 1962 and it is still officially alive though apparently non operational. Nevertheless, an entire generation has been educated under the notion that a group of bureaucrats can arbitrarily decide not only about the prices of consumer goods, but also their availability, if at all, to the Cuban population. The most dramatic example of the consequences of this regime is the severe deterioration of all buildings in Cuba, after more than three decades that the Cuban government denied the access to basic means of maintenance to the regular consumer.

The need to liberalize prices in order to restore equilibrium to supply and demand relations is indispensable to recover the Cuban economy and to install a market system. This however must be explained to the population to avoid the uncertainties that Russia suffered in this regard during the winter of 1992. Even though the current liberalization of some markets in Cuba may help in this direction, the population needs to understand why prices may remain flexible and change with external and internal economic conditions. Part of the state paternalism in Cuba is reflected in the expectation by a significant segment of the public that the state should always protect the common citizen from the vagaries of the economy.

Public enterprises, on the other hand, never had to worry about adapting their production decisions to varying prices. In fact, these enterprises have developed as institutional puppets of the Central Planning Agencies that work under the assumption that they know everything.

Therefore, re-educating the general public about the advantages of price flexibility and free supply and demand also requires some attention to functioning under these radically different conditions. This may sound very obvious and even naive to those lucky ones that have only lived in a free market environment, but it represent a revolutionary change for those that were born in a CPE.

Competition and Planning

A closely related topic is that of the advantages of a competitive economy versus central planning. In the Marxist world, market economics is equivalent to chaos, where the free enterprise system impedes the improvement of the standard of living of the common citizen because there is not a "rational allocation of resources". The fallacy is based on the notion that the state can always look for the public good much better than a system based on private property and economic freedom.

Marx's obsession with his theorem about the falling rates of profit under capitalism, blocked him from understanding the importance of a legal system working in a democratic society. But whatever his reasons, many still believe that competition is detrimental to the general economic welfare since there is a great deal of redundancy among enterprises and resources, plus the fact that competition is inherently destructive. Planning, the argument follows, is necessary to reduce the chaos introduced by competition and only the state can be in charge of such a task.

The evidence about which system is more efficient is overwhelming but there is always the need to support the evidence over more theoretical foundations. The education campaign, for the audiences that can handle abstract discussions of the topic, must be focused on the fact that redundancy in itself is a desirable outcome of competition. On the one hand, it avoids monopoly and all its undesirable consequences, on the other, it provides more stability of supplies because if a supplier fails to deliver there are other sources to rely on. Competition also encourages the constant improvement of the quality of the traditional products and the development of new ones. But competition, to be beneficial, must exist in an environment of freedom of enterprise and consumer sovereignty.

Labor Productivity and Employment Security

One of the thorniest issues in the transition towards a market economy is how to provide job security. Many socialist workers will definitely miss their job security in a market economy, though they never knew how much it cost in terms of economic stagnation and chronic poverty. Nevertheless, in the Cuban case, where the collapse of the economy demonstrated that job security can be an illusion even in a CPE, the educational effort required in this front may be minimal after all the adjustments that are currently taking place in the country.

In any case, a public education program should emphasize: The dependence of the standard of living on the level of real salaries; the latter as a function of productivity; and the need to protect the levels of productivity by letting enterprises reduce employment when economic conditions—or specific behaviors by some workers—demand such an action.

International Trade and Exploitation

Cubans are aware of their economic dependence from the world economy, possibly today more than ever. The government, however, in its failure to manage the economy and its enterprises efficiently, blames the world economy for the poverty of the country through what they call "unequal terms of trade." This condition, they say, is the main instrument of exploitation of the country by foreign powers.

These notions should be quickly dispelled by showing how intelligent economic policies can be highly beneficial to small countries. The examples of Holland, Switzerland, Denmark, Chile, and the Asian success stories must be widely disseminated in Cuba to foster the development of a market economy and contribute to its success through an export-oriented culture.

THE ELEMENTS OF AN EDUCATION STRATEGY[6]

A public education program in support of the transition to a market economy should distinguish among different audiences since their requirements and capabilities vary widely. The main audiences should be the following:

1. The general public

2. The opinion makers

3. Government officials

4. University professors and students of economics, business, law, and related disciplines

5. Legislators

6. Workers and administrators in selected enterprises

---

6. Although this section is written with the Cuban case in mind, the similarities with what other countries require may overwhelm the differences.

7. Union leaders

8. Primary, secondary and other non-university teachers

9. Primary, secondary, and other non-university students

This campaign should be designed and administered by personnel that can project the effort as a serious one and not as an exercise in propaganda. The public's minor suspicion of propaganda will inflict irreparable damage to the credibility of the effort and turn it wasteful at best. The program execution should not be overseen on a day-to-day basis by any political appointee of the government in charge. The design of the program must avoid addressing specific conflicts that may arise during its implementation in other sectors of the economy, even though it has to be prepared to approach highly controversial issues in a sobber and intelligent manner.

The most important audience is the **general public** and it should receive top priority in this program. This campaign should be implemented over a long period of time, with a variety of activities to be performed through the communication media of the country, including radio, television, and newspapers. The detailed formats will not be discussed here but should include ample public participation in radio and television round tables, talk shows, and interviews with experts that can answer telephone calls. These programs should also publicize other education activities of a more specific or specialized nature, and the availability of reading material that could be made available as part of the education program.

An indispensable complement to the program addressing the general public is the education of **opinion makers** and journalists of all persuasions. This part of the effort requires that some of the individuals in charge of the education campaign be given significant access to the media, not only as guests but also as hosts, producers, and directors of the programs to be delivered to the public.

Government officials, new and old, including those in top positions, should participate in regular and intensive seminars and workshops about relevant aspects of a market economy. This part of the education program should have a general component and a specific component according to the sector in each case. For instance, the material to be offered to the judiciary will differ in many aspects to the material to be offered to the officials working in economic institutions that survive the initial restructuring of the state bureaucracy. It would be advisable to produce some material for readings. With time this will become indispensable as the needs for the transition process are better defined and understood.

University professors and students of various disciplines follow in importance in the education program. This audience, however, plays a critical role in the short and long run. For the short run, seminars and workshops should be established to deal with the initial issues of the transition to a market economy, But they are also the professors and the future professionals that will be in charge of studying and operating a market economy, therefore a long-run program to change study programs and curricula should be put in place simultaneously, as well as the availability of the corresponding books and journals.

A transition to a market economy requires the participation of **legislators** in order to enact the laws—and finally the constitutional framework—needed in a market economy. The complexity of the task in their hands is impossible to exaggerate and they should work with the maximum understanding possible if a market economy will ever work in Cuba. They will be easy victims of old preconceptions and the political demagoguery that may inflict serious harm to the effort to build new economic and legal systems. Legislators should be subjected to intensive seminars and workshops focusing on the effects of legislative initiatives on the economic affairs of the nation.

All enterprises must change their management style and culture to operate in the much more sophisticated environment of a market economy. **Workers and managers** of these enterprises, even long before any possibility of privatization appears, must participate in education campaigns that would also have a general economic component and a specific one dealing with general business administration practices inherent to a market economy. It is critical to address issues like the following: a) the importance of profits and its relation to worker productivity, salaries, and the economy; b) the need for a management system capable to respond effectively to macroeconomic and market conditions; c) the need for management flexibility and factor mobility to achieve efficiency; and d) the relationships among labor productivity, salaries, and standard of living and how the economic prosperity of a nation depends on the efficiency of its enterprises and not on labor security.

Union leaders would be included in a program similar to the one just described, but perhaps with some adaptations to their roles and institutions. It is important to take into account that one of their main concerns is employment security on the one hand, and on the other that they have been subjected to a traditional paternalistic role by the state and by a social-democratic influence that advocates for a "mixed" economy and heavy state intervention. Perhaps this is the time to look for a more modern concept of trade unionism in which more attention is given to improve the training of the worker and his adaptability to a continuously changing economy.

Teachers and students other than university's should be included in the educational program on a long-run perspective. This will have to be done, however, during the early stages of the transition to a market economy, since socialist dogma of the current curricula must be replaced by more liberal subject matter as soon as possible. This will be the ideal moment to introduce economic education as part of the regular offerings of the schools system at all levels.

Other audiences which remain and must be incorporated to the program include security forces, police, the military, and the judiciary. They require special treatment because their deep exposure to indoctrination from the past and their need to integrate themselves into the new economic system. Another important sector of the population to be specifically addressed with tailor-made programs is the agricultural worker and the small farmer. Their integration to a market economy is essential, but their accessibility is difficult for educational purposes; radio may have to be the main vehicle for this group.

CONCLUSIONS

Few countries have undertaken economic education as a major endeavor in support of their economic systems. The United States and the United Kingdom have been the leaders in this field, though other countries have made significant efforts. In the U.S. the existence of the National Council on Economic Education covers several decades and their audiences range from young students to college professors of economics. The Council is today increasingly active in some ex-Soviet republics, a welcome development suggesting that some have discovered the importance of economic education in the establishment of market economies. Yet more efforts are necessary to facilitate this process and avoid losing the ground gained for economic and political freedoms since 1989. Donor agencies and international financial institutions should become more sensitive to this need and dedicate resources to this type of effort. Decades of indoctrination were necessary to install the systems that are already disappearing, but they have left a legacy that must be eliminated more quickly than what can be achieved by a policy of benign neglect. As a market economy is much more complex than a CPE, it require knowledge and understanding of its participants and main beneficiaries.

Raising the level of economic understanding of the general public will contribute to reducing the uncertainties of the transition to market economies in all the countries involved. It will also help to adjust expectations to the immediate realities of each of the countries, especially in Cuba where accumulated needs for over more than three decades is leaving a legacy of an impatient population.

REFERENCES

Heilbroner, Robert L., *The Worldly Philosophers*, Sixth Edition. New York: Simon and Schuster, Inc., 1992.

Pomfret, John, "The Big Leap into Capitalism," *The Washington Post* (October 25, 1994).

Reid, T.R., *The Washington Post* (October 22, 1994).

Appendix A:
THE RULES OF THE GAME

Néstor Enrique Cruz

Those of us who are naturalized citizens of the United States took an oath to the Constitution of our adopted country. Those of us who are lawyers took a further oath to the Constitution, upon admission to the Bar. Those of us who are natural-born citizens, by virtue of that fact, took an implicit oath upon birth. Those of us who are members of the Association for the Study of the Cuban Economy, therefore, in one way or another, have subscribed to the principles enshrined in that document, which is not merely a collection of words, but rather a reality for which many people have shed blood. I will not try to improve on the Gettysburg Address, since that would be impossible. I do suggest, however, that once in a while we read the best ever-written 250 words.

This introduction is the background for this short work. Upon reflection, it appears to the author that in 1994 ASCE may very well be embarking on a journey of some importance to Cuba and the United States. I suggest we start our journey within a framework akin to the Constitution, to the Rules of Ethics of the Bar, and to some basic principles subsidiary to the aforementioned, but not in any way less important. I have thought of seven, but I am sure our members can think of more.

MAJORITY RULE

Majority rule is axiomatic. It needs no further proof. There are some nuances, however, worth mentioning. ASCE is a representative, not a direct, democracy. It means that the officers, your servants, will do their best; but, it also means that they will use their independent judgment. Therefore, your representa-tives will and must take unpopular decisions. Luckily for the members we have term limits; but, please let the officers do their work, with your input, and they will try to do right by the membership. I imagine some economists will point to principal and agent problems, to Public Choice theory, and to Arrow's impossibility theorem. However, let us not get too technical or too pessimistic. We are small, we are friends and colleagues, and we are as far away from each other as the next phone. Therefore, let me postulate the Cruz Law (please ask me about the Cruz Curve and the Cruz Circle during question and answer): In a small organization composed of people of good will working for a worthy goal Public Choice theory does not apply, with my apologies to Professor Buchanan of George Mason University, seven miles away from my office.

FREEDOM OF DISSENT

The officers do want plenty of dissent. That is guaranteed by the First Amendment. The officers, however, do not want stridency because it is not polite and we want to be "nice" to each other, or as our member Emilio Cueto, Esquire would spell it: "nais." Worthy dissent is responsible. José Martí put it: "Liberty is not license." Oliver Wendell Holmes, one of the author's favorite U.S. Supreme Court justices put it: "Do not shout FIRE! in a crowded theater." He was, of course, speaking symbolically. Words are powerful and because of the Second Law of Thermodynamics they can reduce to rubble an edifice which might have taken years to build.

DUE PROCESS OF LAW

Due Process exists in one way or another in every civilized country or organization. All it means is that everyone has the opportunity to be heard at least once. Because of my personal preference for arbitration instead of litigation, I think once is enough provided the hearing is fair and impartial, and the decision-maker gives a concise statement of the reasons for his or her decision. Let us make ourselves heard; but, let us also respect the finality of decisions so we do not get bogged-down in fights that benefit no one. Obviously, there will be decisions of such importance that the hearing process will take longer, but finality is indispensable to a well-run country or organization.

CIVILITY

Most lawyers, including the author, are argumentative fools some of the time. Believe or not, however, the Bar is making a concerted effort to reintroduce civility to the practice of law. It will be difficult, but the problem is too generalized to blame only lawyers. Please remember what Paul Krugman said about Laura Tyson last year at Anaheim. Also remember the temper tantrums of many athletes. So, let us be good sports.

INCLUSIVENESS

Inclusiveness, in our context, means several things, but at a minimum I would suggest it means total respect for the views of those with whom we do not agree and a rebuttable presumption that every member of ASCE acts in good faith according to his or her own world-view. I am assuming, however, that we are working towards a constitutional democracy in Cuba, with room for private initiative, a goal conceded even by many ex-communist leaders in Eastern Europe and Russia. The best person to illustrate this principle is our out-going President, Dr. Jorge Pérez-López, always willing to compromise, to take the middle of the road, and to recognize that extremes are pernicious. Let do as he does. He does it very well.

SIMPLICITY

The late Irving Younger, Samuel S. Leibowitz Professor of Trial Technique at Cornell Law School, wrote an article in 1976 published in the *American Bar Association Journal* (Volume 62, May issue, at page 632) titled "In Praise of Simplicity," which was truly pioneering. Economists will appreciate this law review article, especially econometricians, because he invokes the principle of parsimony, which, I understand is quite important in multiple regression in order to get an honest RSQUARED. I prefer to remember the aforementioned principle as Occam's Razor, because I first encountered it in philosophy class in college. It is also my understanding that Milton Friedman, one of my favorite economists along with Samuel Bowles (I will let the reader figure out that apparent contradiction), believes heartily in Occam's Razor. The point, of course, is that the legal profession, which sometimes takes as a first principle that the Law and everything connected with it ought to be as complicated as possible, is finally realizing that complex law is not law at all, but rather a recipe for unpredictability, instability, uncertainty, and, of course, eventually, anarchy. There is definitely such a thing as too much law and it is my observation, based on the Cruz Principle, that our country is now on the diminishing marginal returns part of the curve. I would, therefore, suggest that in running ASCE we keep operations simple, non-bureaucratic, and agile. By all means let us not run things as the government does. I do believe in government, perhaps in big government for certain things, but I do not believe in complicated, non-entrepreneurial government.

HUMILITY

Dr. Alicia Juarrero is a professor of Philosophy in the Washington area. She has done a great deal of good work in the philosophical underpinnings of law and democracy, including publishing her findings in respected law reviews like that of the University of Texas Law School. She also happens to be a trusted friend and colleague of many ASCE members. One of her fine observations is that for democracy to work there must be humility on the part of all members of the polity. The author is not precisely sure how this would apply in practical terms to the operations of ASCE, but certainly there is a lot of truth to her observation in that one often finds awesome the ability of many who are more competent than oneself.

This short work is a call for unity within diversity. The thought is not original. E PLURIBUS UNUM is written on the seal of the United States.

Appendix B:
AUTHORS AND DISCUSSANTS

José F. Alonso is a Senior Economic Researcher with the United States Information Agency, Radio Martí Program. He has a B.A. degree and an M.A. in Economics from Catholic University of America, where he completed all the academic requirements towards a Ph.D. in International Economics (1974). From 1972 to 1985 he served as international economist and commodity analyst in sugar, gold, metal machinery and other commodities at the International Price Division, U.S. Bureau of Labor Statistics. He conducted numerous studies of the Cuban economy, particularly the sugar industry, health sector, and monetary and fiscal affairs. He has published numerous articles and analyses of Cuba's economy, included in the *Free Market Cuba Business Journal* and other publications.

José Alvarez is a Professor of Food and Resource Economics at the University of Florida's Everglades Research and Education Center, where his research and extension programs deal with farm management and production economics. He received his Ph. D. in Food and Resource Economics from the University of Florida. He is the Principal Investigator of a research project intended to estimate the economic impact (benefits and costs) of future trade between the United States and Cuba on the agricultural economy of the State of Florida.

Amparo E. Avella holds a Ph. D. in Geography from the University of La Habana. She served as Senior Professor at the University of La Habana and worked as a National Researcher for the National Council of Science and Technology of Mexico (CONACyT). She is currently working as an Environmental Scientist on the staff of Environmental Site Assessments Inc., a Miami-based environmental consulting company.

B. Ralph Barba is registered as a Professional Geologist in the State of Florida and is the President and CEO of Environmental Site Assessments Inc., an environmental and engineering consulting firm based in Miami. He has worked with three major oil companies, Gulf Oil, Chevron and Exxon Latin America, and has performed many contamination assessments and remedial systems in several states and Puerto Rico.

Ernesto F. Betancourt is a consultant to the UNDP on institutional development and has done consulting work for the World Bank, IDB, AID and the OAS on that subject throughout Latin America. He also lectures on analysis of revolutionary propensity and is author of *Revolutionary Strategy: A Handbook for Practitioners,* Transaction Publishers. He has an MPIA from the University of Pittsburgh, majoring in economics and social development. He has been Director of VOA's Radio Martí program, Director of Organization Development and Director of Finance and Budget at the Organization of American States, and Managing Director of the Cuban Bank of Foreign Trade. He was Castro's representative in Washington during the revolution against Batista.

Roger R. Betancourt is Professor of Economics at the University of Maryland-College Park. He received his Ph. D. from the University of Wisconsin-Madison. Many of his contributions to analysis of capital utilization and shift-work systems are summarized in the entry on "Capital Utilization" in J. Eatwell, M. Milgate, and P. Newman (eds.), *The New Palgrave Dictionary of Economics*, The Stockton

Press, 1987. He has been a Visiting Professor and Scholar at the University of Washington and at IN-SEAD (Fontainebleau, France). His current research interest is the economics of distribution systems.

Evaldo A. Cabarrouy has a Ph. D. in Economics from the University of Texas at Austin, with concentrations in the fields of macroeconomics, monetary economics, international finance and economic development. He is a Professor of Economics and Finance at the University of Puerto Rico, Río Piedras Campus. A former advisor to the Governor of Puerto Rico on economic development, his current research interests are in comparative economic development policy.

Rolando H. Castañeda is currently a Senior Operations Officer working with Chile and Peru at the Inter-American Development Bank (IDB) where he has held different positions since 1974. Before joining the IDB, he worked as an economist at the Organization of American States; the Rockefeller Foundation at the University of Cali, Colombia; the University of Puerto Rico at Río Piedras; and the Puerto Rico Planning Board. He has an M.A. and is a Ph.D. candidate at Yale University, majoring in monetary policy and econometrics.

Juan C. Consuegra-Barquín, Esq., is an Attorney at Law with a practice in Guaynabo, Puerto Rico. He graduated with a B.A. from the University of Puerto Rico (1989) and received a J.D. from The Inter-American University Law School of Puerto Rico (1992) . He also holds a Masters degree in International and Comparative Law from the Georgetown University Law Center (L.L.M., 1993).

Néstor E. Cruz, Esq., is Of Counsel to the Washington, D.C. corporate law firm of Carr, Morris & Graeff, P.C. and President of St. George's Associates, a legal and management consulting firm. He graduated from Malvern Preparatory School (1961), Villanova University (B.A. in Science, 1966), the Cornell Graduate School of Management (M.B.A., 1969), and Cornell Law School (J.D., 1970). He is a member of the Board of Editors of *The Florida Bar Journal* and has published several law review articles

in the *A.B.A. Journal* and the *Labor Law Journal*, among others.

Sergio Díaz-Briquets is a Vice President of Casals and Associates, a Washington-based consulting firm. He was Research Director of the Congressional Commission for the Study of International Migration and Cooperative Economic Development, and earlier held appointments with the International Development Research Centre (IDRC), Population Reference Bureau, and Duquesne University. A recipient of a Ph.D. in Demography from the University of Pennsylvania, he has published numerous articles and books dealing with Cuba and other topics.

Ricardo A. Donate-Armada is an Associate Actuary with Towers Perrin in Rosslyn, Virginia, where he specializes in international benefits issues affecting U.S. multinationals. He graduated from the Massachusetts Institute of Technology with a B.S. in Physics (1992) and has been an Associate of the Society of Actuaries since 1989. He is the author of a study of the Cuban retirement and pension system.

Maida Donate-Armada has Licenciaturas in History (1969) and Sociology (1977) and a Doctorate in Psychological Sciences (1988) from the University of La Habana. During her stay in Cuba, she worked as a Senior Researcher for the Cuban Internal Demand Institute (1983-1993). Her professional experience includes working as a Marketing Researcher for Sigma Dos, S.A. in Madrid (1994-1995). She is the author of the monograph titled *Methodology for the Study of Living Conditions* (1990). She is currently completing a study of suicide, funded by the Cuban-American National Council, comparing the suicidal behavior of Cubans and Cuban-Americans.

Oscar A. Echevarría is Chairman and CEO of Czarnikow-Rionda, a New York-based sugar trading house, and of EISCA, a consulting firm based in Venezuela. He received his Ph.D. in Economics from Georgetown University.

Juan Carlos Espinosa is a doctoral candidate at the Graduate School of International Studies at the University of Miami and currently holds the Emilio Moreau Bacardí Fellowship for Cuban Studies. He was previously the recipient of a North-South Center

Fellowship (1993-1995). Espinosa holds an M.A. in International Studies (1995) from the University of Miami, a B.A. in International Relations (1981) from Florida State University, and a Certificate in Slavic Studies (1981) from the University of Zagreb. He is presently co-editor of *The Journal of Latin American Affairs*, editor of the *Boletín del Instituto Cubano de Economistas Independientes (ICEI)*, and main editor of the Occasional Paper Series of the Cuban Studies Association at the University of Miami.

Robert E. Freer, Jr., Esq. is a member of the Bar of the Commonwealth of Virginia and of the District of Columbia. He is the Senior Partner of Freer & McGarry, P.C., an international law firm in Washington D.C.

Ralph J. Galliano is the President of the Institute for U.S. Cuba Relations in Washington D.C. As Editor of the U.S.*Cuba Policy Report, he provided comprehensive Capitol Hill coverage of the passage of the Cuban Liberty and Democratic Solidarity (LIBERTAD) Act. A graduate of The George Washington University's School of Public and International Affairs, he has written on the issue of expropriated properties, U.S.-Cuba claims, and the settlement process. Galliano provided assistance in the area of U.S. Cuba claims to the Atlantic Council's Road Map for Restructuring Future U.S. Relations with Cuba and is a member of the Council's Task Force on Claims and Standing Group on the Western Hemisphere.

Antonio Gayoso has a Licenciatura in Economics from the University of Villanueva (Havana) and received a B.S. in Business Administration and an M.A. in International Trade and Finance from the University of Florida. He is also a Ph. D. candidate in Agricultural Economics at the University of Florida. He has held several positions at the U.S. Agency for International Development (USAID) and at the U.S. Department of State, having served as Director of the Human Resources Directorate in the Bureau of Science and Technology at USAID. He is currently the Director of the North American Regional Bureau of the World Council of Credit Unions. His academic experience includes serving as Assistant Professor in the Department of Agricultural Eco-

nomics at the University of Florida, and as Professor at American University. Earlier he worked as a Junior Economist in the Cuban Ministry of Finance.

Ernesto Hernández-Catá is currently Deputy Director of the International Monetary Fund's Western Hemisphere Department. Previously he served as Deputy Director of the IMF's European II Department, in charge of relations with Russia and several other states of the former U.S.S.R. He received a Licence from the Graduate Institute of International Studies, Geneva, Switzerland (1967), and both a Masters Degree (1970) and a Ph.D. (1974) in Economics from Yale University. Has held numerous positions in the IMF, ranging from Desk Economist for Mexico, and later the United States in the Western Hemisphere Department: Chief of the North American Division; Senior Advisor of the Research Department; and Deputy Director of the Research Department, in charge of the IMF's *World Economic Outlook*. He also served as an Economist in the Division of International Finance of the Board of Governors of the Federal Reserve System and held teaching positions at American University and School of Advanced International Studies at Johns Hopkins University. He was the recipient of a Yale University Fellowship (1967-71) and a National Science Foundation Grant (1969-70).

Armando M. Lago has a Ph.D. (1966) and an M.A. (1964) in Economics from Harvard University, where he served as a Teaching Fellow (1963- 65) and as a Brookings Fellow (1963-65). He was an Adjunct Associate Professor of Regional and Urban Economics at Catholic University of America (1968-76) and an economic consultant with Stanford Research Institute (1965-1967) and Operations Research, Inc. (1967-1971). He was a Vice-President of Resource Management Corporation (1972-1975), and since 1975 has been President of Ecosometrics, Inc. One of the four original incorporators of ASCE and its Treasurer from 1990 to 1994, he was elected to a two-year term (1994-1996) as President of ASCE. Dr. Lago has been the Chairman of the Greater Washington Ibero-American Chamber of Commerce (1986-89) and a member of the Board of Director OF HUMAN RIGHTS (1974-1994). He is also co-author of *The Politics of Psychiatry in Revolutionary Cuba* (Transaction Publishers, 1991).

Manuel Lasaga, an international economics and finance consultant, is the President of STAT-INFO, an international consulting company headquartered in Miami. His professional experiences include assignments with Southeast Bank in Miami, Citicorp in New York City, and with Wharton Econometric Forecasting Associates in Philadelphia. He has served on the Board of Governors of the Greater Miami Chamber of Commerce, and has been President of the Economic Society of South Florida and member of the Board of Economists of The Miami Herald. He holds an M.A. and a Ph. D. degrees in Economics from the University of Pennsylvania and is an Adjunct Professor of International Economics and Finance at Florida International University.

José Carlos Lezcano graduated with a Licenciatura in Physical Geography from the University of La Habana (1984). His specialty is in Coastal and Oceanic Climatology. His experience includes working for ten years at Cuba's Institute of Meteorology (Instituto de Meteorología), which is part of the Cuban Academy of Sciences. He has worked for Clima-Centro, Inc. and for International Consulting and Training for Productivity (INCAT), and is also the Coordinator of The Caribbean Environmental Group in Miami.

Luis Locay received his Ph.D. in economics from the University of Chicago in 1983. He is currently Associate Professor in the Department of Economics at the University of Miami. He was previously Assistant Professor of Economics at the State University of New York at Stony Brook. His areas of specialization include development, economic demography, and applied macroeconomics.

Alberto Luzárraga has a Ph.D. in Civil Law from the University of Villanova (Havana), a CPA degree from the University of Havana and a Master of Business Administration from the University of Miami. With more than 30 years of experience in the commercial and investment banking business he has specialized in the Latin American area and particularly in investments related to privatizations as well as in-

vestments in emerging companies in those markets. Presently, he is Chairman of the Amerinvest Group Inc., a merchant banking concern specialized in equity investment in the Americas. President of the Cuban American Research Group (CARG), a not for profit organization, whose membership consists of professionals from different industries; CARG's purpose is to contribute to the study of Cuba's problems and future solutions.

Ambassador Alberto Martínez Piedra is Professor of Economics at The Catholic University of America. He received a degree in Political Economy at the Universidad Complutense de Madrid (1957) and a Ph. D. in Economics from Georgetown University (1962). He was Deputy U.S. Ambassador to the Organization of American States (1982-1984), U.S. Ambassador to Guatemala (1984-1987) and Special Assistant to the U.S. Mission to the United Nations (1987-1988). His research interests include economic development and business ethics.

George Plinio Montalván, currently an international economic and management consultant working principally with the Inter-American Development Bank, was Chief Economist at the Organization of American States, where he was employed for almost 20 years. Prior to that, he did economic research at Brookings Institution. He is a founding member of ASCE, served on its Executive Committee during the 1990-92 period, and has edited the Papers and Proceedings of ASCE's Annual Meetings, *Cuba in Transition*. Other recent publications include *Latin America: The Hardware and Software Markets* (INTERSOL, 1991), and *Promoting Investments and Exports in the Caribbean Basin* (OAS, 1989). He has a B.A. and M.A., and is a Ph.D. candidate in Economics from the George Washington University.

C. Richard Nelson is the Director of the International Security Program at the Atlantic Council of the United States. He taught international relations at George Mason University and the Industrial College of the Armed Forces. He graduated from the U.S. Military Academy and served in the Army. He has an M.A. in Far Eastern Studies from the University of Michigan and a Ph. D. in International Relations from Kansas University.

Silvia Pedraza is Associate Professor of Sociology at the University of Michigan, Ann Arbor. She is the author of *Political and Economic Migrants in America: Cubans and Mexicans* (University of Texas Press, 1985), as well as of an edited collection of readings with Ruben G. Rumbaut, *Origins and Destinies: Immigration, Race and Ethnicity in America* (Wadsworth, 1985). She is presently a member of the Council of the American Sociological Association, and was previously Chair of its Section on Racial and Ethnic Minorities. She is also the author of "Immigration Research: A Conceptual Map," *Social Science History* (1990) and "Women and Immigration: The Social Consequences of Gender," *Annual Review of Sociology* (1991)

Lázaro Peña Castellanos is Assistant Researcher in the Department of Global Macroeconomics Issues at the Centro de Investigaciones de Economía Internacional (CIEI) of the University of La Habana. Professor Peña is researching problems associated with the structural transformations of the Cuban economy, especially in the agricultural sector. A graduate in Economics from the Universidad de La Habana, he has conducted graduate work on international development and the agricultural sector in Milan, Italy.

Lorenzo Pérez is currently Assistant Director at the Western Hemisphere Department (WHD) of the International Monetary Fund in charge of Maritime Division (covering Barbados, Jamaica and Venezuela). He has been at the IMF since 1978, where he has worked in the Exchange and Trade Relations Department, the European Department covering various Latin American and European countries. Previously he held positions at the U.S. Department of the Treasury and the U.S. Agency for International Development. He also taught economic development at George Washington University. He has a Ph.D. in Economics from the University of Pennsylvania. He is a founding member of ASCE and served on its Executive Committee from 1990-1992 and 1994-1996.

Jorge F. Pérez-López is an international economist with the Bureau of International Labor Affairs, U.S. Department of Labor. His writings on international economics issues --especially on the Cuban economy-- have appeared in professional journals and several edited volumes. He is the author of *The Economics of Cuban Sugar* (University of Pittsburgh Press, 1991), *The Cuban Second Economy: From Behind the Scenes to Center Stage* (Transaction Publishers, 1995), and editor of *Cuba at a Crossroads* (University Press of Florida, 1995). He received his Ph.D. from the State University of New York at Albany. He is a former President of ASCE.

Joseph M. Perry is Professor of Economics at the University of North Florida, where he has been a faculty member since 1971. He was previously a member of the economics faculty of the University of Florida. Dr. Perry received his Ph.D. in Economics from Northwestern University in 1966, after completing undergraduate studies at Emory University and Georgia State University. His recent research has focussed on regional economic development, with specific reference to Central American and Caribbean nations, and their trade relationships with the United States.

Joaquín P. Pujol is currently Assistant Director in the Exchange and Trade Relations Department of the International Monetary Fund (IMF), with responsibility for the evaluation and review of all macroeconomic programs supported by the IMF. He served previously in various capacities in the Western Hemisphere Department (WHD) of the IMF including as Chief of the Mexico Latin Caribbean Division and Assistant Director to the WHD Department. He is a graduate of the Wharton School and pursued post-graduate studies in economics and Regional Science at the University of Pennsylvania. Prior to joining the IMF he taught economics at the Wharton School and did research on economics and econometrics for the National Bureau of Economic Research, the Foreign Policy Research Institute, the Regional Science Institute and the Economic Research Unit of the University of Pennsylvania. He was the recipient of various fellowships from the University of Pennsylvania and the Organization of American States. He is one of the founders of ASCE and has served as its secretary since its inception.

Carlos N. Quijano is currently a consultant on international economics. He studied at the Universidad of Villanueva (Havana) and the University of

Miami (Florida); subsequently pursued graduate studies in economics at Columbia University. He was an Economic Advisor and Special Assistant for International Economic and Monetary Affairs to the Ministry of Finance in Cuba (1959-60); Economic Advisor at the Central Planning Board and the Ministry of Commerce of Cuba (1960-61); Economic Analyst for W.R. Grace & Co. (1962-66); and Senior Economist at the Organization of America States (1966-67). He joined the World Bank in 1968 where he served as Senior Economist for several Latin American countries (1968-73); Resident Representative in Colombia (1973-76); Special Representative for Interamerican Organizations (1976-78); Senior Advisor Office of the Vice-President for Latin America and Caribbean Region (1980-93). While on leave from the Bank, he was Director of the Cooperation Centre at the World Economic Forum in Geneva, Switzerland (1979-80). He has been a Research Fellow at the Bureau of Business and Economic Research, University of Miami; and Senior Associate at Saint Anthony's College, Oxford University.

Mario A. Rivera is an Associate Professor, School of Public Administration, University of New Mexico. He holds a Ph.D. from the University of Notre Dame.

José Antonio Rivero is President and CEO of Amerop Sugar Corporation, as well as President and CEO for Sugar Import and Distribution of Amerop Chile, S.A. He served as President of Industria Azucarera Nacional in Santiago, Chile (1988-1991), and President and CEO of Aguirre Sugar Company of Puerto Rico and New York (1970-1980). In addition to his extensive consulting practice, he served as Manager of Central Manuelita Cía. Azucarera S.A. and Compañía Agrícola Palmira, S.A. in Cienfuegos, Cuba. He received B.S. degrees in both Mechanical and Electrical Engineering from the University of Miami (1953) and an MBA from the University of Miami (1963).

Jorge Luis Romeu is an Associate Professor of Statistics and Computers in the Department of Mathematics of SUNY-Cortland (NY). He is also an Adjunct Professor of Operations Research in the Manufacturing Engineering Program of Syracuse

University. He worked as a Research Engineer with the Illinois Institute of Technology Research Institute (IITRI) in Rome (NY), where he analyzed software engineering and reliability data. He taught simulation modeling in Mexico, as a Fullbright Fellow, and in Spain and the United States. He received a Ph. D. in Operations Research from Syracuse University and has published over twenty papers dealing with applied statistics in engineering and social sciences in refereed journals and proceedings. Romeu is a Fellow of the Royal Statistical Society and a member of the American Statistical Association and the Operations Research Society of America.

Jorge A. Sanguinetty is founder and President of DevTech Systems, Inc., a Washington, D.C.-based international and domestic economic consulting firm. He received his Ph.D. in economics from the City University of New York. He has over thirty years' experience in research, teaching, management, and consulting in economic policy design and implementation at the macro and sector levels. Dr. Sanguinetty is a founding member of ASCE and a frequent guest speaker and writer on Cuban affairs and transitional economies.

Rafael E. Saumell-Muñoz is an Assistant Professor of Spanish at Sam Houston State University in Huntsville, Texas. He holds an MA degree in French language and literature from the Universidad de la Habana (1978) and a Ph.D. in Spanish from Washington University, St. Louis, Mo. (1994). From 1975 to 1981, he served as screenwriter, TV producer, and adviser to the President of the Instituto Cubano de Radio y Televisión. In 1988, he left Cuba after serving a five year sentence for political activities. While in Cuba, published articles on literature and mass media in *El Caimán Barbudo* and *Unión*. Recently, published in the United States in the following publications: *Revista Iberoamericana, Revista de Estudios Hispánicos, Revista Monográfica.*

Joseph L. Scarpaci Jr., is an Associate Professor of Urban Affairs and Planning at the College of Architecture and Urban Studies of Virginia Tech University, Blacksburg, Virginia. He received an M.S. in Geography from Pennsylvania State University (1978) and a Ph. D. in Geography from the University of

Florida (1985). He was a Director of Latin American Studies at the University of Iowa (1987-1989). He is the co-author of a forthcoming book titled *Havana: Two Faces of an Antillian Metropolis* (Wiley, 1996, with Roberto Segre and Mario Coyula).

Jeffrey W. Steagall is Assistant Professor of Economics at the University of North Florida. Dr. Steagall received his Ph.D. in Economics from the University of Wisconsin-Madison (1990). His undergraduate studies were completed at St. Norbert College. He is an international trade and finance specialist, with particular interest in the trade relationship of developing countries.

Matías F. Travieso-Díaz, Esq., is a partner in Shaw, Pittman, Potts & Trowbridge. He received a B.S. (1966) and an M.S. (1967) in Electrical Engineering from the University of Miami, a Ph.D. in Electrical Engineering from the Ohio State University (1971) and a J.D. from Columbia Law School (1976). Between 1966 and 1973, he worked as an electrical engineer at Florida Power and Light Co., the Ohio State U. Electroscience Lab., and the North American Rockwell and Martin Marietta Corp. Mr. Travieso-Díaz joined Shaw, Pittman in 1976, concentrating on civil litigation with a particular emphasis on administrative and judicial proceedings involving nuclear power plants. He has been involved also in international transactions and currently heads the Cuban Project started by that firm to monitor events in Cuba as it moves to a free market economy. He is a member of the D.C. Bar, the U.S. Court of Appeals for the Fifth District, the U.S. District Court for DC, the American Bar Assoc., the International Bar Assoc., the Federal Bar Assoc., the Inter-American Bar Assoc., and the Hispanic Bar Assoc.

Roberto J. Vichot received his Ph. D. in Political Science from Purdue University (1984). He has been a Visiting Assistant Professor at Texas A&I University (Kingsville), and an Assistant Professor of Political Science at Texas A&M University. He is currently a Visiting Assistant Professor of Political Science at Florida International University. Vichot is the author of journal articles on international law, philosophy of law and human rights, philosophy of science, and of book chapters on the works of José Ortega y Gasset and Miguel de Unamuno. He is currently conducting research on Latino political culture, Cuban nationalism, and the Post-modernist interpretation of sovereignty and power.

Louis A. Woods is Associate Professor of Geography and Economics at the University of North Florida, where he has been a faculty member since 1972. Dr. Woods received his Ph.D. in Geography from the University of North Carolina at Chapel Hill (1972) after completing undergraduate studies in Geography at Jacksonville University. He also completed postgraduate work in Economics at East Carolina University. His recent research has focussed on the determinants of regional economic development, and the constraints imposed by environmental concerns. He has also written widely on the economic development of Belize.

Appendix C:
ACKNOWLEDGEMENTS

We want to take this opportunity to acknowledge the continued financial support provided to ASCE's activities by the following sponsoring members:

Acosta, José D.	Law and Econ Consultant	Miami, FL.
Alverio, Michael	ALVEMAC Representations	Caguas, PR.
Arellano, Victor		Coral Gables, FL
Asón, Elías R.	Empresas Fonalledas	San Juan, PR.
Batista-Falla, Agustín	Neder Finanz NV	Curacao, N.A.
Batista-Falla, Víctor	Publisher-Editor	Madrid, Spain
Belt, Juan A.B.	USAID	Guatemala City
Betancourt, Roger	University of Maryland	College Park, MD.
Blamberg, Margaret	Tate & Lyle	New York, NY.
Carbonell-Cortina, Néstor	Pepsi-Cola	Somers, NY.
Carta, Alvaro L.	Sugar Consultant	W.Palm Beach, FL.
Cisneros, Frank G.	MARMAN USA, Inc.	Tampa, FL.
Cox, Tom	U.S. Cuba Business Council	Washington, DC.
Crespo, Nicolás	Lat. Amer. Hospitality and Consulting	Miami, FL.
Crews, Eduardo T.	Bristol-Myers Squibb	New York, NY.
CXS de Mexico		Jacksonville, FL.
de la Hoz, José	United Trading Group	Coral Gables, FL.
de Lasa, José M., Esq.	Abbott Laboratories	Abbot Park, IL.
Delgado, Natalia, Esq.	Jenner & Block	Chicago, IL.
Díaz, Manuel L.	Republic Int'l Bank of NY	Miami, FL.

Echevarría, Oscar E.	BME INTERFUNDING	Caracas, Venezuela
Falcoff, Mark	American Enterprise Inst.	Washington, DC.
Falk, Dr. Pamela S.		New York, NY.
Fernández, Carlos J.	KPMG Peat Marwick	Miami, FL.
Fernández, Emilio A.	Pulse Electronics, Inc.	Rockville, MD.
Fernández, Ernesto	CXS de Mexico	Jacksonville, FL.
Fernández, Matías A.	Technology Park Group	San Juan, PR.
Fernández-Morell Andrés	VELCO	San Juan, PR.
Freer Jr., Robert E., Esq.	Freer & Mc Garry	Washington, DC.
García Aguilera, Carolina	C & J Investigations	Miami, FL.
Gayoso, Antonio	CUNA	Washington, DC.
Giral, Juan A.	Consultant	Washington, DC.
Gómez-Domínguez, Luis A.	Hialieah-Dade Dev. Inc.	Miami, FL.
Gómez Martín, Leopoldo	GMCS Corporation	Miami, FL.
Gutiérrez, Alfredo	Morgan Guaranty	Sao Paulo, Brazil
Harper, George R.	Steel, Hector & Davis	Miami, FL.
Hernández-Catá, Ernesto	International Monetary Fund	Washington, DC.
Herrera, Jorge R.	Merril Lynch	Coral Gables, FL.
Herrero, Dr. José A.	Consultant	San Juan, PR.
Juvier, Osvaldo A.	Duke Energy Corp.	Charlotte, NC.
La Sociedad Económica	Economic Research	Paris, France
Lasa, Luis R.	Bacardi Imports, Inc.	Miami, FL.
Leiseca, Sergio A.	Baker & McKenzie	Miami, FL.
Linde, Armando	IMF	Washington, DC.
López, Albert	The Tandem Group	Washington, DC.
López, Roberto I.	Citrus Products, Inc.	Tampa, FL.
Loredo, Jorge	Intel Medical Systems	Miami, FL.
Luis, Luis R.	Scudder, Stevens & Clark	Boston, MA.

Luzárraga, Alberto	Cuban American Research Group	New York, NY.
Maidique, Modesto A.	Florida Int'l University	Miami, FL.
Martínez, Enrique F.	Rohm and Hass Co.	Coral Gables, FL.
Martínez, Herminia	The World Bank (IBRD)	Washington, DC.
Masvidal, Sergio J.	American Express Bank, Ltd.	Miami, FL.
Mayer, Alfonso	General Cigar Corp.	New York, NY.
Menéndez, Benjamín F.	General Cigar Corp.	Miami, FL.
Miranda, José E.	Kelly Tractor Co.	Miami, FL.
Mizaurrieta, José A.	Inter-American Partners, Ltd.	New York, NY.
Montaner, Carlos A.	Union Liberal Cubana	Madrid, España
Monto, Edward A.	Houston Industries Energy	Houston, TX.
Montoulieu, Carlos F.	U.S. Dept. of Commerce	Washington, DC.
Morán, Ricardo J.	Consultant	Washington, DC.
Morris, Roy Esq,	Carr, Morris & Graeff, PC	Washington, DC.
Muller, Juan Antonio	INTERFIN, C.A.	Caracas, Venezuela
O'Connell, Richard	Private Investor	Paris, France
Padial, Carlos M.	Padial & Associates, Inc.	Baton Rouge, LA.
Palomares, Carlos	CITIBANK, Florida	Miami, FL.
Pazos, Felipe	Banco Central de Venezuela	Caracas, Venezuela
Perry, Joseph M.	Univ. of North Florida	Jacksonville, FL.
Piedra, Lino	Chrysler Corporation	Washington, DC.
Pino, Jorge E.	META	Miami, FL.
Quijano, Carlos N.	World Bank (IBRD)	Washington, DC.
Ricardo, José M.	Ricards Int'l Inc.	Chantilly, VA.
Rivas, Carlos	Martí, Flores, Prieto & Wachtel	San Juan, PR.
Rivero Cervera, José A.	Amerop Sugar Corporation	Miami, FL.
Roca, Rubén	The Rouse Company	Columbia, MD.
Rodríguez, José Luis	Trans-Tech-Ag. Corp.	Ft. Lauderdale, FL.

Rodríguez, Ricardo	Smith Barney	New York, NY.
Rodríguez-Vázquez, Claudio	Sparrow Trading, Corp.	Coral Gables, FL.
Sabater, Julio	Universal Comm. Enterp.	Elizabeth, NJ.
Sánchez, Federico F.	Interlink Group	San Juan, PR.
Sánchez, Nicolás	College of The Holy Cross	Worcester, MA.
Sanguinetty, Jorge	Development Technologies, Inc.	Miami, FL.
Seigle, Carlos & Diana	Rutgers University	Newark, NJ.
Travieso-Díaz, Matias F.	Shaw, Pittman, Potts & Trowbridge	Washington, DC.
US-Cuba Business Council		Washington, DC.
Vallejo, Jorge I.	Vallejo & Vallejo	San Juan, PR.
Vega, Sr. Juan Antonio	Latin Finance, Inc.	Coconut Grove, PR.
Villalón, Manuel F.	Aga Associates, Inc.	Hato Rey, PR.
Werlau, Maria Cañizares	Orbis, S.A.	Chatham, NJ.
Zayas-Bazán, Eduardo	East-Tenn. State University	Johnson City, TN.